WINDOWS SERVER 4:

Security, Troubleshooting, and Optimization

Wayne Dalton

Scott Fuller

Bob Kolosky

Joel Millecan

Carey Nachenberg

Karanjit S. Siyan, Ph.D.

Lance Skok

Steve Tate

New Riders Publishing, Indianapolis, IN

Windows NT Server 4:
Security, Troubleshooting, and Optimization

By Wayne Dalton, Scott M. Fuller, Bob Kolosky, Joel Millecan, Carey Nachenberg, Karanjit S. Siyan, Ph.D., Lance Skok, and Steve Tate

Published by:
New Riders Publishing
201 West 103rd Street
Indianapolis, IN 46290 USA

Printed in the United States of America 1 2 3 4 5 6 7 8 9 0

Library of Congress Cataloging-in-Publication Data

CIP data available upon request

Warning and Disclaimer

This book is designed to provide information about Windows NT Server 4. Every effort has been made to make this book as complete and as accurate as possible, but no warranty or fitness is implied.

The information is provided on an "as is" basis. The authors and New Riders Publishing shall have neither liability nor responsibility to any person or entity with respect to any loss or damages arising from the information contained in this book or from the use of the disks or programs that may accompany it.

Publisher	Don Fowley
Publishing Manager	Julie Fairweather
Marketing Manager	Mary Foote
Managing Editor	Carla Hall

Product Development Specialist
Jack Belbot

Acquisitions Editors
Pete Bitar
Jeff Durham

Software Specialist
Steve Flatt

Senior Editor
Sarah Kearns

Development Editor
Joe Casad

Project Editor
Dayna Isley

Copy Editors
Margo Catts,
Keith Cline

Technical Editor
Lance Skok

Acquisitions Coordinator
Stephanie Layton

Administrative Coordinator
Karen Opal

Cover Designer
Sandra Schroeder

Cover Production
Aren Howell

Book Designer
©Christopher Zacharow/SIS

Production Manager
Kelly Dobbs

Production Team Supervisors
Laurie Casey, Joe Millay,
Regina Rexrode

Graphics Image Specialists
Will Cruz, Tammy Graham,
Dan Harris, Oliver Jackson,
Clint Lahnen

Production Analysts
Jason Hand
Erich J. Richter

Production Team
Daniel Caparo, Christopher
Morris, Eric L. Puckett, Elizabeth
SanMiguel, Megan Wade

Indexer
Craig Small

About the Authors

Wayne Dalton resides in South Africa where he has been active in computer science for over ten years. In 1995 he joined a Microsoft Authorized Technical Education Center (ATEC) in Johannesburg (Windows Academy) as an instructor. After obtaining MCSE and MCT certification, he was appointed as the ATEC General Manager (July 1996). He is certified to teach all Microsoft operating systems (Windows, Windows 95, Windows NT) as well as the BackOffice products (SQL, SNA, SMS, IIS). His training experience also includes presenting papers at a South African conference and teaching in Germany, Nigeria, and Mozambique. Wayne is currently pursuing a Masters Degree (MSc in Computer Science) as well as a Certified NetWare 4.x Engineer qualification.

Scott M. Fuller is president of IDEAS, a computer consulting group specializing in law firms. Scott has an extensive background in system design, operations, operations management, and technical training for a wide variety of clients. He has contributed to several books, including *Learn Windows 95 in a Day, Upgrade to Windows 95 Quick & Easy, Learn Timeslips in a Day, Learn CompuServe in a Day, Learn Prodigy in a Day*, and *Inside Windows 95 Deluxe Edition.*

Bob Kolosky is a senior product analyst at Symantec Corporation. He has worked in the antivirus business unit at Symantec for the past two years with an emphasis on Windows NT products. He has been writing product documentation and reference material for the past five years.

Joel Millecan has been involved in the growth of the computer industry since learning BASIC programming in 1971. He currently specializes in network and telecommunication systems, with a strong focus on Windows NT, Novell NetWare, and various Unix operating systems. Joel considers the task of keeping pace with the rapid growth of technology, both hardware and software, an enjoyable responsibility.

Carey Nachenberg is a Principal Software Engineer at Symantec Corporation. He researches, designs, and develops new antivirus technologies for the award winning Norton Antivirus line of products. Carey has worked at Symantec for six years as a software engineer and architect on Norton Commander, Norton Desktop for DOS, and Norton Antivirus. He holds Bachelors and Masters degrees in Computer Science and Engineering from the University of California at Los Angeles. His Masters thesis covers polymorphic computer virus detection.

Kiranjit S. Siyan, Ph.D., is president of Kinetics Corporation. He has authored international seminars on Solaris & SunOS, TCP/IP networks, PC Network Integration, Windows NT, Novell networks, and Expert Systems using Fuzzy Logic. He teaches advanced technology seminars in the United States, Canada, Europe, and the Far East. Dr. Siyan has published articles in *Dr. Dobbs Journal, The C Users Journal*, and *Databased Advisor*. He is actively involved in Internet research. Dr. Siyan has been involved with Windows NT since 1992. He holds a Ph.D. in Computer Science. He is a Microsoft Certified Professional for Windows NT and holds an ECNE certification for Novell-based networks. You can reach him at his e-mail address: *karanjit@siyan.com.*

Lance Skok is a Senior Systems Engineer for Inacom Information Systems in San Antonio, Texas. He is a Microsoft Certified Systems Engineer and a Novell Master CNE. He has been heavily involved with PCs since 1980 and has skills in programming, networking, and systems integration. You can reach him at *lskok@netfix.com.*

Steve Tate is a computer professional with ten years of experience using, supporting, and conducting seminars on microcomputers. Steve draws on his wide experience in networking and personal computers to relate technology to his audience, whether novice or expert. His enthusiastic style and technical depth earn high marks from students. His company, Tate Consulting, specializes in providing consulting services supporting Microsoft BackOffice products. Steve is a Microsoft Certified Systems Engineer (MCSE) and Microsoft Certified Trainer (MCT).

Trademark Acknowledgments

All terms mentioned in this book that are known to be trademarks or service marks have been appropriately capitalized. New Riders Publishing cannot attest to the accuracy of this information. Use of a term in this book should not be regarded as affecting the validity of any trademark or service mark.

Acknowledgments

Bill Matsoukas, Lance Skok, and Barrie Sosinsky deserve special thanks for helping us out in a pinch. Their ability to work under tight deadlines helped make this book possible.

The people at New Riders Publishing also deserve recognition. The time and energy that was put into publishing this book is to be commended. Carla Hall, Sarah Kearns, Gina Brown, Jennifer Eberhardt, Noelle Gasco, Carrie Peterson, Cliff Shubs, Karen Walsh, and Molly Warnes went beyond the boundries of their job titles to ensure the completion of this project. The support of this staff is truly invaluable.

Contents at a Glance

Table of Contents

Part II: Troubleshooting

7   The Boot Process   121

8   Troubleshooting Windows NT Security   137

Part 4: Appendixes

PART

Security

Defining Security

A secure network does not exist; nor does a secure computer. The only secure computer is one that is unplugged, locked in a secure vault that only one person knows the combination to, and that person died last year. When you move beyond that scenario, you must expect lapses in security.

The question is how much "insecurity"—for lack of a better term—are you willing to accept? The next question is to what do you want to apply security? Are you trying to keep people from using your CPU processor? Are you trying to keep them from seeing your data? Are you trying to keep them from ruining your hardware? What, exactly, are you attempting to keep safe?

Although the Windows NT operating system was written with security in mind, it inherently contains a few loopholes and inconsistencies that can be exploited to the benefit of a wily hacker.

Although Windows NT has a few security loopholes, compare Windows NT to a DOS-based operating system, which has no security whatsoever. Considered in that light, Windows NT turns out to be one of the most secure operating systems that is still considered usable.

What happens when you connect a secure computer to a network, though? Suddenly individuals are allowed to access data and perform operations without the necessity of sitting at the keyboard. A network provides so many advantages over a stand-alone computer that stand-alones are virtually dinosaurs of the past. At the same time, however, the benefits bring disadvantages. Those disadvantages are risks—you are allowing someone into your system and trusting that they will respect your system and its data.

This chapter looks at ways of reducing the risks to which you expose your system. Understand, however, that no system is entirely foolproof. The first step in risk reduction is to comprehend the different levels of security that can be applied to operating systems.

Understanding Security Levels

The Trusted Computing Standards Evaluation Criteria (also known as the Orange Book), established by the United States Department of Defense, concludes that one cannot simply say that a computer is secure or not secure. Instead, it says that different levels of security can be assigned to an operating system. All these levels are based upon the *trust* you have in the operating system. A highly trusted system prevents intruders from entering the system, whereas a less trusted system has more possibilities of an intruder coming in unnoticed.

Four different levels of security are represented by letters ranging from A to D. Within each level of security, a number can be used to subdivide the level further, as in A1, A2, and so on. DOS is representative of a D1-level operating system. DOS has no security whatsoever; whoever is sitting at the keyboard has complete access to everything on the system. The concept of file ownership and permissions is virtually nonexistent in DOS—all the files are owned by the current user.

At the other end of the spectrum, an A1 level is virtually the machine locked in the vault without power or users. Everything else falls somewhere in between.

C-level operating systems have more security than D-level systems, and have a means by which a user is identified before he or she is allowed to access and manipulate files. Standard Windows NT, without any features other than logins, passwords, and file ownership concepts represents C1 security. C2 is a step higher than C1 and includes the capability to keep users from executing commands if they lack certain criteria, as well as the capability to audit every action that takes place.

The Windows NT Resource Kit contains a utility called CSCONFIG.EXE. This utility enables you to compare your current configuration with the C2 requirements and helps you make any necessary changes so your systems can comply with C2 requirements.

B-level operating systems must offer futher security restraints—including an inability for the owner of a file to change the permissions of it. Very few operating systems, and certainly not those readily available in the commerical market, meet any of the B-level requirements.

Deciding How Much Security to Implement

Although some experts issue the blanket statement that you can never have enough security and that the best thing you can do is implement more, more, more security, these generalities could not be further from the truth. Security, inherently, makes it harder to enter a system by providing additional locks that users must pass. Unfortunately, legitimate users must pass those locks as well. Every security measure installed creates more work for someone. In the instance of applying additional passwords, additional work is required by all users to further identify themselves before being allowed to do the transactions they want to do. With auditing, which may be invisible to the end user, the system administrators must assume additional tasks; they must define rights, maintain log files, and audit them on a regular basis.

Figure 1.1 shows a crude representation of the security spectrum. At one end is no security whatsoever; the system is easy to use by virtue of the fact that no constraints are placed on users or administrators.

At the other end of the spectrum is maximum security—again referring to the unplugged machine locked in a vault. At this end, the system is as secure as it can be, but so difficult to use that no one wants to. The slide in the middle is moveable so that it can be custom-tailored to each site.

Ease of use

Slide

Maximum security

Figure 1.1
The security spectrum.

Because absolutes rarely exist in life and little can be shown with a straight line, figure 1.2 presents the same information in a more realistic manner. The left side of the graph tracks the number of computer problems relating to security measures (including both user and administrator problems), whereas the bottom represents the amount of security implemented. When no security is implemented, no problems occur. As soon as security is implemented, the number of problems begins to increase. The term "problems" is used to represent legitimate complaints as well as additional workload.

In figure 1.2, notice that the line does not grow in a linear fashion; this is known instead as an *indifference curve*. As a small amount of security is implemented, only a few problems occur. It is, in fact, possible to implement more security without affecting the number of problems too significantly. When the security measures begin to tighten significantly, the number of problems begins to increase at a rapid pace.

Figure 1.2

Graphing security measures and the number of problems they generate.

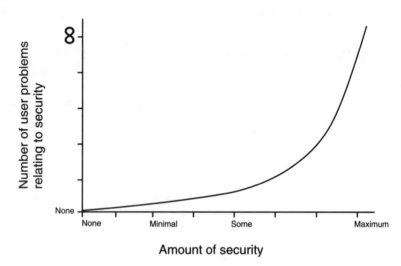

Amount of security

Just looking at this chart, however, is not enough to formulate an answer as to how much security to implement. For one thing, you need to define what you are trying to secure. This ties in to the earlier question of what are you trying to protect. Is the cost of protecting that entity worth doing so? For example, it can be costly to prevent someone from deleting the operating system from a machine. Is it worth it? Most operating systems can be reinstalled within a short period of time—a day at the very most. After you buy an operating system and install it, no changes are made to it beyond that, so you can always go back and restore it to the way it was when you installed it.

What about your hard drive? Can you protect it from someone driving a tank through the front door and blasting it with artillery shells? The answer is yes, you can, but is it worth the cost of constructing a bunker? Probably not. Most hard drives can be formatted, and reconstructed—again within a day usually.

What you cannot recover, and what your biggest investment is in, is your data. You can run to the computer store and buy an operating system. You can run there and buy a hard drive. But you cannot run to the store and buy a copy of your data that has been in the process of being defined since the day you opened your doors for business. That is what you should devote your time and talents to protecting (and backing up).

With regard to that data, the next item that needs to be investigated is the possibility of a system intrusion that could affect that data. Figure 1.3 shows a simple graph charting the possibility for intrusion against the amount of security implemented. This example is for a small business and is not indicative of a giant firm. With no security whatsoever, the potential for intrusion is unlimited. Implementing some security measures reduces this risk significantly, whereas implementing maximum security all but eliminates it.

The actual representation of the graph shown in figure 1.3 is different for every organization. It depends on the number of users accessing the system, the value of the data (the more valuable, the more incentive to try to break in), and how access is allowed (must users log in here, or are they granted access to everything on the system by virtue of logging into another host).

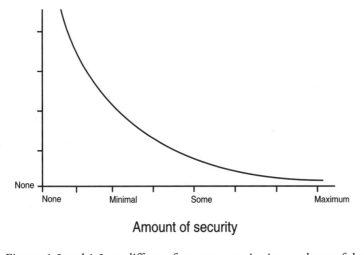

Figure 1.3
Weighing the amount of security against the possibility of intrusion.

Figures 1.2 and 1.3 are different for every organization, and one of the key jobs of management and administration is to define what each graph looks like for their organization. After those two items (potenial for intrusion and number of problems created) have been defined, they can be weighed against each other, as in figure 1.4, to find the equilibrium point at which they meet.

In figure 1.4, an equilibrium point is found by weighing the possibility of intrusion against the number of user problems inherent in implementing security measures. That equilibrium point denotes the point at which the company works the most effectively. The potential for intrusion is curtailed somewhat by the implementation of security measures, yet users are inconvenienced only slightly.

The amount of inconvenience the users tolerate is offset by the gains that come from reducing the possibility for system intrusion. Understanding where the equilibrium lies is essential in planning what measures to take. If the implemented measures fall on either side of the equilibrium, as shown in figure 1.5, then full realization is not obtained.

Within figure 1.5, point A represents a conservative attempt at security. The users are not inconvenienced significantly and, at the same time, the potential for system intrusion is still great. Not enough preventive measures have been taken, and intruders can more easily access this system than should be the case. The flip side of this is reflected in point B. Here, security measures have been liberally applied. The possibility of system intrusion is significantly reduced, yet users are required to go through more steps than they should—possibly entering multiple passwords and being forced to log out exactly at 5:00 p.m. The thing to note is that with implementation falling to either side of the equilibrium point, a loss in potential is generated. Falling on the A side, you lose the potential to provide adequate security to protect your system. Falling on the B side, you lose the potential to get more productivity from users by requiring them to deal with more security measures than they should.

Figure 1.4

Finding the equilibrium point.

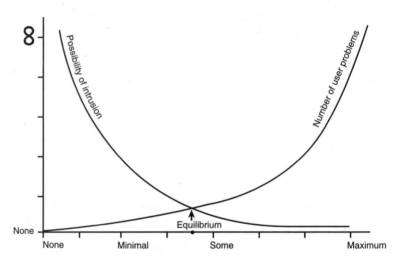

Amount of security

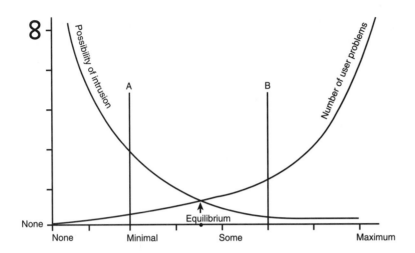

Figure 1.5
Points of nonequilibrium

One last note regarding the amount of security to implement is that after you define your equilibrium point, you should always be cognizant of factors that can cause it to change. Firing a number of analysts can create an outside body of disgruntled ex-employees who would like to break into your system. Possessing knowledge about the way your system is configured and works, they have enhanced skills that would enable them to break into your system, and the entire possibility of intrusion shifts to the right, as depicted in figure 1.6.

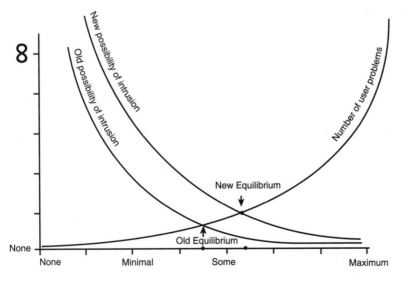

Figure 1.6
A shift in the possibility of intrusion changes the equilibrium point.

Fig 11 6

The shifting in the indifference curve depicted in figure 1.6 causes the equilibrium point to shift to the right also. More security measures should be implemented to counter the shift. The security measures can be installed locally and across the network—depending on your actual scenario.

Conclusion

This chapter has provided an introduction to security in Windows NT 4. You have briefly examined different levels of security. This chapter has also provided you with guidelines to follow when deciding how much security to implement.

Security: Firewalls and Related Issues

Designing and building a firewall is more an art of applying the correct firewall technology to a network than simply adding a firewall product onto the network. This chapter discusses some concepts associated with firewalls and describes some built-in Windows NT security features that provide firewall capabilities. Because understanding basic firewall concepts is important to the proper selection and implementation of firewalls, study the firewall concepts that comprise the early parts of this chapter.

Examining the Importance of Implementing a Firewall

Earlier this year the Defense Department announced that its computer systems were attacked 250,000 times in 1995. What is even more disturbing is the fact that most of these attacks went undetected. The majority of the detected attacks were against computer systems that housed sensitive and classified information. Two-thirds of the attacks were considered successful, resulting in lost, stolen, or modified data.

Corporate espionage is at an all time high and is still on the rise. Most companies are not prepared to deal with corporate invaders. Some companies still do not realize how the threat affects them. This fact remains—there are many unscrupulous people in cyberspace, and they are continually hacking away at security systems. Some people who may not be so unscrupulous outside cyberspace transform into first-rate hackers after they begin to prowl the Internet.

The FBI's National Computer Crime Squad recommends the use of firewalls to guard against computer crime. This chapter discusses some basic firewall concepts and describes how you can implement firewall security on your Windows NT 4 network.

Note   The FBI also recommends the following measures in conjunction with a firewall:

- Log in banner warning against unauthorized access

- Keystroke-level monitoring

- Trap and Tracing service from telephone company

- Caller ID

- Data encryption

Understanding Basic Firewall Concepts

A *firewall* is a system (either software or hardware) that enforces an access control policy between two or more networks. The firewall can be as advanced as your network security standards require. The network on the inside of the firewall is referred to as a *trusted network*, and the network on the outside of the firewall is an *untrusted network*. Firewalls are commonly used to shield trusted networks from unauthorized access via the Internet and to limit access from the trusted network to the Internet.

Firewall Logical Construction

The diagram in figure 2.1 illustrates the basic design of a model firewall.

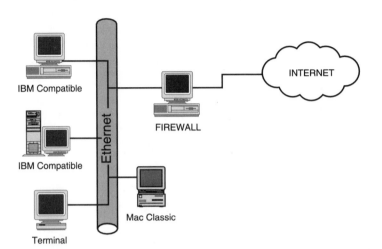

IBM Compatible

Ethernet

FIREWALL

IBM Compatible

Terminal

Mac Classic

INTERNET

Figure 2.1

This firewall is filtering traffic between the Internet and the network.

The single basic function of a firewall is to block unauthorized traffic between two or more networks. This is usually referred to as *filtering* traffic. Filtering can be viewed as either permitting authorized access or denying unauthorized access to a network.

Firewalls know what traffic to block because they are configured with *access control policies*, a set of rules that is applied to network traffic that the firewall "sees." The network administrator that implements access control polices for the firewall can choose to set these policies from two points of view:

■ She can deny access to all traffic except for defined authorized traffic.

■ She can allow access to all traffic except for defined unauthorized traffic.

The appropriate approach to access control policies depends on the goals of the network security policy.

Note   Network security is a two-way street. Firewalls are usually used to secure traffic leaving as well as entering the trusted network. Companies often limit Internet access from their internal (trusted) network.

Exploring the Two Types of Firewalls

Originally there were two types of firewalls. Today these two types have overlapped to the point that distinction between the two has become somewhat difficult. However, there are still two fundamental types of firewalls: Network Level and Application Level. This sections explores both types.

Network-Level Firewalls

Network-level firewalls operate at the IP packet level. At the very least, these firewalls have a single IP interface to the untrusted network and a single IP interface to the trusted network. They filter traffic by interpreting their access control policy against incoming and outgoing IP packets.

Network-level firewalls filter traffic based on any combination of source address, destination address, and Transport Control Protocol (TCP) port assignment in each IP packet. For example:

1. The access control policy for a given firewall says that IP address 121.23.67.101 may not access the Internet.

2. The host workstation with IP address 121.23.67.101 attempts to send a packet to a host on the Internet.

3. The firewall examines the packet and checks the IP address against the access control policy.

4. The packet is rejected by the firewall. This usually means that the packet is thrown away, a status message is returned to the sender, and often the unauthorized access attempt is written to a log file.

The previous example is a simple scenario. Access control policies for a network-level firewall can be much more complex. A host may be limited to Internet access only to certain hosts and only through certain TCP ports.

Note   Network-level firewalls are specialized IP routers. They are very fast and are transparent to the trusted network. Because network-level firewalls function as an IP router, they are assigned an IP address.

Modern network-level firewalls have become increasingly sophisticated. They can maintain internal information about the packets passing through them, including the contents of some of the data streams. The sections that follow describe the following types of network-level firewalls:

- Simple Router

- Bastion Host Firewall

- Screened Host Firewall

- Screened Subnet Firewall

Each of these network-level firewall types offers different levels of security and types of security control. The choice for your network depends on your network security requirements.

Bastion Host Firewall

Another type of network-level firewall is a bastion host. The term bastion refers to the central security system for a network. A bastion host computer acts as a drawbridge on a fortress.

The *bastion host* is a computer with at least one connection to the untrusted network and one connection to the trusted network. When access is granted to a host from the untrusted network by the bastion host, all traffic from that host is allowed to pass unfettered. Figure 2.2 illustrates the configuration of a bastion host protecting a network.

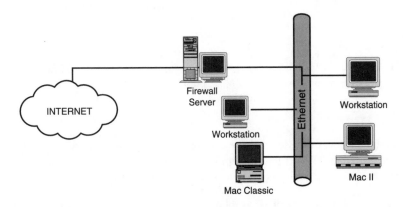

Figure 2.2

A simple implementation of a bastion host firewall provides a drawbridge to the trusted network.

Bastion hosts are generally used as part of a more sophisticated firewall. One can think of them as building blocks for more advanced firewalls.

The disadvantages of the bastion host firewall are as follows:

- After an intruder passes through, he has direct access to the protected network.

- Protection is not advanced enough for most network applications.

Screened Host Firewall

Another slightly more sophisticated example of a network-level firewall is the *screened host.* This firewall uses a router with at least one connection to the untrusted network and a connection to the bastion host. The router serves as a preliminary screen for the bastion host. The screening router sends all IP traffic to the bastion host after it filters the packets. The router is configured with a set of *filter rules,* a list of IP addresses that are allowed to access the trusted network. Only the traffic that conforms to the filter rules is forwarded to the bastion host computer. All other network traffic is filtered out before it gets to the bastion host.

The screened host decreases the amount of traffic sent to the bastion host and simplifies the bastion host's filtering algorithms. Figure 2.3 depicts the implementation of a screened host firewall.

Figure 2.3

The screening router filters all IP traffic and then directs it into a single host computer.

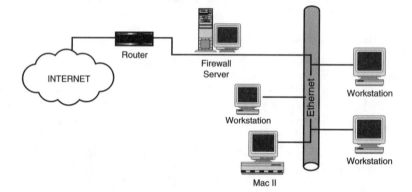

> **Note**   The filtering capability of a router depends on the manufacturer and the model. Most routers have at least a limited amount of filtering capability, but you cannot assume that a given router can be configured with a filter list.

After the traffic passes the filtering processes of the screening router, it passes onto the bastion host for further scrutiny. The bastion host may use application-level functions to block or allow the traffic from the outside network to continue on to the protected network.

The disadvantages of the screen host firewall are as follows:

■ The single screen host can become a traffic bottleneck.

■ If the host system goes down, the entire gateway goes down with it.

Screened Subnet Firewall

A screen subnet firewall uses one or more additional routers and one or more additional bastion host computers. In a *screened subnet firewall,* access to and from the trusted network is secured by using a network of screened bastion host computers. Each of the screened bastion hosts is the "drawbridge" to a subnet of the trusted network (see fig. 2.4).

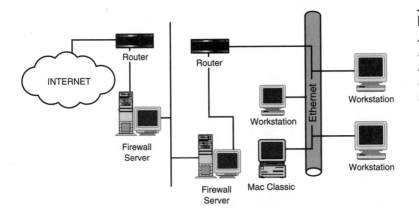

Figure 2.4

A screened subnet firewall is a network of screened host computers in between the protected network and the outside network.

A screened subnet firewall can also be constructed by using a single bastion host computer and two screening routers.

Because screened host firewalls do not allow traffic to pass directly between the outside network and the protected network, the IP addresses of the hosts on the networks are not seen by each other.

The disadvantages of screen subnet firewalls are as follows:

■ They can be more expensive than a simple bastion host firewall because you must have a router port and bastion host for each subnet on the trusted network.

■ Implementation is more labor intensive because configuration of the bastion hosts is more complex. This complexity grows geometrically with the addition of each subnet.

Application-Level Firewalls

Application-level firewalls are hosts running proxy servers located between the protected network and the outside network. Viewed from the client side, a proxy server is an application that services network resource requests by emulating the target resource. The proxy server "pretends," for example, that it is the database server that an application is accessing, when in reality the proxy server is communicating with the database server on behalf of the application. Viewed from the network resource side, the proxy server is accessing network resources by emulating the client.

Application-level firewalls do not allow traffic to pass directly between networks. They also perform elaborate logging and auditing of the traffic. Because the proxy applications are software components running on the network firewall, the firewall host computer is a good place to log events and manage access control policies.

Application-level firewalls can also be used as network address translators. Traffic goes in one side of the firewall and out the other after passing through an application that effectively masks the origin of the initiating connection by passing the traffic along with the firewall IP address. The application can be coded or configured to pass along any IP address.

Application-level firewalls tend to provide more detailed audit reports and tend to enforce stricter security models than network-level firewalls because they are tracking users and applications, as well as IP packet parameters.

In some cases, having an application in the way may impact performance, making the firewall less transparent. When using application-level firewalls, speed is of the essence.

Note   Microsoft has developed an application proxy firewall, code named Catapult, which provides far more enhanced functionality. Catapult is a proxy server that integrates directly with the Windows NT 4 operating system and the Internet Information Server. Catapult is available for download from Microsoft's web site and may be an ideal solution for your NT Internet server application proxy firewall needs.

Proxy Server Host

A proxy server host computer can be designed as an application gateway firewall that mediates traffic between the trusted network and the untrusted network. Proxy servers are application specific. One must code proxies into the applications, and the proxy server must be set up to use the kind of proxy that is being used in the proxy application. Figure 2.5 shows the basic design of a proxy server firewall computer.

Figure 2.5

The proxy server host has total control of data passed between the proxy client and proxy server.

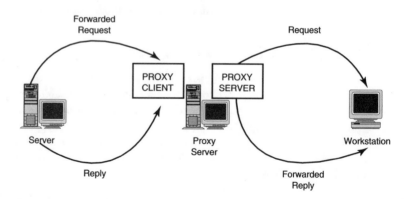

Proxy servers should be written to provide a fail-safe mode of firewall operation. If an invalid proxy is used to contact the proxy server, then the proxy server rejects this communication rather than shutting down the entire gateway.

The disadvantages of the proxy server host firewall are as follows:

- Required use of custom proxy applications can be expensive.

- Proxy applications written incorrectly can cause the gateway to shut down.

Dual-Homed Gateway

Another example of a application-level firewall is the dual-homed gateway. The dual-homed gateway (acting as a network firewall) does not allow any TCP/IP traffic to pass through. This effectively blocks all IP traffic between the trusted network and the untrusted network. Host computer A on network A can access application A on the dual-homed gateway computer, and host computer B on network B can access application B on the dual-homed gateway computer. The two applications both access the same data that resides on the dual-homed gateway computer, but no network traffic between the two systems is allowed.

Three types of network dual-homed gateways are possible with the addition of either an Application forwarder, a Mail forwarder, or a News forwarder.

A Dual-Homed Gateway with an Application Forwarder

Adding an application forwarder to a dual-homed gateway enables users to obtain services. This design is very similar to the proxy server host mentioned earlier in the section "Proxy Server Hosts" (see fig. 2.6).

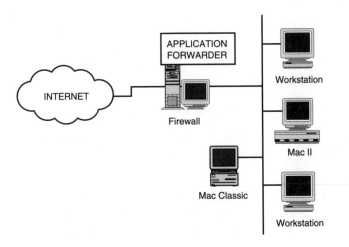

Figure 2.6

You can obtain services through the application forwarder.

A Dual-Homed Gateway with a Mail Forwarder

With a dual-homed gateway acting as a mail forwarder, mail from one network can be safely passed to the protected network (see fig. 2.7).

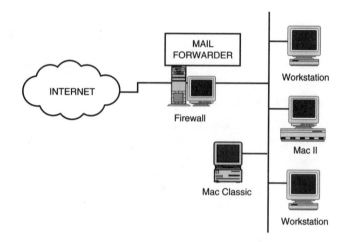

Figure 2.7

A dual-homed gateway with a mail forwarder passes mail traffic safely between networks.

A dual-homed gateway with a news forwarder enables news (such as NNTP) to be forwarded from one network to the other.

Dual-Homed Gateway Construction

A dual-homed gateway is constructed of a host computer with two network interface boards. The host system is a depository of network data (and possibly network applications, depending on design) and should be designed with this in mind. The dual-homed gateway should have adequate disk storage and should be part of the network backup strategy.

In order for a dual-homed gateway to work effectively as a firewall, routing between its interface cards must be disabled. This forces data exchanges at the application-level. If a firewall allows network-level traffic, then the protected network security is compromised.

Several factors can weaken security with a dual-homed gateway, including the following:

- File permissions are not set correctly. Incorrect file permission may allow unauthorized access to system files that control, among other things, access policies and routing configurations. File permissions are often set incorrectly when backup files are restored.

- Unix shell scripts can breach the IP routing being disabled. Unix shell scripts can issue commands that, when run in a supervisory capacity, can enable IP routing. This allows untrusted network traffic to bypass the dual-homed gateway applications.

■ A compromised user account from the trusted network may be used to log on to the dual-homed gateway from the untrusted network. Users should never be allowed to log on to the gateway computer directly. This is a design flaw that can be easily avoided.

■ Users on the untrusted network can learn about the trusted systems through release notes from applications left on the dual-homed gateway.

Circuit Gateway

The *circuit gateway firewall* is a host computer running a gateway application that facilitates communication between network resources and the user application using Transmission Control Protocol (TCP) ports. Figure 2.8 shows a circuit gateway configuration.

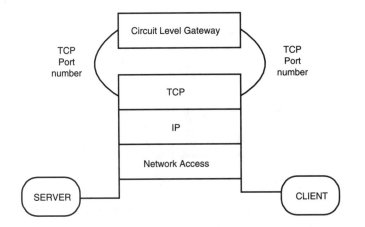

Figure 2.8

Circuit gateways create a circuit between the TCP port number end points.

Circuit gateways generally support only TCP/IP applications. Because circuit gateways operate at the application level, special client software might have to be implemented in order to facilitate application-to-application communication.

The disadvantages of the circuit gateway are basically by-products of the design itself and are as follows:

■ A special user interface may be required.

■ Installation of applications can be very time-consuming.

■ Use of circuit gateways on large networks consisting of many different hardware configurations can be difficult.

■ Every packet processed by a circuit gateway is processed twice, placing an additional traffic load on the network and a performance load on the applications.

NT TCP/IP Security

Windows NT 4 includes TCP/IP Security, which enables you to control the types of network traffic that reach your NT Server. You can limit access to the NT Server by permitting or denying connectivity to specific Transmission Control Protocol (TCP) Ports, User Datagram Protocol (UDP) Ports, and Internet Protocol (IP) Protocols. In essence, TCP/IP Security enables you to restrict connectivity to the NT Server by filtering ports and protocols and can be thought of as a built-in, configurable firewall.

Implementation of TCP/IP Security on NT Server is generally used on servers directly connected to the Internet.

TCP/IP Security Configuration

As a prerequisite to configuring TCP/IP Security, the TCP/IP Protocol must first be installed, configured, and operational. The first step in configuring TCP/IP Security is to enable the Security option. The option to enable TCP/IP Security is located in the TCP/IP Protocol Advanced IP Addressing dialog box.

To open the TCP/IP Protocol Advanced IP Addressing dialog box and enable the Security option, follow these steps:

1. Open the Control Panel by clicking the Start button, Settings, Control Panel.

2. Double-click the Network Applet, located in the Control Panel.

3. Within the Network Applet, select the Protocols tab, and select the TCP/IP Protocol. Click the Properties button.

4. You see the Microsoft TCP/IP Properties screen. Select the IP Address tab and click the Advanced button.

5. You see the Advanced IP Addressing dialog box (see fig. 2.9). Check the box labeled Enable Security.

6. After you check the Enable Security option, the Configure button becomes fully visible and available for selection. Click the Configure button to display the TCP/IP Security dialog box.

The TCP/IP Security dialog box (see fig. 2.10) is comprised of the following four sections:

- ■ **Adapter.** Specifies the network adapter for which you want to set up TCP/IP Security

- ■ **TCP Ports.** Transmission Control Protocol Ports

- ■ **UDP Ports.** User Datagram Ports

- ■ **IP Protocols.** Internet Protocol Protocols

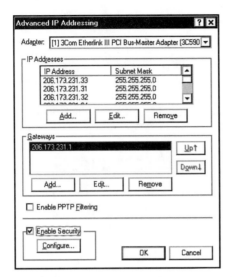

Figure 2.9

Enable the security option through the TCP/IP Properties Advanced IP Addressing dialog box.

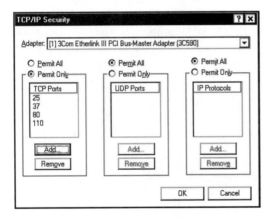

Figure 2.10

Sample settings shown in the TCP/IP Security dialog box.

To configure Security, select the Network Adapter for which you want to apply security filtering. If you have multiple network adapters installed in your computer, verify that you have selected the correct adapter.

The remaining three sections of the TCP/IP Security dialog box—TCP Ports, UDP Ports, and IP Protocols—are the essential configuration options of the TCP/IP Security implementation. For more information on TCP Ports, UDP Ports, and IP Protocols, see the section "Ports and Protocols" found later in this chapter. You have two basic choices for each section: Permit All or Permit Only.

- **Permit All.** Enables all connections to pass through to the server.

- **Permit Only.** Enables you to specify which ports are allowed connectivity and pass-through to the server. If you specify this option, you must then explicitly specify which ports or protocols are to be allowed connectivity. Ports and protocols are specified in decimal format.

By default, the Permit All option is selected for all three port and protocol sections. If you select the Permit Only option for a section, the associated Add button becomes visible and available for selection. To add specific ports or protocol numbers to the Permit lists, select the Permit Only option for the desired port or protocol section and click the Add button. Figure 2.11 shows the Security Add dialog box for the TCP Ports section.

Figure 2.11

The Security Add dialog box is used to add permitted TCP ports.

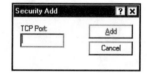

Ports and Protocols

When implementing TCP/IP Security, you should have an understanding of the ports and protocols used by your NT Server. Your NT Server might have many ports and services in operation that must be added to the Permit list for proper operation. Be aware that if you enable Security and add ports to a Permit list, an unintentional omission renders an existing service, which relies on a specific port or protocol, non-operational.

A Port, Protocol, and Service Reference

```
# RFC 1060 (Assigned Numbers)
#
# Format:
#
# <service name> <port number>/<protocol> [aliases...]
[#<comment>]
#
echo          7/tcp
echo          7/udp
discard       9/tcp        sink null
discard       9/udp        sink null
systat        11/tcp
systat        11/tcp       users
```

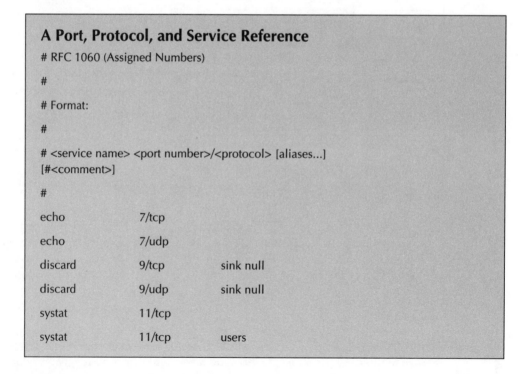

daytime	13/tcp		
daytime	13/udp		
netstat	15/tcp		
qotd	17/tcp	quote	
qotd	17/udp	quote	
chargen	19/tcp	ttytst source	
chargen	19/udp	ttytst source	
ftp-data	20/tcp		
ftp	21/tcp		
telnet	23/tcp		
smtp	25/tcp	mail	
time	37/tcp	timserver	
time	37/udp	timserver	
rlp	39/udp	resource	# resource location
name	42/tcp	nameserver	
name	42/udp	nameserver	
whois	43/tcp	nicname	# usually to sri-nic
domain	53/tcp	nameserver	# name-domain server
domain	53/udp	nameserver	
nameserver	53/tcp	domain	# name-domain server
nameserver	53/udp	domain	
mtp	57/tcp		# deprecated
bootp	67/udp		# boot program server
tftp	69/udp		
rje	77/tcp	netrjs	
finger	79/tcp		
link	87/tcp	ttylink	

continues

supdup	95/tcp		
hostnames	101/tcp	hostname	# usually from srinic
iso-tsap	102/tcp		
dictionary	103/tcp	webster	
x400	103/tcp		# ISO Mail
x400-snd	104/tcp		
csnet-ns	105/tcp		
pop	109/tcp	postoffice	
pop2	109/tcp		# Post Office
pop3	110/tcp	postoffice	
portmap	111/tcp		
portmap	111/udp		
sunrpc	111/tcp		
sunrpc	111/udp		
auth	113/tcp	authentication	
sftp	115/tcp		
path	117/tcp		
uucp-path	117/tcp		
nntp	119/tcp	usenet	# Network News Transfer
ntp	123/udp	ntpd ntp	# network time protocol (exp)
nbname	137/udp		
nbdatagram	138/udp		
nbsession	139/tcp		
NeWS	144/tcp	news	
sgmp	153/udp	sgmp	
tcprepo	158/tcp	repository	# PCMAIL
snmp	161/udp	snmp	
snmp-trap	162/udp	snmp	

print-srv	170/tcp		# network PostScript
vmnet	175/tcp		
load	315/udp		
vmnet0	400/tcp		
sytek	500/udp		
biff	512/udp	comsat	
exec	512/tcp		
login	513/tcp		
who	513/udp	whod	
shell	514/tcp	cmd	# no passwords used
syslog	514/udp		
printer	515/tcp	spooler	# line printer spooler
talk	517/udp		
ntalk	518/udp		
efs	520/tcp		# for LucasFilm
route	520/udp	router routed	
timed	525/udp	timeserver	
tempo	526/tcp	newdate	
courier	530/tcp	rpc	
conference	531/tcp	chat	
rvd-control	531/udp	MIT disk	
netnews	532/tcp	readnews	
netwall	533/udp		# for emergency broadcasts
uucp	540/tcp	uucpd	# uucp daemon
klogin	543/tcp		# Kerberos authenticated rlogin
kshell	544/tcp	cmd	# and remote shell
new-rwho	550/udp	new-who	# experimental

continues

remotefs	556/tcp	rfs_server rfs	# Brunhoff remote filesystem
rmonitor	560/udp	rmonitord	# experimental
monitor	561/udp		# experimental
garcon	600/tcp		
maitrd	601/tcp		
busboy	602/tcp		
acctmaster	700/udp		
acctslave	701/udp		
acct	702/udp		
acctlogin	703/udp		
acctprinter	704/udp		
elcsd	704/udp		# errlog
acctinfo	705/udp		
acctslave2	706/udp		
acctdisk	707/udp		
kerberos	750/tcp	kdc	# Kerberos authentication—tcp
kerberos	750/udp	kdc	# Kerberos authentication—udp
kerberos_master	751/tcp		# Kerberos authentication
kerberos_master	751/udp		# Kerberos authentication
passwd_server	752/udp		# Kerberos passwd server
userreg_server	753/udp		# Kerberos userreg server
krb_prop	754/tcp		# Kerberos slave propagation
erlogin	888/tcp		# Login and environment passing
kpop	1109/tcp		# Pop with Kerberos
phone	1167/udp		
ingreslock	1524/tcp		
maze	1666/udp		

nfs	2049/udp		# sun nfs
knetd	2053/tcp		# Kerberos de-multiplexor
eklogin	2105/tcp		# Kerberos encrypted rlogin
rmt	5555/tcp	rmtd	
mtb	5556/tcp	mtbd	# mtb backup
man	9535/tcp		# remote man server
w	9536/tcp		
mantst	9537/tcp		# remote man server, testing
bnews	10000/tcp		
rscs0	10000/udp		
queue	10001/tcp		
rscs1	10001/udp		
poker	10002/tcp		
rscs2	10002/udp		
gateway	10003/tcp		
rscs3	10003/udp		
remp	10004/tcp		
rscs4	10004/udp		
rscs5	10005/udp		
rscs6	10006/udp		
rscs7	10007/udp		
rscs8	10008/udp		
rscs9	10009/udp		
rscsa	10010/udp		
rscsb	10011/udp		
qmaster	10012/tcp		
qmaster	10012/udp		

Understanding NT Network Firewall Guidelines

One of the most common methods of implementing a firewall involves reconfiguring the network router. This method involves disabling SMB services over TCP/IP. If you have a router, you can disable UDP ports 137 and 138, and TCP port 139. These ports are used for NetBIOS over TCP/IP. If you have a direct dial-up connection to the Internet, you can remove the binding between the Server, Workstations and NetBIOS services, and the TCP/IP protocol. The bindings between these services and the NetBEUI protocol can be retained to allow remote file access to the gateway machine from within your internal LAN.

After you secure the gateway machine, you should secure the internal network. The simplest way to do this is to disable routing on the NT gateway machine. Install a firewall on the gateway machine to allow Internet access to users on your internal LAN.

Creating a Pseudo-Firewall

Windows NT 4 enables you to modify network bindings to create a pseudo-firewall implementation. This method of creating a pseudo-firewall involves unbinding protocols and is generally only recommended for use on smaller networks.

The purpose of a pseudo-firewall is to prevent outside users on the Internet from accessing the Windows NT SMB/NetBIOS protocol services. Because SMB/NetBIOS services are used by Windows NT 4, shutting off access to these protocols, for use by Internet users, effectively blocks unauthorized access to native Windows NT 4 file and print sharing. When running SMB/NetBIOS services exclusively over the non-routed NetBEUI transport on your internal LAN, outside Internet users are blocked from accessing these services. This method implements an effective firewall without the cost of a dedicated firewall machine.

Windows NT 4 has two basic types of networking services:

- **TCP/IP protocol services.** Examples include World Wide Web, FTP, Gopher, SMTP, and Telnet.

- **SMB/NetBIOS protocol services.** Examples include native NT file and print sharing.

The TCP/IP protocol services are primarily used to communicate with the Internet. In a pseudo-firewall implementation, all the network workstations on your internal LAN must run TCP/IP client software, but not TCP/IP services. A designated gateway machine must run the TCP/IP services that will be accessible from the Internet.

Network bindings are enabled and disabled from within the Network Applet, located in the Control Panel. After opening the Network Applet, select the Bindings tab to display the Network Bindings dialog box (see fig. 2.12).

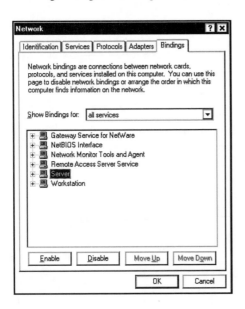

Figure 2.12

Use the Network dialog box to disable network bindings.

Following are lists of bindings that must be enabled and disabled on all the computers on your internal LAN to implement the pseudo-firewall:

Disable session bindings:

NetBIOS	TCP/IP
Workstation	TCP/IP
Server	TCP/IP

Enable transport layer bindings:

NetBEUI	Network Adapter: internal network
TCP/IP	Network Adapter: internal network
TCP/IP	Modem RAS Connection: external Internet gateway

Enable session layer bindings:

NetBIOS	NetBEUI
Workstation	NetBEUI
Server	NetBEUI

Conclusion

This chapter examined firewall concepts and designs and various issued related to overall network security. Reviewing these different firewall designs can help in the implementation of a firewall in a Windows NT 4 network system.

Computer Viruses and Windows NT

computer viruses are no longer an urban myth. Current estimates place the total number of viruses at or above 10,000, with between three and six new viruses written each day. This chapter describes the major classes of viruses, explains how they work, and details their behavior under Windows NT.

A computer virus is a program that performs self-replication by using files or boot sectors as its medium of propagation. Some viruses perform an activity in addition to replicating (known as a payload), such as displaying a message on a computer monitor, seeking out and deleting specific files, or formatting a hard drive. However, this behavior is not a prerequisite for a virus.

Most viruses are written in assembly language, a low-level language one step removed from the machine language of the computer chip. A few viruses have been written in higher-level languages, such as C or Pascal, but using such languages typically results in undesirably bulky viruses. Macro viruses, written to target data files with macro capabilities, are an exception to this pattern.

Fortunately, as of the time of this writing, no viruses have been discovered that specifically target and infect the Windows NT operating system. However, many of today's DOS and Windows viruses can infect and propagate under Windows NT. Table 3.1 shows a summary of the major types of viruses.

Table 3.1
Various Types of Viruses

Virus Type	Approximate Total #	# In the Top-10 "In-the-Wild"	Approximate # "In-the-Wild"
Boot viruses	400	8	100
DOS file-infecting viruses	8,000	1	200
Windows 3.1 viruses	20	0	1
Windows 95 viruses	1	0	0
Macro viruses	100	3	35

The following sections briefly describe the major classes of viruses. Later sections in this chapter detail how these viruses function specifically under Windows NT.

Boot Viruses

Every floppy disk has a boot record, or FBR. The boot record occupies the first sector on the disk and contains information that describes the contents of the floppy disk to the operating system. The boot record also contains a *boot strap routine,* a machine language program designed to load the operating system from the disk. When a computer is started with a floppy disk in the primary drive, the computer retrieves the boot record from the disk and executes its boot strap routine. The boot strap routine then loads the rest of the operating system, if one is present, from the disk. A message such as Non-system Disk. Insert a new disk and press any key. might also appear.

Users frequently make the mistake of leaving disks in floppy drives. This seemingly benign error actually represents the sole vector of infection for the boot record virus. Boot viruses understand that the computer always loads and executes the boot strap routine when booting from floppy disks. Consequently, boot viruses replace the original floppy boot strap program with a viral boot strap program. This enables the virus to gain control of the system as soon as the computer starts. The virus then can infect the hard drive, destroy data, and wreak havoc on the computer. If the floppy disk boot strap routine is infected, the following sequence of events allow the virus to spread:

1. The computer is turned on or rebooted.

2. The computer detects a floppy disk in the primary floppy drive. It loads the boot record from the floppy disk and executes its boot strap routine, which is the viral boot strap routine.

3. The viral boot strap routine locates the (first) hard drive on the computer and infects its Master Boot Record or one of its partition's boot.

4. The viral boot strap routine installs itself as a memory-resident program in the computer's memory.

5. The viral boot strap routine loads a backup copy of the *original* boot strap routine and executes it.

6. The disk boots normally.

7. The memory-resident virus infects additional floppy disks as they are accessed.

Each physical hard drive has exactly one *Master Boot Record* (MBR). Like the floppy boot record, the MBR also has two primary components. The first is a *partition table*, which denotes the allocation of all sectors on the drive and their respective partitions. Many application programs (and the operating system itself) make use of the information stored within the partition table in order to understand the disk's characteristics, such as how many partitions (logical drives) exist on the drive.

The second component of the MBR is a *boot strap routine*. During a system reset, a standard MBR boot strap routine first determines which partition is the *active partition* (the one from which the user wants to boot). The MBR loads and transfers control to the active partition's *Partition Boot Record* (PBR). The PBR, like the floppy boot record, then loads the operating system present on the partition.

The Master Boot Record boot strap routine is the most common target for floppy boot viruses. Most floppy boot record viruses infect hard drives by replacing the MBR boot strap routine with a viral boot strap routine. If the MBR boot strap routine is infected, the following sequence of events allows the virus to execute:

1. The computer is turned on or rebooted.

2. The computer has no floppy disk in the primary drive. The computer loads the Master Boot Record and executes its boot strap routine. This is the viral boot strap routine.

3. The viral boot strap routine installs itself as a memory-resident program in the computer's memory.

4. The viral boot strap routine loads a backup copy of the original (uninfected) MBR boot strap routine and executes it.

5. The original MBR boot strap routine locates the active partition and loads its Partition Boot Record.

6. The MBR boot strap routine transfers control to the PBR boot strap routine.

7. The PBR loads and executes the operating system stored on the active partition.

8. The memory-resident virus infects floppy disks as they are accessed.

The Master Boot Record is the single most common target for boot viruses on the hard drive, but the Partition Boot Record(s) are less commonly infected. The Partition Boot Record is most closely related to the Floppy Boot Record. Each partition (logical drive) on the physical hard drive has its own Partition Boot Record. The PBR contains a series of bytes that comprise the *BPB* or BIOS Parameter Block. These bytes describe the geometry and contents of the logical drive. The PBR also contains a boot strap routine that is charged with loading and executing the operating system present on the logical drive.

Some floppy boot-record viruses infect hard drives by replacing the PBR's boot strap routine with a viral boot strap routine. These viruses typically only infect the PBR of the current active partition (the bootable partition), because this constitutes the most likely partition that will actually boot giving the virus a chance to spread. If the PBR boot strap routine has been infected, the following sequence of events allows the virus to execute:

1. The computer is turned on or rebooted.

2. The computer has no floppy disk in the primary drive. The computer loads the Master Boot Record and executes its boot strap routine.

3. The MBR boot strap routine determines which partition (logical drive) is active. The MBR boot strap routine locates and retrieves the PBR from the active partition.

4. The MBR then executes the PBR boot strap routine. Remember, the PBR contains the viral boot strap routine.

5. The viral boot strap routine installs itself as a memory-resident program in the computer's memory.

6. The viral boot strap routine loads a backup copy of the original (uninfected) PBR boot strap routine and executes it.

7. The original PBR loads and executes the operating system on active partition.

8. The memory-resident virus infects floppy disks as they are accessed.

DOS File-infecting Viruses

The most common executable files used under DOS are COM, EXE, and SYS files. COM and EXE files are used for standard DOS programs, and SYS files are used for system device drivers. Although viruses have targeted each of these file formats, to date, reports of SYS file infections have been rare. The basic file virus replicates by attaching a copy of itself to an uninfected executable program. The virus then modifies the new host program so that when you execute the program, the virus executes first.

A *file-infecting virus* gains control of the computer when the user or operating system executes an infected program. The infected program is usually modified so that the virus immediately usurps control. After the virus machine code begins executing, it can immediately seek out and infect other executable programs on the computer (this is called *direct action infection*), or it can establish itself as a memory-resident addition to the operating system. As a resident program, the virus can then infect subsequent executable files as the operating system or other programs execute, copy, or access them for any reason.

After either type of virus has had a chance to do its mischief, it transfers control back to the host program. The host program can then execute normally, and the user is unaware of the infection.

The *direct action file virus* attempts to infect one or more programs as soon as an infected program is launched. After the virus has completed its infection, it relinquishes control of the computer to the host program.

DOS provides system services to efficiently and systematically traverse the many files and directories present on a drive. The direct action virus uses these services to locate new files to infect, the same way that a file-finding program might locate files that contain a certain text-string.

The *memory-resident file virus* works in a manner similar to its boot record cousins. When an infected program launches, the virus installs itself as a memory-resident addition to the operating system. From this point, any time the user or another program makes a request to the operating system to execute or access a file, the virus intercepts the request and takes control of the computer.

The resident virus can then infect program files as the user references them. If the virus is memory-resident at the time the user references files, the virus gains control at the time of this DOS request. As the virus learns of the service request, it can infect the specified program and then pass the original request along to DOS. DOS then runs the (newly infected) program normally.

Windows 3.1 Viruses

Today, the number of Windows 3.1 viruses is small but growing. Windows viruses come in the same direct action and memory resident flavors as the DOS-based viruses previously described. The difference between DOS and Windows viruses is their infection targets. DOS viruses infect standard COM, EXE, and SYS files; Windows viruses are designed to infect only Windows New Executable (NE) EXE files.

A *Windows NE file* is a new type of EXE file that actually contains two independent program components. The first component of the NE file is a standard DOS executable program. This DOS executable can actually be up to 640 KB in size, like any other DOS program; however, this DOS program is typically a stub program that displays a `This program requires Microsoft Windows.` message. If you launch a Windows NE executable from DOS or from a DOS box (a window that has a DOS session running in it) under Windows 3.1, this DOS stub executes and runs as a standard DOS program would.

The second part of the NE executable file is the Windows executable. This part of the file has its own unique format, executable code, and resources that specify how the program operates under Windows. If the program is launched from within Windows, this part of the program is loaded and executed. Therefore, Windows viruses spread by modifying this component of the NE file.

Note that such a NE file could actually be simultaneously infected by a DOS virus and a Windows virus. If such a file were executed from DOS, then the DOS component, and hence the DOS virus, would launch. Conversely, if the file were run from Windows, then the Windows component, and hence the Windows virus, would execute.

The Tentacle virus is currently the only Windows 3.1 virus that has been found "in-the-wild." This virus was recently distributed over the Internet and has been found at numerous sites around the world. Later sections in this chapter discuss how this and other Windows 3.1 viruses function under Windows NT.

Windows 95 (32-bit) Viruses

As of this writing, only a single Windows 95 virus has been constructed. This virus was dubbed "Boza" by virus researcher Vesselin Bontchev because of its poor design and programming. Boza infects 32-bit, Portable Executable (PE) files used by Windows 95 and Windows NT. The PE format has many things in common with the Windows 3.1 NE format; however, it differs enough that viruses designed to infect one cannot work with the other.

Like the NE format, PE files contain two independent program components. The first component is a standard DOS executable program. Once again, this DOS program is typically a stub program that displays a `This program requires Microsoft Windows.` message. If a

Windows NE executable is executed from DOS, this DOS stub executes and runs as a standard DOS program would. The second part of the PE executable file is the 32-bit Windows executable. This part of the file has its own unique format, executable code, and resources that specify how the program operates under Windows 95 or Windows NT. If the program is launched from within Windows 95 or from a DOS box under Windows 95, this part of the program is loaded and executed. Windows 95 viruses can spread by modifying this component of the PE file.

Most 32-bit Windows programs written for Windows 95 run just fine under Windows NT. However, the Boza virus is an exception. Boza detects whether or not it is running under Windows 95 or NT and refuses to execute if it is being launched from Windows NT. While Boza restricts itself in this way, there is no guarantee or reason why future viruses will do so.

In addition to the new Portable Executable file format, Windows 95 and NT also introduce several new types of executable files. However, no viruses have been constructed to infect these other types of files.

Macro Viruses

Today's word processing and spreadsheet applications provide robust macro facilities that can be used to augment and enhance the application's working environment. Many of the older applications had simple macro systems. The user could record a sequence of operations within the application. They could then tell the application to associate this sequence of operations with a specific keystroke. Later, the user could perform the same sequence of operations by hitting the specified key. This permitted the user to perform redundant or complex operations with ease.

Newer applications provide much more complex macro systems. Today's applications enable the user to write entire macro programs that run within the word processor or spreadsheet environment. These macro programs can do everything that their simple counterparts could do and more. In addition, modern applications enable these macros to be "attached" directly onto word processing and spreadsheet files. For example, you can program a special macro for a given Excel file, give this file to your friend, and then your friend can use your macro with the Excel file on their computer.

The ability to tote macros around with a data file is a very powerful feature. Unfortunately, such a facility also makes it possible to create macro viruses. Today's word processing and spreadsheet files not only contain data, clip art, and text, but they also contain executable macro programs. And where there are executable programs, viruses can flourish.

When a user loads a word processor or spreadsheet data file into an application, the application also loads any macros that are attached to the file. If one or more of the macros meet certain criteria, the application executes these macros as soon as they are loaded. Macro viruses rely on this auto-execution facility to gain control of the application's macro system as soon as an infected file is loaded. After the virus has been loaded and executed, it waits for the user to edit a new document.

The second the user edits and saves a new document, the macro virus kicks into action. The macro attaches its viral macro programs to the new document and allows the application to save the document normally. In the blink of an eye, the virus has spread to another file, doing so in a completely discrete fashion; the user is given no indication of the infection. If this new file is opened on another computer, the virus loads, is launched by the application, and finds other unsuspecting files to infect.

Finally, most computer viruses are written in *assembly language*, an arcane, machine-specific programming language. This assembly language construction limits their ability to run on many different types of computers and makes them difficult to program. Macro viruses, however, have no such constraints. Macro programming languages are well documented and easy to program.

More Types of Viruses

The following sections describe several major categories of viruses based on their behavior. These classes of viruses are singled out because their behavior and ability to infect may be affected when running under Windows NT.

Multipartite Viruses

Multipartite viruses infect boot records and program files by using both mechanisms to spread. For example, when you run an application infected with a multipartite virus, the virus activates and infects the hard disk's Master Boot Record. Then, the next time you boot the workstation, the virus activates from the MBR and starts infecting floppy disks and program files. Only a small number of computer viruses have multipartite functionality because of relative complexity involved. The common One-Half virus is an example of such a virus. One-Half also employs stealthing techniques and is polymorphic or mutating (see the following section for more information).

Stealth Viruses

Stealth viruses attempt to conceal their presence from the user. Most stealth viruses conceal themselves only while the virus is active in memory and hooked into the operating system as a memory resident program. These viruses actively intercept system requests that might reveal information about the viral infection and alter the system service output to conceal their presence.

Stealth viruses are typically classified as having size stealth capabilities, read stealth capabilities, or both. Size stealthing applies exclusively to file infecting viruses. When a virus infects a program file, the virus usually attaches a copy of itself onto the target program file. This results in the target file growing in size by the length of the virus. Because a user might notice such a difference in file size, the size stealthing virus masks the size increase. (Believe it or not, some users, especially antivirus researchers, do remember the size of certain executable files on their system.)

By examining the infected file's contents, a user can see the virus and the changes it has made to the program. This type of stealthing is somewhat like hiding during a game of hide and seek by placing a lampshade over your head. However, most users don't examine the binary contents of their program files, and if they don't notice any change in the overall computer performance or in the size of their programs, they probably won't notice the viral infection.

With read stealthing, when the operating system or another program makes a request to read an infected boot record or file, the virus intercepts the request and provides the requester with the original, uninfected contents. The Stoned.Monkey virus, for example, uses read stealthing. This read stealthing works properly under DOS, Windows 3.1, and Windows 95. If a user executes a disk editing utility to examine the MBR contents where Stoned.Monkey hides, she won't find any evidence of infection. Stoned.Monkey's memory resident handler is called any time the disk is accessed, and it checks to see whether any attempts are being made to read the MBR. If so, the virus provides a backed up copy of the original item in place of the infected copy. This stealthing can be defeated by specially written tools and antivirus programs, but goes undetected by the average disk utility.

Read stealthing also conceals viruses in program files. Usually, the read stealthing file virus possesses size stealthing capabilities as well; it would be useless for a program to hide content changes to an infected file, yet still show the increased file size. For example, the Tremor virus uses both read stealthing and size stealthing to conceal its presence in infected files.

Most stealth viruses can conceal their presence only while resident and active in the computer's memory. If they are not installed as a memory-resident program, any infection is visible. This is why most antivirus manufacturers instruct users to boot from a write-protected, uninfected floppy disk before scanning for, or repairing, virus infections.

Companion Viruses

Companion viruses only infect program files; however, they are unique because they don't attach themselves to existing program files. Instead, the companion virus infects by creating a new file and causing DOS to execute this new program rather than the original one.

Companion viruses use numerous strategies. One such virus creates a COM file with the same file name and in the same directory as an existing EXE file.

When a user types the name of a file to execute at the DOS prompt and both a COM and EXE file of the same name reside in the same directory, the DOS command interpreter (COMMAND.COM, for example) always executes the COM file and ignores the EXE file.

This type of companion virus, for example, could create a file named FORMAT.COM in the DOS directory, knowing that FORMAT.EXE is a popular and frequently executed file that also resides in the DOS directory. The average user could easily overlook the addition of a new file with such a name. In addition, some companion viruses actually conceal the file by changing its attribute to hidden.

This technique ensures that when a user attempts to execute the FORMAT program, DOS loads the companion virus rather than the original program. Finally, the companion virus runs the original FORMAT.EXE program and the user is unaware of the infection.

Viruses in Windows NT

The Windows NT operating system constitutes a paradigm shift from other Microsoft operating systems. It differs from other current PC operating systems in a number of ways, which are listed in the following:

- ■ Windows NT does not rely on a resident DOS kernel for system services.

- ■ Windows NT supports three different file systems: a FAT-based file system, the new NTFS file system, and the MAC file system (on NT servers). A new OLE file system is also under development.

- ■ Windows NT does not rely on the computer's ROM BIOS disk drivers and comes with protected-mode, NT-specific software drivers to perform all low-level disk access functions.

- ■ Windows NT automatically prevents all DOS programs executed in DOS boxes from directly writing to hard drives.

The remainder of this chapter describes how each of the major types of viruses described above function under Windows NT, given the differences between it and previous Microsoft operating systems.

The following virus classes are detailed: MBR viruses (on floppy and hard drive), PBR viruses (on floppy and hard drive), direct action file viruses, memory resident file viruses, multipartite viruses, companion viruses, macro viruses, Windows 3.1 viruses, and Windows 95 viruses. Finally, the possibility of native Windows NT viruses are discussed.

Note	Boot record viruses, Windows 3.1 viruses, and Windows 95 viruses do not function properly on non-Intel–based Windows NT installations (such as a DEC-Alpha or Power PC). Only DOS-based file viruses executed with an emulated 80×86 DOS box function properly.

Master Boot Record (MBR) Viruses under Windows NT

MBR viruses are typically acquired in two different ways. The first method involves booting off of an infected floppy disk. The second method involves running a dropper program from a DOS session that directly "drops" the virus onto the MBR of the hard drive; multipartite computer viruses sometimes attempt this type of infection.

MBR Infection by Booting Off of an Infected Floppy Disk

The Windows NT operating system is still susceptible to infection from a floppy disk. Because NT does not have control of the computer during system boot-up, booting from an infected floppy enables the virus to infect the MBR of any of the physical drives on the system using the usual techniques. This vector of infection is quite common, and we can expect to see more of this type of infection in the future.

MBR Infection by Running a Dropper Program or Multipartite Virus

Dropper programs and multipartite viruses infect the MBR of the hard drive by using BIOS or DOS services to directly write to the hard drive. Because Windows NT prevents all such writes from within an NT DOS box, this type of infection is completely prevented while NT is running.

However, if the computer in question has the ability to dual-boot to DOS or Windows 95, then the user could boot to one of these operating systems and execute the dropper program or multipartite virus normally.

Note	Although DOS-based virus dropper programs are completely neutered under Windows NT DOS boxes, native Windows NT programs can be constructed to modify the contents of the hard drive Master Boot Record.

The NT Boot-up Process with MBR Infection

After a virus is present in the MBR, future system reboots enable the virus to become memory resident in the usual fashion. In addition, if the virus contains any type of payload that is triggered during boot-up, this trigger mechanism functions just as it would under a DOS or Windows 95 system. The virus has the same control because the Windows NT operating system has not yet loaded; therefore, the virus executes as a real-mode program with full access to the entire PC. Thus, viruses such as Michelangelo and One-Half are still able to cause significant damage to Windows NT systems.

Upon boot-up, after the virus has installed itself in memory, it passes control to the original system MBR, which then transfers control to the Windows NT boot-record. This boot record then loads the Windows NT loader which loads the rest of the operating system. During this loading process, NT switches into protected mode and installs its own protected-mode disk drivers. These protected-mode drivers are used for all further disk operations; consequently, the original BIOS disk drivers and any virus that hooked into these drivers are never activated or used in any way.

Accordingly, after Windows NT starts using its own drivers, the resident MBR virus is effectively stopped in its tracks. Furthermore, unlike Windows 95, Windows NT does not support a compatibility that allows disk requests to be sent to the original real-mode disk drivers (and potentially a virus). These Windows NT characteristics have the following implications.

- MBR viruses are unable to infect other floppy disks after Windows NT has loaded.

- Under DOS and Windows 95 systems, some viruses (such as the Ripper virus) have the ability to hook into direct disk services (provided by the computer's BIOS) and maliciously alter data during disk accesses. Under Windows NT, the virus is still able to alter bytes retrieved or stored to the disk while the original BIOS disk drivers are used during boot-up. Thus, all components of the operating system that are read from disk before the protected-mode disk drivers are employed may become corrupted. However, as soon as the operating system starts using the protected mode disk drivers, the virus is disabled and can do no further damage.

- During boot-up, the One-Half virus encrypts sectors on the hard drive before it transfers control to the original Master Boot Record. On DOS, Windows 3.1, and Windows 95 systems, the One-Half virus dynamically decrypts these sectors as they are accessed by the operating system. This occurs because these operating systems rely on the original BIOS interrupt handlers to access the hard drive. However, because Windows NT cuts the virus off entirely after its protected mode drivers are loaded, all encrypted sectors are retrieved by the Windows NT disk handlers and are not dynamically decrypted by the virus's handlers. Hence, programs that access encrypted sectors retrieve the encrypted data rather than the original content.

■ Stealth boot viruses are unable to function properly after NT has loaded because the virus's resident disk handlers are never given control. This makes these viruses easy to detect but can cause other problems (see next item).

■ Stealth MBR viruses such as Stoned.Empire.Monkey (which garble the partition table in the infected MBR sector) cause infected drives to be inaccessible to Windows NT. This occurs because Windows NT reads the partition table from the MBR in order to determine what logical drives are present on the system using its protected mode disk drivers. Because the protected mode drivers are used, the Monkey virus's stealth mechanism is bypassed and the virus is unable to present the original partition table. Hence, Windows NT reads a garbled partition table and is unable to identify the logical drives on the system. Under DOS and Windows 95 systems, the active stealth capabilities of the virus enable it to provide the operating system with the original partition table information.

■ If the virus does not modify the partition table of the MBR, then Windows NT should behave normally, assuming the virus has no payloads that trigger during system boot-up.

■ On a typical DOS system, a multipartite virus would work in the following manner: The virus is present in the MBR of the hard drive. During boot-up, the virus installs itself as a memory resident handler. After DOS has loaded, every file that is accessed by the user is infected by this resident handler. In contrast, on a Windows NT system, if the MBR becomes infected with such a virus, the virus is not able to infect files because Windows NT never utilizes the virus's resident handlers. Instead, Windows NT uses its own protected mode handlers.

Partition Boot Record Viruses under Windows NT

You typically acquire Partition Boot Record viruses in one of two different ways. The first method involves booting off of an infected floppy disk. The second method involves running a dropper program from a DOS session that directly drops the virus onto the boot record of the active partition; multipartite computer viruses sometimes attempt this type of infection.

Like MBR viruses, Partition Boot Record viruses are unable to replicate under Windows NT. The PBR virus is disabled because during the boot-up process, NT switches into protected mode and installs its own protected-mode disk drivers. These protected-mode drivers are used for all further disk operations; consequently, the original BIOS disk drivers and any virus that hooked into these drivers is never activated or used in any way.

Boot Record Infection by Booting Off an Infected Floppy Disk

The Windows NT operating system is still susceptible to this type of infection. Because NT does not have control of the computer during system boot-up, booting from an infected floppy allows the virus to infect the boot record of the active partition on the system using the usual techniques. This vector of infection is quite common, and we can expect to see more of the same in the future.

Boot Record Infection by Running a Dropper Program or Multipartite Virus

Dropper programs and multipartite viruses infect the boot record of the hard drive by using BIOS or DOS services to directly write to the hard drive. Because Windows NT prevents all such writes from within an NT DOS box, this type of infection is completely prevented while NT is running.

However, if the computer in question also has the ability to boot to DOS or Windows 95, then the user could boot to one of these operating systems and execute the dropper program or multipartite virus normally.

Again, while DOS-based virus dropper programs are completely neutered under Windows NT DOS boxes, native Windows NT programs can be constructed to modify the contents of the active Partition Boot Record.

Damage Due to Boot Record Virus Infection

As described, hard drives can still become infected with boot record viruses by booting off of an infected floppy disk. Boot record viruses infect Partition Boot Records by relocating the original PBR to a new (and hopefully unused) location of the drive and then replacing the original boot record with the viral boot record. Usually, PBR viruses place the original, uninfected boot record at the end of the infected drive.

Depending on the type of file system that is being used on the Windows NT boot partition, different problems may arise. They are outlined in the following section.

Damage Due to Boot Record Virus Infection on FAT Systems

The following may occur if a FAT system is infected with a Boot Record virus:

■ If the virus places the original boot record at the end of the drive and does not take steps to protect this sector, Windows NT or another operating system may inadvertently overwrite the saved boot record. This causes the system to crash during boot-up because the virus will inevitably try to load and execute the original (corrupted) boot record. The same behavior may also occur under DOS and Windows 95. Some viruses avert this problem by marking the reserved sector as "bad" or as "used." The virus could also decrease the size of the last partition (by altering the partition table in the MBR) so that the specified sector is inaccessible to the operating system.

■ If the virus corrupts or replaces the contents of the BPB (BIOS Parameter Block) within the Partition Boot Record and relies on stealth functionality to hide these changes, Windows NT is unable to access the drive after the protected-mode disk drivers are in use. This is analogous to the Stoned.Empire.Monkey problem described earlier.

■ Standard Partition Boot Record viruses should not cause any additional problems on FAT-based, Windows NT systems. The virus is completely disabled as soon as the NT protected-mode drivers are loaded and in use.

Damage Due to Boot Record Virus Infection on NTFS Systems

During installation of a bootable NTFS partition, the Windows NT installer places an operating system loader program on the sectors immediately following the NTFS boot record. When the Windows NT Partition Boot Record is loaded and executed by the MBR during system boot-up, it immediately rereads itself and these additional boot strap sectors into memory and transfers control to them. The NTFS boot record and these additional sectors comprise a multisector boot strap program that is capable of loading and launching the bulk of the Windows NT operating system.

If a boot record virus infects the NTFS boot record, it effectively overwrites the first sector of the multisector boot strap program, causing important routines and data to be lost. Following is the sequence of events in the NTFS boot-up process with a boot record infection:

1. The computer is turned on or rebooted.

2. During the NTFS boot-up, the computer loads and executes the original MBR. The MBR boot strap routine then loads and transfers control to the viral Partition Boot Record of the active NTFS partition.

3. The virus then installs itself in memory and transfers control to the original NTFS Partition Boot Record, which is retrieved from the end of the physical drive where the virus stored it.

4. At this point, a small routine in the uninfected NTFS boot record attempts to load the entire NTFS boot strap program (comprised of what should be the original NTFS boot record *and* the following sectors). However, the first sector of the multisector boot strap program has been replaced by the viral PBR. Thus, a corrupted copy of the boot strap program is loaded and executed. This corrupted copy consists of the viral PBR followed by the remaining original boot strap sectors.

5. Executing this corrupted program results in a system crash and Windows NT fails to start up.

Most Partition Boot Record viruses cause an NTFS-based, Windows NT system to crash during boot-up. However, if the boot record virus has stealth capabilities, Windows NT might be able to properly load.

The following describes the boot-up sequence if a stealth PBR virus has infected the drive:

1. The computer is turned on or rebooted.

2. During the NTFS boot-up, the computer loads and executes the original MBR boot strap routine. The MBR boot strap routine then loads and transfers control to the *viral* Partition Boot Record of the active NTFS partition.

3. The virus then installs itself in memory and transfers control to the original NTFS Partition Boot Record boot strap routine that is retrieved from the end of the physical drive where the virus stored it.

4. At this point, the uninfected boot strap attempts to load the entire multisector NTFS boot strap program (comprised of what should be the original NTFS boot record *and* the following sectors). The virus's resident handler intercepts the load request and substitutes the original boot record for the viral boot record. It also loads the other boot strap sectors as requested.

5. Control is transferred to the multisector boot strap program and Windows NT boots normally.

Windows NT Installation with Existing Boot Record Infection

You can install Windows NT within an existing DOS/Windows 95 FAT-based partition, which gives the user the option of either booting into Windows NT or into the old DOS or Windows 95 operating system. Windows NT provides this dual-boot service by making a backup copy of the DOS/Windows 95 boot record during its installation and saving this backup copy to a file called BOOTSEC.DOS in the root directory of the DOS/Windows 95 partition. Windows NT then replaces the boot sector of the FAT-based drive with the Windows NT boot sector.

Each time the user reboots the system, the Windows NT loader asks the user which operating system they would like to start. If the user requests a boot-up into DOS or Windows 95, then the Windows NT loader loads and executes the original boot record contained in the BOOTSEC.DOS file and boots the computer into a standard DOS/Windows session.

Unfortunately, if the boot record of the DOS/Windows 95 partition is infected with a virus before Windows NT is installed, a copy of this virus is placed within the BOOTSEC.DOS file during installation. Consequently, each time the user boots the system into DOS or Windows 95, the virus gains control of the system. In addition, because the virus is not located within the boot record of the drive, it is not detected by Windows NT-unaware antivirus tools.

To fix this problem, the user must use a disk editor to locate the original DOS/Windows 95 Partition Boot Record that was saved by the virus (presumably at the end of the drive). The user must then replace the BOOTSEC.DOS file with this non-viral PBR.

MBR and Boot Record Viruses—The Bottom Line

Viruses such as Michelangelo and One-Half are capable of doing damage during the boot-up process but are completely disabled after Windows NT starts using its protected mode disk drivers. Thus, infection of floppy disks or files (in the case of a multipartite virus) are prevented in all instances (that is, in DOS boxes, and so on).

Viruses that do not save the active Partition Boot Record's BPB information or the Master Boot Record's partition table can prevent NT from booting or make certain drives inaccessible. Furthermore, all non-stealth boot record viruses (such as the extremely common Form virus) that infect bootable NTFS partitions corrupt the multisector operating system boot strap loader and cause Windows NT to crash during boot-up. When booting from an infected floppy disk, buggy virus infection mechanisms can also cause data loss under all file systems supported by NT.

DOS File Viruses under a Windows NT DOS Box

Most DOS file viruses function correctly under a Windows NT DOS box. As previously mentioned, file viruses typically come in two flavors: direct action viruses and memory resident viruses. These two types of viruses have different behaviors under Windows NT.

Direct Action File Viruses under a Windows NT DOS Box

Direct action file viruses function in exactly the same manner as they do under a standard DOS or Windows 95 system. These viruses typically use the standard DOS system services that are thoroughly emulated in Windows NT DOS boxes.

Some older or poorly written direct action viruses might employ behaviors that cause them to crash or work improperly under a Windows NT DOS box. However, such a case is the exception rather than the rule.

Memory Resident File Viruses under a Windows NT DOS Box

In most cases, memory resident file viruses are able to stay memory resident within the confines of a Windows NT DOS box. After the virus is resident within a given DOS box, it is able to infect any programs accessed or executed within that DOS box, assuming the user who launched the virus has the correct access to modify the target program.

The virus is unable to spread to other DOS boxes—each DOS box has its own protected memory space. However, nothing prevents a user from executing infected programs in several DOS boxes. Thus, several independent copies of the virus can be active and infectious at once.

Furthermore, if the virus in question has infected the command shell (that is, CMD.EXE or NDOS.COM) used in Windows NT DOS boxes, then every time the user opens a new DOS box, he automatically launches the memory resident virus into the box's memory space.

Windows NT emulates most DOS functionality within its DOS boxes, and in some ways provides more compatible support than Windows 95 DOS boxes. Memory resident viruses, which hook into the DOS system services within a DOS box, can gain control and are able to infect files any time the system services are utilized by DOS or other programs.

For example, when a user executes a DOS program on a standard DOS machine (that is, not Windows NT/95), the command shell (COMMAND.COM or NDOS.COM, for example) generates an EXECUTE PROGRAM system service request to the DOS kernel. Many viruses intercept this system service in order to infect program files as they are executed by the user. Windows NT provides the same functionality in its DOS boxes and enables viruses to intercept this system service and infect at will.

Furthermore, Windows NT enables users to launch native Windows applications directly from the DOS box's command line. Under the *NDOS* command shell, any Windows (NT/95/3.1) program that is launched from a DOS box's command line causes the *NDOS* command interpreter to generate an EXECUTE PROGRAM system service request.

Thus, if a memory resident virus were to hook into the EXECUTE system service, it could potentially infect these Windows programs as they are executed. However, the vast majority of DOS viruses are incapable of correctly infecting native Windows executable programs. If such a virus were to infect the DOS stub component of the NE/PE file, it would inadvertently overwrite and corrupt the Windows component of the program located at the end of the file.

The default command shell (CMD.EXE) that ships with Windows NT does not generate the EXECUTE system service request when Windows executables are launched from a DOS box; memory resident computer viruses are unable to infect native Windows programs launched from a CMD.EXE based NT DOS box.

Stealth File Viruses under a Windows NT DOS Box

Most memory resident, stealth file viruses function properly within Windows NT DOS boxes. However, some stealth viruses might function improperly if they use undocumented DOS functionality that is not fully supported by Windows NT DOS boxes.

However, such a stealth virus is only able to conceal its changes from programs executing within the same DOS box as the virus. For instance, if a Windows 3.1, 32-bit Windows, or DOS program running in another DOS box accesses an infected file, the virus's resident stealth handler does not activate and consequently fails to conceal the viral changes.

Companion File Viruses under a Windows NT DOS Box

Companion file viruses come in both resident and direct action varieties. These viruses should function properly under a Windows NT DOS box in most instances (refer to "Memory Resident File Viruses under a Windows NT DOS Box" and "Direct Action File Viruses under a Windows NT DOS Box" earlier in this chapter). Again, if the virus employs undocumented DOS functionality, it may not work properly inside of a Windows NT DOS box.

Companion viruses rely on the functionality of the DOS command interpreter in order to spread. This reliance may also cause some companion viruses to fail if the command interpreter used in the NT DOS box differs significantly from the standard COMMAND.COM interpreter assumed by most viruses. (The default Windows NT command interpreter has no such incompatibilities.)

Damage by File Viruses under a Windows NT DOS Box

Windows NT provides file-level access control, which prevents protected files from becoming modified by DOS-based file viruses. The access control provided by Windows NT is significantly more robust than DOS's simple read-only attribute and cannot be bypassed by DOS programs.

However, if an infected program is run by a system operator with root privileges or the Windows NT system is set up without access control, the virus can modify all files to which the operator has access.

If we assume that the typical Windows NT configuration does not employ NT's security features, then viruses are able to damage files as they do on a standard DOS system. For instance, viruses that corrupt program files unintentionally during the infection process are still able to do so under Windows NT DOS boxes. On the other hand, file viruses that attempt to trash the hard drive by using direct disk access are thwarted under Windows NT because all direct access to hard drives is prevented by Windows NT.

Although Windows NT prevents DOS programs from writing directly to hard drives, it does *not* prevent DOS programs from directly writing to floppy disks—multipartite DOS viruses launched from within a DOS box may be capable of infecting or damaging floppy disks.

Luckily, when launched in a DOS box or on a standard DOS system, most multipartite viruses attempt to infect the hard drive's MBR or Partition Boot Record in order to gain control during boot-up. Because Windows NT prevents direct hard drive writes from within a DOS box, these viruses are effectively neutered.

File Virus Infections under Windows NT

DOS-based file viruses only function properly within a DOS box under Windows NT. Under all other circumstances, these viruses fail to function correctly and are non-viral in nature.

DOS File Viruses under Windows NT—System Susceptibility During Boot-up

If one of the files responsible for Windows NT boot-up becomes infected with a DOS-based computer virus, Windows NT is likely to fail to load properly. This occurs because DOS-based viruses require the DOS kernel in order to function, and DOS is necessarily absent during Windows NT boot-up (because NT does not utilize DOS in its operation). The absence of the DOS kernel during the boot-up process, therefore, causes infected executables to crash after the infected program executes.

DOS File Viruses—The Bottom Line

Most DOS file viruses propagate under Windows NT DOS boxes as they do on standard DOS systems. The built-in Windows NT file and directory protection prevents infection of protected files; however, the system must be explicitly configured to provide this protection. Unfortunately, many users may be unaware of, or inconvenienced by, this protection and disable it.

Multipartite viruses (viruses that infect files and boot sectors) are no longer able to infect hard drive boot records or master boot records from within DOS boxes. If the virus relies on this behavior for propagation, it will be neutered by Windows NT's direct-disk access restrictions. However, multipartite file viruses are still able to infect floppy disk boot records if they are so inclined (although this behavior is rare).

DOS file viruses only function within DOS boxes. Although it is possible for native Windows NT system files to become infected (by direct-action viruses search for files all over the hard drive), the infected system files are likely to fail to function properly and cause the machine to crash during Windows NT boot-up.

If a resident DOS file virus is launched from within a DOS box, only files referenced from within the infected DOS box can potentially become infected. Thus, any Windows NT antivirus product that executes outside of a DOS box (such as a 32-bit Windows app) can safely scan the computer without the possibility of infecting clean files; memory scanning is not necessary to properly detect and repair virus infections.

Windows 3.1 Viruses under Windows NT

Most of the native Windows 3.1 viruses function under Windows NT as they do under Windows 3.1 because Windows NT was designed to faithfully execute Windows 3.1 programs.

At least one Windows 3.1 virus uses DPMI (DOS Protected Mode Interface) in order to hook into the standard Windows system services and establish itself as a memory resident Windows TSR. The Ph33r virus hooks into the Windows 3.1 EXECUTE PROGRAM system service and is notified every time a Windows 3.1 program is executed by the user or another Windows 3.1 process. Upon notification, the Ph33r virus can infect the Windows 3.1 executable file before it is executed.

Viruses that hook into these services also function under Windows NT as they do under Windows 3.1. However, under Windows NT, the Windows 3.1 TSR virus previously described is only notified about the execution of standard Windows 3.1 executables. For instance, if a user launches a native 32-bit Windows NT/95 application, the Windows 3.1 subsystem under Windows NT (and any Windows 3.1 TSRs hooked into its system services) is not made aware of the 32-bit program's execution. Consequently, only Windows 3.1 executables launched on the Windows NT system are susceptible to infection or corruption by traditional, resident Windows 3.1 viruses.

Furthermore, Windows NT enables the user to specify whether each Windows 3.1 application is launched in either a common Windows 3.1 memory area or in its own separate memory area. This functionality is provided so that users can prevent misbehaving Windows 3.1 applications from interfering with each other. If the user loads an infected Windows 3.1 application in its own memory area, then the resident virus does not receive notification of system service requests (such as EXECUTE PROGRAM requests) from other Windows 3.1 applications. Such a virus is effectively neutered.

Direct action Windows 3.1 viruses spread normally in most cases; Windows NT faithfully emulates all the standard Windows 3.1 services that may be used to locate and modify programs.

Macro Viruses under Windows NT

All macro viruses written for applications that run on Windows 3.1 or Windows 95 function correctly under Windows NT if the host application works correctly under Windows NT. For example, because Word for Windows version 6.0⁺ works both on Windows 95 and Windows NT, the Concept virus works correctly under both platforms as well.

The file-level protection provided by Windows NT can be used to prevent unauthorized use of documents (limiting potential infection); however, these macro viruses can still be spread through electronic mail or publicly accessible files on a network.

Macro viruses continue to propagate under Windows NT systems. Given the necessity of information-sharing in the enterprise environment, the macro viruses may surpass their file and boot-record cousins as the most common viral threat.

Native Windows NT Viruses

Windows NT presents a much greater challenge to virus writers. First, the basic Windows NT operating system requires at least 12 MB of conventional RAM, a high-speed microprocessor, and tens of megabytes of hard drive space. Most currently sold machines are not powerful enough to provide a bare-bones Windows NT setup for software development. Consequently, virus writers may not be able to afford the appropriate hardware to develop complex, native Windows NT viruses.

Unfortunately, these same virus writers might be able to afford a Windows 95-based computer. Such a computer can also be used to develop simple, 32-bit Windows viruses capable of infecting both Windows 95 and Windows NT.

In addition to the Windows NT hardware requirements, the native Windows NT/95 executable file formats are also more complex than those found in DOS. Windows 3.1 also employs similar executable file formats that might account for the much smaller number of native Windows viruses. Furthermore, far less documentation is available on the 32-bit file formats, requiring virus writers to spend time reverse engineering their file structure.

Finally, the Windows 3.1 architecture permits Windows applications to call standard DOS system services directly, as if they were DOS applications. This permits virus writers with only a superficial understanding of the Windows 3.1 operating system to create viruses by using standard DOS-based virus algorithms.

The Windows NT and Windows 95 operating systems do not allow 32-bit applications to use the DOS system services, although Windows 3.1 programs running in these environments are allowed to use these services. Therefore, virus writers have to gain a fairly detailed understanding of the Windows 32-bit API in order to create native Windows NT/95 viruses.

This probably reduces the number of native Windows NT/95 viruses encountered in the short term. However, as more detailed documentation is published in popular books and magazines, and as virus authors freely distribute their creations, native 32-bit Windows 95 and NT viruses will undoubtedly increase in number.

Summary of Viruses under NT

The Windows NT operating system is definitely susceptible to DOS-based computer viruses. In many instances, Windows NT prevents viruses from spreading as they do under DOS or Windows 95; however, these same viruses can still intentionally or unintentionally cause significant damage to the Windows NT operating system, its programs, and its data. As previously described, DOS-based viruses can be split into two categories: boot record viruses and file viruses.

The Windows NT architecture severely limits the functionality of boot viruses, should the MBR or boot record of the hard drive become infected. If Windows NT *is* able to start up on an infected system, the infecting boot virus is never activated because NT's protected mode disk drivers are used instead of the viral disk drivers. Thus, standard boot viruses are unable to propagate under the Windows NT operating system. Unfortunately, these viruses can still cause serious damage to NT systems, as shown in the following list:

- Boot viruses can affect the boot-up process, causing Windows NT to crash.

- They can inadvertently damage data within the Windows NT partition.

- Boot viruses can make certain drives inaccessible from within Windows NT.

- They can still trigger and intentionally cause damage during the boot-up process, before Windows NT gains control of the computer.

In addition, if Windows NT is installed on top of a DOS or Windows 95 partition, it provides the user with a special mechanism for dual booting between the Windows NT and DOS/Windows 95. In order to provide this dual boot functionality, Windows NT maintains a copy of the original DOS/Windows 95 boot record (present on the drive before Windows NT installation) and uses this copy in the DOS/Windows 95 boot-up process.

Unfortunately, if the boot record of the DOS/Windows 95 partition is infected before Windows NT installation, the copy of the boot record maintained by Windows NT also contains this infection. Furthermore, the copy of the boot record is stored within a file (not in the traditional boot area of the hard drive); therefore, non-Windows NT-aware antivirus tools are unable to detect and repair this infection, leaving the system vulnerable to any boot record virus present on the system at the time Windows NT is installed.

As Windows 95 and Windows NT become the predominant operating systems on PCs, you can expect to see a reduction in the number of boot virus infections because these operating systems subvert their primary method of infection. However, for the time being, these viruses can still cause serious damage to Windows NT systems, and traditional tools might not be able to recover from infection.

Most of the DOS-based and Windows 3.1-based file viruses function properly under Windows NT. Under the NTFS file system, Windows NT enables the user to protect files on a per-file or per-directory basis; however, this security feature might have little effect on DOS/Windows 3.1-based file viruses. Specifically, the following holes are still open to viruses under Windows NT:

- FAT-based partitions cannot be safeguarded by this type of protection.

- The typical end-user has no reason to enable this protection.

- A virus executed in a user's account can still infect all files owned by that user, even though those files may be protected and inaccessible to other users of the Windows NT system.

Currently, DOS/Windows 3.1 file viruses are unable to infect native Windows NT executable files, although they may unknowingly do so and cause damage. In addition, a hybrid file virus can be written to infect both DOS and 32-bit Windows executable files. In fact, this basic concept has already been observed: the recently released Ph33r virus has the ability to infect both DOS and Windows 3.1 executable files.

The new macro viruses also function properly under Windows NT. These viruses do not rely on the underlying operating system to propagate and therefore have no difficulty infecting any Windows NT machine that supports Win Word or other macro-capable products.

Finally, although no native Windows NT viruses exist today, their future appearance is unquestioned. Even though Windows NT provides a significant amount of memory and file protection, native VDD-based (Virtual Device Driver) viruses will have the ability to modify memory, infect or damage files, and directly access both hard drives and floppy disks. They will be able to intercept any system service and infect programs or floppy disks at will. In short, they will have the same capabilities as their DOS cousins on an unprotected DOS machine.

Preventative Measures

The following list details a number of simple precautions you can take to reduce your chances of getting a virus under Windows NT. Following each precaution are one or more scenarios that can be averted by using the described technique. Finally, each precaution is also accompanied by a resolution section that helps simplify the recovery effort if your computer contracts a virus.

1. Before installing Windows NT, scan your computer with an NCSA-certified antivirus program (see table 3.2).

Table 3.2
NCSA-Certified Antivirus Programs

Product	Company	URL
Norton Antivirus for Windows NT	Symantec	www.symantec.com
VirusScan for Windows NT	McAfee	www.mcafee.com
InocuLAN for Windows NT	Cheyenne	www.cheyenne.com

■ **Scenario.** Your computer currently has a DOS or Windows 95 partition with an infected Partition Boot Record. You install Windows NT on your DOS/Windows 95 partition and configure it to allow dual boot into either operating system.

■ **Result.** During installation, Windows NT places the original (infected) DOS/ Windows 95 Partition Boot Record into the BOOTSEC.DOS file in the root directory of the partition. After the boot record has been placed in this file, the virus has a haven where it can infect disks under DOS/Windows 95. Because antivirus programs look for boot viruses within boot records and not files, the virus is not detected after installation.

■ **Resolution.** Scanning the drive before Windows NT installation prevents this scenario from occurring. If such a scan is not performed before installation, the BOOTSEC.DOS file can be fixed manually by using a disk editor. Alternatively, uninstall Windows NT, use an antivirus program to remove the virus from the PBR, and then reinstall Windows NT.

2.　Configure your computer (in the CMOS setup) such that it boots from the hard drive, *not* from floppy disks. In addition, scan all floppy disks with an antivirus program.

■ **Scenario.** You inadvertently leave an infected floppy disk in drive A and later reboot your computer.

■ **Result 1.** The computer attempts to boot from the floppy disk, infecting your hard drive with a PBR or MBR virus. If a virus such as the Stoned.Empire. Monkey virus infects your hard drive's MBR, Windows NT is unable to access the drive partition table and fails to boot.

■ **Result 2.** If you have a bootable NTFS partition, a PBR virus (such as the Form virus) causes Windows NT to crash during boot-up. This occurs because during the infection of the PBR, the virus overwrites the PBR with its own viral code, corrupting the first sector of the multisector NT boot strap program.

■ **Result 3.** Booting off of an infected Michelangelo disk causes the Michelangelo virus to infect your hard drive MBR. (The Michelangelo virus is known for its destructive payload that activates on March 6; the virus writes garbage bytes over the first section of the hard drive.) Even though Windows NT fully prevents the Michelangelo virus from replicating after it has infected the hard drive, the Michelangelo virus is fully able to corrupt the contents of the hard drive *before* Windows NT has had a chance to load during boot-up.

■ **Resolution.** Changing the CMOS settings of your computer prevents virtually all infection by boot record viruses. If such configuration is not possible, results 1 and 2 can be fixed with an antivirus program. The destructive nature of result 3 can only be fixed by reformatting and restoring critical files from backup.

3.　Make sure to create Windows NT Emergency Disks when installing Windows NT. If you have not created emergency disks, use the RDISK.EXE program found in the WindowsNT\System32 directory to create these disks. Keep these disks updated any time you make changes to your system configuration.

■ **Scenario.** You inadvertently boot from an infected floppy disk, infecting your hard drive with a PBR or MBR virus.

■ **Result.** Windows NT subsequently fails to boot. You are not able to access any of your files on NTFS partitions. Files on DOS/Windows 95 partitions might be accessible from these operating systems.

■ **Resolution.** Use your emergency disks to remove the virus infection. Because of inadvertent virus corruption of Windows NT boot areas, these emergency disks might provide the *only* means to fix some infections.

Note   The One-Half virus is a multipartite, "in-the-wild" virus that infects the MBR of hard drives. Each time the user reboots or resets the computer, the virus gains control during the boot process and encrypts two additional cylinders of the hard drive.

Although the Windows NT Emergency Disk can remove the virus from the Master Boot Record, it is unable to decrypt those sectors of the hard drive that the virus has already garbled. Therefore, you should always scan your computer with an antivirus program before using any generic emergency tools. An updated antivirus program can identify the virus strain exactly and take the appropriate steps to remove the virus and undo all reversible virus-specific damage.

4. Configure your Windows NTFS partitions so they employ file and directory level protection for critical files.

■ **Scenario.** The user executes a file-infecting virus under a Windows NT DOS box.

■ **Result.** The virus infects or corrupts critical system files and other executable files. Important data might also be inadvertently corrupted by the virus.

■ **Resolution.** All protected files and directories are immune to damage by viruses running under DOS boxes. Use an antivirus program to detect and remove virus infections from unprotected files.

5. Use an on-access antivirus scanner to protect yourself against macro and other viruses. The on-access scanner runs in the background and constantly searches for viruses each time you access files and disks. (All three products listed in table 3.2 provide on-access scanning.)

■ **Scenario.** You receive an e-mail that contains an infected document file or executable file as an attachment.

■ **Result.** When the attachment is viewed or executed, the virus can gain control and attempt to replicate or damage the computer.

■ **Resolution.** If you are using an on-access scanner, the scanner immediately detects the virus as the file is viewed or executed. If you are not using an on-access scanner, employ a standard on-demand scanner to scan all incoming files and disks. All e-mail attachments should be saved to disk and scanned before being used.

Conclusion

Windows NT 4 is less susceptible to viruses than MS-DOS, Windows 3.1, or Windows 95, but Windows NT is by no means immune from attack. The droves of emerging macro viruses are able to spread under Windows NT just as on other operating systems. In addition, boot viruses, while unable to spread, can still cause significant damage to Windows NT volumes. Dual-boot systems are particularly vulnerable, but users with single-boot Windows NT implementations should also take precautions. This chapter discussed some of the basic virus classes and described how they work within Windows NT. The final section, "Preventative Measures," outlined some recommendations for how you can protect your system.

Security and the Registry

The Windows NT Registry is the central repository (database) for the entire operating system. The Registry contains hardware configuration data, application configuration data, service and device driver configuration data, and network protocol and adapter card settings.

The Registry under Windows NT also takes the place of many individual files that exist under Windows 3.x or Windows 95. Such files include AUTOEXEC.BAT, CONFIG.SYS, WIN.INI, SYSTEM.INI, and PROTOCOL.INI.

The Registry physically exists in the %SystemRoot%\ System32\Config directory as a collection of individual files known as hives. The Registry appears, however, as a single cohesive unit when viewed with either regedit.exe or regedt32.exe.

Regedt32.exe enables you to set access permissions, audit, and take ownership of Registry keys or hives. Regedit.exe, however, has more robust searching capabilities for quick Registry searching and editing. Other programs included in Windows NT enable you to edit very specific portions of the Registry. For example, System Policy Editor enables you to edit certain Windows NT configuration settings such as Automatic Logon, Enabling the Logon banner at startup, and enabling or disabling the Shutdown button in the Windows NT Logon dialog box.

The Registry files themselves are locked by Windows NT while the system is running. You cannot open the files (locally or remotely), nor can you rename or delete the files. Therefore, the Registry itself is fairly secure. However, users may still remove hives in user profiles that are not currently loaded. With an NTFS file system, you can prevent users from removing these hives by restricting access for the Everyone group to Read or No Access for the entire %SystemRoot%\System32\Config directory.

Note   You should only change access permissions for user profile hives because the permissions for the other hives are maintained automatically by the system and should not be altered manually.

Five Effective Policies for Maintaining Registry Security

To maintain a secure Registry, administrators must utilize effective security policies. This section discusses five measures that can help administrators meet their security needs.

Installing Windows NT on an NTFS Volume

When setting up a Windows NT server, restricting access to the files that comprise the Registry is extremely important. One of the most effective ways to restrict access to these files is to install Windows NT, and consequently the Registry, on an NTFS volume.

While running Windows NT, the Registry files cannot be manually read, modified, renamed, or deleted, regardless of the host volume type (FAT or NTFS). However, if the Registry files are stored on a FAT-based volume, a user can easily boot from a DOS floppy disk and edit or modify these files by using readily available DOS tools. In addition, given the lack of file protection on FAT volumes, a user might inadvertently or deliberately delete one or more Registry files.

Configuring Your PC's CMOS

As previously mentioned, the easiest way to access the contents of a computer is to boot from a standard DOS floppy disk and then use disk editing tools to examine or modify the contents of the hard drive. Luckily, such an attack can be easily prevented on most PCs.

In order to prevent unauthorized access to your machine via floppy disk, change the computer's CMOS configuration so the computer cannot boot from floppy disks. This option is standard on today's PCs and can prevent a host of problems (including infection by boot record viruses). After disabling floppy boot-up, you should password protect the CMOS configuration. This prevents attackers from restoring the original CMOS configuration and re-enabling floppy boot-up. Should you have a hard disk failure, or another system problem, and you need to boot from a floppy disk, you can re-enable the floppy boot-up capability by going back into the CMOS configuration.

Installing a Single Operating System on the Windows NT Machine

By installing a single operating system on the Windows NT machine, users cannot boot to an alternate operating system and examine or modify restricted information. When multiple operating systems are installed on the same machine, the machine becomes more vulnerable and the possibility that the information contained in the other operating system's area could be read, modified, or deleted increases significantly.

Restricting Access to All Windows NT Installation Files

In some instances, keeping a copy of the Windows NT installation CD on the hard drive may be convenient. If these files are present on the drive, they should be restricted from non-administrator personnel.

If no copy of the installation CD is kept on the hard drive, a user can install a second copy of Windows NT on the computer in a different Windows directory. This new Windows installation, by default, would have none of the original registry security restrictions supported by the first NT installation. It would, however, still retain the NTFS file permissions. The user can then dual-boot into the second instance of Windows NT and gain access to any and all files present on the machine, including the original Registry, as the user is an administrator for the second instance of Windows NT.

Configuring Windows NT to Use a Zero-Second Start-Up Menu Delay

If you do intend to run multiple operating systems on your Windows NT machine, but do not want casual users to access these other operating systems, set the time-out in the NT boot menu to zero seconds. This forces users to boot into Windows NT and also prevents them from launching NT with non-standard configurations. This setting also prevents users from accessing the Registry contents by booting into an alternate operating system where security may not be enforced.

Limiting Access to the Registry

One of the most important ways to protect the Registry is to assign Administrator access only to those who absolutely need it. Also, make sure you only put regedit.exe and regedt32.exe on workstations that are to be used in remote Registry administration. Typically, you only need regedit.exe or regedt32.exe on a Server or Domain Controller or on the administrator's workstation. You may also put access restrictions on regedit.exe and regedt32.exe to prevent users from starting either of these programs. You must first have Windows NT installed on an NTFS partition, however. You can set Everyone to Read and Administrators to Full Control; this permits only Administrators to execute the program (see fig. 4.1).

Figure 4.1

Edit file access permissions by using the File Permissions dialog box.

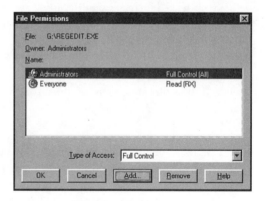

You can also use the System Policy Editor to configure your system to not permit any Registry editing tools, but doing this overrides the administrator being able to use regedit.exe or regedt32.exe. You may also specify a listing of executables that are authorized to run on the system, which prevents third-party tools, or other editing tools, from accessing the Registry.

Backing Up and Restoring the Registry

The single most important thing you can do to protect the Registry is to back up the Registry and pertinent system files on a regular basis. You can do this by running the Repair Disk Utility (RDISK.EXE), as shown in figure 4.2, or the Windows NT Backup Utility (BACKUP.EXE). You may also back up the Registry files with your favorite third-party backup utility for Windows NT 4, as long as you have Backup privileges.

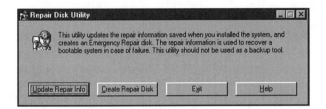

Figure 4.2

By using Windows NT's Repair Disk Utility dialog box, you can create an Emergency Repair disk.

The Emergency Repair disk is not a bootable disk, but is merely for restoring vital system information in the event of loss or corruption. You have to run the Windows NT 4 setup program to actually restore the information contained on the rescue disk.

To manually save specific hives or Registry keys, you may select the Export Registry File option from regedit.exe (see fig. 4.3).

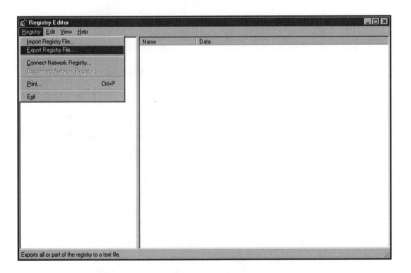

Figure 4.3

Save a registry file by using regedit.exe.

You may also use the Save Key or Save Subtree As options from regedt32.exe (see fig. 4.4).

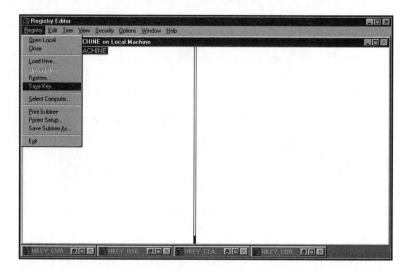

The Save Key option saves the information contained in a Registry key and in all its subkeys as a file. A file created by using Save Key can be loaded into the Registry (with Load Hive) or can be restored (with Restore). To use the Save Key command, you must have Backup privileges.

Note   On the FAT file system, the saved file name cannot have an extension.

The Save Subtree As option saves the contents of the currently selected key as a text file, including all subkeys and value entries for that key.

To import a saved file back into the Registry, select Import Registry File from regedit.exe, or Load Hive from regedt32.exe, and give the path to the saved Registry file you want to restore.

Remote Registry Editing

Today's business environment relies heavily on networking many PCs. Unfortunately, such networking can often cause security holes. This is one reason for restricting access to the Windows NT 4 Registry on any and all Windows NT machines across the network. In order for an administrator to view or modify a remote Registry, she needs to know the user's computer name. Select the Connect option from the Registry menu. After the Connect Network Registry dialog box appears, enter the machine name you want to connect to (see fig. 4.5). Setting security via the Registry, therefore, is extremely easy for an administrator on any Windows NT Server or Workstation located almost anywhere on the network. In fact, the administrator can even configure machines that are off-site and connected over RAS; however, such machines must be connected at the time of configuration.

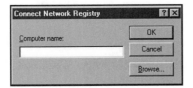

Figure 4.5

Connect to a remote registry through the Connect Network Registry dialog box.

After the Registry is loaded, you can edit just as you would if you were editing your local Registry (see fig. 4.6).

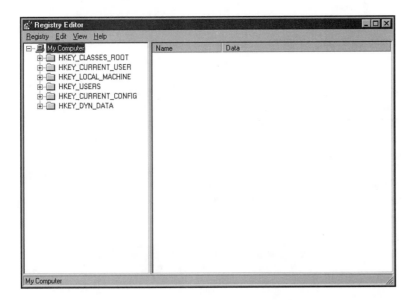

Figure 4.6

Windows NT 4 Registry Editor with registry loaded.

After the remote Registry is loaded, you can then restrict access on particular Registry keys.

In addition, installing software on a network of which an administrator or MIS department is not aware can cause many problems. The most difficult issues to resolve stem from non-standard software and unusual use of the network. Installation of non-standard software could potentially introduce viruses into the individual workstation and the entire network. Controlling the Registry—or disabling Registry editing with System Policy Editor—can help eliminate many of these security issues.

User Profiles and the Registry

A helpful tool for securing the network from most internal problems is the System Policy Editor. The System Policy Editor is broken into two parts: Default Computer and Default User. This tool sets local and network permissions for users, the use of their computers, and how they can view, browse, and connect to resources on the network (see fig. 4.7).

Figure 4.7

You can edit the system policy by using the System Policy Editor.

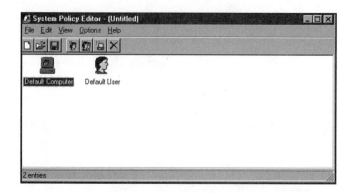

Default User settings enable an administrator to set a variety of restrictions on the user. Display options such as resolution settings, color scheme, screen savers, wallpaper, setting custom desktop icons, and a custom Start Menu and Network Neighborhood can be easily configured. The administrator can hide network drive connections in My Computer and set limitations to users' desktops. He can also disable the Run command and all execution of DOS programs. The most important feature with respect to Registry security is the capability to disable Registry editing tools.

For security reasons, Registry editing should be disabled while policies are being added or modified. Checking the Disable Registry editing tools under System/Restrictions in the Default User Properties dialog box is easiest (see fig. 4.8).

Figure 4.8

Editing the default user policy.

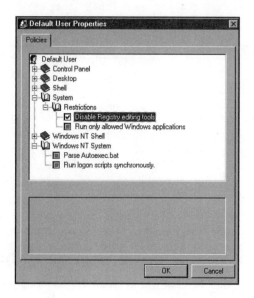

The System Policy Editor's Default Computer settings enable the administrator to control user policy updates, network connections, and RAS connection settings; these settings can be used to limit external access to your intranet. The administrator can also use this tool to gain access to hidden file shares on various users' hard drives.

In addition, administrators can disable users' ability to browse network resources such as printers and network volumes. The administrator can also configure Windows NT 4 to delete cached user profiles after the user logs out. This prevents subsequent users from viewing data used during a previous session.

Using all options is probably more security than your network needs. You should outline the details of the security needed before implementation.

Security restrictions can be configured for individual users as well as for groups of users. Group policies are typically used on large networks. For example, you might put all of MIS in one group, created in User Manager, called MIS. An administrator could also establish groups for marketing, accounting, and so on. When group policies are implemented and a particular user of a group needs special changes to her policy, an individual policy can be created that overrides the group policy (see fig. 4.9).

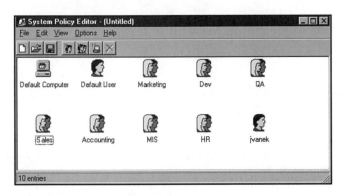

Figure 4.9

Create multiple user and group policies with System Policy Editor.

Again, all these options are stored in the Registry, but editing this information manually is not recommended.

Roaming user profiles are an excellent way to have several user folders follow the user from computer to computer. The Start menu, desktop, personal, Application data, favorites, recent documents, Sendto, and templates folders are stored remotely so a user can log on to any one of the connected workstations and work productively. When a user logs on, the folders are downloaded from their remote location. When logging off the network, all new data and program information is uploaded back to the Primary Domain Controller for synchronization.

One technique that can be used in this type of environment is enabling the deletion of the cached copies of user profiles. Use the System Policy Editor and select Delete cached copies of roaming profiles under the Default Computer settings. This ensures that other users cannot gain access to files that previous users left on the computer (see fig. 4.10). In addition, this forces the Domain Controller to properly authenticate a user before permitting access to any network resources.

Figure 4.10

Editing the default computer policy.

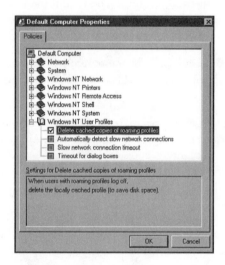

Setting Access Permissions on Registry Keys

You may assign access permissions on a per-key or per-hive basis. You may also assign access rights to Registry keys regardless of the file system of the partition where the Registry files are stored. Figure 4.11 shows the default permissions for the \\HKEY_LOCAL_MACHINE \SOFTWARE Registry hive.

Figure 4.11

Set access permissions on registry subkeys with the Special Access dialog box.

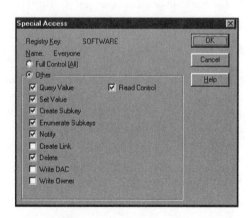

The rights you can assign to each Registry key are as follows:

- **Query Value.** Right to read a value entry from a key

- **Set Value.** Right to set value entries in a key

- **Create Subkey.** Right to create subkeys on a selected key

- **Enumerate Subkeys.** Right to identify the subkeys of a key

- **Notify.** Right to audit notification events from a key in the Registry

- **Create Link.** Right to create a symbolic link in a particular key

- **Delete.** Right to delete the selected key

- **Write DAC.** Right to write a discretionary ACL (Access Control List) to a key

- **Write Owner.** Right to take ownership of a key

- **Read Control.** Right to gain access to the security information on the selected key

Keep in mind that applications that run during normal system operation are launched in the context of the user who is currently logged in (unless a Windows NT Service launches the application). Therefore, you must be careful not to limit the access to certain Registry keys too much. For example, if a member of the Users group runs Microsoft Word, and the access permissions for \\HKEY_LOCAL_MACHINE\SOFTWARE have been limited to Read or No Access for Users, then Word will either be unable to start or will be unable to save some of its configuration data. You should, therefore, only restrict problematic users from specific Registry keys that you suspect are under attack, or unwantedly viewed or changed.

If you change permissions on a Registry key, you should also enable auditing for that key for failed access attempts. Auditing helps determine which applications have problems accessing the Registry under the new access permissions. For more information about auditing the Registry, please see the section titled "Auditing the Registry."

Note   You should also make sure you back up the Registry before making any changes.

After you change any permissions, you should log on in a variety of user and administrative accounts and test the system to make sure the new access permissions do not interfere with the system or its applications.

The following list reflects the major Registry hives and some subkeys and the default access permissions assigned to each.

Registry Hierarchy
\\HKEY_LOCAL_MACHINE

Administrators—Full Control

Everyone—Read

SYSTEM—Full Control

\HARDWARE

Administrators—Full Control

Everyone—Read

SYSTEM—Full Control

\SAM—Security Account Manager (This is an alias to the \SECURITY\SAM key.)

Administrators—Full Control

Everyone—Read

SYSTEM—Full Control

\SECURITY—Contains Local Security Policy

Administrators—Special Access:

Write DAC

Read Control

SYSTEM—Full Control

\SOFTWARE

Administrators—Full Control

CREATOR OWNER—Full Control

Everyone—Special Access:

Query Value

Set Value

Create Subkey

Enumerate Subkeys

Notify

Delete

Read Control

SYSTEM—Full Control

\Microsoft

Administrators—Full Control

CREATOR OWNER—Full Control

Everyone—Special Access:

Query Value

Set Value

Create Subkey

Enumerate Subkeys

Notify

Delete

Read Control

SYSTEM—Full Control

\Windows

Administrators—Full Control

Everyone—Full Control

SYSTEM—Full Control

\Windows NT

Administrators—Full Control

CREATOR OWNER—Full Control

Everyone—Read

Power Users—Special Access:

Query Value

Set Value

Create Subkey

Enumerate Subkeys

Notify

continues

continued

        Delete

        Read Control

    SYSTEM—Full Control

\SYSTEM

    Administrators—Special Access:

        Query Value

        Set Value

        Create Subkey

        Enumerate Subkeys

        Notify

        Delete

        Read Control

        Everyone—Read

    SYSTEM—Full Control

\CurrentControlSet

    Administrators—Full Control

    CREATOR OWNER—Full Control

    Everyone—Read

    SYSTEM—Full Control

\Control

    Administrators—Full Control

    CREATOR OWNER—Full Control

    Everyone—Read

    SYSTEM—Full Control

\Services

    Administrators—Full Control

    CREATOR OWNER—Full Control

Everyone—Read

SYSTEM—Full Control

\\HKEY_CURRENT_USER

Administrators—Full Control

%USERNAME%—Full Control (The currently logged in user always has Full Access to his/her own subkeys.)

SYSTEM—Full Control

\\HKEY_USERS

Administrators—Full Control

%USERNAME%—Read (except for your own user entry, which has Full Control)

SYSTEM—Full Control

\\HKEY_CLASSES_ROOT (This is an alias to \SOFTWARE\Classes key.)

Administrators—Full Control

CREATOR OWNER—Full Control

Everyone—Special Access:

Query Value

Set Value

Create Subkey

Enumerate Subkeys

Notify

Delete

Read Control

SYSTEM—Full Control

\\HKEY_CURRENT_CONFIG

Administrators—Full Control

CREATOR OWNER—Full Control

Everyone—Read

SYSTEM—Full Control

continues

continued

\Software

Administrators—Full Control

CREATOR OWNER—Full Control

Everyone—Special Access:

- Query Value

- Set Value

- Create Subkey

- Enumerate Subkeys

- Notify

- Delete

- Read Control

SYSTEM—Full Control

\System

Administrators—Special Access:

- Query Value

- Set Value

- Create Subkey

- Enumerate Subkeys

- Notify

- Delete

- Read Control

Everyone—Read

SYSTEM—Full Control

\CurrentControl

Administrators —Full Control

CREATOR OWNER—Full Control

Everyone—Read

SYSTEM—Full Control

Auditing the Registry

Occasionally an administrator might want to find which users or applications are using or modifying one or more of the Registry keys. This knowledge can be useful in rooting out a would-be attacker or determining why an application is malfunctioning. Consequently, Windows NT 4 provides powerful Registry auditing capabilities. Specifically, it enables the administrator to log up to eight different types of access to an arbitrary set of Registry keys.

The Registry auditing facility can be configured to log only failed key accesses or successful key accesses. Although both types of logging functionality are available, it usually is a good idea to restrict key auditing to log only failed attempts. Restricting key auditing reduces the volume of log entries because untold numbers of requests to access the various Registry keys are made during the typical Windows session. Administrators can choose to audit the following events:

- **Query of a value.** A log entry is added when a user, an application, or the operating system opens a key with the intent of querying a sub-value.

- **Modification of a value.** The audit system creates a log entry any time a key is opened in order to modify one of its values.

- **Creation of a subkey or value.** A log entry is added when a key is opened with the intent of creating a new sub-value.

- **Enumeration of subkeys.** The audit system logs any attempt to open a key in order to enumerate its subkeys.

- **Notification of key changes.** Windows NT 4 applications can request notification if a key or any of its subkeys are modified. Windows NT 4 can be configured to log the opening of keys when such notification is requested.

- **Creation of a symbolic link from one key to another.** Registry keys can be symbolically linked to each other. The audit system can be configured to log when keys are opened for symbolic linking.

- **Deletion of a key.** The audit system can be configured to log all Registry key deletions.

- **Modification of the DAC (Discretionary Access Control List).** Windows NT 4 enables administrators to restrict access to a given key to an arbitrary list of users. NT can be configured to log any changes to this access list for a specified key.

- **Determination of ownership.** Windows NT can be configured to log all requests to determine ownership of a given key.

In order to configure Registry auditing, the operator must be logged on as a member of the Administrators group for the particular computer that is to be audited. All auditing policies are enforced on a per-computer basis; therefore, the administrator must repeat the following steps to enable Registry auditing for each computer in question:

1. Turn on auditing within the User Manager or User Manager for Domains. In the User Manager, the administrator must configure Windows NT 4 to perform auditing on File and Object Access. This can be accomplished by choosing Audit from the Policies menu. The administrator can configure auditing for both successful and failed access attempts (see fig. 4.12).

Note   If auditing is configured for successful Registry operations, the event log may be filled with large numbers of irrelevant entries.

Figure 4.12

Turn on auditing of File and Object Access through the Audit Policy dialog box.

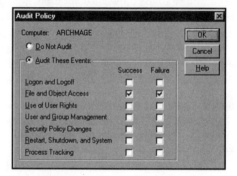

2. Use the Auditing command in the Registry editor to specify the users and groups whose activities are to be audited. The administrator can assign different auditing lists on a per-key basis. To configure a specific Registry key, select the desired key in the Registry Editor and then choose Auditing from the Security menu. Finally, complete the dialog box (see fig. 4.13).

Figure 4.13

You can enable auditing of particular registry subkeys.

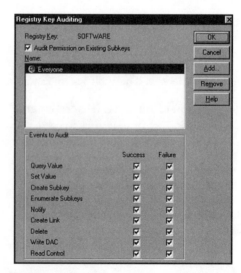

In order to view the Audit Log, launch the Windows NT 4 Event Viewer, which is located in the Administrative Tools program group, and select the desired computer. Then choose the Security command from the Log menu.

Enabling Auditing of Registry Subkeys

Auditing a Registry key is appropriate in several situations. First, auditing can be useful when monitoring an untrusted user or application. If the administrator suspects a user of trying to modify a certain keys' values in the Registry, the administrator can audit all accesses to the key and its contents.

In addition, auditing access to Registry keys can be used to detect misbehaving applications that may be erroneously or maliciously altering Registry items. You may do this by configuring Windows NT 4 to monitor both successful and failed accesses to the key in question. Alternatively, one could first restrict access to the specific key (via regedt32.exe) and then configure the system to audit only failed access attempts on the key and its contents.

Registry key auditing can also be useful if the administrator has added a new key or key value and wants to see what applications are attempting to access or update its contents. You can use Registry key auditing to quickly determine what applications or components of Windows NT 4 are affected by the addition or change of the key in question (see fig. 4.14).

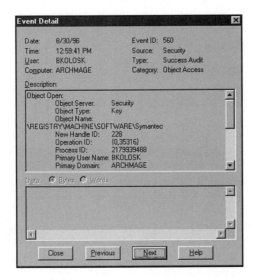

Figure 4.14

The Event Detail dialog box enables you to view security event log details.

In the Description window in the Event Detail dialog box, you can see which key is being accessed, by which user, and to which domain the user belongs. You can also see the type of access requested for each Registry key (see fig. 4.15).

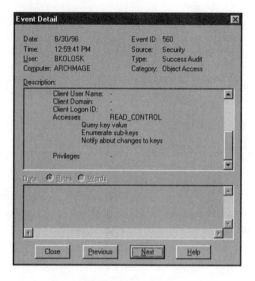

Figure 4.15

*View Registry key access
details in the Event Detail
dialog box.*

Again, you should use Registry key auditing when updating the permission on a specific key. Applications or the operating system itself may need to have access to a key; therefore, changing the key's permission can have a large effect on the overall operation of the computer.

After changing Registry key permissions, use the User Manager to enable Registry key auditing. The administrator should then indicate that he wants to track failed attempts for File and Object Access. Finally, the administrator should make sure that the modified key has auditing enabled in the Registry Editor.

Registry Keys and System Security

As mentioned earlier, the Registry is central to the security of Windows NT 4. All persistent security information for the system is stored within this secure, hierarchical database. Only system-wide, global security parameters are stored in the Registry. Security parameters for other persistent objects (such as folders and files) are stored with the objects as an attribute and are governed by what the particular file system in use supports.

As one of the primary design criteria for Windows NT 4, system security permeates every component and feature of the operating system. Several applications that are part of Windows NT 4 provide the capability to view and modify security parameters that are applicable to its functionality. Among these applications are the following:

■ **User Manager For Domains.** This program provides the means to add and modify users on the system and also enables you to access several global security settings such as security policies for Accounts (see fig. 4.16), User Rights, and Audits.

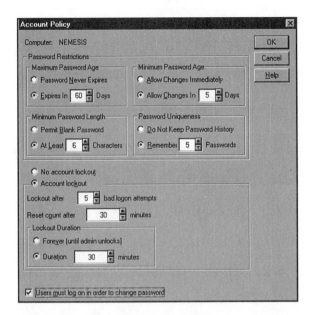

Figure 4.16
You can configure the system account policy.

■ **System Policy Editor.** The policy editor is a wealth of access to a large number of the more esoteric Registry key settings controlling features of Network, Printers, Remote Access, Shell, System (see fig. 4.17), and User Profiles.

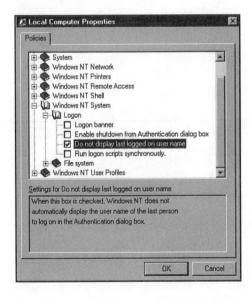

Figure 4.17
Use the System Policy Editor to access Registry keys that control system features.

■ **Remote Access Administrator.** RAS Admin enables you to assign the remote access rights for individual users. By using this application, the administrator can configure which users are permitted to dial in or dial out and whether or not they can receive a callback from the RAS server (see fig. 4.18).

Figure 4.18

Configuring remote access permissions.

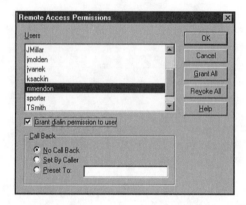

■ **File Manager.** Though somewhat obsolete now that Explorer has come to Windows NT, File Manager is still useful (necessary in fact) when creating, removing, and setting the various permissions (see fig. 4.19) and file type associations for Macintosh shared volumes.

Figure 4.19

Configure directory permissions on Machintosh volumes through the Macintosh View of Directory Permissions dialog box.

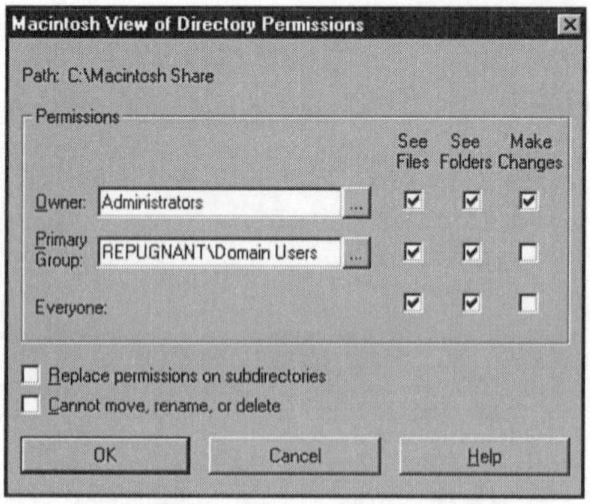

Security information is spread throughout the Registry, sometimes found in logical, reasonable places, sometimes not.

The fact that most of the security information for the system is stored in binary format should be enough to keep anyone from wanting to sift through the Registry with regedit.exe or some other Registry editing tool. Managing the security aspects of your system with the appropriate application is far easier, and much safer.

Although regedit.exe can be used to configure various items relating to system security, doing so is similar to using a sector editor to manage the files on your hard disk. Regedit.exe has no knowledge of the data type, classification, or hierarchy of any entry in the Registry. It cannot validate data entry or pop up a warning message for any invalid or incorrect entries that you make.

If you make a typographical error when editing a Registry key, you may not find out until after your system has crashed and your users can't log on and access the files. You may spend a great deal of time trying to track down the problem. The Windows NT 4 documentation, online help, and Resource Kit all say the same thing, and it's worth reiterating here: Don't edit the Registry directly unless it is absolutely necessary.

Securing Removable Volumes

The multi-user, multitasking nature of Windows NT 4 presents a special problem when you use removable media devices such as floppy disks and CD-ROM drives. Another user or a background process can gain access to the media that you have inserted into a removable drive to work on during an interactive logon session at the server. If you are not currently logged into the system, no network user or application running in the background can gain access to your removable drives.

To eliminate this security risk, Windows NT 4 provides a method of assigning the exclusive use of removable media drives to the user currently logged on to the system interactively. The user has exclusive use of the drives until logging out of the system.

To activate exclusive access to the logged on user, the following two keys must be added to the Registry under the \\HKEY_LOCAL_MACHINE\SOFTWARE\Microsoft\Windows NT\CurrentVersion\Winlogon key (see fig. 4.20):

- ■ AllocateFloppies

- ■ AllocateCdRoms

Both of these keys are the String data type and the values should be set to 1 to activate the feature and 0 to disable it. Though not a requirement of the C2 security specification, an application called C2 Configuration Manager included with the Windows NT 4 Resource Kit can also add and set these keys. The C2 Configuration Manager evaluates your system's C2 compliance (see fig. 4.21). For an explanation of C2 Security, please refer to Appendix C, "The NCSC Security Rating System."

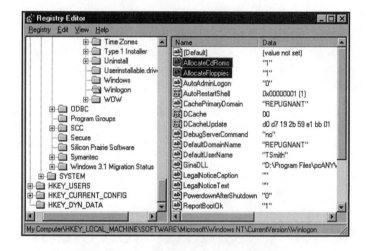

Figure 4.20

Add registry keys through the Registry Editor.

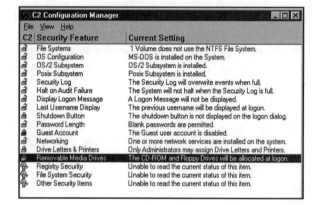

Figure 4.21

The C2 Configuration Manager enables you to evaluate your system's C2 compliance.

Conclusion

Windows NT 4 provides excellent security for most network operations. Providing the right amount of security is up to your business needs. Some companies have very relaxed security policies, while others, including government agencies, have a need for very strict security. Just remember, before you make any major changes to security, or the Registry in general, you should back up the Registry and store it in a safe location.

5

The Windows NT Security Subsystem

Windows NT has received high marks for its C2-compliant security. This chapter examines how Windows NT can limit access to specific files and directories. But first the chapter looks at how the operating system secures access to the computer itself. In Windows NT, security starts at the front door.

> **Note**   Windows NT Resource Kit has an excellent utility: C2CONFIG.EXE, which is a C2 Security Manager. C2CONFIG.EXE examines your computer and shows you which C2 requirements are met. If you are concerned with security, or if you are just curious to see exactly what C2 security entails, you should check out this utility.

Logging On to Windows NT

The first thing a new user of Windows NT notices is the Welcome dialog box; until the user logs on from this screen, there's no way to access anything else on the machine. This section examines this logon process, referred to here as WinLogon, after its executable WINLOGON.EXE.

WinLogon Overview

Users must log on to Windows NT in order to use a Windows-NT based computer. The logon process is mandatory—you cannot bypass it. After a user successfully logs on to Windows NT, an access token is generated. This access token contains the user's security identifier and group identifiers, as well as the user rights granted through the User Rights policy in User Manager or User Manager for Domains.

The access token identifies the user and all processes spawned by the user. No action can take place on a Windows NT system without somebody's access token being attached to it.

WinLogon Process

If no one is logged on to a Windows NT system, a floating window appears with the message `Press Ctrl+Alt+Del to log on`. By default in Windows NT, Ctrl+Alt+Del is the operating system's Security Attention Sequence (SAS). The SAS is the signal to the operating system that someone is requesting access to the security subsystem, perhaps to log on or off, change a password, or lock the workstation. After the SAS is triggered, all user-mode applications pause until the security operation completes or cancels.

Why Ctrl+Alt+Del?

For most people with any kind of a background in Microsoft operating systems, Ctrl+Alt+Del seems an unlikely choice for a logon key sequence. In MS-DOS, for instance, that key sequence instantly reboots the computer, destroying any data in memory at the time. Two good reasons, however, justify Ctrl+Alt+Del being used as the SAS. One comes from a security standpoint, and the other arises from compatibility.

Any logon sequence for Windows NT has to be secure, meaning no other program can be executing at the same time or else a danger exists that the user's logon information could be stolen and misused. Unix is famous for *Trojan Horse* programs, which look just like the logon sequence for the operating system, but actually write the user's user name and password to a file before logging the user on to the system. After the SAS is triggered in Windows NT, all user-mode programs stop. No program can trap the SAS sequence; it is the sole property of the security subsystem. If a user presses Ctrl+Alt+Del, he can be assured that his information is secure.

Still, any key sequence could have been chosen as long as it met the criteria in the preceding paragraph, and that's when compatibility issues arise. Windows NT supports MS-DOS–based applications, Windows 3.x-based applications, Windows 95-based applications, Windows NT-based applications, OS/2-based applications, and POSIX-based applications. If you excluded every key sequence used by all these programs, you would not be left with very many options for a unique SAS. In fact, you'd probably only be left with a single one: Ctrl+Alt+Del. It's a fairly safe bet that no other programs out there use this key sequence.

The user then sees a Logon Information dialog box, the familiar screen that asks for your user name and password.

The user name and password entries, of course, change from user to user; this is how Windows NT identifies users. The user name is not case-sensitive, but the password is. C2 security precludes Windows NT from displaying the password as it is typed, so be careful to check the state of the Caps Lock key before typing the password. Asterisks echo your password as you type.

After you click on the OK button, the WinLogon process takes the information you supplied and passes it down to the security subsystem, which checks your user name and password against the entries in the Security Account Manager (SAM) hive of the Registry. If both user name and password match a single entry in the SAM, the security subsystem constructs an access token for your current session. This is the only time that a user's access token is ever updated. The WinLogon process receives the access token and passes it to the Win32 subsystem, which starts the operating system's shell. The shell receives a copy of the access token, as does every process spawned from the shell. This enables Windows NT to interrogate any executing process for adequate security rights and permissions. It also enables an administrator to audit the actions a user takes on the system.

GINA

Although the retail version of Windows NT continues to use Ctrl+Alt+Del as the Security Attention Sequence, the operating system was designed so that the SAS, in fact the entire WinLogon process, could be replaced. All the logon components are located in a file known generically as the Graphical Identification and Authentication (GINA) module, and known specifically as MSGINA.DLL. You can replace this file under certain conditions.

The SAS can be changed, but it must still be trapped by the security subsystem. Choosing the F1 key as the SAS, for example, is a poor choice because no other application will ever be able to receive the F1 keypress again.

The SAS, however, does not have to be a keyboard combination at all. In the case of an ATM running Windows NT, it could be the insertion of an ATM card. It could be a finger on a touchscreen. In the future, custom vendors may adapt Windows NT to fit their own security needs.

The GINA also needs to check for some proof of ID (such as a password, PIN number, fingerprint, retina scan, and so on) to start the shell. This provides just another example of Windows NT's modularity.

If the user ID and password do not match an entry in the SAM database, access is denied.

Controlling WinLogon

You can fine-tune the WinLogon process in a number of ways to make it more or less secure, depending on your needs. All these options may be manually set in the Registry; you can find them under HKEY_LOCAL_MACHINE\SOFTWARE\Microsoft\WindowsNT\ CurrentVersion\Winlogon.

You can also fine-tune the logon process by using the Windows NT System Policy Editor. A thorough discussion of System Policy Editor is beyond the scope of this book, but it is important to note that you can configure certain logon-related Registry parameters (including some of the parameters discussed in the following sections) from System Policy Editor. Under Local Computer Properties (in Registry mode) or Default Computer Properties (in Policy mode), select Logon under the Windows NT System branch (see fig. 5.1).

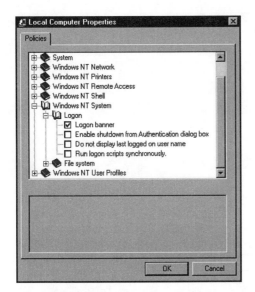

Figure 5.1
*Set logon properties in
System Policy Editor.*

Your options are as follows:

- **Logon banner.** Enables you to specify a caption and a text string that appears prior to logon (see the following section titled "LegalNotice").

- **Enable shutdown from Authentication dialog box.** Enables you to shut down the system from the logon dialog box (see the following section titled "ShutdownWithoutLogon").

- **Do not display last logged on user name.** Tells Windows NT not to display the last logged on user name in the logon dialog box (see the following section titled "DontDisplayLastUserName").

- **Run logon scripts synchronously.** Specifies whether Windows NT should wait for completion of logon scripts before starting the user's shell. You can also choose this value as a Default User setting (in Policy mode) or a Local User setting (in Registry mode).

To configure the logon interface directly, you can set the following parameters in the subkey HKEY_LOCAL_MACHINE\SOFTWARE\Microsoft\WindowsNT\CurrentVersion\ Winlogon. Sometimes the values in question are not present by default; you must add them. The following sections describe some logon-related Registry settings.

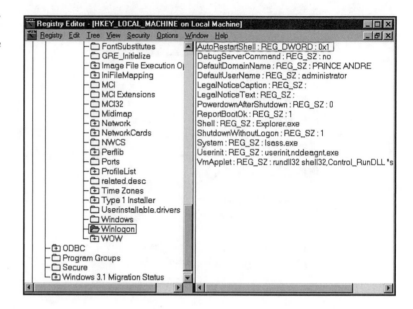

Figure 5.2

You can find the Winlogon subkey in Registry Editor.

NoPopupsOnBoot

Sometimes things just break, and Windows NT is no exception. If something goes wrong during the system boot and load phases, and a service cannot start, Windows NT displays this message at log on: One or more services failed to start. Please see the event log for details.

In certain environments, this message might be considered a breach of security; to an educated intruder, this might indicate a chink in Windows NT's armor that can be exploited. To keep this message from appearing, add a value called NoPopupsOnBoot of type REG_DWORD, and set it equal to 1. The events continue to be logged and are viewable with Event Viewer, but no messages display on-screen.

LegalNotice

A few years back, a much-publicized case involved a hacker who broke into one of the federal government's computer systems and yet was acquitted because the logon screen said Welcome. He was just trying to accept an invitation. Government clients made it quite clear to Microsoft that there had better be a way to put a warning or disclaimer message on the screen if the Welcome message was to remain.

There are actually two different Registry entries for the Legal Notice: LegalNoticeCaption and LegalNoticeText. The caption is what appears in the title bar, and the text is an actual warning message that appears in the window.

The end result is that when users press Ctrl+Alt+Del to log on, they must acknowledge and dismiss the Legal Notice window before they can enter their user names and passwords.

To delete the Legal Notice, you need to delete the entries for both LegalNoticeCaption and LegalNoticeText.

DontDisplayLastUserName

By this point, you have probably noticed that Windows NT remembers the name of the last person who logged on to the system and displays it the next time the SAS is triggered to log on again. This is a convenience for workstations where the same person logs on all the time, but it can be a security risk in some environments. After all, if a hacker knows your user name, that's half the information necessary to break into your system.

You can change this behavior so Windows NT does not display the user name of the user who logged on last. The Registry value is, appropriately enough, DontDisplayLastUserName. This value is not present in the Registry by default; you need to add it with a type of REG_SZ and a value of 1. Remember that the Registry is spelling- and punctuation-sensitive; don't add spaces or an apostrophe, or it won't work. Setting this value to 0, or just deleting it altogether, re-enables the display.

AutoAdminLogon

For many home users, the mandatory logon is just an annoying inconvenience. If you don't need the security provided by the logon process, you can bypass it and have the operating system automatically log you on at the system boot.

Several keys are involved with this entry, beginning with AutoAdminLogon, which must be manually added with a type of REG_SZ and a value of 1. Because the system automatically logs the user on, the default user name and password must be provided as well. The entries for these items are, appropriately, DefaultUserName and DefaultPassword. If the user is a member of a domain, the DefaultDomainName entry must be supplied as well.

An important note about AutoAdminLogon: you're throwing security out the window. Not only can anyone who knows how to turn on the computer log on to your system, but the password is stored as clear text in the Registry. In other words, if the computer is on a network, a user can discover the password by using RegEdit from another machine. If you must use AutoAdminLogon, do it with a non-administrative account.

Also, the word *automatic* in *automatic logon* means instant and always. Without intervention, no one can ever log on to the machine as any user other than the DefaultUserName. Logging off is ineffective; you end up instantly logged back on. The only way to override the AutoAdminLogon process is to hold the Shift key down when booting or logging off.

ShutdownWithoutLogon

It may seem odd that the capability to shut down the system is a user right that can be assigned or removed. After all, what keeps a user from just shutting off the power if he can't do a clean shutdown?

Yet, in a situation where a machine may be used as a public kiosk in which the power switch has been removed or sealed off, this user right becomes the only way to shut down a Windows NT computer. By default, Windows NT has three methods for shutting down a Windows NT computer. You can choose the Shut Down command from the Start menu, or you can trigger the SAS by pressing Ctrl+Alt+Del from your current session. These two methods require that a user log on to Windows NT first.

You may have already noticed, however, that a Shutdown button appears on the WinLogon screen and does not require the user to log on at all. Although this button appears by default, you can disable it. The Registry value is ShutdownWithoutLogon, and it needs to be changed from 1 to 0 to disable the Shutdown button. By default, this feature is enabled on Windows NT Workstation, but disabled on Windows NT Server.

PowerdownAfterShutdown

In the preceding kiosk example, shutting down the workstation does not actually turn off the power. The power switch itself is inaccessible. There is a way to have Windows NT itself turn off the power, but it requires a Plug and Play system BIOS to do so. Change the Registry entry PowerdownAfterShutdown from 0 to 1, and a new entry appears on the Shutdown Computer dialog box: Shutdown and Power off. If you're not certain whether your system can perform the powerdown, try it. If it can't do it, your system just performs a Shutdown and Restart.

Logging On to a Domain

If your Windows NT computer is a member of a domain, you need to pay special attention to the Domain box on the WinLogon screen. The Domain box answers the question, "Which account database is my account from?" For workstations in a workgroup, there is no choice; the box has a single entry (the name of the workstation). In a domain environment, however, Windows NT workstations have at least two entries in the Domain box: the name of the workstation and the name of the domain. Generally speaking, after a computer joins a domain, the Domain box should always show the name of that domain.

If a computer is a member of a domain, the WinLogon process is replaced with the NetLogon process. NetLogon functions similarly to WinLogon, except that it also enables users to log on to a database contained on another machine in the network. After a domain member boots and initializes the NetLogon service, NetLogon broadcasts on the network to find a domain controller for its domain. The first machine to respond is cached in the Registry. This is the domain controller to which NetLogon refers logon requests. This process of finding a proxy domain controller is called *discovery*.

The following happens when a user attempts to log on to a domain:

1. The user types in her user name and password and chooses the domain in the Domain box.

2. NetLogon passes the authentication request to the domain controller discovered during the boot process.

3. If the user name and password exactly match a single entry in the domain account database, the domain controller reports the match to the requesting computer.

4. The requesting computer grants access after receiving notice of authentication.

As you have probably noticed, this process is almost identical to WinLogon, except that it takes place on two machines rather than a single machine.

Locking Windows NT

Windows 3.x and Windows 95 have the capability to password-protect a screen saver, enabling a computer to remain on and executing, while preventing others from accessing the console.

A few problems arise, however, with this model. First, screen savers can take up precious CPU cycles and prevent background operations from executing efficiently. Second, anyone can shut off the machine, reboot it, and access anything on the drive or desktop. Third, in case of an emergency, an administrator cannot override the password-protection to access the desktop.

Windows NT retains password-protection for screen savers, but it also offers a more powerful and secure option: locking the computer.

To lock a Windows NT-based computer, a user must trigger the SAS from within a Windows NT session. A security dialog box appears with Lock Workstation as an option (see fig. 5.3).

Figure 5.3

The Windows NT Security dialog box enables you to lock the workstation.

Choosing the Lock Workstation button serves notice to onlookers that the computer is inaccessible until either the same user who locked the computer unlocks it, or until an administrator overrides the lock. To unlock the computer, the user who locked it must enter her Windows NT password; this differs from the custom passwords assigned to screen savers. An administrator can override the lock by entering the administrator's user name and password.

When a computer is locked, all processing continues in the background unimpeded, but nothing is visible on-screen except for the Workstation Locked message (see fig. 5.4).

Figure 5.4

The Workstation Locked message appears when a computer is locked.

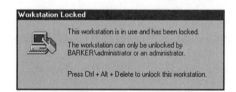

> **Note**   The Lock Workstation feature is available in both Windows NT Server and Windows NT Workstation.

Because no screen saver is active, no CPU cycles are wasted rendering flying toasters. After the computer is unlocked, everything on the desktop at the time it was locked reappears in a refreshed state. The exception to this is when an administrator overrides the lock. In so doing, the administrator logs off the previous user and logs on as the administrator. All programs end, and any unsaved data may be lost. You should not use the administrative override unless absolutely necessary.

Conclusion

This chapter briefly described the Windows NT logon processes and showed how you can configure the logon interface from System Policy Editor and the Registry. This chapter also described the Windows NT Lock Workstation feature.

NTFS File System Security

very partition must be formatted with a supported file system before it can be addressed by Windows NT. Windows NT supports three file systems: FAT, NTFS, and CDFS. CDFS is a read-only file system for CD-ROMs; therefore, it is immediately ruled out for hard disk partitions. That leaves a choice of two. To make the best decision (and this is an important decision), you need to understand the advantages and limitations of each file system.

FAT File System

The venerable File Allocation Table (FAT) file system is still alive and kicking under Windows NT. Originally invented for MS-DOS, FAT is now supported by Windows NT, Windows 95, and OS/2, making it the most universally accepted and supported file system. For this reason alone, you should seriously consider using FAT for your partitions.

If you loathe FAT because it has always forced you to use short file names (eight characters plus a three-character extension), think again: Windows NT 3.5 overcame the 8.3 limitation on FAT partitions and provided users the capability to create files with up to 255 characters in their names. (Short file names are still maintained for compatibility with legacy applications and dual-boot systems.) Even spaces are now allowed, as are multiple extensions. Windows NT preserves the case of file names so that they are displayed exactly as you originally typed them. FAT is not case-sensitive, however, so you don't have to worry about remembering the case(s) used in a particularly long file name. Some file name restrictions are still present, however. These characters are still off-limits for file names:

/ \ [ ] : ; | = . ^ * ?

How'd They Do That?

Admit it. You're wondering how long file names can work with FAT under Windows NT while not totally confusing your MS-DOS installation in the process, aren't you?

Here's how Microsoft's programmers did it: the actual File Allocation Tables are essentially unaltered; linked lists of 8.3 entries are still the core of the FAT file system. Windows NT works around this limitation by concatenating multiple 8.3 segments into a single long file name. For each of the 13 characters in the long file name (LFN), Windows NT uses a single directory entry with a pointer to the next directory entry (with the next 13 characters) if needed. After the LFN is complete, Windows NT generates a short 8.3-compliant file name to be used as an MS-DOS compatible alias.

After a directory listing is requested, Windows NT concatenates the multiple directory entries into complete LFNs and displays the entire LFN on the screen. MS-DOS does not know how to build the LFNs, so when using MS-DOS–based applications under Windows NT, or when booted to MS-DOS on a multiboot computer, only the 8.3 aliases are visible. This is not surprising: why should an older operating system be capable of duplicating the tricks of a new one? What's surprising is that MS-DOS does not just list all the pieces of an LFN as individual directory entries as one might suspect. In fact, performing a directory list under MS-DOS (even in versions released prior to Windows NT) results in a very clean 8.3-compliant list.

Here's the secret: each piece of an LFN is marked with the system, hidden, read-only, and volume attributes. The last one is the kicker. Files and directories cannot be marked as volumes because volume is an attribute reserved for an entire partition. Volumes are never marked system, hidden, and read-only; hidden, system, and read-only files are never marked as volumes. When MS-DOS sees all these attributes on a single file, it freaks. It cannot comprehend what it is seeing, so it pretends those entries don't exist.

The disk utilities included with MS-DOS (SCANDISK.EXE, DEFRAG.EXE, CHKDSK.EXE) continue to work on LFN-enabled FAT partitions without any problems. Microsoft would probably love for you to believe that this is sophistication on the part of MS-DOS, but it's actually due to ignorance; these utilities can't comprehend what they're seeing.

Be aware, however, that other third-party disk utilities are not so easily fooled. Norton Disk Doctor, for example, raises a red flag if it sees files marked system, hidden, read-only, and volume; it offers to fix the problem files. Don't let it do so! Best case scenario is losing your long file names, and the worst case scenario is losing the files themselves.

To be safe, do not use any non-Microsoft, MS-DOS–based disk utilities on an LFN-enabled FAT partition when booted under another operating system. Windows 95-based disk utilities should be safe because Windows 95 uses the same technique for creating its long file names.

If all these precautions scare you, you do have a means of turning off long file names on FAT partitions altogether. This is an all-or-nothing deal; there is no way to turn off long file names for one partition but enable them on another partition. To disable LFNs, change the Win31FileSystem value under HKEY_LOCAL_MACHINE\System\CurrentControlSet\Control\FileSystem and set it equal to 1. To re-enable LFNs, change the same entry to 0.

Date and time tracking has been improved for FAT as well. In the past, the only date associated with a FAT file was the date the file was last modified. When a file changed, a new date was stamped on it. Under Windows NT, however, the last modification date is joined by the original creation date and the last access date. These attributes are available on all Windows NT-supported file systems.

File names and dates do not present an issue any longer, but that should not be your sole reason for using FAT because all Windows NT-supported file systems support long file names. Other advantages encourage the use of FAT; however, it has the lowest overhead (less than 1 MB, compared to an average of 5–10 MB for NTFS). It is typically the most efficient file system for small partitions (under 200 MB). It's also required for the system partition on a MIPS-based or Alpha-based computer (a firmware requirement, not a software requirement).

Here's another point in FAT's advantage: it is not possible to undelete files under Windows NT under any circumstances. If a partition is formatted with the FAT file system, however, the user may boot from an MS-DOS system disk and use the MS-DOS undelete command to restore the deleted files under MS-DOS. This is not possible with NTFS because MS-DOS does not support NTFS.

> ### Deleting versus Recycling
>
> At one time or another, every Windows NT user curses Microsoft for not enabling a file
> to be undeleted (although there really isn't a choice if the operating system is C2-
> compliant). At least under Windows NT 4, you can use a feature borrowed from
> Windows 95 called the *Recycle Bin*. The Recycle Bin stores all deleted files for a time in
> case the user wishes to restore them. Did Microsoft wimp out of its "no undelete"
> pledge? Not really.
>
> The Recycle Bin is actually a hidden directory on the hard disk. If files are *deleted* by
> using the Explorer shell, they are actually just copied to the Recycle Bin directory. If the
> files were truly deleted, they would be removed from the hard disk.

If FAT is so wonderful, why consider any other file system? The answer is simple. FAT really is
not so wonderful. Witness:

- **FAT is slow.** FAT uses an unsorted linked list directory structure. As files are added to a
  directory, they are appended to the end of the directory list. As more files are added,
  Windows NT takes longer to find files at the end of the list. Even at the file level, when
  data is added to an existing file, FAT links the file sector by sector, often fragmenting the
  disk in the process. For partitions greater than 200 MB in size, FAT performance
  degrades quickly.

- **FAT is small.** The maximum file, directory, or partition size is only 4 GB. At one time
  this seemed ridiculously vast, but now we can see the day when 4 GB may be too small
  for our computing needs. Because Windows NT does not support any FAT compression
  software, including Microsoft's own DriveSpace and DoubleSpace, the 4 GB barrier is
  pretty easy to reach.

- **FAT is insecure.** You cannot protect FAT resources with Windows NT user-level
  security.

- **FAT is unsafe.** If the power fails during a disk transaction, the FAT file system may be
  left in a corrupt state, resulting in cross-linked files or orphan clusters.

These limitations are overcome by NTFS.

NTFS File System

The New Technology File System (NTFS) was introduced with Windows NT 3.1 and from
the beginning was designed to fully exploit the features and capabilities of Windows NT.

Like FAT, NTFS can handle long file names, up to 255 unicode characters. (*Unicode* is a method of including all foreign language characters in a single character set.) NTFS also maintains a short, 8.3-compliant file name for compatibility with legacy applications.

NTFS far outshines its competition in several areas:

- **NTFS is big.** This is a 64-bit file system, which means that NTFS files and partitions can be inordinately large—up to 16 exabytes in size. How large is an exabyte? Over 1 billion gigabytes, or 264 bytes. Theoretically, no one manufactures a 16 EB drive so far, at least no one has admitted it. If you still need a little more elbow room, you can compress an NTFS partition and almost double (on average) your available free space. You can compress an entire partition or just individual files or directories within a partition. This chapter discusses NTFS compression in more detail later.

- **NTFS is secure.** Individual files and directories can be protected with user-level security. Access or attempts to access NTFS resources can be audited.

- **NTFS is robust.** NTFS supports sector sparing, also known as *hot fixing*. If a sector fails on an NTFS partition, NTFS attempts to write the data to a good sector (if the data is still in memory) and map out the bad sector so that it will not be re-used. NTFS keeps a transaction log as it works. If the power were to fail, leaving NTFS in a possibly corrupt state, the CHKDSK command executed when the system boots would attempt to redo the transaction (in the case of a delete, for example) or undo the transaction (in the case of a file write where the data would no longer be in memory).

- **NTFS is fast.** In general, files don't get fragmented with NTFS. After a file is committed to disk, NTFS always finds a contiguous run of disk space for the file (if one is available). The only instance in which files become fragmented is if the drive is almost full and there is not a contiguous run of space large enough for the file, or if a saved file is modified and expanded.

- **NTFS scales well.** Because of the overhead involved, you may be better off going with FAT for smaller partitions, but when partitions exceed 400 MB (on average), NTFS begins to shine when its performance is compared to its competitors. Take that 400 MB figure with a grain of salt, however. Actual performance is due more to the number of files than the size of the files.

Sound good? Be aware of these possible drawbacks:

- **NTFS has a lot of overhead.** Typically, NTFS requires somewhere in the range of 4.5–10 MB for the file system itself. For this reason, floppy disks cannot be formatted with NTFS.

- **NTFS is only available to a Windows NT-based operating system.** If your computer boots between Windows 95, for instance, and Windows NT, you cannot access your NTFS partition under Windows 95.

■ **NTFS is case-sensitive.** Sometimes. Sometimes it's not. Remember that Windows NT is POSIX-compatible. POSIX requires that its file systems provide case-sensitivity. So when a POSIX application performs a transaction against an NTFS partition, NTFS is temporarily case-sensitive. In other words, you can create three files named posix.doc, Posix.Doc, and POSIX.DOC in the same directory without error. At all other times (including for native Windows NT applications), NTFS is not case-sensitive, which means you could not selectively delete Posix.Doc and be assured that you were not actually deleting POSIX.DOC. If you are using POSIX-based applications, you should create a separate NTFS partition for those applications and perform any file management on those partitions with a POSIX-based file management utility.

How Is NTFS Constructed?

On an NTFS partition, everything is an object. An *object*, you may recall, is something that has properties and actions that can be performed on it. A file's name is a property, for example, as is its creation date, and even its data. NTFS is designed so that programmers can add their own properties (also called *streams*) to the file system.

This has already been done, in fact. Windows NT Server includes an add-on called Services for Macintosh. One of the Macintosh services enables Macintosh clients to store files on a Windows NT Server NTFS partition. If you are familiar with the Macintosh platform, you may be aware that Macintosh files have two *forks*: a data fork (which is considered to be the contents of the file) and a resource fork (which contains information used by the Mac Finder, such as an associated application). NTFS adds a new stream for Mac files to handle the resource fork, and in so doing is capable of serving the same files to both PC and Mac clients. Macintosh clients request and receive both forks; PC clients only request and receive the data fork.

Representing files and directories as objects creates an extensible file system with some incredible potential for the future. If you are a developer, imagine creating a source-code stream so that you can include the source-code *inside* your executable file.

How do you create and access these multiple streams? Currently you can't, at least not through the GUI interface. If you're a programmer, you can write to a specific API, but if you're a user or administrator, you can try this sneaky command-line demo. Type the following lines from the command prompt:

echo This is the main data stream > Streamdemo.txt

type Streamdemo.txt

Nothing exciting here, but you should see the text you just typed (This is the main data stream) echoed back to your screen. Then type these lines at the command prompt:

echo This is a hidden stream > Streamdemo.txt:NewStream

> **type Streamdemo.txt**
>
> **more < Streamdemo.txt:NewStream**
>
> The type command should echo your original entry, but the more command should echo your last *hidden* entry. This is a backdoor approach; in fact, the reason you switched to the more command from the type command is because the type command does not support the ":" stream syntax!

Comparing the File Systems

The following table provides a quick summary of the differences between file systems:

Table 6.1
Differences between FAT and NTFS

Feature	FAT	NTFS
File Name Length	255	255
8.3 File Name Compatibility	Yes	Yes
File Size	4 GB	16 EB
Partition Size	4 GB	
2 TB (NT)	16 EB	
Directory Structure	Linked List	B-tree
Local Security	No	Yes
Transaction Tracking	No	Yes
Hot Fixing	No	Yes
Overhead	1 MB	>2 MB (avg. 4.5–10)
Required for RISC-based computers	Yes	No
Accessible from MS-DOS/Windows 95	Yes	No

continues

Table 6.1, Continued
Differences between FAT and NTFS

Feature	FAT	NTFS
Accessible from OS/2	Yes	No
Case Sensitive	No	POSIX only
Case Preserving	Yes	Yes
Compression	No	Yes
Efficiency	<200 MB	>400 MB
Windows NT Format	Yes	Yes
Convertible	To NTFS only	No
Fragmentation Level	High	Low
Format Floppy Disk	Yes	No
Extensible Attributes	No	Yes
Creation/Modification/ Access Dates	Yes	Yes

Ownership of NTFS Resources

Every NTFS file and directory has one account designated as its owner. The owner of a resource is the only account guaranteed the right to access a resource, modify its properties, and secure it from outside access.

By default, the owner of a resource is the user who created the resource. Only one user can own a resource at any given point in time. Only one exception is made to this rule: a user who is a member of the Administrators group cannot be the sole owner of any resource. Any resource created by an administrator is co-owned by the entire Administrators group. This is part of a checks-and-balances security model in Windows NT that ensures that an administrator cannot irrevocably hoard power and resources. This is yet another reason why administrators should not use an administrator-level account for day-to-day operations.

To view the owner of any file or directory, follow these steps:

1. Select the file or directory in My Computer or Windows NT Explorer.

2. Choose Properties from the File menu.

3. Click on the Security tab (see fig. 6.1).

4. Click on the Ownership button (see fig. 6.2). If you have the Take Ownership of File and Directories user right, you can take ownership of the file.

Remember that only NTFS resources have owners.

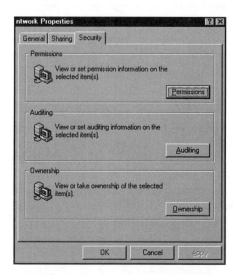

Figure 6.1

The File Properties Security tab appears.

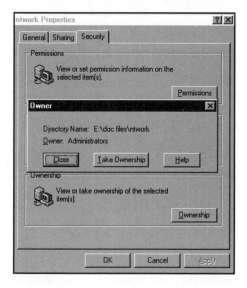

Figure 6.2

The Owner dialog box displays the owner of the file.

You can also take ownership away from the current owner by using the Owner dialog box (refer to fig. 6.2). Usually, only administrators can revoke ownership rights. Administrators can always take ownership of any resource because they have been granted the user right Take

Ownership of File and Directories in the User Rights Policy. Removing administrators from this list removes the right of administrators to take ownership of files and directories that they did not create. Adding another user or group to this list gives this right to that user or group. You should not change this right at all; administrators require this right in order to have a C2-compliant security system.

If you are not an administrator, you may still be able to take ownership if the current owner has granted you permission to take ownership (this mechanism is discussed shortly). The important concept to grasp for now, however, is that ownership is taken, never given. Owner-ship involves responsibility, and that responsibility can never be forced on anyone, even by an administrator. Implications of this rule will surface shortly.

Securing NTFS Resources

NTFS resources can be secured by their owners. The permissions on a file or directory are just another attribute (or stream) attached to the file. This security attribute is called an Access Control List (ACL). Each ACL contains a series of Access Control Entries (ACEs), and each Access Control Entry references a specific user or group SID and a type of access to grant or deny that SID. This section examines the process Windows NT uses to check a user's creden-tials against the Access Control List. First, it is important to learn how permissions are assigned to the ACL to begin with.

Discretionary Access

Who gets to assign permissions to a resource? The owner of the resource. Who is the owner of the resource? The user who created it. In other words, unlike other operating systems, security is not the sole domain of the administrator. If you create a file, you, and not the administrator, get to secure it. In fact, users can easily lock administrators out of their resources, which makes sense in many environments.

Picture a typical company network: memos, reports, and routine documents as well as salary information, personnel files, and other sensitive data. Should the administrator or the MIS department have access to these files just because they run the network? Of course not. In these cases, the users who created and work with these files are the best ones to judge who should and should not have access.

This type of access control is called discretionary access, and it is a hallmark of C2-level security. If it seems dangerous that administrators can be locked out of files and directories, know that there's always a spare key. An administrator can always take ownership of any resource. After the administrator owns the resource, he can modify the permissions on the resource so that he can access it. Just remember that, as previously mentioned, ownership can be taken, but it can never be given, and that goes for giving back, too. After the administrator is the owner of the resource, he cannot return ownership to the original user without that user explicitly taking ownership. That's just as it should be for legitimate situations in which a user might be absent from work when a critical file needs to be accessed. But it puts the administrator in an awfully sticky situation if no important situation requires access.

Permissions versus User Rights

Resource permissions are not the same as user rights. User rights are tasks that you can perform on the system as a whole; these rights are stored with your account information in the Registry. NTFS permissions are stored with the resource itself in the ACL property discussed earlier.

It's important to understand the difference between rights and permissions; this difference explains why it is not possible to view the resource permissions assigned to a user the way you can view trustee assignments in other operating systems (Novell NetWare, for example). Displaying all the permissions assigned to a user requires searching all the NTFS files and directories on all NTFS partitions on shared directories of other workstations and servers on the network and searching for incidences of the user's SID or group SIDs on the ACL of each of those files.

Directory-Level Permissions

Permissions can be placed on both directories and files. If permissions are placed on both directories and files, you must resolve the permissions to figure out the effective permissions for a user. Start with directory permissions.

The owner of a directory may grant a user the following permissions:

- **No Access.** Restricts the user from accessing the directory by any means. The directory appears in the directory tree; instead of a file list, however, the message You do not have permissions to access this directory displays.

- **List.** Restricts the user from accessing the directory, although the user may view the contents list for the directory.

- **Read.** The user may read data files and execute program files from the directory, but no changes of any sort can be made.

- **Add.** The user may not read or even view the contents of the directory, but may write files to the directory. If you write a file to the directory, the message You do not have permissions to access this directory displays, but files may still be saved or copied into this directory.

- **Add & Read.** The user may view and read from the directory and save new files into the directory. Existing files, however, may not be modified in any way.

- **Change.** The user may view and read from the directory and save new files into the directory. In addition, existing files may be modified and even deleted. The user may change attributes on the directory and even delete the entire directory. This, by the way, is as much permission as you should ever assign to anyone.

- **Full Control.** The user may view, read, save, modify, and delete the directory and its contents. In addition, the user may change permissions on the directory and its contents, even though the user may not be the owner of the resource. The user also has permission to take ownership at any time.

What actually happens with all these levels of permissions is a combination of six basic actions that can be performed against a resource:

- Read (R)

- Write (W)

- Execute (X)

- Delete (D)

- Change Permissions (P)

- Take Ownership (O)

The following table shows a breakdown of the permission levels mentioned in the previous list of potential user permissions:

Table 6.2
User-Permission Levels

Level	Directory Permissions	File Permissions
No Access	None	None
List	RX	Unspecified
Read	RX	RX
Add	WX	Unspecified
Add & Read	RXWD	RX
Change	RXWD	RXWD
Full Control	RXWDPO	RXWDPO

Two custom levels of permissions also exist: Special Directory Access and Special File Access, both of which enable the owner (or any user granted the P permission) to custom-build an access control entry by using any combination of the six basic actions previously mentioned. To custom-build an access control entry for a group or user, click on the Permissions button in the Security tab of the Properties dialog box. Select the group or user and choose Special Directory Access in the Type of Access box. Choose the appropriate permissions in the Special Directory Access dialog box (see fig. 6.3).

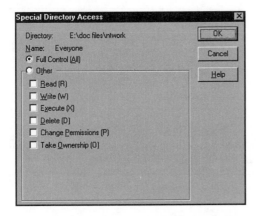

Figure 6.3

You can choose levels of permissions in the Special Directory Access dialog box.

If an NTFS partition is created, the default permissions are set so that the Everyone group has Full Control. You may want to change this at the root directory level. See the Special Considerations section at the end of this chapter, however, before doing so.

If a new directory or file is created on an NTFS partition, the resource inherits the permissions on its parent directory.

File-Level Permissions

NTFS can store permissions for files as well as directories. For files, the permission levels are not quite as varied as they are for directories:

- **No Access.** The user may not access this file at all, although the file name and basic attributes are still displayed in Explorer and My Computer.

- **Read.** The user may read this file if it is a data file, or execute it if it is a program file. The user may not modify this file in any way.

- **Change.** The user may read or execute this file. In addition, the user may modify or delete this file.

- **Full Control.** The user may read or execute, write to, and delete this file. In addition, the user may change permissions on the file and may even take ownership away from the current owner.

Table 6.3 shows the breakdown for file permissions.

Table 6.3
Breakdown of File Permissions

Level	Permissions
No Access	None
Read	RX
Change	RXWD
Full Control	RXWDPO

As with Directory permissions, a Special Access level enables anyone with the ability to change permissions to custom-build an access control entry for a user or group.

Setting Permissions

To set permissions on a file or directory, first select the resource in Explorer or My Computer and then choose Properties from the File menu. Click on the Permissions button in the Security tab of the Properties dialog box. The File Permissions dialog box appears (see fig. 6.4).

Figure 6.4

Set permissions through the File Permissions dialog box.

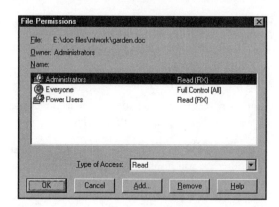

To remove a user or group from the ACL, select the user and choose the Remove button. To add a user or group to the ACL, choose the Add button in the File Permissions dialog box. The Add Users dialog box appears, which includes a list of all the groups in your account database (see fig. 6.5).

To grant access to a specific user, you need to choose the Show Users button; otherwise, only the group names are displayed to make it easier to search through the list. Choose the users and groups you want to add to the ACL individually or collectively, and then choose the Add button to enter their names in the Add Names box at the bottom of the dialog box. Don't try to set the access level here unless all these accounts will be granted the same access level (because that's what this Type of Access setting does—it's all or nothing). After you choose the OK button, you receive another chance to individually modify the permission level for each account on the ACL.

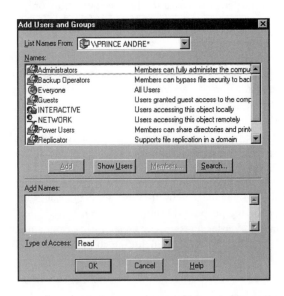

Figure 6.5

Add a user or group through the Add Users and Groups dialog box.

Setting permissions for a directory brings up a slightly different dialog box (see fig. 6.6).

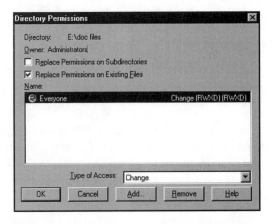

Figure 6.6

Set permissions for a directory through the Directory Permissions dialog box.

Two additional options present themselves here: Replace Permissions of Subdirectories and Replace Permissions on Existing Files. By default, only Replace Permissions on Existing Files is selected, which means that the permissions to be applied to the directory will be applied to the files within the directory, but not to subdirectories or files within subdirectories.

Selecting only the Replace Permissions on Subdirectories check box modifies the permissions on all directories in the directory tree, but not on any files within those directories, even in the top-level directory.

Selecting both options applies these permissions to the entire directory tree and its contents, and setting neither option changes the permissions on the top-level directory only.

Local Groups

When working with user rights, it is usually sufficient to assign rights to users and built-in groups. When assigning resource permissions, however, adding individual users may be too time-consuming and adding built-in groups may be too inclusive. You may have a directory, for example, that contains meeting minutes for a project on which you are working. You would like to grant permissions to the people on the project team, but over 30 people are on the team. Assigning permissions to all 30 people would take a long time, and assigning permissions to Users would give access to far too many people.

It's time to introduce a new level of user management in Windows NT: local groups. Local groups can be created by any user for any purpose (Headquarters, Marketing, Vice-Presidents, Portland, Engineering); furthermore, after local groups are created, they can be used again and again. By creating a local group called MyProject, and including all the project team members, you need to grant only a single set of permissions for each meeting report.

Local Groups versus Built-In Groups

Local Groups are similar to built-in groups in that both types of groups can contain many users to address a single purpose. In fact, technically, the built-in groups in Windows NT Workstation *are* local groups. A *local group* can be defined as a group used to assign rights and permissions to the local system and local resources.

Local and built-in groups are also similar in structure. Both types of groups can contain local users, domain users and global groups, and users and global groups from trusted domains The only type of account that cannot be placed inside a local group is another local group.

Local and built-in groups differ in their intended purpose. The built-in groups are pre-defined and pre-assigned to specific rights and capabilities for system management. They are not intended to be used for managing access to resources. Local groups are impractical for managing the system (would you really want to grant administrative or backup rights to a project team?), but are ideal for assigning permissions to files and directories.

The only other difference between the two types of groups is that built-in groups are permanent members of a computer's account database, whereas local groups can be created and deleted at will.

Defining Local Groups

As with any type of account, you create local groups in User Manager for Domains. First select the user accounts that you would like to include in the local group (remember to hold down the Ctrl key to select multiple accounts). Then from the User menu, choose New Local Group. The New Local Group dialog box appears (see fig. 6.7).

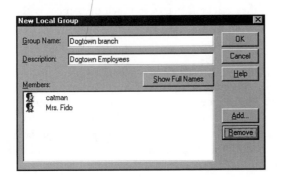

Figure 6.7

Create local groups in the New Local Group dialog box.

Enter a name for the group (this is required) and a description (optional). The users you selected before issuing the New Local Group command should already be listed in the Members box. To add additional users, choose the Add button. The Add Users and Groups dialog box appears (see fig. 6.8).

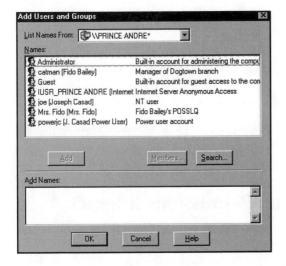

Figure 6.8

Only individual users for a local group appear in the Names list in the Add Users and Groups dialog box.

Notice that only users and global groups are displayed, not local groups. As previously mentioned, local groups cannot be nested, so User Manager does not even tempt you. Choose the users you want to add individually or collectively and use the Add button to enter their names in the Add Names box. Choose OK to return to the New Local Group dialog box.

If you accidentally choose a user who does not belong in the group, use the Remove button to delete the account from the group. Otherwise, choose OK to add the local group to the account database.

Managing Local Groups

After you create your local groups, they can be managed in much the same way that your user accounts are managed. You should be aware, however, of a few idiosyncrasies about local groups:

- You cannot rename a group after it has been created, and there really is no good reason why. Groups are referenced throughout the system by their Security Identifiers (SIDs), just as users are. Microsoft's programmers probably just never got around to adding this feature to the code. You can copy a local group and give the new group a new name (in fact, you'd have to), but that really isn't the same as renaming. None of the permissions granted to the original group would apply to the new copy. A solution for this one just doesn't exist.

- You cannot disable a group after it has been created. This is a bit easier to understand because the proper implications of a disabled group might be unclear. Should members of that group be unable to log on? Or should the group's permissions and rights just not apply while it is disabled? This would be a thorny issue to introduce. In the meantime, to temporarily disable the effects of a group on the system, remove all the users from the group. Do not delete the group and re-create it later or your new group will have a new SID and a brand new set of default rights and permissions; all the old properties will be irrevocably lost.

- If you do want to delete a group, be aware that you will only be deleting the group itself, not the users within the group. The container effect stops here. Select the group in User Manager for Domains and choose Delete from the User menu.

- You can add or remove members from the group at any time by selecting the group in User Manager for Domains and then choosing the Properties command from the User menu.

How User and Group Permissions Interact

At this point, you have probably realized that users are likely to be in many different groups. Abigail's user account, for example, may be a member of the Users' group, the Marketing group, the Department Manager's group, the Philadelphia group, and the Project X group. Each of these user and group accounts are likely to be granted permissions to resources at one time or another, and it is quite likely that occasionally some of the accounts might appear on the same Access Control List. In such scenarios, how do you resolve the permissions granted to a user's user account and group accounts?

User and group permissions are cumulative; neither takes precedence over the other. If the Marketing group is given Read Access to a file, and the Department Manager's group is given Change access to the same file, Abigail (who is a member of both groups) has Change access because Change already includes the R and X permissions that Read incorporates.

The one exception to this rule is the No Access permission. No Access overrides all other permissions granted to a user or the user's groups, regardless of where the No Access is assigned. If Abigail was granted Read Access to a file, for example, but Marketing was granted No Access, Abigail would not be able to access the file. There is—and it cannot be emphasized enough—no way to override a No Access permission.

At first glance, this seems a bit worrisome. Assume, for example, that Beth is thinking about leaving the company and is updating her resume (on her lunch hour, of course). She does not want anyone else to have access to this file, so she assigns the following permissions to the file:

Beth: Full Control

Everyone: No Access

You have probably guessed the result, and you are right: Beth cannot access her resume because she is a member of the Everyone group, and the No Access assigned to Everyone overrides the Full Control assigned to her own account. Is there an easy way for Beth to retain sole access to her resume, or does she need to create a group called Everyone But Me and assign it No Access (thinking about how long that would take in a large company sends shudders)? An easy way exists, and it means making the ACL read:

Beth: Full Control

You do not have to specify No Access for a user or group to exclude them from an ACL. The rule in Windows NT is that if you are not on the list, you do not get in. Now, this brings up another question: why does Windows NT include the No Access command at all if it isn't even necessary to exclude access? Because No Access is intended as a negator to remove permissions from a user or group that may already have been implicitly added to the ACL through membership in another group. Beth, for example, may not care if her co-workers in the Marketing Department know she is thinking of leaving the company, but she wants her supervisor to remain ignorant. She can set the following permissions on her resume's ACL:

Beth: Full Control

Marketing: Read

Abigail: No Access

Because Abigail is a member of the Marketing group, she would have received Read Access to Beth's resume if she had not been excluded by a direct No Access.

How Directory and File Permissions Interact

Now things get just a little bit more complicated; on an NTFS partition permissions are likely to be on both directories and files. Fortunately, this situation is pretty easy to resolve, although a few odd situations might occur.

Simply put, file permissions override directory permissions. Even if Abigail had Full Control over the directory that contained Beth's resume, she would not be able to read Beth's resume if her account had been granted No Access over that file. Likewise, it is possible to grant a user Read access to a directory and yet still grant full control over a single file within that directory. Only that one file would be able to be modified within that directory.

This can lead to some misleading scenarios. Sam may not want anyone to view the contents of his private directory, for example, so he assigns the directory this ACL:

> Sam: Full Control

If Beth tries to view this directory, the You do not have permission to access this directory message appears. Yet Sam may still want to occasionally grant Beth access to one or two of his files. One day, he grants Beth Read Access to a document in his private directory. Beth can read that file, but how can she access it? She can't view the directory contents in Explorer, and when she does a File/Open in an application, she cannot view the directory contents there either. To access the file, Beth must type the full path to the file from the application in which she wants to view it. That is the only way she can read that file.

File Delete Child

Another odd scenario: Sam decides to grant Everyone Full Control to his private directory, but instead applies Read permissions to Everyone for the individual files within the directory. Sam believes (correctly) that although users can copy and save files in his directory, they cannot change the ones already there because those files have Read permissions only. Sam also believes (correctly) that no one else can change permissions on the existing files because those files have Read permissions only. Sam also believes that no one can delete his existing files because those files have Read permissions only. On this last count, he's wrong.

In addition to the six basic permissions (RXWDPO) granted with Full Control, there is a seventh, implicit permission called File Delete Child (FDC). FDC is included for POSIX compatibility, and it grants a user Full Control over a directory and the capability to delete a top-level file within that directory, *even if that user does not have delete permissions to the file itself!* Only top-level files can be deleted, not subdirectories or files within subdirectories.

Is there a workaround? Yes, but you must grant Special Directory Access to use it. If you grant Special Directory Access and choose all six permissions instead of granting Full Control to a directory, the user to whom you granted this level of access does not possess the FDC permission. It looks as if you are really just assigning the equivalent of Full Control, but you are doing so minus File Delete Child. Don't waste time searching for File Delete Child in the Explorer interface—it's not there. It is an implicit permission granted only when Full Control is granted over a directory. An even better workaround is to never grant anyone Full Control over anything, unless you grant it to yourself as the owner. Do you want anyone else to have the power to change permissions on the file and lock you out? And even worse, do you want someone to have the ability to take ownership of the file at the same time so that you can't even change permissions back to what they were? A good rule of thumb is to never grant anyone any permissions higher than Change. That's already high enough because a user with Change access can delete the resource itself.

Special Considerations for the Boot and System Partitions

After Windows NT itself is installed on an NTFS partition, an administrator might be tempted to try to exclude users from accessing the Windows NT installation directory tree to prevent necessary files from being deleted or overwritten. If you examine the Access Control List for that directory, however, you won't see the customary Everyone/Full Control that you normally find on NTFS resources. The critical entry on the ACL is the SYSTEM/Full Control ACE. Do not, under any circumstances, remove or modify this ACE from the list or else Windows NT crashes, and you cannot restart the operating system successfully.

If this does happen, don't panic. You can use the Emergency Repair Disk to strip the permissions from the Windows NT installation directory tree.

Copying and Moving Files

The same rules that applied for the Compressed attribute on NTFS resources apply to Access Control Lists as well. When copying a file within or between partitions, a new instance of that file is being created, and it inherits the ACL of its new parent directory. The same effect results if a file is moved between partitions (remember that a move between partitions is really a copy followed by a delete). If a file is moved within a partition, however, the ACL does not change because the file itself is never altered—only the source and target directories change.

Putting It Together

Now that the elements are in place, it's time to examine how Windows NT makes the decision of whether to grant access to an NTFS resource.

When a user logs on to a Windows NT-based computer, the Security Accounts Manager generates an access token for the user's current session. The access token contains, among other things, the user's SID and group SIDs.

If a user requests access to an NTFS resource, the Security Reference Monitor (a component of the security subsystem) examines the SIDs contained in the user's access token. The Security Reference Monitor then parses the Access Control List starting at the top looking for references to any of the SIDs contained in the user's access token. The search continues until meeting one of the following conditions:

- The Security Reference Monitor encounters a Deny (the internal representation of No Access) for any SID in the user's access token. At this point, the search stops, and access is denied.

- The Security Reference Monitor encounters an Allow for any SID in the user's access token. If the Allow specifies the type of access sought by the user, the search stops and access is granted. If the Allow specifies some, but not all the permissions requested, the search continues until all permissions are accumulated, at which point access is granted. If the Allow specifies none of the permission requested by the user, the search continues.

- The Security Reference Monitor reaches the end of the Access Control List without accumulating all the requested permissions. Access is denied. No partial access is granted.

This process is interesting in that it only works if Denies are placed at the top of the ACL. If any Allows preceded a Deny on the ACL, a user can achieve access even if No Access had been granted to one of the SIDs in his access token because the search stops after the requested permissions have been accumulated and before the No Access is encountered.

Luckily, Windows NT does place all Denies before all Allows. At least all the built-in applications and interfaces work this way. A programmer can, however, write her program such that Denies can be placed anywhere within an ACL. This is done to provide maximum compatibility and flexibility in porting existing custom applications to Windows NT. You should not have anything to worry about with any professionally sold Windows NT application. You should make certain, however, that any programmer you hire for custom development knows how to structure Access Control Lists.

Handles

After the Security Reference Monitor approves the user's access to the file resource, the system creates a handle to that resource. Remember that no user-mode process in Windows NT can access a resource directly. The handle is entered in the object table of the process that requested the access. The object table contains the list of handles to all resources in use by that process along with the permissions granted through each handle. When transactions are performed against an open resource, the security subsystem checks the permissions in the object table rather than parsing the entire ACL again. This provides a bit of performance boost. It also means that a user's permissions over a file do not refresh until the file is closed and reopened, generating a new handle. In other words, you may grant a user Change permissions to a file. The user opens the file with the requested and granted Change permissions, and while the file is in use, you decide to change the user's permissions to Read. Although the ACL changes immediately, the security subsystem is not checking the ACL any longer because the user has an open handle to the file. The user must close and re-open the file for the new permissions to take hold.

Access Tokens Don't Refresh

Similar to handles, access tokens are generated only when a user logs on. Any changes made to a user's rights and group memberships, for instance, do not take effect until the user logs off and back on again. Consider that you can't prevent a user who is logged on as a member of the Marketing group from accessing a resource by removing him from the group. His access token still reflects Marketing membership until the next time he logs on.

Conclusion

This chapter discussed NTFS file system security. The first part of the chapter described the differences between the FAT and NTFS file systems. The chapter then took a closer look at ownership and NTFS file and directory permissions.

Troubleshooting

7

The Boot Process

The Windows NT boot process is one of the most crucial processes that your system undergoes. If a problem occurs during booting, your system may be left in an unusable state, which can be disastrous if this happens to a mission critical file server. This chapter discusses the Windows NT boot process as well as some common boot problems. To troubleshoot the boot process, you must have a thorough understanding of what takes place during each step of the boot process. This chapter focuses primarily on the Intel x86 platform boot process, although an overview of the boot process on RISC-based systems is given.

Boot Process Overview

A successful startup of Windows NT involves many steps. These steps include the following:

1. Power On Self Test (POST)

2. Hard drive boot sequence

3. Windows NT boot loader process

4. Selection of the operating system

5. Hardware detection

6. Kernel loading

7. Kernel initialization

Although the boot process on Intel x86-based systems differs from the boot process on RISC-based systems, each share some similarities. Because of hardware dissimilarities, the initial boot loader phases differ between x86 and RISC platforms. After the initial boot loader phase, much of the boot process is the same between the different platforms. Figure 7.1 shows a graphical representation of the boot process and illustrates the differences between the Intel boot process and the RISC boot process.

Figure 7.1

The boot process on RISC-based systems differs from that of Intel x86-based systems.

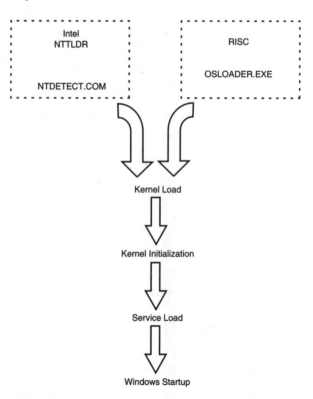

Intel Boot Process

The start of the Intel x86 boot process consists of the following steps:

- ◼ POST

- ◼ Loading of the Master Boot Record

- ◼ Executing the Partition Boot Record

- ◼ Executing NTLDR

- ◼ Executing NTDETECT

The following sections discuss each of these events in greater detail.

POST

When the system is first powered on, all system components must be tested and initialized before the boot process can take place. This Power-On Self Test is referred to by the acronym POST.

In the first step of POST, the CPU is set to real mode and the code located at location F000:0000h is executed. This code checks the amount of memory installed and verifies that all required hardware is installed and functioning properly. Next, any ROMs located on adapter cards, such as a SCSI adapter, are executed. After all hardware has been initialized, BIOS INT 19h is invoked. This is the interrupt that calls the bootstrap loader.

INT 19h first checks if a disk is in the floppy drive. If so, the system tries to boot from a floppy disk. If no floppy is present, the Master Boot Record (MBR) of the hard disk is read and loaded into memory.

Master Boot Record

The Master Boot Record is the first sector on the hard drive. It is always located on track 0, head 0, sector 1. The MBR contains a small amount of executable code as well as the partition table for the disk. The MBR is created when the first partition on the hard drive is created. The purpose of the Master Boot Record is to determine where the active system partition is located and to transfer control to the boot loader of that partition.

After the Master Boot Record is loaded into memory by POST, the code is then executed. This code searches the hard drive partition table to locate the active system partition. After the active system partition is located, the MBR loads and executes the code located in sector 0 of this partition. This sector is referred to as the partition boot record.

Partition Boot Record

The partition boot record contains the first Windows NT specific code thus far and is always located on the same physical disk as the MBR. The length of the partition boot record varies depending on the type of file system on the partition. For FAT volumes, the boot record is only one sector long. On NTFS volumes, the boot record is sixteen sectors long. The extra sectors are needed for NTFS volumes because of the extra code that is required to be able to recognize the NTFS file system.

The partition boot record is responsible for two functions. First, the code located in the partition boot record must be able to recognize enough of the file system to be able to find NTLDR. Secondly, NTLDR must be loaded into memory and executed.

NTLDR

The Windows NT boot loader, NTLDR, enables the user to select the preferred operating system, and then initiates the booting of that operating system. NTLDR gets its name from condensing "NT loader." The execution of NT loader can be recognized by the clearing of the screen and the following message being displayed:

```
OS Loader V4.0
```

The following files are required by NTLDR:

- **BOOT.INI.** The BOOT.INI file contains information on the names and locations of the different bootable operating systems installed. Also within this file is the default operating system selection and the selection time-out period.

- **NTBOOTDD.SYS (if loading Windows NT from a non-INT13 SCSI device).** NTBOOTDD.SYS is a SCSI device driver and is only required if NTLDR must boot Windows NT from a SCSI drive that does not have the BIOS enabled. The NTBOOTDD.SYS is actually a renamed copy of the SCSI device driver for the particular SCSI adapter installed in the system. Remember, if the BOOT.INI file uses the scsi() syntax, the NTBOOTDD.SYS file is required.

- **NTDETECT.COM.** NTDETECT.COM is responsible for detecting the installed hardware and is discussed later in greater detail.

- **BOOTSECT.DOS (if the system is configured to dual boot).** The BOOTSECT.DOS contains the boot sector of the operating system that was installed prior to Windows NT. The file is named BOOTSECT.DOS even if the second operating system is something other than DOS, such as OS/2.

When NTLDR first starts, it switches the processor from real mode to 32-bit flat memory mode. This must be done because Windows NT is a 32-bit operating system. Next, before the load process can continue, the appropriate mini-file system must be started. The code for the

FAT and NTFS mini-file system is contained within NTLDR. This mini-file system is required for reading, writing, and changing directories on the system boot drive. Next, the BOOT.INI file is read, and then the boot loader screen is displayed. You are then prompted to pick the operating system you want to boot.

If an operating system other than Windows NT is selected, NTLDR loads BOOTSECT.DOS and passes control to it. Otherwise, NTDETECT.COM is loaded and executed.

NTDETECT

The execution of NTDETECT.COM can be recognized by the following displayed message:

```
NTDETECT V4.0  Checking Hardware . . .
```

NTDETECT is responsible for collecting a list of currently installed components and passing the information back to NTLDR. NTDETECT detects the following devices:

- Computer ID

- Bus Type

- Keyboard

- Video

- Floppy Disks

- Serial Ports

- Parallel Ports

- Pointing Device

Note   If NTDETECT does not detect any required hardware, it will NOT report any problems.

After NTDETECT has completed, the screen clears and the following message is displayed:

```
OS Loader V4.0
```

```
Press spacebar now to invoke Hardware Profile/Last Known Good menu.
```

The process that occurs after the executing of NTDETECT.COM depends on if Windows NT has been configured with another Hardware Profile or if the user has pressed the spacebar to load the Last Known Good configuration. If either of these conditions are met, NTLDR displays the Hardware Profile/Configuration Recovery Menu. Otherwise, NTLDR proceeds to load by using the default configuration.

> **Note**   If you have a need to boot Windows NT using different hardware configurations, then you should create a Hardware Profile for each configuration. A perfect example of this would be for a laptop. One Hardware Profile can be used to boot without a docking station, and another for booting with support for the additional docking station hardware.

The Hardware Profile/Configuration Recovery Menu enables you to select the Hardware Profile you want to use or to boot with The Last Known Good Control Set. The Last Known Good Control Set is a saved version of the configuration information that was used during the last successful boot of Windows NT. Regardless of the choice you make, NTLDR then proceeds to the kernel load phase of the boot process.

RISC Boot Process

Windows NT systems based on the Alpha, MIPS, or Power PC processors follow a slightly different boot process. This RISC boot process consists of the following steps:

1. POST

2. Execution of OSLOADER

3. Selection of the operating system

4. Loading of the kernel

5. Initialization of the kernel

Because systems based on these processors can vary, the following sections are meant to be a brief overview of how the boot process takes place.

POST

The POST routine on a RISC-based boot process performs much of the same tasks as the POST for x86 systems. The amount of memory is checked as well as whether the needed hardware components are present. After POST is completed, the resident ROM firmware reads the boot precedence table from nonvolatile RAM (NVRAM). The particulars of the boot process that occur next depend on the platform (Alpha, PowerPC, or MIPS). In general, the RISC-based system loads and executes OSLOADER.

OSLOADER

The RISC-based version of NTLDR is OSLOADER. OSLOADER also performs the functions of NTDETECT.COM and BOOTSECT.DOS. The RISC-based equivalent to the BOOT.INI is the environment variables contained within Non Volatile Random Access Memory (NVRAM).

OSLOADER prompts the user to select an operating system. The following is an example of what might appear on the screen of an Alpha-based computer:

```
RC Multiboot Alpha AXP Version 3.5-11
Copyright (c) 1993 Microsoft Corporation
Copyright (c) 1993 Digital Equipment Corporation
Boot Menu:
        Boot Windows NT Server Version 4.0
        Boot an alternate operating system
        Run a program
        Supplementary menu
Use the arrow keys to select, then press Enter.
Seconds until auto-boot. Select another option to override: 9
```

After selecting to boot Windows NT, OSLOADER proceeds with the kernel load phase of the boot process.

Kernel Load

Operating systems contain a core set of software instructions from which the higher level functions are based. This core set of code is referred to as the system kernel. The kernel load and processes that follow occur on both Intel and RISC-based systems. The first step is the loading, but not initialization, of the kernel (NTOSKRNL.EXE) and the Hardware Abstraction Layer (HAL.DLL). You will see several dots appear at the top of the screen during this process. The hardware information obtained by NTDETECT.COM is passed to NTOSKRNL.EXE. In the case of RISC-based systems, this hardware information is read from NVRAM.

A copy of the system hive, HKEY_LOCAL_MACHINE\SYSTEM is then loaded into memory. The control set is then loaded from ControlSet00x, where x is the value of either "Default" or "LastKnownGood" in the HKEY_LOCAL_MACHINE\SYSTEM\Select subkey.

If you select any load option other than the Last Known Good Configuration, then the boot loader loads the control set specified by the value of "Default" in the HKEY_LOCAL_ MACHINE\SYSTEM\Select subkey. If you select the Last Known Good Configuration, the control set specified by the value "LastKnownGood" in HKEY_LOCAL_MACHINE/ SYSTEM\Select is loaded. The value "Current" in the Select subkey is then set to the number of the control set loaded.

Next, HKEY_LOCAL_MACHINE\SYSTEM\CurrentControlSet\Services is scanned for drivers that contain a start value of 0. This value, which is normally assigned to low level hardware device drivers, indicates that the driver should be loaded, but not initialized before the kernel. The order in which these drivers are loaded is determined by the drivers Group value. The List value in subkey HKEY_LOCAL_MACHINE\SYSTEM\ CurrentControlSet\Control\ServiceGroupOrder contains the order in which these groups will be loaded. The drivers loaded during this phase are loaded by using BIOS INT 13h calls or by the NTBOOTDD.SYS driver. In the case of RISC-based systems, these drivers are loaded using firmware calls.

After these drivers have been loaded into memory, the boot loader then initializes NTOSKRNL.EXE and passes control to it.

Kernel Initialization

The kernel initialization phase is easily recognized because the screen turns blue and a message similar to the following appears:

```
Microsoft(R) Windows NT(TM) Version 4.0 (Build 1345)
1 System Processor (32 MB Memory)
```

After NTOSKRNL.EXE has successfully initialized and has control, it creates the HKEY_LOCAL_MACHINE\HARDWARE key from the information that was passed to it by the boot loader. All the information in this key is created fresh at each system startup.

The HKEY_LOCAL_MACHINE\SYSTEM\Clone control set is then created by the kernel by making a copy of the control set that is pointed to by the value of Current in the HKEY_ LOCAL_MACHINE\SYSTEM\Select subkey. The Clone control set is intended to be a copy of the data used to configure the computer and therefore is never modified.

The low level device drivers that were loaded in the kernel load phase are now initialized, and the Registry is once again searched for device drivers. This time, drivers with a start value of 1 are loaded and initialized. Again, the load order is determined by the Group value of the driver. The HKEY_LOCAL_MACHINE\SYSTEM\CurrentControlSet\Control\ ServiceGroupOrder subkey contains the load order of each group. The drivers loaded during this phase are not loaded by using BIOS or firmware calls like they were in the kernel load phase. Instead, they are loaded by using the device drivers that were previously initialized.

Service Load

After the device drivers are initialized, the Session Manager (SMSS.EXE) is started. The Session Manager is responsible for starting and loading the services, as well as the higher-level subsystems. The Session Manager handles tasks as defined under HKEY_LOCAL_MACHINE\SYSTEM\CurrentControlSet\Control\Session Manager. Some of the tasks and registry entries for Session Manager are listed in the following:

- BootExecute item
- Memory Management key
- DOS Devices key
- SubSystems key

Each of these are discussed in more detail in the following paragraphs.

BootExecute

The BootExecute data item contains a list of commands that Session Manager runs before it loads any services. By default, the only program that is executed is AUTOCHK.EXE. If a Windows NT system was not shut down properly, on the next boot AUTOCHK.EXE will scan the partitions for any problems and attempt to correct them.

Memory Management

The Memory Management key contains the information required for the Session Manager to set up the page files that are required by the Virtual Memory Manager. The Virtual Memory Manager function is to manage the memory subsystem so that each application can be allocated a nonconflicting block of memory. The following are some sample item settings used by Session Manager:

   NonPagedPoolSize : REG_DWORD 0

This specifies the size of the nonpaged pool of memory in bytes. The value 0 specifies to use the default size based on physical memory. The maximum for this value is 80 percent of physical memory.

   PagedPoolSize : REG_DWORD 0

This specifies the size of the paged pool of memory in bytes. The value 0 specifies to use the default of 32 MB.

   PagingFiles : REG_MULTI_SZ : c:\pagefile.sys 32

This specifies the location and size of each page file. This can contain multiple values.

DOS Devices

The DOS Devices key contains a list of devices for which Session Manager creates symbolic links. These links are used to direct certain classes of commands to the correct component in the file system.

AUX : REG_SZ : \DosDevices\COM1

MAILSLOT : REG_SZ : \Device\MailSlot

NUL : REG_SZ : \Device\Null

PIPE : REG_SZ : \Device\NamedPipe

PRN : REG_SZ : \DosDevices\LPT1

UNC : REG_SZ : \Device\Mup

SubSystems

Next, the subsystems listed under the Required item of HKEY_LOCAL_MACHINE\ SYSTEM\CurrentControlSet\Control\Session Manager\SubSystems are started. The subsystem that is listed is CSRSS.EXE, which is the Windows subsystem. This subsystem controls all I/O and video access.

Windows Start

The Windows subsystem starts several other subsystems, such as WINLOGON.EXE. WinLogon is the subsystem that controls the local login process. WinLogon then starts LSASS.EXE, the Local Security Authority (LSA). The LSA handles all user mode security validations and it must function in order to use the system. At this point, the logon dialog box appears. The logon dialog box is the first line of security. At this point, the user must supply a valid account and password in order to enter the system.

Even though you are prompted with the ability to login, the system is still in the boot process. The Service Controller, SCREG.EXE is the next process to be executed. The Service Controller searches the Registry for all services that have a start value of 0x2. The order in which these services are started is controlled by each service's values contained in DependOnGroup and DependOnService. If a service has a DependOn value set, the service is not started until the Group or Service listed has been successfully started.

The final step of the boot process occurs as soon as a user successfully logs on. The Clone control set is then copied to the LastKnownGood control set.

Troubleshooting the Boot Process

Now that the Windows NT boot process has been examined, troubleshooting boot problems should be much easier. The following sections take a look at some common problems that can occur as well as how to correct these problems.

Problems During POST

If the POST routine is unable to locate or recognize the primary hard drive, you may receive the following message:

```
Non-System disk or disk error
Replace and press any key when ready
```

An incorrect setting in CMOS is a common cause of this problem. If the system's battery becomes low, CMOS may loose setup information. Check your computer's CMOS setup and verify that the correct parameters are set for the hard drive that it installed. If you have an IDE hard drive installed, the CMOS must be set to reflect the correct drive parameters. If you are booting from a hard drive that is connected to an adapter with an on board BIOS, such as a SCSI adapter, the hard drive type in CMOS is generally set to Not Installed.

The previously listed message might also be caused by the following:

- The hard drive power cable is disconnected.

- The hard drive data cable is disconnected or connected incorrectly.

- A physical problem exists with the hard drive, such as a crashed drive.

- A nonbootable floppy is accidentally left in the floppy drive.

You should verify that none of the above items are the problem. If you suspect one to be the cause, correct the problem and try to boot the system again.

Master Boot Record Problems

The Master Boot Record is responsible for the following functions:

- Reading the Partition Table from the same sector

- Determining the location of the partition boot sector

- Loading and executing the code located in the partition boot sector

If the Master Boot Record cannot accomplish any of these, an error message is displayed. But what happens if no error message appears? If the systems hangs up after POST and does not display an error message, the Master Boot Record may be corrupt. To replace the Master Boot Record, boot the system from the floppy drive by using DOS 5.0 or greater. Then, issue the following command at the a:\ prompt:

```
fdisk /mbr
```

This rewrites the Master Boot Record, but does NOT rewrite the Partition Table. The Partition Table contains the information for all the partitions located on the hard drive. The following error message indicates that the Partition Table is corrupt:

```
Invalid Partition Table
```

This is a very serious problem! If you have not saved a copy of the MBR (see the following section, "Pre-Failure Precautions"), the only way to correct this problem is by using a low-level disk editor and manually re-creating the partition table. Re-creating the partition table is a very complex task and goes beyond the scope of this chapter. If you must undertake this task, check the *Windows NT Resource Guide.* This guide goes into great detail on the partition table.

Partition Boot Record Problems

If the Master Boot Record cannot locate the active boot partition, you may receive an error such as the following:

```
NO ROM BASIC
SYSTEM HALTED
```

This error is typically remedied by using FDISK to set the active partition. If the partition boot record needs to be repaired, you can use the Emergency Repair Disk. Initiate Emergency Repair Disk by starting the Windows NT Setup and then selecting Repair when prompted. Only the Inspect boot sector option should be selected, as shown in the following text:

```
[ ]   Inspect Registry files
[ ]   Inspect startup environment
[ ]   Verify Windows NT system files
[X]   Inspect boot sector
      Continue (perform selected tasks)
```

This process replaces the partition boot sector if it detects that the code in that sector no longer references NTLDR.

NTLDR Problems

Because NTLDR performs many functions, the opportunity arises for many problems to occur. Some common errors and techniques to correct them are examined here. One potential problem could be that NTLDR is missing from the active partition. If the active partition is FAT, you might receive the following error:

```
Couldn't find NTLDR.
```

Or, if the active partition is NTFS, you might receive the following error:

```
A kernel file is missing from the disk.
```

If either of these messages appear, the NTLDR file is missing from the active partition. If you suspect that some of the boot loader files may be missing or corrupt, you can replace them by running the repair process as previously described. To have Windows NT Setup only check the boot loader files, check the Inspect startup environment option, as shown by the following text:

```
[ ]  Inspect Registry files
[X]  Inspect startup environment
[ ]  Verify Windows NT system files
[ ]  Inspect boot sector
     Continue (perform selected tasks)
```

Choosing the Inspect startup environment box checks NTLDR, NTDETECT.COM, and BOOT.INI and repairs any files necessary.

One useful troubleshooting tool in NTLDR is the ability to display information on the kernel and driver names while they are being loaded. This tool is useful if you suspect that a driver is missing or corrupt. To activate this feature, place the /sos switch on the Windows NT entry in the BOOT.INI. The following is an example entry:

```
multi(0)disk(0)rdisk(0)partition(1)\WINNT="Windows NT Server 4.00" /sos
```

After activating this option, and after NTDETECT has completed, you see output similar to the following:

```
multi(0)disk(0)rdisk(0)partition(1)\winnt\System32\ntoskrnl.exe
multi(0)disk(0)rdisk(0)partition(1)\winnt\System32\hal.dll
multi(0)disk(0)rdisk(0)partition(1)\winnt\system32\config\system
multi(0)disk(0)rdisk(0)partition(1)\winnt\system32\c_1252.nls
multi(0)disk(0)rdisk(0)partition(1)\winnt\system32\c_437.nls
multi(0)disk(0)rdisk(0)partition(1)\winnt\system32\l_intl.nls
multi(0)disk(0)rdisk(0)partition(1)\winnt\FONTS\vgaoem.fon
multi(0)disk(0)rdisk(0)partition(1)\winnt\System32\Drivers\atapi.sys
multi(0)disk(0)rdisk(0)partition(1)\winnt\System32\Disk.sys
multi(0)disk(0)rdisk(0)partition(1)\winnt\System32\CLASS2.SYS
multi(0)disk(0)rdisk(0)partition(1)\winnt\System32\Ntfs.sys
```

This output lets you know exactly what drivers are loading and in what order. If the boot process fails during this part of the load process, the output can help identify which driver may be causing the problem.

Another feature of NTLDR is the Last Known Good Configuration. This option is very useful if a new driver is installed that causes the system to stop booting. Activating this option starts Windows NT by using the last configuration that was known to have loaded successfully. To boot by using this feature, press the space bar after the following message is displayed:

```
Press spacebar now to invoke Hardware Profile/Last Known Good menu.
```

This message appears right after NTDETECT completes. You only have this option for a few seconds, so make sure you pay close attention. After pressing the spacebar, the Hardware Profile/Last Known Good menu appears. To boot by using the Last Known Good option, you must press L.

Prefailure Recommendations

You can take several steps to ensure that you can repair any boot problems. Make sure that you have a current Emergency Repair Disk. This can be created by using the rdisk (Repair Disk) command. Figure 7.2 shows the rdisk utility.

Figure 7.2

The rdisk utility is used to update the repair information and create an emergency repair disk.

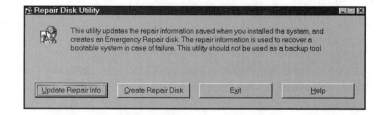

An emergency repair disk can be created by using the following steps:

1. Select the Start menu and select Run.

2. Enter **rdisk** at the prompt and press enter.

3. Click on the Update Repair Info button.

4. Select Yes to update the repair information.

5. Select Yes to create an emergency repair disk.

6. Insert a disk in drive A and select OK.

You should update the repair information and create an Emergency Repair Disk after any system changes are made. Examples of system changes are:

- Creating or modifying partitions by using Disk Administrator

- Converting a partition from FAT to NTFS

- Adding or removing a device to or from the system

Another useful tool is DiskSave, which is located on the *Windows NT Resource CD.* By using DiskSave, the Master Boot Record and the partition boot sector can be saved or restored. Note that this utility backs up and restores not only the Master Boot Record code, but also the Partition Table. If you would like to keep all of your recovery information in one place, save the MBR and partition boot record on the Emergency Repair Disk.

Conclusion

The Windows NT boot process consists of many steps, and this chapter has explained these steps in detail. You need to understand the events in the boot process in order to troubleshoot any problems that may occur during booting. This chapter also examines some common problems and their solutions. If the exact problem you are experiencing has not been discussed here, you should at least be on your way to pinpointing the problem and finding a solution.

Troubleshooting Windows NT Security

*A*nyone who has ever used Windows NT and obtained the frustrating error message `"Access is denied"` *(as depicted in figure 8.1) has surely asked the question, "Why did that happen?" The answer to this question is not straightforward, and one has to go back to the early days of Windows NT development to understand how the security architecture is put together.*

Figure 8.1

An example of a security-related error message, which indicates that Windows NT has refused access permission to a user.

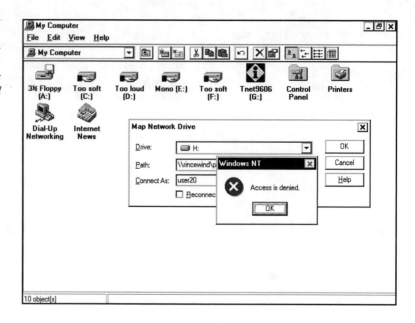

In the summer of 1988, Bill Gates and Dave Cutler discussed the creation of Windows NT. Even then, one of their major design goals for this new operating system was security. This meant that security was cast into the foundations of the Windows NT operating system, making it an integral part of the kernel.

The problem, however, was how to put the security into the operating system and retain system-wide reusability of the security data structures. The solution, of course, was to use objects.

Despite this pervasive use of objects, Windows NT 4 is not really an object-oriented operating system. Objects are only used for the NT Executive data structures that specifically require protection. This meant that every object could be provided with an access control list, which could dictate who could gain access to this security object.

This use of objects permitted the Windows NT development team to focus object protection centrally within the Windows NT design, and comply with C2 security specifications.

This chapter examines Windows NT 4 security and answers questions about Windows NT 4 resource security problems. The chapter is divided into two sections, the first of which looks at a method of troubleshooting this type of problem. In order to develop a logical and successful approach to security troubleshooting, one must first understand how Windows NT 4 security is put together. The first part of this chapter, therefore, highlights the salient features of Windows NT 4's security architecture.

The second part of this chapter describes the tools available to help you isolate and rectify security-related problems. Although numerous utilities are available for this task—either direct from Microsoft or via third-party developers—the tools covered in this chapter illustrate the application of the methodology introduced in the first part of this chapter.

If you are currently administrating a Windows NT 4 network or you are simply interested in how Windows NT security problems can be avoided or detected, this chapter will be of interest to you. This chapter provides sufficient theoretical and technical coverage of the various security-related aspects of Windows NT 4 to be a sufficient method and toolset for troubleshooting Windows NT 4 security.

Methodology

Helen Custer, in her book *Inside Windows NT*, states, "Windows NT includes a uniform security architecture that meets the requirements for a U.S. government rating. For the corporate environment, it provides a safe environment to run mission-critical applications."

Today, networks are used to share key information and resources among many users who work with organizations of varying sizes. Often these information or resource repositories are intended to be secure (that is, access is restricted to specific individuals). The capability of corporate networks to prevent unauthorized access to information is pivotal to the security and competitiveness of any organization.

Windows NT Server 4 is currently being evaluated for C2 security compliance as articulated in the U.S. Department of Defense's National Computer Security Center publication *Trusted Computer System Evaluation Criteria* (also known as the Orange Book). The most important requirements of C2-level security are:

- Identification and authentication. Each user must be uniquely identified to the operating system before being allowed to access the system. Identification is achieved by means of unique logon credentials (user name and password). Furthermore, the system must be able to use these unique credentials to generate a unique user identifier and to track user activity via this unique user identifier.

- Discretionary access control. The owner of any resource, such as a directory, must be able to control access to that resource.

- Auditing. System administrators must be able to audit security-related events and the actions of individual users. Furthermore, access to this audit data must be limited to authorized administrators.

Some military institutions have even more stringent security requirements. For this reason, Windows NT has been designed to evolve toward Class B2 security, also known as Mandatory Access Control. Protecting objects, therefore, includes the use of discretionary access control, identification and authentication, auditing, and eventually mandatory access control.

To be effective, troubleshooting must look for problems in each of the three major aspects of Windows NT security: identification and authentication, discretionary access control, and auditing. To solve problems relating to these areas, one must first fully understand the mechanisms that make them work. Understanding how they work often exposes how they do not work or, at the very least, explains the reason behind specifically observed behavior (for example, Access is denied).

The troubleshooting methodology described in this chapter is dependent upon the thorough understanding of how users are identified and authenticated by the Windows NT 4 operating system. Because it may also be necessary to keep track of users who gain lawful access to a Windows NT server, this methodology also includes a quick look at auditing and how it can be used to solve security problems.

Following one or more of the general pathways described in this chapter enables you to track down security errors, user difficulties, or even breaches of network security. After you understand how Windows NT security is put together, the nature and symptoms of the problem suggests which path to follow.

If the root cause of the problem relates to Windows NT security, checking how a particular object consumer—a user, for example—is identified or authenticated, evaluating the discretionary access to that particular object, or auditing the behavior of both the object consumer and the object itself easily isolates and solves Windows NT 4 security troubleshooting problems.

Identification and Authentication

When working in a secure operating system environment, being able to consistently and uniquely identify yourself to the system is crucial because your security context governs your ability to do specific operations (such as gain access to a server share, or open a handle to a file, and so on) within the operating system. User identification, and subsequent authentication, is one of the major security concerns in a networked operating system like Windows NT 4.

User identification and authentication are discussed in the following sections in order to highlight the underlying mechanisms that make them work. After you understand these mechanisms, you can resolve their problems better and more quickly.

User Identification

Users are identified to the system by a unique security ID. Security IDs are unique across time and space, meaning that there is no possibility (statistically speaking) of having two identical security IDs.

Furthermore, if a unique security ID is lost through deletion of an account, the security context of that user is also lost. This particular situation is to be avoided at all costs (usually by disabling the user account for a period, before eventually deleting it), because Windows NT uses this security ID to identify a user within the operating system (an important building block of Windows NT security).

Re-creating the same user account (via User Manager for Domains) causes an entirely new security ID to be generated, and Windows NT does not recognize the previous and current accounts as being the same user (even if exactly the same user particulars were furnished during the user account creation). This is because of the highly unique nature of the security ID.

A security ID (and the associated security context) plays the same role, within Windows NT security, as one's passport (and associated entry/exit visa) does during international travel. Your passport identifies you uniquely to the authorities, while your visa dictates the terms of your stay within a foreign country.

Your security context, therefore, is the range of system-wide permissions and privileges that have been associated or assigned to your specific security ID. Because the security ID of a user is lost when the account is deleted, it is impossible to regenerate exactly the same security ID by re-creating the user account (using User Manager for Domains). This implies that because your security context is focused on your security ID, your security context is also lost when your user account is deleted.

In this discussion of user identification, the specific aspects covered include security identifiers, loss of security context, access tokens, the logon process, and passwords.

Security Identifiers

In the Windows NT 4 Registry, it is possible to trace a user by using the unique security ID assigned during the creation of the user account. Figure 8.2 shows that HKEY_LOCAL_MACHINE\SOFTWARE\Microsoft\Windows NT\CurrentVersion\ProfileList enumerates the security IDs of all the users who have user profiles and are defined in the security accounts manager database. Furthermore, the ProfileImagePath entry contains the physical location of the user profile.

Furthermore, figure 8.2 provides an example of how the ProfileImagePath Registry entry can be used to match the unique security ID (located just below the ProfileList Registry key) to the "replicate" user's profile (%SystemRoot%\Profiles\replicate).

A security ID is a statistically unique number. In other words, a security ID value used to represent a specific user should never be used at a later date to represent another user. All security IDs are created by using a combination of user information, time, date, and domain information. Security IDs are represented by using the following format:

S-1-X-Y^1-Y^2-..........-Y^n

- According to Microsoft, the prefix S-1 indicates that this is a revision 1 security ID. This may indicate future enhancements or revisions to the security ID. It is generally expected that the Windows NT Directory Services will be extended in future releases of Windows NT (such as Cairo) and that the security ID will be revised.

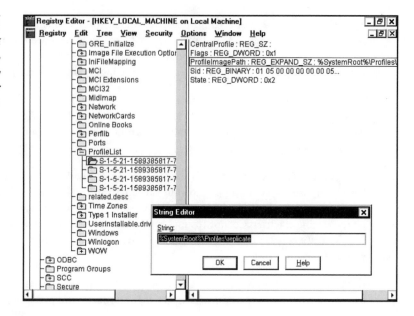

Figure 8.2

The Windows NT 4 Registry can be used to match a unique security ID to a corresponding user profile.

- The X is the value representing the identifier authority.

- The values Y^1-Y^2-..........-Y^n represent the security ID's sub-authority values.

The identifier authority value is probably the most important information contained in a security ID because this value identifies the agency that issued the security ID. Typically the identifier authority represents a corporation or large organization.

Similarly, sub-authority values identify sub-agencies involved in issuing the security ID. For example, Microsoft's Internet security framework involves the issuing of security certificates, which are needed for client authentication and access control. The security ID sub-authority values could identify a certificate authority that could be partly responsible for issuing a Windows NT security ID.

A Windows NT system has some predefined, well known security IDs. A well known security ID is a security ID whose value is constant across all Windows NT systems. In addition, some well known security IDs are universal across all systems.

Loss of Security Context

A security ID is a highly unique value, and this value is used to accurately and consistently identify Windows NT security objects, in particular users.

If, however, this unique security ID is lost, the security context of that object is also lost. This can have serious repercussions on the security administration of the afflicted network. The only way to lose a unique security ID is to delete the corresponding security object, such as a user account.

Figure 8.3

When deleting a user account, a warning is issued to indicate the imminent loss of the security ID associated with this user account.

For example, suppose a user who has a Windows NT account leaves his job at a particular company. Later this user returns to a different job at the same company. When this user left the first time, the administrator deleted his user account. Now Windows NT no longer accepts this user's security credentials as valid. When the user returns, the administrator creates a new account, and Windows NT generates a new security ID for that account. The new security ID does not match the old one, so the user now has a brand-new security context within Windows NT—that is, the old security context is lost.

When this user logs on, Windows NT creates an access token to identify this user to the Windows NT security subsystem. This access token includes the new security ID for the user, as well as other security IDs for the groups to which the user belongs, plus other information (such as the user's name and the groups to which that user belongs). In addition, every process that runs on behalf of this user has a copy of this access token (which now contains a brand new security ID for this newly created user).

Windows NT 4 refers to the security IDs within a user's access token whenever he tries to access an object. The security IDs are compared with the list of access permissions for the object, to ensure that the user has sufficient permission to access the object. Because the security ID reflected in the access control list of the object is definitely not the same as the security ID contained within the user's access token, the user is denied access to the object by the Windows NT security subsystem. In other words, in this example, the user has lost his security context because of his loss of security ID.

Access Tokens

Before a user can do anything on a Windows NT system, she must log on to the system by supplying a user name and password. Windows NT uses the user name for identification and the password for validation. The following procedure illustrates the interactive logon process for Windows NT 4.

The initial logon process for Windows NT is interactive, meaning that the user must type information at the keyboard in response to a dialog box that the operating system displays on the screen. Windows NT grants or denies access based upon the information provided by the user.

Access tokens are discussed in more detail later in this chapter.

The Logon Process

The WinLogon process consists of nine steps that provide a Windows NT user with an access token and a logon session with the operating system. The process of interactive logon is explained in the following steps:

1. The user presses Ctrl+Alt+Del to gain the attention of Windows NT 4. This key combination before logon protects against Trojan Horse-type programs that impersonate the operating system and trick users into disclosing their user name and password.

2. When the user provides a user name and a password (security credentials), the logon process calls the Local Security Authority.

   The Local Security Authority (LSA) ensures that the user has permission to access the system, and forms the center of the Windows NT security subsystem. It generates access tokens, manages the local security policy, and provides interactive user authentication services. The LSA also controls audit policy and logs the audit messages generated by other members of the security subsystem.

3. The Local Security Authority runs the appropriate authentication package. All user authentication in Windows NT 4 occurs using the LsaLogonUser API. LsaLogonUser actually authenticates users by calling an authentication package. The default authentication package that comes with Windows NT 4 is the MSV1_0 Authentication Package. The MSV Authentication Package uses the security accounts manager database as its database of users, and it supports pass-through authentication of users in other domains by using the NetLogon service.

4. The authentication package checks the user accounts database to see whether the account is local. If it is, the user name and password are verified against those held in the user accounts database. If not, the requested logon is forwarded to an alternate authentication package.

5. When the account is validated, the Security Accounts Manager returns the user's security ID and the security IDs of any global groups to which the user belongs.

6. The authentication package creates a logon session and then passes the logon session and the security IDs associated with the user to the Local Security Authority.

7. If the logon is rejected, the logon session is deleted and an error is returned to the logon process. Otherwise, an access token is created, containing the user's security ID and the security IDs of Everyone and other groups. The access token also contains user rights assigned to the collected security IDs. This access token is returned to the logon process with a Success status.

8. The logon session calls the Win32 subsystem to create a process and attach the access token to the process, thus creating a subject for the user account.

   The Windows NT security model must ensure that the programs that a user runs have no more access to objects than the user does. So, if a user is granted only read access to a file, then when he or she runs a program, that program cannot write to the file.

   A subject is the combination of the user's access token plus the program acting on the user's behalf. Windows NT uses subjects to track and manage permissions for the programs each user runs. When a program or process runs on the user's behalf, it is said to be running in the security context of that user. The security context controls what access the subject has to objects or system services.

9. For an interactive Windows NT session, the Win32 subsystem starts the Windows NT 4 shell (systray.exe) for the user.

After the validation process, a user's shell process (the process in which Explorer is started for the user) is given an access token. The information in this access token is used as a security reference for anything the user does or any process that runs on the user's behalf. Even threads that belong to any of the user's processes inherit a copy of this access token.

Because Windows NT can identify users and knows what each user is allowed to do, it can compare the access control list for the object with the user's access token to determine what kinds of accesses, if any, are allowed for each user.

Passwords

User records are stored in the security accounts manager database. Each user has two passwords with which it is associated: the LAN Manager compatible password and the Windows NT 4 password. Each password is stored doubly encrypted in the Security Accounts Manager database.

The LAN Manager password is computed by encrypting a secret key with the clear text password by using DES encryption. In using data encryption, a plain text message can be encoded so it appears like random nonsense and is very difficult to transform back to the original message, without the secret key.

DES encryption is a symmetric algorithm, which is the most common type of encryption algorithm. It is known as symmetric because the same key is used for both encryption and decryption. Symmetric algorithms are very fast.

The Windows NT 4 password is based on the Unicode character set and is computed by using the RSA encryption algorithm. The RSA public-key cipher is popular for both encryption and signatures.

Although both the Lan Manager and Windows NT 4 versions of the user password are maintained (for compatibility reasons), only the Windows NT 4 version of the password is affected if the password is set or changed from a Windows NT client. All the existing user interface limits do not permit Windows NT 4 passwords to exceed 14 characters.

Passwords do not travel across the network during Windows NT 4 authentication. Instead, a random string is sent to the client. The client encrypts the string, based on the user's entered password, and passes the result to the server. The server does the same encryption at its end, using the password it has on file for the user and comparing the string it develops to the string returned by the client. If they match, access is granted.

User Authentication

User authentication makes use of the user identification concepts discussed in the preceding section in order to provide a user legal access to both the operating system and its resources.

Two aspects of user authentication are discussed in this section: pass-through authentication and impersonation. Although it can be seen as being part of the user authentication role, discretionary access control is discussed later in this chapter to provide a natural division in the presentation of user authentication theory.

Pass-Through Authentication

In figure 8.4, the user provides Windows NT with some logon credentials (step 1). Although the user is physically located in Domain_B, his user account has been created in Domain_A (step 2). The user is therefore providing logon credentials that cannot be authenticated within the local domain (step 3). The logon request is passed (by the NetLogon service) to a domain controller in the trusted domain (step 4), where the account is successfully authenticated and an access token can be awarded to this user (step 5).

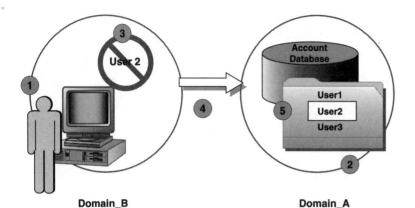

Figure 8.4

The process of pass-through authentication permits a user to log on within a domain without having a user account defined within that domain.

The NetLogon service implements pass-through authentication in three basic steps: by selecting the domain to pass the authentication request to, by selecting the server within the domain, and by actually passing the authentication request to the selected server.

Selecting the domain is straightforward. The domain name is passed to LsaLogonUser. The domain name is processed as follows:

■ If the domain name matches the name of the security accounts manager database, the authentication is processed on that machine. The name of the Security Accounts Manager database on a Windows NT workstation that is a member of a domain is considered to be the name of the Windows NT machine. The name of the security accounts manager database on a Windows NT domain controller is the name of the domain. All logons to Windows NT machines, that are not members of a domain, are processed locally.

■ If the domain name specified is trusted by this domain, the authentication request is passed to the trusted domain. Because the list of trusted domains is readily available on Windows NT 4 domain controllers, this comparison is trivial. On a Windows NT 4 workstation, the request is always passed to the primary domain of the workstation, enabling the primary domain to determine whether the specified domain is trusted.

■ If the domain name specified is not trusted by this domain, the authentication request is processed on the machine being connected to, as if the domain name specified were that domain name. NetLogon does not differentiate between a nonexistent domain, an untrusted domain, and an incorrectly typed domain name.

The Windows NT 4 domain controller also confirms that the account exists locally. If so, the request is processed locally; otherwise, the domain controller tries to determine whether a trusted domain has the account. It does this by sending a mail slot message to each trusted domain. Each trusted domain responds indicating whether it defines the account specified.

The request is passed to the first domain that responds affirmatively. If no domain responds affirmatively, this NULL domain is treated as an untrusted domain and the request is processed locally. If more than one domain responds affirmatively, only the first response is used.

The NetLogon service picks a server in the domain by a process called discovery. A Windows NT 4 workstation finds the name of one of the Windows NT 4 domain controllers in its primary domain. A Windows NT 4 domain controller finds the name of a Windows NT 4 domain controller in each trusted domain.

Subjects and Impersonation

An objective of 'the Windows NT 4 security model is to ensure that the programs a user executes have no more access to objects than the user does. If, for example, a user is granted only read access to a file, when he executes a program, that program cannot write to the file because the program has only inherited read permission from the user.

A subject is the combination of the user's access token plus the program acting on the user's behalf. Windows NT 4 uses subjects to track and manage permissions for the programs each user executes. When a program or process runs on the user's behalf, it is said to be running in the security context of that user. The security context, therefore, controls what access the subject has to objects or system services.

The client-server model of Windows NT 4 defines two classes of subjects within its security architecture:

- **A Simple Subject.** A simple subject is a process that was assigned a security context when the corresponding user logged on. It is not acting in the capacity of a protected server (see Server Subject), which may have other subjects as clients.

- **A Server Subject.** A server subject is a process implemented as a protected server (such as the Win32 subsystem), and it is capable of having other subjects as clients. A server subject typically has the security context of a client when acting on its behalf.

Generally, when a subject calls an object service, through a protected subsystem, the subject's token is used by the service to determine who made the call and to decide whether the caller has sufficient access authority to perform the requested action.

Windows NT 4 enables one process to take on the security attributes of another through a technique called impersonation. Using impersonation, the server can change its security identity to that of the client. A server typically has more permissions to access system objects and resources (such as databases on the server) than the client requesting the specific service.

For example, when a request is delivered to the server through a named pipe, the server changes its security identity to the security identity of the client. This limits the server to only those permissions granted to the client rather than its own permissions. This has the effect of increasing the security of named pipes.

Discretionary Access Control

All Windows NT 4 resources are represented as objects that can be accessed only by authorized Windows NT 4 services and users. An object in Windows NT 4 is defined as a set of data used by the system and the set of actions that manipulate that data.

This definition can be applied to any object used by the system, including memory, printers, or processes. Windows NT 4 objects include directories, symbolic links, printers, processes, network shares, communication ports, devices, windows, files, and threads.

A file object, for example, consists of data stored in a file and a set of functions that enables you to read, write, or delete data in that file.

In this section, the implementation and application of discretionary access are discussed. Some topics restate material in previous sections, but here are focused on the discussion of discretionary access. The topics under discussion include access tokens, security IDs, access control lists, access control entries, permission checking and its optimization, and the security reference monitor.

Access Tokens

When a user's process attempts to access any object, Windows NT 4 checks the user ID and list of groups in the user process's access token against the object's access control list (see fig. 8.5). This check determines whether the user is granted the requested access to the object. The access token is permanently attached to each of the user's processes and serves as the process's identity card when it attempts to use system resources. Access tokens are objects and have attributes and services just like any other system object.

User
  RINCEWIND\wayne

Groups:
  Administrators
  Everyone
  Domain

Special privileges:
  seCreateTokenPrivilege

Figure 8.5
Windows NT uses an access token to uniquely identify the user and the groups to which the user belongs.

Security IDs

Although user and group identifications are represented here as names, the computer actually stores this information as a security identifier and group security identifiers.

A security identifier is a unique identifier used to represent a user, and a group security identifier is a unique identifier used to represent a group or some type of security authority. Security identifiers are used within access tokens and access control lists instead of user names or group names. A security identifier is represented as a unique number.

When users are identified by security identifiers, each instance of the account name has a unique security identifier, even though the same user account name may have been created multiple times on the same computer. For example, if you have a user account for User 1, delete it and then create a new account for User 1 by using the same name. The new account does not have access to the same resources as the old account. Although the account name is the same, the security identifier is different.

Access Control Lists

All functions used to access an object, such as opening a file, are directly associated with a specific object. In addition, the users and groups that are permitted to use the function are also associated with the object. Only users with the appropriate rights are allowed to use functions on an object. As a result, functions from one process cannot access objects that belong to another process.

This characteristic of objects provides built-in security. Access to each object is controlled through an access control list. The access control list contains the user (and group) accounts that have access and permissions to the object. When a user wants to access an object, the security subsystem checks the user's security identifier, and group membership, with the access control list to determine whether or not the requested object access is permitted.

Administrators and users with Change Permissions enabled can use the CACLS.EXE command (located in the \system32 directory) to show or modify access control lists for directories and files.

If you query access control lists for directories, the output is a listing of the permissions on the directory and the files inside the directory (see fig. 8.6). A screen shot, using this utility, is displayed in figure 8.7.

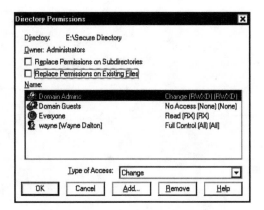

Figure 8.6

The Directory Permissions dialog box displays the permitted user and group access assigned to this directory object.

Under Windows NT 4 Explorer in the Directory Permissions dialog box (refer to fig. 8.6), the first set of parentheses contains directory permissions, and the second set contains file permissions. However, when using the CACLS utility, this information is displayed differently; the first listing of a group or user contains the file permissions whereas the second listing contains the directory permissions.

A full list of the CACLS syntax can be obtained by executing the CACLS utility from the command prompt with the /? Switch. The following is the short form of the syntax:

CACLS <file name|folder> [/t] [/e] [/c] [/g user:perm] [/r user [...]][/p user:perm [...]] [/d user [...]]

Some examples may help to clarify the syntax and usage of this utility:

1. To revoke a user's rights to a file or folder, use the following CACLS syntax:

   cacls <file name|folder> /e /r <user name>

   /e = edit ACL

   /r = revoke user rights

2. To grant a user specific rights to a file or folder, use the following CACLS syntax:

   cacls <file name|folder> /e /g <user name>:<permission>

   /g = grant specified user rights

3. To replace a user's rights to a file or folder, use the following CACLS syntax:

   cacls <file name|folder> /e /p <user name>:<permission>

   /p = replace specified user rights

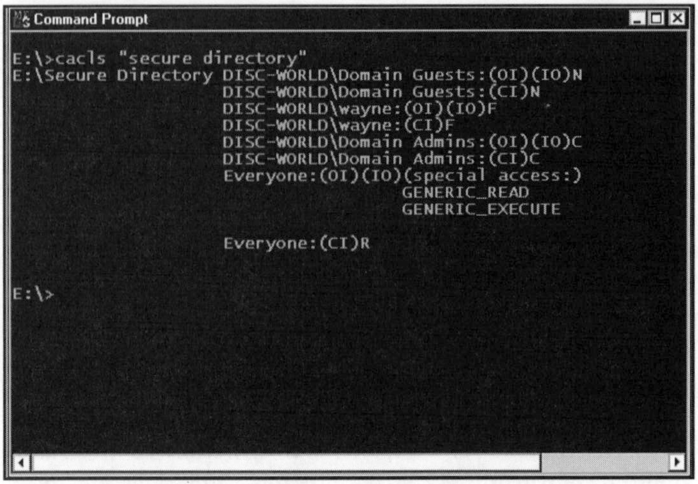

Figure 8.7

*The CACLS.EXE utility
provides access control
information about files
and directories.*

In figure 8.7, the CACLS utility was executed within a directory called \secure directory, and the various access control entries (within this directory's access control list) have been displayed. The format of the output is as follows:

<directory name>   <user/group>:<file permission>

                      <user/group>:<directory permission>

Each set of access control flags is followed by a single character that indicates the nature of the object access. For example, the "C" in DISC-WORLD\Domain Admins:(OI)(IO)C means that the Change right has been assigned to this directory for the DISC-WORLD\Domain Admins global group. The complete list of access rights are:

- N = None

- R = Read

- C = Change (write)

- F = Full control

The letters in parentheses in figure 8.7 represent the access control flags set for the object and container (in this case, the "secure directory" directory object). These access control flags, for file and directory permissions, are discussed next.

File Permissions

Two file permission indicators are evident in CACLS output:

- OI = MSG_CACLS_OBJECT_INHERIT

  The OI access control flag is applicable to permissions for files copied to or created in this directory. It means that this access control entry is inherited by noncontainer objects, such as files created within the container object to which the access control entry is assigned.

- IO = MSG_CACLS_INHERIT_ONLY

  The IO access control flag is applicable to permissions for files copied to or created in this directory. It means that this access control entry does not apply to the container object but to objects contained by it.

Normally both references are present in CACLS output.

Directory Permissions

- CI = MSG_CACLS_CONTAINER_INHERIT

  The CI access control flag is applicable to permissions for the directory and directories copied to or created in this directory. It means that this access control entry is inherited by container objects, such as directories.

- NP = MSG_CACLS_NO_PROPAGATE_INHERIT

  The NP access control flag is displayed when a permission is not to be inherited. This means that the MSG_CACLS_OBJECT_INHERIT and MSG_CACLS_ CONTAINER_INHERIT bits are not propagated to an inherited ACE.

A directory's ACL normally contains at least two ACEs. If CACLS output contains only one ACE, permissions for the other ACE have not been specified. NT Explorer, in this case, displays the ACE as "(Not Specified)".

Access Control Entries

Every user of the system needs to have a user account that can be added to resource access control lists. This requirement, for a user account, also applies to applications and services that need to access resources. When an administrator grants access to a resource, the user account is added to the access control list for that resource along with any specific permissions.

Figures 8.6 and 8.7 illustrate the assignment of access permissions using the NT Explorer (fig. 8.6) and the CACLS.EXE utility (fig. 8.7). The correlation between these two figures is easily seen because the assigned access permissions (to \Secure Directory) are identical.

For example, figure 8.6 highlights the fact that the Domain Admins global group has been granted Change (RXWD)(RXWD) rights to the directory. Figure 8.7 depicts the identical directory access permission as DISC-WORLD\Domain Admins:(OI)(IO)C.

Each entry in the dialog in figure 8.6, and each pair of entries in the CACLS output in figure 8.7, is called an access control entry. Each entry identifies a user or group and the permissions that have been granted or denied for the object. An access control entry is added to the access control list for each user or group that is granted or denied access to an object.

Entries that deny access are listed first in the access control list, and entries that permit access are listed next. The only time this order is changed is when a company has written its own application that edits the access control list of a resource. In this case, a company can place the access control entry anywhere in the access control list.

Access to resources begins with the user logging on. Windows NT 4 requires that users log on before they can access any resources. When a user successfully logs on, she receives an access token that remains with the user process until logging off. Each time the user attempts to access a resource, the access token is compared to the resource access control list to determine whether access is granted or denied.

Checking Permissions

Windows NT 4 requires each user to provide a unique user name and password to log on to a computer. This mandatory logon process cannot be disabled.

When a user logs on to Windows NT 4, the security subsystem creates an access token for the user. The access token includes information such as the user's name and the groups to which the user belongs. Access to the system is allowed after the user has received this access token. During the time a user is logged into a system, she is identified to the system by this access token.

Windows NT 4 compares the information in the access token to the information in the access control list to determine whether access should be granted. When a user attempts to access a resource on the system, the security subsystem compares the user's access token to the access control list to validate or deny the requested permission to the resource. The security subsystem follows these steps:

1. Starting at the top of the access control list, the security subsystem checks each Access Control Entry to see whether it explicitly denies the user (or any of the groups that appear in the user's access token) the type of access that is being requested.

2. The security subsystem checks to see whether the type of access requested has been explicitly granted to the user or any of the groups in the user's access token.

3. The security subsystem repeats step 1 and 2 for each entry in the access control list either until it has encountered a deny or until it has accumulated all the necessary permissions to grant the requested access.

4. If neither a deny or a grant appears in the access control list for each of the requested permissions, the user is denied access.

Optimizing Permission Checking

When Windows NT 4 grants access to an object, what it really does is give the user's process a pointer (handle) to the object. A handle is an identifier used internally by the system to identify and access a resource. The system also creates a list of allowed permissions called the list of granted access rights. This information is then stored in the user's process.

In this way, an access control list is checked only when the object is initially opened. Subsequent actions performed on an opened object are checked against the list of granted access rights that have been stored in the user's process table for that handle.

The Security Reference Monitor

The security reference monitor is the Windows NT 4 component that determines whether a process should be granted rights to access an object (see fig. 8.8). It determines access rights by comparing the process's access token with the access control list of the object the process is trying to open. This section examines how the comparison process used by the security reference monitor impacts Windows NT 4 support.

When an open resource connection request, such as net use, is passed to the network redirector (which forms part of the Windows NT 4 installable file system), it does not use the token to check access control lists. The redirector, with help from components such as the security reference monitor and local security authority, maps the token back to the user credentials that were originally passed to the WinLogon process when the local user logged on (that is, the time when this token was generated).

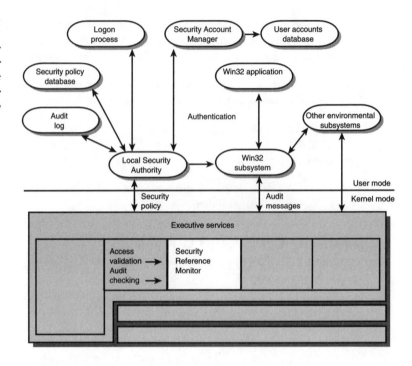

Figure 8.8

*The security reference
monitor is responsible for
access validation and audit
checking within the
Windows NT 4 security
model.*

Auditing User Activity

To keep track of selected user activity, one can audit certain security events and log output into a security log. This auditing can be enabled by using the Audit Policy dialog box (see fig. 8.9) provided by the User Manager for Domains utility.

When administering domains, the Audit policy affects the security logs of the domain controller and of all servers in the domain because they share the same Audit policy. When administering a computer running Windows NT 4 Workstation or a Windows NT Server (as an application server), this policy affects only the security log of that computer.

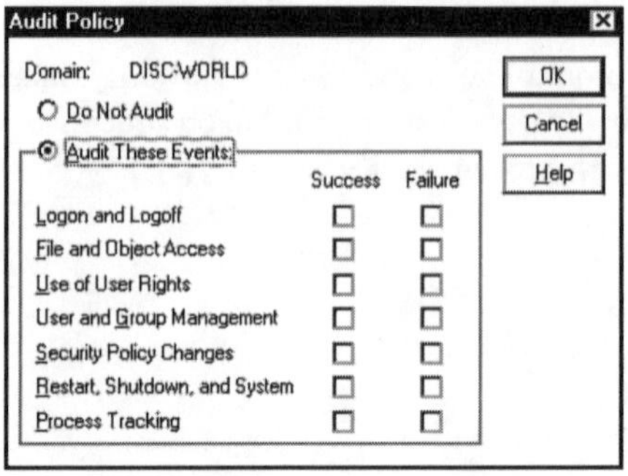

Figure 8.9

*User Manager for
Domains can be used
to enable auditing via
the Auditing Policy
dialog box.*

Because the security log is limited in size, selecting every possible logging option does not allow for a long duration of security auditing. The maximum size of each computer's security log is defined in Event Viewer. Entries in a security log can be reviewed by using Event Viewer (see fig. 8.10).

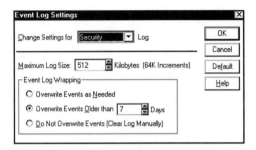

Figure 8.10

The Event Viewer utility can be used to set the size of the security event log through the Event Log Settings dialog box.

Windows NT 4 includes auditing features you can use to collect information about how your system is being used. These features also enable you to monitor events related to system security, to identify any security breaches, and to determine the extent and location of any damage. The level of audited events is adjustable to suit the needs of your organization.

Some organizations need little auditing information whereas others would be willing to trade some performance and disk space for detailed information that can be used to analyze the system. When you enable auditing, however, each audit check the system performs has some small performance overhead.

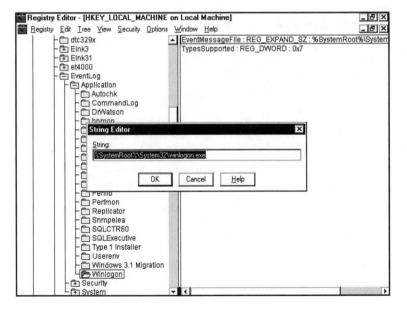

Figure 8.11

Windows NT 4 applications and services must be registered in the Registry before they can start reporting to the Event Log.

Tracking Security Events

Windows NT 4 can track events related to the operating system itself and to individual applications. Each application can define its own auditable events. Definitions of these events are added to the Registry when the application is installed on your Windows NT 4 system.

You can locate the event message files (the location of Event Viewer messages for a specific application) in the HKEY_LOCAL_MACHINE\SYSTEM\CurrentControlSet\Services\ EventLog key. This key is divided into three separate subkeys—Application, Security, and System—and each application is registered beneath the applicable entry.

Figure 8.11 depicts the corresponding registry value for the WinLogon application (as contained in the String Editor dialog box in figure 8.11), which is located beneath the \EventLog\Application Registry key. This means that this application (%systemroot%\ system32\winlogon.exe) reports to the Application log (located in\system32\config\ AppEvent.evt) as WinLogon (the exact name of the Registry key displayed in figure 8.11).

Audit events are identified to the system by the event source module name and an event ID. In addition to listing events by event ID, the security log in Event Viewer lists them by category. The following categories of events are displayed in the Security Log. (Those in parentheses are found in the Audit Policy dialog box of User Manager.)

Table 8.1
Description of Auditing Categories

Category	Meaning
Logon/Logoff (Logon and Logoff)	These events describe a single logon or logoff attempt, whether successful or unsuccessful. Included in each logon description is an indication of what type of logon was requested or performed (that is, interactive, network, or service).
Object Access (File and Object Access)	These events describe both successful and unsuccessful accesses to protected objects.
Privilege Use (Use of User Rights)	These events describe both successful and unsuccessful attempts to use privileges. They also include information about when some special privileges are assigned. These special privileges are audited only at assignment time, not at time of use.
Account Management (User and Group Management)	These events describe high-level changes to the user accounts database, such as User Created or Group Membership Change. Potentially, a more detailed, object-level audit is also performed. (See Object Access events.)

Category	Meaning
Policy Change (Security Policy Changes)	These events describe high-level changes to the security policy database, such as assignment of privileges or logon capabilities. Potentially, a more detailed, object-level audit is also performed. (See Object Access events.)
System Event (System)	These events indicate something affecting the security of the entire system or audit log occurred. System shutdown and restart are also included with (but are separate to) system events.
Detailed Tracking (Process Tracking)	These events provide detailed subject-tracking information. This includes information such as program activation, handle duplication, and indirect object access.

Using Events to Track Users and Files

One of the most important aspects of security is determining who is responsible for the actual operations of security interest—file writes or security policy change, for example. Although a thread that requests access to a resource is identified by the user ID, the thread may be impersonating someone else. In this case, logging events by user ID may be misleading and may not be useful in finding the perpetrator in the case of a security breach.

To solve this problem, two levels of subject identification are used in Windows NT 4 auditing and in the security log. These are the user ID (also called the primary ID) and the impersonation ID (also called the client ID). These two IDs are used to determine who is performing auditable actions.

In some cases, however, a security administrator wants to see what is happening with each process. To meet this need, auditing information also includes a subject's process ID where possible.

When process tracking is enabled (through the Audit Policy dialog box of User Manager), audit messages are generated each time a new process is created (see figure 8.12). This information can be correlated with specific audit messages to see not only which user account is being used to perform auditable actions, but also which program is running.

Many audit events also include a handle ID, which can associate the event with future events. For example, when a file is opened, the audit information indicates the handle ID assigned. When the handle is closed, another audit event with the same handle ID is generated (figure 8.13 illustrates this process). With this information, you can determine exactly how long the file remained open. This could be useful, for example, when you want to assess damage following a security breach. Figure 8.13 is included to illustrate how IDs can be used to track file usage.

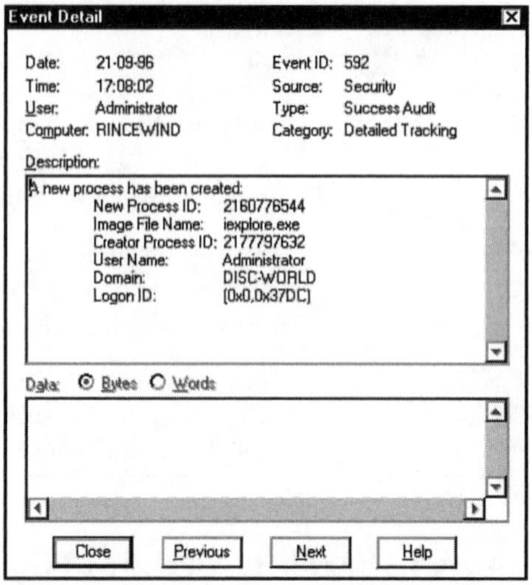

Figure 8.12

Process tracking is possible by using the Event Detail dialog of the Event Viewer (Security Log) utility.

```
Event Detail                                              ×

Date:      21-09-96            Event ID:  592
Time:      17:08:02            Source:    Security
User:      Administrator       Type:      Success Audit
Computer:  RINCEWIND           Category:  Detailed Tracking

Description:
A new process has been created:
        New Process ID:    2160776544
        Image File Name:   iexplore.exe
        Creator Process ID: 2177797632
        User Name:         Administrator
        Domain:            DISC-WORLD
        Logon ID:          (0x0,0x37DC)

Data:  ⊙ Bytes  ○ Words



        Close      Previous      Next      Help
```

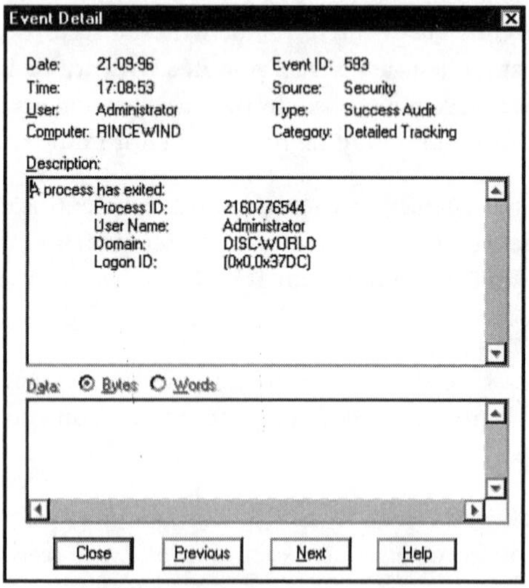

Figure 8.13

Tracking file activity is possible by using the Event Detail dialog of the Event Viewer (Security Log) utility.

```
Event Detail                                              ×

Date:      21-09-96            Event ID:  593
Time:      17:08:53            Source:    Security
User:      Administrator       Type:      Success Audit
Computer:  RINCEWIND           Category:  Detailed Tracking

Description:
A process has exited:
        Process ID:        2160776544
        User Name:         Administrator
        Domain:            DISC-WORLD
        Logon ID:          (0x0,0x37DC)

Data:  ⊙ Bytes  ○ Words



        Close      Previous      Next      Help
```

The following list shows some of the information that Windows NT 4 tracks within a process's access token. This information also is used for auditing.

■ The security ID of the user account used to log on

■ The group security IDs and corresponding attributes of groups to which the user is assigned membership

- The names of the privileges assigned to and used by the user, and their corresponding attributes

- Authentication ID, assigned when the user logs on

Tools

The three major aspects of Windows NT 4 security—identification and authentication, discretionary access, and auditing—are presented in the first part of this chapter. Together, they form the components of a strategy to solve security-related problems. How these components are used and what tools are available to assist, forms the thrust of this section.

The toolset presented is divided among these three central aspects, and where possible, examples are presented to clarify their application.

Identification and Authentication

Problems with identifying and authenticating users in a Windows NT environment invariably arise from incorrect credentials (user name and password) or from mismatching of the parameters associated with user identification and authentication.

This section covers the various tools and concepts relating to the identification and validation of a Windows NT 4 user. This is not a trivial task, and requires a sound understanding of how a user is identified to the system, and how the system in turn validates this user during the logon process.

The focus of this section, therefore, is the logon process and when it can fail. The User Manager for Domains utility plays a central role during the problem solving phase of user authentication and validation.

User Identification

Windows NT 4 makes use of mandatory logon, thereby forcing users to identify themselves to the system. This practice ensures that only valid users are able to log onto the system. If you do not supply credentials that are recognized by the local security authority of a particular workstation or domain, you are not permitted to gain access to the system (see fig. 8.14).

Troubleshooting problems of this nature, therefore, is a simple matter of ensuring that proper credentials are supplied during the logon process. To determine proper credentials for a particular user, an administrator must view the Security Accounts Manager's database via the User Manager for Domains Utility.

Figure 8.14

When incorrect logon credentials are furnished, Windows NT 4 does not permit access to the system.

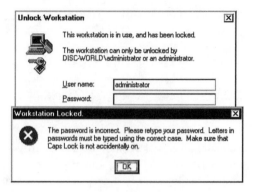

If a user's logon credentials are rejected (as in figure 8.14), then either the correct user name (or spelling of the user name) should be determined by editing the user account using User Manager for Domains or a new password must be provided using the same utility (see fig. 8.15). (Remember that passwords are case-sensitive and have a maximum length of 14 characters.)

Figure 8.15

When a user is experiencing problems with a logon, User Manager can be used to verify the correct spelling of a user name or to provide a new password for the user account.

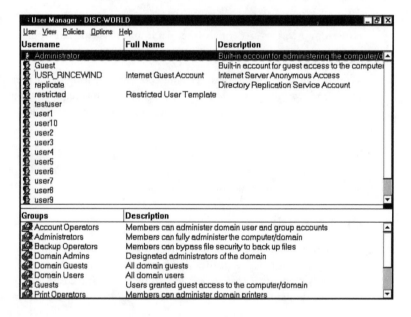

Losing Your Unique Security Identifier

Earlier in this chapter, a reference was made to the problems attendant to deleting and re-creating a user. This is a classic problem associated with the way in which Windows NT 4 user accounts are created. Figure 8.3 shows the warning message Windows NT 4 provides when any user account is deleted.

Deleting and re-creating user accounts is not recommended. In fact, the immediate removal of user accounts is unnecessary. Rather, Windows NT user accounts should be disabled; this prevents the total loss of the unique security Identifier associated with this account and ensures that the security context of this user is not completely lost (see fig. 8.16).

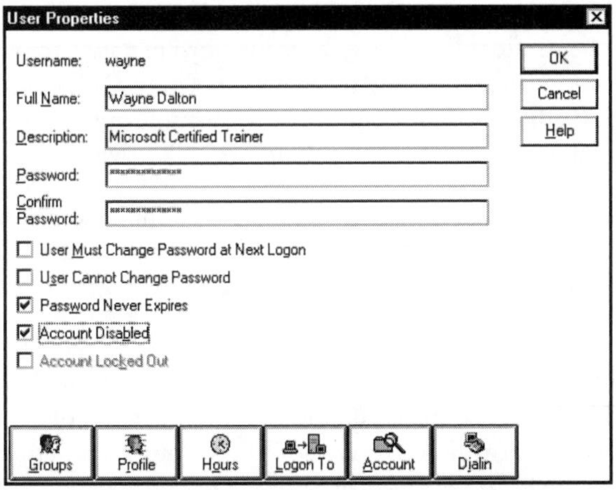

Figure 8.16
The User Manager for Domains utility can be used for disabling a user account.

One common practice is to find replacements for personnel who leave a company. The high turnover of personnel in the information technology industry has necessitated this human resource practice. Windows NT 4 accommodates this industry quirk by allowing specific user accounts to be disabled for a period of time (until a replacement for the employee can be found) and then renamed to reflect the new employee's own name.

The result of disabling and then renaming user accounts is that, although the actual employees may come and go, the security context for the various user accounts is always retained. This not only ensures that security account administration is greatly simplified, but also ensures that the Windows NT 4 security remains consistent. This rather simple way of reducing the overhead associated with turnover and ensuring consistent Windows NT 4 security is invaluable in large corporate network environments.

Presenting Your Credentials

On a stand-alone Windows NT 4 workstation or application server, logging on requires valid credentials that can be found in the security accounts manager database on the local machine.

When logging on to a domain, however, the logical location of the user credentials is of paramount importance. The use of the word logical in this instance refers to the conceptual point of authentication for any user, and implies that the physical location of any user within a domain model is irrelevant.

Often, a user (who is a member of a resource or trusting domain) is validated by a domain controller in an entirely different (master or trusted) domain. Because the user is not physically located within the master or trusted domain, but merely authenticated within this domain, the authenticating domain is referred to as the user's logical location.

For example, a user may work in one particular physical location (Cape Town, for example), but the user account used to authenticate this user may be maintained in a user accounts database in another physical location (Johannesburg, for example). This is typical of the Windows NT 4 domain models (as discussed in Chapter 13, "Domain Planning and Implementation") that are implemented in modern corporate Windows NT networks.

The trick is to establish where the user is to be authenticated and then supply the name of the domain that contains the appropriate user account in its security accounts database. The point is that you cannot log on to a domain unless you have a valid user name and password in that domain's security accounts database.

A hypothetical corporation, called Acme Widgets, has corporate headquarters in New York (U.S. sales region) and Rome (European sales region). Houston, Boston, and London also have regional offices. The Windows NT 4 network has been installed by using the multiple-master domain model as illustrated in figure 8.17.

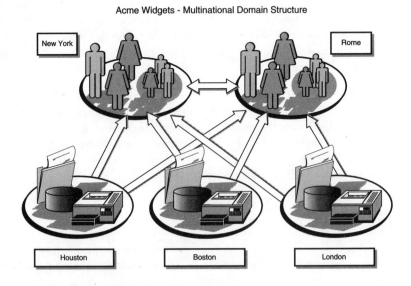

Figure 8.17

The Acme Widgets multiple-master domain model provides enterprise users global access to resources, while maintaining a single user account and login for every user.

Acme Widgets - Multinational Domain Structure

New York

Rome

Houston   Boston   London

In figure 8.17, a user in any of the five domains in this model can make use of a single logon account and gain enterprise-wide access to resources. At issue is how to provide the proper security credentials in order to ensure successful user identification.

A user who lives in Boston and works for the U.S. sales group is authenticated by the trusted domain responsible for account management in the U.S. sales region (New York). Therefore, when prompted for logon credentials, the user must provide New York for the domain (or logical location of user account).

User Authentication

Windows NT 4 has three forms of authentication. These include interactive logon authentication (via the keyboard), which was discussed earlier in this chapter—see the section titled "The Logon Process"—remote logon authentication, and pass-through authentication.

After the correct credentials have been supplied to the WinLogon process, these credentials must be authenticated before access can be granted to the Windows NT 4 Executive services and any resources they protect.

Remote Logon Authentication

Access to resources is not only applicable to local resources, but also to resources that are maintained and advertised by other computers on the same network. Access to these remote resources must also be controlled in the same way in which local resources are protected, and remote logon authentication can also present problems similar to those experienced with local resource authentication. Despite this apparent difference in authentication methods, the way in which Windows NT 4 handles them is almost identical.

Troubleshooting remote logon authentication must, therefore, proceed in a similar manner as local logon authentication problems are resolved. The basic requirement is a valid user account and password; for remote logon authentication it must be local to the remote Windows NT 4 computer that has the targeted resource. In other words, the user credentials on the local and remote Windows NT 4 computers must be identical for seamless access to the appropriate resource.

If the common credentials are not identical, Windows NT 4 attempts to resolve the missing credential. For example, if the user names are the same but the passwords are different, Windows NT 4 prompts the user for a password (see fig. 8.18). After this password has been provided and checked, access to the resource is permitted. If neither the user name nor the password match, access to this remote resource is denied.

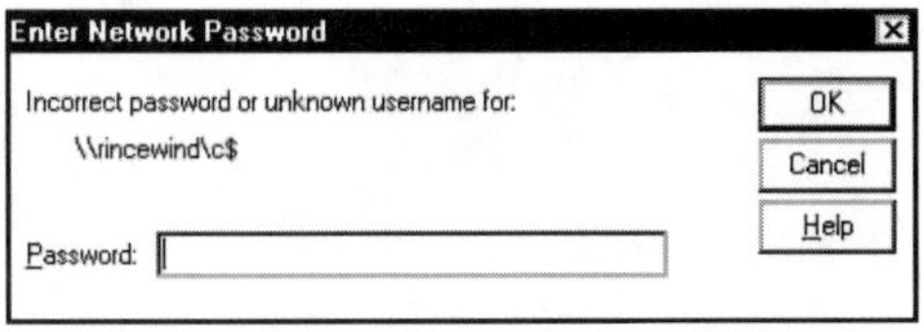

Figure 8.18

If incomplete remote logon credentials are supplied, Windows NT 4 prompts the user for the missing password.

Pass-Through Authentication

Pass-through authentication is a function of the NetLogon service, requiring the presence of at least two domains and a trust relationship between them. Problems relating to pass-through authentication, therefore, invariably originate from problems with the implementation of a Windows NT 4 domain.

In Chapter 13, troubleshooting the planning and implementation of a domain model was covered in detail. Problems of this nature include trust relationship issues, such as direction of the trust, initial password, broken trust, and so on, and the logical point of authentication, such as location of account domains versus resource domains, domain name specified in WinLogon dialog, and so on.

To troubleshoot pass-through authentication, an administrator must typically verify the appropriate trust relationship, as well as determine that the user account has been correctly created in the appropriate accounts domain.

Figure 8.16 (shown earlier in the chapter) illustrates the multiple-master domain model for the Acme Widget corporation. When a user in the Boston domain logs on, the logon authentication request is sent to the New York domain for two reasons. First, New York is the U.S. regional headquarters and has the necessary centralized expertise to administrate the U.S. sales region effectively. Second, the user account has been defined in the security accounts manager database in the New York domain.

For user authentication to be successful, the following three tasks must be correctly carried out:

1. The trust relationship between the Houston and New York domains must be correctly established. A trust relationship can be verified by using User Manager for Domains.

2. The user account for the user who is being authenticated must be created by using User Manager for Domains on any of the domain controllers within the New York domain. This is possible only if the primary domain controller is switched on and available.

3. The user must correctly specify the user name, password, and domain name during the logon phase (the WinLogon process). The user name and password must match those credentials supplied by the administrator when the account was created in the New York domain. The domain name in this example is New York. This can be visually verified when the user types in the necessary logon credentials during the WinLogon process.

Discretionary Access Control

After a user gains legal access to a Windows NT 4 machine, the operating system must be able to validate her access to the underlying objects and resources for which this user has specific access rights and privileges.

In the section "Tracking Security Events" earlier in this chapter, you learned that users can be tracked and validated via their access tokens or by a process of server impersonation. This implies that access can be gained to a security object directly (by means of the user access token) or indirectly (by means of server impersonation).

Either way, a user can experience problems when trying to access a system or user object, and a method is required to find out why this problem has occurred. The two common problem areas are the access token (associated with the user) and the access control list (associated with the object being accessed).

The process of troubleshooting problems of this type, therefore, involves finding out what effective rights the user has to the associated object, as well as finding out what access is permitted with respect to the associated object. The process consists of three steps:

1. Determine the user's effective rights.

2. Determine whether the effective user rights (as determined in the preceding step) give the user sufficient permission to gain the access to the object that is being requested (read access, for example).

3. If both steps 1 and 2 have been completed successfully, the Security Reference Monitor grants the desired access rights to the object. Otherwise, access is denied.

Effective User Rights

The effective rights that a particular user has to an object are governed by two specific concepts. The first is the cumulative user and group rights assigned to a security object. The second is the most restrictive nature of local and network rights assigned to a security object. The most common problems in this area stem from the peculiar relationship between these various types of security rights.

User and Group Rights are Cumulative

User and group rights are cumulative. In other words, the effective rights of a user are the accumulation of rights assigned directly to the user account, as well as any rights assigned to groups to which this particular user is a member. An exception to this rule is the No Access permission. The No Access permission overrides all other rights.

An example of how these cumulative rights are derived is tabulated in the following table:

Table 8.2
Cumulative User and Group Rights

User/Group	Assigned Rights to E:\SecureDirectory
wayne	Full Control
Domain Admins	Change (RXWD)
Domain Users	Change (RXWD)
Effective Rights	Full Control

To construct this table and establish the effective rights of a particular user or group to a security resource, you must complete the following steps:

1. To determine what user and group rights are applicable, an administrator must use the User Manager for Domains utility to determine what groups the particular user (in this case, for user wayne) belongs to (see fig. 8.19).

Figure 8.19

User Manager for Domains can be used to determine group membership of any Windows NT user, by using the User Properties dialog box and the associated Groups button.

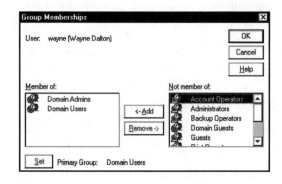

2. After these groups are identified, they can be entered on the left-hand side of the table (refer to table 8.2), and an administrator can use Windows NT 4 Explorer (to view the properties of the subdirectory) to determine the assigned permissions to this resource for every applicable User/Group in the table (see fig. 8.20).

In conclusion, figure 8.20 proves that user wayne is a member of the Domain Users and Domain Admins groups. Figure 8.20 shows that these groups (Domain Users and Domain Admins) both have Change rights (RXWD) to E:\Secure Directory, and that user wayne (Wayne Dalton) has Full Control rights to the same directory object.

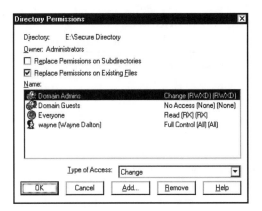

Figure 8.20

The security permissions assigned to E:\Secure Directory can be determined by using the Directory Permissions dialog box of the Directory Properties menu.

Table 8.2 combines this user/group security information and displays user wayne's effective rights to the directory object (which is Full Control). It should be noted that, if user wayne were a member of Domain Guests, the effective rights to this directory object would be No Access.

Local and Network Rights Are Most Restrictive

Windows NT 4 server advertises its resources through the process of sharing. Most utilities (such as NT Explorer, Print Manager, and so on) have the ability to advertise directories and printers to clients using a server "share."

Assuming that user wayne could obtain access to this resource (E:\Secure Directory) across the network via server share, the permissions set on the share would also come into play.

In this case, the same process would be followed (as tabulated in table 8.2) to determine the effective rights to the server share. Assume, for example, that the effective rights to this share is Read (RX). Further, assume that the effective user and group rights are in fact Change (RXWD).

Because local (effective user and group rights to the NTFS file/directory) and network (effective user and group rights to the server share) rights are most restrictive, user wayne obtains the most restrictive effective rights (tabulated in table 8.3) of Read (RX).

Table 8.3
Most Restrictive Local and Network Rights

Object	Effective Rights
Local Rights	Change (RXWD)
Network Rights	Read(RX)

continues

Table 8.3, Continued
Most Restrictive Local and Network Rights

Object	Effective Rights
Effective Rights	Read (RX)

Permitted Object Rights

After the effective rights of a user have been ascertained, the local security subsystem must compare these effective user rights to the permission level being requested by the user on the security object. The local security subsystem never permits security access to an object that exceeds the user's effective rights to that object.

Setting the permissions to an object can be achieved by using a plethora of different utilities, either programmatically or directly. In the current example, Windows NT 4 Explorer can be used to assign specific NTFS directory- and file-level permissions. In the event of an access error, Windows NT 4 Explorer can also be used to determine or verify these assigned permissions.

A fast way to resolve resource access problems is to use the CACLS and WHOAMI utilities (WHOAMI is a resource kit utility). The basic idea is to visually determine the effective rights of both the user and the resource in order to determine where this particular user is losing the necessary permissions to access this resource.

For example, a user is trying to access a subdirectory (E:\SecureDirectory) located on an NTFS permission. The user obtains an error message (see fig. 8.21), informing the user that access has been denied.

The first step is to collect information on what effective rights the user has to this resource. The appropriate steps are documented as follows:

```
E:\>cacls Secure Directory
E:\Secure Directory DISC-WORLD\Domain Guests:(OI)(IO)N
                     DISC-WORLD\Domain Guests:(CI)N
                     DISC-WORLD\Domain Users:(OI)(IO)C
                     DISC-WORLD\Domain Users:(CI)C
                     DISC-WORLD\wayne:(OI)(IO)F
                     DISC-WORLD\wayne:(CI)F
                     DISC-WORLD\Domain Admins:(OI)(IO)C
                     DISC-WORLD\Domain Admins:(CI)C
                     Everyone:(OI)(IO)(special access:)
                                         GENERIC_READ
                                         GENERIC_EXECUTE
                     Everyone:(CI)R
```

```
E:\>cacls Secure Directory\*.*
Access is denied.

E:\>whoami
DISC-WORLD\TestUser
```

It is possible to use a utility called IFMEMBER.EXE, supplied with the Windows 4 NT Resource Kit, which determines whether a user belongs to a group. The syntax of this utility is

```
ifmember [groupname1] [groupname2 ...] [groupnameN]
```

The mystery is solved, however, when it becomes obvious that the TestUser is a member of the

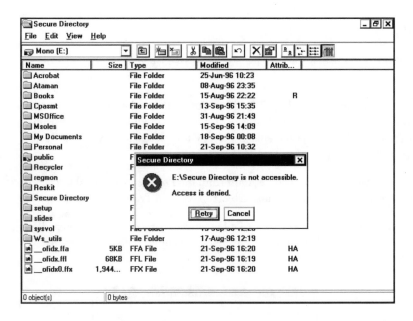

Figure 8.21

The Windows NT 4 security subsystem does not permit access to a resource unless sufficient user permissions have been assigned.

global group Domain Guests and that this group has been assigned No Access to the specified resource (E:\Secure Directory). The solution lies in removing the user from the offending group or in explaining to the user why he is not obtaining permission to access this specific resource.

Auditing

Reacting to a situation in the security environment is not always desirable—that is, waiting for the user to bring a security problem to the attention of an administrator. However, being proactive about security problems is often desirable, especially in high-risk environments in which security breaches can be costly.

To this end, Windows NT 4 provides a significant degree of security auditing, which enables the administrator to track specific security events. Auditing is discussed in the "Auditing User Activity" section earlier in this chapter.

Security Events

After auditing has been enabled, the administrator must monitor the Event Viewer (Security Log) for possible signs of problems or security breaches. Trying to cover every conceivable scenario or problem is an almost impossible task, so a number of examples that illustrate various types of auditable security events are included in this section.

Example 1: Tracking File and Object Access

In this example, auditing is enabled as follows (assuming you are logged on as an administrator):

■ From NT Explorer, right-click on the .TXT file and then choose the Properties menu item. From the Security tab, select the Auditing button. Assign Full Control permission to the user accessing the .TXT file and enable auditing for Success and Failure of Read and Write events.

■ From User Manager for Domains, choose Audit from the Policies menu. Enable auditing for Success and Failure of File and Object Access and Process Tracking.

From NT Explorer, the user double-clicks the .TXT file (which is associated with Notepad), writes data to the file, saves it, and then closes it. This results in audit events, as shown in figures 8.22 and 8.23.

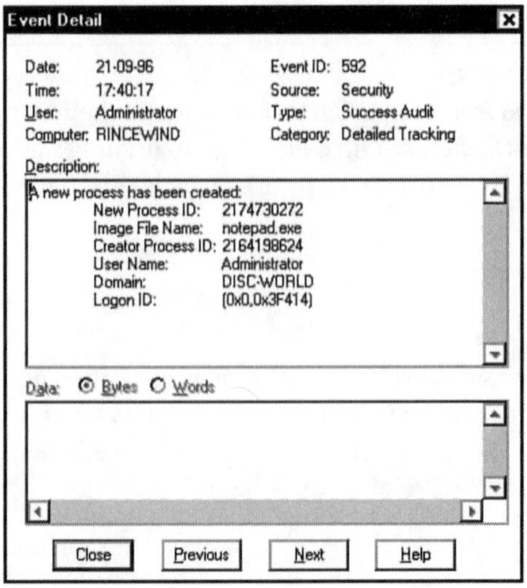

Figure 8.22

Opening Notepad.exe causes a Success Audit event (Detailed Tracking) to be written to the Security Log, which is visible through the Event Detail dialog.

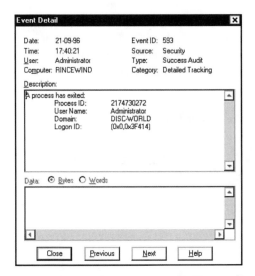

Figure 8.23

Closing Notepad.exe causes another Success Audit event (Detailed Tracking) to be written to the Security Log, which is visible through the Event Detail dialog.

Example 2: Use of User Rights

In this example, auditing is enabled by using User Manager to enable auditing for Success and Failure of Use of User Rights.

When the user tries to change the system time, only one event is generated, as shown in figure 8.24.

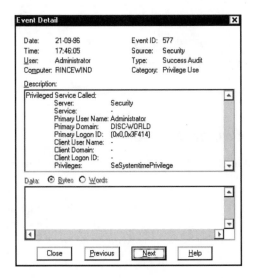

Figure 8.24

Setting the system time causes a Success Audit event (Privilege Use) to be written to the Security Log, which is visible through the Event Detail dialog.

The event shown in figure 8.24 indicates that a privileged service was called and that a server component named Kernel has called an audit check on the primary user name of the user. The audit type is a Success Audit, meaning that the user successfully exercised the right to use the SeSystemtimePrivilege (that is, the right to change the system time).

Example 3: User and Group Management

In this example, a new user account is added to the user accounts database. Auditing is enabled in User Manager by specifying both Success and Failure of User and Group Management. This generates seven audit events, as shown in figure 8.25.

Figure 8.25

Creating a user causes a Success Audit event (Account Management) to be written to the Security Log, which is visible through the Event Detail dialog.

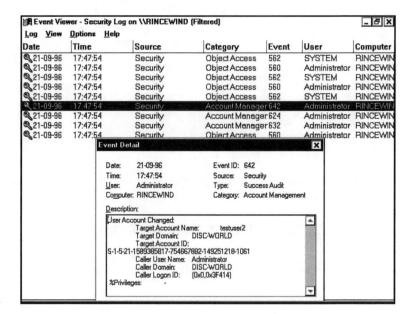

Example 4: Restart, Shutdown, and System

In this example, auditing is enabled in User' Manager for both Success and Failure of Restart, Shutdown, and System (see fig. 8.26).

In this example, a number of events were generated. Note, however, that the number of events generated is related to the number of trusted systems that you start when the system is restarted. This number may vary if you replicate this scenario on your own Windows NT computer.

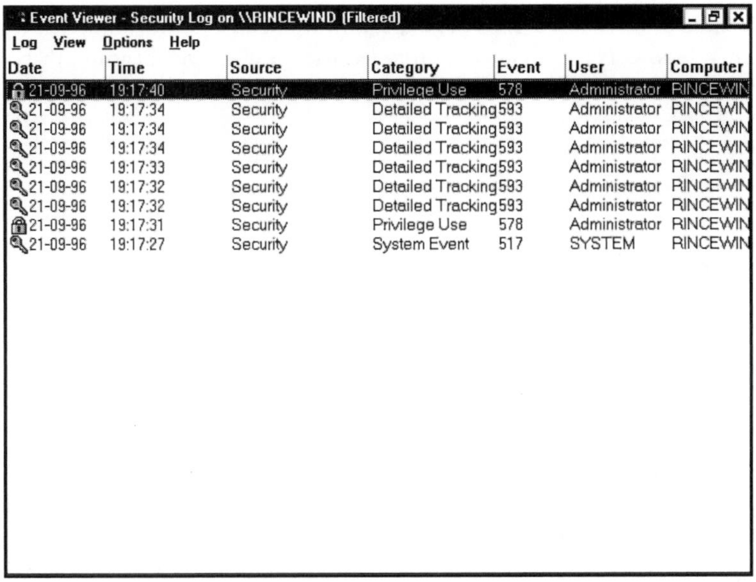

Figure 8.26

Shutting Down the System causes a Success and Failure Audit events to be written to the Security Log, which is visible through the Event Detail dialog.

Conclusion

Security permeates every aspect of Windows NT 4, and it is virtually impossible to use this operating system without being subjected to this design objective. This is, of course, not altogether such a bad idea. Being able to switch security on and off at will is not at all desirable in today's secured network environments.

This chapter presented a basic methodology and tool set that provide an administrator with a strategy for making sense of Windows NT 4 security problems. The Windows NT 4 operating system is designed to operate in C2-certified environments, and it is from the basic requirements of this level of security that this methodology derives its focus.

The capability to identify and authenticate system users, to provide discretionary access to system resources, and to audit system access and resource usage are three fundamental requirements for any C2-certifiable environment. A troubleshooting methodology, therefore, needs to be able to verify that each of these aspects has been successfully negotiated by any user (and administrator) of the system.

In answering the questions, "Has the user been correctly identified to the system and authenticated by the system?" and "Are my effective rights sufficient to gain the requested resource access?" the administrator is propelled toward the source of the Windows NT 4 resource security problem. Apart from the standard user and group management utilities, the administrator can call on the built-in auditing capabilities of Windows NT 4 to assist in tracking some of the more difficult security-related problems.

The methodology presented in this chapter is not a recipe, however, and a healthy understanding of the way in which Windows NT 4 resource security has been implemented ensures that this methodology can be successfully applied.

The Registry

*W*indows NT Server 4 is a complex system of devices and
services that are designed to provide a stable, robust,
and scaleable platform for mission-critical applications
and data. This multifaceted operating system, however,
can be compartmentalized into various distinct
components. These components include the hardware
on which the operating system is installed, the user
security and resource protection it embodies, the
application software it will execute, and the various
system services it provides.

This concise description, however, belies the real depth
and complexity of the burden placed on the typical
system administrator who is tasked to install, configure,
and support the network. In Windows NT 4, the

Registry helps simplify this support burden by providing a secure, unified database that stores configuration data in a hierarchical form.

Troubleshooting Windows NT 4 through the Registry is not recommended for most administrators. However, the Registry does provide a centralized repository of configuration information that can prove useful in this regard. You can troubleshoot Windows NT 4 in other ways, and the Registry should be regarded as a last resort.

The reason for this is that the Registry plays a central role in the operation of a Windows NT 4 server. Making an error when updating the Registry will most probably lead to problems with the afflicted NT server. Typical problems are a failure to boot, incorrect or unpredictable results from system and user services (for example, user applications, system threads, subsystems and executive services, and so on), or a general failure to operate.

This chapter provides an overview of the Registry so that anyone attempting to use it to troubleshoot can understand how it works and obtain a good idea of how to use the Registry better. In earlier versions of Windows NT, for example, the Registry was the only source of advanced system tuning and configuration. Gradually, this advanced functionality was incorporated into the administrative interfaces of later Windows NT releases.

One good example of this type of manual Registry configuration is the enabling of TCP/IP routing in Windows NT Advanced Server (Windows NT Server version 3.1). Today, in Windows NT 4 (since Windows NT 3.50), enabling IP routing is implemented as a check box in the appropriate Control Panel interface.

However, despite this obvious improvement in user-friendliness and configuration reliability (that is, using GUI tools tends to be less error prone than using the Registry Editor), modifying the appropriate Registry entry to enable IP routing was still relatively easy. The real benefit of the Registry, therefore, is that it is maintained in a single location. This relieves the administrator from tracking down configuration information distributed throughout the operating system. Instead, the necessary information is located in a single, centralized database and can be made available to the following processes and operating system functions:

- **Setup.** Setup programs for applications or hardware add new configuration data to the Registry. For example, new information is added when you install a new video card or change the settings for your network card.

- **Recognizer.** The Hardware Recognizer places hardware configuration data in the Registry. This volatile hardware information includes a list of hardware detected in your system. On Intel x86-based computers, this is done by NTDETECT.COM and the Windows NT 4 kernel. On RISC-based computers, hardware configuration data is provided by the ARC firmware.

- **Windows NT kernel.** During system startup, the Windows NT 4 kernel extracts information from the Registry, such as the device drivers the operating system needs to load and the order in which these device drivers need to be loaded. The Windows NT 4 kernel also passes information about itself, such as its version number, to the Registry.

- **Device drivers.** Device drivers send and receive load parameters and configuration data to and from the Registry. This is similar to the way in which the DEVICE= statement in the CONFIG.SYS file passes parameters to DOS-based device drivers, and to the way in which it provides non-invasive configuration information to operating systems (such as Windows 95) during Plug and Play processes. A device driver must report the system resources that it uses (for example, its hardware interrupts) so that the operating system can add this information to the Registry. Applications and device drivers can read this configuration information to assist with smart installation and configuration (such as Plug and Play).

- **Administrative tools.** The administrative tools (for example, Control Panel applets and the Administrative Tools program group) can be used to modify configuration data. The Registry Editor is helpful for viewing and occasionally making detailed changes to the system configuration. You can also use the Windows NT 4 Diagnostics program (WINMSD.EXE) to view configuration information stored in the Registry.

As can be seen from the previous list, the Registry plays a pivotal role in Windows NT 4 installation, configuration, and troubleshooting support. A thorough understanding of this Registry database, and how it can be used to assist in troubleshooting Windows NT 4, is therefore essential. This chapter describes the Registry and shows how to use the information in the Registry for troubleshooting and configuration maintenance.

Registry Components

Until recently, configuration files, such as WIN.INI, were the only way to configure Windows applications and operating system functions. Today, the Windows NT 4 Registry replaces these .INI files. Each key in the Registry is similar to the bracketed heading in an .INI file, and entries under the heading are analogous to values in the Registry.

One limitation of the older .INI file approach is that these files are flat text files, which are unable to support nested headings or contain data other than pure text. Registry keys, on the other hand, can contain subkeys that can be nested to provide finer detail and a greater range to the possible configuration information for a particular operating system aspect.

Furthermore, Registry values can also consist of executable code, as well as provide individual preferences for multiple users of the same computer. The ability to store executable code within the Registry extends its usage to operating system and application developers. The ability to store user-specific profile information enables the operating system to be tailored for each individual user.

The Registry Editor, a tool shipped with Windows NT 4, displays each of the predefined keys on the local computer, while providing an administrator with the ability to modify the contents of the Registry directly (see fig. 9.1). In Windows NT 4, you can use two Registry editors to look at information in the Registry:

- ■ Regedt32.exe has the most menu items and more choices for the menu items. You can search for keys and subkeys in the Registry.

- ■ Regedit.exe enables you to search for strings, values, keys, and subkeys. This feature is useful if you want to find a specific value or string.

For ease of manipulation, the Registry is divided into five separate and distinct tree structures that represent the Registry database in its entirety.

Some of these subtrees are called hives. A *hive* is a discrete body of keys, subkeys, and values that is rooted at the top of the Registry hierarchy. A hive is mapped to a single file and a .LOG file. These files are in the *winnt_root*\system32\config directory9. Each of these keys are discussed in the following sections.

Figure 9.1

The Windows NT Registry Editor provides access to each of the predefined keys on the local computer.

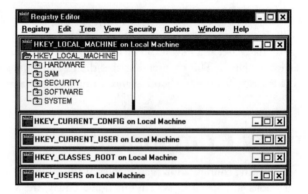

HKEY_CURRENT_USER

This Registry key contains the configuration information for the user that currently has a logged on session with the Windows NT 4 computer (see fig. 9.2). The user's folders, screen colors, and Control Panel settings are stored here. This information is referred to as a *user profile*.

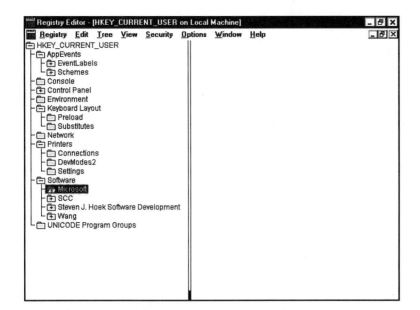

Figure 9.2

*The HKEY_
CURRENT_USER
Registry key is the root
of the configuration
information for the user
who is currently logged on.*

HKEY_USERS

A significant advance in Windows NT 4 is the way user profiles have been implemented. In Windows NT 3.5x, user profiles were stored locally (by default) in the *winnt-root*system32\config directory. In Windows NT 4, they are housed in the *winnt-root*Profiles directory. User-specific information is kept there, as well as common, system-wide user information.

This change in user profile location has been brought about to parallel the way in which Windows 95 handles its user profiles. In earlier releases of Windows NT, the user profile was stored as a single file—either locally in the \Config directory or centrally on a server.

In Windows NT 4, the single user profile has been broken up into a number of subdirectories located below the \Profiles directory. The reason for this is mainly due to the way in which the Windows 95 and Windows NT 4 operating systems use the underlying directory structure to form part of their new user interface.

A user profile is now contained within the NtUser.dat (and NtUser.dat.log) files, as well as the following subdirectories :

- ■ **Application Data.** This is a place to store application data specific to this particular user.

- ■ **Desktop.** Placing an icon or a shortcut into this folder causes that icon or shortcut to appear on the desktop for a particular user.

■ **Favorites.** This folder provides a user with a personalized storage place for files, shortcuts, and other types of information links. A good example to illustrate the use of the Favorites folder is Internet Explorer. When surfing the Web, a user can add a particular web page to her list of favorite pages. The URL (Universal Resource Locator) is then converted to a file format, and this file is saved within the Favorites folder.

■ **NetHood.** This folder maintains a list of personalized network connections. Shortcuts to various network locations can be kept here to facilitate the user's access and re-access to particular network resources.

■ **Personal.** This folder keeps track of personal documents for a particular user. A good example to illustrate the use of the Personal folder is Microsoft Office. When you use an Office product, such as Word or Excel, the Personal folder is presented as the default location for saving and retrieving Office documents.

■ **PrintHood.** Similar to the NetHood folder, the PrintHood folder keeps track of printers rather than network connections.

■ **Recent.** One major advance, introduced by Windows 95, was document-centricity. In previous versions of Windows, a user would first have to search for the appropriate application (Word, for example) before being able to create a document. This process was widely regarded as contrary to the way in which users really dealt with documents. Instead, Windows 95 and Windows NT 4 provide the user with a way to focus on the document rather than on the application that creates it. The Recent folder keeps track of the most recent documents used by the user. To access a document, the user clicks on the Start button and then chooses the document listed under the Documents menu entry located on the Start menu.

■ **SendTo.** The SendTo folder is similar to the Recent folder because it provides a centralized store of shortcuts and output devices (for example, disk drives, mail recipients, printers, and particular applications that print or convert data from one format to another). For example, placing a shortcut to a printer in this folder extends the functionality provided by the SendTo menu item—presented by clicking on a document with the right mouse button.

■ **Start menu.** Introduced by Windows 95, the Start button (and its corresponding Start menu) has presented the user with a small-footprint, concise, and highly-configurable menu system. To extend or enhance the standard Start menu, however, you can add icons and shortcuts to the Start menu folder (as well as the subdirectories below this folder). Subdirectories are presented as menu items on the main Start menu, while entries within these subdirectories are accessible by selecting the appropriate menu items. *Personal groups* are associated with the specific users' \Profiles*user*\Start Menu directory, while *common groups* are associated with the \Profiles\All Users\Start Menu folder.

■ **Templates.** This is a storage location for document templates associated with a particular user.

In short, the shift from a single user profile to this expanded file and directory layout brings Windows NT 4 and Windows 95 closer together, especially in the way they configure the desktop and other preferences for a particular user (see fig. 9.3).

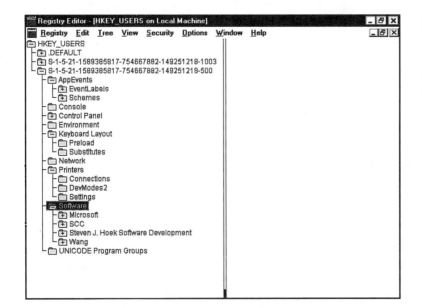

Figure 9.3

The HKEY_USERS Registry key is the root of all user profiles on the computer.

HKEY_LOCAL_MACHINE

The HKEY_LOCAL_MACHINE window contains configuration information particular to the computer (for any user). This information is stored in the *winnt_root*\system32\config directory as persistent operating system files, with the exception of the volatile hardware key (see fig. 9.4).

The information gleaned from this configuration data is used by applications, device drivers, and the Windows NT 4 operating system. The latter usage determines what system configuration data to use, without respect to the user currently logged on. For this reason, the HKEY_LOCAL_MACHINE Registry key is of specific importance to administrators who want to support and troubleshoot Windows NT 4.

HKEY_LOCAL_MACHINE is the most important key in the Registry and contains five subtrees (see table 9.1). The rest of this section describes these subtrees.

Figure 9.4

*The HKEY_
LOCAL_MACHINE
Registry key contains the
configuration data for the
local computer.*

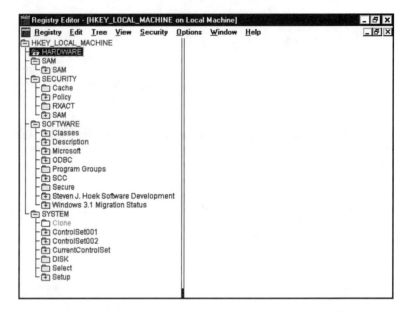

Note You can read information in any of these keys, but you should only add or change information in the SOFTWARE and SYSTEM keys directly by using the Registry Editor utility. In any event, you should not change information in the Registry when you are using it for troubleshooting. Instead, you should use applications such as Control Panel to change Registry information.

The SYSTEM and HARDWARE keys are the most useful for troubleshooting. The HARDWARE key describes the physical hardware in the computer. Because the data in the HARDWARE key is stored in binary form, the best way to view the data is by using Windows NT 4 Diagnostics.

You can use the HKEY_LOCAL_MACHINE subtrees to trace problems relating to services, device drivers, or startup control data.

Table 9.1
The HKEY_LOCAL_MACHINE

Subtree Key Names	Contents
HARDWARE	The database that describes the physical hardware in the computer, the way device drivers use that hardware, and mappings and related data that link kernel-mode drivers with various user-mode code. All data in this subtree is re-created each time the system is started.

Subtree Key Names	Contents
	The Description key describes the actual computer hardware.
	The DeviceMap key contains miscellaneous data in formats specific to particular classes of drivers.
	The ResourceMap key describes which device drivers claim which hardware resources. The Windows NT 4 Diagnostics program (WINMSD.EXE) can report on the contents of this key in an easy-to-read form.
SAM	The security information for user and group accounts and for the domains in Windows NT 4 Server. (SAM is the Security Account Manager.)
SECURITY	The database that contains the local security policy, such as specific user rights. This key is used only by the Windows NT 4 security subsystem.
SOFTWARE	The per-computer software database. This key contains data about software installed on the local computer, as well as various items of miscellaneous configuration data.
SYSTEM	The database that controls system startup, device driver loading, Windows NT 4 services, and operating system behavior.

HKEY_LOCAL_MACHINE\HARDWARE

This subtree contains the volatile hardware data in the Registry that is computed at system startup. This data includes information about hardware components on the motherboard and about the various interrupts that device drivers or hardware devices are hooked into.

The Hardware subtree contains distinct and important sets of data in three subkeys—Description, DeviceMap, and ResourceMap. Applications and device drivers use the Hardware subtree to read information about the system components, store data directly into the DeviceMap subkey, and store data indirectly into the ResourceMap subkey.

These keys are described in the following sections.

The Description Subkey

The Description subkey displays information obtained from the hardware database. This hardware database is created by compiling information obtained from the firmware (on RISC processors), the hardware recognizer (NTDETECT.COM on Intel processors), and the NT Executive (the manager of the interface between the kernel and the environment subsystems).

The DeviceMap Subkey

The DeviceMap subkey contains one or more values to specify the location, in the Registry, of specific driver information appropriate for that kind of hardware component or device.

The value for each Device subkey describes an actual port name or the path for a Service subkey within the HKEY_LOCAL_MACHINE\ SYSTEM\ControlSet*nnn*\Services Registry subkey. In turn, a Registry subkey path within HKEY_LOCAL_MACHINE\ SYSTEM\ ControlSet*nnn*\Services contains information about a particular device driver. This Service subkey contains the information a system administrator might need for troubleshooting and is also the information presented about the device by Windows NT 4 Diagnostics.

ResourceMap Subkey

The ResourceMap subkey maps device drivers to resources that the drivers use. Each ResourceMap subkey contains data reported by the device driver about its use of I/O ports, I/O memory addresses, interrupts, direct memory access (DMA) channels, and so on. Because the data in the HARDWARE subkey is volatile, the ResourceMap subkey is recreated each time you start Windows NT 4. In doing so, an up-to-date map of device information is created.

HKEY_LOCAL_MACHINE\SAM

The HKEY_LOCAL_MACHINE\SAM subtree contains the user and group account information in the Security Account Manager (SAM) database for the local computer. For a computer that is running Windows NT 4, this subtree also contains security information for the domain.

The information contained within the SAM Registry key is what appears in the user interface of the User Manager utility, as well as in the lists of users and groups that appear when you make use of the Security menu commands inWindows NT 4 Explorer.

Use User Manager (Windows NT Workstation 4) or User Manager For Domains (Windows NT Server 4) to add users, remove users, or change information on any account. System administrators can use User Manager or User Manager For Domains to change security information for the local computer or for the domain.

HKEY_LOCAL_MACHINE\SECURITY

The HKEY_LOCAL_MACHINE\SECURITY subtree contains security information for the local computer. This includes aspects such as assigning user rights, establishing password policy, and the membership of local groups, which are configurable in User Manager.

The subkey HKEY_LOCAL_MACHINE\SECURITY\SAM is mapped to HKEY_ LOCAL_MACHINE\SAM, so changes made in one automatically appear in the other. These changes are made using the User Manager (for workstations) and User Manager for Domains (for servers and domain controllers).

HKEY_LOCAL_MACHINE\SOFTWARE

The HKEY_LOCAL_MACHINE\SOFTWARE subtree contains specific configuration information about software on the local computer. The entries under this handle, which apply to anyone using this particular computer, show what software is installed on the computer and define file associations and OLE information. The HKEY_CLASSES_ROOT handle is an alias for the subtree rooted at HKEY_LOCAL_MACHINE\SOFTWARE\Classes.

The HKEY in the Registry components actually means *handle key*, which is used to uniquely identify any part of the Registry programmatically. An application gets a handle to a particular part of the Registry.

This subtree contains, for example, the information you add by using the *Open With* command in Windows NT 4 Explorer, information added during installation for specific Windows-based applications, and information about applications installed with Windows NT 4.

Classes Subkey

The Classes subkey defines types of documents, providing information on file name extension associations and OLE information that can be used by Windows shell applications and OLE applications. HKEY_CLASSES_ROOT displays the same information as stored under this subkey.

Note   The OLE information must be created by the specific application, so you should not change this information by using Registry Editor. If you want to change file name extension associations, use the *Open With* command in Windows NT 4 Explorer.

Description Subkeys

The various HKEY_LOCAL_MACHINE\SOFTWARE*Description* subkeys contain the names and version numbers of the software installed on the local computer. Configuration information, applicable to this installed software, is maintained under the HKEY_ CURRENT_USER\Software subkey.

This configuration information contains references to application-specific settings such as installation directories, user interface settings (such as font face, tool bar and status bar visibility, placement of windows, and so on), Internet plug-ins (for web browsers), and the location and name of various drivers.

During installation, applications record this configuration information in the following form:

HKEY_LOCAL_MACHINE\SOFTWARE\<*CompanyName*>\<*ProductName*>\<*Version*>

Program Groups Subkey

The Program Groups subkey under HKEY_LOCAL_MACHINE\SOFTWARE contains the common program groups—that is, those programs used in common by all users of the local computer. (The program groups for an individual user can be viewed under HKEY_ CURRENT_USER, and the default personal program groups can be viewed in HKEY_ USERS\.DEFAULT.) Each subkey under the Program Groups key is the name of a common program group, and the value contained within each subkey is binary data describing that program group.

If you want to change the content of common program groups, use the menu commands or mouse techniques provided in Windows NT 4 Explorer.

Secure Subkey

The Secure subkey provides a convenient place for applications to store configuration information that should not be changed by anyone except an administrator.

If you have a previous version of Windows (Windows 3.x, Windows for Workgroups) installed on your computer, you are permitted to migrate REG.DAT, groups (.GRP) files, and .INI files to the Windows NT 4 Registry when you first log on to Windows NT 4.

HKEY_LOCAL_MACHINE\SYSTEM

All startup-related data that must be stored (rather than computed during startup) is saved in the System hive. A complete copy of the data is also stored in the SYSTEM.ALT file. The data in HKEY_LOCAL_MACHINE\SYSTEM (commonly referred to as the System hive) is organized into control sets that contain a complete set of parameters for devices and services as described in this section.

Select, ControlSet00x, and CurrentControlSet Subkeys

The Registry, particularly data in the System hive, is essential to starting the system. To help ensure that the system can always be started, a backup copy of the system configuration is kept that enables you to undo any configuration changes that did not have the intended effect.

Say, for example, you make a configuration change such as changing the version of your sound card driver. Unfortunately, this configuration change renders your sound system inoperable. To rectify this situation, you must rollback the configuration changes so the sound system can work again.

Because Windows NT 4 keeps track of previous system configurations (that is, CurrentControlSet*00x*), you can restore an earlier working system configuration to rollback the recent configuration change.

In fact, a clone copy of the current configuration is made during the boot process. After the user successfully logs on to the Windows NT 4 computer, this clone copy is stored as the current system configuration. Furthermore, the *LastKnownGood* system configuration is created and saved for later use. This configuration, which is known to be a good configuration (because the user was able to successfully log on), can be used as a system configuration checkpoint when rolling back a bad configuration.

HKEY_CLASSES_ROOT

The HKEY_CLASSES_ROOT window is a subkey of HKEY_LOCAL_MACHINE\Software. The information stored here is used to open the correct application when a file is opened by using the Windows NT 4 Explorer and for Object Linking and Embedding (OLE).

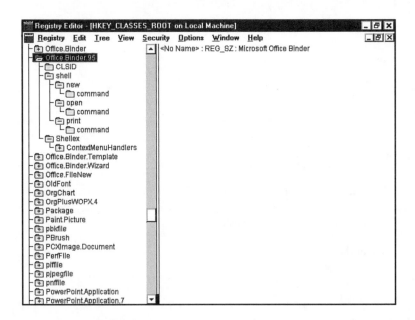

Figure 9.5

The HKEY_CLASSES_ROOT Registry key ensures compatibility with the earlier Windows 3.1 registration database.

Windows NT 4 Explorer is capable of associating a file name extension with a specific application. Windows NT 4 stores these associations in the Registry.

HKEY_CURRENT_CONFIG

The information contained within this subkey is used to configure settings such as the software and device drivers to load or the display resolution to use.

Th HKEY_CURRENT_CONFIG key has a Software and a System subkey, which keeps track of configuration information. An example of this type of information is \System\ CurrentControlSet\Services\S3 subkey that keeps configuration information appropriate to the installed video driver (vertical refresh rate, bits per pixel, maximum resolution, and panning values, for example).

Figure 9.6

The HKEY_ CURRENT_CONFIG Registry key contains information about the hardware profile used by the local computer at system startup.

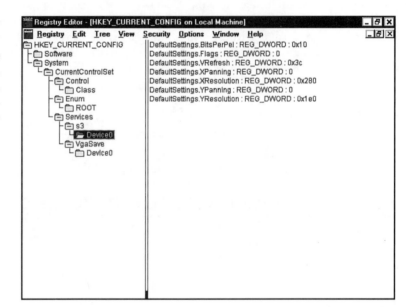

Registry Data Types

Within the Windows NT 4 Registry Editor, you can assign values to new keys or you can alter the appropriate values assigned to the currently selected key. Value entries in the Registry conform to a three-part naming scheme (*name:type:value*):

■ At the left-most side of the value entry pane, the name of the value appears.

■ After the value name, the class or type of the value entry appears. The five Registry data types are discussed in the following list:

■ The REG_BINARY prefix permits valid values of 0 and 1 only. Most hardware component information is stored as this data type, which can be viewed in hexadecimal format in the Registry Editor (or by using WINMSD in an easy-to-read format). Figure 9.7 provides an example of a Registry key value of this data type.

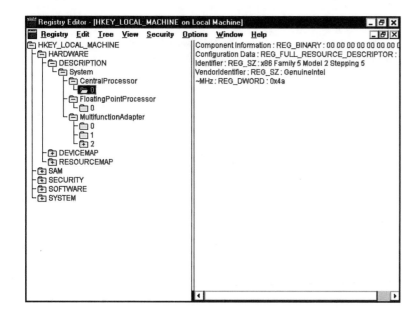

Figure 9.7
The REG_BINARY data identifies a value entry as raw binary data.

■ The REG_SZ prefix is used for a data string value. A component's description is normally of this type and is illustrated in figure 9.8.

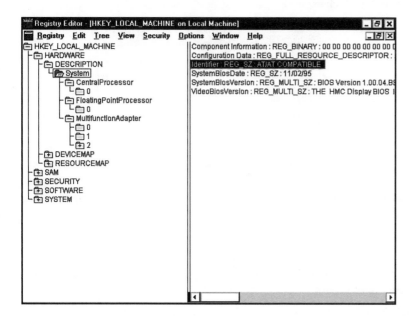

Figure 9.8
The REG_SZ Registry entry identifies a value entry as a data string.

■ The REG_DWORD prefix identifies a value entry as a DWORD entry. A DWORD comprises of four bytes. Many parameters for device drivers and services are of this data type (see fig. 9.9).

Figure 9.9

The REG_DWORD Registry entry identifies a value entry as a four-byte number.

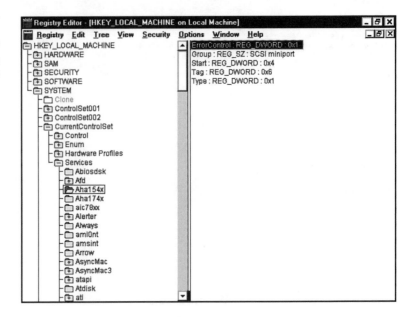

■ The REG_MULTI_SZ prefix identifies a value entry as a multiple string. Values that contain lists or multiple values are of this type (see fig. 9.10). Entries are separated by NULL characters.

Figure 9.10

The REG_MULTI_SZ Registry entry identifies a value entry as a string that can contain lists or multiple values.

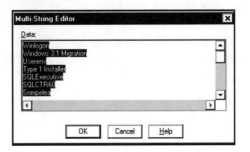

■ The REG_EXPAND_SZ prefix indicates that a value entry is an expandable string (see fig. 9.11). This text contains a variable to be replaced when called by an application.

■ The value itself appears after the class of the entry. Each value class has an editor that bears the same name as the class. These editors are discussed in the section "Modifying the Registry" later in this chapter.

Figure 9.11
This expandable string appears when using the REG_EXPAND_SZ Registry entry.

Finding a Registry Key

As can be seen from the preceding text, the Windows NT 4 Registry is quite complex and vast in its scope. Tracking down specific entries in this Registry can, therefore, be rather difficult or (at the very least) time-consuming. A search tool is what you need.

This section covers two such tools. The Registry Editor (REGEDT32.EXE) can search for specific key values within the Registry. This tool is built into the product, which ships free of charge with Windows NT 4. In addition, a third-party tool developed by Steven J. Hoek provides considerable search capability. This tool is available from the developer (shoek@ix.netcom.com or 72674.326@compuserve.com) for a registration fee of $20.

Windows NT Registry Editor

Windows NT 4 Server supplies an interesting tool called the Registry Editor. This tool comes in two versions, REGEDT32.EXE (32-bit Windows NT Registry tool) and REGEDIT.EXE (32-bit Windows 95 Registry tool useful for searching for keys, values, and data). The REGEDT32.EXE tool is the more useful tool for Windows NT 4.

To run Registry Editor from Windows NT Explorer, double-click Regedt32.exe in the %SystemRoot%\System32 folder. An alternate method is to click on Start and then Run, after which you enter **Regedt32** in the Open text-entry box of the subsequent dialog box. You can search for a key in the Registry by following these steps:

1. Click Find Key in the View menu.

2. In the Find what box, type the name of the key that you want to find (see fig. 9.12).

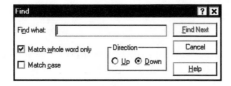

Figure 9.12
Find a Windows NT Registry key by using the REGEDT32.EXE utility.

If you want to find only occurrences that are words by themselves and not part of a larger word, select the Match whole word only check box.

If you want to identify only those keys in the Registry with the combination of uppercase and lowercase letters specified in the Find what box, select the Match case check box.

3. In the Direction box, select the direction you want the search to proceed through the Registry.

   Up searches from the insertion point or the selection to the beginning of the Registry tree or the selected keys.

   Down searches from the selection to the end of the Registry tree or the selected keys.

4. To see the next occurrence of the text that you have specified, click Find Next.

As long as you click Find Next, the search proceeds through the Registry and highlights instances of the key name that you have designated.

Registry Search and Replace Tool

After installation, the third-party search and replace tool (as described in the previous section) becomes fully integrated into the operating system (Windows NT 4 and 95). This integration provides the administrator with a tremendously powerful tool to isolate and fix Registry-based problems (see fig. 9.13).

Figure 9.13

The third-party Registry search and replace utility can be fully integrated into Windows NT.

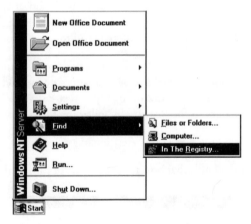

In order to activate a particular search, the target for the search must be defined together with the criteria that will restrict the search. Results of such a search can either be logged to a file or displayed on the screen.

Specific Registry information, although centrally located, can often be distributed throughout the entire Registry database. This distribution of information within the Registry can cause a problem when the data needs to be changed and no GUI interface exists to effect such a change.

The third-party Registry search and replace tool can seek out and replace Registry information with a predefined or user-defined alternative. Figure 9.14 illustrates the search and replace capabilities.

Figure 9.14

General search and replacement criteria can be specified to guide the search and replacement of Registry data.

One weakness of the built-in Registry Editor search capability is that it can only search for a Registry key. The Registry search and replace tool, on the other hand, can search for both Registry values and Registry data (that is, HIVE\KEY\Value=Data) that match the search criteria. The advanced configuration required to make the search work is illustrated in figure 9.15.

Note   A second version of the Registry Editor shipped with Windows NT 4, namely REGEDIT.EXE, does permit an administrator to search for keys, data, and values. It does not, however, permit a replacement of the data that has matched the search criteria.

Once initiated, the progress of any search (and/or replace) can be monitored. The actual key path is displayed in the Progress box, while the search success statistics are maintained in the Statistics box (see fig. 9.16).

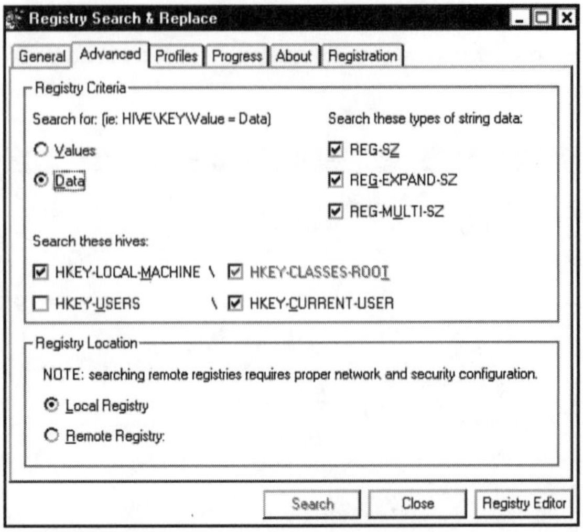

Figure 9.15

The advanced configuration options permit powerful search and replace operations to be launched against the Windows NT Registry.

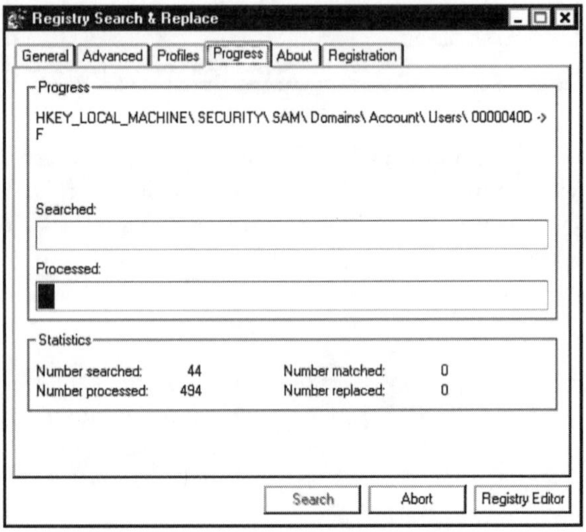

Figure 9.16

The Registry search progress indicator provides feedback on how far the search and replace operation has progressed.

Modifying the Registry

Despite numerous warnings to the contrary, the Windows NT 4 Registry was designed to be directly modified. It can be argued that there are other ways to effect a very large number of these Registry updates via a graphical interface or tool supplied with Windows NT 4. However, some configuration changes have to be made by using direct modification of the Registry.

For the configuration changes that have to be implemented as direct modifications to the Registry, Microsoft has shown that it will eventually implement these Registry change procedures into the graphical interface of the Windows NT 4 administrative tools. Until then, however, you must make these changes via the Registry Editor. This section discusses some of the issues related to making updates to the Registry possible, as well as actually implementing the changes.

Configuring for Updates

When updating the Registry via the Registry Editor consider a few issues to ensure that configuring the Registry is not an unpleasant experience.

Figure 9.17 illustrates the various menu options that you can set to control the manner in which changes will affect the Registry itself. They include the auto refresh function, read-only mode, and delete confirmation. Careful use of these menu options can save an administrator trouble and embarrassment if implemented as safeguards against inadvertent deletions or updates.

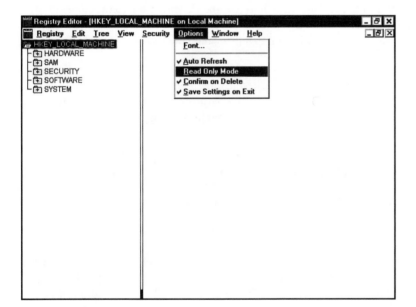

Figure 9.17

You can configure the Registry Editor for updates through various menu options.

Auto Refresh

The Auto Refresh setting ensures that after a Registry entry has been changed, all Registry Editor windows are also updated to reflect changes made to the Registry.

A check mark next to Auto Refresh means that it is in effect. If it is not checked, the Refresh All and Refresh Active commands in the View menu are available. The Refresh Active is quick because it only refreshes the highlighted Registry key, while Refresh All is the manual version of the Auto Refresh option.

You cannot use Auto Refresh while displaying a remote Registry. If you click Auto Refresh while displaying a remote Registry, the manual refresh commands (Refresh All and Refresh Active) are not available. Although Auto Refresh appears to be working as though a local Registry window is displayed, the contents of the remote window will not be refreshed.

Read Only Mode

Read Only Mode protects Registry data by not allowing any changes to be made to Registry keys or value entries. Registry Editor provides the Read Only Mode command to protect your Registry data from accidental but potentially damaging changes.

When you click Read Only Mode, the Registry Editor does not save any changes that you make. A check mark next to this command means that it is in effect.

Confirming a Deletion

To protect' Registry data from accidental deletions, use the Confirm on Delete command when not viewing the Registry in Read Only Mode. If you click Confirm on Delete, Registry Editor presents you with a dialog box asking for confirmation any time that you choose to delete a Registry key or a value entry.

The effect of deleting a key can be quite unpredictable sometimes, especially if you cannot re-establish the deleted value. In most cases, however, the hard-coded defaults for that particular Registry entry apply. These default values are documented in the product administrator guides and in the Microsoft Official Curriculum.

Adding, Deleting, or Modifying Registry Entries

Modifications to the Registry, such as the addition of new data or the modification or deletion of existing data, have to take place according to a strict fashion. The three-part naming scheme, *Name:DataType:Value,* plays a major role in guiding this process.

Name and *Value* depend largely on the nature of the entry and the data type. The data type has to conform with the pre-established types applicable to Registry data. The Registry Editor provides a context-sensitive editor to add or modify Registry data. The various editors are discussed in the following sections.

The String Editor

Many value entries in the Registry are written in a string (REG_SZ) or in an expandable string (REG_EXPAND_SZ) format (see fig. 9.18).

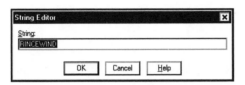

Figure 9.18
The String Editor dialog box provides a convenient method of modifying Registry data stored as character strings.

A *string* is a sequence of characters usually representing readable text. An expandable string usually consists of readable text also, but contains a variable that will be replaced when it is called by an application. For example, in the value entry%SystemRoot%\System32\ Bootok.exe, %SystemRoot% is the expandable portion of the variable that will be replaced by the actual location of the directory that contains the Windows NT 4 system files.

If a value entry in Registry Editor has a REG_SZ or a REG_EXPAND_SZ prefix, you can edit the value entry by using the String Editor.

To invoke the String Editor, follow these steps:

1. Select a value entry of the type REG_SZ or REG_EXPAND_SZ.

2. Click String in the Edit menu or double-click the value entry that you want to edit.

3. Edit the data that is shown in the String box and then click OK.

The Binary Editor

Many value entries in the Registry are written as raw binary data. If a value entry is preceded by the prefix REG_BINARY, the value entry is written as binary data, and you must use the Binary Editor to edit this value entry. However, the Binary Editor can be used to edit any value entry, regardless of the format in which the entry is written.

To invoke the Binary Editor, follow these steps:

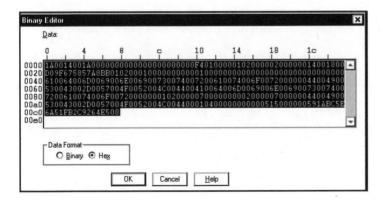

Figure 9.19
The Binary Editor provides a convenient method of modifying Registry data stored as binary numbers. Modifications can be made in binary or hexidecimal format.

1. Click the value entry that you want to edit.

2. Click Binary in the Edit menu.

   If the value entry is of the type REG_BINARY, double-click the value entry.

3. In the Data Format box, click Binary or Hex.

   Binary represents your data as a sequence of binary digits.

   Hex represents your data as a sequence of hexadecimal digits.

4. Edit the data that is shown in the Data box and then click OK.

The DWORD Editor

DWORD refers to data represented by a number that is four bytes long.

If a value entry contains the prefix REG_DWORD, the entry is written in the DWORD format. To edit this data, use the DWORD Editor.

To invoke the DWORD Editor, follow these steps:

Figure 9.20

The DWord Editor dialog box provides a convenient method of modifying Registry data stored as four-byte numbers.

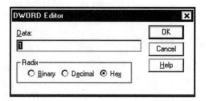

1. Click a value entry of the type REG_DWORD.

2. Click DWORD in the Edit menu.

   Or double-click the value entry in which the REG_DWORD prefix appears.

3. Edit the string that is shown in the Data box.

4. In the Radix box, click Binary, Decimal, or Hex and then click OK.

   ■ Binary displays the data as a binary (base-2) number.

■ Decimal displays the data as a decimal (base-10) number.

■ Hex displays the data as a hexadecimal (base-16) number.

The Multi-String Editor

If a value entry contains the prefix REG_MULTI_SZ, the value entry is written as a multiple string (see fig. 9.21). You can use the Multi-String Editor to edit the value.

Follow these steps to invoke the Multi-String Editor:

Figure 9.21

The String Editor dialog box provides a convenient method of modifying Registry data stored as multiple lists of character strings.

1. Click a value entry of the type REG_MULTI_SZ.

2. Click Multi-String in the Edit menu.

   Or double-click the selected value entry in which the REG_MULTI_SZ prefix appears.

3. Edit the value entry and then click OK.

Location of Registry Hives

The Registry is divided into parts called *hives,* named by a Windows NT 4 developer as an analogy for the cellular structure of a beehive. These hives are mapped to a single file and a .LOG file. These files are in the *winnt_root*\system32\config directory (see fig. 9.22).

Figure 9.22 illustrates the physical location of the various Registry hives (that is, SAM, SECURITY, SYSTEM, and SOFTWARE) and their various log files. Table 9.2 tabulates the relationship between the HKEY_LOCAL_MACHINE Registry key and the corresponding hives that make up this Registry key.

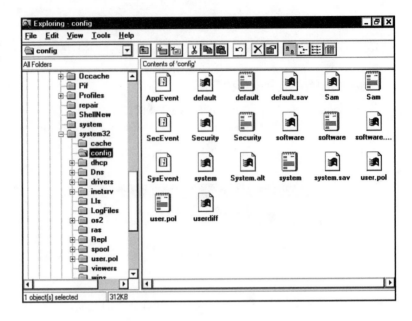

Figure 9.22

The physical location of the Registry hives is in the \system32\config directory.

Table 9.2

The Windows NT Registry Hives

Registry Hive	File Names
HKEY_LOCAL_MACHINE\SAM	SAM and SAM.LOG
HKEY_LOCAL_MACHINE\SECURITY	SECURITY and SECURITY.LOG
HKEY_LOCAL_MACHINE\SOFTWARE	SOFTWARE and SOFTWARE.LOG
HKEY_LOCAL_MACHINE\SYSTEM	SYSTEM and SYSTEM.ALT

Because the SAM, SECURITY, SOFTWARE, and SYSTEM Registry keys map directly to operating system files, they are called hives. The Registry hives are not the only occupants of the \Config directory, however, the other files are not applicable to the discussion and are not covered in this section.

In Windows NT 4, as is the case in Windows 95, user profiles are stored in a separate \Profiles directory. In previous versions of Windows NT (3.1 and 3.5x, for example), the profiles were stored in the *winnt_root*\system32\config directory with the rest of the Registry.

In figure 9.23, the left-side pane has the \Profile directory and the various subdirectories for each of the defined users. In the right-side pane, the various files and folders that constitute the user's local profile are displayed.

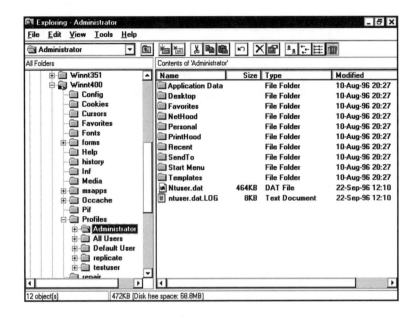

Figure 9.23
*The Windows NT 4 User
Profiles directory structure
is similar to that of
Windows 95.*

Registry Security and Ownership

The Registry plays a central role in the general well-being of a Window NT system. If, for
some reason, access is denied to the Registry, there might be some serious consequences.

For example, Microsoft SQL Server is able to integrate its security completely with Windows
NT 4. This type of security is called *Integrated Security* and is administered by the SQL
Security Manager utility. This utility grants User and Super-User status to the various data-
bases in SQL Server.

If, by some error, all administrative permissions are revoked on a particular SQL Server (for
example, by removing every member from the SQLAdmins group), then the security permissions assigned to the SQL Registry entries may become lost. In effect, a security black hole
occurs.

After all administrative permissions are revoked, nothing works. Trying to reinstall the SQL
Server does not succeed because the Registry keys are still in the Registry and no one has
permission to remove them. The solution for this particular problem is to re-set the permissions to the appropriate Registry keys by using the Permissions menu item.

Permissions

Selecting the Permissions menu option opens the Registry Key Permissions window, which
shows the users who have access to the selected key and the level of access each user has (see
fig. 9.24).

Figure 9.24

With the Registry Key Permissions dialog box the operator has the ability to review security permissions easily.

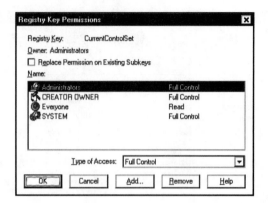

After the Registry Key Permissions dialog box has opened, the following information is applicable:

- **Registry Key.** The name of the Registry key selected as the context for the Registry key permission assigment.

- **Owner.** The group or user who is the creator or owner of this object. This user or group has complete control of this key.

- **Replace Permission on Existing Subkeys.** Allows the security permissions (Access Control List Entries) to be applied to subkeys.

- **Name.** The name of the Windows NT 4 user or group, as defined by User Manager for Domains.

- **Type of Access.** This entry defines the nature of permissible access to the associated Registry keys. The three types of access are as follows:

  - **Read.** Allows keys to be viewed, but does not permit any changes to be made to these keys.

  - **Full Control.** Allows a user to access, edit, or take ownership of a particular Registry key.

  - **Special Access.** Permits customization of the security rights so a security equivalence can be obtained that is not defined by Read and Full Control.

- **Add.** Adds a Windows NT 4 user or group to the Access Control List (ACL) of the associated Registry key. Because of the tight integration, selecting Add brings up the Windows NT 4 accounts database.

- **Remove.** Removes configured entries from the Access Control List of the appropriate Registry key.

Auditing

The Auditing command in Registry Editor lists any changes that have been made to Registry data and identifies the users who have made the listed changes (see fig. 9.25). You can audit both successful and unsuccessful actions.

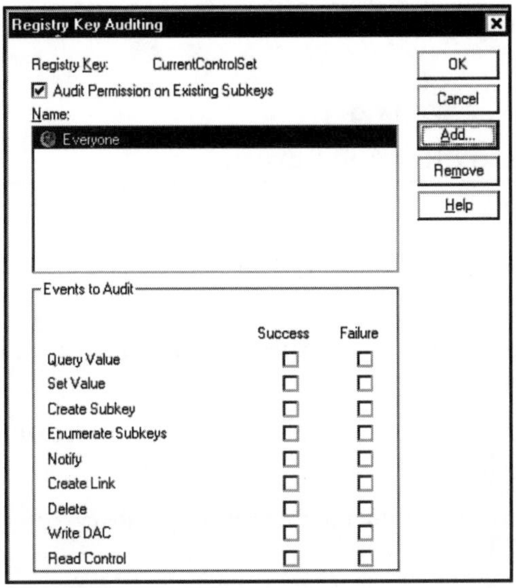

Figure 9.25

The Registry Editor permits auditing of access to particular keys within the Registry.

The advantage of auditing Registry access is to be able to trace what occurs during a particular process in terms of Registry access. If you have reason to believe that your application, for example, is not obtaining proper Registry information (this could be caused by applications not specifically written for Windows NT), you can monitor specific Registry keys to see what happens to them when the application is executed.

To audit a Registry key, you must be logged on as a member of the Administrator's group, or you must have been specifically assigned the right to audit by the system administrator. To audit activity on a Registry key, follow these steps:

1. Launch the Registry Editor and select the particular Registry key that you want to audit.

2. From the Security menu, select Auditing. The Registry Key Auditing dialog box is displayed (refer to fig. 9.25). The names of users that are already being audited appear in the Name box.

3. If you want to audit activity on the subkeys of the key that you selected, click the Audit Permission on Existing Subkeys check box. If this check box is clear, your auditing choices affect only the selected Registry key and its value entries.

4. In the Name box, click the name of a group or user. This displays the auditing events that have already been configured for the selected group or user.

5. In the Events to Audit box, click the Success or Failure check boxes of the activities that you want to audit or stop auditing. The list of possible Registry key events that can be audited are tabulated in table 9.3.

6. Click OK.

Table 9.3
Registry Key Audit Events

Select	In Order To
Query Value	Audit any system activity that attempts to read a value entry from a Registry key.
Set Value	Audit system activity that attempts to set value entries in a Registry.
Create Subkey	Audit the attempted creation of subkeys on a selected Registry key.
Enumerate Subkeys	Audit events that attempt to identify the subkeys of a Registry key.
Notify	Audit notification events from a key in the Registry.
Create Link	Audit events that attempt to create a symbolic link in a particular key.
Delete	Audit attempts to delete a Registry object.
Write DAC	Audit the attempt of a user to gain access to a key for the purpose of writing a discretionary ACL (security permission) to the key.
Read Control	Audit the attempt of a user to access the discretionary ACL on a key.

Taking Ownership

The Owner menu item presents a dialog box that identifies the user who owns the selected key (see fig. 9.26). The owner of a key can permit another user to take ownership of a key. In addition, a system administrator can assign a user the right to take ownership, or a system administrator can take ownership of a Registry key.

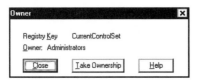

Figure 9.26
*Taking ownership
of a Registry key is
implemented by using the
Registry Editor's Security
menu.*

Taking ownership of a particular Registry key is very useful when troubleshooting. Becoming the owner of a particular Registry key grants you total rights to that key.

Furthermore, granting administrative privileges to a user on an ad hoc basis, simply to enable Registry key access of a specific kind (Registry privileges for the proper functioning of a particular application, for example), is often undesirable.

Instead, the necessary access can be given to the applicable Registry key by taking ownership of that key. In accordance with the principle of least privilege, however, be aware that it can be a complicated and difficult procedure to determine the correct Registry entries to assign the security permissions to. Assigning security access to specific Registry keys should be attempted as a last resort and to a small set of application-related problems.

Disaster Recovery

When gathering honey, one should not kick over the beehive. Wise words, and applicable to the Windows NT 4 Registry. When managing or administrating a Windows NT 4 Server or Workstation, you should not neglect the Registry. In the same way that the bees make honey, the Registry provides the crucial repository of configuration information needed to make Windows NT 4 function.

Ensuring that regular and effective backups of the Registry are made is of paramount importance. The Registry can then be restored in the case of a failure of Windows NT 4 itself or some other catastrophic event, such as the administrator forgetting her password.

This section discusses backing up and restoring the Windows NT 4 Registry and details some of the tools available to assist in this task.

Backing Up Registry Hives

You can make a backup of a Registry hive in four different ways:

■ **Tape Backup.** Windows NT 4 has a built-in data backup facility that is tape-based. Run the Backup application and select the Backup Local Registry option in the Backup Information dialog box to automatically include a copy of the local Registry files in the backup set. This method is preferred for creating backups if you have a tape drive.

■ **Other Backup Utilities.** If you do not have a tape drive, run the REGBACK.EXE program from the Resource Guide disk or use another tool that uses the same techniques to back up Registry files. This utility is discussed in detail later in this section.

■ **The Manual Method.** Start the computer by using a different operating system such as MS-DOS. Then copy all files in the *SystemRoot*\SYSTEM32\CONFIG directory to a safe backup location. For example, use another adjacent installation of Windows NT 4 if the Registry is stored on an NTFS partition, or use MS-DOS if the Registry is stored on a FAT partition.

Some DOS-based NTFS file system readers are available, so a Registry can be read from an NTFS volume in this manner. One such product is the NTFS File System Redirector for DOS/Windows V1.1 (read-only), developed by Mark Russinovich and Bryce Cogswell. Mark can be reached at markr@numega.com, and Bryce can be reached at cogswell@cs.uoregon.edu.

■ **The Save Option.** Use the Save Key command in Registry Editor, which essentially performs the RegBack procedure manually. For each direct subkey of HKEY_LOCAL_MACHINE and HKEY_USERS, when saving to disk, you must choose the Save Key command from the Registry menu, specifying file names that match the key names. For example, save the SYSTEM key to \BACKDIR\SYSTEM. On the FAT file system, the file name should not have an extension.

Don't use Save Key with the Hardware hive, which is volatile. You won't get any data because Save Key cannot save volatile keys to disk.

Restoring Hives from Backup Files

If you have a good set of backup files that you update regularly, you can restore Registry hives that are damaged or missing. You cannot use Registry Editor to fully restore hives because active parts of the Registry require use of the ReplaceKey operation for restoration, which Registry Editor cannot perform.

To restore a damaged system, you must first restore the basic operating system installation. You might do this by using the Emergency Repair disk (created by using RDISK.EXE) to restore your system to what it looked like just after installation or simply by running Windows NT 4 Setup again. Such a restoration results in a system that starts the computer, but lacks changes made since you first set it up. To restore your Windows NT 4 system to the pre-failure state, you must first copy the files from backups by using the Windows NT 4 Backup program for tape backups or by copying from disk backups.

However, you cannot merely copy the backups of Registry hive files because those files are protected while Windows NT 4 is running. After the system and all the additional files such as device drivers are restored, you must restore the Registry. You might do this in one of the following ways, depending on which backup mechanism you used:

- For tape backups, you can use the Windows NT 4 Restore program to restore the Registry. Then restart the computer.

- Start the computer by using an alternate adjacent installation of the operating system (or by using MS-DOS if the system files are on a FAT partition). Copy back the files to the *SystemRoot*\SYSTEM32\CONFIG directory. Then restart the computer by using the regular operating system.

- Use the REGREST.EXE program from the Resource Kit. The RegRest program performs a ReplaceKey API call, which replaces the default files (that the Emergency Repair or Windows NT 4 Setup programs installed) with the backup files, and saves the default files under other file names. Restart the computer after running the RegRest program to see the restored Registry. This tool is discussed in the following section.

Registry Tools

To conclude this section on Windows NT 4 Registry disaster recovery, a list of the various tools is provided as a concise reference. Table 9.4 summarizes the tools provided with Windows NT 4 that you can use to administer the Registry.

Table 9.4
Tools in Windows NT for Registry Management

Tool	Description
Registry Editor	Most Registry management can be done by using this tool
Windows NT Diagnostics	Can be used to view Registry contents in a resource-oriented manner
Backup	Backs up Registry hives as part of a tape backup routine
Emergency Repair disk	Restores default hives to the system in order to make it operational again
Windows NT 4 Explorer	Applies access controls to Registry Editor and hive files

Table 9.5 summarizes the tools on the Resource Guide disk that you can use to administer the Registry. Each tool is discussed in the following sections.

Table 9.5
Tools on the Resource Kit Disk

Tool	Description
REGBACK.EXE	Creates backups of Registry files
REGENTRY.HLP	Documents Windows NT Registry entries
REGINI.EXE	Makes Registry changes by script
REGREST.EXE	Restores Registry hives by using the ReplaceKey function

REGBACK.EXE

The REGBACK.EXE backup batch tool backs up the Windows NT Registry to files, providing a complete snapshot of the Registry. RegBack enables you to back up Registry hives while the system is running and the hive files are open. RegBack does not require a tape drive to be installed.

To use RegBack, you must be logged on as a member of a group that has Backup files and directories privileges. Do not use RDISK.EXE for making a Registry backup because it does not back up all the Registry. RDISK is intended as a last resort for making a system bootable, but not necessarily as it was. The syntax for REGBACK.EXE is as follows:

```
Yes !regback DestinationDirectory
```

As an example, regback c:\gandalf.reg saves all hives in the GANDALF.REG directory. A warning appears if some hives must be backed up manually or if errors occur.

Alternatively, the administrator can manually back up a hive to a named file. The syntax for this operation is as follows:

```
regback filename hivetype hivename
```

> **hivetype.** This parameter must either be machine or users. The backup will fail if this parameter is not machine or users. "Machine" indicates that the information being backed up relates to system-wide information, while "User" indicates the information relates to user-wide information.

> **hivename.** Is the name of an immediate subtree of HKEY_LOCAL_MACHINE or HKEY_LOCAL_USERS. Fails if this is not a hive root.

For example:

```
regback c:\myreg.sav\system machine system
```

This first example backs up the per-machine configuration information contained in the SYSTEM hive, to the file c:\myreg.sav\system.

```
regback c:\myuser.sav\prof users s-1-0000-0000-1234
```

This second example backs up the per-user configuration information contained in the S-1-0000-0000-1234 Registry key to the file c:\myuser.sav\prof.

REGINI.EXE

The REGINI.EXE utility is a character-based console application that you can use to add keys to the Windows NT Registry by specifying a Registry script. To run RegIni from the command prompt, type the following syntax:

```
regini [hivefile hiveroot] [files...]
```

If you use an .INI file to specify the Registry change, the format must locate the key on the first line, followed by the Registry entry value in this format:

```
\Registry\Machine
  System
    CurrentControlSet
      Services
        Elnk31
          Parameters
            Tcpip
              SubnetMask = REG_MULTI_SZ "255.255.0.0"
```

The previous example sets the subnet mask of a 3Com Etherlink III network card to that of a standard Class B IP Address. When configuring changes of this nature to the Registry, you must take care in specifying the correct Registry path.

For example, the successful configuration of the subnet mask relies on the correct Registry name of the network card (that TCP/IP has been bound to) being specified. In this case, Elnk31 indicates that this network card is a 3Com Etherlink III network card. This Registry update will fail if the network card is not a 3Com Etherlink III.

REGREST.EXE

This utility restores Registry hive files from backup copies by using the Win32 ReplaceKey function. You must be logged on as a member of a group that has backup files and directory privileges to use it.

REGREST.EXE has a number of switches. Type **REGREST | more** to get more help about using this utility properly. When using this utility, examine the output to make sure that it does what you want. Of course, the changes take effect only after the system is restarted.

Scenario 1. To restore all active Registry hive files in the CONFIG directory, type the following at the command prompt:

```
regrest newDirectory saveDirectory
```

> **newDirectory.** Specifies the directory for the source of the backed up hive file that will replace a hive file in the CONFIG directory. For each active Registry hive whose file is in CONFIG, RegRest attempts to replace the current file with a like-named file from the newDirectory.

> **saveDirectory.** Specifies the directory to which the old hive files in CONFIG are moved.

For example:

```
regrest c:\gandalf.reg c:\gandalf.old
```

Scenario 2. To manually restore a hive, type the following from the command prompt:

```
regrest newFilename saveFilename hivetype hivename
```

> **newFilename.** Specifies the backup source file name. RegRest renames this file and uses it to replace the old hivename file.

> **saveFilename.** Specifies the file name for saving the old hivename that is being replaced. The old hive file is renamed and moved to this location.

> **hivetype.** Can be either machine or users. Fails if the hivetype is not machine or users.

> **hivename.** The name of an immediate subtree of HKEY_LOCAL_MACHINE or HKEY_LOCAL_USERS. Fails if hivename is not a hive root.

For example:

```
regrest c:\gandalf.reg\system c:\gandalf.old machine system
```

Conclusion

As metioned earlier in this chapter, troubleshooting Windows NT 4 through the Registry is not recommended for every situation. However, the Registry does provide a centralized repository of configuration information that can prove useful in this regard.

You can troubleshoot Windows NT 4 in other ways, and the Registry should be regarded as a last resort. If the last resort arrives, however, then a thorough knowledge of the Registry and practice using the Registry Editor are valuable to the successful configuration of Windows NT Server 4.

10

Windows NT Printing

Troubleshooting Windows NT printing problems is not a simple task, mainly due to the complex nature of printing itself. This complexity stems from the number of variables present in a printing environment, as well as the number of different clients and print devices that Windows NT supports.

Windows NT has a modular printing architecture, which gives it a great deal of flexibility. The modularity of the printing architecture stems from its use of various executables and dynamic linked libraries (DLLs) that make up the various component parts of the printing process (such as the spooler, print processor, and print monitor). Extending or enhancing the functionality of these components, by rewriting and recompiling these executables and DLLs, enhances the overall functionality of the printing process.

Windows NT is able to support a wide variety of client operating systems, applications, data objects, network configurations, spooling options, and print devices. That flexibility comes at a cost, though, because the wide array of possible configurations creates a huge number of possible points of failure.

Successfully troubleshooting Windows NT printing, therefore, depends on being able to quickly identify the general category of failure. The modular composition of the Windows NT printing architecture makes troubleshooting the problem much easier.

Because each major printing task has a corresponding module (DLL or executable), you can easily add or modify these modules to add additional functionality to the printing process. Problems with printing can often be isolated to these specific components.

This chapter covers the troubleshooting of general Windows NT printing in four separate phases. The first phase looks at the actual printing process. A clear understanding of the entire printing process makes troubleshooting much easier. The first section introduces and discusses the various components of the printing process, which include printer drivers, the spooler, the print processor, the router, and the print monitor.

The second phase covers troubleshooting guidelines. Once again, knowledge of Windows NT printing architecture is crucial to effective and successful troubleshooting. This section covers the physical hard disk locations (directories) of the various printing components, as well as some interesting Windows NT registry locations (and some useful registry entries).

The third phase covers some common printing problems experienced in the Windows NT printing environment. These problems include printing from non-Windows applications, distinguishing between creating and connecting to a printer, using separator pages, and working with user security.

The final phase of this chapter covers the built-in Windows NT online printing trouble-shooter. This remarkable aid to troubleshooting answers most general questions about getting started and solving Windows NT-based printing problems.

The Printing Process

Windows NT printing involves nine basic steps. By isolating and analyzing each of these steps, you can determine whether the problem is occurring in that specific process, before it, or after it. After the point of failure is isolated, you can resolve the problem and restore normal printing operations.

This section, therefore, presents the printing process in order to establish a mental model of printing operations within the Windows NT-based network environment.

Figure 10.1 presents a generic model of how a print job, originating from a printing client, goes to a network printer.

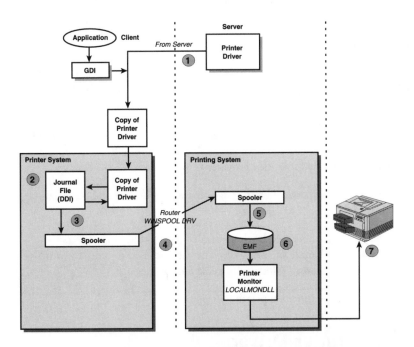

Figure 10.1

*The Windows NT
printing model has a
modular architecture*

Each of the following numbered points corresponds with the number in this figure. The
nine basic steps involved in Windows NT printing are:

1. The printer driver is loaded. During this step, a copy of an appropriate printer driver must
    be made available to the printing process. If a remote printer is in use, then the printer
    driver is copied from the print server to the local client computer. This only works for the
    supported platforms (for example, Windows 95, Windows NT, and so on).

    If the clients in use are not directly supported (such as NetWare or Windows for
    Workgroups clients), then the user is prompted to install the necessary files and drivers
    locally. If, on the other hand, the printer is local to the print server itself, then the local
    copy of the printer is used (which means that no remote copy of the printer driver is
    loaded).

2. The application (for example, Microsoft Word) generates an output file that includes the
    contents and application formatting of the original document. The Graphics Device
    Interface (GDI) generates a metafile version of this application output file, which is
    rendered by the GDI in the language of the printing device (courtesy of the printer driver).
    On computers running Windows NT 4 or Windows 95, the enhanced metafile format
    (EMF) is used.

3. The client side of the spooler makes a remote procedure call to the server side of the spooler,
    spooling the document as a print job to a registry-defined directory on the local hard disk in
    the process. This step is only applicable if the client and server are two separate machines.

4. The server side of the spooler receives the print job from the client and passes this document on to the router.

5. The router determines the type of data format used to render the print job, as received from the spooler, and sends this document to the appropriate print processor. The print processor forms part of the local print provider architecture.

6. The print processor determines the data type of the print job and processes the print job into a format usable by the intended printing device. After the print job has been fully rendered, it is passed back to the local print provider architecture.

7. If applicable, a separator page is created by the page separator processor and placed at the beginning of the print job.

8. After the local print provider is returned by the separator page processor, it selects the appropriate print monitor to handle the print job. The method used to route the print job to the printing device depends on the type of print monitor used.

9. The print job is printed by the intended printing device.

The Windows NT Printer Driver

In the first step of the printing process (refer to figure 10.1), the printer driver is loaded. Because the printer driver is responsible for generating the data stream that makes up a print job, the success of the print job relies on the health of this crucial piece of software. The Windows NT printer driver is implemented as a combination of two dynamic link libraries (or DLLs) and a printer-specific mini-driver or configuration file.

Typically, Microsoft supplies the two dynamic link libraries with Windows NT 4, and the original equipment manufacturer of the printer supplies the mini-driver or configuration file. These three files are as follows:

- **The Printer Graphics Driver.** This dynamic link library consists of the rendering or managing portion of the driver. The printing functions contained within this library are always used by the Graphics Device Interface (GDI). Windows NT provides two printer graphics driver combinations: RASDD.DLL (Universal Raster Printer Graphics Driver) and PSCRIPT.DLL (Universal PostScript Printer Graphics Driver).

- **The Printer Interface Driver.** This dynamic link library consists of the user interface or configuration management portion of the printer driver. An administrator uses this library to configure a printer through Print Manager. Windows NT provides two printer interface driver combinations: RASDDUI.DLL (Universal Raster Printer Interface Driver) and PSCRPTUI.DLL (Universal PostScript Printer Interface Driver).

■ **The Configuration File (mini-driver).** This component contains all the printer-specific information, such as memory, page protection, soft fonts, graphics resolution, paper orientation and size, and so on. It is used by the other two dynamic link libraries whenever they need to gather printer-specific information. Raster mini-drivers are dynamic link libraries (PCL5MS.DLL, for example) and PostScript mini-drivers are Adobe PostScript printer definition files (for example, APLWNTR1.PPD).

These three components of a printer driver (printer graphics driver, printer interface driver, and configuration file) are all located in the *winnt_root*\system32\spool\drivers.directory, according to their Windows NT platforms (w32x86, w32mips, w32alpha, w32ppc) and version numbers (0 = version 3.1, 1 = version 3.5x, 2 = version 4.x). A listing of the directory structure looks similar to the listing below:

```
C:\WINNT400\SYSTEM32\SPOOL
    \DRIVERS
        32x86
            1
            2
        32MIPS
            1
            2
        W32ALPHA
            1
            2
        W32PPC
            1
            2
```

As figure 10.3 illustrates, when sharing a printer locally (which turns the local computer into a print server), Windows NT 4 provides the operator with the opportunity of specifying the full range of supported client platforms. In other words, creating the necessary directory structure (as previously listed) and prompting for the installation of the various platform- and operating system–specific printer device drivers.

These printer drivers are all installed on the print server. When a print job is initiated, the router ensures that the latest version of the appropriate printer driver is copied to the client. The router compares the printer driver on the local computer with the version that is on the print server. If necessary, the client's drivers are updated with the new drivers from the print server.

Figure 10.3

Windows NT 4 supports alternate platform-specific driver installation to enable various clients to print to a Windows NT 4 print server.

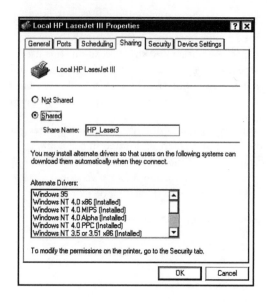

The Spooler

The spooler is a service that acts as an interface between the printing application and the Print Monitor. Spooling of print jobs takes place in a specific directory on the client. This directory (*winnt_root*\system32\spool\PRINTERS by default) can be changed as follows:

■ For all printers:

HKEY_LOCAL_MACHINE\SYSTEM\CurrentControlSet\Control\Print\ PrintersDefaultSpoolDirectory:REG_SZ:<New Spool Path>

■ On a per-printer basis:

HKEY_LOCAL_MACHINE\SYSTEM\CurrentControlSet\Control\Print\ Printers*<printer>*SpoolDirectory:REG_SZ:<New Spool Path>

If a print job gets stuck in the spooler, and an administrator or print operator cannot delete or purge that job, the spooler service can be stopped and restarted. The spooler service can be stopped and restarted by using the Control Panel Services icon, or by manually entering **net stop spooler** and **net start spooler**, respectively. The spooler service is responsible for the following functions:

■ Keeping track of what jobs are destined for which printers.

■ Keeping track of which ports are connected to which printers.

- Routing print jobs to the correct port, as well as managing printer pools.

- Prioritizing print jobs.

The Print Processor

The primary Windows NT print processor is called WINPRINT.DLL and is located in the *winnt_root*\system32\spool\prtprocs*platform* directory. The first action the spooler takes is to establish the specific data type of the current print job (see fig. 10.4).

Figure 10.4

The Print Processor configuration dialog box permits an operator to choose a different set of default data types.

After the spooler has determined the data type of the print job and ascertained that certain pre-conditions have been met, the print job is sent to the appropriate print processor that supports the identified data type. The pre-conditions are as follows:

- The print device is functioning correctly and has not been paused.

- The print device is capable of printing the job (for example, paper orientation and size are correct).

- The print and job schedule times allow for printing.

- No other jobs are of higher priority than the current job.

When the print processor receives the job, it may carry out further rendering. This depends on the specific data type of the job. After the print processor is finished with the print job, the processor passes it back up to the spooler. The print processor supports files of RAW, TEXT, and NT EMF data types.

The new Enhanced Meta File (NT EMF) data type supported by Windows NT 4 provides better response time when printing. Instead of the raw printer data being generated by the printer driver, the Graphical Device Interface generates NT EMF information before spooling.

After the NT EMF is created, control is returned to the user, and the NT EMF is interpreted in the background on a 32-bit printing subsystem spooler thread and sent to the printer driver. This returns control to the user in significantly less time than waiting for the printer calls to be fully interpreted by the printer driver directly.

The first portion of the print job's rendering is done on the client and the last portion is rendered on the print server. This means better performance for very large print jobs because the client application is not tied up for the entire rendering time.

EMF files are more portable than RAW files because EMF files can be printed on any print device, while a RAW file is rendered specifically for one print device model. Furthermore, print jobs using the EMF format are typically smaller than a RAW file that contains the same print job. If the print job comes out garbled, the print processor used for that particular print job may have become corrupted and may not be handling some or all of the data types correctly.

The Router

The *router* is the component that locates the requested printer, copies the printer driver to the local computer, and passes the print job from the client's spooler to the print server's spooler.

As stated earlier, the router compares the printer driver on the local computer with the version on the print server. If the print server has a newer version of the printer driver, it will copy the newer version to the client computer.

The router is implemented as a dynamic link library called WINSPOOL.DRV. (The extension is to ensure that applications that print will see the router and not the printer driver.) This file is located in the *winnt_root*\system32 and *winnt_root*\system directories.

If the router is not functioning properly, a user can expect problems when connecting to a remote printer or when printing to a remote printer. The router is responsible for updating the print driver on the client and for passing the print job to the remote spooler on the print server.

The Print Monitor

The print monitor controls the data stream to one or more printer ports. Writing a print job to the output destination and taking care of port access (opening, closing, configuring, reading from, writing to, and acquiring or releasing) are both responsibilities of the print monitor.

The full list of supported print monitors is listed in the MONITOR.INF file located in the *winnt_root*\system32 directory and is configurable via the print monitor installation dialog box (see fig. 10.5).

In addition, the print monitor has the following duties:

■ Detects unsolicited errors (Toner Low, for example).

■ Handles true end-of-job notification. The print monitor waits until the last page has been printed before notifying the spooler that the print job is finished and that it can get rid of that particular job.

■ Monitors printer status to detect printing errors. If necessary, the print monitor can notify the spooler so that the job can continue or be restarted.

Windows NT provides some standard print monitors. These include print monitors for the following:

■ Local output to LPTx, COMx, remote printer shares, and names pipes (LOCALMON.DLL).

■ Output to Hewlett-Packard network interface printing devices (HPMON.DLL), which can support up to 225 (configured for 64) Hewlett-Packard network interface printing devices. This print monitor requires that the DLC protocol be loaded.

■ Output to Digital (Digital Electronics Company) network port printers (DECPSMON.DLL), supporting both TCP/IP and DECnet protocols. The DECnet protocol does not ship with Windows NT.

■ Output to LPR (Line Printer) Ports (LPRMON.DLL), enabling Windows NT to print directly to Unix LPD print servers or network interface printing devices over the TCP/IP protocol.

■ Output to PJL (Printer Job Language) printing device (PJLMON.DLL). The PJL monitor "speaks" printer job language. Any bi-directional print device that uses PJL can use the PJL Monitor. For example, PJL is the language that implements all the bi-directional communication between an HP LaserJet 5Si (a bi-directional print device) and its print server.

■ Output to Apple Macintosh postscript printers (SFMMON.DLL) for Windows NT servers with services for the Apple Macintosh installed.

Troubleshooting Guidelines

Having considered the processes involved in the Windows NT printing model, this section introduces guidelines for troubleshooting problems experienced with the Windows NT printing process.

The following guidelines can be helpful when trying to isolate printing problems:

1. Check the cable connections and the printer port and verify that the printing device is on and the cables are all securely fitted. This advice might seem simple, but experience has shown that some of the most perplexing problems are caused by the simplest things.

2. Verify that the correct printer drivers are installed and configured properly. This entails establishing the type of printing device (PCL, postscript, and so on) and verifying that the correct driver type has been installed. If necessary, reinstall the printer driver. If a printer driver needs updating, install and configure the new printer driver through the Printers folder.

3. Verify that the printer is selected, either explicitly in the application or as the default printer (see fig. 10.6). Most Windows NT applications have a Printer Setup menu or toolbar button. When printing by means of OLE or another non-direct manner, the operating system needs to have a default printer specified.

Figure 10.6

Setting the default printer entails right-clicking on the appropriate printer icon and selecting the Set As Default menu item.

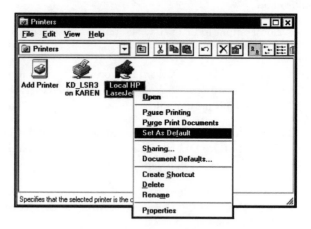

4. Verify that enough hard disk space is available to generate the print job. This is especially true for the logical disk partition (for example, drive C) on which the spooler directory has been configured. By default, this is the system partition (in other words, the *winnt_root* partition).

5. Verify that printing can occur from other applications within Windows NT. Choose the simplest application possible (for example, Notepad) to verify this. If you encounter problems when printing from an application (other than a Win32-based application), then check the appropriate application subsystem (for example, DOS, Win16, POSIX, or OS/2).

6. Print to a file (FILE:) and then copy the output file to a printer port. If this process works, then the problem is spooler- or data transmission-related. If this does not work, then the problem is application- or driver-related.

Hard Disk Location of Printing Components

Windows NT stores printing components on the hard disk in the *winnt_root*\system32\ SPOOL directory. This directory contains the following subdirectories:

■ **\DRIVERS.** This directory stores locally used printer drivers, and a separate directory is maintained for each architecture. An example of this directory structure is as follows:

```
C:\WINNT400\SYSTEM32\SPOOL
  \DRIVERS
     32x86
                1
                2
     32MIPS
                1
                2
     W32ALPHA
                1
                2
     W32PPC
                1
                2
```

■ **\PRINTERS.** This directory stores spool files while a print job is spooling.

■ **\PRTPROCS.** This directory contains the print processors. Again, each architecture has a separate directory. Intel-based computers, for example, have *winnt_root* \system32\ SPOOL\PRTPROCS\W32X86\winprint.dll as their default print processor.

■ **\winnt_root\SYSTEM32.** This directory contains the rest of the components involved in the Windows NT printing process.

Registry Locations of Printing Components

Windows NT printer information is stored in four registration database locations:

- **HKEY_LOCAL_MACHINE\SYSTEM\CurrentControlSet\Control\Print.** This registry key contains system-wide printer configuration parameters such as:

    - **Environment.** This subkey enumerates the printer drivers and print processors according to architecture and operating system version.

    - **Forms.** This subkey contains the various control codes associated with the supported form types (for example, U.S. Legal, U.S. Letter, and so on).

    - **Monitors.** This subkey contains information about the various printer monitor drivers and optional configuration parameters.

    - **Printers.** This subkey contains configuration information about each configured printer listed in the Printers dialog box.

    - **Providers.** This subkey contains configuration information for each print provider hierarchy (for example, LanMan Print Services, NetWare Print Services, and so on).

- **HKEY_CURRENT_USER\Printers.** This registry key contains parameters for the user currently logged on (for example, printer device modes and settings). The default printer and persistent connections are stored in this key.

- **HKEY_CURRENT_USER\Software\Microsoft Windows NT\CurrentVersion\Print Manager.** This registry key contains specific settings for the currently logged-on user, such as the current local and network connected printers.

- **HKEY_CURRENT_USER\Software\Microsoft WindowsNT\CurrentVersion\ PrinterPorts.** This registry key contains the spooler, network, and timeout settings for each of the currently defined printers.

Useful Registry Keys

The following registry entries can be used to control the spooler and printing in general. These options are not exposed in the print server interface and, unless otherwise noted, are set under HKEY_LOCAL_MACHINE\SYSTEM\CurrentControlSet\Control\Print.

FastPrintWaitTimeOut

When printing while spooling, the specific port thread (used to send data to this particular printer port) has to synchronize with the application that is spooling to that particular port.

This value determines how long the port thread will wait before giving up, pausing the job, and moving on to the next job. To control how long the port thread waits, add a REG_DWORD value (in milliseconds). The default is four minutes ($4 \times 60 \times 1000$ milliseconds).

A constant flow of data from spooler to printer is needed to prevent a timeout from occurring. The FastPrintWaitTimeOut, therefore, must be extended if application printing continues to fail or be paused.

FastPrintThrottleTimeout

When printing jobs while spooling is enabled, some printers timeout if they do not receive data for a timeout period (usually about 15 seconds for Postscript). To avoid this problem, one can instruct the spooler to throttle back data being sent to the printer when the FastPrintSlowDownThreshold is reached.

At that point, one byte per FastPrintThrottleTimeout period is sent until more than the threshold is reached again. To control the throttling back of spooler data being sent to the printer, add a REG_DWORD value (milliseconds) to this registry entry. If not specified, the default value is two seconds (2×1000 milliseconds).

FastPrintSlowDownThreshold

The FastPrintSlowDownThreshold is the threshold set to initiate the throttling back of data being sent to the printer. The default threshold is the result of FastPrintWaitTimeout divided by FastPrintThrottleTimeout.

Increasing or decreasing this value delays or expedites the throttling of spooler data sent to the printer, as discussed in the FastPrintThrottleTimeOut section.

PortThreadPriority

The PortThreadPriority enables you to set the priority of the PortThreads. The PortThreads are actually operating system threads that present the printer output to the port. The default is THREAD_PRIORITY_NORMAL.

Increasing the priority of the PortThreads can increase printing performance, but this configuration must be viewed within the context of a multi-threaded environment. A priority increase in one place may mean a priority decrease in another, equally important thread or process.

SchedulerThreadPriority

The SchedulerThreadPriority enables you to set the priority of the scheduler thread, which is responsible for assigning print jobs to the appropriate ports. The default is THREAD_ PRIORITY_NORMAL.

EventLog

Use EventLog to disable or enable Event logging by the spooler. This value is added to HKEY_LOCAL_MACHINE\ SYSTEM\CurrentControlSet\Control\Print\Providers and is 0x1F (informative, warning, and error events will be logged) by default.

The various values (in both hexadecimal and binary formats), as well as their meanings, are shown in the following table. The more astute reader should recognize a relationship between the last three bits of the Bin=*<binary value>* table entry and the logging functionality (that is, informative, warning, and error).

The value, which represents EventLog in the Registry, is implemented as a byte value. The last three bits of this EventLog value are used for configuring the kind of event logging desired (error, warning, and informative logging).

So, for example, a value of 11000 disables event logging completely (last three bits are all zero, effectively disabling all logging) while a value of 11010 enables the logging of warning messages.

In the following table, notice the correspondence between the 1s in the last three bits of the Registry Entry Value, and the Yes/No to the far right side.

Table 10.1
Possible Values of the EventLog Registry Entry

Registry Entry Value	Error	Warning	Information
Hex=0x18, Bin=11000	No	No	No
Hex=0x19, Bin=11001	No	No	Yes
Hex=0x1A, Bin=11010	No	Yes	No
Hex=0x1B, Bin=11011	No	Yes	Yes
Hex=0x1C, Bin=11100	Yes	No	No
Hex=0x1D, Bin=11101	Yes	No	Yes
Hex=0x1E, Bin=11110	Yes	Yes	No
Hex=0x1F, Bin=11111	Yes	Yes	Yes

PriorityClass

This controls the priority class of the spooler. The default value is 0, the value 7 indicates a workstation, and the value 9 is reserved for servers.

DisableServerThread

Setting the DisableServerThread value to True (1) disables the printing browse thread on the affected system. This thread is used to call other printer servers to notify them that this printer exists and will cause additional network traffic. Add the value ServerThreadRunning and set it to 1 to disable the browse thread.

ServerThreadTimeout

This specifies the amount of time the server thread sleeps before it notifies all the other print servers about the printers on the affected system. The default REG_DWORD value ServerThreadTimeout is 10 minutes ($10 \times 60 \times 1000$ in milliseconds).

Note that the default NetPrinterDecayPeriod on other servers is one hour, so if you modify the NetPrinterDecayPeriod to be longer than one hour other servers will forget about this printer when a browse dialog is brought up.

NetPrinterDecayPeriod

The NetPrinterDecayPeriod specifies the amount of time to keep a NetPrinter cached. The *cache* is used to present the list of printers when the browse dialog box is used. The REG_DWORD default for this subkey is one hour ($60 \times 60 \times 1000$ in milliseconds).

Common Printing Problems

Now that the printing model has been sketched as a mental reference point, and the physical printing components have been located and discussed, some common problems relating the Windows NT printing can be examined.

The problems discussed in this section certainly do not represent the entire width and breadth of Windows NT printing problems. Instead, they represent some examples of areas that have caused problems in the past. These include printing from a non-Windows application, deciding whether to create a local printer or whether to connect to a network printer, using and creating separator pages, and securing printer access.

Printing from Non-Windows Applications

Invariably, when printing from MS-DOS, OS/2, or POSIX-compliant non-Windows applications, some additional configuration may be required:

■ If the printing device is locally attached, you only need to configure the application to print to the appropriate port (for example, LPT1:). If the printer has also been created in the Windows NT Printers folder, with a desination address of LPT1:, the spooler will spool the print job from the non-Windows applications.

- If the print job needs to be sent to a remote print server, connect to the remote print server from the command prompt (for example, net use lpt1: \\remote\printer).

- If the non-Windows application generates text output, such as an MS-DOS Editor, no special configuration is required. As long as there is a locally attached printer device, or LPT1: has been redirected to a print server, the application will be able to print.

- If the non-Windows application prints graphics or formatted documents, such as an MS-DOS word processor, the application must have its own vendor-supplied printer driver for the printing device. This is the same printer driver that the application would use when installed on its native operating system.

Creating versus Connecting Printers

Essentially, you can access network printers in two ways. You can either create a printer or connect to a printer. When you create a printer, the driver is installed on your local computer (see fig. 10.7). When you connect to a printer, the printer device driver is copied from the server when it is needed by an application.

Figure 10.7

The Add Printer Wizard dialog box helps you install local printers.

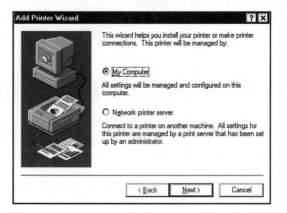

Of course, the decision of whether to create your own local printer or to connect to a remote printer is not always an obvious one (see fig. 10.8). When faced with both options, the correct decision may depend on many factors. To facilitate this decision-making process, the characteristics of each method are tabulated below for reference:

Table 10.2
Connecting Printers versus Creating Printers

Creating a Printer	Connecting to a Printer
You can print from a Windows NT-based computer to any type of NT print server or locally attached printing device. This is the only way to print to a local printing device.	You can print from a Windows NT-based computer to a printer on other server Windows NT-based computers only.
The printer configuration defined on the local computer is used to control printing.	The printer driver and configuration is downloaded to the requesting Windows NT-based computer. You do not need to install a printer driver. Requires print privileges.
Requires Administrator or Power User privileges.	The requesting Windows NT-based computer cannot change the printer
The printer configuration can only be changed by someone with the appropriate privileges.	configuration unless the user has administrative privileges on the print server.
Only current user print jobs can be viewed in the printer window. Good for mixed enviroments where there are different types of print servers (Windows NT-based, Windows for Workgroups, other networks).	All print jobs can be viewed in the printer windows. You only need to know the network address (UNC name) to connect and print. You do not need to know any- thing about what type of printer it is, how much memory it has, and so on.

The method used to establish a printer on a client computer dictates the configuration of the client computer in relation to the printer. Only Windows NT and Windows 95 client computers can actually "connect to" a network printer served by a Windows NT print server. All other client computers must create the printer—that is, they must install the printer driver directly on their hard disks, specify a port, name the printer, and so on. Windows NT and Windows 95 print clients can also create a remote printer served by a Windows NT print server.

Figure 10.8

Connecting to a remote printer is controlled by the printer wizard.

Each method has advantages and disadvantages. Connecting to a remote printer is easier and faster than creating one. If the Windows NT client has connected to a printer, the print job doesn't spool on the client machine, so no spool options are available. (Windows 95 clients always spool locally and again remotely.) The connected client also cannot queue print jobs locally.

Separator Pages

Separator pages are used to separate print jobs on a printer. These pages are often very useful when a number of different users access a single printer, or when a printer pool causes your work to print to more than one printer. In either case, the separator pages act as a banner to identify your print jobs from those printed by other users.

Windows NT supplies three persistent separator-page files (SYSPRINT.SEP, PCL.SEP, PSCRIPT.SEP) in the *winnt_root*\system32 directory. These files are designed for different purposes.

Table 10.3
Windows NT Separator Pages

File Name	Function
SYSPRINT.SEP	A PostScript-compatible separator file that prints a separator page at the beginning of each document. There is some error handling code at the beginning of the SYSPRINT.SEP file.
PCL.SEP	Switches the printing mode to PCL for Hewlett-Packard series printers. It also prints a page before each document.
PSCRIPT.SEP	Switches the printer to PostScript printing, but does not print a separator page before each document.

Rolling Your Own Separator Page

You can set up separator pages only if you have Full Control access permissions. Members of the Administrators, Server Operators, Print Operators, or Power Users group have Full Control permission by default (see fig. 10.9).

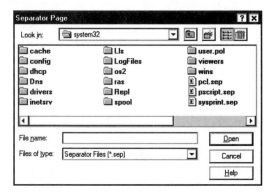

Figure 10.9

Selecting a separator page makes finding a document at the printer easier.

The local print provider has an interpreter that reads the commands from a separator file and produces one or more pages of text (or graphics) as header or burst pages. Separator files are commonly referred to as burst pages, header pages, or banner pages.

The SYSPRINT.SEP and PSCRIPT.SEP files are both compatible with PostScript printing, while PCL.SEP is more suited for dual-language Hewlett-Packard printers (PCL printing).

Although the three standard separator files are already configured and ready for use, they may not necessarily be suitable for every printing occasion. For this reason, you may want to create user-defined separator files. A good starting point is to make a copy of the SYSPRINT.SEP (or any other file) and amend this file according to the specific requirements. To assist in this venture, the following table of escape codes is included for reference:

Table 10.4
Separator Page Escape Codes

Code	Function
\N	Returns the name of the user who submitted the job.
\I	Returns the print job number.
\D	Returns the date the job was printed. The date is formatted according to the setting configured using the International control panel applet.
\T	Returns the time the job was printed. The time is formatted according to the setting configured using the International Control Panel applet.

continues

Table 10.4, Continued
Separator Page Escape Codes

Code	Function
\L*xxxx*	Returns all the characters (*xxxx*) following it until another escape code is encountered.
\F*pathname*	Returns the contents of a file specified by the path name, starting on an empty line. The contents of the file are copied directly to the printer without any processing.
\H*nn*	Sets a printer-specific control sequence, where *nn* is a hexadecimal ASCII code that is sent directly to the printer. The correct values can be found in the appropriate printing device reference guide or manual.
\W*nn*	Sets the width of the separator page. The default is 80 and the maximum value is 256. Any printable characters beyond this width parameter will be truncated.
\B\S	Prints text in single-width block characters until a \U code is encountered.
\E	Ejects the page from the printer. This code can be used to start or end a separator page file. If you get an extra blank page when you print anything, then remove this code from the separator page file's instruction text.
\n	Skips *n* number of lines (0–9). Skipping 0 lines can be used to move printing to the next line.
\B\M	Prints text in double-width block characters until a \U code is encountered.
\U	Turns off block character printing.

The only real problems to expect when designing your own separator pages are syntactic errors in the actual separator page file. Thorough knowledge of the various escape codes is necessary to prevent such errors.

A PCL Example

To illustrate the use of the escape codes, the following example is included for completeness:

```
1 \
2 \H1B\L%-12345X@PJL ENTER LANGUAGE=PCL
3 \H1B\L&l1T\0
4 \H1B\L(19U\H1B\L(s1p16v0s0b16602T
5 \H1B\L&a10L\L\LDate: \D\H1B\L&a60L\LJob: \I\H1B\L&a94L\LTime: \T
6 \9\5
7 \H1B\L(19U\H1B\L(s1p36v0s0b16602T
8 \H1B\L&a17L
```

```
9  \H5C\H5C\LServer\H5C\LShare
10 \9\6
11 \H1B\L(19U\H1B\L(s1p96v1s0b4116T
12 \H1B\L&a10L\N
13 \H1B\LE
```

Each line of code is explained further in the following list:

- **Line 1.** The first line of any separator file is a delimiter character by itself. The separator file interpreter looks for the backslash (\) character on the first line and uses it as the delimiter for its command strings in the rest of the separator file.

- **Line 2.** If you want to send printer language commands, and those commands include unprintable characters, you must send those characters by typing **\H** followed by the character's hexadecimal value. Because most PCL commands begin with an ESC character (hex value 0×1B) and are followed by printable text, many PCL separator file lines begin with \H1B, followed by \L, and then a literal string containing the rest of the PCL command. Remember that PCL commands are case-sensitive. The previous line tells HP print devices with multiple languages (personalities) to switch to PCL.

- **Line 3.** \H1B\L&l1T\0 toggles job separation and moves the cursor down one line.

- **Line 4.** Two PCL commands are in Line 4; the first sets the symbol set, and the second sets the font spacing, size, and name:

```
<ESC>(19U sets symbol set to 19U (Windows 3.1 Latin 1)
<ESC>(s1p sets spacing to 1 (1=proportional, 0=fixed)
16v sets font size to 16 points
0s0b16602T sets font to Arial (Plain)
```

To use a different symbol set, size, or font, you need to change this command. (Spacing is usually defined by the font and is not configurable.) To get a list of the available fonts on an HP 4 Si print device, use its front panel. From the Test menu, choose the PCL TYPE LIST entry and press Enter. The resulting pages include lines that provide the commands to set the font spacing and name.

- **Line 5.** The PCL command <ESC>&a#L sets the horizontal cursor position on the current line to column #. This line positions the Date:, Job:, and Time: labels horizontally at columns 10, 60, and 94, respectively, and prints the current date, the job number, and the time after their respective labels.

- **Line 6.** \9\5 moves the cursor position down 14 lines. The \n separator file command moves the cursor down n lines. Although n must be a single digit (0–9) number, you can move nine lines, and then five lines, to move a total of 14 lines.

- **Line 7.** \H1B\L(19U\H1B\L(s1p36v0s0b16602T re-defines the current font, increasing the size from 16 to 36 points.

■ **Lines 9 and 10.** The separator file code \H5C\H5C\LServer\H5C\LShare and \9\6 sets the left margin at column 17, prints \\Server\Share, and then moves down 15 lines.

You can change the Server and Share strings to the names of your print server and its print share. \9\6 sets the left margin at 17 because this roughly centers the text \\Server\Share horizontally. If your server and share name create a longer or shorter string, you may want to adjust this margin to maintain the centering. There is no separator file command to center text automatically.

■ **Line 11.** \H1B\L(19U\H1B\L(s1p96v1s0b4116T re-defines the current font to 96-point Marigold Windows 3.1 Latin 1 symbol set. This example uses the Marigold font to demonstrate that you can get multiple fonts on the same page. You can, however, change the font setting in the previous code fragment to the font of your choice.

■ **Line 12.** \H1B\L&a10L\N sets the left margin to column 10 and then prints the user's name.

■ **Line 10.** There are two final lines in the file. The first is a PCL printer reset command <ESC>E, and the second is the carriage return-linefeed pair that follows the printer reset command. Do not forget the carriage return-linefeed pair.

The precise output you get when you use the sample separator file varies depending on the values for the date, job number, time, the share specified, and the user's name. However, the basic layout of the page can be described as follows: near the top of the separator page you see one line with the label "date" with a value on the left, the label "job" and a number in the center, and the label "time" and its current value at the right.

The text in this line will be in Arial 16 font. Roughly centered on the page will be the \\Server\Share name in the Arial 36 point font. On the lower half of the sheet, and also centered left to right on the page, will be the user name in a 96-point script font.

User Permissions for a Printer

Printers are objects and have owners just like everything else in the Windows NT environment. In Windows NT 4, a printer object can be assigned specific user access permissions, which is useful when trying to prevent unauthorized usage of a printing device.

A printer object can also be audited to keep track of who makes use of these access privileges, which assists in tracking down attempted or actual misuse of printer access privileges.

Lastly, a printer object can be owned by a group of users, affording an operator a safe way to manipulate security control of printing devices. As an object owner, you have full control of that object. Object ownership, therefore, is a much safer way of providing super-user privileges to certain printer objects without providing super-user privileges to the entire operating system.

The ability to assign user access permissions, or to take ownership of printer objects, can lead to some problems, particularly if you do not assign or revoke permissions in a controlled fashion. Auditing is a good tool to use when trying to troubleshoot security-related Windows NT printing problem. Tracking the successful and unsuccessful events allows an administrator to determine the best course of action to resolve a given situation.

You can secure printers by setting permissions for users who might be connected to the printer on the network or for users who log on locally. In order to assign these permissions, administrative privileges are necessary. By right-clicking on a particular printer's icon and then selecting the Security tab, permissions can be assigned to a printer (see fig. 10.10).

Figure 10.10

Windows NT printer security includes setting and viewing access permissions, auditing, and object ownership.

The four levels of permissions are: Full Control, Manage Documents, Print, and No Access (see fig. 10.11). These permissions allow users the following privileges:

Table 10.5
User Permissions for Windows NT Printers

Function	No Access	Print	Manage Documents	Full Control
Print Documents		X	X	X
Control jobs for the user's own jobs		X	X	X

continues

Table 10.5

User Permissions for Windows NT Printers

Function	No Access	Print	Manage Documents	Full Control
Pause, restart, and delete the user's own documents		X	X	X
Control job settings for all documents			X	X
Pause, restart, and delete all documents			X	X
Share a printer				X
Change printer properties				X
Delete printers				X
Change printer permissions				X

Portions reprinted with permission from Microsoft Corporation.

Figure 10.11

The four levels of printer security permissions control user access to Windows NT printing devices.

Of course, in a secure environment, you often need the ability to keep track of successful and unsuccessful usage of these printer privileges. To do this, auditing must be configured for a particular printer. Figure 10.12 illustrates the various auditing functions.

In particular, auditing unsuccessful access to printer resources is the first step in establishing that there is a problem with the printing environment. Invariably, a printing problem does not have a singular root cause, and you will often have to track down a range of problem areas before actually fixing the problem.

For example, your ability to print to a printer is derived from your Windows NT security context. This security context is derived from the access token issued during the logon and authentication processes.

You may, for example, be a member of the Engineers group, which has print rights to a particular printer. Unfortunately, you are unable to print to this printer despite your membership to the Engineers group.

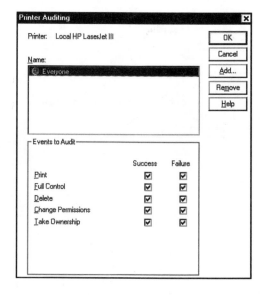

Figure 10.12
Printer events can be audited to keep track of printing device usage on a per-group or per-user basis.

Perhaps the problem is occurring because you also belong to the TonerGuzzler group, which does not have any access to that particular printer. By auditing unsuccessful print events, you can track the true cause of the problem.

The Windows NT Printing Troubleshooter

Windows NT 4 has its own online printing troubleshooter, which is an ideal tool to help you unravel problems experienced when printing documents. This tool follows a question-and-answer approach and leads the user to isolate the problem through a process of verification.

The Windows NT Online Printing Troubleshooter forms part of the online help supplied with the Windows NT Server 4. If you search for Troubleshooting, printing problems in the Windows NT Help index, the Help system finds and loads the Printing Troubleshooter (see fig. 10.13).

The troubleshooter starts by asking "What's wrong?" (see fig. 10.14). This starts the process of finding the root cause of the printing problem you are experiencing. All that is required, at every step, is to select the answer that best suits the prevailing situation.

Figure 10.13

Locating the Windows NT Online Printing Troubleshooter is as easy as looking it up in the online Help index.

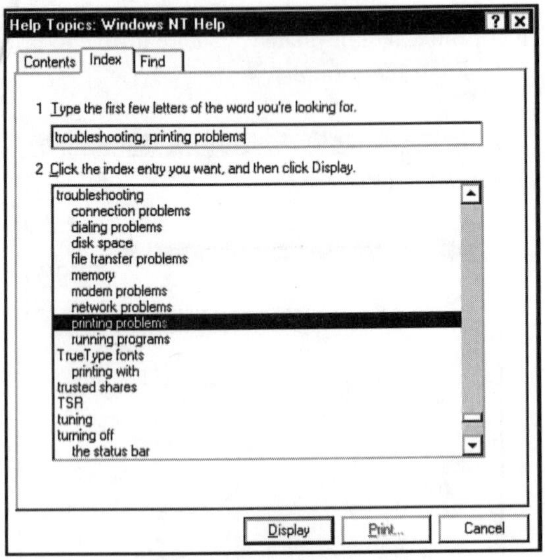

Help Topics: Windows NT Help

Contents | Index | Find

1 Type the first few letters of the word you're looking for.

troubleshooting, printing problems

2 Click the index entry you want, and then click Display.

troubleshooting
    connection problems
    dialing problems
    disk space
    file transfer problems
    memory
    modem problems
    network problems
    printing problems
    running programs
TrueType fonts
    printing with
trusted shares
TSR
tuning
turning off
    the status bar

Display | Print... | Cancel

Figure 10.14

The Windows NT Online Orienting Troubleshooter opening screen.

Windows NT Help

Help Topics | Back | Options

Print Troubleshooter

This troubleshooter helps you identify and solve printer problems. Just click to answer the questions, and then try the suggested steps to fix the problem.

What's wrong?

☐ My document didn't print at all.

☐ My document printed, but it doesn't look right, or it printed only partially.

☐ Printing is unusually slow.

After a period of reading and answering the various questions posed by the Printing Trouble-shooter, a solution will be reached (see fig. 10.15) or the Printing Troubleshooter will run out of ideas and present its dead-end screen (see fig. 10.16).

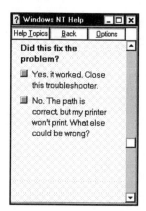

Figure 10.15

A possible solution might look like this.

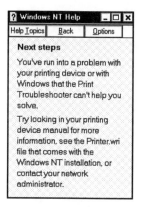

Figure 10.16

A possible dead end might look like this.

One of the finest features of this new-generation troubleshooting tool is its integration into the operating system itself. A good example of this is illustrated in figure 10.17, where the Online Troubleshooter gives the user an opportunity to call up the Printers folder to check the settings of the printer port.

The capability to access online help and to get clear and concise help in troubleshooting a printing problem is a definite high point of the next-generation troubleshooting assistants. Coupled with the capability to call up specific Windows NT tools and dialogs, the Online Printing Troubleshooter is a valuable asset in the fight against printing problems.

Figure 10.17

*The Online Printing
Troubleshooter integrates
completely with the Windows
NT operating system.*

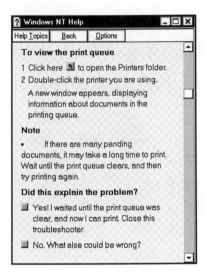

Conclusion

When troubleshooting, no single method can be used in isolation. This is especially true when troubleshooting printing problems.

The printing process, as depicted in figure 10.1, provides the necessary mental model on which to base a troubleshooting strategy, and the troubleshooting guidelines presented throughout this chapter provide a way in which to isolate the problem to a particular application or device.

This chapter also discussed the Windows NT Online Printing Troubleshooter, an integrated Help tool that assists with troubleshooting your printer configuration.

Windows NT Fault Tolerance

In Windows NT 4, Redundant Array of Inexpensive Disks (RAID) fault tolerance (see fig. 11.1) can be implemented in either hardware or software. In a hardware solution, the controller interface handles the creation and regeneration of redundant information. This activity can also be performed in a software solution by using Disk Administrator. RAID fault tolerance supports the Windows NT file system (NTFS) and the File Allocation Table (FAT) file system.

Figure 11.1

RAID fault tolerance is implemented in six distinct levels with RAID levels 0, 1, and 5 supported by Windows NT.

Level 0	Disk striping
Level 1	Disk mirroring
Level 2	Disk striping with error-correction code (ECC)
Level 3	Disk striping with ECC stored as parity
Level 4	Disk striping large blocks; parity stored on one drive
Level 5	Disk striping with parity distributed across multiple drives

RAID levels 0, 1, and 5 are supported by Windows NT Server directly

Windows NT Server offers two specific fault-tolerant RAID strategies (RAID 1 and RAID 5) in a software solution. This chapter presents both approaches and discusses how to recover from media or system failures when either fault-tolerant strategy is implemented.

RAID 1—Mirroring

In RAID 1 (disk mirroring), all data written to the primary disk is also written to a mirrored disk (also referred to as a shadow or twin disk partition), which results in a disk space utilization of only 50 percent (see fig. 11.2). Of course, this is a rather obtuse way of looking at things because the twin disk may very well save the mirrored operating system (and your critical data) in a disaster.

Figure 11.2

RAID 1 provides an identical twin for a selected disk, which is called disk mirroring.

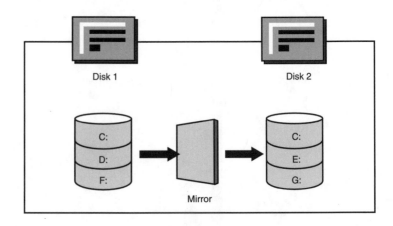

Technically, mirroring is not restricted to a partition identical to the primary partition in size or number of tracks and cylinders, nor to disk drives made by the same manufacturer. In short, you do not have to replace a failed drive with an identical model.

For practical purposes, however, it is highly advisable for the shadow partition to be the same size as the primary partition. The shadow partition should not be smaller than the primary. If the shadow partition is larger than the primary, then the extra space on the shadow drive is left as free space. A mirrored partition and its shadow partition constitute a mirror set.

If a read failure occurs on one of the drives, the system reads the data from the other drive in the mirror set (see fig. 11.3). If a write failure occurs on one of the drives in the mirror set, the system uses the remaining drive for all accesses.

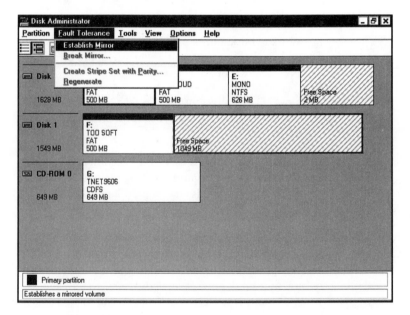

Figure 11.3

Use Disk Administrator to establish a mirror set.

When compared to stripe sets, a mirror-set implementation has a lower entry cost because it requires only two disks.

A stripe set with parity, however, requires three or more disks and more system memory than mirror sets (striping with parity can require up to three times more memory than normal due to parity calculations that need to be carried out). Mirroring also provides the best overall performance and does not show performance degradation during a failure.

The cost-per-megabyte for RAID 1 is higher than for RAID 5. This is because when two 1 GB disk drives are mirrored, the effective storage capacity remains at 1 GB if these two disks are used to create a RAID 1 mirror set.

In RAID 1, however, you can mirror the boot and system partitions, which significantly reduces the amount of time needed to get your Windows NT Server back up if a problem occurs with the hard disk containing your operating system.

The boot partition is generally the partition containing the boot sector, making it a startable partition. The system partition is generally the partition containing the operating system files. The boot and system partitions can be separate partitions or the same partition.

Important Facts about Disk Mirroring

RAID 1 may appear to be a reasonably simple concept to understand and implement, but you should consider some specific concepts and caveats when implementing disk mirroring. The following facts apply to disk mirroring under Windows NT:

- Only Windows NT Server can create and break mirror sets. By design, Windows NT Workstation cannot provide fault tolerance; therefore, you cannot attempt to break or create mirror sets with Windows NT Workstation.

- Mirrors are the only type of Windows NT fault tolerant partition that can be created from existing partitions, which contrasts with volume sets. Stripe sets (with or without parity) must be created from free disk space.

- Mirrors are file system independent. Any partition that uses a file system that Windows NT recognizes or that is blank can be used to create a mirror. These file systems include FAT, NTFS, and HPFS. CDFS is precluded from this kind of partitioning because it is read-only by design.

- Mirrors sets are not dependent on disk geometry. The only requirement is that the mirror set be created by using two logical partitions of similar size (the twin partition should be at least the same size as the primary partition). Mirroring is not restricted to a partition of identical geometry (size, number of heads, cylinders, tracks, sectors, and so on) nor is it restricted to a drive of the same type (IDE, ESDI, SCSI, and so on).

- A single mirror set is limited only to two hard disks. If fault tolerance over more than two disks is needed, use disk striping with parity.

- Mirror sets are invisible to the user. When a mirror set is created, both partitions are assigned the same drive letter.

- Mirroring is the only Windows NT fault tolerant option available for use on boot and system partitions. Mirroring a boot partition is illustrated in figure 11.4.

- The primary and twin partitions must be on separate hard disk drives. They cannot be

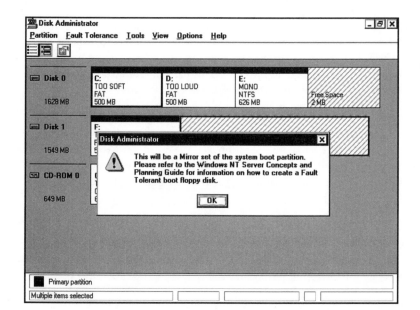

on the same physical hard disk drive. Apart from the physical limitations, having both partitions on the same physical disk is like having all your eggs in one basket.

- The two hard disks containing the primary and mirrored partitions may be on the same or different disk controllers (disk duplexing). Windows NT defines both options as mirroring and makes no distinction.

- If the boot or system partition is mirrored and the primary partition is damaged, the computer can boot off the twin partition by using a fault-tolerant boot floppy disk. This requires a straightforward modification of the BOOT.INI file, on the boot disk, but can require a little more work when using IDE master/slave configurations.

- Only the Windows NT Server installation that created the mirror set can normally recognize the set. Other operating systems cannot recognize the mirrored partition. MS-DOS can identify the partitions of the mirror as non-DOS partitions. Windows NT and other installations of Windows NT Server can identify the primary and mirror partitions as having an "Unknown" file system type in Disk Administrator.

Breaking the mirror set is very often a requirement before the partitions can become visible to other operating systems. Windows NT and other installations of Windows NT Server can recognize a mirror set created by Windows NT Server by restoring disk configuration information.

■ A new installation of Windows NT cannot be installed on an existing mirror set. During the Windows NT setup process, you must select the partition on which to install Windows NT. The Windows NT setup, however, identifies a mirror set as a Windows NT fault tolerant partition. If you attempt to select this partition for installation of Windows NT, a message appears stating that Windows NT does not recognize this partition, and it must be deleted before Windows NT setup can use it.

■ The fault-tolerance driver makes the loss of one partition in a mirror set invisible; you can read from and write to the remaining partition as if the mirror set were healthy. If only one partition of a mirror set is functioning, however, then it is no longer fault tolerant. This vulnerable state means that losing the remaining partition will result in an unrecoverable loss of all data in the mirror set.

■ The status bar in Disk Administrator is a key to determining the condition of a mirror set. When you select one of the partitions of a mirror set, Disk Administrator displays information about the mirror in the lower-left corner of the window. The various condition indicators are explained in the following list:

   ■ [HEALTHY] indicates that the status of the mirror set is healthy (see fig. 11.5).

Figure 11.5

Disk Administrator exposes a HEALTHY mirror set.

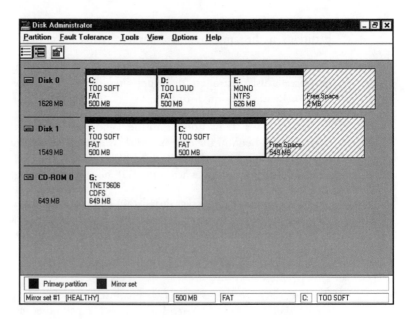

   ■ [NEW] appears immediately after the mirror set has been created in Disk Administrator, but before the system is shut down and actual generation of the mirror begins (see fig. 11.6).

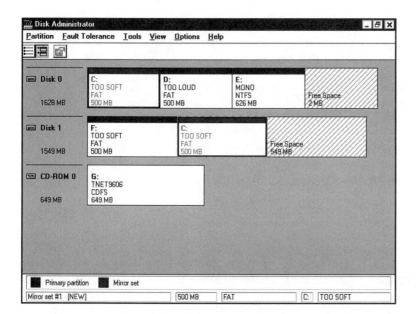

Figure 11.6
When a mirror set is created by using the Disk Administrator, the mirror set is marked as NEW.

■ [INITIALIZING] displays when generation of the mirror set by the system has been started but is not yet complete (see fig. 11.7).

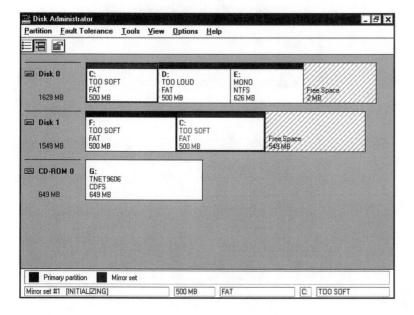

Figure 11.7
After a mirror set is created by using the Disk Administrator, it is marked as INITIALIZING.

- [RECOVERABLE] appears when one of the partitions in the set has been lost, but the other partition is undamaged. This message also appears when one partition loses synchronization with the other.

- [BROKEN] appears when one of the partitions has been lost, and the status of the other partition is unknown. This status is not commonly encountered.

■ When a member of a mirror set fails, no significant loss in performance occurs. When a dynamic failure of the primary partition occurs, performance decreases while Windows NT Server determines that a problem has occurred. After Windows NT Server figures out the problem, the normal system performance is restored.

■ Disk mirroring provides better overall write performance than striping with parity, and better read performance in the event of a drive failure.

This better performance is due mainly to the fact that because two copies of the same data are maintained, data reads can occur from the read/write head closest to the allocation unit that contains the data to be read.

Any progress (including errors) during the entire process of creating a mirror set is reported by Windows NT through the system event log. Figure 11.8 illustrates the successful completion of a mirror initialization or synchronization.

Figure 11.8

The system event log reports the status of a mirror initialization process to the operator through the Event Detail dialog box.

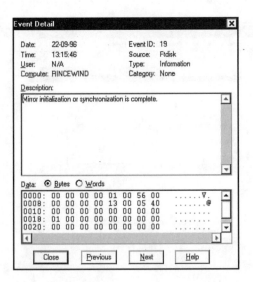

Creating a Fault-Tolerant Boot Disk

To create a fault-tolerance floppy disk for recovering from a failed boot mirror partition, you may need to correct the hardware identifier on the arc path name in the BOOT.INI file.

In the BOOT.INI file, scsi() indicates a SCSI disk drive is connected to a SCSI adapter whose BIOS has not been loaded. However, multi() can indicate a non-SCSI disk drive supported by either the ATDISK.SYS or ABIOSDSK.SYS driver, or a SCSI disk drive supported by a SCSI BIOS that loads when the SCSI adapter detects a bootable device on the lowest SCSI ID on most SCSI adapters.

Intel (x86-based) computers running Windows NT Server use the multi() option as the default hardware identifier for the primary bootable disk drive. This is due to the SCSI BIOS, ATDISK.SYS driver, or ABIOSDSK.SYS driver support.

If the system is using a SCSI adapter and the primary boot drive of a mirror set fails or becomes inaccessible and the SCSI adapter BIOS does not load, the multi() identifier option will fail to locate the healthy mirror drive. As a result, the BOOT.INI file on the fault-tolerance boot disk will require the use of the SCSI option to boot the remaining mirror drive.

The fault-tolerant boot disk is pivotal to the successful recovery of a failed mirror set member, which is especially true when the mirror set includes the system or boot partition. If the partition containing the Windows NT Server system files is mirrored and then lost, you can use a fault-tolerant boot floppy disk to restart Windows NT Server and access the mirror of the lost drive.

A fault-tolerant boot floppy contains the files necessary to boot Windows NT from a mirrored partition. The idea is to think about creating this boot disk before the need for its use arises. In the real world, however, this luxury is often not available. So, because of the importance of having a fault-tolerant boot disk, various ways of creating a fault-tolerant boot disk are discussed in the following sections.

Pre-Failure

When creating a mirror set, creating a fault-tolerant boot disk is common practice (and is recommended). This fault-tolerant boot disk should be able to start the system from the mirrored twin (in the case of the failure of the primary mirrored partition).

The following steps should be followed to create a fault-tolerant boot disk:

1. Format a high-density floppy disk under Windows NT by using the FAT file system. Use the Windows NT GUI (My Computer, NT Explorer), or the command prompt (format a: /fs:fat).

Figure 11.9

Formatting a floppy disk is the first step in creating a fault-tolerant boot disk.

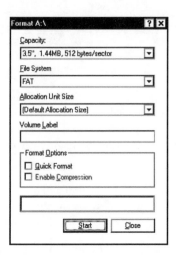

2. Copy NTLDR, BOOT.INI, and NTDETECT.COM onto this floppy disk. If required, you should include a copy of NTBOOTDD.SYS (which is a renamed copy of the device driver for the SCSI controller with its ROM BIOS disabled).

3. The BOOT.INI file must be modified to reflect the ARC naming convention location of the mirrored copy of Windows NT Server. The following examples are copies of two BOOT.INI files (before and after):

```
C:\BOOT.INI
[boot loader]
timeout=20
default=multi(0)disk(0)rdisk(0)partition(1)\WINNT400
[operating systems]
multi(0)disk(0)rdisk(0)partition(1)\WINNT400="NT 4.00 (Beta 2)"
C:\="MS-DOS 6.22"
```

The original BOOT.INI file (C:\BOOT.INI) is used to boot Windows NT normally, while the fault-tolerant version (A:\BOOT.INI) is used to boot from both the original and the twin partition. The following example assumes that two separate IDE drives exist, both of which are connected to the same adapter (or motherboard interface).

```
A:\BOOT.INI
[boot loader]
timeout=20
default=multi(0)disk(0)rdisk(0)partition(1)\WINNT400
[operating systems]
multi(0)disk(0)rdisk(0)partition(1)\WINNT400="NT 4.00 (Beta 2)"
multi(0)disk(0)rdisk(1)partition(1)\WINNT400="NT 4.00 (Fault Tolerant)"
C:\="MS-DOS 6.22"
```

4. Lastly, but most important, the correct functioning of this fault-tolerant boot disk must be verified. To verify that the disk is functioning correctly, you must test the disk.

Please note that after creating your fault-tolerant boot floppy disk, you can perform the following test to re-assure yourself that it will work when needed.

1. Insert the fault-tolerant boot floppy disk and restart the computer. You will be presented with the normal Windows NT dual boot screen.

2. If your boot selection, from Windows NT's dual boot menu, correctly specifies the alternate ARC path to the twin partition, your system should begin to boot and then fail with the following STOP message:

```
***STOP: 0x0000006B (0xC000000D, 0x00000002, 0x00000000, 0x00000000)
PROCESS1_INITIALIZATION_FAILED
```

You may get a different stop message than the one previously listed, but this also indicates that the FT boot floppy is working correctly. The following is an example of what you may expect to be listed:

```
*** STOP: 0x0000001E (0xc0000006,0x801Abe58,0x00000000, 0x00000000)
KMODE_EXCEPTION_NOT_HANDLED
```

To fully test the fault-tolerant boot disk to ensure it will boot from your mirrored drive, disable the primary NT drive by unplugging the power cable from that physical drive.

Post-Failure

If you have lost the primary partition of a mirror set, you cannot start Windows NT Server, and no other Windows NT system is available from which to create a fault tolerant boot floppy, then use the following method to revive your system:

1. Boot to MS-DOS, either through another system or with a floppy on the current system.

2. Copy the first Windows NT Server Setup Disk (for floppy disk installation) to a blank floppy disk. Use any utility that will create a clone image of this disk (for example, diskcopy).

3. Delete all files on the copied disk except NTDETECT.COM and NTLDR._ files.

4. By using Windows NT's expand utility (which uncompresses the original installation files), decompress the NTLDR and rename it to SETUPLDR by executing the command:

```
EXPAND NTLDR._ SETUPLDR
```

5. If the mirrored drive is a SCSI disk requiring a SCSI driver to work with Windows NT, copy and expand the appropriate SCSI driver from the first Windows NT Server Setup Disk and then rename it to NTBOOTDD.SYS.

6. By using a text editor (for example, EDIT.COM), create a BOOT.INI file with an ARC path that points to the Windows NT directory on the mirrored partition. The disk is now ready for use as a fault-tolerant boot floppy.

Booting without a Fault-Tolerant Boot Disk

If the primary or boot drive is mirrored and fails, the twin drive can be made the active bootable drive, even if no fault-tolerant boot disk is available.

The following procedure applies only if the boot partition is mirrored, and works only for Intel (x86-based) platforms with MS-DOS installed (for FDISK.EXE):

1. Remove the power cable from the failed primary drive.

2. Boot from drive A.

3. Use FDISK to make the mirrored twin bootable:

    a. Start FDISK. Make sure you have Fixed Disk Drive 1 selected, which is the twin drive.

    b. Select the second option, Set Active Partition, which prompts you for the particular number of the partition you wish to make active.

    c. Press 1 when you are prompted to enter the number of the partition you want to make active.

    d. When the Partition 1 Made Active message appears, press Esc. FDISK then reboots the system. You should now be able to boot from this hard disk.

Note   The specified offset for the boot indicator assumes that the first physical partition table entry contains the system partition. This may not always be the case.

The system partition has the NTLDR, NTDETECT.COM, and BOOT.INI files on it. Furthermore, it should be marked active.

As can be seen from the following table, the correct offset for any partition's boot indicator can be calculated by adding 16 to the boot indicator offset of the previous partition.

If, for example, partition X has a boot indicator offset of 446, then the offset of partition X+1 is 462.

```
Boot Indicator for Partition 1 = 446 - Hex 01BE
Boot Indicator for Partition 2 = 462 - Hex 01CE
Boot Indicator for Partition 3 = 478 - Hex 01DE
Boot Indicator for Partition 4 = 494 - Hex 01EE
```

Recovering a Mirrored Partition

The sole reason for implementing RAID 1 (disk mirroring) and creating a fault-tolerant boot disk is to be able to recover the system from a media failure involving the system or boot partition. The recovery process depends on what type of device was used to contain the boot and system partitions.

This section examines recovering a mirrored partition on both a SCSI and IDE device.

SCSI Devices

Under some circumstances, the fault tolerance (FT) driver cannot initialize after a failure of a mirrored boot partition (containing Windows NT system files) or system partition (containing NTLDR and boot loader files). Recovery of this failed partition can occur in two ways. Each of these approaches is discussed in the ensuing sections.

Configuring the Hardware

The first way is to physically bypass the failed drive and make the existing mirror the new primary or master device. After the swap has been carried out, Windows NT can be booted from the newly appointed master or primary device. To preserve fault tolerance, the mirror set must be regenerated.

To physically bypass the failed driver, adhere to the following procedure:

1. If the hard disk with the primary system partition has failed, and the mirror set has been established by using a single disk controller, then set the physical SCSI ID on the mirrored drive to zero.

    If the mirror set has been established by using disk duplexing hardware, then swap the drive from the primary controller to the secondary controller.

2. Use a Windows NT fault-tolerant boot disk to point to and boot from the system/boot partition on the mirrored drive. Make sure the BOOT.INI file points to the partition with the Windows NT system files.

    Booting from the fault-tolerant disk is necessary because the mirrored (twin) partition is not yet an active partition.

3. Open Disk Administrator, break the mirror set, and mark the primary system partition on the primary disk (device 0) as Active so that the Windows NT fault-tolerant boot disk is not necessary for the next startup.

4. If the failed drive has been replaced with a new, healthy drive, re-establish the mirror set and enable data regeneration to take place during the next system boot (services load phase).

5. The generation of the mirror can take a while. The actual time taken depends entirely on how large the mirror partition is, the access time of the disk drive subsystem, and the type of central processor (Pentium, for example) driving the creation of the mirror set.

   Even though the mirror set creation process is initiated during the third (services load) phase of the NT boot process, the mirror generation may successfully complete long after the Windows NT server boot process has ended.

Configuring the Software

The second option makes use of the fault-tolerant boot disk to boot from the existing, healthy mirror. Disks are swapped and mirrors are regenerated by using the Disk Administrator, which is the more traditional way of recovering from a failed mirror set.

1. Before breaking the mirror set in Disk Administrator, shut down the server and use the Windows NT fault-tolerant boot disk to point to and boot from the remaining healthy partition (the twin or mirror).

2. Open Disk Administrator, select the mirror set partition, and break the mirror. The healthy partition retains the drive letter previously assigned to the mirror set. The faulty partition, if it is still available, is assigned the next available letter.

3. Delete the faulty partition on primary device or replace the disk drive if necessary. You cannot delete the active boot partition through Disk Administrator in 80×86-based computers; you have to use the Windows NT Setup Disk to delete it.

4. Establish the mirror between the healthy system/boot partition and the raw disk space on the primary device (disk 0). Exit Disk Administrator and save the disk configuration changes.

5. Use the Windows NT fault-tolerant boot disk to start regenerating the mirror set to the primary device (disk 0). Time required for regeneration depends on factors such as disk size, access time, and controller type.

6. Verify that the mirror set is healthy and has completed regenerating, then select the set and break the mirror. You have to do this on 80×86-based computers because the system partition needs to be marked as Active for startup, and Disk Administrator enables you to mark only primary partitions on the primary device (disk 0) as Active.

7. From Disk Administrator, modify the partition drive letters to have the appropriate assignments (C drive on disk 0 and D drive on disk 1). Mark the primary partition on disk 0 as Active.

8. Reboot the system without the Windows NT FT boot floppy and re-establish the mirror from the primary device (disk 0) to the other device (disk 1).

IDE Devices

The IDE specification requires that a working master drive be available at all times to be able to gain access to other IDE drives on the system. When recovering from a failed primary IDE device, you can choose a number of different options. Two specific options are presented in this section; namely, cloning a new master IDE device and promoting a slave to be the new master IDE device.

Creating a New Master

When the primary mirrored partition fails, a complete replacement for this failed master device can be obtained. The failed primary device is removed and replaced by a brand new disk. You then restart Windows NT from the twin (or mirrored partition) by using the fault tolerant boot disk. Disk Administrator is used to regenerate the primary mirrored partition from the twin.

The following steps institute this process:

1. Edit the BOOT.INI file on the fault-tolerant boot disk to point to multi(0)disk(0)rdisk(0)...

2. Verify that the jumper on the IDE hard drive is set to Master.

3. If the replacement drive is not identical to the failed IDE hard drive, you must go into CMOS and use either the auto-detect feature in your CMOS or manually set the new hard drive (Heads/Cylinders/Sectors) parameters.

4. Boot the Windows NT boot disk and load Windows NT.

5. Start Disk Administrator and break the mirror.

6. Establish another mirror by mirroring from the slave hard drive to the master drive. This procedure is essentially the reverse of the procedure used to create the original mirror set.

7. You can now restart Windows NT.

Promoting the Slave

Promoting the slave uses an existing mirrored, slave IDE device and makes it the master device. Booting from this device permits the installation and remirroring of a new slave device. After the slave device has been promoted to a master device, a fault-tolerant Windows NT system is restored.

1. Verify that the BOOT.INI file on the Windows NT fault-tolerant boot disk points to multi(0)disk(0)rdisk(0)...to boot from the primary IDE drive.

2. Remove the hardware jumper from the slave drive and make the Slave device a Master device (to replace the failed Master).

3. If this drive is not identical to the failed IDE hard drive, you must go into CMOS and either use the auto-detect feature in your CMOS or manually set the new hard drive's parameters (Heads/Cylinders/Sectors).

4. Boot the Windows NT from the fault-tolerant boot disk, which has been modified to boot from the twin partition (in step 1). Install a new drive as the slave.

5. Go into Disk Administrator and break the mirror. Windows NT will now automatically reboot when you exit the Disk Administrator utility.

6. Re-establish the mirror by remirroring from this new master IDE device (originally the mirrored slave) to the new slave IDE device.

7. Rebooting Windows NT restores the original fault tolerant system.

RAID 5—Stripe Set with Parity

Striping with parity dedicates the equivalent of one disk for storing the parity stripes, but distributes the parity stripes across all the drives in the group. RAID 5 is an improvement over RAID 4, striping with parity's predecessor, which dedicates a single physical disk for this parity data.

In RAID 5, the data and parity information are arranged on the disk array so that they are always on different disks. In figure 11.10, the first of the four blocks on disk 1 is a parity stripe. On disk 2, the parity stripe is the second block, and so on.

Because the parity stripe is simply the logical exclusive OR (XOR) of all the data values for the data stripes in the stripe, as long as the old data and the old parity values are known, the new parity for a write can be calculated without having to read the corresponding stripes from the other data disks. Thus, only two disks are involved in a write operation—the target data disk and the disk that contains the parity stripe.

The XOR function is a Boolean operation that is normally used to operate on two variables. In this case, it evaluates to TRUE when one of the variables equals FALSE and the other TRUE. If both variables have the same value, XOR evaluates to FALSE. If more than two variables exist, XOR evaluates to TRUE if an odd number of the variables involved equals TRUE.

At least three disks and no more than 32 disks must be in a stripe set with parity. A partition of approximately the same size should be selected from each disk. The disks can be on the same or different controllers.

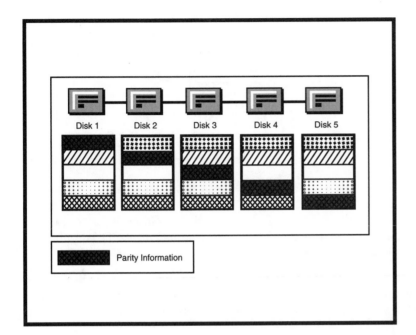

Figure 11.10
RAID 5—striping with parity adds fault tolerance to the normal disk striping (RAID 0) technology by including parity information with the data.

If one of the disks in a stripe set with parity fails, none of the data is lost. When a read operation requires data from the failed disk, the system reads all the remaining good data stripes in the stripe and the parity stripe. Each data stripe is subtracted (with XOR) from the parity stripe; the order isn't important. The result is the missing data stripe.

Recovering a failed member relies on a simple arithmetic principle. In an equation with n variables, if you know the value of $n-1$ of the variables, you can determine the value of the missing variable. Consider the equation $a+b=c$, where c represents the parity stripe. The disk driver (FTDISK.SYS) calculates $c-b$ to determine the contents of a.

A stripe set with parity implementation has better read performance and a lower cost-per-megabyte than a mirror set, but it requires more system memory and loses its performance advantage when a member is missing. RAID 5 is recommended over RAID 1 for applications that require redundancy and are primarily read-oriented. Neither the system partition nor the boot partition can be configured as a stripe set with parity.

Unlike RAID 4, which dedicates a single physical disk for parity data, RAID 5 dedicates the equivalent of one entire disk for storing check data but distributes the parity data over all the drives in the group. As long as the old sector data and the old check data values are known, the new check data for a single sector write can be calculated without having to read the corresponding sectors from the other data disks (see fig. 11.11).

Figure 11.11

The parity data is simply the XOR of all the write data values for the corresponding sector on each of the data disks.

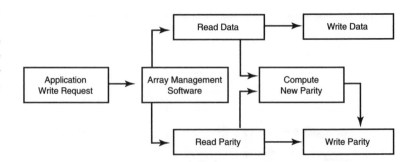

Thus, only two disks are involved in a single sector write operation: the target data disk and the corresponding disk that holds the check data for that sector. The implementation of RAID 5 contrasts with a RAID 3 implementation, which requires all drives in a group to be read and written when a single sector size write occurs. The primary benefit of the RAID 5 distributed check data approach is that it permits write operations to take place simultaneously.

RAID 5 also enables multiple reads to take place simultaneously and is efficient in handling small amounts of information. Depends on the applications users are running, RAID 5 is the preferred option when setting up fault tolerance in Windows NT Server.

Recovering a Stripe Set with Parity

When a member of a stripe set with parity is orphaned, you can regenerate the data for the orphaned member from the remaining members (see fig. 11.12). Select a new area of free space that is the same size as, or larger than, the other members of the stripe set with parity. Then choose Regenerate from the Fault Tolerance menu.

Figure 11.12

The Disk Administrator dialog box shows a restart message.

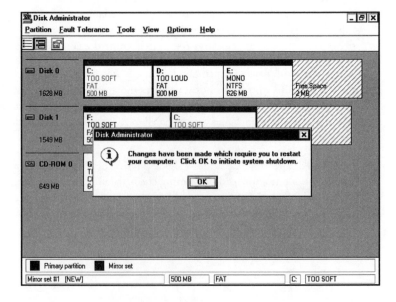

When you restart the computer, the fault-tolerance driver reads the information from the stripes on the other member disks, and then recreates the data of the missing member and writes it to the new member. The following procedure is applicable:

1. Select the recoverable stripe set by clicking on the appropriate logical partition in the Disk Administrator utility.

2. Select an area of free space that is the same size or larger than the partition selected in step 1. The free space selected will be incorporated into the subsequent stripe set (with parity).

   If the stripe set failure is due to a power outage or cabling fault on a single device, however, you can regenerate within the orphaned member of the original stripe set after the hardware state is restored.

3. From the Fault Tolerance menu, choose the Regenerate command.

4. Quit Disk Administrator and restart your computer.

The regeneration process occurs in the background. In Disk Administrator, text associated with stripe set with parity is red until regeneration is complete. This color-coding is exactly the same convention used when creating a mirror set.

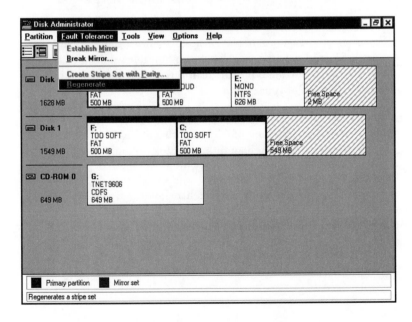

Figure 11.13

Use the Disk Administrator's Fault Tolerance menu to regenerate a stripe set with parity.

Note In the Disk Administrator display, information about the partition is not updated automatically. If you click on the partition, the information for that volume updates. You can also check the Event Log to know when the regeneration is finished.

You can receive the following error message when attempting to regenerate an orphaned drive:

```
The drive cannot be locked for exclusive use...
```

This error occurs if Disk Administrator is not allowed exclusive access to the stripe set with parity. This could be because the page file, or some other system service such as Microsoft SQL Server or Microsoft Systems Management Server, is accessing the drive. You must temporarily shut down these services and relocate the page file to regenerate the stripe set with parity.

Conclusion

Creating fault tolerant partitions (data storage) has been made *very* easy through the Disk Administrator utility. The fault tolerant strategies covered in this chapter and supported by Windows NT Server 4 include disk mirroring (RAID 1) and disk striping with parity (RAID 5).

These two strategies offer various advantages to the administrator who wants to prevent loss of data during a media or system failure. Of course, one day the unthinkable will happen and Windows NT will crash or have a media failure. In particular, this crash or media failure will corrupt or destroy the primary partition of your system.

This chapter presents recovery strategies for both RAID 1 and RAID 5, which will undoubtedly assist a stricken administrator to troubleshoot problems relating to RAID drives. Pivotal to the recovery of mirror sets is the fault tolerant boot disk, and Disk Administrator plays a similar role in the recovery of lost members in a striped set (with parity).

Apart from the various hints and tips offered in this chapter, here is one more piece of helpful advice. When it comes to setting up recovery strategies for fault tolerant parti-tions, make sure the strategies work by aggressively testing your procedures. Test, test, and then test again. When your system crashes, and your data is lost, it is too late.

Dial-up Networking

*M*icrosoft's Remote Access Server (RAS) first shipped
with LAN Manager 2.1 in 1991. It was included
with the Windows NT 3.1 operating system, and has
now been significantly enhanced for Windows NT
3.5 and 4.

RAS features the following features:

- Multiprotocol routing via point-to-point protocol (PPP) support.

- Internet support.

- Improved integration with NetWare networks.

- Increased number of simultaneous connections. Windows NT Server 3.5x and 4 support up to 256 simultaneous connections. The Windows NT Workstation provides a single RAS connection, primarily for personal use or for very small networks.

- Software data compression.

- Data encryption.

- Availability of the RAS APIs.

This chapter covers troubleshooting Windows NT's dial-up networking components. To begin, a troubleshooting methodology or strategy is introduced, covering the various aspects that you should bear in mind when dealing with problems relating to dial-up networking.

The troubleshooting methodology covers areas such as the isolation of hardware problems and conflicts, modem recognition and configuration problems, the applicable Registry entries, and COM ports.

Another major aspect of this chapter is the discussion of the various tools available to assist in troubleshooting Windows NT dial-up networking. These include the Event Viewer, Registry Editor, and logging (modem and PPP) tools. The last section of this chapter deals with the online Modem Troubleshooter, which forms part of the Windows NT online help.

Troubleshooting Methodology

Any troubleshooting methodology or strategy for dial-up networking problems revolves around the process of elimination. You must try to isolate the exact location and nature of the error so that it can be resolved. This process of elimination, however, can be long and arduous.

The troubleshooting methodology discussed in this chapter aims at making this process less arduous and more successful. The aspects covered in this first section, therefore, are designed to take you through a logical step-wise process toward finding and solving dial-up networking problems.

Isolating Hardware Problems and Conflicts

Isolating hardware problems and conflicts invariably involves either the modem itself or the associated COM port (see fig. 12.1). If the COM port is not recognized in the Control Panel Ports applet, there is most likely a hardware problem or a configuration problem.

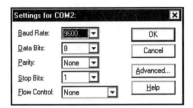

Figure 12.1

COM port settings are accessible via the appropriate Control Panel applet.

External Modems

You should remember the following list when dealing with external modems:

■ If the COM port is on the motherboard or is provided by a serial card, make sure the port is not disabled in the BIOS setup of the machine. Refer to the computer motherboard documentation to obtain information about configuring options in the BIOS setup.

■ Make sure that no other adapters or devices are configured for the same Base I/O Address or IRQ as the COM port to which the modem is attached. This causes a conflict and renders the associated hardware devices inoperable. It may have some other undesirable effects on the underlying operating system.

■ Verify that the serial port is not defective. If the modem or any other serial device fails on a COM port but functions properly on a different COM port on the machine and you have verified the two previous items in the list, the serial port may be defective.

■ Verify that the serial cable is not defective and that it is wired correctly. Search the Dial-up Networking Help File under the topic "Cabling Requirements" for instructions on how to wire the serial cable correctly.

Internal Modems

When dealing with internal modems, you should keep the following list in mind:

■ If the COM port is defined by an internal modem, make sure the jumpers on the modem are configured properly. Internal modems almost always have a jumper on the adapter that configures the modem as a particular COM port. There may or may not be jumpers that enable you to set the Base I/O Address and IRQ to be used by the modem.

■ If the modem is configured for a COM port that already exists on the motherboard or a serial card, you must use the BIOS setup to disable the COM port with the same number as the internal modem. For example, if the internal modem is set to COM1, the physical COM1 port must be disabled in the BIOS setup.

Disabling the COM port in the BIOS would not apply to serial ports located on ISA based adapters. These would have to be configured using manufacturer supplied tools or jumper settings.

■ Make sure that no other adapters or devices are configured for the same Base I/O Address or IRQ as the internal modem.

■ Verify that the internal modem is not defective.

■ Use the Event Viewer utility to diagnose hardware and software configuration problems. Check the System Log of the Event Viewer for error messages of type Serial.

Hardware Conflicts

If the error message indicates a conflict with either the IRQ or Base I/O Address used by the COM port, reconfigure the conflicting device or the COM port to use a different IRQ or Base I/O Address. The Windows NT Diagnostics application (see fig. 12.2) ships with Windows NT and is a good tool to troubleshoot hardware conflicts.

Figure 12.2

By using Windows NT diagnostics, you can review the properties of the resources that are allocated to specific hardware devices.

If possible, you should always attempt to configure the COM port with the industry standard IRQ and I/O Address for the port. This standard is tabulated as shown in table 12.1:

Table 12.1
Industry Standard COM Port Settings

COM Port	IRQ	Base I/O Address
1	4	3F8
2	3	2F8
3	4	3E8
4	3	2E8

Registry Parameter Conflicts

If you see the following error message:

```
Event ID 25—User configuration for parameter SerialX must have PortAddress.
```

in which X is a number greater than or equal to 0, delete the *SerialX* key from the following location in the Windows NT Registry Editor (REGEDT32.EXE):

HKEY_LOCAL_MACHINE\SYSTEM\CurrentControlSet\Services\Serial\Parameters

Duplicate COM Ports

You do *not* need to add a new port in the Control Panel Ports applet to add support for an internal modem. NTDETECT will detect the internal modem and the COM port it is configured to use. If a duplicate port was added by using the Add button in the Control Panel Ports applet, use the Control Panel Ports applet Delete button to remove the duplicate port.

Verifying Modem Recognition

A modem may be detected as a standard modem even though it is a supported modem for which Windows NT 4 contains a driver. A supported modem that is detected as a standard modem functions correctly if you manually select the correct driver. If you are not able to use the modem in HyperTerminal, you will not be able to use the modem in dial-up networking. Before attempting to use HyperTerminal, you must ensure that the dial-up networking Server Service is not running, especially if dial-up networking is configured to enable dial-in on the port you plan to test in HyperTerminal.

HyperTerminal is a new 32-bit communications application that provides asynchronous connectivity to host computers such as online services. HyperTerminal has preconfigured scripts to allow easy access to some popular systems (such as AT&T Mail, CompuServe, MCI Mail, and others). In addition, HyperTerminal can be configured to verify correct modem detection as follows:

1. After installing a modem by using the Control Panel Modem applet, launch HyperTerminal (see fig. 12.3) to determine whether the installed modem software is functioning, the correct modem has been detected, and the Telephony API (TAPI) software is fully functional.

2. Type **AT** in the HyperTerminal window and press Enter. Do not be alarmed if your keystrokes are not echoed to the screen—this is to be expected. You can type **ATZ** in the HyperTerminal windows to get echoed input to the console screen.

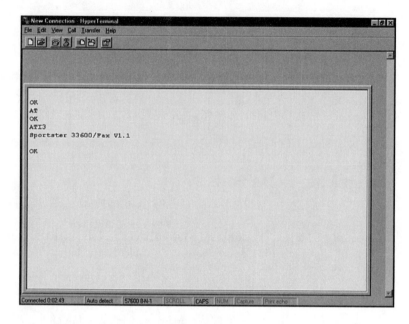

Figure 12.3

Test correct modem detection and installation by using HyperTerminal.

Verifying Modem Dial-out Capability

If your modem is recognized in HyperTerminal but you are not able to dial out, the phone line may be causing the problem. The following steps test to see if this is the problem:

1. Type **ATDT** and the telephone number you are trying to dial in the HyperTerminal window and press the Enter key.

2. Unless the modem's speaker has been disabled, you should hear a dial tone followed by the sound of the modem dialing the number you entered.

These two steps are just a very basic guide aimed at helping you isolate the cause of a modem communications problem, especially one involving the inability to dial out with your modem. Troubleshooting this kind of problem requires an understanding of how your local telephone system works, as well as the language of your modem. Complete coverage of any or both of these aspects is beyond the scope of this chapter.

Verify Modem Is Supported by NT

Windows NT dial-up networking must correctly initialize your modem in order for the modem to function properly. The list of modems supported with dial-up networking can be found in the Windows NT Hardware Compatibility List. Modems not listed in the Hardware Compatibility List may work with dial-up networking, but they are untested and unsupported by Microsoft.

To use an unsupported modem with dial-up networking, try one of the following procedures:

■ Check with the software supplied by your modem manufacturer to see if it has a MODEM.INF file for use with dial-up networking. *MODEM.INF* is the file used by dial-up networking to store the initialization settings and modem responses for all supported modems. The MODEM.INF file is just a plain ASCII file that—if the correct format is adhered to—can be fairly portable.

■ Configure dial-up networking to use the Hayes Compatible 9600 option. If your modem is fully Hayes Compatible, this option should enable dial-up networking to function with your modem. This option, however, may fail to utilize all features supported by your modem (including error control and high speeds).

■ Configure dial-up networking to use a supported modem that your modem can emulate. If you are lucky, your modem vendor might supply useful information, in the modem documentation, about what kinds of modem emulations are possible.

Some unsupported modems use the same settings as a supported modem, especially if the unsupported modem and supported modem are from the same manufacturer. Check the documentation included with the unsupported modem for information on emulation modes of the modem.

■ Create a custom entry in the MODEM.INF for your unsupported modem. This procedure is documented in the dial-up networking help file, RASPHONE.HLP.

One example is the U.S. Robotics 28800 external modem. Windows NT 3.51 cannot correctly detect this modem unless the MODEM.INF file is modified. To do this, change the detection string in the MODEM.INF file (which is displayed by entering the ATI3 modem command in a dial-up terminal session) to match the string that is actually returned by my version U.S. Robotics modem.

This change enables Windows NT 3.51 to automatically detect your modem correctly. Of course, when you upgrade to Windows NT 4, this problem is solved by an updated MODEM.INF file supplied by Microsoft.

Is the Problem a Client or Server Issue?

When troubleshooting, it is helpful to isolate the problem to either the dial-up networking server or the dial-up networking client. The best way to isolate the problem to the server or to the client is to ask the following questions:

■ Are all dial-up networking clients having this problem when attempting to dial the dial-up networking server?

■ Does this dial-up networking client have the same problem when dialing different dial-up networking servers?

If more than one dial-up networking client is having the same problem when dialing a dial-up networking server, yet these clients have no problem connecting to other dial-up networking servers, the problem is most likely the dial-up networking server. If the dial-up networking client has the same problem regardless of the dial-up networking server to which it attempts to connect, the problem is most likely the dial-up networking client.

Another possibility is that both the dial-up networking server and dial-up networking client function properly except when connecting to each other. This problem is usually a modem negotiation problem.

Troubleshooting the Dial-up Networking Client

This section provides a checklist of things to do when troubleshooting dial-up problems on the client. This checklist includes ensuring that the client hardware is functioning, the client hardware and software have been correctly configured, the client has the necessary security privileges on the remote dial-up server, the appropriate network protocols match, the Internet Service Provider has been correctly contacted, and the remote server is up and running.

Modem Initialization Failure

If dial-up networking is unable to dial out because your modem could not be properly initialized, you should receive the error message shown in figure 12.4.

Figure 12.4

Error 651 indicates a modem hardware-related error.

The error message shown in figure 12.4 may result if the initialization string sent to the modem by dial-up networking is incorrect for your modem or if you have a hardware problem with the modem, cable, or serial port on your computer.

You can also use modem command logging to diagnose modem initialization problems when using dial-up. Logging is covered in more detail later in this chapter.

Connection Negotiation Failure

If two modems don't support the same modulation standards, the modems may have difficulty negotiating a connection. If the modem on the dial-up networking client and the dial-up networking server are unable to negotiate a connection, try the following:

- Verify that the dial-up networking server is functioning properly. Make sure other dial-up networking clients are able to connect to the dial-up networking server you are unable to connect to.

- Reduce the speed on the dial-up networking client. Edit the Dial-up Networking Phone Book entry, choose the Modem button, and reduce the initial speed parameter.

- Disable hardware flow control, modem error control, and modem compression. Edit the Dial-up Networking Phone Book entry, choose the modem button, and disable these parameters.

- Try using the same model modem on the dial-up networking server as the dial-up networking client. If the modems conform to the same industry standard, they do not need to be identical, but to be safe, you should try using the same modem on the dial-up networking client as on the dial-up networking server.

When negotiating a dial-up connection, compatibility problems may increase when you attempt to use speeds above 9,600 bits per seconds. This is because different modems achieve higher speeds in different ways.

Dial-In User Validation Failure

The dial-up networking error messages, which appear in figures 12.5 and 12.6, may occur on the dial-up networking client machine if the dial-up networking server is unable to validate dial-in permission for your user account.

Figure 12.5

Error 649 indicates that the current user has been denied Remote Access permission.

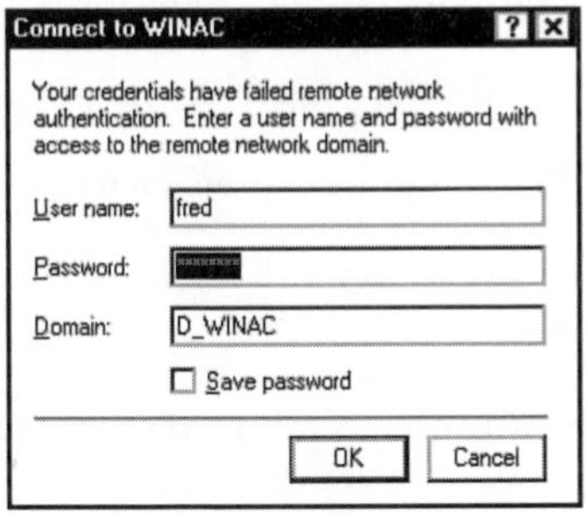

Figure 12.6

Domain account authentication has failed.

Here are some aspects to keep in mind to avoid dial-in validation problems:

- On the dial-up networking server, use the Remote Access Administration utility from the Administrative Tools program group and choose Permissions from the Users menu. Select the account with which you are attempting to dial in and make sure the Grant dial-in permission to user option is selected.

- If your dial-up networking account is different than the account you use to log on to your dial-up networking client machine, you must disable the Authenticate using current user name and password option.

■ If the dial-up networking server has its own local account database, but your account is defined in the remote domain account database, you must specify the name of the remote domain in the Domain field of the Dial-up Networking Authentication dialog box on the dial-up networking client.

■ If your account is defined in a remote domain that is trusted by the dial-up networking server's domain, you must specify the name of the trusted domain that contains your account in the Domain field of the Dial-up Networking Authentication dialog box on the dial-up networking client.

The crux of dial-in validation is matching a user name and a password to a corresponding user account in the Windows NT security accounts database. If you do not have the sufficient security credentials (user names and passwords) on the remote system, you should supply separate security credentials in order to successfully log on to the specific dial-in server.

Network Protocol Mismatch

The golden rule of networking is to ensure that both the client and the server have at least one common transport protocol with which to communicate. When it comes to dial-up networking, however, this can be a common point of communication failure. This is due mainly to the fact that the transport protocols on the portable client are not always supported by the server.

The following dial-up networking error messages may result on the dial-up networking client machine if one or more compatible network protocols could not be negotiated with the dial-up networking server:

Error 629: The port was disconnected by the remote server

Error 733: The PPP control protocol for this network protocol is not available on the server

Error 734: The PPP link control protocol terminated

The following are some aspects to watch out for when configuring transport protocols for use with dial-up networking:

■ Confirm that the network protocols you have enabled on your dial-up networking client for the dial-up networking connection are also enabled on the dial-up networking server. For the dial-up networking connection to complete successfully, at least one protocol requested by the dial-up networking client must be enabled as an allowed dial-up networking dial-in protocol on the dial-up networking server.

■ If you are using the NetBEUI protocol, make sure the machine name of your dial-up networking client is not the same machine name as another computer on the remote network.

■ If you are using the TCP/IP protocol and you have selected the option to use a server-assigned IP address for your dial-up networking connection, the dial-up networking server must be configured to assign IP addresses to dial-up networking clients.

Internet Service Provider Problems

Windows NT dial-up networking enables you to connect to third-party PPP servers, which means that you can connect to an Internet service provider (ISP) and gain access to the Internet by using dial-up networking. If you have problems connecting to a third-party PPP server, try the following:

■ Make sure TCP/IP is the only protocol enabled in your Dial-up Networking Phone Book entry for the ISP.

■ Try disabling the Request LCP Extensions (RFC 1570) option (see the Server tab of the Edit Phonebook Entry dialog box). Some older PPP servers may not support LCP Extensions. Choose the Network button in your Dial-up Networking Phone Book entry for the ISP in order to disable LCP Extensions.

■ Try disabling VJ Header compression to reduce the chance of communication failure with the ISP (which does not support or use compression). Choose the Network button and then the TCP/IP Settings button in your Dial-up Networking Phone Book entry for the ISP to disable VJ Header compression.

■ If the ISP supports only clear-text logins, or some other password authentication protocol (such as MS-CHAP, MD5-CHAP, SPAP, or PAP), select the Accept any authentication including clear text security option. Choose the Security tab of the Edit Phonebook Entry for the ISP and select the Accept any authentication including clear text security option. This is the least restrictive authentication method, which is particularly suitable for connecting to a non-Microsoft server or when you are not overly concerned about passwords.

■ If the ISP supports only PAP, select the After dialing (login) option from the Script tab on the Edit Phonebook Entry dialog box. Enabling this option causes dial-up networking to display a Terminal window after connecting to the ISP's server. The ISP's server prompts for login information; enter the proper commands in response to the ISP's prompts in this window.

These simple guidelines should prove helpful when attempting to dial in to an ISP. If problems persist, however, it is recommended that you contact your ISP for more specific information about their dial-in servers.

Remote Network Connection Failure

When connecting to a remote network server, security-related problems can often prevent user access to the server. The following aspects should be kept in mind when attempting to establish a remote server connection:

■ If you receive Access Denied errors when attempting to connect to resources on the remote network, remember that the credentials (that is, user name and password) you enter in the Dial-up Networking Authentication dialog box are *not* used by the remote network to grant you permission to access remote resources.

The credentials you enter in the Dial-up Networking Authentication dialog box are only used by the dial-up networking server to determine whether your account has been given dial-in permission.

After you have connected to the remote network, the user name and password used to log on to your machine are the credentials that verify whether or not you can make a connection to a remote resource.

You can work around the problem of remote network connection failure in three ways:

1. The first option is to log off and then log on to the remote network after making your dial-up networking connection. (Logging off will not hang up the dial-up networking connection.)

2. A second option is to create a local account on the dial-up networking client machine that has the same user name and password as the account you are using to make the dial-up networking connection. You can then use this account when logging on to your machine.

3. The third option is to specify a different user name in the Connect As field of NT Explorer or via the /User parameter of the NET USE command.

■ If you cannot browse machines on the remote network, but you can connect to them by specifying the server name and share name, make sure that the workgroup name or domain name of your dial-up networking client machine is the same as the remote workgroup or domain to which you are connecting.

Remote network connection failures occur when the security context of this connection is invalid. The examples and solutions provided in this section are not definitive; they simply illustrate how you can overcome this kind of problem.

Other solutions to the problem of remote network connection failures can include the use of user-defined scripts (see the Script tab of the Edit Phonebook Entry dialog box) to supply the proper user name and passwords to the remote server. The crux, however, is to realize that user authentication is at issue and that the proper credentials are needed to make the remote network connection succeed.

Dial-up Networking Server Troubleshooting

An incorrectly configured remote server is one problem a dial-up networking client can face. In this section, the configuration of the server comes into question, and the various factors influencing dial-up networking on the remote access server are discussed. These factors include hardware configuration, transport protocol issues, client interoperability, communication port configurations, and user dial-in permission.

Modem Initialization Failure

If the Dial-up Networking Server service is unable to answer an incoming call because your modem could not be properly initialized, you may observe the following symptoms on the dial-up networking server:

■ In the System Log of the Event Viewer, the following error message appears:

```
Error 20015: The communications device attached to port COMX
is not functioning.
```

■ The Port Status option of the Remote Access Admin utility reports the following error message:

```
Modem Condition: Hardware failure
Line Condition: Line non-operational
```

■ Dial-up networking clients may receive the following error when attempting to connect to a dial-up networking server that is not able to properly initialize its modem:

```
Error 650: The Remote Access Server is not responding
```

These error messages may result if the initialization string sent to the modem by dial-up networking is incorrect for your modem or if you have a hardware problem with the modem, cable, or serial port on your computer.

Invalid TCP/IP Addresses

It is often convenient to establish a pool of IP addresses (and other IP configuration information) for use with dial-up networking. This affords a high degree of ease-of-use to the dial-up clients.

In addition to enabling the TCP/IP protocol for dial-up networking dial-in, you must provide a method of assigning IP addresses to dial-up networking dial-in clients. There are two alternatives to providing IP addresses—DHCP (Dynamic Host Configuration Protocol) and static pools. These alternatives are discussed below:

■ You can use DHCP to assign remote TCP/IP client addresses if a DHCP server is on your network. A DHCP server is simply a Windows NT server with the DHCP Server service installed. The Dial-up Networking Server service leases one or more IP addresses from the DHCP server and caches these leases in its local Registry.

Keep in mind that if you change your address scope in DHCP, the dial-up networking server might continue to assign addresses from the previous scope to dial-up networking dial-in clients. To correct this problem, delete the following HKEY_LOCAL_MACHINE subkey in the Registry Editor on the dial-up networking server:

\SYSTEM\CurrentControlSet\Services\RemoteAccess\Parameters\Ip\DhcpAddress

Stop and restart the Dial-up Networking Server service to enable this change.

■ You can also create a static address pool on the dial-up networking server to assign remote TCP/IP client addresses. You should create this pool so that it includes at least the maximum number of simultaneous dial-in TCP/IP clients plus one address.

The dial-up networking server always uses the first IP address in the defined static pool for the address of its own dial-up networking interface. Make sure dial-up networking clients aren't configured to request this first address, or they will not have connectivity to the remote network after the dial-up networking connection has been made.

Remote NetWare Connection Failure

If your dial-up networking clients are unable to connect to NetWare resources directly (that is, connect to NetWare resources without using Gateway Services for NetWare), configure the manner in which the dial-up networking server allocates network numbers to dial-up networking clients.

Run the Control Panel Network applet and double-click Remote Access Service from the Services tab. Click the Network button and then click the Configure button that corresponds to IPX in the Server Settings section. Select the Allocate Network Numbers option and enter a unique IPX network number in the From field.

Windows for Workgroups Client

The Windows for Workgroups clients can use the RAS NetBIOS gateway to access NetBIOS servers running TCP/IP, IPX, or NetBEUI, but cannot run applications that must use TCP/IP or IPX on the client.

Make sure you have configured your dial-up networking server to allow dial-in access to remote clients that are running NetBEUI.

Third-Party Clients

Third-party PPP clients that adhere to the Request for Comments (RFCs) for the PPP standard should be able to connect to a Windows NT dial-up networking server. Make sure your dial-up networking server is configured to enable any authentication, including clear text. Most third-party PPP clients only support TCP/IP; therefore, make sure your dial-up networking server is configured to enable dial-in access to remote clients running TCP/IP. You should also make sure that you have configured your dial-up networking server to allocate IP addresses to remote dial-in clients.

Multiple Modem Ports

If you are using a multiport serial adapter on your dial-up networking server to enable multiple simultaneous dial-in sessions, you should configure these modem ports to Receive calls only, as opposed to Dial out and receive calls.

To configure the modem ports for Receive calls only usage, run the Control Panel Network applet and double-click Remote Access Service from the Services tab. A list of configured modem ports is displayed. Click the Configure button and the appropriate Configure Port Usage dialog box appears.

Configuring a port to enable dial-out requires a separate memory pool for each dial-out port, meaning resources (such as memory) can become an issue. All ports configured to enable dial-in use the same memory pool, which means that these resources are not an issue.

If you require dial-out on your dial-up networking server, configure one port to dial out and receive calls. Configure all other ports to receive calls only.

Assignment of Dial-In Permissions

In Windows NT 4, the User Manager for Domains (or the User Manager) utility is used to configure dial-in permissions. If your dial-up networking server is a member of a domain, you can grant dial-in permission to domain accounts and to local user accounts (if the dial-up networking server is a Windows NT workstation or a Windows NT server that is not a domain controller). See figure 12.7.

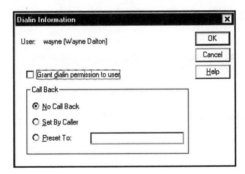

Figure 12.7

Assign user dial-in permissions by using the User Manager for Domains.

If a user account is present in both the domain account database and the local account database of the dial-up networking server, make sure the proper account has been granted dial-up networking dial-in permission.

Troubleshooting Tools

The primary tool in troubleshooting dial-up networking problems is the conversation log between the remote access software and the modem. This section covers how to enable modem communication logging, as well as PPP conversation logging. This section also discusses the Event Viewer and Registry Editor as well as a whole host of Registry entries.

Logging Modem Communications

When dialing up a Windows NT remote access server, capturing the actual commands being sent to a modem in a special log file can be very helpful in troubleshooting hardware problems. This log file captures the initialization dialog between the remote access server software and the modem and should contain entries showing the initialization string, the modem's echoed commands, and the desired positive response of "OK."

In earlier versions of Windows NT server, the logging of such dialog was manually enabled via the Registry by an administrator. The administrator would configure the *HKEY_LOCAL_MACHINE\SYSTEM\CurrentControlSet\Services\ RasMan\Parameters* Registry key. By adding the *Logging:REG_DWORD:0x1* Registry entry, an ASCII file (DEVICE.LOG) was configured to log all the dialog between the dial-up software and the modem in the *winnt_root*\system32\ dial-up networking directory.

In Windows NT Server 4, recording modem communications is enabled in a much easier manner. Logging is enabled by configuring the modem to create a log file through the Control Panel Modems applet.

From the Modems Properties dialog box, choose the Properties button. This causes the modem property dialog box (specific to your modem) to be displayed, from which the Connection tab can be selected. Selecting the Advanced button produces the dialog box shown in figure 12.8.

Figure 12.8

Enabling a modem to record its output to a log file is achieved through the Advanced Connection Settings dialog box of the Control Panel Modems applet.

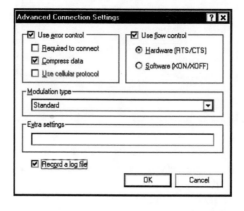

The log file is named according to the name of the modem logging its command sequences and responses (for example, ModemLog_Sportster 28800-33600 External.txt), and the logged file is stored in the *winnt_root* directory. Windows NT Server 4 has identified my modem as a U.S. Robotics Sportster 28.8 (33.6) external modem and logs all the communications dialog into the file referred to earlier.

The first few lines from the previously mentioned log file (ModemLog_Sportster 28800-33600 External.txt) are as follows:

```
08-24-1996 20:09:48.234 - Sportster 28800-33600 External in use.
08-24-1996 20:09:48.234 - Modem type: Sportster 28800-33600 External
```

```
08-24-1996 20:09:48.234 - Modem inf path: mdmusrsp.inf
08-24-1996 20:09:48.234 - Modem inf section: Modem16
08-24-1996 20:09:48.244 - 57600,N,8,1
08-24-1996 20:09:48.244 - 57600,N,8,1
08-24-1996 20:09:48.254 - Initializing modem.
08-24-1996 20:09:48.254 - Send: ATE0Q0V1<cr>
08-24-1996 20:09:48.384 - Recv: <cr><lf>OK<cr><lf>
08-24-1996 20:09:48.384 - Interpreted response: OK
```

As stated earlier, there has been a significant change in the way in which modem logging is enabled in Windows NT Server 4. The following steps are applicable when configuring your modem to enable logging:

1. Hang up any connections and then exit from the Dial-up Monitor.

2. Start the Control Panel application and select the Modems applet.

3. Select the appropriate entry in the displayed list that matches the modem you want to configure for logging.

4. Click the Properties button and then select the Connection tab on the modem property dialog box. The Advanced button appears at the bottom-right side of this dialog box.

5. Click the Advanced button and select the Record a log file check box (refer to fig. 12.8).

6. Choose OK until you close the Control Panel.

Logging begins when you restart Remote Access or start the Remote Access Server service (if your computer is receiving calls). You do not need to shut down and restart Windows NT.

Note   In previous versions of Windows NT Server, the traces from all calls are appended to the device.log file, as long as dial-up networking or the Remote Access Server service is not stopped and restarted. However, in Windows NT Server 4, this process has changed. The ASCII log file is not cleared unless you physically delete it yourself.

Logging PPP Communications

You can create a point-to-point protocol (PPP) log file to help diagnose connectivity problems between a PPP server and a PPP client when one of the computers is a Windows NT Remote Access Service client. You can enable this option by changing a value in the Registry.

To enable PPP logging, follow these steps:

1. Run Registry Editor (REGEDT32.EXE). See figure 12.9.

2. From the HKEY_LOCAL_MACHINE subtree, go to the following key:
   SYSTEM\CurrentControlSet\Services\RasMan\PPP.

3. Select the Logging value.

4. From the Edit menu, choose DWORD.

5. Enter 1 and click OK.

Figure 12.9

PPP logging is enabled through the CurrentControlSet\Services\ RasMan\PPP subkey of the HKEY_LOCAL_MACHINE\ SYSTEM hive.

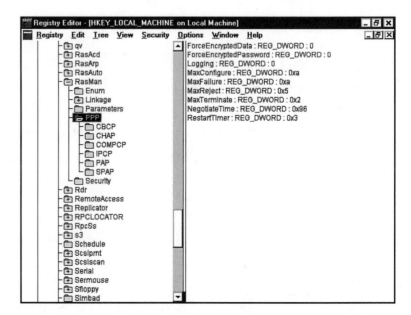

PPP logging is helpful when used with an understanding of the PPP protocol and in conjunction with the following PPP RFCs: 1661 (supersedes 1548), 1549, 1552, 1334, and 1332. Logging information is placed in *winnt_root*\SYSTEM32\Dial-up Networking\PPP.LOG.

The Event Viewer

The Event Viewer is useful in diagnosing dial-up networking problems because many dial-up networking events are logged in the System Log. By default, all server errors, user connect attempts, disconnects, and so on are logged.

Check the System Log for error messages of type "Serial" or source "RemoteAccess" (see fig. 12.10). A logged error message could indicate a hardware or software error.

Figure 12.10

The Windows NT event viewer automatically records system- or application-level errors, providing useful information for isolating modem-related problems.

The Remote Access Service Registry Configuration

The RemoteAccess subkey is created in the Registry when you install dial-up networking on a server by using the Network icon in the Control Panel. The default values in RemoteAccess and its subkeys work well for all Windows NT operations, such as copying files, using network resources, and sending and receiving electronic mail. For some systems, however, you may want to adjust individual parameters to suit your particular performance and security needs.

No value entries are in the Registry for the RemoteAccess key or its subkeys until you add them with new settings. (The only exception is EnableNetbiosGateway, the NetBIOS parameter.) Unlisted value entries are set to their default values, as described in this section.

The Parameters Subkey

The Parameters subkey for the Remote Access Server service has the following Registry path:

HKEY_LOCAL_MACHINE\SYSTEM\CurrentControlSet\
Services\RemoteAccess\Parameters

For changes to take effect, you must stop and restart the Remote Access Server service. The functions and settings of these value entries are described in the following sections.

AuthenticateRetries

The AuthenticateRetries Registry key sets the maximum number of unsuccessful retries allowed if the initial attempt at authentication fails. The initial default value for AuthenticateRetries is 2.

The AuthenticateRetries Registry key has a REG_DWORD data type and can accept values within the range of 0–10.

AuthenticateTime

The AuthenticateTime Registry key sets the maximum time limit within which a user must be successfully authenticated. If the client does not initiate the authentication process within this time, the user is disconnected. The initial default value for AuthenticateTime is 120 seconds.

The AuthenticateTime Registry key has a REG_DWORD data type and can accept values within the range of 20–600 seconds.

CallbackTime

The CallbackTime Registry key sets the time interval that the server waits before calling the client back when the Callback feature has been set. Each client communicates the value of its own callback time when connecting to a Remote Access server. If this value is not communicated (that is, if the client does not communicate a value for the callback time, as with Remote Access 1.0 and 1.1 clients), the value of the CallbackTime parameter becomes the default. The initial default value for CallbackTime is 2 seconds.

The CallbackTime Registry key has a REG_DWORD data type and can accept values within the range of 2–12 seconds.

AutoDisconnect

The AutoDisconnect Registry entry sets the time interval after which inactive connections are terminated. Inactivity is measured by lack of NetBIOS session data transfer, such as copying files, accessing network resources, and sending and receiving electronic mail. You might want to set this value to 0 seconds if clients are running NetBIOS datagram applications. Setting this value to 0 turns off AutoDisconnect. The initial default value for AutoDisconnect is 20 minutes.

The AutoDisconnect Registry entry has a REG_DWORD data type and can accept values within the range of 0–1,000 minutes.

The Parameters\NetBIOSGateway Subkey

The Registry path for these entries is the following:

HKEY_LOCAL_MACHINE\SYSTEM\CurrentControlSet\
Services\RemoteAccess\Parameters\NetbiosGateway

The functions and settings of these value entries are described in the following sections.

DisableMcastFwdWhenSessionTraffic

The DisableMcastFwdWhenSessionTraffic Registry key enables NetBIOS session traffic (for example, Windows NT-based applications) to have priority over multicast datagrams (such as server messages). In other words, multicast datagrams are transferred only when there is no session traffic. Unless you're using an application that depends on multicast datagrams, leave this parameter enabled. The initial default value for DisableMcastFwdWhenSessionTraffic is 1 (enabled).

The DisableMcastFwdWhenSessionTraffic Registry entry has a REG_DWORD data type and can accept values of 0 or 1.

EnableBroadcast

The EnableBroadcast Registry key determines whether broadcast datagrams are forwarded to remote workstations. Broadcast datagrams are not often useful and take up too much bandwidth on a slow link. Unless you're using an application that relies on broadcast datagrams, leave this parameter disabled. The initial default value for EnableBroadcast is 0 (disabled).The EnableBroadcast Registry entry has a REG_DWORD data type and can accept values of 0 or 1.

EnableNetbiosSessionsAuditing

The EnableNetbiosSessionsAuditing Registry key is enabled to record (in the event log) the establishment of NetBIOS sessions between the remote clients and the LAN servers. Enable this parameter to track the NetBIOS resources accessed on the LAN. The initial default value for EnableNetbiosSessionsAuditing is 0 (disabled).

The EnableNetbiosSessionsAuditing Registry entry has a REG_DWORD data type and can accept values of 0 or 1.

MaxBcastDgBuffered

The MaxBcastDgBuffered Registry key sets the number of broadcast datagrams that the gateway buffers for a client. If you're using an application that communicates extensively through multicast or broadcast datagrams, increase this parameter so that the Remote Access server can deliver all datagrams reliably. The initial default value for MaxBcastDgBuffered is 32.

The MaxBcastDgBuffered Registry entry has a REG_DWORD data type and can accept values within the range of 16–255.

MaxDgBufferedPerGroupName

The MaxDgBufferedPerGroupName Registry key sets the number of datagrams that can be buffered per group name. Increasing this value buffers more datagrams per group name but also takes up more virtual memory. The initial default value for MaxDgBufferedPerGroupName is 10.

The MaxDgBufferedPerGroupName Registry entry has a REG_DWORD data type and can accept values within the range of 1–255.

MaxDynMem

The MaxDynMem Registry key sets the amount of virtual memory used to buffer NetBIOS session data for each remote client. Because the Remote Access server is a gateway between the slow line and the LAN, data is stored (buffered) in the Remote Access server's memory when coming from the fast line (LAN) before it is forwarded to the slow line (asynchronous line).

The Remote Access server minimizes the usage of the system's physical memory by locking only a minimal set of pages (about 64KB per client) and making use of virtual memory (up to MaxDynMem) to buffer the rest of the data. So, as long as you have enough space on the hard disk to expand PAGEFILE.SYS, you can increase this value if needed.

If you have an application with a LAN (fast) sender and an asynchronous (slow) receiver and if the sender is sending more data than the Remote Access server can buffer in MaxDynMem, the Remote Access server tries to apply a form of NetBIOS level flow control by not submitting NCB.RECEIVE on the session until it has enough buffer space to get incoming data. For this reason, if you have such an application, you should increase your NetBIOS SEND/ RECEIVE timeouts so that the fast sender can keep pace with the slow receiver. The initial default value for MaxDynMem is 655,350. The MaxDynMem Registry entry has a REG_DWORD data type and can accept values within the range of 131,072–4,294,967,295.

MaxNames

The MaxNames Registry key sets the number of unique NetBIOS names each client can have, with a limit of 255 names for all clients together.

Remote clients running Windows NT and Windows for Workgroups may need as many as seven or eight names each. To accommodate these workstations, set the MaxNames value to 8 and reduce the number of ports on the Remote Access server. If you have Windows NT or Windows for Workgroups clients dialing in to servers running Remote Access version 1.1 or earlier, set this parameter to 8 or greater. The initial default value for MaxNames is 255.

The MaxNames Registry entry has a REG_DWORD data type and can accept values within the range of 1–255.

MaxSessions

The MaxSessions Registry key sets the maximum number of simultaneous NetBIOS sessions each client can have, with a limit of 255 sessions for all clients together. If you have multiple clients connecting simultaneously with each running four or five sessions, decrease the value of this parameter so that the total number of sessions does not exceed 255. The initial default value for MaxSessions is 255.

The MaxSessions Registry entry has a REG_DWORD data type and can accept values within the range of 1–255.

MultiCastForwardRate

The MultiCastForwardRate Registry key governs the multicasting of group name datagrams to all remote workstations. This parameter filters datagrams sent on group names by forwarding them at a specified time interval.

The value –1 disables forwarding. The value 0 guarantees delivery of group name datagrams. The value n forwards datagrams every n seconds, when $1 \leq n \leq 32,676$.

If the EnableBroadcast parameter is set to 0, broadcasts are not forwarded even if the MultiCastForwardRate parameter is set to a positive number. (In this case, only multicast datagrams are forwarded.) The line becomes overloaded. If MultiCastForwardRate is set to –1, broadcasts are not forwarded even if EnableBroadcast is set to 1. (Refer to "EnableBroadcast.")

To save bandwidth for session traffic, filter the datagrams. If you have an application based on multicast datagrams, however, set this parameter to 0. This value guarantees delivery of all datagrams sent on group names from the LAN to the remote client. The initial default value for MultiCastForwardRate is 5.

The MaxSessions Registry entry has a REG_DWORD data type and can accept values of either –1 (disabled), or within the range of 0–32,676 seconds.

NumRecvQueryIndications

The NumRecvQueryIndications Registry key enables a Remote Access client to initiate multiple network connections simultaneously. If a remote client is running a NetBIOS application that does multiple NCB.CALL commands simultaneously, increase this parameter to improve performance. The initial default value for NumRecvQueryIndications is 3.

The NumRecvQueryIndications Registry entry has a REG_DWORD data type and can accept values within the range of 1–32.

RcvDgSubmittedPerGroupName

The RcvDgSubmittedPerGroupName Registry key determines the number of NetBIOS commands of the type Receive Datagram that can be submitted simultaneously per group name on the LAN stack. Keep this setting as small as possible to minimize the amount of memory consumed by system resources. Each datagram command received locks about 1.5K of physical memory in the system. The initial default value for RcvDgSubmittedPerGroupName is 3.

The RcvDgSubmittedPerGroupName Registry entry has a REG_DWORD data type and can accept values within the range of 1–32.

RemoteListen

The RemoteListen Registry key sets the remote NCB_LISTEN capability. The RemoteListen Registry key has an initial default value of 1 (see table 12.2 for details).

Table 12.2
Remote NCB_LISTEN Settings

Value	Meaning
0	Disable. Disables a client's ability to post NCB_LISTEN for any NetBIOS name. Because every RemoteListen posted consumes one session, setting this parameter to 0 saves sessions.
1	Messages. Enables clients to post NCB_LISTEN on Windows NT Server message aliases only. If a remote client is running the Messenger service, it can then receive messages from LAN users, printers, and so on.
2	All. Enables NCB_LISTEN for all remote client NetBIOS names, enabling clients to run NetBIOS server applications. This setting enables all clients to function as NetBIOS servers on the network.

You should leave the RemoteListen parameter set to the default, 1 (messages). Enabling NCB_LISTEN capability on remote clients can significantly drain system resources and, therefore, is not recommended.

If the RemoteListen parameter is set to 2, Remote Access posts an NCB_LISTEN on all NetBIOS names of Remote Access clients. Because the average Windows NT Server workstation has about seven or eight NetBIOS names assigned to it, the total number of NetBIOS names for which an NCB_LISTEN would be posted is 7 or 8×64 (the maximum number of clients per Remote Access server), which exceeds the 255 maximum.

The RemoteListen Registry entry has a REG_DWORD data type and can accept values within the range of 0–2.

SizWorkBufs

The SizWorkBufs Registry key sets the size of work buffers. The default setting is optimized for the server message block (SMB) protocol, the protocol between the workstation and the server running on the Windows NT Advanced Server system. The initial default value for SizWorkBufs is 4,500.

The SizWorkBufs Registry entry has a REG_DWORD data type and can accept values within the range of 1,024–65,536.

The AsyncMac Subkey

This Registry key controls settings and parameters for the remote access MAC driver. The Registry path for these entries is the following:

HKEY_LOCAL_MACHINE\SYSTEM\CurrentControlSet\
Services\AsyncMac*x*\Parameters

For changes to take effect, you must restart the computer.

MaxFrameSize

The MaxFrameSize Registry key determines the maximum frame size. Use smaller frames for noisy links. A lower setting sends less data per frame, slowing performance. Do not change this parameter for previous versions of the Remote Access service. The value is negotiated between the server and Windows NT clients. The initial default value for MaxFrameSize is 1,514.

The MaxFrameSize Registry entry has a REG_DWORD data type and can accept values within the range of 576–1,514.

The \RasMan\PPP Subkey

The Registry path that contains entries for the Point-to-Point Protocol (PPP) service is the following:

HKEY_LOCAL_MACHINE\SYSTEM\CurrentControlSet\Services\ Rasman\PPP

MaxConfigure

The MaxConfigure Registry key indicates the number of Configure-Request packets sent without receiving a valid Configure-Ack, Configure-Nak, or Configure-Reject before assuming that the peer is unable to respond. The initial default value for MaxConfigure is 10.

The MaxConfigure Registry entry has a REG_DWORD data type and can accept any DWORD value.

MaxFailure

The MaxFailure Registry key indicates the number of Configure-Nak packets sent without sending a Configure-Ack before assuming that the configuration is not converging. The initial default value for MaxFailure is 10.

The MaxFailure Registry entry has a REG_DWORD data type and can accept any DWORD value.

MaxReject

The MaxReject Registry key indicates the number of Config-Rejects sent before assuming that the PPP negotiation will not converge. The initial default value for MaxReject is 5.

The MaxReject Registry entry has a REG_DWORD data type and can accept any DWORD value.

MaxTerminate

The MaxTerminate Registry key indicates the number of Terminate-Request packets sent without receiving a Terminate-Ack before assuming that the peer is unable to respond. The initial default value for MaxTerminate is 2.

The MaxTerminate Registry entry has a REG_DWORD data type and can accept any DWORD value.

The Modem Troubleshooter

Windows NT Server 4 has a modem troubleshooter as part of its online help (see fig. 12.11). This troubleshooting assistant is similar to the Printing Troubleshooter discussed in Chapter 10, "Windows NT Printing."

Figure 12.11

The Modem Troubleshooter can be invoked by searching through the Windows NT online help index for the "troubleshooting, modem" string.

The Windows NT Modem Troubleshooter provides advice that is easy to understand. This assistant is also tightly integrated with the host operating system and is capable of calling up appropriate administrative tools to assist in solving modem-related problems. To locate the Modem Troubleshooter, look for Troubleshooting modem problems in the Windows NT Help index (see fig. 12.12).

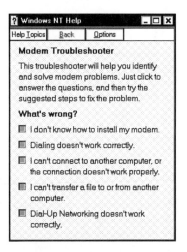

Figure 12.12

The Windows NT online Modem Troubleshooter provides you with an interactive method of identifying and solving modem-related problems.

Of course, the Windows NT online Modem Troubleshooter cannot solve all the possible modem-related problems, but it does provide invaluable assistance in a large percentage of situations where modem troubleshooting is required. Figure 12.13 illustrates a scenario in which the Windows NT online Modem Troubleshooter is unable to provide any real assistance. In this case, the modem vendor's documentation must be consulted.

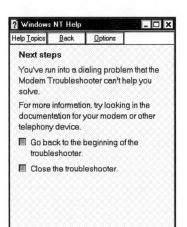

Figure 12.13

The Windows NT online Modem Troubleshooter might not be able to assist you in troubleshooting a modem problem, in which case you must consult the vendor's documentation.

Conclusion

Troubleshooting Windows NT dial-up networking relies heavily upon your ability to successfully isolate the problem area through logging, using the online help, and having a good working knowledge of the necessary computer hardware.

When troubleshooting a problem, it is often helpful to make the basic assumption that whatever you are trying to fix actually does work. Your task is to establish what is making it not work and then rectify whatever is causing the problem. This outlook may appear to be naïve, but it underlines a positive attitude toward troubleshooting in general.

The strategy outlined in this chapter is aimed at providing a focused methodology and tool set to the Windows NT administrator who intends to troubleshoot problems relating to dial-up networking. Because troubleshooting, however, is an art and not a science, the real test of any methodology is in its application. Successful methodologies evolve with practice and application.

Domain Planning and Implementation

*P*ossibly the most crucial part of any Windows NT 4 installation is the planning and implementation of your domain. A domain consists of one or more specialized Windows NT servers (called domain controllers) that have been configured under a single name (called a domain name) and share the same accounts database contained within their Registries. Therefore, when solving problems related to a Windows NT 4 installation, one must undoubtedly investigate and analyze the planning and implementation of that domain.

The domain planning process should take place well before any physical installation—a poorly planned and implemented domain results in a waste of time, effort, and money. Furthermore, a Windows NT 4 installation that proceeds without the proper planning results in frustration and additional effort to redress a situation that could have been avoided. After installation, the proper functioning of the chosen domain model must be verified.

This chapter covers the process of successfully planning and implementing the logical design of your corporate or departmental domain. The emphasis of this chapter, however, is placed firmly on the resolution of any problem that occurs during such an implementation, as well as verification that the chosen domain model has been correctly applied. The aim of this chapter, therefore, is to introduce an approach to problem solving, as well as a tool set that can be used to guide, debug, and verify a successful Windows NT 4 domain model installation.

This chapter is broken down into two sections describing an approach to problem solving, as well as the set of tools required to implement and verify a chosen domain model. If you are about to install a Windows NT 4 network, or already administrate one, then, read this chapter in order to gain some useful insight into planning, debugging, and verifying the current health and future prospects of your Windows NT 4 domain.

An Approach to Solving Domain Model Problems

The first step toward successful installation of Windows NT 4 is ensuring that you have a proper understanding of the underlying domain concepts, as well as a clear idea of how Windows NT 4 is to be implemented within your organization. The choice of your Windows NT 4 domain model is the first major planning decision you need to make. The choice of domain model guides the rest of the process of problem solving, and verifies its successful implementation. The four standard Windows NT domain models are discussed in the next section.

Choosing a Windows NT 4 domain model is not a trivial exercise; however, it does form an important part of this problem-solving method, simply because solving problems related to each different domain model must be approached from a different perspective.

Some tools are available to assist an administrator in this decision-making process (for example, the domain planning tool DOMPLAN.EXE in the Windows NT Resource Kit).

Coupled with this choice of domain model is the prescribed understanding of several concepts that relate directly to Windows NT 4 domains. In this section, an analysis is presented of these domain-related concepts in terms of their role in the installation process. The topics under discussion include "Solving the Workgroup Capacity Problem," "Choosing the Role of the Server," "Local and Global Groups," as well as "Domain Models."

To lay the conceptual foundation, this section begins with an introduction to trust relations and discusses the various domain models, before covering the rest of the aforementioned topics ("Choosing the Role of the Server" and "Local and Global Groups").

Trust Relationships

A *trust relationship* is an administrative mechanism that is used to facilitate the administration of a multidomain Windows NT environment. Windows NT Server 4 enables the user accounts from one domain to be used in another domain.

Two principal role players exist within a trust relationship: the trusted domain (also known as the account or user domain because the user accounts are defined in this domain) and the trusting domain (also know as the resource domain because resource management, as opposed to account management, is done in this domain).

The *trusted domain* is the domain that has made its accounts available to be used within the first domain. These trusted accounts are only available on Windows NT servers and workstations participating in the trusted and trusting domains.

The trust relationship, therefore, is the link between the trusted domain and trusting domain; allowing them to effectively share account information (centrally managed from the trusted domain), while providing global access to resources at the same time. Trust relationships provide the following benefits:

- They provide a secure communications channel between two domains. With a trust relationship, one domain is trusted to manage the user accounts on behalf of both domains participating in the trust relationship.

- They cause the divisions between domains to become invisible. A trust relationship enables administrators to see the network as a single administrative unit, rather than as a collection of LANs that must be managed separately.

- They move centralized administration to the enterprise level, rather than just the domain level. This can be seen by the implementation of the NT domain models, which are discussed in the next section.

Trusts simplify administration by combining two domains into a single administrative unit. When trust relationships are properly established between domains, a user need only log on once (and provide a password) to access any shared resources on the network for which the user account has been granted permissions.

This concept of a single logon and global access to resources is the essential benefit sought after when implementing trust in any of the standard Windows NT domain models. All these domain models (with the exception of the single domain model) need trust relationships. Trust relationships can be set up as one- or two-way relationships:

■ **One-way trust relationship.** In this type of trust relationship, accounts in one domain (the trusted domain) can be given permission to access resources in another domain (the trusting domain). One-way trust relationships are typically used in networks in which user accounts must be centrally controlled in one domain, but resources require distributed control.

■ **Two-way trust relationship.** In this type of trust relationship, accounts and resources are administered in each domain, but can be given permission to access resources in the other domain. In fact, a two-way trust is essentially two one-way trust relationships. From the definition of a one-way trust, one can see that each domain in a two-way trust is both trusting and trusted at the same time.

Domain Models

A *domain model* is a collection of domains, accounts (user and group), and trusts that have been logically ordered into a recognizable form. Adopt a particular domain model to ensure that your Windows NT 4 domain conforms to an international standard that is self-documenting (that is, if implemented correctly, a domain model does not require any documentation to explain its logical organization).

Note   This is very similar to the role that flowchart diagrams played for program source code. Regardless of the language used to code a program, its flowchart diagram essentially provided a declarative document explaining exactly what the program source code was supposed to do.

Four standard domain models can be used in a Windows NT 4 network. Solving problems related to domain models requires an understanding of how each of these models is supposed to work (for example, what number and type of trusts are required, and so on) as well as a capability to verify that a particular model has been properly and completely implemented. Problems might also arise if an unsuitable domain model has been chosen for a given situation.

Each of the domain models must therefore be analyzed according to its logical organization (for example, layout, trusts, groups, and so on) and to its recommended use (number of users, resource control, centralized administration, and so on).

Single Domain Model

The single domain model is possibly the most useful domain model, especially for small- to medium-sized organizations. Typically, the network has only one domain, and all users and global groups are created in this domain.

The single domain, as depicted in figure 13.1, consists of a primary domain controller with one or more backup domain controllers. The primary domain controller and each backup domain controller can support 2,000 to 2,500 user accounts to validate user logons and provide fault tolerance (in the case of Primary Domain Controller failure). The actual capacity of these domain controllers depends on the power of the processor driving them. A very powerful computer (such as a Pentium processor or a symmetric multiprocessor) can support up to 5,000 accounts.

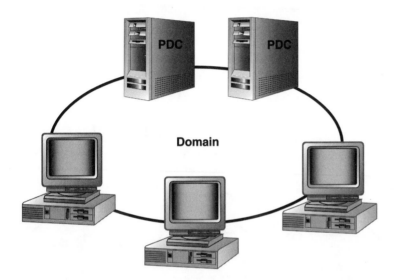

Figure 13.1

The Single Domain Model is the simplest of all domain models and does not require any trust relationships.

A network can use the single domain model if it has a small number of users (up to 26,000) and groups (up to 250) to ensure good performance. The exact number of users and groups depends on the number of servers in the domain and the hardware of the servers. Having a single domain also means that all the network administrators can administer all network servers.

Single-Master Domain Model

When the network needs to be split into domains for organizational purposes, and the network has a small enough number of users and groups (up to 26,000 user and 250 group accounts), the single-master domain model might be the best choice. This model gives you both centralized administration and the organizational benefits of multiple domains.

One domain (the master domain) acts as the central administrative unit for user and group accounts. All other (resource) domains on the network trust this domain. This means that they rely on the master (accounts) domain to administrate the security accounts database on their behalf. If your company has an information technology department that manages your local area network, it makes sense to have the information technology department administer the master domain.

In figure 13.2, all users log on to their accounts in the master domain. Resources, such as printers and file servers, are located in the other domains (Domain_A, Domain_B, and Domain_C). Each resource domain establishes a one-way trust (denoted by the white arrows) with the master domain, enabling users with accounts in the master domain to use resources in all the other domains. The network administrator can manage the entire multiple-domain network and its users and resources by managing only a single domain.

Figure 13.2

The single-master domain model provides a way to centralize account administration while providing distributed control of resources within an enterprise.

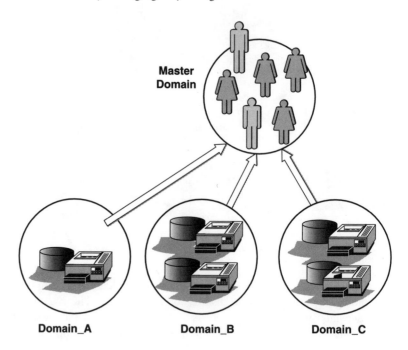

The single-master domain model is particularly suited for:

- **Centralized account management.** User accounts can be centrally managed from the domain controllers, where user accounts can be added, deleted, and modified from a single point.

- **Decentralized resource management or local system administration capability.** Department domains can have their own administrators who manage the resources in the department.

- **Logical resource arrangement.** Resources can be grouped logically, corresponding to local domains, for easier access by the users. This means that a user can find resources according to where they are located (in trusting or resource domains), and not according to where access to these resources is administered (from trusted or master domains).

Multiple-Master Domain Model

In the multiple-master domain model, there are two or more single-master domains. Like the single-master domain model, the master domains serve as account domains—every user and computer account is created and maintained on one of these master domains.

It is important to realize that domain user accounts need not be created in every master domain. The multiple-master domain model provides single enterprise accounts for every user. Each master domain controls a particular aspect of the enterprise (such as departments, geographical regions, and so on), which means that only domain user accounts that are applicable to these departments of geographical regions are maintained in an appropriate master domain's accounts database.

A company's information technology department can centrally manage these master domains. Like the single-master domain model, the other domains on the network are called *resource domains*; they don't store or manage user accounts but do provide resources such as shared file servers and printers to the network.

As can be seen in figure 13.3, every master or accounts domain is connected to every other master domain by a two-way trust relationship (double-headed arrow). Each resource domain trusts every master domain with a one-way trust relationship. The resource domains can trust other resource domains, but are not required to do so.

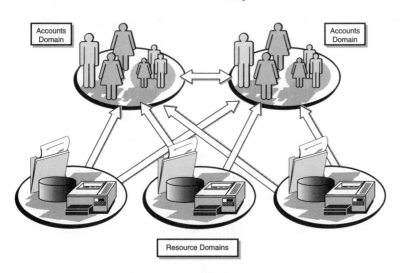

Accounts Domain

Accounts Domain

Resource Domains

Figure 13.3

The multiple-master domain model supports very large organizations that require centralized account administration and decentralized resource management.

Because every user account exists in one of the master domains, and each resource domain trusts every master domain, every user account can be used on any of the master domains. In addition to incorporating all the features of a single-master domain model, the multiple-master domain model accommodates the following:

■ Organizations of more than 40,000 users. The multiple-master domain model is scaleable to networks with any number of users.

■ Mobile users. Users can log on from anywhere in the network, anywhere in the world.

■ Centralized (corporate-wide) or decentralized administration (region-based).

■ Organizational needs. Domains can be configured to mirror specific departments or internal company organizations. A large, multinational organization, for example, might have corporate headquarters in New York, London, and Sydney. Creating master domains in each of these cities (and creating a multiple-master domain model around these domains) mirrors the geographical organization of this multinational company, while providing a single logon and global access to resources at the same time.

■ Backup Domain Controllers can be distributed between sites to facilitate inter-network interaction. It is common for large organizations to own their own wide area network. When it comes to user logon authentication, it is advisable to place your logon servers as close to the users as possible. Placing backup domain controllers, from the master domains, within the trusting domains provides better logon response times.

Complete Trust Model

The complete trust modelis an unusual Windows NT 4 domain model because it contrasts considerably with the other three models already discussed. It can be argued that the single, single-master, and multiple-master domain models are logical extensions of each other (single, to single-master, to multiple-master).

The complete trust model, however, is not a logical extension of any of the previously mentioned models and caters to corporate or departmental requirements that are not met by the first three models.

All trusts in this model are two-way trusts. A two-way trust is different and is depicted with a double-headed arrow. (Notice in figure 13.4 that each domain has account and resource responsibilities.)

The important fact to remember about two-way trusts (apart from the increased complexity of establishing them) is that any two domains participating in a complete trust relationship have both accounts AND resources to manage. This means that the complete trust domain model is suitable for:

■ Organizations of more than 40,000 users. The complete trust model is scaleable to networks with any number of users.

■ Mobile users. Users can log on from anywhere in the network, anywhere in the world.

■ Decentralized administration (region-based). Each component domain controls its own accounts and resources (that is, single domain model), but global access to resources is achieved through the complex arrangements of trusts.

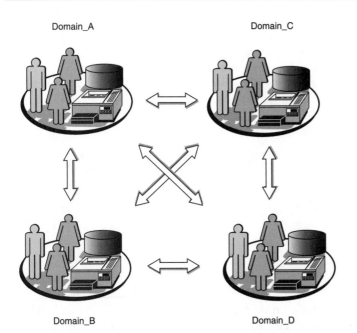

Domain_A Domain_C

Domain_B Domain_D

Figure 13.4

The Complete Trust Model is suitable for organizations of any size that do not have a centralized network management and support infrastructure.

One disadvantage of this model is the initial overhead involved when creating all the necessary trust relationships. A formula can calculate the exact number of trusts needed and is based on the number (n) of participating domains in the model:

```
n(n-1)   : 6 domains, 6(6-1) = 6*5 = 30 trusts
         : 7 domains, 7(7-1) = 7*6 = 42 trusts!
```

For every domain that is added, therefore, a large number of trusts must be added. (In the preceding example, 12 additional trusts are required.) The addition of trust relationships (in reaction to the addition of extra domains) can become a source of overhead expense, and a definite source of potential errors. You need only neglect to establish one or two choice trust relationships, and the entire model ceases to function properly.

When analyzing domain models, the number, nature, and establishment of trusts are crucial factors. In addition, implementing the group strategy across these trust relationships must be done in a complete and correct fashion; otherwise, there is the potential for security- or access-related errors.

Not unlike the problem associated with choosing the role of a Windows NT 4 server (domain controller versus application server), solving problems related to the choice of a domain model relies on prevention rather than cure. Fixing a domain-model problem, therefore, requires a careful analysis and verification of the domain model in question.

Solving the Workgroup Capacity Problem

To solve the complexity and capacity problems associated with a workgroup or a single server in terms of account and security management, Windows NT provides a network management mechanism called the domain.

The Windows NT trust relationship provides an adequate solution to the workgroup or single-server problem, but is limited by a number of other factors, such as the size of the accounts database, the underlying geography and logistics, and the organizational hierarchy of the corporate or departmental information technology infrastructure. A one-way trust relationship is depicted in figure 13.5, in which the arrow points toward the accounts and away from the resources.

Figure 13.5

A one-way trust relationship is a tool that combines two domains into a single administrative unit.

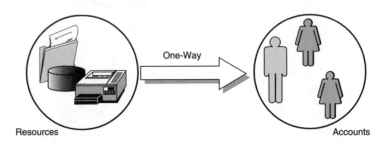

Resources   One-Way   Accounts

The four standard Windows NT 4 domain models (single, master, multiple master, and complete trust) are designed to overcome these difficulties; the simplest and most applicable model is chosen in any given situation. Therefore, the trust relationship between two Windows NT domains is a crucial instrument in the planning and implementation of a corporate or departmental domain model.

Size of the Accounts Database

An exact figure for the maximum size of a domain's account database is difficult to obtain, but Microsoft suggests that the accounts database should not exceed 40 megabytes (although they have tested databases in excess of this size). A single Windows NT 4 domain can accommodate approximately 26,000 user and 250 group accounts.

The figures in table 13.1 show that 26,000 users and 250 groups can easily result in an accounts database of 40 MB:

$(26,000 \times 1.0K) + (26,000 \times 0.5K) + (250 \times 4.0K) = 40$ MB

Table 13.1
Computing the Security Accounts Database Size

Object	Space Used
User account	1.0K
Computer account	0.5K
Group account	4.0K (average group size equals 300 members)

There are cases of far larger account databases, but because the Registry is cached on startup, it may be inadvisable to have an extremely large accounts database. A large database causes a longer boot time for your Windows NT 4 machine.

After the accounts database grows beyond a manageable size, a new or an additional accounts database is needed. This is achieved by creating an entirely new domain. Creating a new domain might require changing to another domain model (for example, from a master domain model to a multiple master domain model). So, if your Windows NT Server 4 begins to take an especially long time to start up, but then continues to run perfectly, you may have a Registry that has become too large.

To establish the actual size of your Registry, you must refer to the virtual memory settings of your Windows NT Server 4. Figure 13.6 shows the steps necessary to view the size of the Registry. As shown in the figure, one is able to specify a maximum size for the Registry. You should, however, exercise caution when specifying a megabyte value for this setting because the Maximum Registry Size (MB) entry defines the page pool size in memory as well as the amount of disk space used by the Registry. This is *not* an allocation (it does not reserve this memory up front), but merely an indication (a desired, future value), and so it does *not* guarantee that this space will always be available to the Registry.

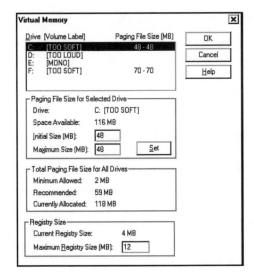

Figure 13.6

The actual size of the Registry can be viewed by using the Virtual Memory dialog box of the Control Panel System applet.

An ever-increasing Registry size eventually necessitates the creation of trust relationships between two or more domains, especially when centralized administration is desired at the time that global access to resources is needed.

Geography and Logistics

Not only the size of the accounts database can necessitate the spawning of another domain within an organization. Changes in the geographical or the logistical layout of a corporation or department can also demand change.

For example, a small company decides to start a branch office in another region. Rather than extend the single domain model across the wide area network and into this new region, this company can simply start another single domain model in the new region.

A crucial factor is how this small company wants to control the administration, security, and resource access within these various domains, and how its control priorities impact network connectivity and bandwidth-oriented performance.

Generally speaking, performance is better if two separate domains are maintained, thereby reducing the wide area network traffic. You should realize, however, that by maintaining two separate domains, the administration and security does become centralized within each region (that is, per domain) and *not* within the company as a whole.

It appears that centralization and performance are mutually exclusive ideals. Gladly, this is not the case. By establishing a trust relationship between these two separate domains, both ideals can be achieved rather eloquently, but it requires careful planning in order to be successful.

Despite the fact that a trust relationship solves this apparent dilemma, it has to be established correctly (particularly the order in which the steps are carried out when establishing the trust relationship), otherwise it becomes a completely separate problem of its own. The factors that you should bear in mind when establishing a trust relationship between two domains are discussed in a later section.

What is important in this example, however, is that the geographical layout of this company (two physical regional locations) and the logistical layout (account domains versus resource domains) necessitates the creation of a trust relationship between the two single domain models.

Organizational Hierarchy

Not all companies organize their information technology staff into the same logical models in terms of a functional hierarchy. Two functional hierarchy models are applicable to Windows NT 4 domains: centralized and de-centralized.

A large corporation, such as a bank or an insurance house, may not have a large number of information technology personnel when compared to its total personnel strength. A centralized approach might be suitable in this case because this relatively small group of highly-skilled computing professionals can be centrally located and trained to support and administer the information technology requirements on behalf of the entire company.

In a smaller company, or in a company that has a large number of information technology professionals in its employ, the de-centralized model might be more suitable. In this model, the highly-skilled computing professionals can be located regionally (or per business unit) and trained to support and administer the information technology requirements on behalf of specific regions or branch offices.

Either way, because centralized administration (single logon) and global access to resources is a consistent goal for all Windows NT 4 domain models, trusts are still necessary to implement any chosen domain model (with the exception of the single domain model). In the hierarchical model, trusts are used to configure a domain model such as the single- or multiple-master domain model; in the non-hierarchical model, trusts are used to configure the complete trust domain model.

Trust Establishment Errors

Many problems can prevent a trust relationship from being successfully established, but they can all be categorized into three groups of error classification: procedural, security, and connectivity.

- **Procedural Errors.** This type of error includes conceptual problems (wrong direction of the trust) and configuration problems (passwords, creating trust in the wrong order, and so on). In a nutshell, your trust is not set up properly.

- **Security Errors.** This type of error includes physical security problems (breaking a trust at one end or invalid user authentication, and so on) as well as connection problems (being already connected to the trusted domain while establishing the trust relationship). In a nutshell, your security is not configured properly.

- **Connectivity Errors.** This type of error includes network errors (for example, the trusted domain controller cannot be found on the network) as well as connectivity failure (for example, the physical network is down, or the network card or some other component is inoperable). In other words, your network connection is not established properly.

The trust relationship between two domains plays a crucial part in the domain planning and implementation phases. Understanding why the trust relationship is important is essential in order to troubleshoot problems with establishing a trust relationship.

Because trusts play a significant role in domains (and their models), it is probable that most domain problems are trust-related. The knack of solving this kind of problem is to determine the type of trust establishment error that is causing the problem. After it is identified, the cause can be isolated and rectified. Identifying the problem, however, is a lot easier than isolating and rectifying it.

Choosing the Role of the Server

A Windows NT 4 server can be installed to serve in any one of three different types of functional roles: primary domain controller, backup domain controller, or application server. The focus when planning and implementing a domain model is invariably on the two domain controller roles—one primary domain controller per domain and zero or more backup domain controllers per domain (depending on the server load expected).

It is important to realize that you cannot easily change the role of an NT server. After you install a Windows NT server as a domain controller in a particular domain, it must remain within that domain unless it is to be completely reinstalled. This fact is often very startling to the uninitiated administrator who discovers, with no small degree of annoyance, that moving a domain controller from one domain to another requires a complete reinstall of that particular domain controller.

The best way to avoid problems when choosing the role of your server is to carefully plan any Windows NT Server 4 installation, no matter how small or insignificant you deem it to be. The biggest implication of making a poor choice of server role is that you will have to reinstall some of the domain controllers.

Consider this example of what can happen if a system is hastily installed. When installing a number of domain controllers, a decision was made to share the servers evenly among the company's domains (one primary and two backup domain controllers per domain). As it turns out, one of the domains experiences a heavier user authentication load than any of the others (after the installation has been completed). You decide to move one of the backup domain controllers from one domain to another to balance the load better within that domain. This domain controller, being moved to balance the load, has to be reinstalled within its new domain.

You should always consider the possibility for growth in any domain configuration (in terms of the number of user and group accounts, as well as the number and location of domains and their controllers), and reevaluate your choices considering this projected growth. This is a time-consuming process, but failing to do so can lead to significant problems.

This domain controller migration problem (which does not affect Windows NT Application Servers) exists for a very good reason. The primary clue to the answer lies within the NT security model—in particular, with unique Security Identifiers.

In figure 13.7, a typical NT Security Identifier is depicted. This highly unique value is calculated every time a new security object is created (for example, when creating a new user, or even a new domain). In other words, when a Primary Domain Controller is installed for the first time (that is, when you establish a new domain), a Windows NT Security ID is associated with the name of this new domain.

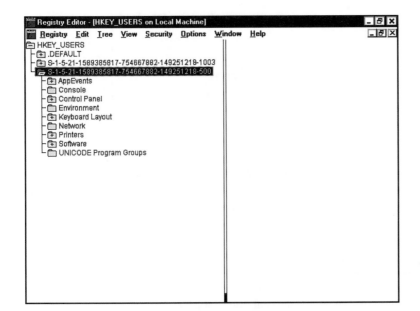

Figure 13.7

Security identifiers are used to uniquely identify users and computers within the Windows NT 4 security environment.

During the installation process, the Primary Domain Controller spends a few seconds trying to detect another Primary Domain Controller with the same domain name. If it succeeds in finding another Primary Domain Controller, then the domain-name registration fails.

Of course, if no such Primary Domain Controller is detected, the domain name is registered and a unique Security ID is associated with it. The Primary Domain Controller of the newly registered domain is now able to complete its installation. It is often necessary to install Backup Domain Controllers for fault tolerance and load balancing among the domain controllers.

When a Backup Domain Controller is installed, it too spends a few seconds trying to establish whether a Primary Domain Controller exists with the same domain name. This time, when a matching Primary Domain Controller is found, the Backup Domain Controller adopts the unique Security Identifier from this Primary Domain Controller as its own. In other words, all domain controllers for a particular domain share a common, unique Security Identifier.

A common misconception is that a domain controller can be moved from one domain to another by changing the domain name. Unfortunately, this procedure (as depicted in figure 13.8) will not be successful for a domain controller. For a Windows NT 4 workstation or Application Server, however, changing the domain name is sufficient to enable the Windows NT machine to join the domain specified.

Figure 13.8

Changing the Windows NT domain name is possible via the Identification Changes dialog box.

The role of a Windows NT 4 server is important when planning and implementing a Windows NT 4 domain because a bad choice can result in having to reinstall a number of them. Unfortunately, reinstallation is the only way to rectify bad choices. In this case, prevention is better than cure.

Local and Global Groups

Apart from the most obvious errors of omission (neglecting to include a user account in the membership list of a group, and so on), a common source of errors is the lack of a systematic method for assigning user permissions. Small accounts databases grow into large accounts databases very quickly and often haphazardly. In the beginning, because it is convenient, security is applied in a direct, ad hoc manner with no adherence to any form of strategy at all. However, after the domain starts to grow in size, the problem of controlling user security and access becomes a big headache.

The adherence to a de jure or de facto standard is therefore an extremely important requirement, as well as documenting this adherence for reference purposes. Often, the only person who really understands your network security is the person who fixes it. More likely than not, the much-needed information is stored in this person's memory and not on paper or disk.

In order to prevent having to assign the same security rights to a dozen or so users individually, a Windows NT administrator can make use of a special security account called a *group*. The group account enables a collection of user accounts to be logically associated with each other for the specific purpose of facilitating security administration and resource allocation.

In other words, security privileges or resource access rights need only be awarded to a particular group once. When user accounts are made members of this group, they each inherit the associated group rights, thereby drastically reducing the associated administrative overhead.

Windows NT 4 security can be viewed from two perspectives. The first has to do with assigning certain domain-wide functionality (for example, Domain Administrator); the second has to do with assigning access to certain resources (for example, Read permission to a network share). Both entail the use of groups, and both should subscribe to a unifying group strategy (adherence to which greatly simplifies the implementation and verification of a domain model).

When solving security problems associated with the use of Windows NT groups, one has to determine whether the group strategy has been adhered to, and how the various network and file system security objects interact.

A Group Strategy

Regardless of whether you adopt the single domain model or a more complex model, the group strategy remains the same. In simple terms, the group strategy can be stated as "Identify the task, create and place users into global groups, place global groups into local groups, and then the local groups can be assigned to resources." This strategy provides a standard template for setting up a security infrastructure within a domain.

For the purpose of explaining the group strategy, consider the following example and the group strategy that applies to it. Each of the five steps that make up the group strategy include a cumulative example of what each step is trying to achieve.

The example, used to explain the application of the group strategy, involves a user named Peter Williamson who is required to run backups on all the servers within a particular Windows NT domain environment. Each step of the group strategy is presented, and its application is explained by referring to this example. The domain model is assumed to be the single domain model, although this strategy can be implemented by using any of the Windows NT domain models.

Note   Windows NT 4 security has only two purposes: to provide chosen users with specific enterprise-wide security privileges (such as administrator, server operator, backup operator, and so on) or to control user access to resources.

Windows NT makes system-wide security privileges available through the various built-in local and global groups (there is no need to create local groups in this case). Examples of built-in local groups include Administrators, Print Operators, Server Operators, Backup Operators, and so on.

Providing access to resources (and controlling this access), however, might require the creation of user-defined global and local groups. One should always attempt to use existing local groups before creating new ones.

1. Identify the Task

   Identify the task at hand, and match existing groups and users to this task. Creating new user accounts (such as peterw, if it does not already exist) and group accounts (such as the global group Domain Backup Operators) might be necessary.

   In our example, the task has been established as "Peter Williamson must backup all servers within the domain." This task identifies two important points: a user account for Peter Williamson is needed (which must be created in step 2 because it does not already exist), and a domain-wide security privilege must be established to permit servers to be backed up (domain-wide security privileges are always provided by means of built-in group accounts—see preceding note).

2. Create Users and Groups in the Domain

   Create user and group accounts at the domain controller (only if necessary because these user and group accounts might already exist).

   For example, Peter Williamson, as stated in step 1, must be able to back up all servers within the domain. Therefore, the domain user account peterw should be created on a domain controller. Furthermore, a global group Domain Backup Operators must be created on the same domain controller because the task (from step 1) dictates a domain-wide privilege (backup servers).

3. Place Users into Global Groups

   Place the appropriate domain user accounts into the applicable domain global groups. These domain global groups export their member domain user accounts into the local groups on the appropriate Windows NT 4 machines.

   Step 3 suggests that we place the domain user account called peterw into the newly created domain global group called Domain Backup Operators. The reason for doing this is to enable the peterw account to be exported to the appropriate NT servers. An explanation (and an example) of why this step is carried out is provided in step 5.

4. Create the Local Groups

   We are now required to create the local groups on every Windows NT 4 computer that is affected by the task at hand (back up all NT servers in the domain). The golden rule is to use existing local groups before creating any new ones.

   In our example, the Backup Operators local group already exists, so in this case it is not necessary to create this local group (see preceding note). In the case of resource access, however, a new user-defined local group might be created during this step (and the necessary file or resource access permissions assigned).

5. Export the Global Groups into the Local Groups

   The final step is perhaps the most important. The first four steps establish a global user and global group on the domain controller, and at the same time establish a local group with local permissions on every Windows NT 4 machine affected by the task at hand (back up all NT servers in the domain).

   To link the global user to the local resource requires placing the domain global group (defined on the domain controller) in the local group (defined on every Windows NT machine affected by the task at hand). This completes the implementation of the group strategy.

In our example, peterw is placed into the Domain Backup Operators global group on the domain controller. The final step in the example, then, is to include the Domain Backup Operators global group into each and every local Backup Operators group on every server that must be backed up by Peter Williamson.

In summary, the Group Strategy is a five step process that must be implemented completely and accurately. It can be used to provide users with specific domain-wide privileges (such as the case with Peter Williamson who obtained domain-wide privileges to backup the servers).

Furthermore, this strategy can be used to provide access to resources. For example, all project managers must have access to the project folder on the central server (Step 1). Therefore, a folder (called Projects) is shared on a single Windows NT 4 server called CENTRAL as \\CENTRAL\PROJECTS. A local group is created on CENTRAL called Project Managers, and this group is provided Change (RXWD) permissions to the \\CENTRAL\PROJECTS share (Step 4).

A domain global group, called Domain Project Managers, is created on a domain controller MASTER, and user accounts are created for each of the project managers (Step 2). The final step is to place the global Domain Project Managers group from MASTER into the local Project Managers group on CENTRAL (Step 5). The group strategy is completely implemented. Notice that this example is different from the original example in that it deals with resource access (and not domain-wide security privileges). This second example also required the creation of local groups, a common practice in this type of scenario (providing resource access).

In some cases, you need to establish the group strategy first (as discussed in the preceding section) and then document it for maintenance purposes. When trying to track down any error of this nature, you should start either at the beginning or at the end of the group strategy and proceed forward or backward through the group strategy procedure, verifying that each stage has been completed successfully.

The group strategy has proven very useful in large, complex security environments where it is not so easy to keep mental track of who belongs to which group, or where people are getting their security rights or access privileges.

The real benefit of using the group strategy (as explained in steps 1 through 5) lies in the ability to vary the membership of the global group in order to change security permissions. For example, the Domain Administrators global group and the local Administrators groups are available on a Windows NT 4 server by default.

Furthermore, the Domain Administrators global group is a default member of every local Administrators group on every Windows NT computer in the domain. So, by creating a domain user account called "wayned" and placing it into the Domain Administrators global group on the domain controller, the user who logs on to the domain as wayned becomes a domain administrator (that is, an administrator on everyone's computer).

Group Security Dynamics

Computers have an annoying habit of doing exactly what you tell them to do. When it comes to security (the application of the group strategy in particular), an administrator's actions can often lead to unanticipated side effects due to the complexities in the security models of today's modern networks.

For example, even when the group strategy is correctly implemented, something as small as placing the wrong user can lead to significant problems. This is especially true when the group strategy is combined with network security (shares and printer permissions) and local security (file system permissions). When implementing the group strategy, even the most insignificant action can cause the subsequent problem-solving equation to become rather complex.

Two simple rules have been devised to help clarify the mystery that surrounds network and local security permissions. Acquiring an understanding of the mechanics of these two rules is important when unraveling the security path from users to resources.

The first rule is that user and group rights are cumulative. The second rule is that local and network rights are most restrictive. These two rules are discussed in the next two sections.

User and Group Rights Are Cumulative

The first rule states that the permissions assigned to a particular user, and the permissions also assigned to the groups (to whom a particular user belongs), are cumulative.

For example, Fred Turner (also known as fredt) is a member of the Programmer and Manager groups. He is assigned specific personal permissions to a resource, as well as permissions based on his membership in the two previously mentioned groups. His effective rights are cumulative, as illustrated in table 13.2.

Table 13.2
The Effective Rights to an Object Are the Cumulative Rights Assigned to the Appropriate User and Group Accounts

Security Object	Assigned Rights to Resource
User: fredt	Read (RX)
Group 1: Programmer	Change (RXWD)
Group 2: Management	Read (RX)
Effective Rights	Change (RXWD)

In the preceding tabulated example, the effective (cumulative) rights are Change (RXWD). However, if any of the assigned rights to this resource were No Access, this assignment would effectively override all cumulative rights. In this case, the effective rights would be No Access.

Local and Network Rights Are Most Restrictive

The second rule states that the permissions assigned to a particular network resource (for example, a shared drive or directory), and the permissions cumulatively accrued to the user (in whose security context the network resource is being accessed) are the most restrictive.

For example, Fred Turner is still a member of the Programmer and Manager groups. His effective local rights are cumulative, and table 13.2 depicts his effective rights to this resource as being Change. However, Fred Turner chooses to access this local resource from a remote machine using server share. The resource in question is shared with Read (RX) permission assigned to this share. Table 13.3 depicts Fred Turner's effective rights to this resource.

Table 13.3
The Effective Rights to an Object Are the Most Restrictive Rights Assigned Locally (User and Group) or to the Network Share

Security Object	Assigned Resource Rights
Effective Local Rights	Change (RXWD) (refer to table 13.1)
Share Permission	Read (RX)
Effective Rights	Read(RX)

In table 13.3, the effective (most restrictive) rights are Read (RX). If any of the assigned rights to this resource were No Access, this assignment would effectively override all cumulative rights.

When solving local and global group security problems, two questions must be asked, "Have I arranged my trusts and group strategy correctly?" and "Have I assigned correct permissions to achieve the expected effective rights?" The group strategy should serve as a simple recipe for setting up the necessary users and groups to achieve a particular goal.

The two rules ("user and group rights are cumulative" and "local and network rights are most restrictive") should provide a formal way of evaluating and verifying the security permissions that have been allocated, to determine whether the effective rights allocated are what we expected them to be.

Solving Domain Planning and Implementation Problems

The application of any problem-solving method requires tools, the focus of this section. The method, described in the preceding section, consists of examining specific aspects of planning and implementing a domain model. These aspects include trust relationships, the role of the server, local and global groups, and the domain models.

These aspects are revisited in this section, this time to look at the various tools available to assist in the application of this problem-solving method.

Trust Relationships Problems

The tools discussed in this part of the chapter are useful in solving problems that arise from incorrectly configured trust relationships between two domains. Some tools (like the Winlogon process and the Event Viewer) are incidental to the problem-solving process because they can be used to detect problems. Other tools, like the User Manager for Domains, can be used directly to redress any error in configuration.

Problems with trusts fall into three categories: procedural, security, and connectivity.

Procedural Problems

Procedural problems occur regularly because they entail errors that occur during the actual establishment of the trust. The different permutations are too vast to document in detail, but three very common problems illustrate how to troubleshoot trust relationship problems of this nature.

To establish a trust relationship, User Manager for Domains is used (see fig. 13.9). A trust relationship must be established by a user with administrator privileges, either by two different administrators (one at each end of the trust) or by a single administrator from within the resource (trusting) domain.

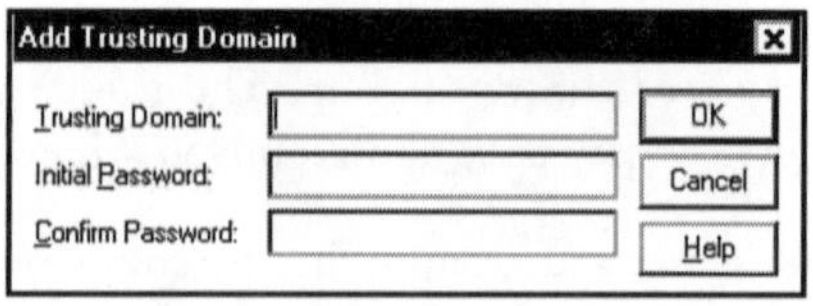

Figure 13.9

Establishing a trust relationship is possible through the Add Trusting Domain dialog box.

Trust Established in Wrong Order

A trust relationship must be established in a particular order. One must first add the Trusting Domains before adding the Trusted Domains. This sets up a secure channel between the two participating domains.

When the trust is established in the opposite order (that is, the Trusted Domain followed by the Trusting Domain), the warning message depicted in figure 13.10 is issued to indicate that the trust relationship cannot be verified immediately. The trust is eventually verified after the secure channel is established, but this takes a long time (approximately 15 minutes).

Figure 13.10

The User Manager for Domains dialog box appears when a trust relationship cannot be verified.

Incorrect Configuration Information

The configuration information needed to establish a trust relationship between domains is the name of the other domain and a password.

The administrator in the trusted domain initially permits the trusting domain to trust by typing in the name of the trusting domain and an initial password, as shown in figure 13.11.

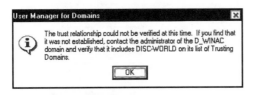

Figure 13.11

Type the name of the trusting domain and the password to permit the trusting domain to trust.

When establishing a trust relationship, a domain name and a password must be provided by both administrators establishing the trust relationship. If you provide incorrect details for any of these required pieces of information, the trust relationship is not verified and will not work. A warning message (refer to fig. 13.10) is displayed.

Trust Established in Wrong Direction

Establishing the trust relationship in the wrong direction is more a conceptual problem than it is a disastrous error. However, the end result is about the same—the trust relationship does not function as advertised. The problem is that the administrator, in this case, switches the trusted and the trusting domains. The trust is established, but in the wrong direction.

This is not a particularly difficult problem to diagnose, and the place to go to verify that this problem has occurred is the Winlogon dialog box, and in particular, the Domain drop-down list on the Winlogon dialog.

Figure 13.12 depicts the similar dialog box (used to unlock the server console), and shows two entries in the Domain drop-down list, the D_WINAC (trusted domain) and DISC-WORLD (trusting domain). The dialog box in figure 13.12 serves to illustrate the choice of domains when a trust relationship has been employed between two domains.

Figure 13.12

The Domain entry can be used to verify the proper establishment of a trust relationship.

Because the D_WINAC and DISC-WORLD domain names are visible and available for selection, you can safely assume that the trust relationship between these two domains is successfully established.

Security Problems

The capability to establish a trust relationship between two Windows NT domains is a powerful network management tool, but it is also potentially dangerous. For this reason, the establishment of a trust relationship has a significant number of security restrictions associated with it.

Apart from its integration into the C2-certifiable security environment provided by Windows NT 4, the establishment of a trust relationship requires a password to be supplied. A further restriction is placed on the capability to establish a trust relationship while maintaining an active connection to the trusted domain.

If these restrictions are not adhered to, or if they are incorrectly applied, problems arise in the establishment of the associated trust relationship.

Trust Relation Is Broken

When a trust relationship is broken at one end, whether it is due to a server going down or someone removing the relationship from User Manager for Domains, it is not enough to add the trust relationship back into the domain from which the relationship was broken. Administrators from the domains involved must remove the trust relationship and recreate the trusts.

When a trust relationship is established between two domains, the password used to create the relationship is immediately changed by the operating system, even if a blank password was used to establish the trust relationship. The domain controllers for both domains know the new password, but the password is hidden from the users.

This password change provides extra security. Because of this, after the trust relationship is broken, the only way to re-establish the trust is to reset it completely on both ends, which serves to reset the password.

After the trust relationship has been set up, a secure channel is created between the two affected domains. After this secure channel has been established (which normally takes a few minutes), the trust relationship has to be broken at both ends if any changes are to be made to this trust relationship. It has been my experience that, prior to the successful establishment of the secure channel, changes can be made to the trust relationship configuration (such as changing the password).

Connection Already Exists

If an open session is already established between the trusted and trusting domains when establishing a trust between two domains, the message shown in figure 13.13 appears.

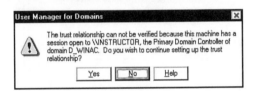

Figure 13.13

An open session between the trusting and trusted domains causes the establishment of a trust relationship to fail.

The trust might be established and working correctly. The reason this message appears is that a session is already established between the domain controllers under a user account. (In this case, a session exists between DISC-WORLD\RINCEWIND and D_WINAC\ INSTRUCTOR.) This session keeps the special trust verification from being sent because the Windows NT 4 Redirector can establish remote sessions under only one user account per remote server.

Connectivity Problems

When establishing a trust relationship between two Windows NT domains, resolution of connectivity errors depends largely on the transport protocol, the physical network layout (for example, WAN, LAN, remote access, and so on), and the general health of the network.

Transport Protocols

Windows NT 4 supports three main-line transport protocols: Netbeui, NWLink, and TCP/IP. Netbeui is ideally suited for local area network traffic, and so problems that occur when using Netbeui as primary transport are invariably due to a failure of the network connection or the remote domain controller.

The two routeable protocols, NWLink (IPX/SPX) and TCP/IP, are dependent on network hardware (routers, bridges, and so on). So when resolving problems when using one of these two as a primary protocol, these hardware devices must be taken into consideration. Check the power supply to these devices, internal configuration parameters, and whether they are functioning correctly.

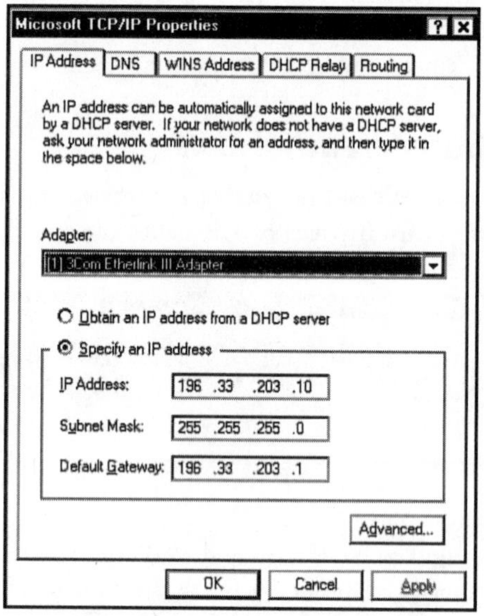

Figure 13.14

Verifying a TCP/IP protocol stack configuration for correctness is done by using the Microsoft TCP/IP Properties dialog box of Protocol tab on the Control Panel Network applet.

After it has been ascertained that all the physical network hardware is functioning correctly, the appropriate protocol stack must be tested. For example, to establish the health of a TCP/IP protocol stack, follow these steps:

1. Check the Configuration Parameter. This entails verifying that the TCP/IP parameters have been correctly assigned. First make a visual inspection (refer to figure 13.14), then do a physical test by using the IPCONFIG and PING utilities:

```
C:\users\default>ipconfig ø
Windows NT IP Configuration
Ethernet adapter Elnk31:
 IP Address . . : 196.33.203.10
 Subnet Mask . . : 255.255.255.0
 Default Gateway . . : 196.33.203.1
```

```
C:\users\default>ping localhost ø
Pinging rincewind [127.0.0.1] with 32 bytes of data:
Reply from 127.0.0.1: bytes=32 time<10ms TTL=128
```

2. Test your own IP configuration:

```
C:\users\default>ping rincewind ø
Pinging rincewind [196.33.203.10] with 32 bytes of data:
Reply from 196.33.203.10: bytes=32 time<10ms TTL=128
```

3. Test connectivity with the default gateway:

```
C:\users\default>ping gateway ø
Pinging gateway [196.33.201.38] with 32 bytes of data:
Reply from 196.33.201.38: bytes=32 time<10ms TTL=127
```

4. Test connectivity with the remote domain controller:

```
C:\users\default>ping instructor
Pinging instructor [196.33.203.1] with 32 bytes of data:
Reply from 196.33.203.1: bytes=32 time<10ms TTL=32
```

Other utilities can test connectivity to the remote domain controller over the wide area network. For more information, refer to the TCP/IP Implementation white paper on Microsoft's FTP site.

Physical Network Layout

The physical layout of the network is important because it determines whether the trusting domain is local or remote to the trusted domain. This also determines the nature of the transport protocol to be used (that is, routeable or not).

If the trusted domain controller is on another network segment, a routeable protocol is required. Furthermore, the chosen transport protocol must be installed on both servers. To test for connectivity on a wide area network, the same procedure can be followed as discussed in the previous sub-section "Transport Protocols" dealing with protocols.

When establishing a trust relationship across a slow (dial-up) link, it is crucial to distinguish between errors caused by a loss of connectivity and errors caused by transport protocol time-outs. The default TCP/IP protocol stack is configured for typical, high-speed, reliable networks. However, the configurable parameters of this protocol must be configured to suit the specific conditions of the network separating the two domains from each other.

Health of the Network

The health of the underlying network is very important because it forms the pathway for the trust and domain traffic to travel along. Network problems largely depend on the physical medium (for example, 10baseT, 10base2, and so on) and the specific network topology (for example, ring, bus, star, and so on).

Although it is very obvious, you need to ensure that the physical network is functioning correctly before spending time trying to isolate the problem on either of the domain controllers. The problem may be a defective network terminator or a non-functioning T-piece. Only after the underlying network is given a clean bill of health should you proceed to check other aspects of the connectivity equation.

Local and Global Groups

Your most useful tool (albeit intangible) for solving problems relating to user and group security is the group strategy that was introduced in the earlier section, "An Approach to Solving Domain Model Problems." This group strategy guides the process of setting up user and group security and is essentially the only worthwhile way to isolate problems in this area.

Step 1—Identify the Error

User and group security are almost always configured to provide one of two types of permissions: security equivalence or access to resources. The aim of this first step is to identify into which category any given error falls.

If the problem is security privileges (that is, being able to back up all the servers in the domain), then you can trace the problem from the built-in local group (in this case, Backup Operators) on all the servers, all the way back to the domain controller where the specific user account (that wants to attain the security equivalence) has been created. The goal is to trace and isolate the break in the group strategy chain (that is, users into global groups, global groups into local groups, and so on).

If the problem is resource access (that is, permission granted to a shared directory or a printer), then you can trace the problem from the appropriate resource on the local machine, all the way back to the domain controller where the specific user account (that wants to attain the resource permission) has been created. Again, the goal is to trace and find the break in the group strategy chain.

Step 2—Trace the Broken Chain

In step 1, the type of error is identified. Now you need to trace the group strategy chain backward until you find the problem or you end up at the user account of the person who originally notified you about the problem. Either way, you know what the problem is by the time you reach the end of this process.

Tracing the chain entails the laborious task of tracing group membership by using the User Manager for Domains utility. For example, let us assume that a user called wayne is supposed to have administrator privileges on the Windows NT domain controller called RINCEWIND. However, when this user logs on, he is unable to do the normal things other administrators can do. He phones you and explains that he is having a problem and goes on to say that you have to fix it.

First of all, this very simple example falls into the security equivalence category, which means that our first port of call is the local administrators group on the domain controller. Figure 13.15 depicts what User Manager for Domains reveals.

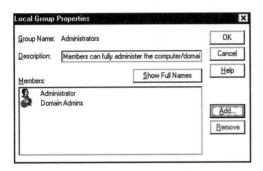

Figure 13.15

Membership of the Local Group Administrators can be verified by using the Local Group Properties dialog box of the User Manager for Domains utility.

The only members of the local administrators group are the user account Administrator (which is not the user in question) and a global group called Domain Admins (placed there by default). Using the information gleaned from this examination of the local group membership, the focus shifts to the contents of the global group.

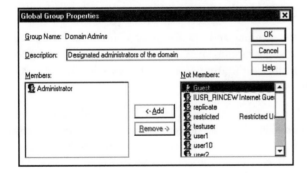

Figure 13.16

Membership List of the Global Group Domain Admins can be verified by using the Global Group Properties dialog of the User Manager for Domains utility.

The solution to the problem is now discovered. The user wayne is not a member of the global group Domain Admins, and so is not a member of the local group Administrators. He therefore lacks administrator privileges on RINCEWIND. This is a simple example, but it is sufficient to illustrate the methodical manner in which the group strategy can be used to troubleshoot user and group problems.

Domain Models

A Windows NT domain model is essentially a pre-defined, logical arrangement of domains and trusts that forms the foundation for the direct application of the group strategy. Solving problems related to the implementation of a domain model, therefore, is simply verifying that the trust relationships have been correctly configured and that the group strategy has been correctly applied.

Obviously, some models are far more complex than others, making them harder to trouble-shoot. Nevertheless, whether solving problems within a single domain model or a complete trust domain model the approach remains exactly the same. The former is just a great deal easier, and the latter is much more difficult.

Solving problems within a domain model implementation should not be impossible if the preceding method and tool set is applied in a methodical and meticulous manner. All the tools covered in this section are shipped with Windows NT Server 4, with the possible exception of one or two from the Windows NT 3.51 Resource Kit.

Conclusion

A definite challenge that computing professionals have to face on an ongoing basis is known as the Competency Gap. This Competency Gap is the gap between what we already know and what we need to know in order to carry out our work successfully.

Education, in part, can help narrow this gap by providing an understanding of the subject (for example, installing a Windows NT 4 domain), and thereby enable computing professionals to develop sufficient insight to easily cope with problems. The other part of the solution, however, is to have a methodical approach to solve these problems.

Solving problems that relate to the planning and installation of Windows NT 4 domains requires in-depth knowledge and understanding of Windows NT 4. Combining this knowledge with a structured approach (such as the group strategy, for example), however, is the only way to ensure a successful problem-solving strategy.

This chapter has provided fundamental concepts and a method to be used when planning and implementing Windows NT 4 domains. It is not, however, a complete and concise answer to everyone's specific Windows NT 4 domain questions, nor was it meant to be. For specific remedies for particular problems, refer to other sources such as Microsoft Technet, the Internet, and the Microsoft Developers Network, to name a few.

Network Monitor

*T*he Windows NT Server Network Monitor, included
with NT Server 4, is an extremely useful and powerful
network diagnostic tool. The Network Monitor enables
you to detect and troubleshoot problems on your Local
Area Network (LAN) by collecting information and
capturing frames from your LAN's data stream.

You can use Network Monitor, for example, to diagnose network hardware- and software-related problems
when two or more computers have communication
problems. Captured network activity can be saved to a
file. If you encounter a serious network problem, you
can send the capture file to a professional network
support organization for analysis assistance. Network
application developers can use Network Monitor to
monitor and debug network applications during the
development.

Collected information and captured frames are viewed in an easy-to-read, graphical display of network statistics.

When using the Network Monitor, you can perform the following:

- Capture network frames

- Display captured frames and set capture filters

- Set capture triggers

- View network statistics

For security reasons, the Windows NT Server Network Monitor captures only network traffic sent to or from the local computer, as well as broadcast and multicast frames. The Systems Management Server (SMS) Network Monitor captures frames sent to or from any computer on your network, edits and transmits frames on the network, and remotely captures frames. The SMS Network Monitor can be used over a dial-up network connection via Remote Access Service (RAS) or from other computers on the network running the Network Monitor Agent (such as computers running Windows NT Workstation and Windows 95).

This chapter provides an overview of the capabilities of the Network Monitor included with NT Server 4.

How the Network Monitor Works

NT Server 4's Network Monitor monitors the data stream on your network, between your NT Server and the computers communicating with it. The SMS Network Monitor has the capability to monitor the entire network data stream.

To use the Network Monitor effectively, you should already have a general understanding of network protocols and the operation of the Windows NT operating system.

Before anything is transmitted across the network, the network software divides the information into smaller segments, called frames or packets. Each frame of information consists of the following:

- The source address of the computer that originated the frame. The source address is a unique hexidecimal number that identifies the computer on the network.

- The destination address of the computer on the network that is intended to receive the frame.

- Protocol Headers from each protocol used to transmit the frame.

- Data being transmitted.

When frames are transmitted on the network, all computers are exposed to the traffic, except on Token Ring and subnetted environments. Under normal conditions, the network card passes only frames addressed to the destination computer to the networking software. If a network card passes all frames that travel over the network to the networking software, the network card is considered to be in promiscuous mode. When the Network Monitor is used with a network adapter that supports promiscuous mode, it copies all the frames detected to a capture buffer. This process is termed *capturing*. For more information, see "Network Monitor Capture Window" later in this chapter.

Operation Basics

The Windows NT Server 4 Network Monitor uses a new Network Driver Interface specification (NDIS) version 4 feature to copy all the frames it detects to its capture buffer. Because the Network Monitor uses NDIS 4 rather than promiscuous mode, you can use the Network Monitor even if your network adapter card does not support promiscuous mode. Networking performance is not degraded when you use an NDIS 4 driver to capture frames. A network adapter card in promiscuous mode can add an approximate 30 percent additional load on the CPU.

The Network Monitor can be used to capture network traffic from another computer with a network adapter capable of promiscuous mode operation. In this case, connect to a Network Monitor Agent running on a computer that has a network adapter card capable of promiscuous mode operation, and use the remote Network Monitor Agent to capture. This process is called *remote capturing*.

If your computer uses multiple network adapters, you can use Network Monitor to collect data from all the network adapters. Accomplish this by either switching between the two adapters or by running multiple instances of Network Monitor.

The amount of information the Network Monitor can capture is limited only to the amount of memory in your computer. Most often, you need to capture only a small amount of the network traffic to have enough information to analyze.

The Network Monitor can use capture filters to help narrow down that information contained within the capture file. The use of capture filters can make the task of locating a specific problem much easier. You can filter frames by source and destination addresses, protocols, protocol properties, or by using a pattern offset. For more information, see "Capture Filters" later in this chapter.

You also can configure the Network Monitor to automatically respond to events or a specific set of conditions on your network during the capture process, based on a capture trigger that you design. A capture trigger can perform a specific action such as starting an executable or batch file. For more information, see "Capture Triggers" later in this chapter.

Supported Protocols

The Network Monitor can detect and capture many types of frames transmitted on the network. The Network Monitor uses Protocol Parsers to identify the protocols used to send a frame on to the network. A *Protocol Parser* is a dynamic link library (.DLL) software component that resides in the Netmon directory. When displaying captured frames in the Frame Viewer window, information about these protocols appears. There is a corresponding Protocol Parser for each protocol that the Network Monitor supports.

To capture data sent in a protocol that the Network Monitor does not support by default, you can use the SMS Network Monitor or add a Protocol Parser to the NT 4 Server Network Monitor. If you add a Protocol Parser, for example, the parser must be copied to the C:\WINNT\System32\Netmon directory. You also need to edit the parser/protocol and netmon initialization files, *parser.ini* and *netmon.ini* respectively. In the parser.ini file, add a corresponding entry for the new parser. In the netmon.ini file, add the necessary information as referenced in the netmon.ini example.

The following is an example of a parser.ini initialization file:

```
;=============================================================================
;    Bloodhound parser/protocol initialization file.
;=============================================================================
[PARSERS]
    FRAME.DLL     = 0: FRAME
    MAC.DLL       = 0: ETHERNET, TOKENRING, FDDI, TMAC, SMT
    LLC.DLL       = 0: LLC, RPL, SNAP, BPDU
    NETBIOS.DLL   = 0: NETBIOS
    SMB.DLL       = 0: SMB
    XNS.DLL       = 0: XNS
    IPX.DLL       = 0: IPX, SAP, RIPX, NMPI, NBIPX, SPX,NWDP, NSP, NDR
    TCPIP.DLL     = 0: IP, ARP_RARP, ICMP, IGMP, UDP, NBT,TCP, DNS, FTP, RIP, DHCP,
    ➥RPC, NFS, OSPF, FINGER
    NCP.DLL       = 0: NCP
    ATALK.DLL     = 0: LAP, AARP, DDP, RTMP, NBP, ATP, PAP,ASP, ZIP, AFP, ADSP
    BONE.DLL      = 0: BONE
    MSRPC.DLL     = 0: MSRPC
    BROWSER.DLL   = 0: BROWSER
    NETLOGON.DLL  = 0: NETLOGON
    PPP.DLL       = 0: PPP, LCP, PPPPAP, PPPCHAP, IPXCP,IPCP, NBFCP, CBCP, CCP,
    ➥PPTP, GRE, PPPML, IPXWAN
    ;TPCTL.DLL    = 0: TPCTL
    VINES.DLL     = 0: VINES_IP, VINES_TL
    TRAIL.DLL     = 0: TRAIL, GENERIC, BOOKMARK, STATS,ODBC, MESSAGE, COMMENT
```

The following is an example of a netmon.ini initialization file:

```
;===============================================================================
;   Microsoft Network Monitor Initialization File.
; Copyright 1992,1993,1994
;
; The following sections are configurable.  You can add ETYPES/SAPS and
; Vendor IDs by following the format described above the section.
;===============================================================================
;   KEY NAME        =LABEL[32], Description[128], value1, value2, value3,  ...
[ETYPES]
ETYPE_Netware_802.2 =Netware 802.2,Raw IPX 802.2, FFFF
ETYPE_LOOP          =Loop,Loop back driver,              9000
ETYPE_3COM_NETMAP   =TCP,3Com's TCP,                     9001
ETYPE_3COM_NETMAPXNS=XNS,3Com's XNS,                     9002
ETYPE_IBM_RT        =IBM RT, ,                           80D5
ETYPE_NETWARE       =Netware,Netware on ethernet,        8137
ETYPE_XNS           =XNS,Xerox Network System,      0600, 0807
ETYPE_3COM_NBP      =3Com NBP,
➡3C00, 3C01, 3C02, 3C03, 3C04, 3C05, 3C06, 3C07, 3C08, 3C09, 3C0A
ETYPE_IP            =IP,Internet's Internet Protocol, 0800
ETYPE_ARP           =ARP,Internet's Address Resolution Protocol,    0806
ETYPE_TRLR0         =TRLR,
➡1000, 1001, 1002, 1003, 1004, 1005
ETYPE_PUP           =PUP, ,                    0200
ETYPE_PUP_ARP       =PUP ARP, ,                0201
ETYPE_SNMP          =SNMP,Simple Network Management Protocol,       814C
ETYPE_APPL_TALK_ARP =Appletalk ARP,Apple's Address Resolution Protocol, 80F3
ETYPE_APPL_TALK_LAP =Appletalk LAP, ,                    809B
ETYPE_VINES_IP      =VINES,Banyan Vines IP Protocol, 0BAD, 80C4
;   KEY NAME          = LABEL[32], Description[128], value1, value2, value3,  ...
[SAPS]
SAP_SNAP            =SNAP,Internet's Snap Protocol,      AA
SAP_IBM_NM          =IBM NM,IBM Network Management,      F4
SAP_IBM_NETBIOS     =NetBIOS,IBM Netbios,               F0
SAP_RPL             =RPL,IBM Remote Program Load,       F8, FC
SAP_UB              =UB,Ungerman-Bass,                   FA
SAP_SNA             =SNA,IBM System Network Architecture, 04, 05, 08, 0C
SAP_NETWARE         =Netware SAP,Netware Service Advertising Protocol,
➡10,E0, FE
SAP_IP              =IP,Internet's Internet Protocol,    06
SAP_XNS             =XNS,3Com's version of Xerox Network System,
➡80
SAP_NULL            =NULL,Null SAP,                      00
SAP_BPDU            =BPDU, ,                             42
SAP_VINES_IP        =VINES,Banyan Vines IP Protocol,    BC, BA
[VENDOR_IDS]
; The Vendor ID numbers can only be 6 characters.  The names should fit in 6 chars
; The Vendor IDs listed here are considered additions to the 650+ that are stored
➡ internally.
; example entry list would look like:
; NumberIDs = 1
; VID0= 002211, MyCard
NumberIDs   =0
```

Default Supported Protocols

The following is a list of protocols supported by the NT 4 Server Network Monitor. The SMS Network Monitor supports additional protocols.

AARP	IP	PAP
ADSP	IPCP	PPP
AFP	IPX	PPPCHAP
ARP_RARP	IPXCP	PPPPAP
ASP	LAP	RIP
ATP	LCP	RIPX
BONE	LLC	RPC
BPDU	MSRPC	RPL
BROWSER	NBFCP	RTMP
CBCP	NBIPX	SAP
CCP	NBP	SMB
DDP	NBT	SMT
DHCP	NCP	SNAP
DNS	NDR	SPX
ETHERNET	NetBIOS	TCP
FDDI	NETLOGON	TMAC
FINGER	NFS	TOKENRING
FRAME	NMPI	UDP
FTP	NSP	XNS
ICMP	NWDP	ZIP
IGMP	OSPF	

Installation

Installation of the Network Monitor and the Network Monitoring Agent is performed from within the Network applet, located in the Control Panel. The following steps outline the installation procedure used to install the Network Monitor and the Network Monitor Agent:

1. Open the Control Panel.

2. Double-click the Network applet, located in the Control Panel.

3. Within the Network applet, select the Services tab, and click the Add button.

4. Select Network Monitor Tools and Agent from the list of available services and then click the OK button.

5. Setup will ask you for the location of your NT distribution files. Use the default location, or type a new location, and click the Continue button.

6. Setup copies the necessary files to your computer and configures, restores, and reviews binding information. Click the Close button to continue.

7. You must shut down and restart your computer for the changes to your system to effect.

After restarting your computer, the Monitoring Agent applet is located in the Control Panel, and the Network Monitor is located in the Administrative Tools folder.

Starting the Network Monitor

The Network Monitor is located in the Administrative Tools folder, and may be run from there; you may also start the program from the command prompt. If you start the Network Monitor from the command prompt, a number of command line switches can be used to change the operational characteristics of the program.

When running the Network Monitor from the command prompt, you will find it very useful to begin the command line with the START command. The START command starts a program or command in a separate window; you have greater control of the Network Monitor when using it. When using the START command, for example, you can set the priority of the program with either /LOW, /NORMAL, /HIGH, or /REALTIME.

The following is a list and explanations of command line switches for the START command:

"title"	Title to display in window title bar
path	Starting directory
I	The new environment will be the original environment passed to the cmd.exe and not the current environment.
MIN	Start window minimized
MAX	Start window maximized
SEPARATE	Start 16-bit Windows program in separate memory space
SHARED	Start 16-bit Windows program in shared memory space
LOW	Start application in the IDLE priority class
NORMAL	Start application in the NORMAL priority class
HIGH	Start application in the HIGH priority class
REALTIME	Start application in the REALTIME priority class
WAIT	Start application and wait for it to terminate
B	Start application without creating a new window. The application has ^C handling ignored. Unless the application enables ^C processing, ^Break is the only way to interrupt the application.
command/	If it is an internal cmd command or a program batch file then the command processor is run with the /K switch to cmd.exe. This means that the window will remain after the command has been run. If it is not an internal cmd command or batch file then it is a program and will run as either a windowed application or a console application.
Parameters	These are the parameters passed to the command or program.

Nonexecutable files may be invoked through their file association just by typing the name of the file as a command. (WORD.DOC, for example, launches the application associated with the .DOC file extension.) See the ASSOC and FTYPE commands for how to create these associations from within a command script.

When executing a 32-bit GUI application, CMD.EXE does not wait for the application to terminate before returning to the command prompt. This new behavior does not occur if executing within a command script.

When executing a command line, whose first token is CMD, without an extension or path qualifier, START then replaces CMD with the value of the COMSPEC variable, and thus avoids picking up random versions of CMD.EXE when least expected.

When executing a command line whose first token does *not* contain an extension, CMD.EXE uses the value of the PATHEXT environment variable to determine which extensions to look for and in what order. Following is the default value for the PATHEXT variable:

`.COM;.EXE;.BAT;.CMD`

Notice that the syntax is the same as the PATH variable, with semicolons separating the different elements. When executing a command, if there is no match on any extension, START looks to see whether the name, without any extension, matches a directory name. If it does, the START command launches the Explorer on that path. If done from the command line, it is the equivalent to doing a CD /D to that path.

To start the Network Monitor from the command prompt, you must first change to the Network Monitor's directory, for example, C:\WINNT\System32\Netmon. Then type the following command:

START NETMON [*options*]

The following is a list with explanations of command line switches for the Network Monitor:

/REMOTE *remotename*	Starts the Network Monitor with a connection to the remote Network Monitor Agent that you specify.
/NET *number*	Starts the Network Monitor with a connection to the network number that you specify.
/CAPTUREFILTER *path*	Starts the Network Monitor with a designated capture filter loaded.
/DISPLAYFILTER *path*	Starts the Network Monitor with the designated display filter loaded.
/QUICKFILTER *type,address*	Starts the Network Monitor with the capture ON, with filters on the address specified.
/AUTOSTART	Starts the Network Monitor with capture ON.
/AUTOSTOP	Stops the Network Monitor when the capture buffer becomes full.
/BUFFERSIZE *number*	Starts the Network Monitor with a buffersize specified, in bytes.

Configuring Network Monitor and the Monitoring Agent

Configuration of the Network Monitor is primarily performed within the Network Monitor program itself. The associated configuration component that configures the Network Monitoring Agent is called the Monitoring Agent. The Monitoring Agent is an applet, and is located within the Control Panel (see fig. 14.1).

Figure 14.1

The Monitoring Agent applet in the Control Panel.

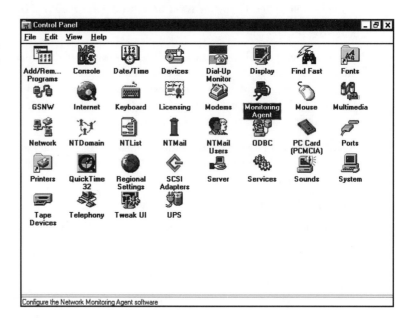

Monitoring Agent

The Monitoring Agent, located in the Control Panel, is used to set, change, capture, and display passwords for the Network Monitor and the Network Monitor Agent. It also is used to describe network cards and to reset the Network Monitor to installation defaults. Figure 14.2 shows the Network Monitoring Agent configuration window.

Capture and Display Passwords

You can use the Monitoring Agent applet in the Control Panel to change the capture password for the Network Monitor Agent and to display the password for Network Monitor. It is highly recommended that you use passwords for the Network Monitor and Agent. When you use capture and display passwords, you safeguard your network data from unauthorized access. If the Network Monitor is installed on your computer with the Monitoring Agent service running and if no password is set, anyone using the SMS Network Monitor can connect to your computer and use it to capture from your network.

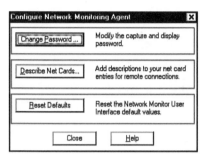

Figure 14.2
Configure Network Monitoring Agent dialog box.

If you use a capture password, only authorized users can capture statistics from the network and display captured data. If you use a display password, only authorized users can open previously saved capture (.CAP) files.

If you install both the Network Monitor and the Network Monitor Agent, the capture and display passwords apply to both components. Figure 14.3 shows the Network Monitor Password Change window.

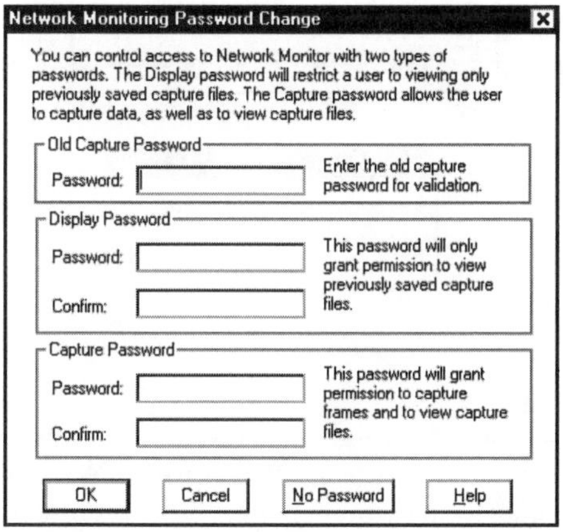

Figure 14.3
The Network Monitoring Password Change dialog box.

Describing Network Cards

The Network Monitoring Agent has an option to describe network cards. You will find this option to be extremely valuable, especially when multiple network cards are installed in the computer. When using the SMS Network Monitor to remotely access the Network Monitor Agent running on your computer, for example, having a description makes it easy to identify which network card and which computer is being used to capture frames. Figure 14.4 shows the Describe Net Cards dialog box.

Reset Defaults

The Reset Defaults option can be used to reset the Network Monitor settings to installation defaults. When learning or experimenting with Network Monitor filtering options, even the veteran Network Monitor user can, at times, find the configuration options overwhelming. If the Network Monitor is not capturing or displaying the data that you expect, most often the best course of action will be to reset to defaults and then reconfigure. You will find the option to be of great value, especially during the process of learning how to use the Network Monitor. Figure 14.5 shows the Reset Defaults confirmation dialog box.

Figure 14.4

The Describe Net Cards dialog box.

Figure 14.5

The Reset Defaults confirmation box.

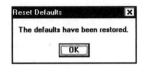

Network Monitor

Operation of the Network Monitor is centered around the process of capturing. Capturing occurs when a network card passes on a subset of network frames to the Network Monitor. The Network Monitor stores these frames in the capture buffer. If the capture buffer over-flows, the most recent frame added to the buffer replaces the oldest frame. To prevent the capture buffer from overflowing and to make frame analysis easier, you use a capture filter. The capture filter enables you to capture only those frames that meet parameters you define. To have a running capture respond to events on your network as soon as they are detected, you can design a capture trigger.

The following sections discuss the operation of the Network Monitor, working with the capture window, and creating capture filters and triggers.

Network Monitor Capture Window

When frames are captured from the network, statistics about the frames display in the Network Monitor Capture window.

Frames captured from the network are copied to the Network Monitor's capture buffer. The capture buffer is reserved storage area in memory. Information about these captured frames displays in the Network Monitor capture window, as the frames are captured. The capture process can be controlled by choosing Start, Stop, Stop and View, Pause, or Continue from the Capture menu.

The Network Monitor Capture window includes the following panes:

Graph	Graphical representation of the activity currently taking place on the network
Session Stats	Statistics about individual sessions currently taking place on the network
Station Stats	Statistics about the sessions participated in by the computer running Network Monitor
Total Stats	Summary statistics about the network activity detected since the capture process was started

Figure 14.6 shows the Network Monitor Capture Window, with sample capture statistics.

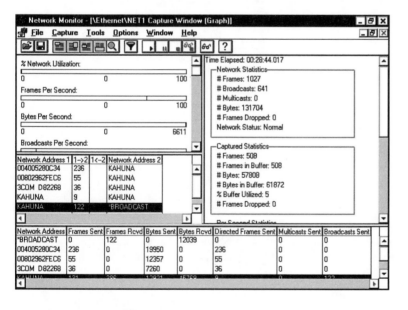

Figure 14.6
The Network Monitor Capture Window.

Capture Buffer Settings

Captured frames are stored in the capture buffer. When the capture buffer becomes full, each new frame replaces the oldest frame in the buffer.

The following four factors affect the rate in which capture buffer will be filled:

Capture Buffer Size	Can be set from within the Network Monitor or set from the command line
Frame Size	Set within the Network Monitor
Capture Filter	Can be set from within the Network Monitor or set from the command line
Volume of Network Traffic	Cannot be adjusted

The Network Monitor can display session statistics from the first 100 unique network sessions that it detects. If you have more than 100 network sessions that you need to monitor, you can reset the statistics and view information on the next 100 network sessions. To reset statistics, click on Clear Statistics, located on the Capture menu.

Figure 14.7 shows the Capture pull-down menu.

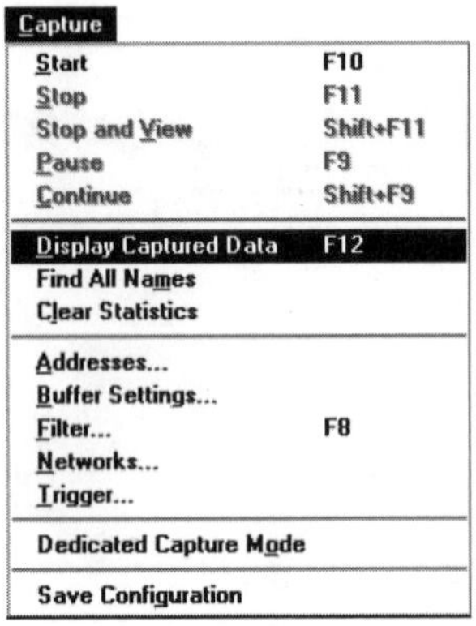

Figure 14.7

The Network Monitor Capture pull-down menu.

Capture	
Start	F10
Stop	F11
Stop and View	Shift+F11
Pause	F9
Continue	Shift+F9
Display Captured Data	F12
Find All Names	
Clear Statistics	
Addresses...	
Buffer Settings...	
Filter...	F8
Networks...	
Trigger...	
Dedicated Capture Mode	
Save Configuration	

Capture Buffer Size

During the capture process, the capture buffer is stored in memory, not on disk. The capture buffer can be saved to disk after the capture has been stopped. Even though the Network Monitor can use virtual memory to store a capture buffer, you run the risk of dropping frames if the Network Monitor accesses virtual memory.

To ensure that frames are not dropped, you should use a capture buffer large enough to retain the necessary information needed for analysis—but not exceeding available real memory limitations. The default maximum capture buffer size is 8 MB less than the amount of RAM installed on your computer.

If you notice an increase in the Dropped Frames count located in the Capture Window Total Stats pane, your first course of action should be to reduce the size of the capture buffer. If this does not reduce the Dropped Frames count, you can place the Network Monitor in dedicated mode. For more information, see "Capture Filters." Figure 14.8 shows the Capture Buffer Settings dialog box.

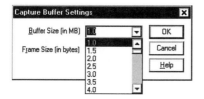

Figure 14.8

Setting the capture buffer size in the Capture Buffer Settings dialog box.

Frame Size

When you are interested in capturing the frame information only, and not necessarily the data being transmitted, you can reduce the frame size to match the size of the frame header. This reduces the overall size of the capture buffer. If you are interested in only the data in the frame header, for example, set the Frame Size (in bytes) to the size of the header frame. The Network Monitor discards the frame data as it stores frames in the capture buffer. Figure 14.9 shows Capture Buffer Settings, which may be selected.

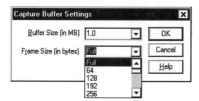

Figure 14.9

Setting the frame size in the Capture Buffer Settings dialog box.

Capture Filters

Capture Filters are relatively easy to design. A capture filter is used when desiring to keep the content of the capture file limited to specific criteria. A capture filter functions much like a database query and is used to specify the types of network information you want to monitor. If you want to see only a specific subset of computers or protocols, for example, you can create an address database. You can use the address database to add addresses to a filter and then save the filter to a file. By filtering frames, you save time and buffer resources. If you frequently use the Network Monitor, you should get into the practice of saving specific capture filters for later re-use.

To create a capture filter, you must specify decision-related statements in the Capture Filter dialog box. The Capture Filter dialog box displays the filter's decision tree, which is a graphical representation of a filter's logic. When you include or exclude information from your capture specifications, the decision tree reflects these specifications.

Often, to diagnose a problem related to a specific computer, you need to capture frames that originate from the specific computer. To be able to do this, you must know the addresses of the computers on your network. The Network Monitor can associate a computer's hexadecimal address with a name that is more familiar. After the name associations are made, you can save the names to an address database (.ADR) file that you can use to design capture filters and display filters. For more information, see "Displaying Captured Data" and "Designing a Display Filter" later in this chapter. Figure 14.10 shows the Capture Filter dialog box.

Figure 14.10
The Capture Filter dialog box.

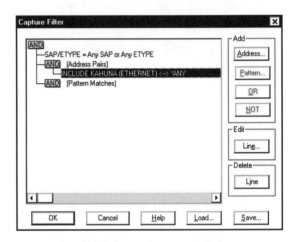

You will notice that in addition to setting a sufficient buffer size and capture filter, you can place the Network Monitor into Dedicated Capture mode. When you place the Network Monitor in Dedicated Capture mode, the Network Monitor Capture window statistics are replaced by the Dedicated Mode dialog box (see fig. 14.11).

Figure 14.11
The Dedicated Mode dialog box.

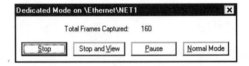

When the Network Monitor is in Dedicated Capture mode, the Network Monitor does not have to update and display the capture windows statistics. The load on the CPU is greatly reduced; therefore, the chances of dropping frames are reduced. It is recommended to use this option on a busy computer.

Protocol Filtering

The Network Monitor has the capability to capture frames transmitted using a specific protocol. To capture frames sent using a specific protocol, specify the protocol on the capture filter SAP/ETYPE= line. To capture only IP frames, for example, you must disable all other protocols and then enable IP ETYPE 0x800 and IP SAP 0x6. By default, all the protocols that the Network Monitor supports are enabled. Figure 14.12 shows the Network Monitor Capture Filter SAPs and ETYPEs configuration window.

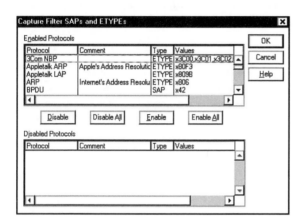

Figure 14.12

The Network Monitor Capture Filter SAPs and ETYPEs dialog box.

Address Filtering

To capture frames from specific computers on your network, specify one or more address pairs in a capture filter. You can monitor up to four specific address pairs simultaneously. When using the SMS Network Monitor, the address pairs can be any computers on the network. The address pairs do not need to include the address of the computer running the Network Monitoring Agent.

An address pair consists of the following:

■ The addresses of the two computers between which you want to monitor traffic. An address is a hexadecimal number that identifies a computer on the network.

■ Arrows that specify the direction of traffic you want to monitor.

■ INCLUDE or EXCLUDE keyword that indicates how the Network Monitor should respond to a frame that meets a filter's criteria.

When using EXCLUDE statements, EXCLUDE statements are evaluated first, regardless of the sequence in which statements appear in the Capture Filter dialog box. If a frame meets the criteria specified in an EXCLUDE statement in a filter containing both an EXCLUDE and INCLUDE STATEMENT, the frame is discarded. The Network Monitor will not test the frame by INCLUDE statements to see if it meets that criteria also. If you want to capture all the traffic from Bill's computer except the traffic from Bill to Programming, for example, use the filter addresses in the following example:

```
Addresses:
include    Bill    ANY
exclude    Bill    Programming
```

In the preceding example, if no include lines are entered, ANY is used by default. Figure 14.13 shows the Network Monitor Capture Filter Include line in the Address Expression configuration window.

Figure 14.13

The Network Monitor Capture Filter Include line in the Address Expression configuration window.

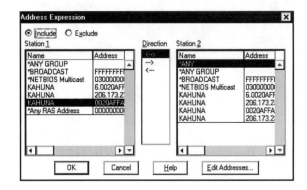

Data Pattern Filtering

Pattern filtering is an advanced feature of the Network Monitor. When you specify a pattern match in a capture filter, you can perform the following:

- Limit captures to only those frames containing a specific pattern of ASCI or hexadecimal data.

- Explicitly specify how many bytes into the frame the pattern must occur. The number of bytes specified is known as an offset.

When you filter captured frames based on a pattern match, you must specify where the pattern occurs in the frame. You must specify in which direction the count for the pattern will start, from the beginning or the end. If your network media has a variable size in the media access control (MAC) protocol, such as Ethernet or Token Ring, you should specify to count from the end of the topology header. Figure 14.14 shows the Network Monitor Capture Filter, Pattern Match dialog box.

Capture Triggers

A *capture trigger* is a set of conditions that initiate an action. When the conditions of the trigger are met, the trigger fires. Before using Network Monitor to capture data from the network, for example, you can set a trigger to stop the capture or to execute a program or command file when the trigger criteria is met. You can also specify the conditions under which the actions will occur.

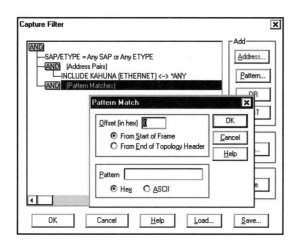

Figure 14.14
The Network Monitor Capture Filter, Pattern Match dialog box.

You can use one of the following trigger types to specify the condition that starts the trigger:

Nothing	Select this option to specify that no trigger is initiated. This condition is the default.
Pattern Match	Select this option to initiate the trigger when the specified pattern occurs in a captured frame.
Buffer Space	Select this option to initiate the trigger when a specified amount of the capture buffer is filled.
Pattern Match Then Buffer Space	Select this option to initiate the trigger when the pattern occurs and is followed by a specified percentage of the capture buffer.
Buffer Space Then Pattern Match	Select this option to initiate the trigger when the specified percent age of the capture buffer fills and is followed by the occurrence of the pattern in a captured frame.

When a trigger action is met, you can specify to have one of the following actions occur:

No Action	Select this option to specify that no action is taken when a trigger condition is met. This is the default. When you select No Action, the computer beeps when the trigger condition is met.
Stop Capture	Select this option to stop the capture process when the trigger condition is met.

Execute Command Line

Select this option to run a program or batch file when a trigger condition is met. If you select this option, you must provide a command or the path to a program or batch file.

Figure 14.15 shows the Network Monitor Capture Trigger dialog box with default settings.

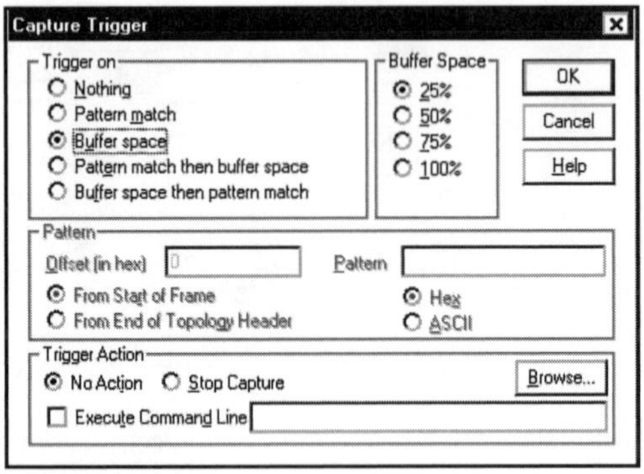

Figure 14.15

The Network Monitor Capture Trigger dialog box.

Saving Captured Data

When you save captured data, the data in the capture buffer is written to a capture (.CAP) file. The capture file can be retrieved for later analysis. You should make it a regular procedure to save your capture files for the following reasons:

■ When you start another capture, the current capture will be lost unless you save the capture to a file.

■ You may want to analyze the data at later time.

■ You may need to document a network problem or network usage.

In addition to choosing a file name, when saving captured data to a file, you can specify the range of frames you want to save. If the data you want to save is found within a small range of frames, you can select the range of frames to reduce the size of the saved capture file. The Network Monitor calculates the total number of frames in the capture buffer and displays the total in the Range option of the Save Data as window. Figure 14.16 shows the Network Monitor Save Data as window, with a sample range from 1 to 166.

Capture files can be opened later and viewed in the Frame Viewer window. For more information, see "Displaying Captured Data" later in this chapter.

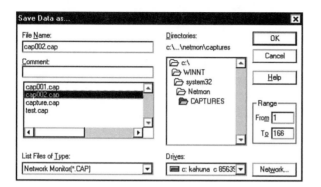

Figure 14.16
Network Monitor saving captured data.

Network Monitor Security

For reasons of security, the Windows NT Server 4 Network Monitor captures frames, including broadcast and multicast frames, sent only to or from the local computer. The SMS Network Monitor has the capability to capture frames sent to or from any computers on the network. Network Monitor also displays overall network segment statistics for broadcast frames, multicast frames, network utilization, total bytes received per second, and total frames received per second.

The Network Monitor uses a new network driver interface specification (NDIS) version 4 feature to copy all the frames it detects to its capture buffer.

To help protect your network from unauthorized use of Network Monitor installations, Network Monitor has the following security related features:

- Password protection

- The capability to detect other installations of the Network Monitor on the LAN segment.

Password Protection and Network Monitoring Detection

The Network Monitor has a configuration option that enables the use of passwords for the processes of capturing and displaying captured data. The Monitoring Agent applet, located in the Control Panel, is used to set passwords for the Network Monitor. Unique passwords can be set for each process, both Capture and Display. If you set the same password for both processes, for example, when a user runs the Network Monitor and enters the password, access to the Capture and Display processes will be granted. If you set unique passwords for each process, for example, users given the Capture password only will not be allowed to display the captured data. The use of passwords to access Network Monitor's capture and display processes is optional. To protect the integrity of data on your network, the use of passwords for the Network Monitor Capture and Display processes should be considered mandatory.

To protect your network from unauthorized monitoring, the Network Monitor can detect other installations of the Network Monitor on the LAN segment. The Network Monitor also detects the presence of other Network Monitor Agents and the Windows NT Performance Monitor capturing data remotely on your network.

When Network Monitor detects other Network Monitor installations on the network, it displays the following information about them:

- Name of the computer

- User name accessing the computer

- Operational state of the Network Monitor running on the remote computer (either Driver Installed, Running, Capturing, or Transmitting)

- Network adapter address of the remote computer

- Version number of the Network Monitor running on the remote computer

The capability of the Network Monitor to locate other installations of the Network Monitor is not guaranteed. Some kinds of network architecture can inhibit the Network Monitor from detecting another. If an installation is separated from yours by a router that does not forward multicasts, for example, your installation will not be able to detect that installation of the Network Monitor.

Displaying Captured Data

The Network Monitor displays captured data in the Frame Viewer window, which is an easy-to-read graphical interface to the raw data. The Frame Viewer window simplifies data analysis.

To display captured information in the Frame Viewer window, choose Stop and View from the Capture menu while the capture is running. Alternatively, you can open a previously saved capture (.CAP) file.

The Frame Viewer window includes the following panes:

Detail	Frame content, including the protocols used to transmit it
Hex	A hexadecimal and ASCII representation of the captured data
Summary	General information about the captured frames, presented in the order in which they were captured

Figure 14.17 shows the Network Monitor Frame Viewer Window, with sample captured data.

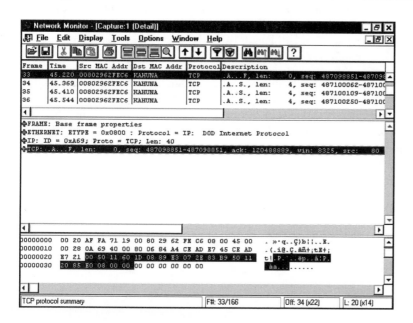

Figure 14.17
*The Network Monitor
Frame Viewer window.*

Designing a Display Filter

Display Filters are extremely useful and make the task of analyzing captured data easier. A Display filter functions much like a database query and is used to specify the types of network information you want to display. A display filter operates on data that has been previously captured and will not affect the Network Monitor capture buffer content.

When designing a display filter, expression/decision statements in the Display Filter dialog box must be specified. Information in the Display Filter dialog box is depicted in the form of an expression/decision tree, which is a graphical representation of a filter's logic. When modifying a display filter, the expression/decision tree will become a visible reference for the modifications.

When using a display filter to determine which frames to display, you can configure the filter by the following criteria:

Address	The default is ANY <—> ANY. Address filter lines are used to specify the computer addresses, from which you want to display data.
Protocol	Protocol lines are used to specify the desired protocols or protocol properties.
Property	The Property option, is used to specify property instances that match your display criteria. Three configuration components can be chosen.

Three configuration components can be chosen: Protocol Property, Relation, and Value. A Protocol Property is a data field within a protocol header. A Relation specifies the correlation between the Protocol Property and its possible Value. A Value displays the possible value to which the highlighted Property is compared. Figure 14.18 shows the Network Monitor Display Filter dialog box configured as default.

When adding to the display filter, you can add only one expression/decision statement at a time. If you specify an expression/decision statement and proceed to select another category, the previously selected expression/decision statement will be lost. To save the specified expression statement, each time an expression/decision statement is added, you must click the OK button. Newly added expression/decision statements will be added to the expression/ decision tree.

Figure 14.18

The Network Monitor Display Filter dialog box.

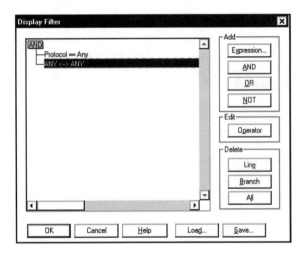

As discussed in the "Capture Filters" section of this chapter, capture filters are limited to four address filter pairs. Display filters are not restricted by the same limitations. With display filters, multiple logical Expressions of AND, OR, and NOT can also be used. Figure 14.19 shows the Network Monitor Display Filter, Expression window.

Display Filtering by Address

To display frames from specific computers on your network, specify one or more address pairs in a display filter. You can display many specific address pairs simultaneously. When using the SMS Network Monitor, the address pairs can be any computers on the network. The address pairs do not need to include the address of the computer running the Network Monitoring Agent.

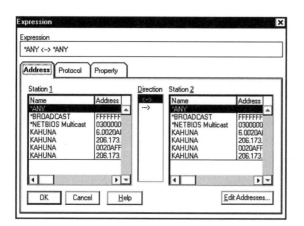

Figure 14.19

The Network Monitor Address Filter, Expression window.

An address pair consists of the following:

■ The addresses of the two computers between which you want to display traffic. An address is a hexadecimal number that identifies a computer on the network.

■ Arrows that specify the direction of traffic you want to monitor.

Display Filtering by Protocol

Frames can be displayed by specifying the protocol type. To display frames sent using a specific protocol, specify the protocol on the display filter Protocol == line. To display only IP frames, for example, disable all protocols and then enable IP and IPCP. By default, all the protocols that Network Monitor supports are enabled. Figure 14.20 shows the Network Monitor Display Protocol Filter configuration window.

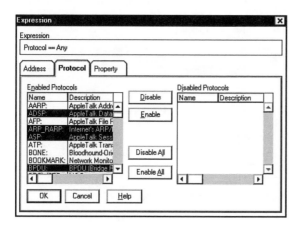

Figure 14.20

The Network Monitor Display Protocol Filter window.

Display Filtering by Protocol Property

When setting the criteria for Protocol Property, three possible components or elements of information define a protocol's purpose. Protocol properties differ from one protocol to another. To filter by protocol property, click on Expression within the Add area in the Display Filter dialog box. Click on the Property tab and then specify the protocol property, relation, and value to filter.

If a capture file is large and contains thousands of IP protocol frames, for example, a property filter can be used to further limit the selection of displayed IP protocol frames to match a specific property. To examine only those frames in which the IP protocol was used to create a directory on your computer, you can single out frames where the SMB command property is equal to *make directory*.

To accomplish the preceding example, follow this procedure:

1. From the Display Filter screen, double-click on the entry on the expression/decision tree that you want to modify, or click on the Expression button to create a new expression/decision.

2. Select the Protocol tab. Within the Protocol list, choose the IP protocol.

3. Select the Property tab (see fig. 14.21). Within the Protocol: Property list, select *SMB* Protocol. Within the Relation list, select == (equals). Within the Value field, enter **make directory**.

4. To save the expression/decision, click on OK.

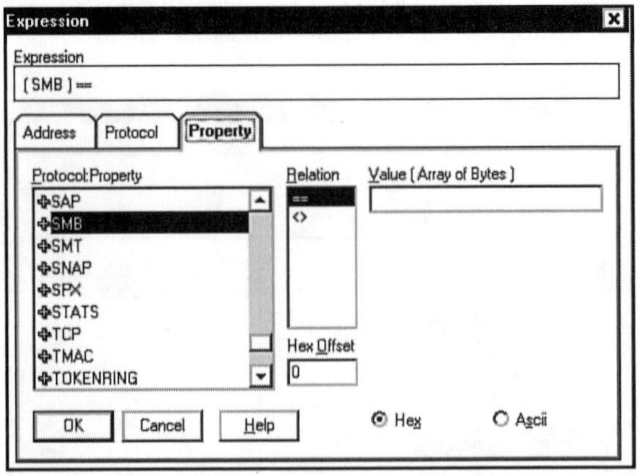

Figure 14.21

Network Monitor Protocol Property Filter sheet tab.

Network Monitor Help

The Network Monitor Help, contained within the program itself, contains procedures to guide you through the tasks relating to the information covered in this chapter. Two types of additional Help are available: Property and Protocol.

Online Property Help is located on the Help pull-down menu. Property Help contains a protocol command reference. To obtain Property Help, a Property must be selected in the Detail pane.

Protocol Help includes an introduction to the SMB protocol and also includes the contents of the SMB protocol specification. Figure 14.22 shows the Network Monitor Help pull-down menu.

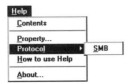

Figure 14.22
The Network Monitor Help pull-down menu.

Conclusion

In this chapter, you learned about the advanced configuration issues related to Network Monitor. Many of the concepts needed to understand the configuration of the Network Monitor were discussed.

The configuration procedures discussed in this chapter should suffice for the majority of installation situations.

Optimization

Windows NT and Performance Tuning

As with any computer solution, the performance of your applications on Windows NT depends on the marriage of hardware and software on your system. A good match of the two provides you with a cost-effective computing solution. However, a mismatch results in either inefficient use of resources or inadequate performance. In many environments, performance optimization is an art known only by experts that requires knowledge of little-known configuration parameters.

Fortunately, Windows NT 4 has many self-optimizing characteristics that do not require user intervention. A typical installation with some simple planning by the administrator gets decent performance without configuring obscure parameters in the Registry. Windows NT 4 also provides a useful tool, the Performance Monitor, for monitoring and analyzing activities within your system.

However, the choices that you make about the hardware on which you run your application make a tremendous difference in performance. If you experience a performance problem such as slow response time on a network application, how do you know where the problem lies? Should you get a faster processor? More memory? Or move some of your data from one disk to another? After you understand how to monitor and interpret performance data provided by Windows NT 4, you can make informed choices about the hardware on which to run your applications.

This chapter provides you with a basic understanding of the steps involved in getting the best possible performance from Windows NT Server. Two related chapters provide additional information: Chapter 16 covers capacity planning, and Chapter 17 is a tutorial on the Performance Monitor.

Defining Performance Optimization

Optimal performance is simple to define: to complete a task in the shortest amount of time. Optimizing the performance of a system is a matter of arranging the resources of the system in such a way that the desired task is finished as quickly as possible. It means getting the best results with the hardware and software you have.

Optimization of a task on your system, then, consists of measuring and analyzing the resource demands created by the task in order to determine what can make your system finish the task in a shorter period of time.

Before you can get optimal performance from your system, however, you need to answer a very important question: What task or tasks on the system are most important? Do you want to optimize the utilization of the hardware or the speed of a particular application or service? The answers to these questions determine what you should measure and how to decide whether your performance is optimal.

Performance Objectives

The first step in optimizing system performance is defining your performance objective. On a file server, for example, the objective might be to service requests from clients for files as quickly as possible. By measuring the number of bytes transferred to all the server's clients across the network in a given period of time, you can tell whether the changes you made to the system's configuration made performance better or worse.

On the other hand, what is optimal performance for a primary domain controller that is responsible for replicating a large account database to many backup domain controllers? In this case, the objective might be to achieve synchronization of the account database throughout the WAN in a timely manner with the minimum amount of network traffic. To know whether performance is optimal, you need to measure two things: the amount of time it takes for changes to the account database to be implemented on all domain controllers and the amount of network traffic generated by the domain synchronization.

Optimizing performance of a database server might include this objective: "Provide the fastest response time for queries against the customer service database." If your goal is to make the database task complete as quickly as possible, regardless of the impact on other processes on the system, optimization can result in non-database tasks running more slowly than before.

Yet another performance goal might be to make the most efficient use of resources to get the greatest amount of work completed by all processes on the system. To achieve this goal, you need to optimize overall throughput and efficiency, making sure that processes do not get blocked by bottlenecks created by other processes.

After you have optimized performance of your application (that is, after you've gotten the best performance from the hardware and software you have), the next question is whether that level of performance meets your business goals. You may have the best performance possible with your existing system, but to get adequate performance you may need to upgrade one or more components, such as memory, disk, or processor.

The best way to pinpoint what can be done to improve performance is to measure it. Gathering data on how your system performs under various circumstances gives you the necessary information to make appropriate changes to your system.

Self-Tuning in Windows NT

One of Microsoft's design goals for Windows NT is that a user should not have to make changes to Registry settings to get good performance. One problem when optimizing performance with any operating system is that what is considered to be optimal configuration changes as the demands on the system fluctuate. For example, how large should the paging file be? At one point in the day, a large paging file might be optimal, whereas a few hours or minutes later a smaller paging file might be optimal.

Asking users and administrators to make frequent configuration changes is not practical, and yet leaving a static configuration would inevitably lead to inefficiencies. Microsoft decided to let the operating system itself evaluate settings—such as the size of the disk cache and paging file—and adjust them dynamically as resource demands change.

As a result, Windows NT does most of the optimizing of overall system performance without requiring manual changes to Registry parameters. For example, Windows NT dynamically adjusts the balance between the size of the disk cache and the amount of RAM used for applications in response to resource demands on the system.

Reasons to Monitor Performance

Although there is little to tune within Windows NT 4 itself, you should monitor system performance for several reasons.

Optimizing Specific Tasks

If you have a particular application on your server that you want to optimize, monitoring system performance can tell you if changing your hardware enables your application to run faster. It can also uncover contention by multiple applications for resources.

For example, if you are setting up a database server, performance data can tell you whether you have excess capacity to handle additional work, or whether you have a resource shortage that is affecting performance. If other applications are competing for the same resources as your database application, you can move the other applications to another server that is less busy.

Troubleshooting Performance Problems

One of the most difficult kinds of performance problems to troubleshoot is diagnosing transient network problems. A sudden increase in interrupts generated by a malfunctioning network card can bring server performance to a screeching halt as the processor handles all the interrupts. If you monitor key indicators of network performance (number of errors, number of interrupts processed), you can be alerted of problems as they occur.

Planning for Future Needs

Another reason to monitor performance is because monitoring allows you to detect changes in the way that the server is being used by users. If users are using a file server more frequently to store very large files, for example, the increased demands for file services can be measured and documented.

By anticipating changes in demand for the server's resources, you can take appropriate action before performance suffers.

Planning your hardware needs for servers is covered in Chapter 16, "Capacity Planning."

Configuration Changes That Affect Performance

You can, however, change many things that affect overall system performance. All strategies described in the following sections have the effect of shifting the demands for resources to achieve higher throughput.

Adding or Upgrading Hardware Components

An obvious way to affect the performance of your system is to add or change hardware components. The benefits you obtain from changing the hardware depend on how your application uses resources on the system.

If the processor is the bottleneck on your system, you could enhance system performance by one or more of the following processor upgrades:

■ Upgrade the speed of the processor

■ Add another processor (for example, two Pentium processors on a SMP system)

■ Add a co-processor if your application can use it

■ Upgrade the secondary cache

Another hardware component that can dramatically affect performance is system memory. Keep in mind the following two key points regarding memory and Windows NT:

■ Add more RAM. Having adequate RAM reduces the need for paging memory to and from the hard disk.

■ Shadowing of the ROM BIOS in RAM does not improve performance under Windows NT 4, so disabling this feature can make more memory available to the system.

Some common configuration changes that affect disk performance include the following:

■ Replace slow disks with faster ones

■ Use NTFS for partitions larger than 400 MB

■ Use a defragmentation tool if disks become fragmented

■ Use a controller with the highest possible transfer rate and best multitasking functionality

■ Isolate disk I/O intensive tasks on separate physical disks or disk controllers

■ Create a stripe set to gain the advantage of simultaneous writes to multiple disks if your hardware can support it

Changes to the network components that affect performance include the following:

■ Get a network card with the widest data bus available on your system. For example, if your system has a PCI bus, use a PCI network adapter instead of an ISA adapter. This consideration is especially important for network servers.

■ Divide your network into multiple networks, attaching the server to each network with a different adapter. Allocating the server requests across the two separate interfaces can reduce congestion at the server.

To improve the performance of a fault tolerant system, consider the following configuration changes:

■ If you are using software-based fault tolerance (striping with parity or RAID 5), use a hardware-based solution instead. Using RAID 5 implemented in hardware relieves the processor of calculating the parity information.

■ If the goal is the greatest availability of data, you could consider mirroring (via Windows NT fault tolerant drivers) two hardware-based RAID 5 arrays. There are also solutions for Windows NT 4 for mirroring entire servers, such as Octopus from Octopus Technologies.

Removing Unnecessary Software Components

To optimize your system, you can remove any software components that are using precious processor and memory resources. These software components fall into three categories: device drivers, network protocols, and services.

Device Drivers

Any drivers loaded into memory that are not used should be removed. For example, if you have a SCSI driver loaded for a non-existent adapter, remove it. If you have an extra network adapter installed, but it is not currently connected to the network, remove the driver.

> **Warning** Be extremely careful when removing or disabling components in Windows NT 4. Removing the wrong components can make your system unstable or prevent it from booting. If you remove one of NT's standard drivers by mistake, you can run the Windows NT 4 Setup program (WINNT.EXE or WINNT32.EXE) to refresh the system files.

Network Protocols

Remove any unnecessary network protocols. For example, if all your systems can communicate by using NWLink, remove NetBEUI. Loading protocols that are not needed increases network traffic and processing overhead without improving performance.

You can remove the bindings for a protocol selectively, rather than remove the entire protocol component, by using the Bindings option in Control Panel Network (as shown in fig. 15.1).

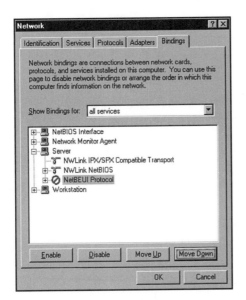

Figure 15.1

The Bindings option in Control Panel Network enables you to unbind network components from each other.

In figure 15.1, the symbol beside NetBEUI Protocol indicates that it has been unbound from the Server service. This server will no longer service file and print requests that come via NetBEUI.

Services

Any services that this server does not need to provide should be disabled or configured to start manually. If a server will not be providing print services, for example, you can disable the Spooler service.

The list of installed services is displayed by double-clicking the Services option in the Control Panel (see fig. 15.2).

Figure 15.2

The Services dialog box displays a list of services and their current status. By disabling unneeded services, you can free up wasted processor and memory resources.

Tip

You can start and stop services from the command prompt. For example, to stop the Spooler service, type **net stop spooler**. To start the Spooler service, type **net start spooler**. You can combine the net start command with the AT command to start and stop services as needed, either locally or on another system by typing **at \\myserver 12:00 net start spooler**. This technique is useful when certain services are needed across slow WAN links only at certain times of the day, such as directory replication. To control the way the service behaves, you can create a batch file that uses REGINI (from the Windows NT Resource Kit) to modify the Registry and then start the service with the new settings.

Replacing Inefficient Software

It may not be possible to make a particular application run faster if your system has applications or drivers that make inefficient use of system resources. A poorly coded application or device driver can adversely affect performance of the entire system.

If your performance monitoring uncovers a software component that makes unacceptably large resource demands, the solution is to replace the offending software.

Changing Windows NT Performance Parameters

A few settings in Windows NT are relatively easy to change and can make a substantial difference in performance. These changes can be made via the Control Panel.

Optimizing the Paging File

The virtual memory manager in Windows NT is responsible for managing all the memory pages on the system, including physical memory (RAM) and virtual memory (the paging file). When an application makes a reference to a page of memory that is not currently located in physical RAM, a page fault occurs. Excessive paging activity dramatically affects overall system performance. Adding RAM reduces the need for paging, so when in doubt, add more RAM!

You can set the size of the paging file by changing the Virtual Memory setting on the Performance tab in Control Panel. When the system is started, Windows NT creates a paging file (PAGEFILE.SYS) and sets its size to the minimum value in the Virtual Memory dialog box (see fig. 15.3). The Virtual Memory Manager then monitors system activity and can increase the size of the paging file up to the maximum value if it determines that paging would be more efficient.

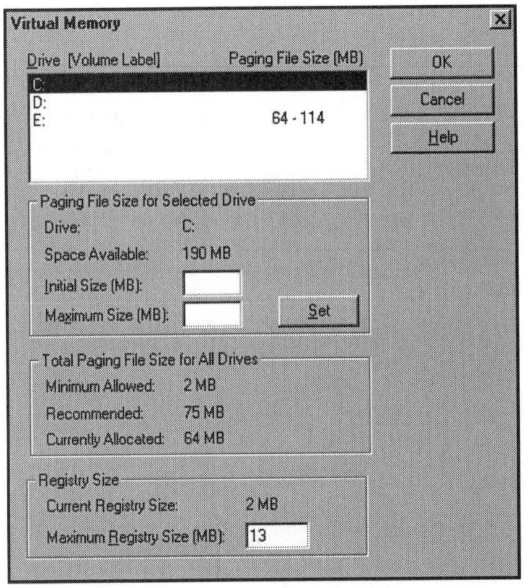

Figure 15.3

The Virtual Memory dialog box contains settings for the size and location of the paging file.

The paging file can be located on one or more local hard disks. If you specify a paging file size for more than one disk (for example, 30 MB on C and 30 MB on D), then the Virtual Memory Manager writes memory pages to the paging files on both physical disks.

Some general recommendations regarding the virtual memory settings are as follows:

■ Consider spreading the paging file across multiple disks if your hardware supports writing to those disks at the same time.

■ Move the paging file to the disk(s) with the lowest amount of total disk activity.

■ If you plan to use Windows NT's Recovery feature, which saves the contents of memory in a file on disk if a stop error occurs, then your swap file has to be larger than the amount of physical RAM present on the system.

■ Monitor the size of the paging file under peak usage and then set the minimum size to that value. Making the minimum paging file size large enough eliminates the need for virtual memory manager to increase its size (and saves processor cycles).

■ To determine the amount of RAM to add to reduce paging activity, use a tool such as Performance Monitor or Process Viewer to determine the amount of memory needed by each application. Remove applications (noting their working set sizes) until paging activity is within acceptable limits. The amount of memory freed up by terminating those applications is the amount of physical RAM that is needed on the system.

Use of the Performance Monitor and Process Viewer are described in the "Measuring System Performance" section later in this chapter.

Optimizing the Server Service

Another setting that can affect performance is the configuration of the Server service. You can access the Server dialog box by selecting Server on the Services tab in Control Panel Network and then choosing Properties (see fig. 15.4). By default, Windows NT Server 4 is configured to work best as a file server for 64 or more users. Changing the Server service settings adjusts the amount of RAM and other resources that are allocated for the server service to use. Table 15.1 provides a description of each setting.

Figure 15.4

The configuration of the Server service adjusts the resources used to handle remote file and print requests.

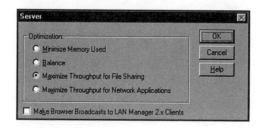

Table 15.1
Server Service Optimization

Setting	Description
Minimize Memory Used	Up to 10 remote users
Balance	Up to 64 remote users
Maximize Throughput for File Sharing	64 or more users, large file cache (for file servers)
Maximize Throughput for Network Applications	64 or more users, small file cache (for application servers)

Optimizing Other Services

Other services on your system may have Registry settings that need adjustment for optimal performance. Table 15.2 lists some common values for standard Windows NT services that are good starting points for evaluation.

If you have installed additional services on your system, research the Registry parameters associated with those services for performance enhancement opportunities.

Table 15.2

Some Common Registry Values for Standard Windows NT Services

Service	Value
Net Logon	Pulse
	Pulse Concurrency
	Pulse Maximum
	Replication Governor
Directory Replication	Interval
	Guard Time
Computer Browser	Hidden
	IsDomainMaster
	MaintainServerList
Spooler	DefaultSpoolDirectory
	PriorityClass

Rescheduling Resource-Intensive Tasks

Demands for resources on a server often fluctuate widely at different times of day. A server running an accounting package has its greatest demands at the end of an accounting period. A logon server typically experiences a spike in authentication requests at the beginning of the day. Print servers often experience heaviest demands during late morning and late afternoon. Shifting some of the demand from the peak period to other times can help alleviate the load on the server. In addition, any task that competes for resources with your primary application should be scheduled for non-peak hours.

> **Tip**
>
> Changing the relative priority of tasks can make a big difference when you have multiple applications running.
>
> Normally, Windows NT gives the foreground application more processor time than background applications. You can change this behavior by setting the Application Performance on the Performance tab in Control Panel. For example, if you set the performance boost for the foreground application to "None," foreground and background applications are scheduled with the same relative priority.
>
> Whether or not you want to boost the performance of the foreground task depends on what else you are doing on the system. On a file server, you do not
>
> *continues*

want user mode tasks to slow down the file services, so you should set the boost to "None." However, on a workstation running an application in user mode, you would want the user mode application to be more responsive, so you would set the performance boost to "Maximum."

You can also adjust the priority at which an application runs by using the start command to launch it. For example, entering **start/low mybatch.bat** at a command prompt starts the batch file with a low priority.

> **Warning**   Starting a task with the /realtime switch can cause severe degradation of performance of other tasks.

For example, if you have a batch job that is processor-intensive, do not schedule it to run on a domain controller at 8:00 a.m., when most users are logging on and logon authentication demands are at their greatest. Shift demands for resources to times when there is a surplus of the resource available.

Moving Tasks to Another System

If you find that you cannot resolve a resource shortage in an acceptable way on your system, you may be able to move the demand to another machine that has idle resources. For example, if you have two applications on a file server, both of which are I/O intensive, you may be able to improve performance of both applications by moving one of them to another file server that is less busy.

In a client/server application, you may also be able to spread out the load of your application by running portions of it using the idle processing capacity of other systems on the network.

Considerations Before Making Changes

Before you can make any of these changes, you first have to do some detective work. You have to be able to isolate which resource on the system is acting as the bottleneck. Then you have to discover the source of the demand for that resource.

For example, if you find that the processor is busy 100% of the time while a certain task is being performed, you cannot conclude that you need a faster processor. You have to determine *why* the processor is busy. For example, if your system has a memory shortage, the processor could be busy handling the increased need to manage virtual memory. Alternatively, your task could have invoked another process that was processor-intensive and consumed all available processor cycles.

This kind of investigative work requires a measurement tool that can tell you what is really going on with your system.

Measuring System Performance

Windows NT 4 was designed to be measured. The operating system itself maintains information about various aspects of your system's performance, such as the rate at which data is being written to a disk or the amount of memory in use. Examining these pieces of information, called *counters*, can tell you about what your system is doing.

Tools that are available to measure performance include the following (each is explained in detail in the following sections):

- Performance Monitor

- Process Viewer (PVIEWER)

- Process Resource Monitor (PMON)

Performance Monitor

By far the most useful tool for measuring performance on NT systems is the Performance Monitor. The Performance Monitor is installed into the Administrative Tools program group by default. With Performance Monitor you can perform the following tasks:

- Measure the demand for resources on your system

- Identify bottlenecks in your system performance

- Monitor the behavior of individual processes

- Monitor the performance of remote systems

- Generate alerts to inform you that an exception condition has occurred

- Export performance data for analysis using other tools

Figure 15.5 shows an example of a Performance Monitor chart measuring various aspects of a system's performance.

Performance Monitor is an essential tool for monitoring your system. You can use it to gather everything from general indicators of system health to detail on individual processes on the system.

Chapter 17 contains an introductory tutorial to the Performance Monitor.

Figure 15.5

The Performance Monitor graphically displays processor, memory, and disk performance during a 30 MB copy operation.

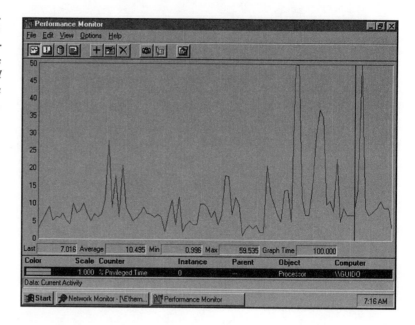

Process Viewer (PVIEWER)

Process Viewer provides a useful collection of information about processes running on Windows NT 4, including system processes. For each process running on your system, Process Viewer enables you to view the following:

- Amount of memory being used by the process

- Amount of privileged and user mode processor time used by each thread of the process

- Base priority of the process

Process Viewer gives you a snapshot of the resource usage of any process. Figure 15.6 shows the information displayed by Process Viewer about all processes, and figure 15.7 shows the memory usage of Performance Monitor (PERFMON.EXE) reported by Process Viewer.

The Process Viewer program is PVIEWER.EXE and is part of the Windows NT Resource Kit. To run it, double-click the Process Viewer icon in the NT Resource Kit program group.

Tip   In addition to using the Process Viewer to display information about running processes, you can use it to kill processes that cannot be ended using the Task Manager. Run Process Viewer, select the process from the list, and click on the Kill Process button.

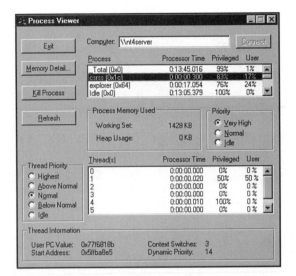

Figure 15.6
The Process Viewer dialog box displays processes currently running on the system, including details on memory usage and priority.

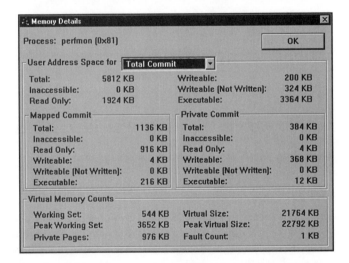

Figure 15.7
The Memory Details dialog box displays memory usage by the Performance Monitor program (PERFMON.EXE).

Process Resource Monitor (PMON)

The Process Resource Monitor was originally part of the Win32 Software Development Kit and is now part of the utilities on the Windows NT Workstation Resource Kit CD-ROM. It displays a useful snapshot of the memory and processor for the entire system. It shows global memory statistics at the top of the display, and then shows processor usage, memory usage, page faults, priority, and number of threads on a per process basis.

Figure 15.8 shows a sample of the output of PMON.EXE.

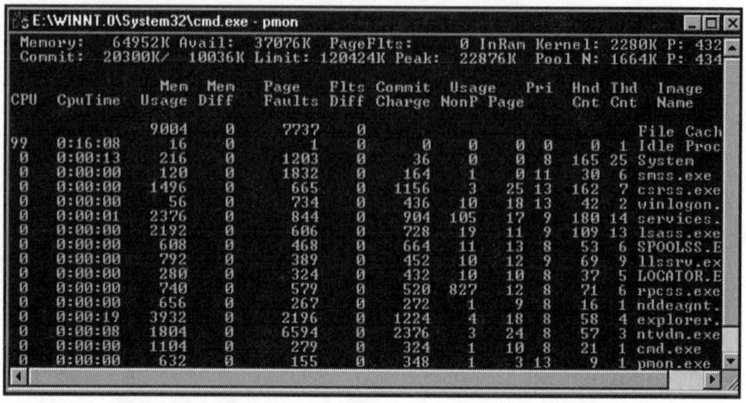

Figure 15.8

The Process Resource Monitor (PMON) displays a summary of memory and processor usage by all process running on the system.

```
E:\WINNT.0\System32\cmd.exe - pmon                                      _ □ ×
Memory:   64952K Avail:  37076K  PageFlts:        0 InRam Kernel: 2280K P: 432
Commit:   20300K/  10036K Limit: 120424K Peak:    22876K Pool N: 1664K P: 434

          Mem   Mem        Page   Flts Commit  Usage    Pri Hnd Thd  Image
CPU CpuTime Usage Diff      Faults Diff Charge NonP Page      Cnt Cnt Name
            9004     0       7737    0                            File Cach
99  0:16:08   16     0          1    0     0     0    0   0    0   1 Idle Proc
 0  0:00:13  216     0       1203    0    36     0    0   8  165  25 System
 0  0:00:00  120     0       1832    0   164     1    0  11   30   6 smss.exe
 0  0:00:00 1496     0        665    0  1156     3   25  13  162   7 csrss.exe
 0  0:00:00   56     0        734    0   436    10   18  13   42   2 winlogon.
 0  0:00:01 2376     0        844    0   904   105   17   9  180  14 services.
 0  0:00:00 2192     0        606    0   728    19   11   9  109  13 lsass.exe
 0  0:00:00  608     0        468    0   664    11   13   8   53   6 SPOOLSS.E
 0  0:00:00  792     0        389    0   452    10   12   9   69   9 llssrv.ex
 0  0:00:00  280     0        324    0   432    10   10   8   37   5 LOCATOR.E
 0  0:00:00  740     0        579    0   520   827   12   8   71   6 rpcss.exe
 0  0:00:00  656     0        267    0   272     1    9   8   16   1 nddeagnt.
 0  0:00:19 3932     0       2196    0  1224     4   18   8   58   4 explorer.
 0  0:00:08 1804     0       6594    0  2376     3   24   8   57   3 ntvdm.exe
 0  0:00:00 1104     0        279    0   324     1   10   8   21   1 cmd.exe
 0  0:00:00  632     0        155    0   348     1    3  13    9   1 pmon.exe
```

Detecting Bottlenecks

After you understand the tools needed to measure your system's performance, you are ready to use the data to determine how to improve it.

This section presents a simple strategy for detecting the part of your system that has become the performance bottleneck.

Bottleneck: The Limiting Resource

The term *bottleneck* is a descriptive term that comes from a familiar phenomenon. If you take a bottle filled with your favorite beverage and turn it upside down, the rate at which the liquid pours out of the bottle is dependent on one thing: the width of the neck. In this sense, the limiting characteristic of the bottle—the characteristic that prevents a faster rate—is the neck of the bottle. If the neck were wider, you could pour the contents of the bottle more quickly.

The bottleneck on your system is the resource that limits the rate at which your system can complete a task. If the resource were faster or you had more of it, the system would finish the task sooner. For example, if your task uses processor, network, and disk resources, but mostly spends time using the disk, then the disk is the bottleneck. After you know what the bottleneck is, you can resolve it by changing or reallocating your resources (by adding a faster hard disk, for example).

The simplest way to detect the bottleneck on your system is to examine the amount of time consumed by the various components of your system in completing the task. The component that used the most time to complete its portion of the task is the bottleneck.

Imagine, for example, that you determined, using the Performance Monitor, that while Windows NT was executing your task, it consumed .5 seconds of processor time, .1 second accessing the network, and .8 seconds accessing the disk. During most of the time the task is running, the processor and network are sitting idle waiting for the disk. After you add a faster hard disk, the disk access is down to .4 seconds, but the processor still takes .5 seconds. The processor is the new bottleneck.

Overall Performance Indicators

A reasonable place to start in monitoring performance for a server in Windows NT is to watch a number of general counters in Performance Monitor. These counters can provide a great deal of insight into the performance of the system as a whole. If you are not sure what to monitor, start with these and then gather more detail as you determine which component is the bottleneck. Four counters that can give you a good indicator of overall system performance are listed in table 15.3.

Table 15.3
Counters That Provide an Indicator of Overall Performance

Object	Counter
Processor	%Processor Time
Memory	Pages/sec
Physical Disk	% Disk Time
Server	Bytes Total/sec

Tip You can use the Performance Monitor to monitor these four basic counters on your system on a regular basis, including logging the activity to disk. If you have multiple servers to monitor, you can monitor all of them from one Performance Monitor session by adding counters from each of the systems. For more information, see "Monitoring Remote Systems" in Chapter 17, "Using Performance Monitor."

Using the Processor Counters

The following are useful counters for the processor object. When looking at the processor, remember that high levels of processor activity can result from two situations other than handling a processor-intensive task:

- There is a severe memory shortage and the processor is busy managing virtual memory (swapping pages of memory to and from the disk).

- The system is busy handling a large number of interrupts.

In either of these cases, replacing the processor with a faster one would not address the real problem.

Some useful counters to watch for the processor object include the following:

- **%Processor Time.** Measures the amount of time the processor spends executing a non-idle thread. In effect, it is the percent of time that the processor is busy. If the average value exceeds 80%, then the processor could be the bottleneck.

- **Interrupts/sec.** Measures the number of interrupts handled by the processor per second. An increase in the number of interrupts can indicate hardware failures in I/O devices such as disk controllers and network cards.

- **System: Processor Queue Length.** Measures the number of threads waiting in the queue for an available processor. Generally, if the number of threads in the queue is greater than 2, there is a problem with processor performance.

Using the Memory Counters

In general, the symptoms of a memory shortage on the system are a busy processor (managing the virtual memory) and a high level of disk activity on the disk containing the page file (accessing the disk to read and write memory pages).

Counters to watch include the following:

- **Pages/sec.** This counter measures the number of times a memory page had to be paged in to memory or out to the disk. An increase in this value indicates an increase in paging activity.

- **Available Bytes.** This counter measures the amount of physical memory available. When this value falls below 1 MB, excessive paging is occurring.

Using the Physical Disk Counters

Before you can use Performance Monitor to monitor disk activity, you have to enable the disk performance counters. Otherwise, all values for the disk counters will report zeroes in Performance Monitor.

To turn on the disk performance counters, log on as a user with administrative privileges and type **diskperf -y**. After you have turned on the disk performance counters, you can monitor the following:

- **Physical Disk: %Disk Time.** Reports the percentage of the time that the physical disk was busy reading or writing.

- **Logical Disk: %Disk Time.** Reports the percentage of time that the logical disk (for example, the C drive) was busy. To monitor the total activity of all the partitions on a single disk drive, use the Physical Disk: %Disk Time counter.

- **Logical Disk: Disk Queue Length.** Measures the number of read and write requests waiting for the disk to become available. If this counter is greater than 2, disk performance is suffering.

Using the Server Counters

The Server component is responsible for handling all SMB-based requests for sessions and file and print services. If the Server service becomes the bottleneck, requests from clients will be denied and will be forced to retry, creating slower response times and increased traffic.

Watch these two counters for the Server object:

- **Bytes Total/sec.** Measures the number of bytes sent to and received from the network. It provides an overall indicator of how much information is being handled by the server service. When the combined total of this counter for all your servers nears the maximum throughput for your network medium, you have run out of network capacity and need to subdivide the network.

- **Pool Nonpaged Failures and Pool Paged Failures.** Measures the number of times that a request from the server to allocate memory fails. These failures are indicators of a memory shortage.

Establishing Baseline Performance Data

Many of the counters provided by Performance Monitor cannot be interpreted without some baseline data to which to compare it. For example, the number of bytes read per second from the disk vary tremendously depending on the type of drive and controller that you have. However, the historical data for these counters can provide a basis for comparison.

You should log performance from your servers, at various times of the day, on a regular basis. Then if you do confront a performance problem, you can look at the historical data to see how the demands on the server have changed over time. For example, if you see changes in the percent of free space on the disk or the number of bytes being handled by the Server component, you can make appropriate adjustments in the hardware before a performance problem develops.

Conclusion

With the correct combination of hardware and software, Windows NT Server 4 requires very little tuning. However, determining the correct hardware for your needs is critical in getting the best performance. Knowing how to interpret performance data for your system helps you understand how changes to your hardware affect performance.

Capacity Planning

Everyone has experienced a shortage of capacity at one time or another—a needed resource in short supply at a critical moment.

Imagine, for example, that you need to move some boxes from your office to a location in another city that is one day's drive away. You hire some movers and a truck to do the job. After they arrive, however, you discover that the truck they brought is too small in which to fit all the boxes—you will need to make two trips (consequently, the delivery will be late). Not to be undone by this turn of affairs, you hire another truck. Unfortunately, you have a new problem: the first truck is blocking the driveway, and the second truck cannot begin loading until the first one has left. The boxes finally arrive at their destination, and your boss is not very sympathetic and asks, "Why did you get the large instead of the extra large?"

Capacity planning is an important part of network management. It prevents your network from running over capacity, which can stall your mission-critical applications.

In a networked environment, many variables affect the applications' ability to complete the work. The network infrastructure needs to be adequate and well designed. Application software has to be configured appropriately for your environment. The hardware on which you run Windows NT Server can make a dramatic difference in performance. Capacity planning is the task of anticipating the interaction of these components so that critical resources are available when needed.

Capacity planning is meant to answer questions such as

- Am I reaching the saturation point of my network?

- Is my server able to handle the increased workload if there are additional services added to it? What happens if I increase the number of clients?

- How do I need to subdivide my network to remove network bottlenecks?

- How can I configure my applications to eliminate unnecessary network traffic?

This chapter attempts to teach you how to approximate the impact of adding specific Windows NT-based services to your network. You also learn how to use the Network Monitor tool to observe the actual impact of your changes.

The Capacity Planning Process

Capacity planning is an ever-moving target. Just about the time you think you have a solution that meets your business needs, one of two things changes: the needs of the organization or the technology. To stay one step ahead, you need a methodology for estimating demand and a tool for detecting changes in network usage.

Steps to a Successful Capacity Plan

Planning for the introduction of new applications or services consists of the following steps:

1. Determine the demand for network services, such as logon and authentication, file and print services, WINS, and DHCP.

2. Determine the demand for application services, such as Web servers, database servers, and other client/server applications.

3. Optimize the delivery of the above services (determine hardware requirements for servers, minimize network traffic, and maximize performance of critical applications).

4. Forecast demand for the network and servers based on the needs analysis performed in steps 1 and 2.

5. Measure actual traffic generated by the applications and services identified in the analysis.

6. If necessary, restructure your environment.

7. When in production, monitor the network performance levels on an ongoing basis to identify changes in demand or performance problems.

This chapter provides background information that you need to optimize and estimate the network load of common Windows NT Server services. Applications (such as database servers and web servers) have their own optimization and capacity planning parameters. The process of optimizing these applications is the same as for the basic Windows NT Server network services: capture the traffic in a test environment, change your configuration to optimize the application, and then capture the traffic again until the network performance is optimized. Many server-based applications have significant tuning and optimization configuration options that must be carefully explored and tested before you can project how the application will work in a production environment.

Tip	After you have estimated your network capacity requirements, make certain that you at least double your estimate! You need the excess capacity to handle peak demands and unanticipated changes to your environment.

Determining the Demand for Network Services

The first step is to understand the applications that demand resources on the network. The following sections provide information on the basic Windows NT Server network services, how to optimize them, and the amount of traffic they generate.

Logon and Authentication Services

Whenever a client logs on to a domain or connects to a Windows NT system, a user authentication takes place in which the user's identity is checked against a security database (locally or on a domain controller). This section details the types of user authentication that occur on Windows NT systems, and then covers the options you can configure that affect their performance.

Types of Authentication

Windows NT offers four types of authentication:

- **Local logon.** A logon to a computer from its console using an account that exists in the local account database. No network traffic is generated.

- **Remote logon.** A request to create a session with the server received from a remote user on the network. If the account exists on the server being accessed and the user has adequate rights on the system, a session is established.

- **Domain logon.** A request from a client to a domain controller to validate a user's account in the domain database. This type of logon can also include processing of logon scripts and user profiles.

- **Pass-through authentication.** Occurs when the server being accessed (locally or remotely) cannot validate the user's identity using its own local account database. Instead, the server needs to pass through the request to an authority that can verify the account. A pass-through authentication occurs when:

  - A user logs on at a workstation that is a member of a domain by using a domain account.

  - A user connects to a server that is a member of a domain by using a domain account.

  - A user connects to a server that is a member of a domain by using an account from a trusted domain (this requires two pass-throughs: the first from the server to its domain controller, and the second from the domain controller to a domain controller in the trusted domain).

  - An authentication request fails at a BDC because of a password mismatch (the BDC verifies the password with the PDC before denying the request).

The Logon Process

In a single domain environment, the process of logging on to the domain consists of the following steps:

1. The client locates a logon server, either via a broadcast to the NETLOGON mailslot or via WINS (if configured as a WINS client).

2. All available logon servers respond (if via broadcast), or the WINS server responds with a list of up to 25 logon servers (if via the WINS client).

3. The client sends a logon request to all identified logon servers.

4. The client selects the first response from the logon servers in step 3 and continues the logon process with that server.

5. Logon scripts, user profiles, and system policies are processed at the client.

6. The client terminates its session with the server.

The domain model that you select has an impact on the performance of this process.

The Effect of Domain Design on Performance

In general, the number of domains required by an organization is determined by how the system is managed. Although operational considerations such as the location of domain controllers are affected by the network design and location of the systems, a domain is essentially an administrative unit of control—a group of systems that share a command account database. A domain can be as small as a single system or as large as one that spans the globe with thousands of user accounts. The number of domains that you need is determined by the number of separate account databases that are needed to achieve the desired security administration context.

In a single domain model, a single domain account database is used by all Windows NT systems in the network. A single group of administrators manage a single, shared account database. All users log on with accounts stored in a single account database.

In the master domain model, the domain database is partitioned into several separate account databases that can be managed independently of each other. A single domain database (the master domain) contains the user logon accounts for all users. Servers are grouped into resource domains, however, that can be administered by a different group of administrators than the ones in the master domain. Master domain user accounts can be authenticated by servers in the resource domains via pass-through authentication.

Placement of Domain Controllers

In a Local Area Network (LAN) environment, one that has high-speed connections between all the systems, a single domain controller (the Primary Domain Controller, or PDC) can satisfy all client logon requests and all pass-through authentication requests from member servers. At least one backup domain controller is desirable for fault tolerance (users could still log on with domain accounts even if the PDC is down), and a large account database might require multiple domain controllers to handle the amount of authentication traffic.

In addition, if there are slow links in the network, or if it is desirable to segment the logon traffic, a Backup Domain Controller (BDC) should be placed on each remote network.

In an environment that has implemented the master domain model, all users log on with accounts from the master domain. In that respect, the need for domain controllers is the same as it is in a single domain environment. In addition, domain controllers are needed for the resource domains in all locations their accounts are referenced.

To see how pass-through authentication works in this environment, reference the diagram in figure 16.1, where a trust relationship exists in which Domain1 trusts Domain2. A user sits down at computer A to log on with his account from Domain2. The following occurs:

1. System A (an NT workstation) cannot validate the request from its own database, so it passes the request to its domain controller (System B).

2. System B cannot validate the request either, so it passes the request to a domain controller in Domain2, System C.

3. System C sends a response to System B, which responds to System A.

Figure 16.1

If a user logs on at System A using an account from Domain 2, the logon request travels from System A to System B, across the slow link to System C, and back again.

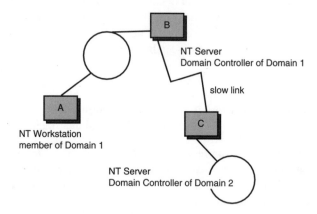

To avoid the pass-through authentication traffic crossing the slow links in your network, use a BDC for the master domain in each location.

Domain Synchronization

If you have multiple domain controllers that are spread out over a Wide Area Network (WAN), the synchronization of the account database becomes a significant issue.

In a Windows NT Server domain, the primary domain controller maintains the master copy of the directory services database; each backup domain controller has a copy. The Windows NT component responsible for keeping these copies of the database synchronized is the NetLogon service. When a domain synchronizes, the PDC sends out a message (called a pulse) to the BDCs to notify them that changes are waiting. The BDCs then connect to the PDC to get the changes.

Although the traffic generated by this process usually only consists of the changes to the database, a full synchronization can occur if the BDC is too far out of date, a new domain controller is installed, or the domain is synchronized in Server Manager. If the database is small, the amount of traffic is minimal. With thousands of user accounts, however, the traffic can easily turn into megabytes of data to transfer.

The key factors to consider when planning the domain synchronization process are

- The number of domain controllers

- The speed of the links between physical locations

- The size of the account database

- The desired amount of time within which the synchronization of the domain must be complete

Domain Controller Hardware Requirements

To handle logon authentication requests most efficiently, you should add enough memory to the domain controllers to accommodate the entire account database in RAM. If memory is a bottleneck, do not use the system as a file or application server; use it as a domain controller only.

The size of the account database depends on the number of user accounts, group accounts, and computer accounts in the domain. Table 16.1 shows the amount of space taken by each of these types of accounts in the database.

Table 16.1
Size of Objects in the Directory Services Database

Object	Space Used
User account	1,024 bytes
Global group account	512 bytes plus 12 bytes per user
Local group account	512 bytes plus 36 bytes per user
Computer account	512 bytes

Thus, an account database with 1,000 users and 1,000 computers would have an account database size of a little more than 1.5 MB.

The size of the Security Accounts Manager (SAM) database is limited by the maximum size of the Registry. The Registry can not exceed 80 percent of the PagedPoolSize (the paged pool is the set of memory pages used by the operating system components that can be paged to disk). Because the PagedPoolSize is limited to no more than 128 MB, the entire Registry, including the SAM database, cannot exceed 102 MB.

Microsoft's guidelines for the hardware configuration of domain controllers is listed in table 16.2.

Table 16.2
Microsoft's Recommended Hardware for Domain Controllers (All Sizes in MB)

Number of Users	SAM Size	Registry Size	PagedPool Size	CPU Needed*	Pagefile Size	RAM
3,000	5	25 (default)	50 (default)	486DX/33	32	16
7,500	10	25 (default)	50 (default)	486DX/66	64	32
10,000	15	25 (default)	50 (default)	P, M, or A	96	48
15,000	20	30	75	P, M, or A	128	64
20,000	30	50	100	P, M, or A	256	128
30,000	45	75	128	P, M, or A	332	166
40,000	60	102	128	SMP	394	197
50,000	75	102	128	SMP	512	256

*P, M, or A = PowerPC, MIPS, or Alpha

Note   Microsoft has tested SAM databases larger than 40 MB; with existing hardware, however, the amount of time needed to load the database into memory during startup is unacceptable in a production environment. Improvements in hardware performance might provide acceptable performance for such large databases in the future.

To put this hardware limitation in perspective, Microsoft recommends a maximum size of the SAM database of 10 MB for Windows NT 3.1. The increase in the recommended maximum to 40 MB is purely due to the availability of new hardware.

How many domain controllers are needed? For a single domain, table 16.3 gives Microsoft's recommendations. The table assumes that high-speed connections exist between the clients and the domain controllers.

Table 16.3
Recommended Number of Backup Domain Controllers

Number of User Accounts	Number of BDCs
<2,000	1
5,000	2
10,000	5
20,000	10
30,000	15

You should, however, seriously consider additional domain controllers. If your database is not large, the processing overhead of being a domain controller is not very much, so you could add the domain controller role to one or more file servers and gain additional fault tolerance on logon authentication (users can still log on if your other domain controllers are down). As the size of the account database gets beyond 1,000 users, however, performance becomes a major issue.

Another consideration is the physical topology of your network and its available capacity. If clients have to cross a slow link to log on, and that link is consumed by some other network task, user logons could fail. The solution is to locate a BDC on the other side of the link to service logon requests.

Configuring the NetLogon Service

To configure the behavior of the NetLogon service, you can change the Registry values for the following key:

`HKEY_LOCAL_MACHINE\SYSTEM\CurrentControlSet\Services\NetLogon\Parameters`

Several of the values may need to be adjusted for remote backup domain controllers in a WAN environment. Options to configure include:

- **Pulse.** The interval at which the NetLogon service looks for new changes to the database and sends a pulse (change notice) to the BDCs (default: five minutes).

- **PulseMaximum.** The interval at which the NetLogon service sends a pulse to the BDCs to verify the synchronization level, regardless of whether there are new changes to the database (default: two hours).

- **PulseConcurrency.** The number of BDCs to which pulses are sent concurrently. A higher value increases the amount of network bandwidth required at each synchronization (default: 10).

- **ReplicationGovernor.** Limits the amount of bandwidth the domain synchronization process can consume. Forces the NetLogon service to sleep between calls and use smaller buffers to enable other network traffic to pass (default: uses up to 100 percent of available bandwidth until synchronization is complete).

Directory Replication Service

The Directory Replication service in Windows NT Server is used to synchronize directories and files among multiple Windows NT systems. You designate a system as the export server and then configure your other NT systems as import servers. The Directory Replication service then ensures that the directories on the export server match exactly with those on the import servers. As files are changed, added, or deleted from the export computer, they are changed, added, or deleted from all the import computers.

This service is extremely useful for maintaining certain kinds of read-only files that need to be made accessible by a large number of systems. Directory Replication can be used to replicate logon scripts, mandatory user profiles, and other relatively small files that need wide distribution. Directory Replication is not designed, however, for distributing large numbers of files with ensured delivery; for that kind of job, you need a software distribution application such as the Systems Management Server that is part of Microsoft BackOffice.

The Registry parameters for the Directory Replication service are located in the following key:

`HKEY_LOCAL_MACHINE\SYSTEM\CurrentControlSet\Services\Replicator\Parameters`

To control the amount of directory replication traffic, you can change the following values:

- **Interval.** Interval at which the export server checks to see whether the export directory tree has changed (default: five minutes).

- **Pulse.** Number of times the import computer repeats the change notice after the initial announcement (default: two times).

File Services

The Windows NT Server file and print services are provided by the Server service. To provide adequate file services performance, it is important to size the amount of RAM and disk space on the server.

The general rule of thumb on memory for Windows NT Server is this: the more the better! Windows NT uses all available RAM for applications and caching of the disks automatically. This is important for file servers because the bottleneck on file servers is typically the disk (and a lack of memory to cache disk requests).

The base operating system requires 16 MB of RAM. You need to add to that amount enough RAM to enable all applications executing on the server to be resident in RAM (that is, not paged to disk) and to enable all open data files to be present in the cache. The total memory required is the sum of the three: 16 MB + total data files opened by clients + total executables being run from the server. This amount enables most disk requests to be satisfied from pages of memory resident in RAM.

The disk space requirement for a file server consists of the applications that will be stored on the server plus a budgeted amount of space per user (again, you need to at least double your estimates!). The boot partition needs enough space for the operating system and a generous swap file (150 MB + RAM + 12 MB). If you have basic productivity applications stored on the server (250 MB), for example, and allow 10 MB of personal storage for your 200 users (2 GB), you should estimate space for the server at 4.5 GB for data (2.25 GB × 2).

The memory and disk performance counters need to be monitored closely on file servers because changes in user habits can quickly change the demands on the server.

The Browser Service

The Browser service enables a Windows NT system to maintain a list of available servers on the network and provide the list to clients when needed. Every workgroup on every subnet has a system playing the role of master browser for that subnet. In a domain, a master browser resides on each subnet, with the primary domain controller as the domain master browser responsible for maintaining a domain-wide list.

The browsing process takes place on every installed protocol. Servers announce themselves on every protocol, and clients request browse lists on every protocol. A major savings in the overhead for browsing can be realized, therefore, if you limit the number of protocols being used on the network.

Another process that produces network traffic is the election process. If a master browser is no longer available, an election takes place to determine a new master browser. By configuring a system on each subnet to be the preferred master browser, you can reduce the traffic generated by elections.

You can also configure servers so that they do not announce themselves on the network. To turn off these announcements, enter the following command at the command prompt on the server:

```
net config server /hidden:yes
```

TCP/IP Related Services

Two services available on Windows NT Server that support TCP/IP environments are the Dynamic Host Configuration Protocol (DHCP) Server service and the Windows Internet Naming Service (WINS) Server service. The configuration of these services can have a significant impact network traffic.

Dynamic Host Configuration Protocol

The Dynamic Host Configuration Protocol (DHCP) is a mechanism by which network clients using the TCP/IP protocol can get an IP address from a server dynamically instead of having a user-configured address. An administrator configures the DHCP server with a set of valid IP addresses, along with a lease length. Clients can then lease addresses from the server. After the client's lease expires, the address can be returned to the pool and leased to another client.

The process of leasing an address from a DHCP server consists of the following major steps:

1. The client broadcasts a request for an IP address from a DHCP server.

2. The DHCP server offers the client an address.

3. The client accepts the offer.

4. The DHCP server acknowledges the transaction and specifies a lease length for the address.

DHCP configuration issues:

- If the lease length is too short, there is too much DHCP renewal traffic as clients renew leases.

- If the lease length is too long, addresses will not be returned to the pool when unused. If there is a shortage of addresses, this creates a problem.

- Changes to the DHCP scope do not affect current DHCP clients until their leases expire. (You can force a client to release its address and get a new one by entering **ipconfig /release** and then **ipconfig /renew** at a Command Prompt.)

- Scopes of addresses specified on DHCP servers cannot overlap and cannot include addresses already used by hosts on the network.

- Configuring as many IP options as possible via DHCP minimizes the amount of client configuration.

Windows Internet Naming Service

The Windows Internet Naming Service (WINS) provides IP address to NetBIOS name resolution. WINS maintains a dynamic database of IP addresses and their associated NetBIOS name registrations. Rather than using LMHOSTS files, clients can query a WINS server for IP addresses. This feature enables clients to log on to a Windows NT domain even if there is no domain controller on the local subnet. The client queries the WINS server for the addresses of domain controllers and logs on using directed datagrams.

A WINS Proxy Agent is a system that monitors network traffic for non-WINS client address resolution broadcasts. When a non-WINS client makes such a broadcast, the WINS Proxy Agent queries the WINS server and then responds to the original broadcast with the requested host IP address.

WINS configuration issues:

- Ensure that there are enough WINS servers on the network to satisfy client name resolution requests.

- Make certain that the WINS server has adequate RAM to maintain the WINS database in RAM for best performance.

- Manage the push/pull of the WINS database between WINS servers carefully, ensuring that frequency is often enough to provide the needed functionality without generating needless traffic.

- Locate WINS proxy agents at appropriate locations on the network. Each network segment that has non-WINS clients should have a WINS proxy agent.

Network Services Summary

Table 16.4 is a summary of the configuration options to review for each Windows NT Server network service. Table 16.5 shows the approximate amount of traffic generated by various network functions. The numbers given for number of frames and number of bytes are just examples captured on a specific network; the numbers vary depending on your network media and server configuration.

After you have optimized these services, you can predict the incremental impact of adding clients or services to the network.

You can gather performance statistics like these by using the Network Monitor and Performance Monitor.

Table 16.4
Changes That Can Be Made to Windows NT Network Services to Affect Network Utilization

Service	Configurations to Review
Domain Synchronization	Modify the Registry settings on the BDCs for the following values: ReplicationGovernor, Pulse, PulseMaximum, and PulseConcurrency.
	Review domain model for possible changes to domains and trust relationships.
	Monitor synchronization of remote BDCs to ensure they are complete within the desired timeframe without excessive bandwidth utilization.
Logon	Use WINS for resolution of address for domain controllers.
	Limit the number of network protocols installed.
	Ensure that all domain controllers have adequate RAM and CPU for the size of the directory services database.
	If domain controllers are functioning as other kinds of servers (file servers, application servers), monitor performance to ensure that spikes in demand for other services do not affect logon availability. Move applications to another server if necessary.
	Ensure that all clients have a high-speed network connection to a domain controller in their domain and all trusted domains.
Pass-Through Authentication	Minimize the number of domains if possible.
	Minimize the number of loaded network protocols.
	Minimize the number of trusts active on the network.
	Ensure that pass-through authentication does not have to go through slow links; position BDCs of trusted domains on each network where the accounts have to be referenced.
Directory Replication	Modify the Registry settings for the Interval and GuardTime values to accomplish the desired frequency of replication.
	Restrict replication to a small number of read-only files. Place other files in a shared location on a server.

Service	Configurations to Review
WINS	Make certain that each client and server is registered in WINS to minimize broadcasts for IP address to NetBIOS name resolution.
	Locate WINS servers so that each client has a high-speed network connection available to its primary WINS server (that is, minimize WINS queries across slow links).
	Adjust the replication of the WINS database between Push and/or Pull partners.
	Use WINS proxy agents where appropriate.
DHCP	For ease of administration, use DHCP to lease addresses instead of manually assigning them.
	Make certain that no DHCP scopes overlap.
	Configure as many TCP/IP configuration options as possible with DHCP.
	Set the longest practical lease length on each network to minimize renewal traffic.
Browser	Limit the number of workgroups on the network.
	Limit the number of network protocols installed.
	Configure the following Browser Registry values: MasterPeriodicity and BackupPeriodicity.
	Configure a system to be a preferred master browser on each subnet where no NT domain controllers exist.
	Configure systems that have minimal resources so that they do not maintain a list of servers MaintainServerList=no).
	Disable the server announcements on systems that do not need to appear in the browse list.
	Monitor the browse servers by using the Browser Monitor utility in the Windows NT Resource Kit.

*Portions reprinted with permission from Microsoft Corporation.

Table 16.5
Sample Network Traffic Generated by NT Server Network Services

Service	Description	Frames	Bytes	Frequency
DHCP	Acquire IP Address	4	1,368	Once per client
	Renew IP Address lease	2	684	Every startup and at 1/2 Lease Life
WINS	Registration	2	214	Once per service or application at startup
	Renewal	2	214	Once per service or application every 1/2 TTL
	Resolution	2	196	Varying frequencies
Logon Validation	Preparation	15	2,000	Once per user logon
	Validation sequence	4	760	Once per user logon
	Session breakdown	5	360	Once per user logon
	Scripts, policies, profiles		varies	Once per user logon
Browser	Host Announcement	1	243	Once per "server" computer every 12 minutes
	Local Master Announcement	1	250	After each Announcement Request or Election
	Workgroup Announcement	1	250	Every 15 minutes
	Elections	many	235	After each computer capable of becoming the master browser initializes

Service	Description	Frames	Bytes	Frequency
	Finding a backup browser	2	450	Once per browsing computer at initial browse attempt
File Sessions	Address resolution	2	120	At each attempt to communicate with another TCP/IP host (when aged from ARP cache)
	TCP Session	3	180	Once per first connection to each target TCP host
	NetBIOS Session	2	186	Once per first NetBIOS connection to a target computer
	SMB Protocol Negotiation	2	350	Once per first SMB connection to a target computer
	Connection Sequence	2	350	Once per network resource access
	Session Disconnection	5	360	Once per final connection to TCP host has been disconnected
Directory Services Database	Finding the PDC	4	545	Once per BDC bootup
Synchronization	Establish session	11	1,200	Every synchronization event
	Establish secure channel	8	1,550	Every synchronization event
	Verify the databases	6	1,350	Every synchronization event

continues

Table 16.5, Continued
Sample Network Traffic Generated by NT Server Network Services

Service	Description	Frames	Bytes	Frequency
	PDC Update notice	1	400	Every synchronization event
Establishing a Trust Relationship		100	15,000	Once per each trust relationship created
Importing Trusted Accounts		100	24,000 bytes of traffic for 11 trusted accounts	Each attempt to import a trusted account into a trusting domain
Pass-Through Authentication		20	3,700	Once for the first attempt to access a resource on a trusting computer, or logon to a trusted domain from a trusting computer
Directory Replication	Announcement	1	340	Once per importing domain or server for every update of the export tree
	Establish session	9	1,300	Once from each import server every update event
	Verify directory	22	3,700	Once from each import server every update event
	Update directory		varies	Once from each import server every update event

Service	Description	Frames	Bytes	Frequency
WINS Replication	Database verification	12	900	Once per update request to each replication partner
	Database update	14	2,100 varies	Once per update request to each replication partner

Forecasting Demand

After you have identified the services that need to be delivered, the next step is to measure and analyze the actual activity on the network. Two tools that provide the information you need are Performance Monitor and Network Monitor.

Network Trend Analysis by Using Performance Monitor

Performance Monitor can give you some basic statistic information on overall network traffic, including the percent of network utilization and the number of broadcasts and multicasts.

The Network Segment object and its counters become available to measure after you install the Network Monitor Agent, as shown in figure 16.2. If your system has multiple network interfaces, each interface appears as a separate instance and can be monitored separately. The counters that you can monitor include:

- %Multicast frames

- %Network utilization

- Broadcast frames received/second

- Multicast frames received/second

- Total bytes received/second

- Total frames received/second

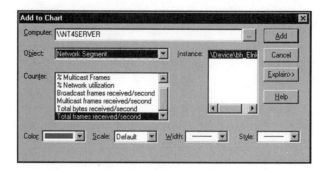

These counters provide overall indicators of the volume of traffic on your network. The %Network utilization tells you what percentage of the bandwidth of the physical network is in use, and the Total bytes received/sec tells you the throughput.

Note   To install the Network Monitor Agent and make these counters available, open Control Panel, Network, and then choose the Services tab. Choose Add and then choose Network Monitor Agent from the list of possible components.

It is a good idea to watch the utilization of your network on an ongoing basis to detect changes in network traffic. To capture the data that you need for basic trend analysis, use the logging capabilities of Performance Monitor to create a log of network demand and save it to disk. Log the activity at various times of the day to get a picture of the peaks and valleys in network demand. For more information on how to log activity on remote systems, see the section titled "Monitoring Performance on a Remote Computer" in Chapter 17, "Using Performance Monitor."

The data that you log can be exported from Performance Monitor and then imported into a spreadsheet or database program for further analysis. An effective graph of the increase in network activity is useful when you need to convince your manager to buy new network hardware.

Tip   An effective and inexpensive way to display the network activity on all your networks without any dedicated hardware is to install the Network Monitor Agent (which comes with Windows NT) on a system on each network. You can then use the Performance Monitor to display the activity on each network by adding counters to your chart or report for each computer.

To minimize the performance drain on the system running Performance Monitor, use the Report view, add as few counters as possible, and increase the update interval (every 20 seconds would be reasonable).

Capturing Data with Network Monitor

The other tool that you can use to provide information on network activity is the Network Monitor, a software-based network traffic and protocol analysis tool included in Microsoft Systems Management Server and Microsoft BackOffice. A version of the Network Monitor is included with Windows NT Server 4; however, it has limited capabilities. It does not capture all network traffic. It can be used to capture only the activity to and from a particular server. Although this chapter describes the more powerful SMS Network Monitor tool's capabilities, the steps to capture and view network traffic are the same for both.

By using the Network Monitor, you can

- Capture network traffic

- Generate statistics on network utilization

- Analyze network conversations between systems

- Examine the network packets generated by a specific network service

In addition to using Network Monitor to analyze network traffic for capacity planning impacts, there are two other good reasons to get to know this tool:

- It is an invaluable tool for troubleshooting network problems. If a network application is not working, for example, you can use Network Monitor to look at the actual frames being sent between the client and the server. Or, if you are experiencing some other network problem, and Microsoft's Product Support cannot troubleshoot it over the phone, they may ask you to capture and send them a *trace* of the network (that is, a network capture by using Network Monitor). Developers can use these traces—that would otherwise require a site visit—to pinpoint the exact nature of a problem remotely.

- It also is a great learning tool. If you want to see how the networking components really work in Windows NT, capture some traffic and then analyze it. To analyze the performance of the Browser service (which is responsible for maintaining a list of available servers on the network), examine the browser traffic. If you are not certain how often servers are announcing their presence on the network, for example, you can use Network Monitor to examine the actual Browser-related traffic on the network and see each server announcement as it is generated.

Figure 16.3

The Network Monitor window after capturing data.

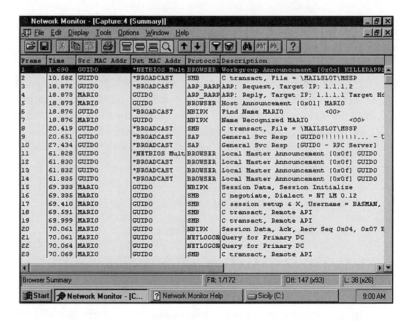

For more information on how to use Network Monitor, see "Using Network Monitor" later in this chapter.

Tip

A good way to observe the actual behavior of your servers and clients is to set some representative systems on an isolated test network that emulates your production environment. You can then use the Network Monitor to capture and analyze the network traffic. The limited number of frames generated on a small test network makes it easier to isolate and measure changes in traffic in your test configurations. Often, you discover traffic that you need to eliminate, such as client broadcasts to resolve IP addresses. You can then extrapolate your experience in the test environment to the larger number of clients and servers on the production network.

Analyzing and Modifying the Design

After capturing network traffic and statistics on a test network, the next step is to optimize traffic for the various services present on your test network. You are looking for traffic that can be reduced or enhanced by changing the configuration of either the physical network or the software components involved.

The contents of the network trace provide information on how the software components are working. Are servers announcing themselves correctly to enable browsing? Are clients that need addresses from a DHCP server able to locate a server? How are IP addresses being resolved for host names? Looking at the individual frames in the network trace provides this information.

The first thing to determine is whether your test environment met all your production requirements. Questions to ask include the following:

- Can users log on to all domains where they have accounts without excessive pass-through authentications?

- How long does synchronization of the domain really take with a full-size directory services database? Does synchronization complete in an acceptable amount of time for servers on remote networks?

- How is name resolution handled? WINS, DNS, LMHOSTS, or ARP? Can broadcast traffic be reduced?

- Can routers forward DHCP requests (BOOTP)? Are clients able to lease valid addresses?

- Does internetwork browsing work? What is the overhead?

- What is the memory utilization on domain controllers after a full-sized directory services database is loaded?

At this point, you need to ask, "What can I change that will make a difference in performance?" A number of potential strategies for optimizing the basic NT network services were listed in table 16.4. In addition to these Windows NT optimization issues, you should consider the physical layout of the network—whether it matches the capacity and speed requirements of your applications. In particular, at this stage, you need to consider the impact of subdividing the network or addition of other kinds of network devices to determine whether they will enhance network performance enough to justify the cost.

Some additional strategies that could be used to address various performance problems include

- Changing the number and location of domain controllers, WINS servers, DHCP servers, and other application servers.

- Testing performance of applications by using other protocols. If your systems are currently using IPX/SPX, for example, test your application by using TCP/IP as the network protocol to compare the performance. There can be significant differences in the amount of data and number of frames transferred depending on the network protocol used for file operations.

- Subdividing the existing physical network into multiple IP (logical) networks.

- Installing additional routers, gateways, or bridges.

■ Relocating servers, applications, or clients to other networks to balance traffic demands or to locate clients closer to the servers they access.

■ Change the network bandwidth available to clients or servers by installing new interfaces or relocating specific servers to a high-speed backbone.

If the network configuration needs to be modified to support your new applications, now is the time to test the new configuration to see the impact made by the changes.

Ongoing Reporting and Analysis

After your applications are in production, you need to evaluate the network performance on a regular basis to determine how the demand for network services has changed. The Performance Monitor and Network Monitor are again the best tools for the job.

To support your ongoing network analysis, you should

■ Set up a Network Monitor Agent on each network.

■ Log network segment statistics to disk at regular intervals on each network and then consolidate them for analysis.

■ Configure Performance Monitor on your desktop or some other management console to monitor key indicators on the production servers, including the Network Segment object counters mentioned earlier in this chapter. Define Alerts in Performance Monitor for exception conditions.

■ Periodically capture a trace on each network and review the various protocols and applications to determine whether they are still optimized.

■ Export the logged data from Performance Monitor and update your performance history in a spreadsheet or database application. Report and graph trends on a regular basis.

Using Network Monitor

How the Network Monitor Works

The Network Monitor consists of two components that can be installed on the same system or on two different systems:

■ **Network Monitor Agent.** A software component that works with the network interface driver to capture network frames into a buffer (installed on the system where the network traffic is captured).

■ **Network Monitor.** The user interface used to initiate and configure network captures and display the results (installed on the system where the capture results are to be displayed).

To capture all the frames on the network, the network interface has to support a promiscuous mode. A list of supported network cards is available on Microsoft TechNet or on Microsoft's web site.

Installing Network Monitor

To install the Network Monitor Agent on a Windows NT System:

1. Run the Control Panel and then choose Network. The Network Settings dialog box appears.

2. Choose Add Software.

3. Select Network Monitor Agent from the list of available components and choose OK.

After closing the Control Panel, a prompt appears for you to restart the computer. The Network Monitor Agent is now installed as part of the network components on the system. After restarting the system, you are ready to install the Network Monitor user interface on the system that displays the network data.

Note   Certain versions of Network Monitor work on Windows for Workgroups and Windows 95 clients. These are found on the Systems Management Server CD in the NETMON directory.

To install the Network Monitor tool:

1. Insert the Microsoft Systems Management Server CD or the Microsoft BackOffice CD containing the SMS directory into your CD-ROM drive.

2. Locate the SMSSETUP directory on the CD. It is either SMSSETUP off the root directory (SMS CD) or the \SMS12\SMSSETUP directory (BackOffice CD).

3. Run Setup.

4. When prompted for which components of SMS to install, choose Admin Tools.

5. Choose Custom. Remove all the suggested components (such as the SMS Administrator) from the list except for the Intel Network Monitor. Choose OK.

After setup completes, you are ready to run the Network Monitor from the Systems Management Server program group.

Capturing Data

After you start the Network Monitor, it displays the Capture window, which reflects the contents of the Network Monitor Agent's capture buffer. At this point, no data is being captured. To start capturing data, choose Start from the Capture menu (or press F10). The Network Monitor application then instructs the Network Monitor Agent to begin capturing network frames. As data is captured, activity appears in the Capture window showing statistics on the network activity as shown in figure 16.4.

Figure 16.4

The Network Monitor window shown after a capture.

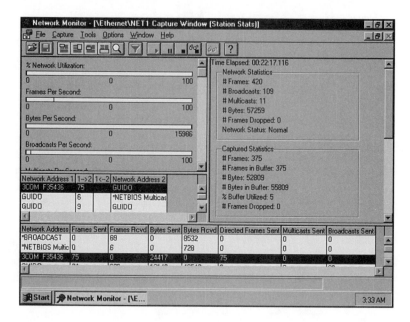

While the capture is running, each frame on the network is copied into a capture buffer on the system running the Network Monitor Agent. When the buffer is full, the capture stops automatically. To change the size of the buffer from the default size of 1 MB, choose Buffer Settings from the Capture menu and then type a new size. Be careful not to set the buffer size larger than the amount of physical RAM on the system or else network frames can be dropped while the contents of memory is paged out to disk.

Before you can look at the actual data, however, you have to stop the capture. To stop the capture process, choose Stop from the Capture menu.

<table>
<tr><td>Tip</td><td>

You might find that Network Monitor cannot capture all the frames on your network (indicated by the number of Frames Dropped), depending on the capabilities of your network card and other activity on your system. To minimize the number of dropped frames, choose Dedicated Capture Mode from the Capture menu. Network Monitor runs minimized with little screen update.

If frames are being dropped even when using Dedicated Capture Mode, consider running Network Monitor at a higher priority with the START command, or upgrade your network adapter. To start the Network Monitor at the highest possible priority, enter the following at a command prompt:

```
start /realtime netmon
```

Running Network Monitor at the real-time priority negatively affects performance of other tasks on the system, so you do not want to use this technique on a server. Instead, use an idle client system to perform the network capture.

</td></tr>
</table>

Understanding the Display

The Capture window in Network Monitor is divided into four areas, or panes, displaying statistical information about the captured traffic. These four areas are (clockwise from upper left) as follows:

- **Graph pane.** Contains a series of bar charts showing the five counters for the Network Segment object: %Network utilization, Frames per second, Bytes per second, Broadcasts per second, and Multicasts per second. The black line that appears in the bar chart shows the peak value attained by that counter during the capture.

- **Total Statistics pane.** Displays summary statistics for the network capture for the network statistics, capture statistics, and per second statistics.

- **Station Statistics pane.** Displays statistics for each network address captured, including the number of frames and bytes sent and received.

- **Session Statistics pane.** Displays statistics for network conversations between two addresses (source address and destination address).

<table>
<tr><td>Tip</td><td>

Double-clicking on a column heading in the Station Statistics or Session Statistics panes sorts the display in descending order. To see which network address sent the most bytes on the network during the capture, for example, double-click on the heading of the Bytes Sent column in the Station Statistics pane.

</td></tr>
</table>

Resolving Hardware Addresses to Computer Names

The network addresses displayed in the Capture window are the hardware addresses (or MAC or NIC addresses) of the network interfaces. The Network Monitor can search the frames in the capture for any frames that include computer names and then display the name rather than the hardware address. To do this, choose Find All Names from the Capture menu. Network Monitor adds any names that it finds to an address database. You can display or edit the names in the database by choosing Addresses from the Capture menu.

Tip	If you already have a database of hardware addresses for your network, you can load these addresses into Network Monitor's database by choosing the Load button in the Addresses dialog box.

Saving the Captured Data To Disk

To save your captured data for later analysis, choose Save As from the File menu. Capture files have a .CAP extension by default. Capture files are binary files that contain the frames from the capture.

Another way to save the capture is to use the Print command from the File menu and then choose the File option to put the captured data in a text file (see fig. 16.5).

Figure 16.5

The Print dialog box shown with the Advanced options displayed.

Viewing Captured Data

After you have finished capturing data, you can view the contents of the frames by choosing Display Captured Data from the Capture menu (or press F10, or click on the button on the toolbar that looks like a pair of glasses). The Capture window displays a list of the captured frames, showing the source and destination addresses, the protocol used, and a description of the frame contents.

To get more details about a particular frame, double-click on the frame in the list. The window splits into three panes (see fig. 16.6). The Detail pane parses the frame into its component parts, and the Hex pane shows each byte in hexadecimal notation.

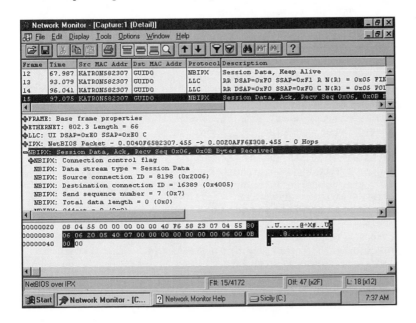

Figure 16.6

The display of captured data, showing the Summary, Detail, and Hex panes.

The following is the Detail information for a single frame in the Network Monitor:

```
Network Monitor trace Thu 10/03/96 07:42:12 c:\Capture1.TXT

**********************************************************************************************************************

Frame   Time   Src MAC Addr   Dst MAC Addr   Protocol   Description
Src Other Addr   Dst Other Addr   Type Other Addr
15      9.194  NT351SERVER    *NETBIOS Multi BROWSER     Get Backup List Request
[0x09]

  FRAME: Base frame properties
      FRAME: Time of capture = Oct 3, 1996 6:41:14.714
      FRAME: Time delta from previous physical frame: 1187 milliseconds
      FRAME: Frame number: 15
      FRAME: Total frame length: 153 bytes
      FRAME: Capture frame length: 153 bytes
      FRAME: Frame data: Number of data bytes remaining = 153 (0x0099)
  ETHERNET: 802.3 Length = 153
      ETHERNET: Destination address : 030000000001
          ETHERNET: .......1 = Group address
          ETHERNET: ......1. = Locally administered address
      ETHERNET: Source address : 00A024896844
          ETHERNET: .......0 = No routing information present
          ETHERNET: ......0. = Universally administered address
```

```
        ETHERNET: Frame Length : 153 (0x0099)
        ETHERNET: Data Length : 0x008B (139)
        ETHERNET: Ethernet Data: Number of data bytes remaining = 139 (0x008B)
LLC: UI DSAP=0xF0 SSAP=0xF0 C
    LLC: DSAP = 0xF0 : INDIVIDUAL : IBM NetBIOS
    LLC: SSAP = 0xF0: COMMAND : IBM NetBIOS
    LLC: Frame Category: Unnumbered Frame
    LLC: Command = UI
    LLC: LLC Data: Number of data bytes remaining = 136 (0x0088)
NETBIOS: Datagram (0x08), NT351SERVER    <00> -> REMOTE        <1D>
    NETBIOS: Length = 44 (0x002C)
    NETBIOS: Signature = 0xEFFF
    NETBIOS: Command = Datagram (0x08)
    NETBIOS: Destination Name = REMOTE        <1D>
        NETBIOS: SMB Name Type = Program defined (1D)
    NETBIOS: Source Name = NT351SERVER    <00>
        NETBIOS: SMB Name Type = Workstation (00)
    NETBIOS: NetBIOS Data: Number of data bytes remaining = 92 (0x005C)
SMB: C transact, File = \MAILSLOT\BROWSE
    SMB: SMB Status = Error Success
        SMB: Error class = No Error
        SMB: Error code = No Error
    SMB: Header: PID = 0x0000 TID = 0x0000 MID = 0x0000 UID = 0x0000
        SMB: Tree ID      (TID) = 0 (0x0)
        SMB: Process ID   (PID) = 0 (0x0)
        SMB: User ID      (UID) = 0 (0x0)
        SMB: Multiplex ID (MID) = 0 (0x0)
        SMB: Flags Summary = 0 (0x0)
            SMB: .......0 = Lock & Read and Write & Unlock not supported
            SMB: ......0. = Send No Ack not supported
            SMB: ....0... = Using case sensitive pathnames
            SMB: ...0.... = No canonicalized pathnames
            SMB: ..0..... = No Opportunistic lock
            SMB: .0...... = No Change Notify
            SMB: 0....... = Client command
        SMB: flags2 Summary = 0 (0x0)
            SMB: ...............0 = Understands only DOS 8.3 file names
            SMB: ..............0. = Does not understand extended attributes
            SMB: ..0............. = No paging of IO
            SMB: .0.............. = Using SMB status codes
            SMB: 0............... = Using ASCII strings
    SMB: Command = C transact
        SMB: Word count = 17
        SMB: Word parameters
        SMB: Total parm bytes = 0
        SMB: Total data bytes = 6
        SMB: Max parm bytes = 0
        SMB: Max data bytes = 0
        SMB: Max setup words = 0 (0x0)
        SMB: Transact Flags Summary = 0 (0x0)
            SMB: ...............0 = Leave session intact
            SMB: ..............0. = Response required
```

```
         SMB: Transact timeout = 1000 (0x3E8)
         SMB: Parameter bytes = 0 (0x0)
         SMB: Parameter offset = 0 (0x0)
         SMB: Data bytes = 6 (0x6)
         SMB: Data offset = 86 (0x56)
         SMB: Setup word count = 3
         SMB: Setup words
         SMB: Mailslot opcode = Write mailslot
         SMB: Transaction priority = 1
         SMB: Mailslot class = Unreliable (broadcast)
         SMB: Byte count = 23
         SMB: Byte parameters
         SMB: Path name  = \MAILSLOT\BROWSE
         SMB: Transaction data
     SMB: Data: Number of data bytes remaining = 6 (0x0006)
  BROWSER: Get Backup List Request [0x09]
     BROWSER: Command = Get Backup List Request [0x09]
     BROWSER: Get Backup List Requested Count = 4 (0x4)
     BROWSER: Backup Request Token = 3 (0x3)
```

Using a Filter

When you capture data in Network Monitor, every frame is captured by default, regardless of whether it is relevant to what you are testing. You can have Network Monitor sift through the frames and limit what is displayed by using a Filter. Filters can be applied after you capture the data, or you can define them before you perform the capture to reduce the amount of data collected. In figure 16.7, only frames that are broadcasts for one of the listed protocols appear after the filter is applied.

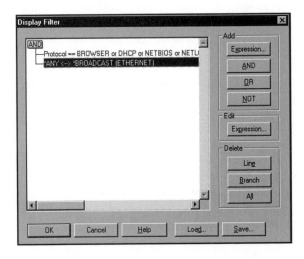

Figure 16.7

A filter enables you to limit your view of the capture to the frames that you specify.

To create a Filter, choose Filter from the Display menu (or press F8). The Display Filter dialog box appears (refer to fig. 16.7). You can limit what is displayed by creating expressions telling Network Monitor what to display. You can filter the data by specifying the addresses, protocols, or any data contained within the frame. To add an expression to the filter, choose Expression. The Expression dialog box appears, enabling you to choose the specific criteria for the filter (see fig. 16.8).

Figure 16.8

The Expression dialog box enables you to select the network frames you want to display based on the destination address, protocol used, or other information contained within the frame.

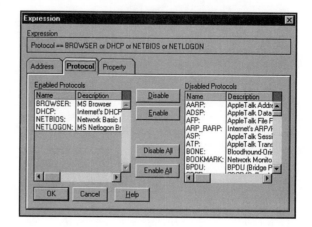

Filters can be saved to disk and then loaded when needed from the Display Filter dialog box. Filters have a .DF extension by default.

Tip

If you are viewing the captured data with a filter applied, you have a new option available in the Save As dialog box: the Filtered option. If you turn on this check box, only the frames displayed are saved to disk; all other frames are ignored.

If you have a specific focus for your capture, such as the conversation between two systems or the traffic generated by a specific application, you can create a filter and then use the filter to capture only the data that you want instead of all the network frames. Using a filter this way can dramatically cut down on the size of the buffer needed by Network Monitor, especially on busy networks.

You create a filter for the capture process in the same way that you create a display filter. Choose Filter from the Capture menu and then create the expressions that you need to select the type of frames to capture.

Capturing Data on a Remote System

To capture the network activity on a remote network, you need to first install the Network Monitor Agent on a system on that network. On Windows NT systems, the Network Monitor Agent is installed as a service set to start manually. Before you can capture data on the remote system, you must make certain that this service is started. You have three options for starting the service:

■ Use Control Panel Services to list the available services, select the Network Monitor Agent, and choose Start.

■ At a command prompt, type **net start nmagent** and then press Enter.

■ In Server Manager, select the system on which Network Monitor Agent is installed, choose Services from the Computer menu, select the Network Monitor Agent, and then choose Start.

After the service has been started, you are ready to connect to the agent from Network Monitor. Choose Networks from the Capture menu to display a list of network interfaces on this system. To specify a different system to perform the capture, select REMOTE from the list, and then choose Connect. The Connect to Network Monitoring Agent dialog box appears (see fig. 16.9). Type the agent's computer name and an update frequency, and then choose Connect. You are now ready to start capturing data on that remote computer.

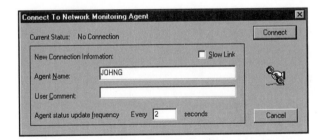

Figure 16.9

The Connect to Network Monitoring Agent dialog box enables you to capture the activity on remote networks by connecting to a Network Monitor Agent on that network.

No visible sign appears on the capturing computer that a capture is running. The summary information is sent from the agent to the system running the Network Monitor at whatever update frequency is specified. Upon exiting from Network Monitor, the session with the agent is disconnected and the data in the capture is discarded, so be certain to save the capture to a file before exiting if you want to keep it.

Conclusion

With careful planning, testing, and analysis, you can optimize the performance of the network services provided by Windows NT. The tools that will provide you with the data that you need to evaluate your configuration are the Network Monitor and the Performance Monitor. Both are essential tools in any administrator's toolkit. For more information on the Performance Monitor, turn to Chapter 17, "Using Performance Monitor."

Using Performance Monitor

Windows NT keeps statistics on the usage of various objects on your system, such as the processors, memory, disks, and network interfaces. These statistics are through the Win32 API, so any Win32 application can know the status of resources on your system.

The Performance Monitor tool provided with Windows NT collects this performance information provided by the operating system and displays it in a graphical user interface that you can customize to suit your needs. Gathering and analyzing these statistics are essential parts of any capacity planning or performance optimization you may want to do. If you need to know what your system is doing, and how you can make it perform better, you will find Performance Monitor an indispensable tool.

This chapter teaches you how to collect and view performance data about Windows NT systems. You will also find several hands-on exercises that you can perform on any Windows NT system to get familiar with the features of Performance Monitor. The best way to use this chapter is to try out the tools and options at your system as you read about them.

Getting Started

After you install Windows NT, an icon for the Performance Monitor is created by default in the Administrative Tools program group. After you start Performance Monitor (PERFMON.EXE), the Performance Monitor window appears as a chart with no current activity being monitored (see fig. 17.1).

Figure 17.1

The opening Performance Monitor Chart window appears.

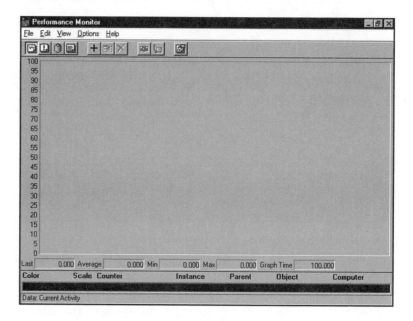

It is now up to you to choose what you want to measure and when to measure it. For example, do you want to watch your system's activity in real time, or do you want to have Performance Monitor save the data to disk periodically so you can review it later? Do you want to monitor all the ups and downs of a system's performance, or would you rather have Performance Monitor notify you only when there are performance problems?

As you use Performance Monitor, follow these basic steps:

1. Choose the type of window you want to use (Chart, Report, and so on).

2. Add objects or counters to be monitored.

3. Set options for Performance Monitor to use such as the resolution (frequency) of your monitor, location of the log file, and so on.

4. Save your configuration in a Settings file so that you can recall it when needed.

5. Start the data collection process.

6. Stop the data collection process.

7. Analyze the results.

Choosing a View

Performance Monitor has four different types of windows that can be selected from the View menu. Each is designed for a different purpose (see table 17.1).

Table 17.1
Performance Monitor Windows

View	Purpose
Chart window	Display counter data as a line graph or histogram
Alert window	Define and monitor Alert conditions based on monitoring criteria (for example, send an Alert if disk space is low)
Log window	Save performance data in a log file on disk
Report window	List counters with their current values

Tip	You can move quickly among these four views by using the first four buttons on the toolbar, or by using these shortcut keys:
	Ctrl+C Chart window
	Ctrl+A Alert window
	Ctrl+L Log window
	Ctrl+R Report window

These four windows (Chart, Alert, Log, and Report) are described and illustrated in the sections that follow.

Other Display Options

Some general options affect the Performance Monitor window regardless of which view you are using. Table 17.2 describes these settings, which are located in the Options menu.

Table 17.2
Performance Monitor Options

Option	Function
Menu and Title	Toggles display of menu bar and title bar
Toolbar	Toggles display of the Toolbar
Status Bar	Toggles display of the Status Bar at the bottom of the Performance Monitor window
Always on Top	Keeps the Performance Monitor window on top of other windows, even if it is not the active window

Tip

You can keep a copy of Performance Monitor running on your desktop without taking up a lot of space. From the Options menu, turn off Menu and Title, Toolbar, and Status Bar. Choose Chart from the Options menu, and turn off the Legend check box. The result is a very sparse looking Performance Monitor with just the data displayed (see fig. 17.2).

To bring back the title bar and menus, double-click on the chart or press Ctrl+M. If you want to keep the Performance Monitor display on top even if another application is active, press Ctrl+P or choose Always on Top from the Options menu.

Figure 17.2
Performance Monitor with display options set to take as little screen space as possible.

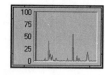

Creating a Chart

The Chart view displays counter information as a line graph or as a histogram. After you add counters to the chart, a line graph appears in the Chart view for each one, along with an entry in the legend at the bottom of the window.

The Chart window displays 100 data points of information. The default for the Chart view is to update the display one time per second; therefore, by default, the window displays 100 seconds of information.

Creating a chart in Performance Monitor consists of adding counters and setting the chart options. As soon as you add counters, Performance Monitor starts sampling those counters and displays the information in the Chart window.

Adding Counters

To add a counter to your chart and start collecting data, choose Add to Chart from the Edit menu. The Add to Chart dialog box appears (see fig. 17.3).

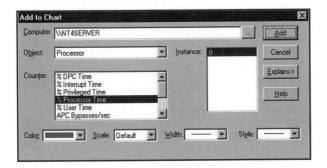

Figure 17.3
The Add to Chart dialog box appears.

Which Computer?

The first decision to make in this dialog box is which computer you want to monitor. By default, the local computer is selected. To monitor an object on a remote system, you can type computer name in the form \\computername, or you can click on the ellipsis button to get a browse list of systems on the network.

Note   For more information on monitoring remote systems, see "Monitoring Remote Systems," later in this chapter.

Which Object?

The question now becomes, what should I monitor? Windows NT provides statistics on the objects listed in table 17.3 on every NT system. Depending on your hardware and software, additional objects may be available to monitor. If you have a server component running, for example, the Server object is available to monitor. Application software programs designed for Windows NT can add their own objects and counters that can be monitored in Performance Monitor.

Table 17.3
Windows NT Default Objects That Can Be Monitored

Object	Description
Cache	File system cache
Logical Disk	Disk partitions (C:, D:, and so on)
Memory	Random Access Memory
Objects	System software objects
Paging File	Paging file used for virtual memory
Physical Disk	Hardware disk unit
Process	Software object that represents a running program
Processor	System CPU
Redirector	File system driver for network resources
System	System-wide counters
Thread	Software object inside a process

Which Counter?

Each object on your system has specific counters associated with it that provide information about the object. The Processor object, for example, has counters for such things as what percentage of the time the processor is busy, how much of the processor activity is in privileged mode versus user mode, and so forth. The Memory object has counters such as the amount of free memory and the number of page faults.

A brief description of a counter measure is available via the Explain button. After you choose Explain, the dialog box expands to display a definition of the selected counter (see fig. 17.4).

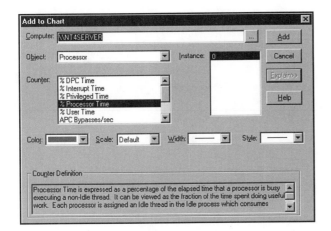

Figure 17.4

The Add to Chart dialog box after choosing Explain with the Explain text displayed.

If you are not certain which counter to measure, you cannot go too far wrong by using the default counter for each object (for example, Processor:%Processor time or Memory:Pages/sec). The default counter is the one that Microsoft feels best represents the overall performance of the object. If you determine that the processor is busy by using the Processor:%Processor time counter, you can then dig deeper into the other Processor counters to see *why* it is busy.

Which Instance?

Finally, you may need to select an Instance if your system has more than one of the object you are monitoring. If your system has more than one processor, for example, the Processor object has a separate instance for each processor. The first processor is Instance 0 (zero), the second processor is Instance 1, and so forth. If your system has two physical disks, then the first hard disk is Instance 0, and the second is Instance 1.

After you have made all the appropriate selections in the dialog box, choose Add to add the counter to the chart and start displaying data. If you added the Processor:%Processor time counter, your chart looks similar to the one shown in figure 17.5

Tip

To select multiple counters or multiple instances simultaneously, select the first counter and then use one of the following techniques:

■ To add to the current selection, hold down the Ctrl key and select additional counters or instances.

■ To select a range of counters or instances, hold down the Shift key and select the last item in the range.

Figure 17.5

The Chart window with one counter added (Processor:%Processor time). With an average value of x%, this is not a busy system.

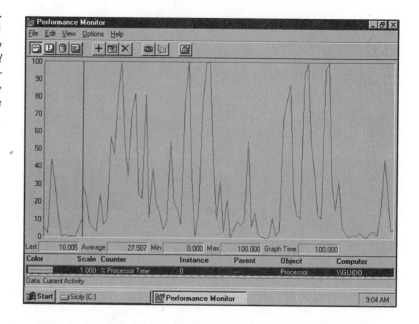

> **Note** If you are having trouble identifying which line in your chart goes with which counter, select the counter in the legend area and then press the Backspace key. The selected counter's line or bar in the Chart window will be highlighted. Pressing the Backspace key again toggles off the highlight.

Turning On Disk Counters

If you add any of the disk-related objects to your chart (Physical Disk, Logical Disk) you may get a flat line at zero, with no activity showing for any disk access.

This phenomenon occurs when the disk performance counters are not turned on by default in Windows NT. Turning on the counters adds a small amount of overhead on every disk access. Although the counters add slightly to the system overhead on 386-based processors (up to 1.5 percent on a 20 MHz 386), the impact of enabling the counters on a 486 or higher is insignificant.

To turn on the disk counters, use the DISKPERF command. The syntax of DISKPERF is

```
diskperf -y \\computername
```

(You need only to supply the \\computername if you are enabling the counters on a remote system.)

Upon running DISKPERF, you receive the following response from the system:

```
Disk Performance counters on this system are now set to start at boot.
This change will take effect after the system is restarted.
```

DISKPERF changes the data for the Start value for the DiskPerf service from 4 (disabled) to zero (start at boot) in the Registry in the following path:

```
HKEY_LOCAL_MACHINE\SYSTEM\CurrentControlSet\Services\DiskPerf
```

> **Note** You must be a member of the local Administrators group on the machine on which you want to enable the disk performance counters.

Setting Chart Options

Each one of the four views (Chart, Alert, Log, and Report) has options that you can set that affect only that view. The Chart command in the Options menu enables you to set general options for the chart such as the type of chart (line graph or histogram), display of grid lines and labels, and the maximum value for the vertical axis.

The type of chart you use depends on what you are monitoring. The line chart is appropriate when you want to see changes in a particular counter over time. The histogram is useful when you want to compare a counter to other counters. The other options are primarily formatting questions that are up to your preference for the particular chart you are viewing.

By far, though, the most significant setting in this dialog box is the interval setting.

Adjusting the Update Interval

The Periodic Update interval determines how often Performance Monitor takes a snapshot of the objects that you have selected. The resolution of the picture that develops depends on how often you take the snapshots.

To change the interval between samples, choose Chart from the Options menu (see fig. 17.6). Type a new interval (in seconds) in the Interval text box and then choose OK.

Figure 17.6

*To set the sample frequency
for the chart, choose Chart
from the Options menu
and type a value for the
number of seconds between
samples in the Interval
text box.*

The Interval that you choose can make a big difference in the data reported by Performance Monitor. If you do not sample the data often enough, you risk missing important system events that happen entirely between samples. If you sample too frequently, you create additional overhead on the system that you are monitoring, affecting both the data that is collected and the overall performance of the system. The more remote the systems that are doing the monitoring are and the more counters that are being monitored, the more this effect is increased.

Saving Your Configuration in a Settings File

After taking the time to configure everything exactly as you want it, including all the counters and options you want in each view, you do not want to reconfigure your environment from scratch each time you run Performance Monitor. Instead, save your selections in a Settings file that can be loaded into Performance Monitor whenever you need it.

In the File menu are two different options for saving your configuration. Save Settings saves your environment for your current view (Chart, Alert, Log, or Report) only, without saving the others. Save Workspace saves your environment for all the views.

Table 17.4 shows the default extensions for each kind of Settings file. Although these are the default extensions, Performance Monitor enables you to use any extension you want for any type of settings file.

Tip | If you need to make minor changes to a Settings file, such as the computer names of the systems being monitored, you can edit the Settings file directly by using SETEDIT.EXE in the Windows NT Resource Kit.

Table 17.4
Default Extensions for Performance Monitor Settings Files

Extension	Contains Settings For
.PMC	Chart view
.PMA	Alert view
.PML	Log view
.PMR	Report view
.PMW	Workspace (all views)

After Performance Monitor starts, it looks in its working directory for a file named _DEFAULT.PMC for its default settings. If no file by that name is found, Performance Monitor starts up the same window size and location as when you last ran it, with no counters loaded.

You can have your settings in place and ready to use when you start Performance Monitor by adding the name of the settings file to the PERFMON command. To use a settings file called MONDAY.PMW, for example, type

```
perfmon monday.pmw
```

Tip

To specify the settings for your workspace to be the default whenever you start Performance Monitor, save your workspace as _DEFAULT.PMC. Even though Workspace files normally have a .PMW extension, this works fine!

Monitoring Remote Systems

To monitor counters on a remote system across the network, run Performance Monitor and then specify the computer name you want to collect data from when you add each counter. To monitor performance on a system called \\myserver, for example, choose Add to Chart from the Edit menu and then type **\\myserver** in the Computer text box. Performance Monitor retrieves the information from the remote system at each interval and displays the results.

You can remotely monitor the performance of any Windows NT system as long as the user account you are using has the "Access this computer from network" right on the system.

Only administrators, however, can run the Performance Monitor at the real-time priority class and enable the disk counters with the DISKPERF command. For more information on the disk counters, see "Turning On Disk Counters" earlier in this chapter.

> **Tip**
>
> If you need to enable the disk counters on a machine over the network, type
>
> ```
> diskperf -y \\servername
> ```
>
> where \\servername is the name of the machine on which you are enabling the counters. You can then reboot the machine remotely by using a tool such as the Shutdown GUI (SHUTGUI.EXE) in the Windows NT Resource Kit.

You can start Performance Monitor with a remote system selected by default by using the -c switch. To start Performance Monitor with the computer MYSERVER as the default, for example, type the following at the command prompt:

```
perfmon -c \\myserver
```

> **Note**
>
> Monitoring a remote system creates overhead for Performance Monitor on both the machine running PERFMON and the machine being monitored. An alternative is to run PERFMON as a service on the system that you want to monitor. You can then log the data locally on that system and look at the log it generated sometime later. For more information, see "Running Performance Monitor as a Service" later in this chapter.

Hands-On: Creating a Chart

Exercise 1: Getting the Chart Set Up

1. If the disk counters have not been enabled on your system (or you are not certain whether they are), enable them by entering the following from a command prompt:

   ```
   diskperf -y
   ```

2. Shut down and restart your system.

3. Log on with an administrative account and start Performance Monitor.

4. From the Edit menu, choose Add to Chart. The Add to Chart dialog box appears.

5. Choose Processor from the list of objects, choose %Processor Time from the list of counters, and then choose Add. Note the line graph appearing in the Chart window.

6. Add the following counters to your chart. When finished, choose Done.

   Logical Disk:%Disk Time

Memory:Pages/sec

Server:Bytes Total/sec

7. Select the Processor:%Processor Time counter in the legend. Notice the values for this counter in the value bar showing the minimum, maximum, and average values.

8. Generate some processor activity by minimizing and maximizing some windows. Note the effect on the processor in the chart display.

9. Save your settings for the chart in a settings file. From the File menu, choose Save Chart Settings As. Type **EX1.PMC** and then press Enter.

Exercise 2: Performance Monitor Overhead

1. Remove all counters from the preceding exercise except for Processor:%Processor Time.

2. From the Edit menu, choose Add to Chart and select the Process object. Note that the Instance box lists all running processes, including the Performance Monitor itself (PERFMON). Select the %Processor Time object and select the PERFMON instance, and then choose Add.

3. While you still have the Process object selected, add the Thread Count and Working Set counters for PERFMON to your chart.

4. Note the values for the counters by selecting each counter and examining the value bar for minimum, maximum, and average values that PERFMON is currently consuming. This is the PERFMON overhead on the system.

5. Exit Performance Monitor.

Exercise 3: Detecting a Bottleneck

1. Start the Performance Monitor from a command prompt by using the settings saved in Exercise 1 by entering

```
perfmon ex1.pmc
```

2. Note the baseline values for the four counters still being displayed

Processor:%Processor Time

LogicalDisk:%Disk Time (drive C:)

Memory:Pages/sec

Server:Bytes Total/sec

3. Create a new directory called C:\JUNK and then copy a large directory from one location on drive C: to the new \JUNK directory. As soon as you start the process, switch back to Performance Monitor to watch the action.

4. Examine the graph. Which component on the system was the bottleneck? Which component (if any) was the busiest?

5. Delete C:\JUNK.

Creating a Report

Unlike the Chart window, which displays a graph, Report view displays a simple list of counters and their values. The values are updated at each interval.

The Report window is better than Chart window for monitoring a large number of counters. As you add more counters, it becomes harder and harder to tell what each line represents in the Chart window, whereas the Report window has no such ambiguity. Figure 17.7 shows a sample of a display that is useful in a Report window but that would be difficult to read in a chart.

Figure 17.7

An uncluttered view of major counters on the system in the Report window.

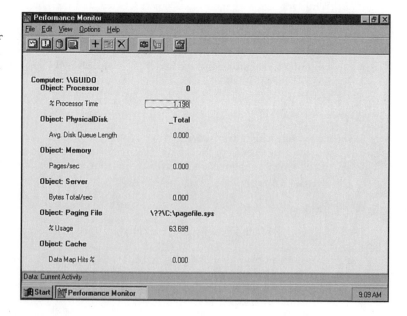

Adding Counters

Adding counters to the Chart window does not add them to the Report window, and vice versa. Each window has its own independent settings.

The actual process of adding counters to a Report is the same as in the Chart window. The only difference is that the counters are displayed as numeric values rather than as lines on a chart.

Tip	Because the Chart window provides a great overview and the Report window displays details well, consider displaying the system's vital signs in a Chart window; leave for the Report window the detailed counters used for exception analysis.

Often it is helpful to add all the counters for an object in Report view. Adding all the counters makes it easy to compare them (see fig. 17.8).

To add all the counters easily from the Add to Report dialog box, drag all their names with the mouse (or press Home and then Shift+End) and then choose Add.

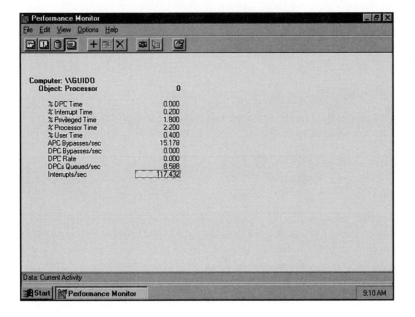

Figure 17.8

A Report can show all the processor counters.

Report Options

Unlike the Chart view, which has several useful options, the Report view has only one option: the update interval value. By default, the update interval is five seconds (the Chart view default is every second). This means that the default Report view has only one-fifth the resolution of the default Chart view.

> **Note**　In addition to defaulting to a lower resolution, the Report view has a little less processor overhead than Chart view because it has to display numeric values only rather than draw a chart.

Hands-On: Creating a Report

Exercise 4: Creating a Report

1. Start Performance Monitor.

2. From the View menu, choose Report.

3. Add the following counters for drive C: (be certain to choose the correct instance):

   LogicalDisk:%Disk Read Time

   LogicalDisk:%Disk Write Time

   LogicalDisk:%Free Space

4. Note that the counters are changing at each interval (every five seconds by default) because the data source indicated on the Status Bar is Current Activity.

5. From the Options menu, choose Report. Change the update interval to one second.

6. Create a \JUNK directory on C:.

7. Start a copy of a large directory to C:\JUNK (at least several megabytes) and then switch back to Performance Monitor to watch the action. As the files are being copied, you will likely see a higher percentage of the time on writes than on reads. This is due to caching of the disk. Because the counters are being updated every second, however, it is difficult to see how the read and write operations relate to each other. As you will see, this view is much more useful when looking at a static log file rather than real-time data collection.

8. Delete C:\JUNK.

Saving Performance Data in a Log

After you add a counter in Chart view or Report view, you begin to see the display of current activity, updated at the interval you specified for that view. These views, however, do not have any way to save the data that they are collecting for analysis later. That is the job of the Log view.

The Log view enables you to specify the objects that you want to observe and the interval at which to record the data (see fig. 17.9). All the counters for each selected object are logged to a file on disk. After you add the Processor object to your log settings, you are instructing Performance Monitor to save all the counters (%Processor Time, %Privileged Time, %User Time, Interrupts/sec, and so on) for all instances of the object (for example, multiple processors).

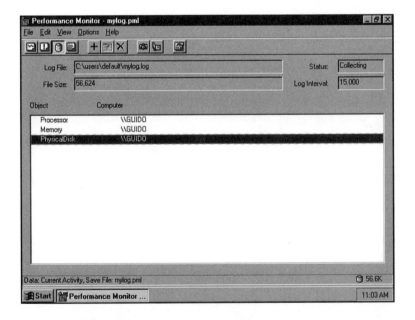

Figure 17.9

Configure the Log window to log performance data to disk for the Processor, Memory, and PhysicalDisk objects.

After the data has been captured to disk, you can retrieve the logged information in any of the other views to perform analysis on the data.

Logging Performance Data to a File

Generating a log of performance data involves four steps:

1. In the Log window, add the objects that you want to log.

2. From the Options menu, choose Log. The Log Options dialog box appears (see fig. 17.10). Specify a file name, location, and update interval.

> **Warning**   Be very careful about the counters that you choose to log and the frequency. The log file can grow very large very quickly.
>
> Logging the Processor, Process, Memory, and Logical Disk objects for an hour with an update interval of every second, for example, produces a log file over 30 MB! Reducing the resolution to an update interval of five seconds cuts the size down to 6 MB.

Figure 17.10

*The Log Options dialog box. Do not set the update interval too small because **all** counters for the selected objects are logged to disk.*

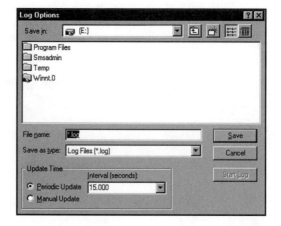

3. In the Log Options dialog box, choose Start Log. As the information is being logged, the size of the log file displays in the Status Bar at the lower-left corner of the Performance Monitor window.

4. After you have the data you need, choose Log from the Options menu, and then choose Stop Log.

Note   You can use DATALOG.EXE to automate the capture process on systems across the network. For more information, see "Running Performance Monitor as a Service," later in this chapter.

Viewing Logged Data

To view the data that you logged to the log file, follow these steps:

1. Choose the view that you want to use (Chart, Alert, or Report).

2. From the Options menu, choose Data From.

3. Select the log file created earlier and then choose OK.

4. Use the Add To choice in the Edit menu to add the counters that you want to view. Only counters for the objects logged can be selected. The data is displayed for analysis.

The process is the same no matter which view or views you use for analysis.

Selecting a Time Window

One of the advantages of logging data for analysis later is that you can change the start and end points of the display of information. You may have logged data from 8:00 a.m. to 10:00 a.m. for example, but you are primarily interested in the activity between 8:30 a.m. and 9:00 a.m. because that is when most users log on. By using a Time Window, you can narrow your focus to display only the data between those two points; Performance Monitor also recalculates the Min, Max, and Average values based on the data included in the Time Window only.

To select a portion of the logged data to view, choose Time Window from the Edit menu. You can then adjust the end points of the data to display (see fig. 17.11).

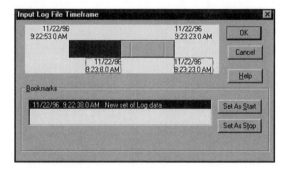

Figure 17.11

Choosing Time Window from the Edit menu displays the Input Log File Timeframe dialog box.

While you are logging the data, you can create bookmarks in the captured data and then refer to those bookmarks in the data by name when specifying the start and end points of the display. If you want to limit your view to when a certain task is running, for example, you can create a bookmark, run the task, and then create another bookmark after the task is complete. Selecting the two bookmarks as the beginning and end points for the display focuses your attention on the task being measured and gives you more useful cumulative data (such as the averages).

Saving the Log Settings

After you finish configuring the Log window with the objects you want to log, you can save your settings the same way as with the other views. Choose Save Settings from the File menu. Log settings are saved with a .PML extension by default.

Exporting Log Data

The data collected in the log can be exported to a text file as tab-separated values (.TSV) or comma-separated values (.CSV), whichever you prefer. To export data, choose a view (Chart, Alert, or Report), add the counters that you want to export, and then choose Export from the File menu. You can then import the data into another program for analysis, such as a spreadsheet or database program.

Hands-On: Creating a Performance Log

Exercise 5: Creating a Log File

1. Start Performance Monitor.

2. From the View menu, choose Log.

3. From the Edit menu, choose Add to Chart. Add the Processor, Memory, and Logical Disk objects to the Log window.

4. From the Options menu, choose Log.

5. In the File name box, type **test.log**. Set the update interval to one second. Choose Start Log to begin logging the objects to the disk.

6. Wait five seconds.

7. Using Program Manager, run the Control Panel from the Main program group. Double-click on the Network icon. Cancel from the Network dialog box and then close the Control Panel.

8. Wait five more seconds.

9. From the Options menu, choose Log. Choose Stop Log to stop the logging of data to the disk and then choose OK to exit.

Exercise 6: Displaying Data from a Log

1. From the View menu, choose Chart to display the Chart window.

2. From the Options menu, choose Data From.

3. Choose Log file, type the name of the log file to open (**test.log**), and then choose OK. The Chart view is now using the data from the log file rather than current activity.

4. Add the following counters to the chart:

   LogicalDisk:%Disk Time

Memory:Pages/sec

Processor:%Processor Time

5. Note the average utilization of the processor (covers the entire time that data was logged).

6. From the Edit menu, choose Time Window.

7. Drag the starting point of the Time Window to just before the increased activity on the chart (a vertical line appears on the chart to show you the cutoff point). Drag the end point of the Time Window to just after the activity and then choose OK. The Chart window now displays only the data collected between those two end points.

8. Note the average utilization of the processor; it has been recalculated to reflect the average for the Time Window. If what you are trying to measure is the peak demand from a task, this is a more useful number than the one for the entire log.

9. Close Performance Monitor and then delete test.log.

Alert and Performance Monitor

Last, but not least, this chapter examines the Alert window. In managing a group of servers, the last thing you want to do is to be watching the Performance Monitor window in hopes that you will spot performance problems. Instead, you can have Performance Monitor notify you automatically, based on criteria you specify. You can even specify a command line that you want to run when the alert condition is detected.

One of the critical resources that you should monitor on file servers, for example, is the amount of free disk space remaining on each logical drive. In the Alert window of Performance Monitor, you can create a new alert for the % Free Space counter, specifying a threshold value (for example, less than 10%). Performance Monitor checks the value for this counter at the interval you specify (every five seconds by default). If the amount of free space is less than 10% at any of those intervals, an alert is generated.

Just as with the other views in Performance Monitor, you need to set the resolution of the alert process by setting the Alert Options (choose Alert from the Options menu).

Setting an Alert in Performance Monitor

You add alert settings in the same way that you add counters to the Chart or Report window. Figure 17.12 shows the Add to Alert dialog box that is displayed when you choose Add to Alert from the Edit menu. Notice that the dialog box includes two new options:

■ **A threshold value (Alert If).** Specify a minimum or maximum threshold by choosing Over or Under and then typing a value in the text box. Make sure that you use the same units of measurement as the counter. For example, % Free Space is a percentage; if you mean 10%, do not type 0.1 for the threshold.

■ **An action to perform (Run Program on Alert).** Typing a command line in the text box causes that command line to execute when an alert occurs. If you want the Performance Monitor to send a message to your beeper when a particular alert occurs, you can specify a command line that would send a message to you via your paging service.

Figure 17.12

Setting an alert on %Processor Time. A value greater 90% generates an alert.

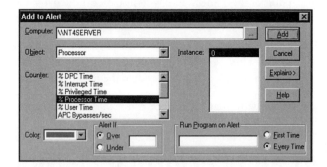

Note   Batch files should not be used in the Run Program on Alert box. See "Triggering Actions When Alerts Occur," which follows.

Table 17.5 contains a list of counters and threshold values that would be useful to monitor with alerts.

Table 17.5
Common Alert Settings with Threshold Values for a File Server

Counter	Threshold
Processor:%Processor Time	>90
System:Processor Queue Length	>2
Physical Disk:%Disk Time	>70
Logical Disk:%Free Space	<10
Memory:Pages/sec	>30
Memory:Available Bytes	<4 MB

Note Be sure to include all relevant instances. For example, if you are monitoring the logical disk object, include all of the instances (drive C:, drive D:, and so on).

How Alerts are Generated

At each update interval specified in the Alert Options, Performance Monitor checks the values of the counters against their threshold values. If a value satisfies the alert condition (for example, the %Free Space is less than ten percent), then Performance Monitor logs an alert in the Alert Log pane of the Alert window. If the alert condition is still present at subsequent update intervals, additional entries are made to the Alert Log.

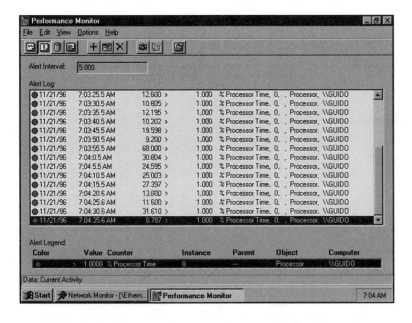

Figure 17.13

The Alert window with multiple alerts recorded in the Alert Log.

Triggering Actions When Alerts Occur

In addition to logging the event in the Alert Log within Performance Monitor, you can choose to do any of the following:

■ **Log alerts to the Windows NT Application Log (viewed with the Event Viewer).** You can turn on this option globally (for all alert settings) by choosing Alert from the Options menu and then turning on the Log Event in Application Log check box.

■ **Send an Alert message to a predefined computer or user on the network.** If you choose Alert from the Options menu, you can turn on the Send network message check box and type a computer name or user name in the Net Name text box to be notified whenever any alert occurs.

The alert recipient name set in Performance Monitor has no relationship to the recipients of the Windows NT alerts you can configure on a per-server basis in Server Manager. Those alerts are generated only by the operating system.

In order for the alert message to be delivered, the target system has to be running the Messenger service (Windows NT) or WinPopUp (Windows 95 and Windows for Workgroups).

■ **Run a command line when a specific alert occurs.** Although the other two actions are global (any alert triggers them), you can type the command line to be executed in the Run Program on Alert text box for the specific setting involved.

Figure 17.14

Set the Options for the Alert window to log events to the NT event log and to notify the user "perfmgr" when alerts occur.

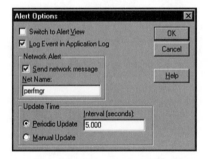

Tip	Do not use batch files that are processed by the command prompt in the Run Program on Alert text box. Performance Monitor passes parameters to the command line that are in Unicode format and include the greater-than and less-than signs (< and >). These symbols are interpreted by the command prompt as redirection of input and output (stdin and stdout), causing your batch file to fail.
	Instead, run a command line that does not use the command prompt. One tool that you can use to create your own executables without the use of batch files is a product from Microsoft called MS Test. Originally designed as a development environment for testing Windows applications, it also serves as a way to automate any Windows task. Another alternative, which requires less programming skill, is WinBatch from WilsonWare.

Changing the Alert Recipient

You can specify the computer name or user name that should receive notification of alerts in the Log Options dialog box. If you prefer to direct the alert messages to a name on the network that is set aside for this purpose, you can register a unique NetBIOS name on the network at the target workstation.

For example, to deliver all alert messages to a special name "perfmgr," first register that name on the network by entering the following at a command prompt:

```
net name perfmgr /add
```

The name "perfmgr" is registered at the computer. Any messages sent to perfmgr now appears as pop-up messages on this computer.

Alerts on Logged Data

If you have saved performance data in a log file, you can use the Alert window to help you analyze the data and highlight problems. From the Options menu, choose Data From and then select the log file. Performance Monitor loads all of the data into memory. If you then create some alert settings, Performance Monitor generates alerts in the Alert Log for all of the history just as if it had been monitoring it live.

Hands-On: Creating Alerts

Exercise 7: Creating an Alert

1. At the command prompt, type **net name perfmgr /add** and press Enter.

2. In Performance Monitor, choose Chart from the View menu. Add the Logical Disk:%Free Space counter for drive C: to the chart. Notice the amount of space that is currently free on the drive.

3. Choose Alert from the View menu.

4. Choose Alert from the Options menu. Turn on the Log Event in Application Log check box. Turn on the Send network message check box, type **perfmgr** in the Net Name box, and choose OK.

5. From the Edit menu, choose Add to Alert.

6. Choose the Logical Disk object and then select the %Free Space counter and the Instance for drive C:. In the Alert If box, choose Under, and type **10** in the text box (this represents ten percent). Choose Add and then choose Done.

7. Create a C:\JUNK directory.

8. Copy enough files into the C:\JUNK directory so that the amount of free space is less than ten percent. In a few seconds you should receive a pop-up message for the alert, and the Alert Log should include an alert entry for the %Free Space counter.

9. Delete the C:\JUNK directory. Wait a few seconds to see if any alert messages are generated (you should not get any alerts because the alert condition is no longer true).

10. Copy the same files back to the C:\JUNK directory. You should receive the alert again.

11. Close Performance Monitor.

Performance Monitor Tips

In this section, you learn tips and techniques in Performance Monitor that can make you an expert. You learn how to

■ Use keyboard shortcuts

■ Reduce the overhead used by Performance Monitor

■ Run multiple instances of Performance Monitor (and understand why you would want to do this)

■ Run Performance Monitor as a service

■ Simulate a memory shortage on your system

Using Keyboard Shortcuts

Table 17.5 contains a list of useful shortcut keys in Performance Monitor.

Table 17.5
Performance Monitor Shortcut Keys

Key	Function
BackSpace	Highlight current selection in legend
Ctrl+P	Always on top
Ctrl+U	Update now
Ctrl+E	Bring up time window
Tab	Add to command from the Edit menu
Ctrl+C	Chart window
Ctrl+A	Alert window

Key	Function
Ctrl+L	Log window
Ctrl+R	Report window
Ctrl+O	Options menu
Ctrl+W	Save Workspace
Ctrl+B	Create bookmark
Ctrl+M	Display or hide menu and title bars
Ctrl+T	Display or hide toolbar
Ctrl+S	Display or hide status line
Ctrl+F12	Open file
Shift+F12	Save file
F12	Save As file
F1	Help

Reducing the Overhead Used by Performance Monitor

The Performance Monitor tool is not free when it comes to system performance. As soon as you start to measure performance, you have changed it. Running the Performance Monitor tool creates additional demand for system resources such as processor, memory, and network. The amount of extra overhead depends on a number of factors:

- **The frequency of data collection.** The more often that you sample the values of the counters, the more work you are asking the system to do, just to report them. Setting the update interval to one second, for example, creates twice the overhead of setting the interval to two seconds. Thus, the more often you sample the performance data, the more you degrade the performance of the system you are measuring.

- **The number of objects to be measured.** After you add an object to be reported from a remote system, performance monitor gets all the counters for that object, even if you choose to display only some of them. You need to be especially careful about monitoring the Thread object; even a standard install of Windows NT has more than 100 threads for the operating system alone.

- **The location of log files.** If you are monitoring disk activity and you are logging the data, the location of the log file can affect the results. To remove this factor, you can put the log file on another disk. Remember, however, that if you decide to log the data to a network disk, you affect the network performance.

Running Multiple Instances of Performance Monitor

You can run multiple instances of Performance Monitor on your system. It is useful to do this if you are monitoring several objects on multiple systems; you can run a separate Performance Monitor window for each object (one for Processor, one for Memory, and so on), making it easier to compare the activity on those machines if you do not have a mixture of data types in the chart.

Another reason to run more than one instance of Performance Monitor is to display more than one view of the data at a time. You might want one window to display a chart, for example, while another window displays a report (see fig. 17.15).

Figure 17.15

Two Performance Monitor windows: one with a Chart and one with a Report.

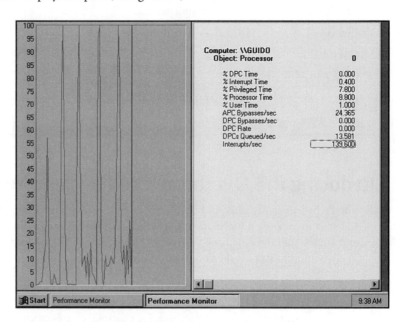

Running Performance Monitor as a Service

Monitoring a server from a remote workstation has a cost associated with it in terms of processor overhead on the system running Performance Monitor and network activity. It also requires that you be logged on at a Windows NT system running the tool for any data to be collected.

Both of these limitations of Performance Monitor are solved if you run it as a service so that it runs regardless of anyone being logged on. Data can be logged to the local hard disk, avoiding any additional network traffic. You can even configure your system so that Performance Monitor starts automatically when the system starts.

To run Performance Monitor as a service, you need two utilities from the Windows NT Resource Kit: DATALOG.EXE and MONITOR.EXE. Datalog is the monitoring service itself. The monitor program is used to install the service and then to control how the service runs.

To install DATALOG.EXE as a service, place a copy of it and monitor.exe in the <winntroot>\system32 directory and then enter the following at a command prompt:

```
monitor setup
```

After the service is installed, you can start and stop the service by using the monitor command. Table 17.6 provides a list of switches for MONITOR.EXE.

Table 17.6
Switches for the Monitor Command

Switch	Function
setup	Installs DATALOG.EXE as a service and modifies the Registry
filename.pmw	Workspace file containing Performance Monitor settings (objects to log, alert definitions, and so on)
start	Starts the service
stop	Stops the service
pause	Pauses the service, stops logging
continue	Continues the service, continues logging
automatic	Starts the service automatically at boot
manual	Sets the start up of the service to manual (use monitor to start it)
disable	Disables the service (monitor commands are ignored)

To configure the service to use a particular workspace settings file (including the counters to log), type

```
monitor \\myserver myworkspace.pmw
```

To start the service manually, type

```
monitor \\myserver start
```

You can schedule the service to start and stop by using the Schedule service and the AT command:

```
at \\myserver 8:00 "monitor start"
at \\myserver 9:00 "monitor stop"
```

Alternatively, you can configure the service to start automatically when the system is started:

```
monitor \\myserver automatic
```

Simulating a Memory Shortage

To create a memory shortage on your system to see how it responds, tell Windows NT to use less than the total physical memory. To do this, use the MAXMEM switch in BOOT.INI. The second line in the following BOOT.INI causes Windows NT to use only 16 MB of RAM, no matter how much physical RAM is installed:

```
[boot loader]
timeout=30
default=multi(0)disk()rdisk(0)partition(1)\WINNT
[operating systems]
multi(0)disk(0)rdisk(0)partition(1)\WINNT="Windows NT Server"
multi(0)disk(0)rdisk(0)partition(1)\WINNT="Windows NT 16 MB" /MAXMEM=16
```

Note   A tool included in the Windows NT Resource Kit called Response Probe enables you to create a synthetic workload on your system. You can then watch how your system reacts to the increased demands for resources. For information on how to use Response Probe, see Appendix C of *Optimizing Windows NT* by Russ Blake.

Conclusion

In this chapter, you have learned how to use the Performance Monitor to display and log performance data in Windows NT. As you have seen, there is a wealth of information about your system available through the Performance Monitor.

Every administrator should invest the time needed to learn this essential tool and set up automated tracking of performance of their servers.

Supporting Windows NT Server Clients

The Windows NT Server supports a number of different client computers, such as MS-DOS, Windows 3.x, Windows 95, Windows NT, OS/2, and Macintosh. This chapter discusses the network client architecture, protocols, and APIs used to access Windows NT Server resources.

You will learn about the Network Client Administrator tool and how to use this tool to install and configure different clients to access a Windows NT Server.

Examining the Architecture of Network Clients

To support a large number of different clients, the networking software supplied by Microsoft for clients follows a general networking model. The network client architecture consists of a number of components that can be understood best in terms of the OSI model.

Looking at Windows NT Clients and the OSI Model

Figure 18.1 shows a networking model for Windows NT clients. The following are the network components on the client:

- Network adapters

- Network drivers

- Client network protocol stacks

- Network APIs

- The Redirector

Figure 18.1

Network client architecture.

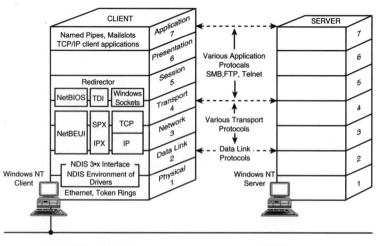

The network adapters can be considered as part of layers 1 and 2 of the OSI model, and are the physical aspects of the network on the client workstation.

Network Drivers

The network drivers provided by Microsoft are written using the NDIS interface (Network Driver Interface Specification) enabling multiple protocols to communicate with one or more network adapters. The NDIS drivers for most popular cards are shipped with Windows NT. You can think of the NDIS drivers as the interface between layers 2 and 3 of the OSI model. In reality, NDIS drivers implement portions of layers 2 and 3 of the OSI model. Figure 18.2 shows the NDIS interface; the NDIS driver has a wrapper DLL around it that implements the NDIS interface. Multiple protocols—such as NetBEUI, TCP/IP with Streams, and IPX/SPX—communicate with the NDIS interface.

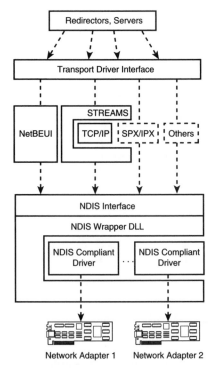

- NDIS shields details of physical networks from transport protocols

- NDIS enables multiple protocol stacks to share a network adapter

- NDIS enables a protocol stack to use multiple network adapters

- NDIS 3.x has been updated to use 32-bit addresses and multiprocessors

Figure 18.2

The NDIS interface.

Client Network Protocol Stacks

The network protocol stacks comprise layers 3, 4, and 5 (optional) of the OSI model. Windows NT ships with the following client protocols:

- NetBEUI

- IPX/SPX (called NWLink IPX Compatible Protocol in Windows NT)

- TCP/IP

A server and its clients must use a common protocol to communicate. To support Macintosh workstations that use the AppleTalk protocol, you must install Services for Macintosh at the Windows NT Server.

Network APIs

If the client is using the NetBEUI protocol, the *Network Basic Input/Output System* (NetBIOS) interface is available to client applications. NetBIOS is a Session level interface used to communicate with other NetBIOS-compliant protocol stacks. Microsoft's implementation of NetBIOS often is called *NetBIOS Frame* (NBF). NetBIOS was developed by Sytek (now part of Hughes LAN Systems) for the IBM Broadband PC Network (PCN).

The network Redirector uses NetBIOS to communicate with other computers running the same interface. NetBIOS establishes logical names for computers on the network and virtual circuits between those logical names, ensuring reliable data transfer.

The *Windows sockets interface*, (WINSOCK) is an implementation of the popular BSD sockets programming interface for TCP/IP networks. The sockets interface was developed for BSD Unix, but has been adopted widely on other Unix and non-Unix platforms. WINSOCK is used by client applications to communicate with the TCP/IP protocol stack. Version 2 of WINSOCK can be used with TCP/IP, IPX, DecNET, and OSI protocols.

Both NetBIOS and WINSOCK are implemented as DLLs in the Windows environment.

The *Transport Driver Interface* (TDI) provides a uniform interface to the various transport protocols that can exist in the Windows NT environment. The TDI provides an interface to the network components at the Session layer of the OSI model. The TDI enables virtual circuits to be established with applications on other computers.

The *Named Pipes* and *Mailslot Application Programming Interfaces* (APIs) are modeled using file system operations such as Open, Read, and Write. However, the operations are not performed on actual files. They are translated as commands to the network transport protocols to communicate with other applications that use the same APIs on remote computers.

On Windows NT, Named Pipes are based on OS/2 APIs but have additional asynchronous support and increased security. The Mailslot APIs on Windows NT are a subset of the Mailslot APIs in OS/2. Mailslots are categorized as *first-class* mailslots, which provide connections-oriented communications, and *second-class* mailslots, which provide connectionless communications useful for messaging and broadcasting applications. In Windows NT, only second-class mailslots are used. Because second-class mailslots are connectionless, messages delivered using this API are not guaranteed to be delivered. Second-class mailslot messages are used by clients to identify other computers and services, and to send notification messages.

Windows NT clients have an added feature for named pipes called *impersonation*. Impersonation enables a server that is servicing a request to change its security ID (SID) to match the requesting client's SID. Impersonation means that the request is carried out by impersonating the client's SID and is therefore permitted to execute only if the client has the authority to execute the request.

Remote access to named pipes and mailslots is provided through the Redirector component.

The Redirector

The *Redirector* is the component that enables a client computer to gain access to resources on another computer as if the remote resources were local to the client computer. The Redirector communicates with other computers using the protocol stack.

Figure 18.3 shows the Redirector's use of the Server Message Block (SMB) protocol in a Windows NT client. The Redirector is implemented as a file system driver and is represented by the object name \Device\Redirector. Requests by a client for a file on a remote computer are sent to the I/O Manager. The I/O Manager calls a driver entry point for the Redirector. The Dispatch routines within the Redirector translate the I/O request to SMB protocol requests. The SMB protocol can translate I/O requests into requests for services on the remote computer.

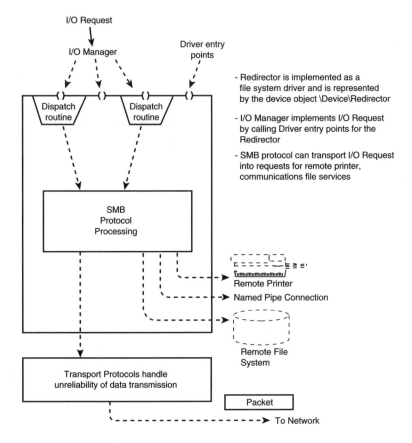

- Redirector is implemented as a file system driver and is represented by the device object \Device\Redirector

- I/O Manager implements I/O Request by calling Driver entry points for the Redirector

- SMB protocol can transport I/O Request into requests for remote printer, communications file services

Figure 18.3
The Redirector and the SMB protocol.

Understanding the Interaction Between a Client and a Windows NT Server

Figures 18.4 and 18.5 show the client-side and server-side view as requests are sent from the client to the computer. In this example, the client is shown issuing a request for a file resource on the server.

Client-side view of network operation (see fig. 18.4):

1. An application issues a request for a file service on the Windows NT Server.

2. In a Windows NT client, the I/O Manager creates an I/O request packet and passes it to the file system driver—in this case, the Redirector. In non-Windows NT clients, the request is sent directly to the Redirector component of the network client software.

3. The Redirector forwards the request for network processing to the network transport drivers.

4. The network transport drivers forward the request to the NDIS drivers.

5. NDIS drivers issue commands to transmit a packet containing the original request to the physical network.

Server-side view of network operation (see fig. 18.5):

6. The NDIS drivers on the server receive the packet from the network adapter.

7. The network transport drivers receive the packet from the NDIS drivers.

8. The request is received by the server module.

9. The server module decides if the request can be satisfied by the local file system. If the request needs to be sent to a gateway service, then the request is sent to that service. An example of a gateway service is Gateway Service for NetWare.

10. The local file system issues a command to the local disk drive on the server.

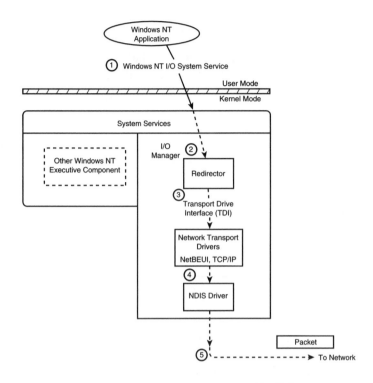

Figure 18.4

The client-side view of network I/O.

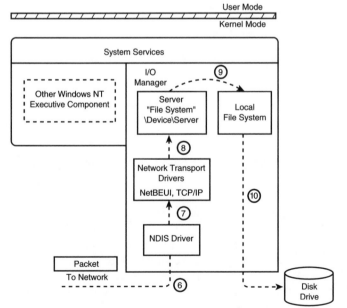

Figure 18.5

The server-side view of network I/O.

The SMB protocol was developed by IBM originally, and then jointly developed by both Microsoft and IBM. The network requests are encoded as Network Control Block (NCB) data structures. The NCB data structures are encoded in SMB format for transmission across the network. SMB is used in many of the Microsoft- and IBM-derived networking software, such as the following:

■ MS-Net

■ IBM PC Network

■ IBM LAN Server

■ MS LAN Manager

■ LAN Manager for Unix

■ DEC PATHWORKS

■ MS Windows for Workgroups

■ Ungermann-Bass Net/1

SMB messages can be categorized into four types:

■ **Session Control.** Used to establish or discontinue Redirector connections with a remote network resource such as a directory or printer.

■ **File.** Used to access and manipulate file system resources on the remote computer.

■ **Printer.** Used by the Redirector to send print data to a remote printer or queue, and to obtain the status of remote print devices.

■ **Message.** Used by applications and system components to send unicast or broadcast messages.

Understanding How Network Drives Are Redirected to the Redirector

DOS, Windows, and Windows NT clients that need to access a directory on a Windows NT Server can do so by using available drive letters such as F, G, and so on. These drive letters are called *network drives*. The client operating system translates these network drive letter references for the Redirector. Figure 18.6 shows how this is accomplished for Windows NT clients. The drive letters such as A, B, ... F are implemented as symbolic links. The drive letter A is a symbolic link to \Device\Floppy0. The drive letter F is a symbolic link to the \Device\Redirector. A reference to the drive letter F, therefore, would be translated to \Device\Redirector, which has directory assignment information for the local drive letter F.

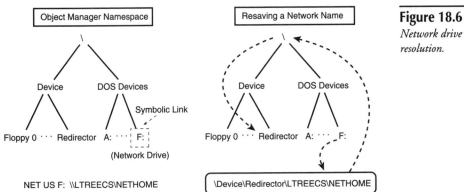

Figure 18.6

Network drive name resolution.

Understanding the Provider Component

To support connections with other network architectures such as NetWare and VINES, the Windows NT network architecture uses the concept of a provider. Figure 18.7 shows the Provider layer, called the *Multiple Provider Router* (MPR), which provides a common interface to access different network resources. In the example in figure 18.7, the MPR can use the Windows NT Redirector, the NetWare Redirector, or some other Redirector. The MPR can be accessed by applications through the *WNet APIs*, which are system calls used by applications to access network resources. Because of the MPR, the WNet APIs work with a variety of network architectures. The WNet API is part of the Win32 subsystem APIs and can be used to connect to multiple networks, browse computers in a workgroup or domain, and transfer data. The Windows NT File Manager is an example of an application that uses WNet API calls for managing network connections and for network browsing.

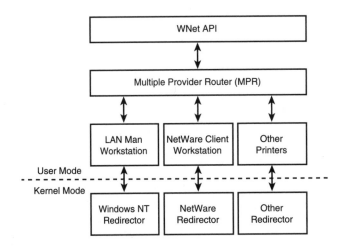

Figure 18.7

Provider architecture.

The WNet API is one of two methods used by applications for accessing network resources. The other method is the Uniform Naming Convention (UNC), which enables access to a network resource on a computer by using a share name defined for the resource. The UNC format is:

```
\\server\sharename\subdir1\subdir2\...\filename
```

To support UNC names, a Multiple UNC Provider (MUP) component is provided that translates requests involving UNC names received from the I/O Manager to one of the UNC providers. During its initialization, Workstation services register with the MUP. MUP maintains a cache of UNC names that it has seen and resolved to a UNC provider. If MUP has not seen a given UNC name for 15 minutes, it sends the UNC name to each UNC provider. MUP tries each UNC provider (Redirector) in the order of the MUPs' registered priorities. When a provider indicates that it can access the UNC resource, the MUP sends the remainder of the command to that provider.

Using Windows NT Server Clients

The following client software is included with Windows NT Server distribution software:

- MS Network Client for MS-DOS

- MS LAN Manager for MS-DOS

- MS LAN Manager for OS/2

- Windows for Workgroups

The Windows for Workgroup software is provided for over-the-network installations. Before installing this software, ensure that you have a valid software license.

In addition to the previously mentioned client software, the Windows NT Server distribution CD-ROM contains connectivity tools such as Remote Access Server for MS-DOS and MS TCP/IP 32-Bit for Windows for Workgroups 3.11.

Figure 18.8 illustrates the different clients included for Windows NT Server.

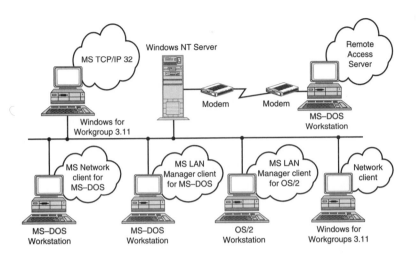

Figure 18.8
Clients for Windows NT Server.

Using the Network Client Administrator Tool

The network client software is included on the Windows NT Server distribution CD-ROM. Before you can install the network client software, you must generate the appropriate boot disks and set up the client software on the Windows NT Server for download and installation. The tool used to accomplish these tasks is the Network Client Administrator. This tool enables you to install the software clients shipped with Windows NT Server. By using the Network Client Administrator, you can accomplish the following tasks:

- Create floppy disk sets for installing network client software.

- Create a shared directory on a Windows NT server that is used to install Windows NT clients, Windows 3.x clients, and Windows NT Server tools.

- Create a network installation startup disk that is used to perform an over-the-network installation of the network client for DOS or Windows for Workgroups on a workstation.

You can use any of the following methods to access the client installation files and to create a network client installation startup disk or disk set:

- Share the CLIENTS directory on the Windows NT Server.

- Share the CLIENTS directory on the CD-ROM device that contains the Windows NT Server distribution CD-ROM.

- Copy network client installation files to the local hard disk on the workstation.

You use the Network Client Administrator to create a shared directory on the Windows NT Server, which contains the aforementioned client software.

To create floppy disks for the network client software installation, use table 18.1 as a guide for the number of disks required. To avoid disk incompatibility problems, ensure that the disks are formatted by using the operating system that is on target workstation. If you are installing the client software on an OS/2 computer, for example, format the disk with the OS/2 version running on that computer.

Table 18.1
Number of Floppy Disks Needed for Installation Files

Software	Installation Disk Set	Network Installation Startup Disk
MS Network Client for MS-DOS and Windows	2	1
MS LAN Manager Client for MS-DOS	4	
MS LAN Manager Client for OS/2	4	
MS TCP/IP 32-Bit for Windows for Workgroups	1	
RAS for MS-DOS	1	

Creating the Share Name for the Client Installation Files

When you install Windows NT Server, Network Client Administrator is installed in the Administrative Tools folder. To create the shared CLIENTS directory, use the Network Client Administrator and the Windows NT Server distribution CD-ROM.

To run the Network Client Administrator tool, follow these steps:

1. Log on as an Administrator user to the Windows NT Server and open the Administrative Tools (Common) Folder.

2. Start the Network Client Administrator tool. The Network Client Administrator dialog box appears (see fig. 18.9).

Figure 18.9

The Network Client Administrator dialog box.

Before you can create client startup or installation disks, you must first perform an on-time configuration of the shared CLIENTS directory. To copy the files to the Windows NT Server to create disk sets, you only need to copy them once by selecting either of the following options:

- Make Network Installation Startup Disk

- Make Installation Disk Set

3. If you choose one of these options, the Share Network Client Installation Files dialog box appears (see fig. 18.10). Use this dialog box to indicate whether you want to share the network client installation files that are on the Windows NT Server distribution CD-ROM, to copy the files to a new shared directory and then share the files, or to specify the share name of the directory to which files have already been copied.

The Path field indicates where the installation files are located. If this is the first time you have selected this Network Client Administrator option, this field should be set to the CD-ROM path.

If you previously installed the network client on a different path, select the Use Existing Path option.

To share the files contained on the Windows NT distribution CD-ROM, select Share Files and type the share name in the adjacent Share Name field. The default name for the CD-ROM share is Clients.

To copy the CD-ROM installation files to a directory and then share the directory, select the Copy Files to a New Directory, and then Share option. This is the preferred option to install client software for a large number of clients. If you select this option, enter information in the Destination Path field for the location of the files to be copied. Additionally, specify the share name in the Share Name field.

Figure 18.10

The Share Network Client Installation Files dialog box.

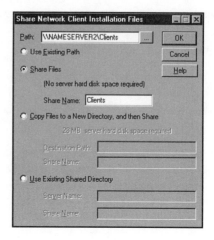

You need approximately 43 MB of disk space on the server if you select the Copy Files to a New Directory, and then Share option.

To use installation files that have been previously copied, select the Use Existing Shared Directory option. If you select this option, specify the server and share name in the Server Name and Share Name fields.

After making your selections, click OK.

The menus that appear next depend on which option you selected in the Network Client Administrator dialog box, and are described in the following sections.

Creating the Network Installation Startup Disk

To create an installation startup disk for MS Network Client for MS-DOS or a Windows for Workgroups client, select the Make Network Installation Startup Disk in the Network Client Administrator dialog box. The installation disk you create with this option starts the client computer, connects to the computer containing the installation files, and initiates the client installation.

To make a network installation startup disk, follow these steps:

1. Create a bootable system disk, preferably formatted on the target client workstation.

2. Start the Network Client Administrator. Select the Make Network Installation Startup Disk option in the Network Client Administrator dialog box. Select Continue. The Share Network Client Installation Files dialog box appears.

3. Specify the shared directory or path containing the client installation files and click OK. The Target Workstation Configuration dialog box appears (see fig. 18.11).

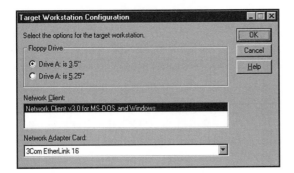

Figure 18.11

The Target Workstation Configuration dialog box for the network startup disk.

4. Select the floppy drive type in the Floppy Drive section. Your choices are Drive A: is 3.5" and Drive A: is 5.25".

In the Network Client box, select the appropriate workstation software. Your choices are Windows for Workgroups and Network Client v3.0 for MS-DOS and Windows.

In the Network Adapter Card field, select the network adapter driver.

Click OK. The Network Startup Disk Configuration dialog box appears (see fig. 18.12).

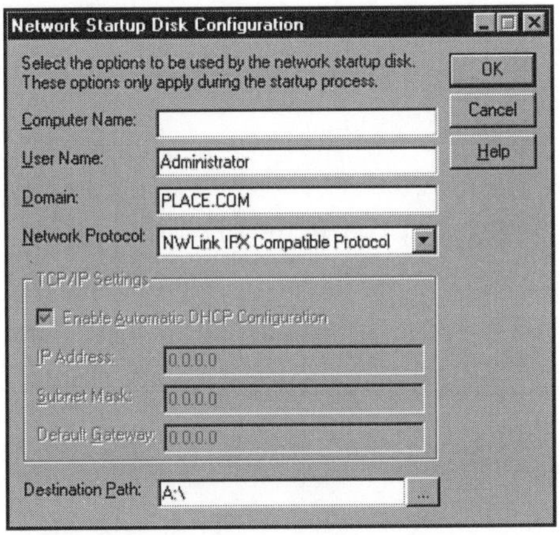

Figure 18.12

The Network Startup Disk Configuration dialog box.

5. In the Computer Name field, enter the computer name for the workstation client. This is a 1- to 15-character computer name that is unique on the network.

In the User Name field, enter the name that identifies the user to the network. This should be a user account in the domain or computer that has at least Read privileges to the shared directory on the server.

In the Domain field, enter the domain name or computer name of the Windows NT Server that contains the installation files.

From the Network Protocol drop-down list, select the network protocol to be used to establish the network connection to the server for client installation. Your choices are NetBEUI, NWLink, or TCP/IP. The network installation disk can use a different protocol than the one used by the installed client software. You must ensure, however, that the server is configured to use the protocol that you select.

If you select the NWLink client, the default frame type selected is 802.2 for Ethernet adapters. This frame type is saved in the \NET\PROTOCOL.INI file on the network installation startup disk. To use a different frame type, such as 802.3 or Ethernet_II, you must manually change the PROTOCOL.INI file.

If you select the TCP/IP protocol, the network installation startup disk is by default configured as a DHCP (Dynamic Host Configurable Protocol) client. The DHCP client obtains its IP address configuration from a DHCP server. If a DHCP server is not set up, you must provide an IP address, subnet mask, and, optionally, a gateway IP address that can be used on the network. You can enter IP address information only if the Enable Automatic DHCP Configuration check box is not enabled.

In the Destination Path field, select the location where startup files are to be copied. This is usually the floppy drive A. If you do not have a bootable system floppy disk formatted for the workstation, you can specify a destination path that is a directory. The Network Client Administrator will copy the network startup files to this directory. You can copy these files to the system disk later.

Select OK.

If you selected a destination path that is a directory, you see a message that the destination drive you selected does not match the drive type in the target workstation. Select OK to acknowledge this message.

The Confirm Network Disk Configuration information box summarizing your selections appears (see fig. 18.13). Confirm your selections by selecting OK.

Figure 18.13

*The Confirm Network
Disk Configuration
dialog box.*

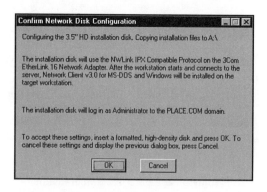

If you selected a destination path that is a directory, you see another message that the target disk is not a system disk. Click OK to acknowledge this message.

6. After the files have been copied successfully, you see a message informing you of this fact. Select OK to continue.

7. Exit the Network Client Administrator dialog box if you have no other client Administrator tasks to perform.

A directory listing of the files created on the startup disk for Network Client for MS-DOS and Windows is shown next for your reference.

```
Directory of A:\net

08/05/96  06:08p      <DIR>              .
08/05/96  06:08p      <DIR>              ..
08/05/96  06:08p                    380  system.ini
08/05/96  06:08p                    443  protocol.ini
05/07/96  01:30a                  4,644  ifshlp.sys
05/07/96  01:30a                  4,468  ndishlp.sys
05/07/96  01:30a                450,342  net.exe
05/07/96  01:30a                 76,234  net.msg
05/07/96  01:30a                123,066  neth.msg
05/07/96  01:30a                  1,531  setup.inf
05/07/96  01:30a                  1,477  wcsetup.inf
05/07/96  01:30a                    840  wfwsys.cfg
05/07/96  01:30a                    622  shares.pwl
05/07/96  01:30a                 29,136  himem.sys
05/07/96  01:30a                120,926  emm386.exe
05/07/96  01:30a                 27,670  nwlink.exe
05/07/96  01:30a                  9,792  elnk16.dos
05/07/96  01:30a                 21,940  protman.dos
05/07/96  01:30a                 13,782  protman.exe
             19 File(s)         887,293  bytes
```

The CONFIG.SYS file installs the helper for the installable file system (IFSHLP.SYS) and sets the LASTDRIVE to Z. Sample contents of the CONFIG.SYS file follow:

```
files=30
device=a:\net\ifshlp.sys
lastdrive=z
```

The AUTOEXEC.BAT file loads the network interface, loads the communications protocols, starts the network client software, connects a drive to the Windows NT Server share directory, and runs the setup program. The following are sample contents of the AUTOEXEC.BAT file (comments have been added for clarity):

```
path=a:\net
a:\net\net initialize          ;Load the network interface
a:\net\nwlink                  ;Load IPX protocol
a:\net\net start               ;Start the client software
net use z: \\NTSB\Clients      ;Connect to the shared directory
echo Running Setup...
z:\msclient\netsetup\setup.exe /$    ;Run setup
```

To connect to a different Windows NT Server, change the computer name in the NET USE command.

When the initial NET INITIALIZE command is executed, the information in the PROTOCOL.INI file is read and processed. The following are sample contents of the PROTOCOL.INI file in the NET subdirectory (comments have been added for clarity):

```
[network.setup]                    ;Network identification section
version=0x3110                     ;Client version number
netcard=ms$elnk16,1,MS$ELNK16,1    ;Associates network adapter with driver
transport=ms$ndishlp,MS$NDISHLP    ;Identifies transports
transport=ms$nwlink,MS$NWLINK      ;
lana0=ms$elnk16,1,ms$nwlink        ;Associates LANA number with IPX/SPX driver
lana1=ms$elnk16,1,ms$ndishlp       ;Associates LANA number with NDIS helper

[ms$elnk16]                        ;Network adapter parameters
drivername=ELNK16$                 ;Driver name for Etherlink Adapter Card
; iobase=0x300

[protman]                          ;Protocol manager parameters
drivername=PROTMAN$                ;Identifies protocol manager
PRIORITY=MS$NDISHLP                ;Sets priority order for protocols

[MS$NDISHLP]                       ;NDIS helper parameters
drivername=ndishlp$                ;Identifies the driver name
BINDINGS=ms$elnk16                 ;Binds NDIS helper to the Etherlink driver

[ms$nwlink]                        ;IPX driver parameters
drivername=nwlink$                 ;Identifies the driver name
FRAME=Ethernet_802.2               ;Specifies frame type
BINDINGS=ms$elnk16                 ;Binds IPX/SPX to Etherlink driver
LANABASE=0                         ;Assigns LANA number to the protocol
```

The network adapter drivers are configured with default settings. If the network adapter does not use the default settings, you must edit the parameters in the configuration files to use the network adapter settings.

Creating an Installation Disk Set

To create an installation disk set for the MS Network client for MS-DOS, LAN Manager for MS-DOS client, LAN Manager for OS/2 client, RAS for MS-DOS, or TCP/IP for Windows for Workgroups, select the Make Installation Disk Set option in the Network Client Administrator dialog box.

Use the installation disk set that is created to install the software on each client computer locally. The RAS for MS-DOS and TCP/IP for Windows for Workgroups can be installed over the network.

To make client disk sets, follow these steps:

1. Start the Network Client Administrator and select the Make Installation Disk Set option in the Network Client Administrator dialog box. Select Continue; the Share Network Client Installation Files dialog box appears.

2. Specify the shared directory or path containing the client installation files and select OK. The Make Installation Disk Set dialog box appears (see fig. 18.14).

Figure 18.14

The Make Installation Disk Set dialog box.

3. In the Network Client or Service box, select the workstation software for which you are creating the installation disk.

   In the Destination Drive box, specify the drive on which to place the disks. You can check the Format Disks option if you want the system to format the disk for you.

   Click OK.

4. You are prompted to enter appropriately labeled disks. If you selected the Format Disk option, the Network Client Administrator quick formats the disk. Next, you see a status of the files that are copied.

5. Follow the instructions on-screen to create the remaining disks in the disk set.

The installation is started by running the SETUP.EXE program found on the first disk. Many of the files in this listing are in compressed format. The files include drivers for some of the popular network adapters; support for Windows; and support for the NetBEUI, NWLink, and TCP/IP protocols at the workstation.

Using the Copy Client-Based Network Administration Tools

To run network administration tools for Windows NT from a Windows NT or Windows 95 workstation, select the Copy Client-Based Network Administration Tools option in the Network Client Administrator dialog box.

You can run tools such as User Manager for Domains on Windows 95 or Windows NT Workstation.

To copy client-based server tools to the Windows NT Server, follow these steps.

1. Start the Network Client Administrator and select the Copy Client-Based Network Administration Tools option in the Network Client Administrator dialog box. Select Continue. The Share Client-based Administration Tools dialog box appears (see fig. 18.15). Use this dialog box to indicate whether you want to share the server tools' installation files that are on the Windows NT distribution CD-ROM, to copy the files to a new shared directory and then share the files, or to specify the share name of the directory to which files have been copied.

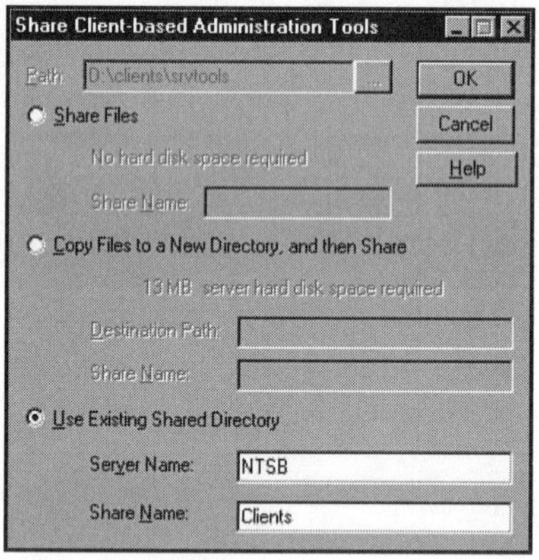

Figure 18.15

The Share Client-based Administration Tools dialog box.

The Path field indicates where the installation files are located. If this is the first time you have selected this Network Client Administrator option, this field is set to the CD-ROM path.

2. If you previously installed the network client on a different path, select the Use Existing Path option.

3. To share the files contained on the Windows NT distribution CD-ROM, select Share Files and type the share name in the Share Name field. The default name for the CD-ROM share is Clients.

4. To copy the CD-ROM installation files to a directory and then share the directory, select the Copy Files to a New Directory, and then Share option. This is the preferred option to install client software for a large number of clients. If you select this option, enter the location of the files to be copied in the Destination Path field. Additionally, specify the share name in the Share Name field.

   You need approximately 13 MB of additional disk space on the server to copy the server tools if you select the Share Files option.

5. To use installation files that have been copied previously, select the Use Existing Shared Directory option. If you select this option, specify the server and share name in the Server Name and Share Name fields.

Figure 18.15 shows that, by default, the Use Existing Shared Directory button is enabled, and the Server Name and Share Name fields under this option have default values. These defaults appear because the client software for generating network startup disks and disk sets was previously copied. To copy the server tools installation files to the Windows NT server, select the Copy Files to a New Directory, and then Share option.

When you select the Copy Files to a New Directory, and then Share option, the Destination Path and Share Name fields are filled with the default values of C:\clients\srvtools and SetupAdm. You can keep the default values or change them. If drive C on the Windows NT Server is a FAT partition with limited space, change the Destination Path to specify another drive.

After making your selections, click OK. A status of the copied files appears.

Copying the Client Distribution Files to the Windows NT Server

When you select the Make Network Installation Startup Disk or Make Installation Disk Set options in the Network Client Administrator dialog box and copy the installation client software on the Windows NT Server, the directory structure of the copied files is shown in figure 18.16.

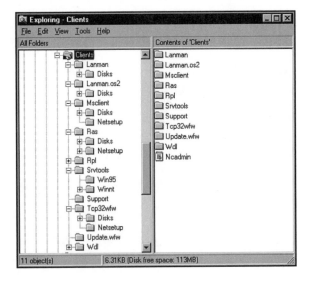

Figure 18.16

Client directory setup of disk sets on Windows NT Server.

Each subdirectory under the Clients directory contains the installation files and disk software for a particular client or service. You can browse the Clients directory to better understand how the installation files are organized.

Installing the Network Client Software and Services

After you set up the share name for the network installation client software on the Windows NT Server, and after you create the network startup disks or client installation disk sets as described in the previous sections, you can proceed with installing the client software.

The sections that follow discuss typical tasks that you perform while installing and verifying the operation of MS-DOS and Windows network client software.

Installing a Network Client for MS-DOS and Windows

You should have created the installation disk set for the network client for MS-DOS and Windows, as described in the section "Creating an Installation Disk Set," earlier in this chapter.

The MS-DOS workstation should meet the following minimum configuration requirements:

- Processor should be Intel 8088 or higher

- RAM in workstation should be at least 640 KB

- At least 1 MB of free space on hard disk

- A network adapter for which network driver support exists

- MS-DOS 3.3 or later

- Optionally, MS Windows running at the workstation

To run Network Client Setup, you must have 429 KB of available conventional memory.

To install the network client for MS-DOS and Windows, follow these steps:

1. Boot up the MS-DOS workstation and examine the CONFIG.SYS and AUTOEXEC.BAT files on the workstation. Remove from these files any references to network driver client software for other networks such as NetWare, VINES, or Lantastic. Remove any components that could occupy additional RAM or conflict with the installation.

Reboot the workstation if you made changes to the CONFIG.SYS and AUTOEXEC.BAT files.

2. Insert the first disk in the MS Network Client for MS-DOS and Windows disk set that you created into a floppy drive and issue the following command:

A:\SETUP

The Setup for Microsoft Network Client v3.0 for MS-DOS screen appears (see fig. 18.17).

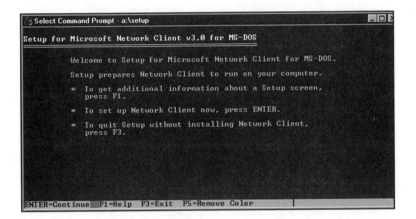

Figure 18.17

The Setup for Microsoft Network Client v3.0 for MS-DOS screen.

3. Press Enter to continue.

A screen appears, prompting you for the location for placing the network client software (see fig. 18.18).

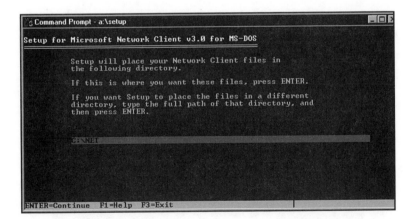

Figure 18.18

Specifying the location for MS-DOS/Windows client software.

4. Enter a location path or accept the default, and press Enter.

The next screen asks you to select a network adapter from the list provided (see fig. 18.19).

Figure 18.19

Network adapter selection.

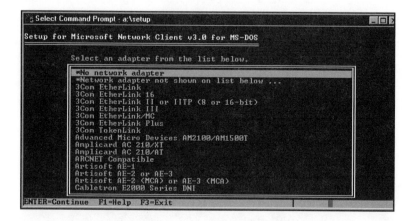

A Set Network Buffers information box shows the default setting, which optimizes network performance by using Network Buffers. This takes more memory and you can choose not to use this option.

Figure 18.20

Network buffers.

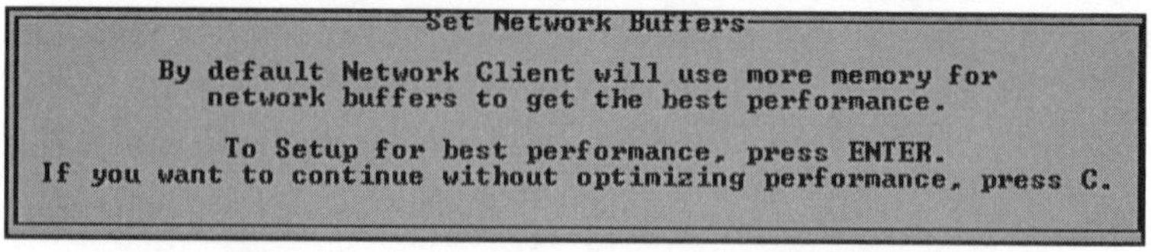

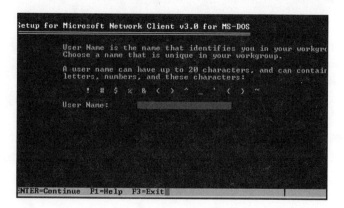

A screen appears, prompting you to enter the user name (see fig. 18.21). The user name you select should be the workstation user's logon name to the workgroup or domain.

Figure 18.21

Specifying the user name for MS-DOS/Windows client software.

5. Enter a user name and press Enter.

   A screen for changing names, setup options, and network configuration appears (see fig. 18.22).

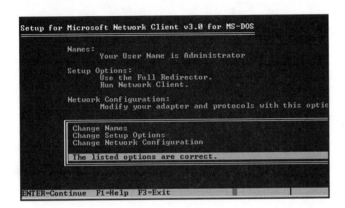

Figure 18.22

The Changing Options screen for MS-DOS/ Windows client software.

6. Select the Change Names option.

   A screen for changing user name, computer name, workgroup name, and domain names appears (see fig. 18.23). The default computer name is assumed to be the same as the user name. If this is not true, change the computer name.

   Change the Workgroup or Domain Name to which the workstation belongs.

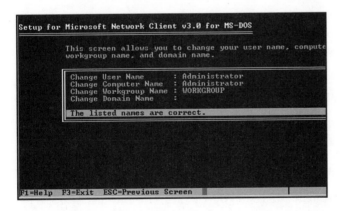

Figure 18.23

The Change Names screen for MS-DOS/Windows client software.

7. Select the The listed names are correct option. The Changing Options screen appears again.

8. Select the Change Setup Option.

   The screen for changing the Redirector, startup, logon, and net pop-up options appears (see fig. 18.24).

Figure 18.24

*The Setup Options screen
for MS-DOS/Windows
client software.*

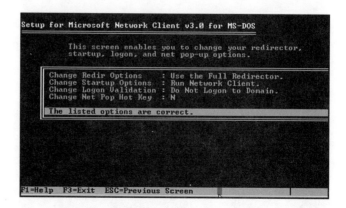

Figure 18.24

*The Setup Options screen
for MS-DOS/Windows
client software.*

You can set the Redirector to be a Full Redirector or a Basic Redirector. The Full
Redirector gives you access to all network client features, such as logging on to Windows
NT and LAN Manager domains and using advanced network options, such as named
pipes. Select this option unless you have memory-constraint problems or do not need the
advanced options, in which case select Basic Redirector. The Basic Redirector uses less
memory and disk but does not encrypt passwords. It provides workgroup functions, such
as connecting to share directories and printers.

If you are using Remote Access Services or MS Windows, or you are logging on to a
domain, select Full Redirector and start it with the following command before starting
Windows:

```
net start full
```

The Windows for Workgroups and Windows NT Workstations have their own built-in
network client, and you should not use the MS-DOS network client on these workstations.

The Startup options (refer to fig. 18.24) can be set up to automatically run networking
functions when the workstation is booted. You can select from the following Startup
options:

■ **Run Network Client.** Starts the network client that prompts you for your logon
   user name for the workgroup or domain.

■ **Run Network Client and Load Pop-Up.** Starts the network client that prompts
   you for your logon user name for the workgroup or domain, and then loads the
   pop-up interface into memory.

■ **Do Not Run Network Client.** The network client will not be started. You must
   type the NET LOGON command at the command prompt to start the network
   client, which then prompts you to log on.

The Change Logon Validation option can be set to log on to a domain or to not log on to a domain. To use the workstation to log on to a Windows NT or LAN Manager domain, select the Logon To Domain option, otherwise select the Do Not Logon To Domain option. The domain name is set in the Change Names.

After the pop-up interface is loaded, you can display it by pressing Ctrl+Alt+N. To change the pop-up key, set the new key in the Change Net Pop Hot Key field. The pop-up key is of the form Ctrl+Alt+*X*, where *X* can be replaced by the letters A to Z. The letter N is the default.

9. After making changes to the Setup Options screen, select the The listed options are correct option. You then return to the Changing Options screen.

10. Select the Change Network Configuration option.

   The screen for installing network adapters and protocol drivers appears (see fig. 18.25). Use the Tab key to move between boxes, and change the network configuration for your network adapter and protocols.

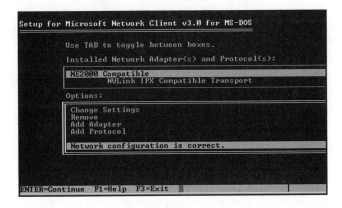

Figure 18.25

Changing the network adapter and protocol drivers screen for MS-DOS/Windows client software.

Figure 18.26 shows a sample configuration that has the SMC EtherCard PLUS adapter drivers and the NWLink IPX, NetBEUI, and TCP/IP protocols selected. Remember that if you select multiple protocols, they will take up more memory, and this could prevent some applications from running.

11. After making the changes, select the option Network configuration is correct. You are returned to the Changing Options screen.

   Select the option Network configuration is correct from the Changing Options screen.

   The Setup program configures your network drivers and copies the software to the workstation. At the completion of the installation, you see the completion screen informing you of the changes that have been made (see fig. 18.27).

Figure 18.26
*The network adapter and
protocol drivers screen for
MS-DOS/Windows
client software.*

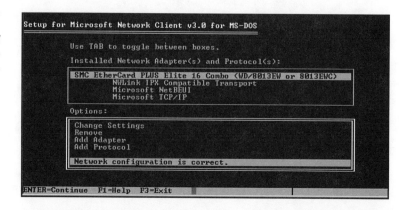

Figure 18.27
*The completion screen for
MS-DOS/Windows
client software.*

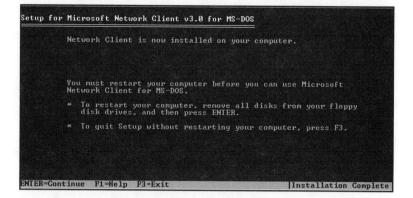

12. Remove the disks and press Enter to reboot the workstation. Alternatively, press F3 to exit without rebooting the workstation.

Verifying Network Client for MS-DOS and Windows

If you selected the drivers and other configuration options correctly, you will see messages indicating that the driver initialized properly. The following is an example working session for logging on to the domain. In this example, the built-in Administrator account was changed to Admin, so the user Admin was typed to log on to the domain:

```
The command completed successful
Standard Microsystems EtherCard Plus MAC Module v1.19
Microsoft(R) NWLINK Version 1.0
Copyright Microsoft 1994. All Rights Reserved.
Type your name, or press ENTER if it is ADMINISTRATOR: Admin
Type your password:********
There is no password-list file for ADMIN.
Do you want to create one? (Y/N) [N]: Y
```

```
Please confirm your password so that a password list can be created: ********
Please enter your password for the domain KINETD:********
The command completed successfully.
```

The password list file is used for workgroup connections. It is stored in the C:\NET directory and referenced in the SYSTEM.INI file in the [Password Lists] section. If you create this password file once, you will not be prompted for it when the workstation boots the next time. Keep in mind that the password file encryption is minimal and offers a security risk because they are stored on the local hard drive.

If you have installed the pop-up interface, press Ctrl+Alt+N to verify the pop-up program interface (see fig. 18.28). You can use this interface to create or delete network drive connections to a shared directory and print resources.

Figure 18.28

The pop-up interface for MS-DOS Client.

To unload the pop-up interface, use the following command:

```
NET STOP POPUP
```

To restart the pop-up interface, use the following command:

```
NET START POPUP
```

The NET.EXE program that implements the NET commands is copied to the C:\NET directory during installation. You can use the NET /? command to see the list of NET commands and learn how to obtain help on them. Table 18.2 shows the NET commands available from an MS-DOS client. You can use this table to test the network client. Using the NET CONFIG command displays information about the workgroup settings. An example of the type of information shown by this command follows:

```
> NET CONFIG
Computer name                \\WKS1
User name                    ADMIN
Software version             3.11
Redirector version           2.51
Workstation root directory   C:\NET
Workgroup                    WORKGROUP
The command completed successfully.
```

Table 18.2
NET Commands on an MS-DOS Client

Command	Description
NET	Loads the pop-up interface into memory and displays it on your screen.
NET CONFIG	Displays information about your workgroup settings.
NET DIAG	Runs the Microsoft Network Diagnostics program to display diagnostic information about your network.
NET HELP	Provides information about commands and error messages.
NET INIT	Loads protocol and network-adapter drivers without binding them to Protocol Manager.
NET LOGOFF	Breaks the connection between your computer and the shared resources to which it is connected.
NET LOGON	Identifies you as a member of a workgroup and re-establishes your persistent connections.
NET PASSWORD	Changes your logon password.
NET PRINT	Displays information about print queues and controls print jobs.
NET START	Starts services or loads the pop-up interface.
NET STOP	Stops services or unloads the pop-up interface.
NET TIME	Displays the time on, or synchronizes your computer's clock with, the clock on a Microsoft Windows for Workgroups, Windows NT, or LAN Manager time server.
NET USE	Connects to or disconnects from a shared resource or displays information about connections.
NET VER	Displays the type and version number of the workgroup Redirector you are using.
NET VIEW	Displays a list of computers that share resources or a list of shared resources on a specific computer.

The Full Redirector configuration consumes a substantial amount of memory. Use the DOS MEM /C command to see how memory is used by the network client. The following example shows a sample of the memory usage of the network DOS client. The memory used by the network client components is in italics. In a practical configuration, you will find it necessary to use memory-optimization techniques such as MEMMAKER, an MS-DOS utility available on versions 5.0 and up. In the configuration example shown here, no attempt was made to load DOS high or to use any other memory-optimization technique:

```
> MEM /C
Modules using memory below 1 MB:
  Name          Total       =   Conventional   +   Upper Memory
  ____        _____          _____            _____
  MSDOS       65,357   (64K)    65,357   (64K)           0   (0K)
  HIMEM        3,792    (4K)     3,792    (4K)           0   (0K)
  IFSHLP       3,968    (4K)     3,968    (4K)           0   (0K)
  COMMAND      6,272    (6K)     6,272    (6K)           0   (0K)
  SMARTDRV    29,024   (28K)    29,024   (28K)           0   (0K)
  PROTMAN        400    (0K)       400    (0K)           0   (0K)
  ELNK3        8,416    (8K)     8,416    (8K)           0   (0K)
  NDISHLP      1,440    (1K)     1,440    (1K)           0   (0K)
  NWLINK      10,144   (10K)    10,144   (10K)           0   (0K)
  PROTMAN      2,560    (3K)     2,560    (3K)           0   (0K)
  REDIR      102,256  (100K)   102,256  (100K)           0   (0K)
  NETPOP      34,832   (34K)    34,832   (34K)           0   (0K)
  Free       385,696  (377K)   385,696  (377K)           0   (0K)

Memory Summary:

  Type of Memory      Total    =    Used    +    Free
  _____       _____        _____        ____

  Conventional       654,336       268,640       385,696
  Upper                    0             0             0
  Reserved                 0             0             0
  Extended (XMS)  15,728,640     2,229,248    13,499,392
  _____        _____    _____    _____

  Total memory    16,382,976     2,497,888    13,885,088

  Total under 1 MB   654,336       268,640       385,696

  Largest executable program size     250,464    (245K)
  Largest free upper memory block           0     (0K)
```

The high memory area is available. The memory configuration example shows that 102 KB of RAM is used by the Full Redirector.

To configure Windows on the MS-DOS workstation to run with the MS-DOS network client, perform the following steps:

1. Start Windows and run Windows Setup from the Main program group.

2. Choose Change System Settings from the Options menu.

3. In the Network Settings dialog box, select Microsoft Network (or 100 percent compatible).

4. Save your changes. If you are asked to insert Windows Setup disks, do so, or specify the directory containing the Microsoft Network device driver.

Updating the MS-DOS Network Client Configuration

To update the MS-DOS Network Client configuration, you can manually edit the network configuration files or run the SETUP.EXE program in the installed directory (usually, C:\NET) on the workstation. Figure 18.29 shows the SETUP.EXE screen for making configuration changes.

Figure 18.29

SETUP for making MS-DOS network client configuration changes.

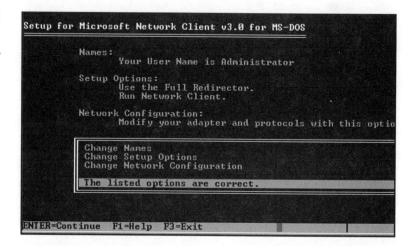

If you do not have enough memory to run SETUP.EXE and unload the network Redirector, if it is running, by using the following command:

```
NET STOP RDR
```

Use the SETUP screen to examine the network client configuration settings, make any desired changes, and save your settings. The procedure for making changes is similar to the steps you take when you use SETUP to create the installation disks.

Examining the Configuration Files for the Network Client

After you install the network client software, you can study the changes made to the workstation configuration files to better understand how the network client operates.

The CONFIG.SYS file should have the following lines added to it for supporting the network client:

```
device=C:\NET\ifshlp.sys
LASTDRIVE=Z
```

These lines load the installable file system helper and set the last drive in the MS-DOS drive configuration table to Z.

The AUTOEXEC.BAT should have the following lines added to it to run the network client:

```
C:\NET\net initialize      ;Load network drivers
C:\NET\nwlink              ;Load IPX protocol
C:\NET\net start           ;Start network services
```

If you install the MS-DLC protocol, you must edit the AUTOEXEC.BAT file to add "/ dynamic" to the NET INITIALIZE line. The line should be

```
net initialize /dynamic
```

The MS-DLC protocol requires the NETBIND command. If the NETBIND command does not exist, add it to the line after all lines in AUTOEXEC.BAT that load network drivers. The line simply should be

```
netbind
```

The NWLINK loads the NWLink protocol stack if you selected the IPX protocol during the client installation. Note that the NWLINK supports only the IPX protocol; it does not support the SPX protocol.

The NET START command loads the Redirector in the configuration that was specified when the network client software was installed. The default Redirector to use is specified in the preferredredir statement in the [networks] section of the SYSTEM.INI file.

To start the Redirector in a different mode, you can specify additional options to the NET START command. The general syntax of the NET START command and the options you can use follow:

```
NET START [POPUP ¦ BASIC ¦ FULL ¦ WORKSTATION ¦ NETBIND ¦ NETBEUI]
          [/LIST] [/YES] [/VERBOSE]
  POPUP       Loads the pop-up interface into memory.
              Use this option if the pop-up interface
              is not automatically loaded each time you
              start your computer.
  BASIC       Starts the Basic Redirector.
  FULL        Starts the Full Redirector.
  WORKSTATION Starts the Default Redirector.
  NETBIND     Binds protocols and network-adapter drivers.
  NETBEUI     Starts the NetBIOS interface.
  /LIST       Displays a list of the services that are
              running.
  /YES        Carries out the NET START command without
              first prompting you to provide information or
              confirm actions.
  /VERBOSE    Displays information about device drivers and
              services as they are loaded.
```

To load the basic Redirector instead of the Full Redirector, you can use the following command in the AUTOEXEC.BAT file:

```
NET START BASIC
```

A SYSTEM.INI file is installed in the C:\NET directory. This file is used by the network client at startup. If you use Windows on your workstation, add the statements in this file to your Windows SYSTEM.INI file also. The following is an example of the SYSTEM.INI file (comments have been added for clarity):

```
[network]                           ;Network parameter section
sizworkbuf=1498                     ;Network buffer size in bytes
filesharing=no                     ;Enable workgroup file sharing flag
printsharing=no                    ;Enable workgroup printer sharing flag
autologon=yes                      ;Prompt for user name at startup time
computername=WKS1                  ;Computer name
lanroot=C:\NET                     ;Location of network client files
username=ADMINISTRATOR             ;Last user name to logon
workgroup=WORKGROUP                ;Workgroup name
reconnect=yes                      ;Persistent share connections flag
dospophotkey=N                     ;NET popup hot key (ctrl-alt-N)
lmlogon=1                          ;Domain logon flag
logondomain=KINETD                 ;Target domain
preferredredir=full                ;Redirector to use: may be overridden in DOS
autostart=full,popup               ;Default parms for NET START command
maxconnections=8                   ;Maximum connections if computer is a server

[network drivers]                  ;Network drivers parameters
netcard=smcmac.dos                 ;Name of DOS driver file
transport=ndishlp.sys              ;Name of installable file system helper file
devdir=C:\NET                      ;Device driver directory
LoadRMDrivers=yes

[Password Lists]                   ;Password file listing
*Shares=C:\NET\Shares.PWL
ADMINISTRATOR=C:\NET\ADMINIST.PWL
ADMIN=C:\NET\ADMIN.PWL
```

The PROTOCOL.INI file in the C:\NET directory of the Network Client software contains the network setup, protocol settings, and the Protocol Manager settings. A sample PROTOCOL.INI file for an MS-DOS network client for the SMC network adapter and the NWLink protocol follow for your reference (comments have been added for clarity):

```
[network.setup]                           ;Network descriptions
version=0x3110                            ;Network version number
netcard=ms$w13ew,1,MS$W13EW,1             ;Network adapter driver names
transport=ms$nwlink,MS$NWLINK             ;Network transport driver name for NWLINK
transport=ms$ndishlp,MS$NDISHLP           ;Network transport driver name for NDISHLP
lana0=ms$w13ew,1,ms$nwlink                ;Assigns LANA number to NWLINK protocol
lana1=ms$w13ew,1,ms$ndishlp               ;Assigns LANA number to NDISHLP
```

```
[MS$NWLINK]                          ;NWLINK protocol, adapter driver param-
eters
FRAME=ETHERNET_802.2                 ;Frame type
IOADDRESS=0x3000                     ;Network adapter I/O address
SLOT=3                               ;Network adapter location on bus
DriverName=nwlink$                   ;NWLINK protocol driver name
BINDINGS=MS$W13EW                    ;Binds NWLINK to network adapter driver

[MS$W13EW]                           ;Network adapter driver parameters
DriverName=SMCMAC$                   ;Identifies adapter driver name

[protman]                            ;Protocol manager parameters
DriverName=PROTMAN$                  ;Identifies the protocol manager name
PRIORITY=MS$NDISHLP                  ;Set protocol priorities

[MS$NDISHLP]                         ;NDISHLP parameters
DriverName=ndishlp$                  ;Identifies driver name
BINDINGS=MS$W13EW                    ;Binds NDISHLP to network adapter
```

Installing MS Network Client for MS-DOS Using Network Startup

To install an MS Network client for MS-DOS using the network setup disk, you first should create the network setup disk by using the steps outlined in the section "Creating the Network Installation Startup Disk."

Next, boot the MS-DOS workstation with the network setup disk. You see messages similar to the following:

```
A>a:net\net initialize
Standard Microsystems EtherCard Plus MAC Module v1.19
The command completed successful
A>a:\net\nwlink
Microsoft(R) NWLINK Version 1.0
Copyright Microsoft 1994. All Rights Reserved.
A>a:\net\net start
Type your name, or press ENTER if it is ADMINISTRATOR:
Type your password:********
There is no password-list file for ADMINISTRATOR.
Do you want to create one? (Y/N) [N]: Y
Please confirm your password so that a password list can be created: ********
The command completed successfully.
A>net use z: \\NTSA\Clients
The command completed successfully.
A> echo Running Setup
Running Setup
A>z:\msclient\netsetup\setup.exe /$
    :
    :
```

The last command initiates the installation process and copies the files to the workstation. If the network installation fails at any point, use this listing as a guide for what you should expect to see. If the installation process fails after the network adapter driver is loaded, for example, it could be because you are using the wrong network adapter driver or network adapter parameters. If the network installation fails after the SETUP.EXE command is executed, ensure that you have sufficient rights to access the SETUP.EXE file on the Windows NT Server. You might want to manually execute the network startup and SETUP.EXE commands to see whether you have access to the CLIENTS shared directory on the Windows NT Server.

Installing LAN Manager for MS-DOS Enhanced Clients

If you are integrating the Windows NT Server into existing LAN Manager clients, you can install the LAN Manager for MS-DOS enhanced clients on MS-DOS workstations.

You should have created the installation disk sets for the LAN Manager for DOS clients using the procedure in the section "Creating an Installation Disk Set."

The MS-DOS workstation should meet the following minimum configuration requirements:

- Processor should be Intel 8088 or higher

- RAM in workstation should be at least 640 KB

- At least 4 MB of free space on hard disk

- A network adapter for the network driver support that exists

- MS-DOS 3.3 or later

- Optionally, MS Windows running at the workstation

To install the LAN Manager for an MS-DOS enhanced client, follow these steps:

1. Boot up the MS-DOS workstation and examine the CONFIG.SYS and AUTOEXEC.BAT files on the workstation. Remove from these files any references to network driver client software for other networks such as NetWare, VINES, or Lantastic. Remove any components that could occupy additional RAM or conflict with the installation.

   Reboot the workstation if you made changes to the CONFIG.SYS and AUTOEXEC.BAT files.

2. Place the first disk in disk set that you created into a floppy drive and run the following command:

   `A:\SETUP`

   The Microsoft LAN Manager Setup screen appears (see fig. 18.30).

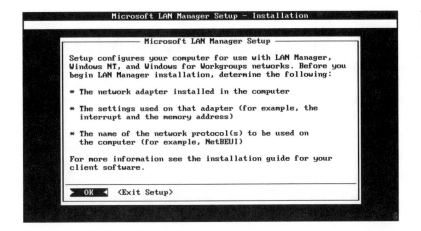

Figure 18.30

The Microsoft LAN Manager Setup screen.

3. Select OK to continue.

A screen appears, telling you how to use the mouse and keyboard in the setup (see fig. 18.31).

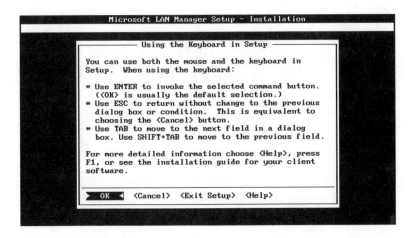

Figure 18.31

Information on the keyboard and the mouse in the setup program.

4. Select OK to continue.

The Install LAN Manager screen appears, telling you about the location of installation files and the target directory (see fig. 18.32). Make any necessary changes.

Figure 18.32
Selecting the location of files.

5. Select OK to continue.

    The Install LAN Manager screen that contains Enhanced or Basic installation options appears (see fig. 18.33).

Figure 18.33
Selecting basic or enhanced clients.

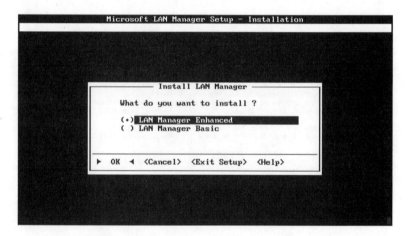

The enhanced client gives you access to all network client features, such as connecting to LAN directories and printers, sending and receiving messages, and using services such as named pipes. Select the Enhanced Client option unless you have memory-constraint problems or you do not need the more advanced options. The basic client provides workgroup functions, such as connecting to share directories and printers. With the Basic Client, you can issue network commands only from the command line.

6. Select the client type, and then select OK to continue.

    You should see the status of the files that are being copied.

When prompted for other disks, such as driver disks, insert them into the floppy drive.

7. After the files are copied, the Network Adapter Drivers screen appears (see fig. 18.34).

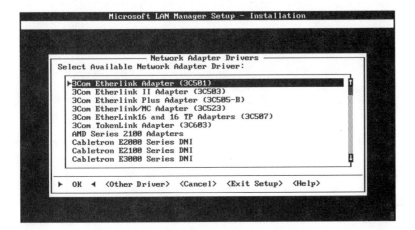

Figure 18.34

The Network Adapter Drivers screen.

Select the appropriate network driver. If you cannot find a compatible driver in the list, select the <Other Driver> option to add other drivers.

8. After selecting the network adapter driver, select OK to continue. A list of protocol choices appears (see fig. 18.35).

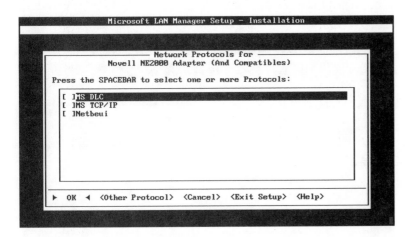

Figure 18.35

LAN Manager protocol choices.

Select the protocol you want to use. To install another protocol, select the <Other Protocol> option to add other protocols.

9. Select OK to continue. The Workstation Configuration screen appears, which lists the network adapters and protocols that you have selected (see fig. 18.36).

Figure 18.36

The Workstation Configuration screen.

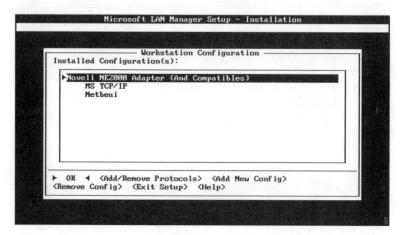

10. Make any necessary network adapter and protocol changes and select OK to continue. If you chose to install MS TCP/IP then the TCP/IP Settings screen appears (see fig. 18.37).

Type the IP Address, Subnet Mask, and Default gateway or enable the DHCP server do this for you.

Figure 18.37

The TCP/IP Settings screen.

```
                    Microsoft LAN Manager Setup - Installation

                    ┌─────────── TCP/IP Settings ───────────┐
                    │                                        │
                    │        IP Address:  [................] │
                    │       Subnet Mask:  [................] │
                    │   Default gateway (router):  [........]│
                    │   Number of NetBIOS sessions:  [6..]   │
                    │                                        │
                    │   [X] Enable automatic DHCP configuration│
                    │                                        │
                    │       WINS Primary Server:  [........] │
                    │        WINS Backup Server:  [........] │
                    ▶ OK ◀  <Cancel>  < dvanced... >  <Help>  │
                    └────────────────────────────────────────┘
```

The Workstation Settings form appears next (see fig. 18.38).

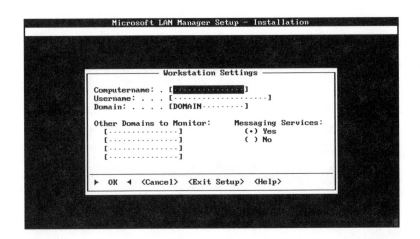

Figure 18.38

The Workstation Settings form.

Enter the Computername, Username, and Domain.

In the Other Domains to Monitor field, enter the names of the domains in which this workstation can participate. This enables the NET VIEW command to list the servers in the specified domains. Other domains can be used only with enhanced client services.

The Messaging Services option enables workstations to send and receive messages. The default is Yes.

11. After changing the workstation settings, select OK to continue. The Support for the Windows Environment screen appears (see fig. 18.39).

    Choose Yes if you have Windows installed and need to use network services from Windows.

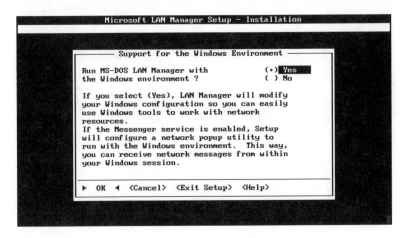

Figure 18.39

The Support for the Windows Environment screen.

12. If you selected Yes for installing Windows-related files, the Windows Directory screen appears. Enter the name of the Windows directory at the workstation and select OK.

To run LAN Manager with Windows, the setup program modifies certain configurations in Windows. The Windows Directory screen appears asking for the Windows path and directory (see fig. 18.40)

Figure 18.40

Windows Directory screen.

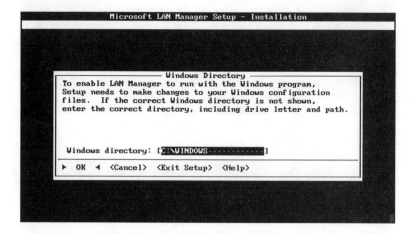

13. If you selected the Messaging Services, you are given a choice of when to run the messaging services (see fig. 18.41).

Figure 18.41

The Messaging Popups screen.

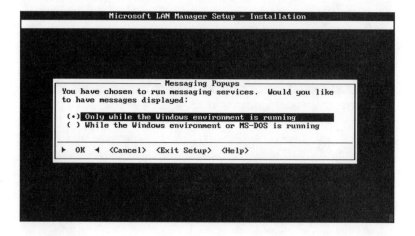

14. After making your messaging selections, select OK to continue. The Memory Management screen appears if setup detects extended memory (see fig. 18.42), and you are asked whether you want setup to maximize application memory. The default choice is Yes, and you should allow setup to optimize memory usage.

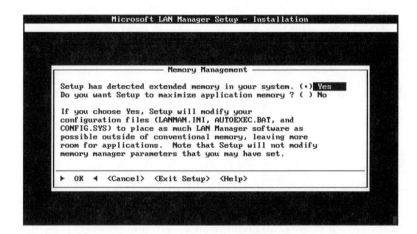

Figure 18.42

The Memory Management screen.

15. Select OK to continue. The Configuration Complete screen appears.

    Select <Review> to review your configuration settings. This displays all the configuration screens one by one.

    Select <Save> to save your configuration changes.

16. Follow the instructions on-screen to insert the driver disks.

17. At the completion of the installation, you see the Installation Complete screen.

18. Follow the instructions on-screen to exit Setup, or reboot your computer.

The installation procedure adds lines similar to the following in the CONFIG.SYS file:

```
DEVICE=C:\LANMAN.DOS\DRIVERS\DOSUTILS\EMM386.EXE NoEMS
LASTDRIVE=Z
DOS=HIGH,UMB
DEVICE=C:\LANMAN.DOS\DRIVERS\PROTMAN\PROTMAN.DOS /i:C:\LANMAN.DOS
DEVICE=C:\LANMAN.DOS\DRIVERS\ETHERNET\SMCETH\SMCMAC.DOS
```

The first DEVICE statement loads the memory manager driver. The LASTDRIVE statement sets the size of the DOS drive table to handle drive letters up to Z. The DOS=HIGH,UMB statement loads DOS high and in the upper memory blocks. The second DEVICE statement loads the NDIS protocol manager. The last DEVICE statement loads the network adapter driver.

You will find lines similar to the following added in the AUTOEXEC.BAT file by the installation procedure:

```
SET PATH=C:\LANMAN.DOS\NETPROG;%PATH%
NET START WORKSTATION
LOAD NETBEUI
```

The PATH statement adds the LAN Manager program directory to the PATH statement. The NET START statement starts the workstation client service. The last command loads the NETBEUI protocol.

The PROTOCOL.INI file in the C:\LANMAN.DOS directory contains protocol configuration information for the LAN Manager client for MS-DOS. A sample PROTOCOL.INI for the LAN Manager client follows (comments have been added for clarity):

```
[PROTMAN]                          ;Protocol manager parameters
  DRIVERNAME = PROTMAN$            ;Identifies the protocol manager name
  DYNAMIC = YES                    ;Tells protman to dynamically load protocols
  PRIORITY = NETBEUI               ;Sets priority for protocol services

[NETBEUI_XIF]                      ;NetBEUI protocol parameters
  Drivername = netbeui$           ;Identifies NetBEUI protocol name
  SESSIONS = 6                     ;Number of concurrent sessions max
  NCBS = 12                        ;Network control blocks
  BINDINGS = "SMCETH_NIF"          ;Binds NetBEUI to SMC driver
  LANABASE = 0                     ;Assigns LANA number to NetBEUI

[SMCETH_NIF]                       ;Network adapter parameters
    drivername = SMCMAC$           ;Identifies the network adapter driver name
;    enable these setting if card does not support soft setup
;    irq = 3
;    ramaddress = 0xd000
;    iobase = 0x280

    receivebufsize = 1024          ;Receive buffer size in bytes
```

The LANMAN.INI file in the C:\LANMAN.DOS directory contains the LAN Manger client configuration information. A sample LANMAN.INI for the LAN Manager client follows (comments have been added for clarity):

```
;**************************************************************;
;                                                             ;
;**              Microsoft LAN Manager                      **;
;**          Copyright Microsoft Corp., 1993                **;
;**************************************************************;
;                                                             ;

[networks]                              ;Network parameters
  netservices = chknet, minses          ;Network services to be started
```

```
[workstation]                                    ;Workstation parameters
  wrkservices = encrypt,messenger,minipop        ;Workstation services to start
  computername = WKS1                            ;Computer name
  domain = domain_A                              ;Logon domain name
  othdomains = KINETD                            ;Other domains
  numdgrambuf = 4                                ;
  lanroot = C:\LANMAN.DOS                        ;Location of network client files

[netshell]
  user name = Administrator                       ;Last user to logon

[version]                                        ;Client version information
  lan_manager = 2.2c.0                           ;Client version number

[messenger]                                      ;Message services parameters

[services]                                       ;Network services parameters
  chknet      = netprog\chknet.exe               ;The rest of these lines
  minses      = netprog\minses.exe /n            ;define the various workstation
  workstation    = netprog\netwksta.exe          ;components that are loaded
  messenger     = services\msrv.exe              ;to provide network services
  netpopup      = services\netpopup.exe          ;and utilities
  encrypt       = services\encrypt.exe
  minipop       = services\minipop.exe
```

You can use any of the NET commands described in table 18.2 to test the operation of the network client.

You can use the NET CONFIG command, for example, to verify your LAN Manager client configuration:

```
> NET CONFIG Workstation
Computer name                   \\WKS1
User name                       ADMINISTRATOR
Software version                3.11
Redirector version              2.20
Workstation root directory      C:\LANMAN.DOS

Workstation Domain                                       Domain_A
Logon Domain                                                Domain_A
Other Domains

The command completed successfully.
```

If you installed the Windows components during the LAN Manager client installation, you can start Windows to verify the client installation. You should see the WinPopup icon if you enabled messenger services. Figure 18.43 shows an example use of the WinPopup application.

Figure 18.43
*The LAN Manager client
WinPopup interface.*

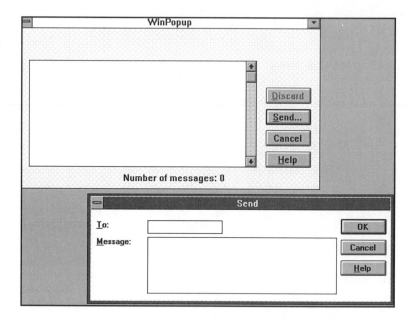

Installing Client-based Server Administration Tools

In addition to performing Windows NT Server administration by logging on locally to a
Windows NT Server, you can perform many of these tasks from a Windows 95 or Windows
NT workstation. The following 32-bit Windows tools are available:

- **User Manager for Domains.** Used for administering domain accounts.

- **User Profile Editor.** Used for administering server-based user profiles.

- **Event Viewer.** Used for viewing the Windows NT Server event log.

- **Server Manager.** Used to manage Windows NT Server resources.

- **Remoteboot Manager.** Used for administering remoteboot clients.

- **Remote Access Administrator.** Used for administering remote access services.

- **DHCP Manager.** Used for DHCP administration.

- **WINS Manager.** Used for WINS server administration.

Setting Up Server Tools on a Windows NT Workstation Client

One of the most commonly used Windows NT Server tools is the User Manager for Domains. This tool and other server-based tools are not included with Windows NT Workstation. To use a Windows NT Workstation to perform server and domain administration, install the Windows NT Server tools on Windows NT Workstation clients.

To install the Windows NT Server tools on Windows NT Workstation clients, follow these steps:

1. Install the client-based tools on a Windows NT Server, as outlined in the previous section, "Using the Copy Client-Based Network Administration Tools."

2. Log in as an Administrator user to a Windows NT Workstation.

3. Use File Manager to set up a connection to the \clients\srvtools directory on the Windows NT Server. The default share name for this directory is SetupAdm. Alternatively, you can use the following command:

   NET USE *X*: *servername*\SetupAdm

   Substitute an unused drive letter for *X* and the server computer name for *servername*.

4. Locate and run SETUP.BAT in the \clients\srvtools\winnt directory.

   Figure 18.44 shows the results of executing the SETUP.BAT file.

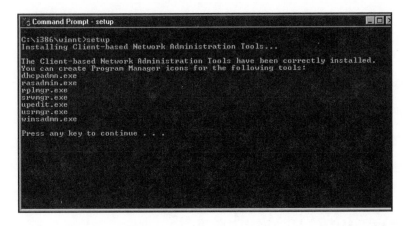

Figure 18.44

Installing client-based server tools by running SETUP.BAT.

5. When the client-based server tools are installed at the Windows NT Workstation, a program folder and program items are not created automatically. You must create these as a separate step.

Table 18.3 shows the file names of the server-based tools that are copied to the %SystemRoot%\System32 directory. You need these program file names for creating the program items.

Figure 18.45 shows a program group for server tools created on Windows NT Workstation. The Event Viewer program at the Windows NT Server and the Windows NT Workstation is the same.

Figure 18.45

The Windows NT Server Tools group on a Windows NT Workstation.

Table 18.3
File Names for Server-Based Tools

File Name	Server Tool
dhcpadm.exe	DHCP Manager
rasadmin.exe	Remote Access Server Administrator
rplmgr.exe	Remoteboot Manager
srvmgr.exe	Server Manager
upedit.exe	User Profile Editor
usrmgr.exe	User Manager for Domains
winsadmn.exe	WINS Manager

Setting Up Server Tools in Windows 95

You can install the server tools for NT on your Windows 95 workstation. You need about 2.5 MB of disk space to install them.

1. Double-click on the Add/Remove icon in the Control Panel. Choose the Windows Setup tab.

2. Click on the Have Disk button. You can specify a local directory or a share on the network. It is important that the directory you specify contains the srvtools.inf file.

3. Choose OK.

4. Check the Windows NT Server Tools box.

5. Choose Install, then OK.

6. You will need to edit the autoexec.bat to include the Server Tools directory in the path. The default installation copies them to C:\Srvtools.

7. Restart the computer.

   You must be logged on to the network before you can use the NT Server Tools.

   The installation automatically generates the NT Server Tools icons in the NT Server Tools program folder.

Installing Network Client Support for Windows 95 Clients

MS Windows 95 clients have a built-in Client for Microsoft Networks configuration. This client can be used to make connections to any Windows NT Server because the client uses network protocol and Redirector software that is compatible with the Windows NT Server.

During Windows 95 installation, if the installation procedure can recognize a network adapter, it automatically installs the Client for Microsoft Networks. Figure 18.46 shows the network configuration on a Windows 95 workstation connected to a network. The list of components installed includes the Client for Microsoft Networks used by this client. Figure 18.46 also shows that the Client for Microsoft Networks configuration is set to be the primary client used at the workstation.

You can use the Windows 95 workstation to connect to network drives on any Windows NT Server or Windows NT Workstation.

To establish a connection to a Windows NT Server, follow these steps:

1. Right-click on My Computer icon.

2. Select Map Network Drive.

Figure 18.46

The Windows 95 Network Configuration.

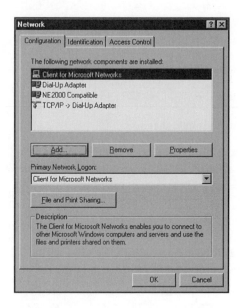

The Map Network Drive dialog box appears (see fig. 18.47).

3. Select the drive to use for mapping from the Drive field and specify the UNC name of the path in the Path field.

4. Figure 18.48 shows an example of drive F mapped to share name SetupAdm on a Windows NT Server named Nameserver1.

5. If you try to connect to an administrative share, you are prompted for a valid password. Figure 18.49 shows an attempt to connect to the Administrator share Admin$ on the Windows NT Server Nameserver1. Notice that you are required to specify a password.

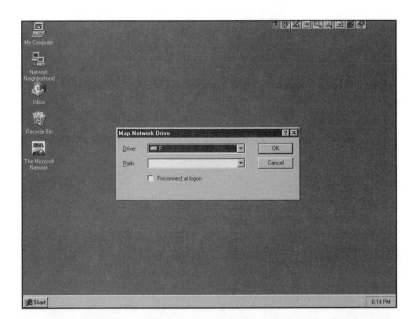

Figure 18.47

The Windows 95 Map Network Drive dialog box.

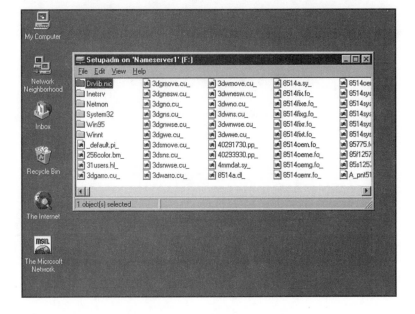

Figure 18.48

Mapping to a share name on a Windows NT Server.

Figure 18.49

Connecting to an Administrator share on a Windows NT Server.

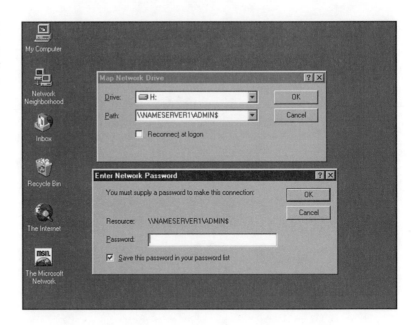

6. To disconnect from a network drive, right-click on the computer name and select the Disconnect Network Drive option. The Disconnect Network Drive dialog box appears (see fig. 18.50). Use this dialog box to select the network drive to disconnect.

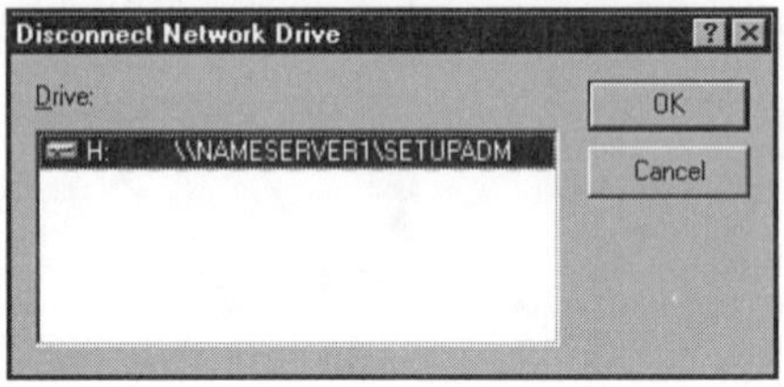

Figure 18.50

The Disconnect Network Drive dialog box in Windows 95.

Supporting Macintosh Clients

Macintosh clients have built-in network client software that enables them to talk to other AppleShare servers. The Macintosh clients communicate with AppleShare servers by using the AppleTalk protocols (see fig. 18.51). The AppleTalk protocols are a suite of protocols built into every Macintosh computer. The network adapters used on a Macintosh network can be LocalTalk, a proprietary networking technology; or a standards-based technology such as Ethernet, Token Ring, and FDDI. These are called EtherTalk, TokenTalk, and FDDITalk, respectively.

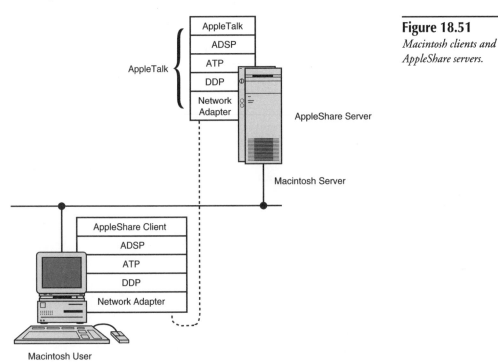

Figure 18.51

Macintosh clients and AppleShare servers.

Windows NT Server can support Macintosh clients by emulating an AppleShare server. Emulation of the AppleShare server is supported by the AppleTalk protocols on the Windows NT server (see fig. 18.52). This emulation is implemented by Services for Macintosh in Windows NT. Windows NT Server also includes a special network client for Macintosh computers. The client can be downloaded by logging on as a Guest user to the Windows NT Server by using the AppleTalk protocols.

Figure 18.52
Windows NT Server support for AppleTalk clients.

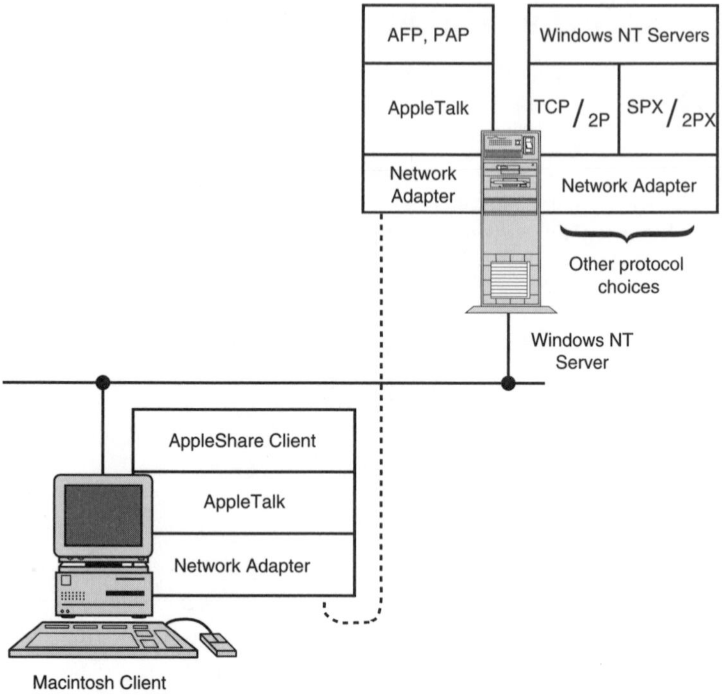

The Services for Macintosh provide you with the following benefits:

- **File sharing.** For AppleShare clients, and between Macintosh and non-Macintosh clients.

- **Print sharing.** Enables PCs and Macintosh computers to share printers.

- **Simplified administration.** You can use a common server—the Windows NT Server—as both an NT server and an AppleShare server.

- **AppleTalk routing support.** The Windows NT server with multiple network adapters can provide routing at the Datagram Delivery Protocol (DDP) layer for AppleTalk computers.

There are three steps involved in setting up services for the Macintosh:

1. Install Services for Macintosh on the Windows NT Server.

2. Configure Macintosh Accessible volumes.

3. Set authentication services for Macintosh Client.

Installing Services for Macintosh on Windows NT Server

To set up Services for Macintosh, follow these steps:

1. Log on as an Administrator to the Windows NT Server.

2. Open the Control Panel.

3. Double-click on the Network icon.

   The Network dialog box appears (see fig. 18.53).

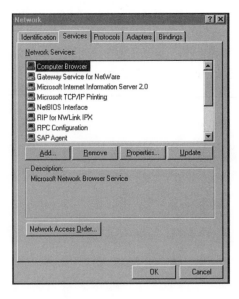

Figure 18.53
The Network Services tab.

4. Choose the Add button.

   The Select Network Service dialog box appears (see fig. 18.54).

5. Select Services for Macintosh from the list.

6. Click the OK button. The Windows NT Setup dialog box appears.

7. Enter the path for the Windows NT Server distribution files, then select Continue.

8. If you have not set up NTFS, an information dialog box appears, reminding you to do so. You do not have to install NTFS before you add the Macintosh Service (see fig 18.55). Setup copies the necessary files and configures the Windows NT Server registry.

9. Select the Properties button.

   The Microsoft AppleTalk Protocol Properties dialog box appears (see fig. 18.56).

Figure 18.54

The Select Network Services dialog box.

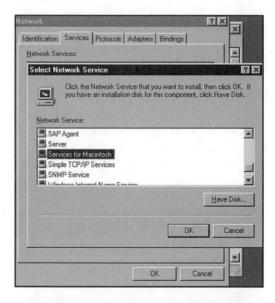

Figure 18.55

The Macintosh Service Setup Message.

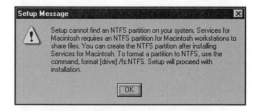

Figure 18.56

The Microsoft AppleTalk Protocol Properties dialog box.

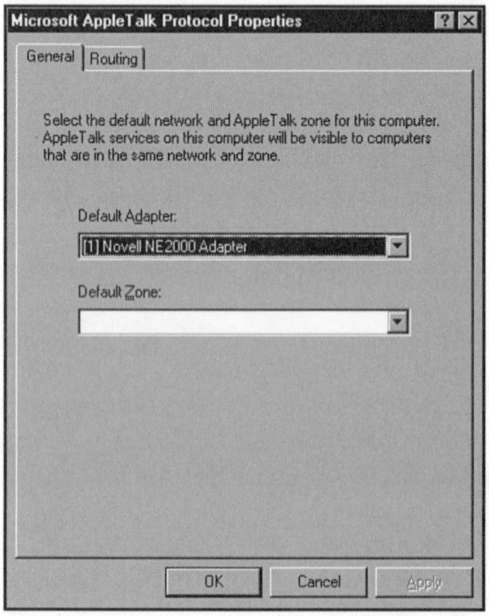

10. Select the network adapter information from the Network drop-down list and select the zone name of the AppleTalk network from the Zone drop-down list.

Zones are similar to the workgroup concept in Windows NT networks. Although Microsoft documentation says that zones are similar to domains, zones are closer in concept to workgroups. Zones are used primarily to simplify browsing operations, which is typically the reason for using Windows NT workgroups. Zones do not have user accounts, and you do not log on to zones. You can assign multiple zone names to a physical network segment.

A *physical network segment* is a network that does not contain routers. If routers exist on the physical network segment, they represent the boundary of the physical network segment.

For simpler networks, a single zone name is associated with a physical network segment. If you have multiple zone names for a physical network segment, select a default zone name for the segment.

If no AppleTalk routers or AppleShare servers exist on the network, and this is the first Windows NT Server on which you are configuring Services for Macintosh, no zone names are defined. In this case, select the Routing tab and set the Enable Routing option to set the Windows NT Server as an AppleTalk router. Normally, an AppleTalk router has multiple network adapters. You can have a computer act, however, as a *seed* for information on zones and network numbers associated with the physical network attached to a Windows NT Server's network interface. A *seed router* is a supplier or source of information on the network numbers and zone names associated with the network.

11. Select the Routing tab and check the Enable Routing box (see fig. 18.57).

Enable the Use this router to seed the network check box option so you can enter values for other fields.

In the Network Range section, enter a range of unique network numbers associated with the network segment. Network numbers are used by AppleTalk routers to identify a physical network segment. AppleTalk Phase I protocols supported only 254-nodes per network. When the currently used AppleTalk Phase II was introduced, the 254-node limitation per network segment was removed by enabling additional network numbers to be associated with a physical network segment. Windows NT 4 only supports the AppleTalk phase II protocols.

If you have only one network number assigned to the network segment, enter the same number in the Start and End fields.

Figure 18.57

The Microsoft AppleTalk Routing Configuration dialog box with the Routing tab shown.

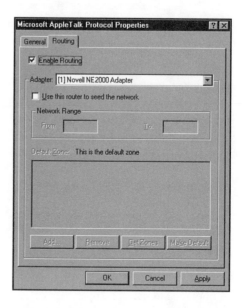

In the Zone Information section, enter zone names for the network attached to the Windows NT Server network interface. The previously added zone names appear in the Zone list. Use the Zone list to specify the default zone. The first zone name you enter becomes the default zone name.

Figure 18.58 shows some sample settings for the AppleTalk Routing Configuration dialog box with the Routing tab shown.

Figure 18.58

Sample settings for a Microsoft AppleTalk Routing Configuration dialog box with the Routing tab shown.

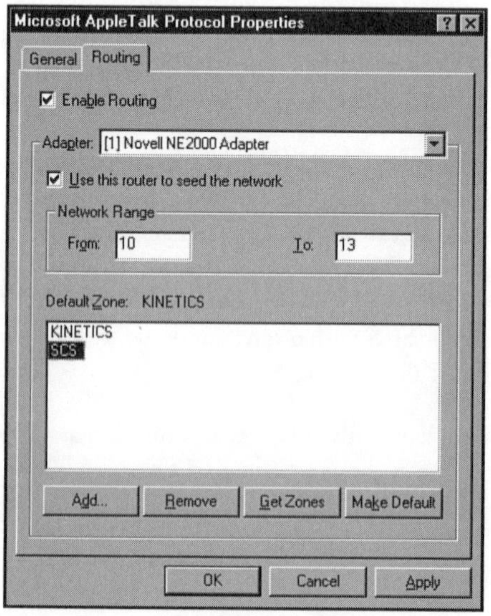

Select OK to return to the AppleTalk Protocol Configuration screen. Notice that you can now set the Zone field by using the new zones you have added.

12. Select OK. A message should appear, telling you that AppleTalk Protocol was configured successfully.

13. Select OK. You are returned to the Network Settings Change dialog box.

14. Select Yes.

15. Restart the Windows NT Server so that your changes will take effect.

After the Services for Macintosh are installed and the Windows NT Server restarts, you need to configure the volumes on the Windows NT Server that will be accessible to Macintosh clients.

To configure Macintosh-accessible volumes, follow these steps:

1. Log on as an Administrator to the Windows NT Server.

2. Open the Control Panel.

An icon for MacFile appears as a result of successfully installing Services for Macintosh (see fig. 18.59).

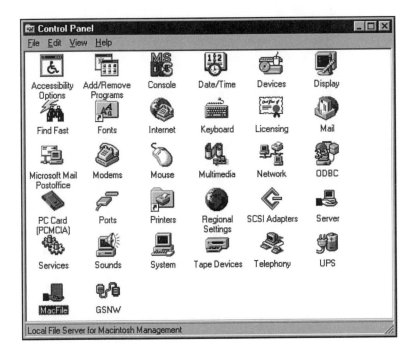

Figure 18.59

Changes to the Control Panel for Macintosh file configuration.

3. Double-click on the MacFile icon.

The MacFile Properties dialog box appears (see fig. 18.60).

Figure 18.60
*The MacFile Properties
dialog box.*

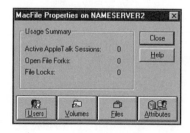

4. Select the MacFile Attributes button.

The MacFile Attributes dialog box appears (see fig. 18.61).

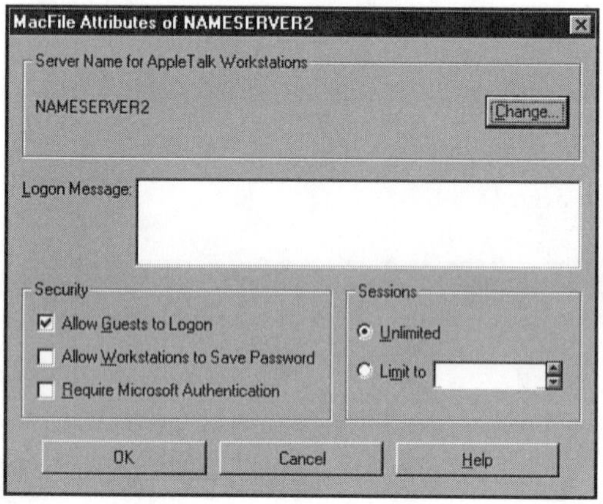

Figure 18.61
*The MacFile Attributes
dialog box.*

Type text in the Logon Message box to change the welcome logon message.

Select the options in the Security box to change the logon options. After installing the Microsoft authentication files on the Macintosh clients, you can select the Require Microsoft Authentication option.

Select the options in the Sessions box to enable unlimited sessions (default) or a limited number of sessions to the Windows NT Server. You might want to limit the number of sessions to limit the level of activity of Macintosh clients.

5. Open Explorer and verify that you have the Microsoft UAM folder in the NTFS partition (see fig. 18.62). This directory was created as a result of installing Services for Macintosh. This directory contains the authentication files for Macintosh clients, so they can log on by using Microsoft's logon authentication, which provides encrypted passwords. These passwords are difficult to decrypt even if they are captured by protocol analyzer devices. By default, the AppleShare servers implemented for Macintosh support only clear text (unencrypted) passwords.

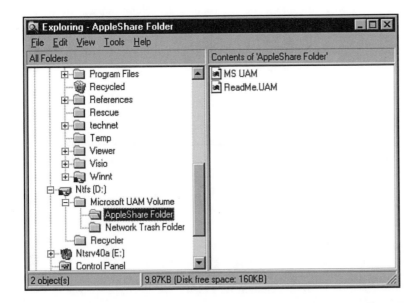

Figure 18.62

The Microsoft UAM folder viewed from Explorer.

Setting Authentication Services for Macintosh Clients

You can set up authentication services for AppleShare by downloading the authentication files from the Windows NT Server. Microsoft's authentication services are an extension of AppleShare services and provide a more secure logon to a Windows NT Server emulating an AppleShare server. Microsoft authentication encrypts passwords and stores them on the Windows NT Server.

By using the Microsoft authentication on a Macintosh client, users can specify the domain they can log on to and change their passwords.

To install the configuration files, follow these steps:

1. Select Chooser from the Macintosh Apple menu. The Chooser dialog box appears.

2. Select the AppleShare icon.

   Select the zone in which the client resides from the AppleTalk Zones list. A client can reside only in a single zone even if other zones overlap on the cable segment.

3. From the list of servers displayed for the zone, select the Windows NT server acting as an AppleShare server and then select OK. The Sign-In dialog box appears.

4. Select the Guest or Registered User option. Then select OK. The Server dialog box appears.

5. Select the Microsoft UAM Volume option. Then select OK.

6. Close the Chooser dialog box. An icon for the Microsoft UAM volume appears on the Microsoft desktop.

7. Open the Microsoft UAM volume. The Microsoft UAM Volume window and the AppleShare folder inside the window appear.

8. Drag the AppleShare folder to the System folder.

   If you already have an AppleShare folder inside the System folder, you are asked if you want to overwrite it. If this is another valid folder, such as a NetWare UAM folder used by Macintosh clients to access a NetWare server, you should not overwrite it. You can drop the Microsoft UAM folder into the existing AppleShare folder inside the System folder.

9. Restart the Macintosh workstation.

10. The next time you log on, select the Windows NT server as you did earlier. This time, you see a Sign-on dialog box asking you to select the logon method.

    If the Macintosh workstation is running System 7.1 or later, and the Cleartext and Guest options are disabled at the AppleShare server, you see only the choice for the Microsoft authentication logon method. In earlier systems, you would see both choices: the Cleartext and the Microsoft authentication logon, regardless of the fact that the Cleartext and Guest options are disabled at the AppleShare server.

11. Select Registered User and Microsoft Authentication.

    Enter your user name and password and select OK. A list of Macintosh-accessible volumes appears.

12. Select a volume to access its contents.

If a volume icon is grayed out, you might not have the correct privileges to access it, or you already might be logged in to that volume.

Managing Macintosh Users, Volumes, and Files on Windows NT Server

You can use the MacFile icon in the Control Panel to manage Macintosh client users who have made connections to the Windows NT Server.

To manage the user connection properties, follow these steps:

1. Log on as an Administrator user to the Windows NT Server.

2. Double-click on the MacFile icon in the Control Panel.

   The MacFile Properties dialog box appears. This properties dialog box displays the active AppleTalk sessions, number of open file forks, and file locks.

3. Select the Users button.

   The Macintosh Users screen appears (see fig. 18.63). You can use this screen to disconnect specific user connections or to send messages to the Macintosh users.

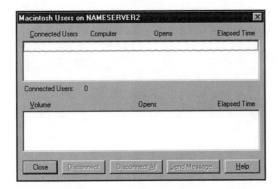

Figure 18.63

The Macintosh Users dialog box for Windows NT Server.

   Select Close to return to the MacFile Properties dialog box.

4. Select the Volumes button.

   The Macintosh-Accessible Volumes dialog box appears (see fig. 18.64). You can use this screen to monitor Macintosh users connected to a specific volume, the amount of time they have been connected, and whether or not the volume is being used. You can also disconnect specific user connections.

Figure 18.64

The Macintosh-Accessible Volumes dialog box for Windows NT Server.

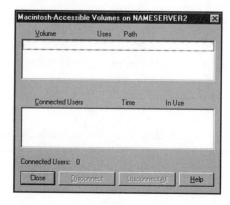

Select Close to return to the MacFile Properties dialog box.

5. Select the Files button.

The Files Opened by Macintosh Users dialog box appears (see fig. 18.65). You can use this dialog box to monitor the files opened by Macintosh users, the permissions they have to a specific file, the number of locks for a specific file, and the directory path to the file. You also can close a fork opened by the Macintosh users.

Figure 18.65

Files Opened by Macintosh Users dialog box on Windows NT Server.

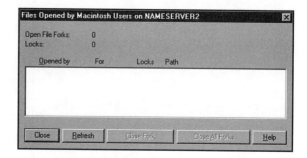

Select Close to return to the MacFile Properties dialog box.

6. Select Close to exit the MacFile Properties dialog box.

Conclusion

Windows NT Server supports a number of different clients, including MS-DOS, Windows 3.x, Windows NT, OS/2, and Macintosh. This chapter discussed the network client architecture, protocols, and APIs that are used to access Windows NT Server resources.

This chapter also discussed the different options available in the Network Client Administrator tool for setting up installation files for network clients. You also learned how to configure different types of network clients to access a Windows NT network.

PART

Appendixes

Planning Network Security

This appendix contains general guidelines for designing and implementing a security system for your network.

Examining Security Controls

You can use two basic types of security controls to protect a computer network system: internal controls and external controls. The majority of this chapter discusses internal controls, but for purposes of being complete, the external controls are discussed also.

Internal Controls

Internal controls consist of the controls internal to the computer system itself. Passwords, firewalls, and data encryption are examples of internal controls. Internal controls are effective only if accompanied by some level of external controls as well.

External Controls

External controls cover the part of the system that the system cannot address itself. The three general categories of external controls are as follows:

- Physical

- Personnel

- Procedural

Physical controls refer to the physical security measures that protect the computer system. Locked doors, air conditioned rooms, and keyboard locks are examples of physical controls. As intra-networking becomes more commonplace, the role of physical controls continues to diminish.

Personnel controls refer to the techniques and policies that an employer uses in deciding who to trust with the organization's computer system. As an employee gains a higher level of access to the computer system, the scrutiny of the employee should be increased. This can range from interviews with previous supervisors to polygraph tests. All this depends on the particulars of the installation.

Procedural controls refer to the measures taken to ensure that the information on the computer system is accessed only by those who require access. This is known in military circles as a "need to know" policy. Procedural controls also cover how new software is installed and how the system is maintained.

Internal and External—Hand-in-Hand

Internal and external controls should function together to create a complete security system. Although it is possible to trade off one for the other, most of the time internal and external controls complement one another. It would not do much good for a crucial NT file server to be password protected, for example, if it was left in an unprotected hallway for anyone to steal or damage.

The general rule of thumb is that if an exposure can be eliminated by either an internal or external control, the internal control should be used. External controls are usually more expensive and harder to implement. In addition, procedure controls are notoriously error prone because they rely on people.

Examining the Approaches to Network Security

Every network security issue has two approaches. A security administrator can deny access to everyone and grant permissions to resources as needed, or she can grant access to all and restrict specific resources as required. The criteria for the access or restriction is unique to every installation.

The following two sections describe allowing access and denying access as well as using these two paradigms cooperatively.

Allowing Access

Allowing a user access to a resource is an act of inclusion. The criteria that enables the user access should match the nature of the resource being shared.

The payroll system, for example, should be accessed only by the users who work in the payroll department. On a Windows NT server, the system administrator creates a group of users called payroll and grants that group access to that resource. If a new employee (Matthew) is hired for the position of payroll clerk in the payroll department, he is added to the payroll group and automatically has the same level of access as anyone else in that group. This is the act of inclusion.

One potential pitfall with the inclusion concept occurs, for example, when Matthew is transferred out of the payroll department to the general ledger department. At the new department, Matthew is granted access to the general ledger system by his inclusion in another group called general ledger. The potential problem becomes a real problem if someone forgets about the inclusion of Matthew in the payroll group, and his access is not taken away. Now, inadvertently, access has been given to the payroll system to someone outside the payroll group.

To prevent this from happening, procedures should be defined for granting users access to a group. Procedures should be implemented, for example, that require a user's entire security profile to be analyzed and updated each time he is transferred. Also, if possible and supported by the operating system, safeguards should be programmed into the software that require users to be removed from other groups when they are added to new groups.

The Windows NT security system offers another way to avoid this potential problem: the No Access security attribute. The No Access attribute overrides all other security attributes. Any user assigned this attribute for a given resource may not access that resource regardless of any other permissions assigned. Consider the result of Matthew's transfer to a different department if all groups except users in the payroll department were assigned the No Access attribute for the payroll system. This security practice is exclusion and in this example can be coordinated with inclusion to "plug" a security hole.

Denying Access

To deny a user access to a network resource is an act of rejection. Rejecting the user's access is based on a set of criteria. This criteria matches the restrictions placed on the shared resource.

As in the previous example, access might be denied to the payroll system if an authorized user were trying to access the system at three o'clock in the morning. In this case, the system administrator might set after hours as one of the criteria for denial of access. This is an example of granting access to a resource and then restricting that access with a different type of denial.

Handling Exceptions

Often the two approaches in network security, described previously, work together. As in the example of the payroll system, you both allow access and deny access to the same resource as part of the protection to that resource. This is an excellent way to handle exceptions. Exceptions are the biggest catches when looking at network security. Often the security of a network resource is all planned out, and someone throws in an exception that foils the plan. At this point, the exception needs to be examined in the light of the two approaches to network security and worked out.

For example, users that run the aforementioned payroll system may be located in a secure section of their building. It would therefore be wise to not only limit access to the payroll system to payroll department employees but to also restrict access to the payroll system by authorized users to workstations located in the secure area of the building.

Designing a Network Security Policy

Every organization that has a network with outside or interdepartmental connectivity should have a network security policy. A *network security policy* is a statement of the network security requirements for that site. A network security policy is the blueprint from which you design and build the network's defenses against intruders—both internal and external. A good network security policy is an essential part of building effective network firewalls.

It is important to identify significant network security issues before implementing firewalls. Of course, identifying these significant network security issues is easier said than done. Identification involves discussing network services with all appropriate users and determining which resources you are going to allow users to access and which ones will be restricted because of security risks.

An effective network security policy should balance the concerns of network administrators with the practical needs of network users. The policy should cover all the potential security risks while not impairing the use of the network.

The following sections discuss suggested steps in creating an effective network security policy.

Step One: Identifying Security Issues at the Installation

To have an effective network security policy, you must identify all the important network security issues associated with a network installation. The consideration of the issues should extend beyond the current situation to encompass the future plans for the network.

To start a network security policy, you should ask several questions:

- What resources must be protected?

- How important are each of these resources?

- Who are the potential "intruders"?

- How likely is the threat?

- What is needed to guard against this possible intrusion?

- Does the cost of defense balance with the likelihood of the threat and the value of the resource?

You should involve the entire MIS staff and department heads in answering these questions because these people have knowledge of the day-to-day interworkings of the computer system or their department and can offer valuable insight. If department heads are part of the initial fact-finding process, they won't feel as if something foreign is being pushed into their department. Because they were involved in the beginning of the process, they feel that the new network security policy is partially their idea. This helps a great deal with their acceptance of the security policy and its successful implementation.

The use of an outside consultant can also be useful in this step. An outside consultant can offer insight and suggestions that she has seen at other installations. Additionally, a consultant should be aware of the latest approaches and technologies in computer security.

At this step, the different network resources are reviewed in light of the two approaches to network security. A decision must be made as to which approach the network security policy will take with respect to the different network security issues.

While reviewing the different network resources, you must be certain to include all the resources. Leaving anything out of the consideration can weaken the overall security plan and can cause an inaccurate risk analysis. The following basic list identifies the areas you should consider:

- Hardware

- Software

- Data

- People

- Documentation

- Supplies

Step Two: Risk/Cost Analysis

You can perform a risk analysis of the network system in several ways. The method discussed in this section uses a simple cost/risk matrix. The *cost/risk matrix* is simply a ranked list of known security risks, their likelihood of occurring, and their cost exposure. This method does not produce a detailed list of probable or expected losses. However, this method shows management the high risk exposures that can be addressed in a cost effective manner.

Start by listing all the security risks that have been identified by the MIS team or consultant. The exposures on the list should be ranked on a scale from 1 to 100. The higher the likelihood of a particular exposure, the higher the score. The risk of a user cracking the system administrator's password and reconfiguring a gateway receives a low score. Conversely, the risk of tampering with an unprotected stand-alone computer system that monitors all long distance calls receives a very high score.

Next, rank the exposures again—this time according to the cost of the loss on a scale from 1 to 100. By using the previous examples, the cost of the correcting the gateway settings would most likely be low. The loss of long distance phone tracking could be high. At this point, you should consider all the factors carefully to ensure that there is an accurate cost estimate.

Finally, the list is ranked a third time—this time according to the cost to implement corrective procedures for each exposure on a scale from 1 to 100. When several corrective procedures can do the job, you should pick the least expensive option.

Now each of the of these exposures are plotted on a three-dimensional graph to show the matrix. If the list is produced on a spreadsheet program, plotting the exposures should be quick and easy.

At this point, you see all the exposures and how they rate on the three different axes. Of particular interest are the exposures of highest risk and of lowest corrective measure cost. They should be addressed first.

Step Three: Implementation

After the cost/risk analysis is completed, it should be fairly easy to decide which measures should be implemented first. Depending on the scope of what needs to be done and the budget to do it with, you should start with the corrective measures that apply to the exposures of highest risk and of lowest corrective measure cost. These are generally policy changes.

Generally speaking, firewalls are also found in this area of the graph. Firewalls can protect many large areas of concern and potential exposures for comparatively low cost. They provide an excellent starting point for the initial security changes. The first things that you implement should have a big effect for relatively low cost for a few reasons:

- Other departments will see faster progress and be more cooperative as the implementation progresses.

- Management will see progress and feel as though the money is being spent wisely.

- If the whole budget has not been received, having fast initial progress should help in getting the rest of the budget.

- If the budget gets cut later, the most important exposures are protected.

After the first wave of security devices and policies are implemented, you can now roll out the next or the rest of the security measures that seem practical or are needed.

It is important that these security measures do not disrupt the workflow of the users. If you make the system "unfriendly" in order to have a complete lock-down of system security, you have failed. Remember that balance between security and practical user needs is important to the success of the security system. The overall goal in this process is to make the security checkpoints and barriers as transparent as possible to the end user.

Step Four: Periodic Review and Update

An important step to include in the network security policy is a fixed (and recurring) time frame for review of the entire policy. As new hardware and software is added to the network, security requirements change. If a predefined time and procedure for reviewing the security design is not established, it probably never will be. The review period will obviously be different for every organization. It should, however, be done at least once each year, regardless of the size of the organization.

In this final step, you should also designate a group of people in the organization to serve as a security review team. This team of employees can make the process of reviewing the network security policy easier and more effective. Depending on the complexity of the original network security policy, you might consider using an outside consultant in this process. The review team should review the network security plan for the following concerns:

- New exposures

- Old exposures that no longer exist

- Security violations since the last review

RFC 1244—The Site Security Handbook

The following document is RFC 1244—The Site Security Handbook from the Internet Task Force. This is the original document first written in July 1991 that is commonly looked to as the working administrators' bible.

This handbook is the product of the Site Security Policy Handbook Working Group (SSPHWG), a combined effort of the Security Area and User Services Area of the Internet Engineering Task Force (IETF). This FYI RFC provides information for the Internet community. It does not specify an Internet standard. Distribution of this memo is unlimited.

Contributing Authors

The following are the authors of the Site Security Handbook. Without their dedication, this handbook would not have been possible.

Dave Curry (Purdue University), Sean Kirkpatrick (Unisys), Tom Longstaff (LLNL), Greg Hollingsworth (Johns Hopkins University), Jeffrey Carpenter (University of Pittsburgh), Barbara Fraser (CERT), Fred Ostapik (SRI NISC), Allen Sturtevant (LLNL), Dan Long (BBN), Jim Duncan (Pennsylvania State University), and Frank Byrum (DEC).

Editors' Note

This FYI RFC is a first attempt at providing Internet users guidance on how to deal with security issues in the Internet. As such, this document is necessarily incomplete. There are some clear shortfalls; for example, this document focuses mostly on resources available in the United States. In the spirit of the Internet's "Request for Comments" series of notes, we encourage feedback from users of this handbook. In particular, those who utilize this document to craft their own policies and procedures.

This handbook is meant to be a starting place for further research and should be viewed as a useful resource, but not the final authority. Different organizations and jurisdictions will have different resources and rules. Talk to your local organizations, consult an informed lawyer, or consult with local and national law enforcement. These groups can help fill in the gaps that this document cannot hope to cover.

Finally, we intend for this FYI RFC to grow and evolve. Please send comments and suggestions to:

`ssphwg@cert.sei.cmu.edu.`

1. Introduction

1.1 Purpose of this Work

This handbook is a guide to setting computer security policies and procedures for sites that have systems on the Internet. This guide lists issues and factors that a site must consider when setting their own policies. It makes some recommendations and gives discussions of relevant areas.

This guide is only a framework for setting security policies and procedures. In order to have an effective set of policies and procedures, a site will have to make many decisions, gain agreement, and then communicate and implement the policies.

1.2 Audience

The audience for this work are system administrators and decision makers (who are more traditionally called "administrators" or "middle management") at sites. This document is not directed at programmers or those trying to create secure programs or systems. The focus of this document is on the policies and procedures that need to be in place to support any technical security features that a site may be implementing.

The primary audience for this work are sites that are members of the Internet community. However, this document should be useful to any site that allows communication with other sites. As a general guide to security policies, this document may also be useful to sites with isolated systems.

1.3 Definitions

For the purposes of this guide, a "site" is any organization that owns computers or network-related resources. These resources may include host computers that users use, routers, terminal servers, PC's, or other devices that have access to the Internet. A site may be an end user of Internet services or a service provider such as a regional network. However, most of the focus of this guide is on those end users of Internet services.

We assume that the site has the ability to set policies and procedures for itself with the concurrence and support from those who actually own the resources.

The "Internet" is those set of networks and machines that use the TCP/IP protocol suite, connected through gateways, and sharing a common name and address spaces [1].

The term "system administrator" is used to cover all those who are responsible for the day-to-day operation of resources. This may be a number of individuals or an organization.

The term "decision maker" refers to those people at a site who set or approve policy. These are often (but not always) the people who own the resources.

1.4 Related Work

The IETF Security Policy Working Group (SPWG) is working on a set of recommended security policy guidelines for the Internet [23]. These guidelines may be adopted as policy by regional networks or owners of other resources. This handbook should be a useful tool to help sites implement those policies as desired or required. However, even implementing the proposed policies isn't enough to secure a site. The proposed Internet policies deal only with network access security. It says nothing about how sites should deal with local security issues.

1.5 Scope

This document covers issues about what a computer security policy should contain, what kinds of procedures are need to enforce security, and some recommendations about how to deal with the problem. When developing a security policy, close attention should be made not only on the security needs and requirements of the local network, but also the security needs and requirements of the other interconnected networks.

This is not a cookbook for computer security. Each site has different needs; the security needs of a corporation might well be different than the security needs of an academic institution. Any security plan has to conform to the needs and culture of the site.

This handbook does not cover details of how to do risk assessment, contingency planning, or physical security. These things are essential in setting and implementing effective security policy, but this document leaves treatment of those issues to other documents.

We will try to provide some pointers in that direction.

This document also doesn't talk about how to design or implement secure systems or programs.

1.6 Why Do We Need Security Policies and Procedures?

For most sites, the interest in computer security is proportional to the perception of risk and threats. The world of computers has changed dramatically over the past 25 years. Twenty-five years ago, most computers were centralized and managed by data centers. Computers were kept in locked rooms and staffs of people made sure they were carefully managed and physically secured. Links outside a site were unusual.

Computer security threats were rare, and were basically concerned with insiders: authorized users misusing accounts, theft and vandalism, and so forth. These threats were well understood and dealt with using standard techniques: computers behind locked doors, and accounting for all resources.

Computing in the 1990's is radically different. Many systems are in private offices and labs, often managed by individuals or persons employed outside a computer center. Many systems are connected into the Internet, and from there around the world: the United States, Europe, Asia, and Australia are all connected together. Security threats are different today. The time honored advice says "don't write your password down and put it in your desk" lest someone find it. With world-wide Internet connections, someone could get into your system from the other side of the world and steal your password in the middle of the night when your building is locked up.

Viruses and worms can be passed from machine to machine. The Internet allows the electronic equivalent of the thief who looks for open windows and doors; now a person can check hundreds of machines for vulnerabilities in a few hours.

System administrators and decision makers have to understand the security threats that exist, what the risk and cost of a problem would be, and what kind of action they want to take (if any) to prevent and respond to security threats.

As an illustration of some of the issues that need to be dealt with in security problems, consider the following scenarios (thanks to Russell Brand [2, BRAND] for these):

- A system programmer gets a call reporting that a major underground cracker newsletter is being distributed from the administrative machine at his center to five thousand sites in the US and Western Europe.

  Eight weeks later, the authorities call to inform you the information in one of these newsletters was used to disable "911" in a major city for five hours.

- A user calls in to report that he can't login to his account at 3 o'clock in the morning on a Saturday. The system staffer can't login either. After rebooting to single user mode, he finds that password file is empty.

  By Monday morning, your staff determines that a number of privileged file transfers took place between this machine and a local university.

  Tuesday morning a copy of the deleted password file is found on the university machine along with password files for a dozen other machines.

  A week later you find that your system initialization files had been altered in a hostile fashion.

- You receive a call saying that a breakin to a government lab occurred from one of your center's machines. You are requested to provide accounting files to help trackdown the attacker.

  A week later you are given a list of machines at your site that have been broken into.

- A reporter calls up asking about the breakin at your center. You haven't heard of any such breakin. Three days later, you learn that there was a breakin. The center director had his wife's name as a password.

- A change in system binaries is detected. The day that it is corrected, they again are changed. This repeats itself for some weeks.

- If an intruder is found on your system, should you leave the system open to monitor the situation or should you close down the holes and open them up again later?

■ If an intruder is using your site, should you call law enforcement? Who makes that decision? If law enforcement asks you to leave your site open, who makes that decision?

■ What steps should be taken if another site calls you and says they see activity coming from an account on your system? What if the account is owned by a local manager?

1.7 Basic Approach

Setting security policies and procedures really means developing a plan for how to deal with computer security. One way to approach this task is suggested by Fites, et. al. [3, FITES]:

■ Look at what you are trying to protect.

■ Look at what you need to protect it from.

■ Determine how likely the threats are.

■ Implement measures which will protect your assets in a cost-effective manner.

■ Review the process continuously, and improve things every time a weakness is found.

This handbook will concentrate mostly on the last two steps, but the first three are critically important to making effective decisions about security. One old truism in security is that the cost of protecting yourself against a threat should be less than the cost recovering if the threat were to strike you. Without reasonable knowledge of what you are protecting and what the likely threats are, following this rule could be difficult.

1.8 Organization of this Document

This document is organized into seven parts in addition to this introduction.

The basic form of each section is to discuss issues that a site might want to consider in creating a computer security policy and setting procedures to implement that policy. In some cases, possible options are discussed along with some of the ramifications of those choices. As far as possible, this document tries not to dictate the choices a site should make, since these depend on local circumstances. Some of the issues brought up may not apply to all sites. Nonetheless, all sites should at least consider the issues brought up here to ensure that they do not miss some important area.

The overall flow of the document is to discuss policy issues followed by the issues that come up in creating procedures to implement the policies.

Section 2 discusses setting official site policies for access to computing resources. It also goes into the issue of what happens when the policy is violated. The policies will drive the procedures that need to be created, so decision makers will need to make choices about policies before many of the procedural issues in following sections can be dealt with. A key part of creating policies is doing some kind of risk assessment to decide what really needs to be protected and the level of resources that should be applied to protect them.

Once policies are in place, procedures to prevent future security problems should be established. Section 3 defines and suggests actions to take when unauthorized activity is suspected. Resources to prevent secruity breaches are also discussed. Section 4 discusses types of procedures to prevent security problems.

Prevention is a key to security; as an example, the Computer Emergency Response Team/ Coordination Center (CERT/CC) at Carnegie-Mellon University (CMU) estimates that 80% or more of the problems they see have to do with poorly chosen passwords.

Section 5 discusses incident handling: what kinds of issues does a site face when someone violates the security policy. Many decisions will have to made on the spot as the incident occurs, but many of the options and issues can be discussed in advance. At very least, responsibilities and methods of communication can be established before an incident. Again, the choices here are influenced by the policies discussed in section 2.

Section 6 deals with what happens after a security violation has been dealt with. Security planning is an on-going cycle; just after an incident has occurred is an excellent opportunity to improve policies and procedures.

The rest of the document provides references and an annotated bibliography.

2. Establishing Official Site Policy on Computer Security

2.1 Brief Overview

2.1.1 Organization Issues

The goal in developing an official site policy on computer security is to define the organization's expectations of proper computer and network use and to define procedures to prevent and respond to security incidents. In order to do this, aspects of the particular organization must be considered.

First, the goals and direction of the organization should be considered. For example, a military base may have very different security concerns from a those of a university.

Second, the site security policy developed must conform to existing policies, rules, regulations and laws that the organization is subject to. Therefore it will be necessary to identify these and take them into consideration while developing the policy.

Third, unless the local network is completely isolated and standalone, it is necessary to consider security implications in a more global context. The policy should address the issues when local security problems develop as a result of a remote site as well as when problems occur on remote systems as a result of a local host or user.

2.1.2 Who Makes the Policy?

Policy creation must be a joint effort by technical personnel, who understand the full ramifications of the proposed policy and the implementation of the policy, and by decision makers who have the power to enforce the policy. A policy which is neither implementable nor enforceable is useless.

Since a computer security policy can affect everyone in an organization, it is worth taking some care to make sure you have the right level of authority on the policy decisions. Though a particular group (such as a campus information services group) may have responsibility for enforcing a policy, an even higher group may have to support and approve the policy.

2.1.3 Who is Involved?

Establishing a site policy has the potential for involving every computer user at the site in a variety of ways. Computer users may be responsible for personal password administration. Systems managers are obligated to fix security holes and to oversee the system.

It is critical to get the right set of people involved at the start of the process. There may already be groups concerned with security who would consider a computer security policy to be their area. Some of the types of groups that might be involved include auditing/control, organizations that deal with physical security, campus information systems groups, and so forth. Asking these types of groups to "buy in" from the start can help facilitate the acceptance of the policy.

2.1.4 Responsibilities

A key element of a computer security policy is making sure everyone knows their own responsibility for maintaining security.

A computer security policy cannot anticipate all possibilities; however, it can ensure that each kind of problem does have someone assigned to deal with it. There may be levels of responsibility associated with a policy on computer security. At one level, each user of a computing resource may have a responsibility to protect his account. A user who allows his account to be compromised increases the chances of compromising other accounts or resources.

System managers may form another responsibility level: they must help to ensure the security of the computer system. Network managers may reside at yet another level.

2.2 Risk Assessment

2.2.1 General Discussion

One of the most important reasons for creating a computer security policy is to ensure that efforts spent on security yield cost effective benefits. Although this may seem obvious, it is possible to be mislead about where the effort is needed. As an example, there is a great deal of publicity about intruders on computers systems; yet most surveys of computer security show that for most organizations, the actual loss from "insiders" is much greater.

Risk analysis involves determining what you need to protect, what you need to protect it from, and how to protect it. It is the process of examining all of your risks, and ranking those risks by level of severity. This process involves making cost-effective decisions on what you want to protect. The old security adage says that you should not spend more to protect something than it is actually worth.

A full treatment of risk analysis is outside the scope of this document. [3, FITES] and [16, PFLEEGER] provide introductions to this topic. However, there are two elements of a risk analysis that will be briefly covered in the next two sections:

1. Identifying the assets

2. Identifying the threats

For each asset, the basic goals of security are availability, confidentiality, and integrity. Each threat should be examined with an eye to how the threat could affect these areas.

2.2.2 Identifying the Assets

One step in a risk analysis is to identify all the things that need to be protected. Some things are obvious, like all the various pieces of hardware, but some are overlooked, such as the people who actually use the systems. The essential point is to list all things that could be affected by a security problem.

One list of categories is suggested by Pfleeger [16, PFLEEGER, page 459]; this list is adapted from that source:

1. Hardware: cpus, boards, keyboards, terminals, workstations, personal computers, printers, disk drives, communication lines, terminal servers, routers.

2. Software: source programs, object programs, utilities, diagnostic programs, operating systems, communication programs.

3. Data: during execution, stored on-line, archived off-line, backups, audit logs, databases, in transit over communication media.

4. People: users, people needed to run systems.

5. Documentation: on programs, hardware, systems, local administrative procedures.

6. Supplies: paper, forms, ribbons, magnetic media.

2.2.3 Identifying the Threats

Once the assets requiring protection are identified, it is necessary to identify threats to those assests. The threats can then be examined to determine what potential for loss exists. It helps to consider from what threats you are trying to protect your assets.

The following sections describe a few of the possible threats.

2.2.3.1 Unauthorized Access

A common threat that concerns many sites is unauthorized access to computing facilities. Unauthorized access takes many forms.

One means of unauthorized access is the use of another user's account to gain access to a system. The use of any computer resource without prior permission may be considered unauthorized access to computing facilities.

The seriousness of an unauthorized access will vary from site to site. For some sites, the mere act of granting access to an unauthorized user may cause irreparable harm by negative media coverage. For other sites, an unauthorized access opens the door to other security threats. In addition, some sites may be more frequent targets than others; hence the risk from unauthorized access will vary from site to site. The Computer Emergency Response Team (CERT—see section 3.9.7.3.1) has observed that well-known universities, government sites, and military sites seem to attract more intruders.

2.2.3.2 Disclosure of Information

Another common threat is disclosure of information. Determine the value or sensitivity of the information stored on your computers. Disclosure of a password file might allow for future unauthorized accesses. A glimpse of a proposal may give a competitor an unfair advantage. A technical paper may contain years of valuable research.

2.2.3.3 Denial of Service

Computers and networks provide valuable services to their users. Many people rely on these services in order to perform their jobs efficiently. When these services are not available when called upon, a loss in productivity results. Denial of service comes in many forms and might affect users in a number of ways. A network may be rendered unusable by a rogue packet, jamming, or by a disabled network component. A virus might slow down or cripple a computer system. Each site should determine which services are essential, and for each of these services determine the affect to the site if that service were to become disabled.

2.3 Policy Issues

There are a number of issues that must be addressed when developing a security policy. These are:

1. Who is allowed to use the resources?

2. What is the proper use of the resources?

3. Who is authorized to grant access and approve usage?

4. Who may have system administration privileges?

5. What are the user's rights and responsibilities?

6. What are the rights and responsibilities of the system administrator vs. those of the user?

7. What do you do with sensitive information?

These issues will be discussed below. In addition you may wish to include a section in your policy concerning ethical use of computing resources. Parker, Swope and Baker [17, PARKER90] and Forester and Morrison [18, FORESTER] are two useful references that address ethical issues.

2.3.1 Who is Allowed to use the Resources?

One step you must take in developing your security policy is defining who is allowed to use your system and services. The policy should explicitly state who is authorized to use what resources.

2.3.2 What is the Proper Use of the Resources?

After determining who is allowed access to system resources it is necessary to provide guidelines for the acceptable use of the resources. You may have different guidelines for different types of users (i.e., students, faculty, external users). The policy should state what is acceptable use as well as unacceptable use.

It should also include types of use that may be restricted. Define limits to access and authority. You will need to consider the level of access various users will have and what resources will be available or restricted to various groups of people.

Your acceptable use policy should clearly state that individual users are responsible for their actions. Their responsibility exists regardless of the security mechanisms that are in place. It should be clearly stated that breaking into accounts or bypassing security is not permitted. The following points should be covered when developing an acceptable use policy:

■ Is breaking into accounts permitted?

■ Is cracking passwords permitted?

■ Is disrupting service permitted?

■ Should users assume that a file being world-readable grants them the authorization to read it?

■ Should users be permitted to modify files that are not their own even if they happen to have write permission?

■ Should users share accounts?

The answer to most of these questions will be "no."

You may wish to incorporate a statement in your policies concerning copyrighted and licensed software. Licensing agreements with vendors may require some sort of effort on your part to ensure that the license is not violated. In addition, you may wish to inform users that the copying of copyrighted software may be a violation of the copyright laws, and is not permitted.

Specifically concerning copyrighted and/or licensed software, you may wish to include the following information:

■ Copyrighted and licensed software may not be duplicated unless it is explicitly stated that you may do so.

■ Methods of conveying information on the copyright/licensed status of software.

■ When in doubt, DON'T COPY.

Your acceptable use policy is very important. A policy which does not clearly state what is not permitted may leave you unable to prove that a user violated policy.

There are exception cases like tiger teams and users or administrators wishing for "licenses to hack"—you may face the situation where users will want to "hack" on your services for security research purposes. You should develop a policy that will determine whether you will permit this type of research on your services and if so, what your guidelines for such research will be.

Points you may wish to cover in this area:

■ Whether it is permitted at all.

■ What type of activity is permitted: breaking in, releasing worms, releasing viruses, etc..

■ What type of controls must be in place to ensure that it does not get out of control (e.g., separate a segment of your network for these tests).

- How you will protect other users from being victims of these activities, including external users and networks.

- The process for obtaining permission to conduct these tests.

In cases where you do permit these activities, you should isolate the portions of the network that are being tested from your main network. Worms and viruses should never be released on a live network.

You may also wish to employ, contract, or otherwise solicit one or more people or organizations to evaluate the security of your services, one of which may include "hacking." You may wish to provide for this in your policy.

2.3.3 Who Is Authorized to Grant Access and Approve Usage?

Your policy should state who is authorized to grant access to your services. Further, it must be determined what type of access they are permitted to give. If you do not have control over who is granted access to your system, you will not have control over who is using your system. Controlling who has the authorization to grant access will also enable you to know who was or was not granting access if problems develop later.

There are many schemes that can be developed to control the distribution of access to your services. The following are the factors that you must consider when determining who will distribute access to your services:

- Will you be distributing access from a centralized point or at various points?

  You can have a centralized distribution point to a distributed system where various sites or departments independently authorize access. The trade off is between security and convenience. The more centralized, the easier to secure.

- What methods will you use for creating accounts and terminating access?

From a security standpoint, you need to examine the mechanism that you will be using to create accounts. In the least restrictive case, the people who are authorized to grant access would be able to go into the system directly and create an account by hand or through vendor supplied mechanisms. Generally, these mechanisms place a great deal of trust in the person running them, and the person running them usually has a large amount of privileges. If this is the choice you make, you need to select someone who is trustworthy to perform this task. The opposite solution is to have an integrated system that the people authorized to create accounts run, or the users themselves may actually run. Be aware that even in the restrictive case of having a mechanized facility to create accounts does not remove the potential for abuse. You should have specific procedures developed for the creation of accounts. These procedures should be well documented to prevent confusion and reduce mistakes. A security vulnerability in the account authorization process is not only possible through abuse, but is also possible if a mistake is made. Having clear and well documented procedure will help ensure that these mistakes won't happen. You should also be sure that the people who will be following these procedures understand them.

The granting of access to users is one of the most vulnerable of times. You should ensure that the selection of an initial password cannot be easily guessed. You should avoid using an initial password that is a function of the username, is part of the user's name, or some algorithmically generated password that can easily be guessed. In addition, you should not permit users to continue to use the initial password indefinitely. If possible, you should force users to change the initial password the first time they login. Consider that some users may never even login, leaving their password vulnerable indefinitely. Some sites choose to disable accounts that have never been accessed, and force the owner to reauthorize opening the account.

2.3.4 Who May Have System Administration Privileges?

One security decision that needs to be made very carefully is who will have access to system administrator privileges and passwords for your services. Obviously, the system administrators will need access, but inevitably other users will request special privileges. The policy should address this issue. Restricting privileges is one way to deal with threats from local users. The challenge is to balance restricting access to these to protect security with giving people who need these privileges access so that they can perform their tasks. One approach that can be taken is to grant only enough privilege to accomplish the necessary tasks.

Additionally, people holding special privileges should be accountable to some authority and this should also be identified within the site's security policy. If the people you grant privileges to are not accountable, you run the risk of losing control of your system and will have difficulty managing a compromise in security.

2.3.5 What Are The Users' Rights and Responsibilities?

The policy should incorporate a statement on the users' rights and responsibilities concerning the use of the site's computer systems and services. It should be clearly stated that users are responsible for understanding and respecting the security rules of the systems they are using. The following is a list of topics that you may wish to cover in this area of the policy:

- What guidelines you have regarding resource consumption (whether users are restricted, and if so, what the restrictions are).

- What might constitute abuse in terms of system performance.

- Whether users are permitted to share accounts or let others use their accounts.

- How "secret" users should keep their passwords.

- How often users should change their passwords and any other password restrictions or requirements.

- Whether you provide backups or expect the users to create their own.

- Disclosure of information that may be proprietary.

- Statement on Electronic Mail Privacy (Electronic Communications Privacy Act).

- Your policy concerning controversial mail or postings to mailing lists or discussion groups (obscenity, harassment, etc.).

- Policy on electronic communications: mail forging, etc.

The Electronic Mail Association sponsored a white paper on the privacy of electronic mail in companies [4]. Their basic recommendation is that every site should have a policy on the protection of employee privacy. They also recommend that organizations establish privacy policies that deal with all media, rather than singling out electronic mail.

They suggest five criteria for evaluating any policy:

1. Does the policy comply with law and with duties to third parties?

2. Does the policy unnecessarily compromise the interest of the employee, the employer or third parties?

3. Is the policy workable as a practical matter and likely to be enforced?

4. Does the policy deal appropriately with all different forms of communications and record keeping with the office?

5. Has the policy been announced in advance and agreed to by all concerned?

2.3.6 What Are The Rights and Responsibilities of System Administrators Versus Rights of Users

There is a tradeoff between a user's right to absolute privacy and the need of system administrators to gather sufficient information to diagnose problems. There is also a distinction between a system administrator's need to gather information to diagnose problems and investigating security violations. The policy should specify to what degree system administrators can examine user files to diagnose problems or for other purposes, and what rights you grant to the users. You may also wish to make a statement concerning system administrators' obligation to maintaining the privacy of information viewed under these circumstances. A few questions that should be answered are:

- Can an administrator monitor or read a user's files for any reason?

- What are the liabilities?

- Do network administrators have the right to examine network or host traffic?

2.3.7 What To Do With Sensitive Information

Before granting users access to your services, you need to determine at what level you will provide for the security of data on your systems. By determining this, you are determining the level of sensitivity of data that users should store on your systems. You do not want users to store very sensitive information on a system that you are not going to secure very well. You need to tell users who might store sensitive information what services, if any, are appropriate for the storage of sensitive information. This part should include storing of data in different ways (disk, magnetic tape, file servers, etc.). Your policy in this area needs to be coordinated with the policy concerning the rights of system administrators versus users (see section 2.3.6).

2.4 What Happens When the Policy is Violated

It is obvious that when any type of official policy is defined, be it related to computer security or not, it will eventually be broken. The violation may occur due to an individual's negligence, accidental mistake, having not been properly informed of the current policy, or not understanding the current policy. It is equally possible that an individual (or group of individuals) may knowingly perform an act that is in direct violation of the defined policy.

When a policy violation has been detected, the immediate course of action should be predefined to ensure prompt and proper enforcement. An investigation should be performed to determine how and why the violation occurred. Then the appropriate corrective action should be executed. The type and severity of action taken varies depending on the type of violation that occurred.

2.4.1 Determining the Response to Policy Violations

Violations to policy may be committed by a wide variety of users. Some may be local users and others may be from outside the local environment. Sites may find it helpful to define what it considers "insiders" and "outsiders" based upon administrative, legal or political boundaries. These boundaries imply what type of action must be taken to correct the offending party; from a written reprimand to pressing legal charges. So, not only do you need to define actions based on the type of violation, you also need to have a clearly defined series of actions based on the kind of user violating your computer security policy. This all seems rather complicated, but should be addressed long before it becomes necessary as the result of a violation.

One point to remember about your policy is that proper education is your best defense. For the outsiders who are using your computer legally, it is your responsibility to verify that these individuals are aware of the policies that you have set forth.

Having this proof may assist you in the future if legal action becomes necessary.

As for users who are using your computer illegally, the problem is basically the same. What type of user violated the policy and how and why did they do it? Depending on the results of your investigation, you may just prefer to "plug" the hole in your computer security and chalk it up to experience. Or if a significant amount of loss was incurred, you may wish to take more drastic action.

2.4.2 What to do When Local Users Violate the Policy of a Remote Site

In the event that a local user violates the security policy of a remote site, the local site should have a clearly defined set of administrative actions to take concerning that local user. The site should also be prepared to protect itself against possible actions by the remote site. These situations involve legal issues which should be addressed when forming the security policy.

2.4.3 Defining Contacts and Responsibilities to Outside Organizations

The local security policy should include procedures for interaction with outside organizations. These include law enforcement agencies, other sites, external response team organizations (e.g., the CERT, CIAC) and various press agencies.

The procedure should state who is authorized to make such contact and how it should be handled. Some questions to be answered include:

- Who may talk to the press?

- When do you contact law enforcement and investigative agencies?

- If a connection is made from a remote site, is the system manager authorized to contact that site?

- Can data be released? What kind?

Detailed contact information should be readily available along with clearly defined procedures to follow.

2.4.4 What are the Responsibilities to our Neighbors and Other Internet Sites?

The Security Policy Working Group within the IETF is working on a document entitled, "Policy Guidelines for the Secure Operation of the Internet" [23]. It addresses the issue that the Internet is a cooperative venture and that sites are expected to provide mutual security assistance. This should be addressed when developing a site's policy. The major issue to be determined is how much information should be released. This will vary from site to site according to the type of site (e.g., military, education, commercial) as well as the type of security violation that occurred.

2.4.5 Issues for Incident Handling Procedures

Along with statements of policy, the document being prepared should include procedures for incident handling. This is covered in detail in the next chapter. There should be procedures available that cover all facets of policy violation.

2.5 Locking In or Out

Whenever a site suffers an incident which may compromise computer security, the strategies for reacting may be influenced by two opposing pressures.

If management fears that the site is sufficiently vulnerable, it may choose a "Protect and Proceed" strategy. This approach will have as its primary goal the protection and preservation of the site facilities and to provide for normalcy for its users as quickly as possible. Attempts will be made to actively interfere with the intruder's processes, prevent further access and begin immediate damage assessment and recovery. This process may involve shutting down the facilities, closing off access to the network, or other drastic measures. The drawback is that unless the intruder is identified directly, they may come back into the site via a different path, or may attack another site.

The alternate approach, "Pursue and Prosecute," adopts the opposite philosophy and goals. The primary goal is to allow intruders to continue their activities at the site until the site can identify the responsible persons. This approach is endorsed by law enforcement agencies and prosecutors. The drawback is that the agencies cannot exempt a site from possible user lawsuits if damage is done to their systems and data.

Prosecution is not the only outcome possible if the intruder is identified. If the culprit is an employee or a student, the organization may choose to take disciplinary actions. The computer security policy needs to spell out the choices and how they will be selected if an intruder is caught. Careful consideration must be made by site management regarding their approach to this issue before the problem occurs. The strategy adopted might depend upon each circumstance. Or there may be a global policy which mandates one approach in all circumstances. The pros and cons must be examined thoroughly and the users of the facilities must be made aware of the policy so that they understand their vulnerabilities no matter which approach is taken.

The following are checklists to help a site determine which strategy to adopt: "Protect and Proceed" or "Pursue and Prosecute."

Protect and Proceed

1. If assets are not well protected.

2. If continued penetration could result in great financial risk.

3. If the possibility or willingness to prosecute is not present.

4. If user base is unknown.

5. If users are unsophisticated and their work is vulnerable.

6. If the site is vulnerable to lawsuits from users, e.g., if their resources are undermined.

Pursue and Prosecute

1. If assets and systems are well protected.

2. If good backups are available.

3. If the risk to the assets is outweighed by the disruption caused by the present and possibly future penetrations.

4. If this is a concentrated attack occurring with great frequency and intensity.

5. If the site has a natural attraction to intruders, and consequently regularly attracts intruders.

6. If the site is willing to incur the financial (or other) risk to assets by allowing the penetrator continue.

7. If intruder access can be controlled.

8. If the monitoring tools are sufficiently well-developed to make the pursuit worthwhile.

9. If the support staff is sufficiently clever and knowledgable about the operating system, related utilities, and systems to make the pursuit worthwhile.

10. If there is willingness on the part of management to prosecute.

11. If the system adminitrators know in general what kind of evidence would lead to prosecution.

12. If there is established contact with knowledgeable law enforcement.

13. If there is a site representative versed in the relevant legal issues.

14. If the site is prepared for possible legal action from its own users if their data or systems become compromised during the pursuit.

2.6 Interpreting the Policy

It is important to define who will interpret the policy. This could be an individual or a committee. No matter how well written, the policy will require interpretation from time to time and this body would serve to review, interpret, and revise the policy as needed.

2.7 Publicizing the Policy

Once the site security policy has been written and established, a vigorous process should be engaged to ensure that the policy statement is widely and thoroughly disseminated and discussed. A mailing of the policy should not be considered sufficient. A period for comments should be allowed before the policy becomes effective to ensure that all affected users have a chance to state their reactions and discuss any unforeseen ramifications. Ideally, the policy should strike a balance between protection and productivity. Meetings should be held to elicit these comments, and also to ensure that the policy is correctly understood. (Policy promulgators are not necessarily noted for their skill with the language.) These meetings should involve higher management as well as line employees.

Security is a collective effort.

In addition to the initial efforts to publicize the policy, it is essential for the site to maintain a continual awareness of its computer security policy. Current users may need periodic reminders. New users should have the policy included as part of their site introduction packet. As a condition for using the site facilities, it may be advisable to have them sign a statement that they have read and understood the policy. Should any of these users require legal action for serious policy violations, this signed statement might prove to be a valuable aid.

3. Establishing Procedures to Prevent Security Problems

The security policy defines what needs to be protected. This section discusses security procedures which specify what steps will be used to carry out the security policy.

3.1 Security Policy Defines What Needs to be Protected

The security policy defines the WHAT's: what needs to be protected, what is most important, what the priorities are, and what the general approach to dealing with security problems should be.

The security policy by itself doesn't say HOW things are protected.

That is the role of security procedures, which this section discusses. The security policy should be a high level document, giving general strategy. The security procedures need to set out, in detail, the precise steps your site will take to protect itself. The security policy should include a general risk assessment of the types of threats a site is mostly likely to face and the consequences of those threats (see section 2.2). Part of doing a risk assessment will include creating a general list of assets that should be protected (section 2.2.2). This information is critical in devising cost-effective procedures.

It is often tempting to start creating security procedures by deciding on different mechanisms first: "our site should have logging on all hosts, call-back modems, and smart cards for all users." This approach could lead to some areas that have too much protection for the risk they face, and other areas that aren't protected enough. Starting with the security policy and the risks it outlines should ensure that the procedures provide the right level of protect for all assets.

3.2 Identifying Possible Problems

To determine risk vulnerabilities must be identified. Part of the purpose of the policy is to aid in shoring up the vulnerabilities and thus to decrease the risk in as many areas as possible. Several of the more popular problem areas are presented in sections below. This list is by no means complete. In addition, each site is likely to have a few unique vulnerabilities.

3.2.1 Access Points

Access points are typically used for entry by unauthorized users. Having many access points increases the risk of access to an organization's computer and network facilities.

Network links to networks outside the organization allow access into the organization for all others connected to that external network. A network link typically provides access to a large number of network services, and each service has a potential to be compromised.

Dialup lines, depending on their configuration, may provide access merely to a login port of a single system. If connected to a terminal server, the dialup line may give access to the entire network.

Terminal servers themselves can be a source of problem. Many terminal servers do not require any kind of authentication. Intruders often use terminal servers to disguise their actions, dialing in on a local phone and then using the terminal server to go out to the local network. Some terminal servers are configured so that intruders can TELNET [19] in from outside the network, and then TELNET back out again, again serving to make it difficult to trace them.

3.2.2 Misconfigured Systems

Misconfigured systems form a large percentage of security holes. Today's operating systems and their associated software have become so complex that understanding how the system works has become a full-time job. Often, systems managers will be non-specialists chosen from the current organization's staff. Vendors are also partly responsible for misconfigured systems. To make the system installation process easier, vendors occasionally choose initial configurations that are not secure in all environments.

3.2.3 Software Bugs

Software will never be bug free. Publicly known security bugs are common methods of unauthorized entry. Part of the solution to this problem is to be aware of the security problems and to update the software when problems are detected. When bugs are found, they should be reported to the vendor so that a solution to the problem can be implemented and distributed.

3.2.4 "Insider" Threats

An insider to the organization may be a considerable threat to the security of the computer systems. Insiders often have direct access to the computer and network hardware components. The ability to access the components of a system makes most systems easier to compromise. Most desktop workstations can be easily manipulated so that they grant privileged access. Access to a local area network provides the ability to view possibly sensitive data traversing the network.

3.3 Choose Controls to Protect Assets in a Cost-Effective Way

After establishing what is to be protected, and assessing the risks these assets face, it is necessary to decide how to implement the controls which protect these assets. The controls and protection mechanisms should be selected in a way so as to adequately counter the threats found during risk assessment, and to implement those controls in a cost effective manner. It makes little sense to spend an exorbitant sum of money and overly constrict the user base if the risk of exposure is very small.

3.3.1 Choose the Right Set of Controls

The controls that are selected represent the physical embodiment of your security policy. They are the first and primary line of defense in the protection of your assets. It is therefore most important to ensure that the controls that you select are the right set of controls. If the major threat to your system is outside penetrators, it probably doesn't make much sense to use biometric devices to authenticate your regular system users. On the other hand, if the major threat is unauthorized use of computing resources by regular system users, you'll probably want to establish very rigorous automated accounting procedures.

3.3.2 Use Common Sense

Common sense is the most appropriate tool that can be used to establish your security policy. Elaborate security schemes and mechanisms are impressive, and they do have their place, yet there is little point in investing money and time on an elaborate implementation scheme if the simple controls are forgotten. For example, no matter how elaborate a system you put into place on top of existing security controls, a single user with a poor password can still leave your system open to attack.

3.4 Use Multiple Strategies to Protect Assets

Another method of protecting assets is to use multiple strategies. In this way, if one strategy fails or is circumvented, another strategy comes into play to continue protecting the asset. By using several simpler strategies, a system can often be made more secure than if one very sophisticated method were used in its place. For example, dial-back modems can be used in conjunction with traditional logon mechanisms. Many similar approaches could be devised that provide several levels of protection for assets. However, it's very easy to go overboard with extra mechanisms. One must keep in mind exactly what it is that needs to be protected.

3.5 Physical Security

It is a given in computer security if the system itself is not physically secure, nothing else about the system can be considered secure. With physical access to a machine, an intruder can halt the machine, bring it back up in privileged mode, replace or alter the disk, plant Trojan horse programs (see section 2.13.9.2), or take any number of other undesirable (and hard to prevent) actions. Critical communications links, important servers, and other key machines should be located in physically secure areas. Some security systems (such as Kerberos) require that the machine be physically secure.

If you cannot physically secure machines, care should be taken about trusting those machines. Sites should consider limiting access from non-secure machines to more secure machines. In particular, allowing trusted access (e.g., the BSD Unix remote commands such as rsh) from these kinds of hosts is particularly risky. For machines that seem or are intended to be physically secure, care should be taken about who has access to the machines. Remember that custodial and maintenance staff often have keys to rooms.

3.6 Procedures to Recognize Unauthorized Activity

Several simple procedures can be used to detect most unauthorized uses of a computer system. These procedures use tools provided with the operating system by the vendor, or tools publicly available from other sources.

3.6.1 Monitoring System Use

System monitoring can be done either by a system administrator, or by software written for the purpose. Monitoring a system involves looking at several parts of the system and searching for anything unusual. Some of the easier ways to do this are described in this section.

The most important thing about monitoring system use is that it be done on a regular basis. Picking one day out of the month to monitor the system is pointless, since a security breach can be isolated to a matter of hours. Only by maintaining a constant vigil can you expect to detect security violations in time to react to them.

3.6.2 Tools for Monitoring the System

This section describes tools and methods for monitoring a system against unauthorized access and use.

3.6.2.1 Logging

Most operating systems store numerous bits of information in log files. Examination of these log files on a regular basis is often the first line of defense in detecting unauthorized use of the system.

- Compare lists of currently logged in users and past login histories. Most users typically log in and out at roughly the same time each day. An account logged in outside the "normal" time for the account may be in use by an intruder.

- Many systems maintain accounting records for billing purposes. These records can also be used to determine usage patterns for the system; unusual accounting records may indicate unauthorized use of the system.

- System logging facilities, such as the UNIX "syslog" utility, should be checked for unusual error messages from system software. For example, a large number of failed login attempts in a short period of time may indicate someone trying to guess passwords.

- Operating system commands which list currently executing processes can be used to detect users running programs they are not authorized to use, as well as to detect unauthorized programs which have been started by an intruder.

3.6.2.2 Monitoring Software

Other monitoring tools can easily be constructed using standard operating system software, by using several, often unrelated, programs together. For example, checklists of file ownerships and permission settings can be constructed (for example, with "ls" and "find" on UNIX) and stored off-line. These lists can then be reconstructed periodically and compared against the master checklist (on UNIX, by using the "diff" utility).

Differences may indicate that unauthorized modifications have been made to the system.

Still other tools are available from third-party vendors and public software distribution sites. Section 3.9.9 lists several sources from which you can learn what tools are available and how to get them.

3.6.2.3 Other Tools

Other tools can also be used to monitor systems for security violations, although this is not their primary purpose. For example, network monitors can be used to detect and log connections from unknown sites.

3.6.3 Vary the Monitoring Schedule

The task of system monitoring is not as daunting as it may seem.

System administrators can execute many of the commands used for monitoring periodically throughout the day during idle moments (e.g., while talking on the telephone), rather than spending fixed periods of each day monitoring the system. By executing the commands frequently, you will rapidly become used to seeing "normal" output, and will easily spot things which are out of the ordinary. In addition, by running various monitoring commands at different times throughout the day, you make it hard for an intruder to predict your actions. For example, if an intruder knows that each day at 5:00 p.m. the system is checked to see that everyone has logged off, he will simply wait until after the check has completed before logging in. But the intruder cannot guess when a system administrator might type a command to display all logged-in users, and thus he runs a much greater risk of detection.

Despite the advantages that regular system monitoring provides, some intruders will be aware of the standard logging mechanisms in use on systems they are attacking. They will actively pursue and attempt to disable monitoring mechanisms. Regular monitoring therefore is useful in detecting intruders, but does not provide any guarantee that your system is secure, nor should monitoring be considered an infallible method of detecting unauthorized use.

3.7 Define Actions to Take When Unauthorized Activity is Suspected

Sections 2.4 and 2.5 discussed the course of action a site should take when it suspects its systems are being abused. The computer security policy should state the general approach towards dealing with these problems.

The procedures for dealing with these types of problems should be written down. Who has authority to decide what actions will be taken? Should law enforcement be involved? Should your organization cooperate with other sites in trying to track down an intruder? Answers to all the questions in section 2.4 should be part of the incident handling procedures.

Whether you decide to lock out or pursue intruders, you should have tools and procedures ready to apply. It is best to work up these tools and procedures before you need them. Don't wait until an intruder is on your system to figure out how to track the intruder's actions; you will be busy enough if an intruder strikes.

3.8 Communicating Security Policy

Security policies, in order to be effective, must be communicated to both the users of the system and the system maintainers. This section describes what these people should be told, and how to tell them.

3.8.1 Educating the Users

Users should be made aware of how the computer systems are expected to be used, and how to protect themselves from unauthorized users.

3.8.1.1 Proper Account/Workstation Use

All users should be informed about what is considered the "proper" use of their account or workstation ("proper" use is discussed in section 2.3.2). This can most easily be done at the time a user receives their account, by giving them a policy statement. Proper use policies typically dictate things such as whether or not the account or workstation may be used for personal activities (such as checkbook balancing or letter writing), whether profit-making activities are allowed, whether game playing is permitted, and so on. These policy statements may also be used to summarize how the computer facility is licensed and what software licenses are held by the institution; for example, many universities have educational licenses which explicitly prohibit commercial uses of the system. A more complete list of items to consider when writing a policy statement is given in section 2.3.

3.8.1.2 Account/Workstation Management Procedures

Each user should be told how to properly manage their account and workstation. This includes explaining how to protect files stored on the system, how to log out or lock the terminal or workstation, and so on. Much of this information is typically covered in the "beginning user" documentation provided by the operating system vendor, although many sites elect to supplement this material with local information.

If your site offers dial-up modem access to the computer systems, special care must be taken to inform users of the security problems inherent in providing this access. Issues such as making sure to log out before hanging up the modem should be covered when the user is initially given dial-up access.

Likewise, access to the systems via local and wide-area networks presents its own set of security problems which users should be made aware of. Files which grant "trusted host" or "trusted user" status to remote systems and users should be carefully explained.

3.8.1.3 Determining Account Misuse

Users should be told how to detect unauthorized access to their account. If the system prints the last login time when a user logs in, he or she should be told to check that time and note whether or not it agrees with the last time he or she actually logged in.

Command interpreters on some systems (e.g., the UNIX C shell) maintain histories of the last several commands executed. Users should check these histories to be sure someone has not executed other commands with their account.

3.8.1.4 Problem Reporting Procedures

A procedure should be developed to enable users to report suspected misuse of their accounts or other misuse they may have noticed. This can be done either by providing the name and telephone number of a system administrator who manages security of the computer system, or by creating an electronic mail address (e.g., "security") to which users can address their problems.

3.8.2 Educating the Host Administrators

In many organizations, computer systems are administered by a wide variety of people. These administrators must know how to protect their own systems from attack and unauthorized use, as well as how to communicate successful penetration of their systems to other administrators as a warning.

3.8.2.1 Account Management Procedures

Care must be taken when installing accounts on the system in order to make them secure. When installing a system from distribution media, the password file should be examined for "standard" accounts provided by the vendor. Many vendors provide accounts for use by system services or field service personnel. These accounts typically have either no password or one which is common knowledge. These accounts should be given new passwords if they are needed, or disabled or deleted from the system if they are not.

Accounts without passwords are generally very dangerous since they allow anyone to access the system. Even accounts which do not execute a command interpreter (e.g., accounts which exist only to see who is logged in to the system) can be compromised if set up incorrectly. A related concept, that of "anonymous" file transfer (FTP) [20], allows users from all over the network to access your system to retrieve files from (usually) a protected disk area. You should carefully weigh the benefits that an account without a password provides against the security risks of providing such access to your system. If the operating system provides a "shadow" password facility which stores passwords in a separate file accessible only to privileged users, this facility should be used. System V UNIX, SunOS 4.0 and above, and versions of Berkeley UNIX after 4.3BSD Tahoe, as well as others, provide this feature. It protects passwords by hiding their encrypted values from unprivileged users. This prevents an attacker from copying your password file to his or her machine and then attempting to break the passwords at his or her leisure.

Keep track of who has access to privileged user accounts (e.g., "root" on UNIX or "MAINT" on VMS). Whenever a privileged user leaves the organization or no longer has need of the privileged account, the passwords on all privileged accounts should be changed.

3.8.2.2 Configuration Management Procedures

When installing a system from the distribution media or when installing third-party software, it is important to check the installation carefully. Many installation procedures assume a "trusted" site, and hence will install files with world write permission enabled, or otherwise compromise the security of files.

Network services should also be examined carefully when first installed. Many vendors provide default network permission files which imply that all outside hosts are to be "trusted," which is rarely the case when connected to wide-area networks such as the Internet.

Many intruders collect information on the vulnerabilities of particular system versions. The older a system, the more likely it is that there are security problems in that version which have since been fixed by the vendor in a later release.

For this reason, it is important to weigh the risks of not upgrading to a new operating system release (thus leaving security holes unplugged) against the cost of upgrading to the new software (possibly breaking third-party software, etc.).

Bug fixes from the vendor should be weighed in a similar fashion, with the added note that "security" fixes from a vendor usually address fairly serious security problems.

Other bug fixes, received via network mailing lists and the like, should usually be installed, but not without careful examination. Never install a bug fix unless you're sure you know what the consequences of the fix are—there's always the possibility that an intruder has suggested a "fix" which actually gives him or her access to your system.

3.8.2.3 Recovery Procedures—Backups

It is impossible to overemphasize the need for a good backup strategy. File system backups not only protect you in the event of hardware failure or accidental deletions, but they also protect you against unauthorized changes made by an intruder. Without a copy of your data the way it's "supposed" to be, it can be difficult to undo something an attacker has done.

Backups, especially if run daily, can also be useful in providing a history of an intruder's activities. Looking through old backups can establish when your system was first penetrated. Intruders may leave files around which, although deleted later, are captured on the backup tapes. Backups can also be used to document an intruder's activities to law enforcement agencies if necessary.

A good backup strategy will dump the entire system to tape at least once a month. Partial (or incremental") dumps should be done at least twice a week, and ideally they should be done daily. Commands specifically designed for performing file system backups (e.g., UNIX "dump" or VMS "BACKUP") should be used in preference to other file copying commands, since these tools are designed with the express intent of restoring a system to a known state.

3.8.2.4 Problem Reporting Procedures

As with users, system administrators should have a defined procedure for reporting security problems. In large installations, this is often done by creating an electronic mail alias which contains the names of all system administrators in the organization. Other methods include setting up some sort of response team similar to the CERT, or establishing a "hotline" serviced by an existing support group.

3.9 Resources to Prevent Security Breaches

This section discusses software, hardware, and procedural resources that can be used to support your site security policy.

3.9.1 Network Connections and Firewalls

A "firewall" is put in place in a building to provide a point of resistance to the entry of flames into another area. Similarly, a secretary's desk and reception area provides a point of controlling access to other office spaces. This same technique can be applied to a computer site, particularly as it pertains to network connections.

Some sites will be connected only to other sites within the same organization and will not have the ability to connect to other networks. Sites such as these are less susceptible to threats from outside their own organization, although intrusions may still occur via paths such as dial-up modems. On the other hand, many other organizations will be connected to other sites via much larger networks, such as the Internet. These sites are susceptible to the entire range of threats associated with a networked environment.

The risks of connecting to outside networks must be weighed against the benefits. It may be desirable to limit connection to outside networks to those hosts which do not store sensitive material, keeping "vital" machines (such as those which maintain company payroll or inventory systems) isolated. If there is a need to participate in a Wide Area Network (WAN), consider restricting all access to your local network through a single system. That is, all access to or from your own local network must be made through a single host computer that acts as a firewall between you and the outside world. This firewall system should be rigorously controlled and password protected, and external users accessing it should also be constrained by restricting the functionality available to remote users. By using this approach, your site could relax some of the internal security controls on your local net, but still be afforded the protection of a rigorously controlled host front end.

Note that even with a firewall system, compromise of the firewall could result in compromise of the network behind the firewall. Work has been done in some areas to construct a firewall which even when compromised, still protects the local network [6, CHESWICK].

3.9.2 Confidentiality

Confidentiality, the act of keeping things hidden or secret, is one of the primary goals of computer security practitioners. Several mechanisms are provided by most modern operating systems to enable users to control the dissemination of information.

Depending upon where you work, you may have a site where everything is protected, or a site where all information is usually regarded as public, or something in-between. Most sites lean toward the in-between, at least until some penetration has occurred.

Generally, there are three instances in which information is vulnerable to disclosure: when the information is stored on a computer system, when the information is in transit to another system (on the network), and when the information is stored on backup tapes.

The first of these cases is controlled by file permissions, access control lists, and other similar mechanisms. The last can be controlled by restricting access to the backup tapes (by locking them in a safe, for example). All three cases can be helped by using encryption mechanisms.

3.9.2.1 Encryption (Hardware and Software)

Encryption is the process of taking information that exists in some readable form and converting it into a non-readable form. There are several types of commercially available encryption packages in both hardware and software forms. Hardware encryption engines have the advantage that they are much faster than the software equivalent, yet because they are faster, they are of greater potential benefit to an attacker who wants to execute a brute-force attack on your encrypted information. The advantage of using encryption is that, even if other access control mechanisms (passwords, file permissions, etc.) are compromised by an intruder, the data is still unusable. Naturally, encryption keys and the like should be protected at least as well as account passwords.

Information in transit (over a network) may be vulnerable to interception as well. Several solutions to this exist, ranging from simply encrypting files before transferring them (end-to-end encryption) to special network hardware which encrypts everything it sends without user intervention (secure links). The Internet as a whole does not use secure links, thus end- to-end encryption must be used if encryption is desired across the Internet.

3.9.2.1.1 Data Encryption Standard (DES)

DES is perhaps the most widely used data encryption mechanism today. Many hardware and software implementations exist, and some commercial computers are provided with a software version. DES transforms plain text information into encrypted data (or ciphertext) by means of a special algorithm and "seed" value called a key. So long as the key is retained (or remembered) by the original user, the ciphertext can be restored to the original plain text.

One of the pitfalls of all encryption systems is the need to remember the key under which a thing was encrypted (this is not unlike the password problem discussed elsewhere in this document). If the key is written down, it becomes less secure. If forgotten, there is little (if any) hope of recovering the original data.

Most UNIX systems provide a DES command that enables a user to encrypt data using the DES algorithm.

3.9.2.1.2 Crypt

Similar to the DES command, the UNIX "crypt" command allows a user to encrypt data. Unfortunately, the algorithm used by "crypt" is very insecure (based on the World War II "Enigma" device), and files encrypted with this command can be decrypted easily in a matter of a few hours. Generally, use of the "crypt" command should be avoided for any but the most trivial encryption tasks.

3.9.2.2 Privacy Enhanced Mail

Electronic mail normally transits the network in the clear (i.e., anyone can read it). This is obviously not the optimal solution. Privacy enhanced mail provides a means to automatically encrypt electronic mail messages so that a person eavesdropping at a mail distribution node is not (easily) capable of reading them. Several privacy enhanced mail packages are currently being developed and deployed on the Internet.

The Internet Activities Board Privacy Task Force has defined a draft standard, elective protocol for use in implementing privacy enhanced mail. This protocol is defined in RFCs 1113, 1114, and 1115 [7,8,9]. Please refer to the current edition of the "IAB Official Protocol Standards" (currently, RFC 1200 [21]) for the standardization state and status of these protocols.

3.9.3 Origin Authentication

We mostly take it on faith that the header of an electronic mail message truly indicates the originator of a message. However, it is easy to "spoof," or forge the source of a mail message. Origin authentication provides a means to be certain of the originator of a message or other object in the same way that a Notary Public assures a signature on a legal document. This is done by means of a "Public Key" cryptosystem.

A public key cryptosystem differs from a private key cryptosystem in several ways. First, a public key system uses two keys, a Public Key that anyone can use (hence the name) and a Private Key that only the originator of a message uses. The originator uses the private key to encrypt the message (as in DES). The receiver, who has obtained the public key for the originator, may then decrypt the message.

In this scheme, the public key is used to authenticate the originator's use of his or her private key, and hence the identity of the originator is more rigorously proven. The most widely known implementation of a public key cryptosystem is the RSA system [26]. The Internet standard for privacy enhanced mail makes use of the RSA system.

3.9.4 Information Integrity

Information integrity refers to the state of information such that it is complete, correct, and unchanged from the last time in which it was verified to be in an "integral" state. The value of information integrity to a site will vary. For example, it is more important for military and government installations to prevent the "disclosure" of classified information, whether it is right or wrong. A bank, on the other hand, is far more concerned with whether the account information maintained for its customers is complete and accurate.

Numerous computer system mechanisms, as well as procedural controls, have an influence on the integrity of system information. Traditional access control mechanisms maintain controls over who can access system information. These mechanisms alone are not sufficient in some cases to provide the degree of integrity required. Some other mechanisms are briefly discussed below.

It should be noted that there are other aspects to maintaining system integrity besides these mechanisms, such as two-person controls, and integrity validation procedures. These are beyond the scope of this document.

3.9.4.1 Checksums

Easily the simplest mechanism, a simple checksum routine can compute a value for a system file and compare it with the last known value. If the two are equal, the file is probably unchanged. If not, the file has been changed by some unknown means.

Though it is the easiest to implement, the checksum scheme suffers from a serious failing in that it is not very sophisticated and a determined attacker could easily add enough characters to the file to eventually obtain the correct value.

A specific type of checksum, called a CRC checksum, is considerably more robust than a simple checksum. It is only slightly more difficult to implement and provides a better degree of catching errors. It too, however, suffers from the possibility of compromise by an attacker.

Checksums may be used to detect the altering of information.

However, they do not actively guard against changes being made.

For this, other mechanisms such as access controls and encryption should be used.

3.9.4.2 Cryptographic Checksums

Cryptographic checksums (also called cryptosealing) involve breaking a file up into smaller chunks, calculating a (CRC) checksum for each chunk, and adding the CRCs together. Depending upon the exact algorithm used, this can result in a nearly unbreakable method of determining whether a file has been changed. This mechanism suffers from the fact that it is sometimes computationally intensive and may be prohibitive except in cases where the utmost integrity protection is desired.

Another related mechanism, called a one-way hash function (or a Manipulation Detection Code (MDC)) can also be used to uniquely identify a file. The idea behind these functions is that no two inputs can produce the same output, thus a modified file will not have the same hash value. One-way hash functions can be implemented efficiently on a wide variety of systems, making unbreakable integrity checks possible. (Snefru, a one-way hash function available via USENET as well as the Internet is just one example of an efficient one-way hash function.) [10]

3.9.5 Limiting Network Access

The dominant network protocols in use on the Internet, IP (RFC 791) [11], TCP (RFC 793) [12], and UDP (RFC 768) [13], carry certain control information which can be used to restrict access to certain hosts or networks within an organization. The IP packet header contains the network addresses of both the sender and recipient of the packet. Further, the TCP and UDP protocols provide the notion of a "port," which identifies the endpoint (usually a network server) of a communications path. In some instances, it may be desirable to deny access to a specific TCP or UDP port, or even to certain hosts and networks altogether.

3.9.5.1 Gateway Routing Tables

One of the simplest approaches to preventing unwanted network connections is to simply remove certain networks from a gateway's routing tables. This makes it "impossible" for a host to send packets to these networks. (Most protocols require bidirectional packet flow even for unidirectional data flow, thus breaking one side of the route is usually sufficient.)

This approach is commonly taken in "firewall" systems by preventing the firewall from advertising local routes to the outside world. The approach is deficient in that it often prevents "too much" (e.g., in order to prevent access to one system on the network, access to all systems on the network is disabled).

3.9.5.2 Router Packet Filtering

Many commercially available gateway systems (more correctly called routers) provide the ability to filter packets based not only on sources or destinations, but also on source-destination combinations. This mechanism can be used to deny access to a specific host, network, or subnet from any other host, network, or subnet.

Gateway systems from some vendors (e.g., cisco Systems) support an even more complex scheme, allowing finer control over source and destination addresses. Via the use of address masks, one can deny access to all but one host on a particular network.

The cisco Systems also allow packet screening based on IP protocol type and TCP or UDP port numbers [14]. This can also be circumvented by "source routing" packets destined for the "secret" network. Source routed packets may be filtered out by gateways, but this may restrict other legitimate activities, such as diagnosing routing problems.

3.9.6 Authentication Systems

Authentication refers to the process of proving a claimed identity to the satisfaction of some permission-granting authority. Authentication systems are hardware, software, or procedural mechanisms that enable a user to obtain access to computing resources. At the simplest level, the system administrator who adds new user accounts to the system is part of the system authentication mechanism. At the other end of the spectrum, fingerprint readers or retinal scanners provide a very high-tech solution to establishing a potential user's identity. Without establishing and proving a user's identity prior to establishing a session, your site's computers are vulnerable to any sort of attack.

Typically, a user authenticates himself or herself to the system by entering a password in response to a prompt.

Challenge/Response mechanisms improve upon passwords by prompting the user for some piece of information shared by both the computer and the user (such as mother's maiden name, etc.).

3.9.6.1 Kerberos

Kerberos, named after the dog who in mythology is said to stand at the gates of Hades, is a collection of software used in a large network to establish a user's claimed identity. Developed at the Massachusetts Institute of Technology (MIT), it uses a combination of encryption and distributed databases so that a user at a campus facility can login and start a session from any computer located on the campus. This has clear advantages in certain environments where there are a large number of potential users who may establish a connection from any one of a large number of workstations. Some vendors are now incorporating Kerberos into their systems. It should be noted that while Kerberos makes several advances in the area of authentication, some security weaknesses in the protocol still remain [15].

3.9.6.2 Smart Cards

Several systems use "smart cards" (a small calculator-like device) to help authenticate users. These systems depend on the user having an object in their possession. One such system involves a new password procedure that require a user to enter a value obtained from a "smart card" when asked for a password by the computer. Typically, the host machine will give the user some piece of information that is entered into the keyboard of the smart card. The smart card will display a response which must then be entered into the computer before the session will be established. Another such system involves a smart card which displays a number which changes over time, but which is synchronized with the authentication software on the computer.

This is a better way of dealing with authentication than with the traditional password approach. On the other hand, some say it's inconvenient to carry the smart card. Start-up costs are likely to be high as well.

3.9.7 Books, Lists, and Informational Sources

There are many good sources for information regarding computer security. The annotated bibliography at the end of this document can provide you with a good start. In addition, information can be obtained from a variety of other sources, some of which are described in this section.

3.9.7.1 Security Mailing Lists

The UNIX Security mailing list exists to notify system administrators of security problems before they become common knowledge, and to provide security enhancement information. It is a restricted-access list, open only to people who can be verified as being principal systems people at a site. Requests to join the list must be sent by either the site contact listed in the Defense Data Network's Network Information Center's (DDN NIC) WHOIS database, or from the "root" account on one of the major site machines. You must include the destination address you want on the list, an indication of whether you want to be on the mail reflector list or receive weekly digests, the electronic mail address and voice telephone number of the site contact if it isn't you, and the name, address, and telephone number of your organization. This information should be sent to SECURITY-REQUEST@CPD.COM. The RISKS digest is a component of the ACM Committee on Computers and Public Policy, moderated by Peter G. Neumann. It is a discussion forum on risks to the public in computers and related systems, and along with discussing computer security and privacy issues, has discussed such subjects as the Stark incident, the shooting down of the Iranian airliner in the Persian Gulf (as it relates to the computerized weapons systems), problems in air and railroad traffic control systems, software engineering, and so on. To join the mailing list, send a message to RISKS-REQUEST@CSL.SRI.COM. This list is also available in the USENET newsgroup "comp.risks."

The VIRUS-L list is a forum for the discussion of computer virus experiences, protection software, and related topics. The list is open to the public, and is implemented as a moderated digest. Most of the information is related to personal computers, although some of it may be applicable to larger systems. To subscribe, send the line:

```
SUB VIRUS-L your full name
```

to the address LISTSERV%LEHIIBM1.BITNET@MITVMA.MIT.EDU. This list is also available via the USENET newsgroup "comp.virus."

The Computer Underground Digest "is an open forum dedicated to sharing information among computerists and to the presentation and debate of diverse views." While not directly a security list, it does contain discussions about privacy and other security related topics. The list can be read on USENET as alt.society.cu-digest, or to join the mailing list, send mail to Gordon Myer (TK0JUT2%NIU.bitnet@mitvma.mit.edu). Submissions may be mailed to: cud@chinacat.unicom.com.

3.9.7.2 Networking Mailing Lists

The TCP-IP mailing list is intended to act as a discussion forum for developers and maintainers of implementations of the TCP/IP protocol suite. It also discusses network-related security problems when they involve programs providing network services, such as "Sendmail." To join the TCP-IP list, send a message to TCP-IP-REQUEST@NISC.SRI.COM. This list is also available in the USENET newsgroup "comp.protocols.tcp-ip." SUN-NETS is a discussion list for items pertaining to networking on Sun systems. Much of the discussion is related to NFS, NIS (formally Yellow Pages), and name servers. To subscribe, send a message to SUN-NETS-REQUEST@UMIACS.UMD.EDU.

The USENET groups misc.security and alt.security also discuss security issues. misc.security is a moderated group and also includes discussions of physical security and locks. alt.security is unmoderated.

3.9.7.3 Response Teams

Several organizations have formed special groups of people to deal with computer security problems. These teams collect information about possible security holes and disseminate it to the proper people, track intruders, and assist in recovery from security violations. The teams typically have both electronic mail distribution lists as well as a special telephone number which can be called for information or to report a problem.

Many of these teams are members of the CERT System, which is coordinated by the National Institute of Standards and Technology (NIST), and exists to facilitate the exchange of information between the various teams.

3.9.7.3.1 DARPA Computer Emergency Response Team

The Computer Emergency Response Team/Coordination Center (CERT/CC) was established in December 1988 by the Defense Advanced Research Projects Agency (DARPA) to address computer security concerns of research users of the Internet. It is operated by the Software Engineering Institute (SEI) at Carnegie-Mellon University (CMU). The CERT can immediately confer with experts to diagnose and solve security problems, and also establish and maintain communications with the affected computer users and government authorities as appropriate.

The CERT/CC serves as a clearing house for the identification and repair of security vulnerabilities, informal assessments of existing systems, improvement of emergency response capability, and both vendor and user security awareness. In addition, the team works with vendors of various systems in order to coordinate the fixes for security problems.

The CERT/CC sends out security advisories to the CERT- ADVISORY mailing list whenever appropriate. They also operate a 24-hour hotline that can be called to report security problems (e.g., someone breaking into your system), as well as to obtain current (and accurate) information about rumored security problems.

To join the CERT-ADVISORY mailing list, send a message to CERT@CERT.SEI.CMU.EDU and ask to be added to the mailing list. The material sent to this list also appears in the USENET newsgroup "comp.security.announce." Past advisories are available for anonymous FTP from the host CERT.SEI.CMU.EDU. The 24-hour hotline number is (412) 268- 7090.

The CERT/CC also maintains a CERT-TOOLS list to encourage the exchange of information on tools and techniques that increase the secure operation of Internet systems. The CERT/CC does not review or endorse the tools described on the list. To subscribe, send a message to CERT-TOOLS- REQUEST@CERT.SEI.CMU.EDU and ask to be added to the mailing list.

The CERT/CC maintains other generally useful security information for anonymous FTP from CERT.SEI.CMU.EDU. Get the README file for a list of what is available.

For more information, contact:

> CERT
> Software Engineering Institute
> Carnegie Mellon University
> Pittsburgh, PA 15213-3890
> (412) 268-7090
> cert@cert.sei.cmu.edu.

3.9.7.3.2 DDN Security Coordination Center

For DDN users, the Security Coordination Center (SCC) serves a function similar to CERT. The SCC is the DDN's clearing-house for host/user security problems and fixes, and works with the DDN Network Security Officer. The SCC also distributes the DDN Security Bulletin, which communicates information on network and host security exposures, fixes, and concerns to security and management personnel at DDN facilities. It is available online, via kermit or anonymous FTP, from the host NIC.DDN.MIL, in SCC:DDN-SECURITY-yy-nn.TXT (where "yy" is the year and "nn" is the bulletin number). The SCC provides immediate assistance with DDN- related host security problems; call (800) 235-3155 (6:00 a.m. to 5:00 p.m. Pacific Time) or send email to SCC@NIC.DDN.MIL. For 24 hour coverage, call the MILNET Trouble Desk (800) 451-7413 or AUTOVON 231-1713.

3.9.7.3.3 NIST Computer Security Resource and Response Center

The National Institute of Standards and Technology (NIST) has responsibility within the U.S. Federal Government for computer science and technology activities. NIST has played a strong role in organizing the CERT System and is now serving as the CERT System Secretariat. NIST also operates a Computer Security Resource and Response Center (CSRC) to provide help and information regarding computer security events and incidents, as well as to raise awareness about computer security vulnerabilities.

The CSRC team operates a 24-hour hotline, at (301) 975-5200.

For individuals with access to the Internet, on-line publications and computer security information can be obtained via anonymous FTP from the host CSRC.NCSL.NIST.GOV (129.6.48.87). NIST also operates a personal computer bulletin board that contains information regarding computer viruses as well as other aspects of computer security. To access this board, set your modem to 300/1200/2400 BPS, 1 stop bit, no parity, and 8-bit characters, and call (301) 948-5717. All users are given full access to the board immediately upon registering.

NIST has produced several special publications related to computer security and computer viruses in particular; some of these publications are downloadable. For further information, contact NIST at the following address:

> Computer Security Resource and Response Center
> A-216 Technology
> Gaithersburg, MD 20899
> Telephone: (301) 975-3359
> Electronic Mail: CSRC@nist.gov

3.9.7.3.4 DOE Computer Incident Advisory Capability (CIAC)

CIAC is the Department of Energy's (DOE's) Computer Incident Advisory Capability. CIAC is a four-person team of computer scientists from Lawrence Livermore National Laboratory (LLNL) charged with the primary responsibility of assisting DOE sites faced with computer security incidents (e.g., intruder attacks, virus infections, worm attacks, etc.). This capability is available to DOE sites on a 24-hour-a-day basis.

CIAC was formed to provide a centralized response capability (including technical assistance), to keep sites informed of current events, to deal proactively with computer security issues, and to maintain liaisons with other response teams and agencies. CIAC's charter is to assist sites (through direct technical assistance, providing information, or referring inquiries to other technical experts), serve as a clearinghouse for information about threats/known incidents/ vulnerabilities, develop guidelines for incident handling, develop software for responding to events/incidents, analyze events and trends, conduct training and awareness activities, and alert and advise sites about vulnerabilities and potential attacks.

CIAC's business hours phone number is (415) 422-8193 or FTS 532-8193. CIAC's e-mail address is CIAC@TIGER.LLNL.GOV. 3.9.7.3.5 NASA Ames Computer Network Security Response Team The Computer Network Security Response Team (CNSRT) is NASA Ames Research Center's local version of the DARPA CERT. Formed in August of 1989, the team has a constituency that is primarily Ames users, but it is also involved in assisting other NASA Centers and federal agencies. CNSRT maintains liaisons with the DOE's CIAC team and the DARPA CERT. It is also a charter member of the CERT System. The team may be reached by 24 hour pager at (415) 694-0571, or by electronic mail to CNSRT@AMES.ARC.NASA.GOV.

3.9.7.4 DDN Management Bulletins

The DDN Management Bulletin is distributed electronically by the DDN NIC under contract to the Defense Communications Agency (DCA). It is a means of communicating official policy, procedures, and other information of concern to management personnel at DDN facilities.

The DDN Security Bulletin is distributed electronically by the DDN SCC, also under contract to DCA, as a means of communicating information on network and host security exposures, fixes, and concerns to security and management personnel at DDN facilities.

Anyone may join the mailing lists for these two bulletins by sending a message to NIC@NIC.DDN.MIL and asking to be placed on the mailing lists. These messages are also posted to the USENET newsgroup "ddn.mgt-bulletin." For additional information, see section 8.7.

3.9.7.5 System Administration List

The SYSADM-LIST is a list pertaining exclusively to UNIX system administration. Mail requests to be added to the list to SYSADM-LIST-REQUEST@SYSADMIN.COM.

3.9.7.6 Vendor Specific System Lists

The SUN-SPOTS and SUN-MANAGERS lists are discussion groups for users and administrators of systems supplied by Sun Microsystems. SUN-SPOTS is a fairly general list, discussing everything from hardware configurations to simple UNIX questions. To subscribe, send a message to SUN-SPOTS- REQUEST@RICE.EDU. This list is also available in the USENET newsgroup "comp.sys.sun." SUN-MANAGERS is a discussion list for Sun system administrators and covers all aspects of Sun system administration. To subscribe, send a message to SUN-MANAGERS-REQUEST@EECS.NWU.EDU.

The APOLLO list discusses the HP/Apollo system and its software. To subscribe, send a message to APOLLO- REQUEST@UMIX.CC.UMICH.EDU. APOLLO-L is a similar list which can be subscribed to by sending SUB APOLLO-L your full name to LISTSERV%UMRVMB.BITNET@VM1.NODAK.EDU. HPMINI-L pertains to the Hewlett-Packard 9000 series and HP/UX operating system. To subscribe, send SUB HPMINI-L your full name to LISTSERV%UAFSYSB.BITNET@VM1.NODAK.EDU. INFO-IBMPC discusses IBM PCs and compatibles, as well as MS- DOS. To subscribe, send a note to INFO-IBMPC-REQUEST@WSMR- SIMTEL20.ARMY.MIL.

There are numerous other mailing lists for nearly every popular computer or workstation in use today. For a complete list, obtain the file "netinfo/interest-groups" via anonymous FTP from the host FTP.NISC.SRI.COM.

3.9.7.7 Professional Societies and Journals

The IEEE Technical Committee on Security & Privacy publishes a quarterly magazine, "CIPHER."

> IEEE Computer Society
> 1730 Massachusetts Ave. N.W.
> Washington, DC 2036-1903

The ACM SigSAC (Special Interest Group on Security, Audit, and Controls) publishes a quarterly magazine, "SIGSAC Review."

> Association for Computing Machinery
> 11 West 42nd St.
> New York, NY 10036

The Information Systems Security Association publishes a quarterly magazine called "ISSA Access."

> Information Systems Security Association
> P.O. Box 9457
> Newport Beach, CA 92658

"Computers and Security" is an "international journal for the professional involved with computer security, audit and control, and data integrity."

> $266/year, 8 issues (1990)
>
> Elsevier Advanced Technology
> Journal Information Center
> 655 Avenue of the Americas
> New York, NY 10010

"The Data Security Letter" is published "to help data security professionals by providing inside information and knowledgable analysis of developments in computer and communications security."

> $690/year, 9 issues (1990)
>
> Data Security Letter
> P.O. Box 1593
> Palo Alto, CA 94302

3.9.8 Problem Reporting Tools

3.9.8.1 Auditing

Auditing is an important tool that can be used to enhance the security of your installation. Not only does it give you a means of identifying who has accessed your system (and may have done something to it) but it also gives you an indication of how your system is being used (or abused) by authorized users and attackers alike. In addition, the audit trail traditionally kept by computer systems can become an invaluable piece of evidence should your system be penetrated.

3.9.8.1.1 Verify Security

An audit trail shows how the system is being used from day to day. Depending upon how your site audit log is configured, your log files should show a range of access attempts that can show what normal system usage should look like. Deviation from that normal usage could be the result of penetration from an outside source using an old or stale user account. Observing a deviation in logins, for example, could be your first indication that something unusual is happening.

3.9.8.1.2 Verify Software Configurations

One of the ruses used by attackers to gain access to a system is by the insertion of a so-called Trojan Horse program. A Trojan Horse program can be a program that does something useful, or merely something interesting. It always does something unexpected, like steal passwords or copy files without your knowledge [25]. Imagine a Trojan login program that prompts for username and password in the usual way, but also writes that information to a special file that the attacker can come back and read at will. Imagine a Trojan Editor program that, despite the file permissions you have given your files, makes copies of everything in your directory space without you knowing about it.

This points out the need for configuration management of the software that runs on a system, not as it is being developed, but as it is in actual operation. Techniques for doing this range from checking each command every time it is executed against some criterion (such as a cryptoseal, described above) or merely checking the date and time stamp of the executable. Another technique might be to check each command in batch mode at midnight.

3.9.8.2 Tools

COPS is a security tool for system administrators that checks for numerous common security problems on UNIX systems [27]. COPS is a collection of shell scripts and C programs that can easily be run on almost any UNIX variant. Among other things, it checks the following items and sends the results to the system administrator:

- Checks "/dev/kmem" and other devices for world read/writability.

- Checks special or important files and directories for "bad" modes (world writable, etc.).

- Checks for easily-guessed passwords.

- Checks for duplicate user ids, invalid fields in the password file, etc.

- Checks for duplicate group ids, invalid fields in the group file, etc.

- Checks all users' home directories and their ".cshrc," ".login," ".profile," and ".rhosts" files for security problems.

- Checks all commands in the "/etc/rc" files and "cron" files for world writability.

- Checks for bad "root" paths, NFS file systems exported to the world, etc.

- Includes an expert system that checks to see if a given user (usually "root") can be compromised, given that certain rules are true.

- Checks for changes in the setuid status of programs on the system.

The COPS package is available from the "comp.sources.unix" archive on "ftp.uu.net," and also from the UNIX-SW repository on the MILNET host "wsmr-simtel20.army.mil."

3.9.9 Communication Among Administrators

3.9.9.1 Secure Operating Systems

The following list of products and vendors is adapted from the National Computer Security Center's (NCSC) Evaluated Products List. They represent those companies who have either received an evaluation from the NCSC or are in the process of a product evaluation. This list is not complete, but it is representative of those operating systems and add on components available in the commercial marketplace.

For a more detailed listing of the current products appearing in the NCSC EPL, contact the NCSC at:

> National Computer Security Center
> 9800 Savage Road
> Fort George G. Meade, MD 20755-6000
> (301) 859-4458

```
Version Evaluation
Evaluated Product Vendor Evaluated Class
------------------------------------------------------------
Secure Communications Honeywell Information 2.1 A1
Processor (SCOMP) Systems, Inc.
Multics Honeywell Information MR11.0 B2
Systems, Inc.
```

```
System V/MLS 1.1.2 on UNIX AT&T 1.1.2 B1
System V 3.1.1 on AT&T 3B2/500and 3B2/600
OS 1100 Unisys Corp. Security B1
Release 1
MPE V/E Hewlett-Packard Computer G.03.04 C2
Systems Division
AOS/VS on MV/ECLIPSE series Data General Corp. 7.60 C2
VM/SP or VM/SP HPO with CMS, IBM Corp. 5 C2
RACF, DIRMAINT, VMTAPE-MS,
ISPF
MVS/XA with RACF IBM Corp. 2.2,2.3 C2
AX/VMS Digital Equipment Corp. 4.3 C2
NOS Control Data Corp. NOS
Security C2
Eval Product
TOP SECRET CGA Software Products 3.0/163 C2
Group, Inc.
Access Control Facility 2 SKK, Inc. 3.1.3 C2
UTX/32S Gould, Inc. Computer 1.0 C2
Systems Division
A Series MCP/AS with Unisys Corp. 3.7 C2
InfoGuard Security
Enhancements
Primos Prime Computer, Inc. 21.0.1DODC2A C2
Resource Access Control IBM Corp. 1.5 C1
Facility (RACF)


Version Candidate
Candidate Product Vendor Evaluated Class
- - - - - - - - - - - - - - - - - - - - - - - - - - - - - - - - - - - - - - - - - - - - - - - - -
Boeing MLS LAN Boeing Aerospace A1 M1
Trusted XENIX Trusted Information
Systems, Inc. B2
VSLAN VERDIX Corp. B2
System V/MLS AT&T B1
VM/SP with RACF IBM Corp. 5/1.8.2 C2
Wang SVS/OS with CAP Wang Laboratories, Inc. 1.0 C2
```

3.9.9.2 Obtaining Fixes for Known Problems

It goes without saying that computer systems have bugs. Even operating systems, upon which we depend for protection of our data, have bugs. And since there are bugs, things can be broken, both maliciously and accidentally. It is important that whenever bugs are discovered, a should fix be identified and implemented as soon as possible. This should minimize any exposure caused by the bug in the first place.

A corollary to the bug problem is: from whom do I obtain the fixes? Most systems have some support from the manufacturer or supplier. Fixes coming from that source tend to be implemented quickly after receipt. Fixes for some problems are often posted on the network and are left to the system administrators to incorporate as they can. The problem is that one wants to have faith that the fix will close the hole and not introduce any others. We will tend to trust that the manufacturer's fixes are better than those that are posted on the net.

3.9.9.3 Sun Customer Warning System

Sun Microsystems has established a Customer Warning System (CWS) for handling security incidents. This is a formal process which includes:

- Having a well advertised point of contact in Sun for reporting security problems.

- Pro-actively alerting customers of worms, viruses, or other security holes that could affect their systems.

- Distributing the patch (or work-around) as quickly as possible.

They have created an electronic mail address, SECURITY- ALERT@SUN.COM, which will enable customers to report security problems. A voice-mail backup is available at (415) 688-9081.

A "Security Contact" can be designated by each customer site; this person will be contacted by Sun in case of any new security problems. For more information, contact your Sun representative.

3.9.9.4 Trusted Archive Servers

Several sites on the Internet maintain large repositories of public-domain and freely distributable software, and make this material available for anonymous FTP. This section describes some of the larger repositories. Note that none of these servers implements secure checksums or anything else guaranteeing the integrity of their data. Thus, the notion of "trust" should be taken as a somewhat limited definition.

3.9.9.4.1 Sun Fixes on UUNET

Sun Microsystems has contracted with UUNET Communications Services, Inc., to make fixes for bugs in Sun software available via anonymous FTP. You can access these fixes by using the "ftp" command to connect to the host FTP.UU.NET. Then change into the directory "sun-dist/security," and obtain a directory listing. The file "README" contains a brief description of what each file in this directory contains, and what is required to install the fix.

3.9.9.4.2 Berkeley Fixes

The University of California at Berkeley also makes fixes available via anonymous FTP; these fixes pertain primarily to the current release of BSD UNIX (currently, release 4.3).

However, even if you are not running their software, these fixes are still important, since many vendors (Sun, DEC, Sequent, etc.) base their software on the Berkeley releases.

The Berkeley fixes are available for anonymous FTP from the host UCBARPA.BERKELEY.EDU in the directory "4.3/ucb-fixes." The file "INDEX" in this directory describes what each file contains. They are also available from UUNET (see section 3.9.9.4.3).

Berkeley also distributes new versions of "sendmail" and "named" from this machine. New versions of these commands are stored in the "4.3" directory, usually in the files "sendmail.tar.Z" and "bind.tar.Z," respectively.

3.9.9.4.3 Simtel-20 and UUNET

The two largest general-purpose software repositories on the Internet are the hosts WSMR-SIMTEL20.ARMY.MIL and FTP.UU.NET.

WSMR-SIMTEL20.ARMY.MIL is a TOPS-20 machine operated by the U.S. Army at White Sands Missile Range (WSMR), New Mexico. The directory "pd2:<unix-c>" contains a large amount of UNIX software, primarily taken from the "comp.sources" newsgroups. The directories "pd1:<msdos>" and "pd2:<msdos2>" contains software for IBM PC systems, and "pd3:<macintosh>" contains software for the Apple Macintosh.

FTP.UU.NET is operated by UUNET Communications Services, Inc. in Falls Church, Virginia. This company sells Internet and USENET access to sites all over the country (and internationally). The software posted to the following USENET source newsgroups is stored here, in directories of the same name:

    comp.sources.games

    comp.sources.misc

    comp.sources.sun

    comp.sources.unix

    comp.sources.x

Numerous other distributions, such as all the freely distributable Berkeley UNIX source code, Internet Request for Comments (RFCs), and so on are also stored on this system.

3.9.9.4.4 Vendors

Many vendors make fixes for bugs in their software available electronically, either via mailing lists or via anonymous FTP. You should contact your vendor to find out if they offer this service, and if so, how to access it. Some vendors that offer these services include Sun Microsystems (see above), Digital Equipment Corporation (DEC), the University of California at Berkeley (see above), and Apple Computer [5, CURRY].

4. Types of Security Procedures

4.1 System Security Audits

Most businesses undergo some sort of annual financial auditing as a regular part of their business life. Security audits are an important part of running any computing environment. Part of the security audit should be a review of any policies that concern system security, as well as the mechanisms that are put in place to enforce them.

4.1.1 Organize Scheduled Drills

Although not something that would be done each day or week, scheduled drills may be conducted to determine if the procedures defined are adequate for the threat to be countered. If your major threat is one of natural disaster, then a drill would be conducted to verify your backup and recovery mechanisms. On the other hand, if your greatest threat is from external intruders attempting to penetrate your system, a drill might be conducted to actually try a penetration to observe the effect of the policies.

Drills are a valuable way to test that your policies and procedures are effective. On the other hand, drills can be time-consuming and disruptive to normal operations. It is important to weigh the benefits of the drills against the possible time loss which may be associated with them.

4.1.2 Test Procedures

If the choice is made not to use scheduled drills to examine your entire security procedure at one time, it is important to test individual procedures frequently. Examine your backup procedure to make sure you can recover data from the tapes. Check log files to be sure that information which is supposed to be logged to them is being logged to them, etc. When a security audit is mandated, great care should be used in devising tests of the security policy. It is important to clearly identify what is being tested, how the test will be conducted, and results expected from the test. This should all be documented and included in or as an adjunct to the security policy document itself.

It is important to test all aspects of the security policy, both procedural and automated, with a particular emphasis on the automated mechanisms used to enforce the policy. Tests should be defined to ensure a comprehensive examination of policy features, that is, if a test is defined to examine the user logon process, it should be explicitly stated that both valid and invalid user names and passwords will be used to demonstrate proper operation of the logon program.

Keep in mind that there is a limit to the reasonableness of tests. The purpose of testing is to ensure confidence that the security policy is being correctly enforced, and not to "prove" the absoluteness of the system or policy. The goal should be to obtain some assurance that the reasonable and credible controls imposed by your security policy are adequate.

4.2 Account Management Procedures

Procedures to manage accounts are important in preventing unauthorized access to your system. It is necessary to decide several things: Who may have an account on the system? How long may someone have an account without renewing his or her request? How do old accounts get removed from the system? The answers to all these questions should be explicitly set out in the policy.

In addition to deciding who may use a system, it may be important to determine what each user may use the system for (is personal use allowed, for example). If you are connected to an outside network, your site or the network management may have rules about what the network may be used for. Therefore, it is important for any security policy to define an adequate account management procedure for both administrators and users. Typically, the system administrator would be responsible for creating and deleting user accounts and generally maintaining overall control of system use. To some degree, account management is also the responsibility of each system user in the sense that the user should observe any system messages and events that may be indicative of a policy violation. For example, a message at logon that indicates the date and time of the last logon should be reported by the user if it indicates an unreasonable time of last logon.

4.3 Password Management Procedures

A policy on password management may be important if your site wishes to enforce secure passwords. These procedures may range from asking or forcing users to change their passwords occasionally to actively attempting to break users' passwords and then informing the user of how easy it was to do. Another part of password management policy covers who may distribute passwords—can users give their passwords to other users?

Section 2.3 discusses some of the policy issues that need to be decided for proper password management. Regardless of the policies, password management procedures need to be carefully setup to avoid disclosing passwords. The choice of initial passwords for accounts is critical. In some cases, users may never login to activate an account; thus, the choice of the initial password should not be easily guessed. Default passwords should never be assigned to accounts: always create new passwords for each user. If there are any printed lists of passwords, these should be kept off-line in secure locations; better yet, don't list passwords.

4.3.1 Password Selection

Perhaps the most vulnerable part of any computer system is the account password. Any computer system, no matter how secure it is from network or dial-up attack, Trojan horse programs, and so on, can be fully exploited by an intruder if he or she can gain access via a poorly chosen password. It is important to define a good set of rules for password selection, and distribute these rules to all users. If possible, the software which sets user passwords should be modified to enforce as many of the rules as possible.

A sample set of guidelines for password selection is shown below:

- DON'T use your login name in any form (as-is, reversed, capitalized, doubled, etc.).

- DON'T use your first, middle, or last name in any form.

- DON'T use your spouse's or child's name.

- DON'T use other information easily obtained about you. This includes license plate numbers, telephone numbers, social security numbers, the make of your automobile, the name of the street you live on, etc.

- DON'T use a password of all digits, or all the same letter.

- DON'T use a word contained in English or foreign language dictionaries, spelling lists, or other lists of words.

- DON'T use a password shorter than six characters.

- DO use a password with mixed-case alphabetics.

- DO use a password with non-alphabetic characters (digits or punctuation).

- DO use a password that is easy to remember, so you don't have to write it down.

- DO use a password that you can type quickly, without having to look at the keyboard.

Methods of selecting a password which adheres to these guidelines include:

- Choose a line or two from a song or poem, and use the first letter of each word.

- Alternate between one consonant and one or two vowels, up to seven or eight characters. This provides nonsense words which are usually pronounceable, and thus easily remembered.

- Choose two short words and concatenate them together with a punctuation character between them.

Users should also be told to change their password periodically, usually every three to six months. This makes sure that an intruder who has guessed a password will eventually lose access, as well as invalidating any list of passwords he/she may have obtained. Many systems enable the system administrator to force users to change their passwords after an expiration period; this software should be enabled if your system supports it [5, CURRY].

Some systems provide software which forces users to change their passwords on a regular basis. Many of these systems also include password generators which provide the user with a set of passwords to choose from. The user is not permitted to make up his or her own password.

There are arguments both for and against systems such as these. On the one hand, by using generated passwords, users are prevented from selecting insecure passwords. On the other hand, unless the generator is good at making up easy to remember passwords, users will begin writing them down in order to remember them.

4.3.2 Procedures for Changing Passwords

How password changes are handled is important to keeping passwords secure. Ideally, users should be able to change their own passwords on-line. (Note that password changing programs are a favorite target of intruders. See section 4.4 on configuration management for further information.)

However, there are exception cases which must be handled carefully. Users may forget passwords and not be able to get onto the system. The standard procedure is to assign the user a new password. Care should be taken to make sure that the real person is requesting the change and gets the new password. One common trick used by intruders is to call or message to a system administrator and request a new password. Some external form of verification should be used before the password is assigned. At some sites, users are required to show up in person with ID.

There may also be times when many passwords need to be changed. If a system is compromised by an intruder, the intruder may be able to steal a password file and take it off the system. Under these circumstances, one course of action is to change all passwords on the system. Your site should have procedures for how this can be done quickly and efficiently. What course you choose may depend on the urgency of the problem. In the case of a known attack with damage, you may choose to forcibly disable all accounts and assign users new passwords before they come back onto the system. In some places, users are sent a message telling them that they should change their passwords, perhaps within a certain time period. If the password isn't changed before the time period expires, the account is locked.

Users should be aware of what the standard procedure is for passwords when a security event has occurred. One well-known spoof reported by the Computer Emergency Response Team (CERT) involved messages sent to users, supposedly from local system administrators, requesting them to immediately change their password to a new value provided in the message [24]. These messages were not from the administrators, but from intruders trying to steal accounts. Users should be warned to immediately report any suspicious requests such as this to site administrators.

4.4 Configuration Management Procedures

Configuration management is generally applied to the software development process. However, it is certainly applicable in a operational sense as well. Consider that the since many of the system level programs are intended to enforce the security policy, it is important that these be "known" as correct. That is, one should not allow system level programs (such as the operating system, etc.) to be changed arbitrarily. At very least, the procedures should state who is authorized to make changes to systems, under what circumstances, and how the changes should be documented.

In some environments, configuration management is also desirable as applied to physical configuration of equipment. Maintaining valid and authorized hardware configuration should be given due consideration in your security policy.

4.4.1 Non-Standard Configurations

Occasionally, it may be beneficial to have a slightly non-standard configuration in order to thwart the "standard" attacks used by some intruders. The non-standard parts of the configuration might include different password encryption algorithms, different configuration file locations, and rewritten or functionally limited system commands.

Non-standard configurations, however, also have their drawbacks. By changing the "standard" system, these modifications make software maintenance more difficult by requiring extra documentation to be written, software modification after operating system upgrades, and, usually, someone with special knowledge of the changes.

Because of the drawbacks of non-standard configurations, they are often only used in environments with a "firewall" machine (see section 3.9.1). The firewall machine is modified in non-standard ways since it is susceptible to attack, while internal systems behind the firewall are left in their standard configurations.

5. Incident Handling

5.1 Overview

This section of the document will supply some guidance to be applied when a computer security event is in progress on a machine, network, site, or multi-site environment. The operative philosophy in the event of a breach of computer security, whether it be an external intruder attack or a disgruntled employee, is to plan for adverse events in advance. There is no substitute for creating contingency plans for the types of events described above.

Traditional computer security, while quite important in the overall site security plan, usually falls heavily on protecting systems from attack, and perhaps monitoring systems to detect attacks. Little attention is usually paid for how to actually handle the attack when it occurs. The result is that when an attack is in progress, many decisions are made in haste and can be damaging to tracking down the source of the incident, collecting evidence to be used in prosecution efforts, preparing for the recovery of the system, and protecting the valuable data contained on the system.

5.1.1 Have a Plan to Follow in Case of an Incident

Part of handling an incident is being prepared to respond before the incident occurs. This includes establishing a suitable level of protections, so that if the incident becomes severe, the damage which can occur is limited. Protection includes preparing incident handling guidelines or a contingency response plan for your organization or site. Having written plans eliminates much of the ambiguity which occurs during an incident, and will lead to a more appropriate and thorough set of responses. Second, part of protection is preparing a method of notification, so you will know who to call and the relevant phone numbers. It is important, for example, to conduct "dry runs," in which your computer security personnel, system administrators, and managers simulate handling an incident.

Learning to respond efficiently to an incident is important for numerous reasons. The most important benefit is directly to human beings—preventing loss of human life. Some computing systems are life critical systems, systems on which human life depends (e.g., by controlling some aspect of life-support in a hospital or assisting air traffic controllers).

An important but often overlooked benefit is an economic one. Having both technical and managerial personnel respond to an incident requires considerable resources, resources which could be utilized more profitably if an incident did not require their services. If these personnel are trained to handle an incident efficiently, less of their time is required to deal with that incident.

A third benefit is protecting classified, sensitive, or proprietary information. One of the major dangers of a computer security incident is that information may be irrecoverable. Efficient incident handling minimizes this danger. When classified information is involved, other government regulations may apply and must be integrated into any plan for incident handling.

A fourth benefit is related to public relations. News about computer security incidents tends to be damaging to an organization's stature among current or potential clients. Efficient incident handling minimizes the potential for negative exposure.

A final benefit of efficient incident handling is related to legal issues. It is possible that in the near future organizations may be sued because one of their nodes was used to launch a network attack. In a similar vein, people who develop patches or workarounds may be sued if the patches or workarounds are ineffective, resulting in damage to systems, or if the patches or workarounds themselves damage systems. Knowing about operating system vulnerabilities and patterns of attacks and then taking appropriate measures is critical to circumventing possible legal problems.

5.1.2 Order of Discussion in this Session Suggests an Order for a Plan

This chapter is arranged such that a list may be generated from the Table of Contents to provide a starting point for creating a policy for handling ongoing incidents. The main points to be included in a policy for handling incidents are:

- Overview (what are the goals and objectives in handling the incident).

- Evaluation (how serious is the incident).

- Notification (who should be notified about the incident).

- Response (what should the response to the incident be).

- Legal/Investigative (what are the legal and prosecutorial implications of the incident).

- Documentation Logs (what records should be kept from before, during, and after the incident).

Each of these points is important in an overall plan for handling incidents. The remainder of this chapter will detail the issues involved in each of these topics, and provide some guidance as to what should be included in a site policy for handling incidents.

5.1.3 Possible Goals and Incentives for Efficient Incident Handling

As in any set of pre-planned procedures, attention must be placed on a set of goals to be obtained in handling an incident. These goals will be placed in order of importance depending on the site, but one such set of goals might be:

- Assure integrity of (life) critical systems.

- Maintain and restore data.

- Maintain and restore service.

- Figure out how it happened.

- Avoid escalation and further incidents.

- Avoid negative publicity.

- Find out who did it.

- Punish the attackers.

It is important to prioritize actions to be taken during an incident well in advance of the time an incident occurs. Sometimes an incident may be so complex that it is impossible to do everything at once to respond to it; priorities are essential. Although priorities will vary from institution-to-institution, the following suggested priorities serve as a starting point for defining an organization's response:

- Priority one—protect human life and people's safety; human life always has precedence over all other considerations.

- Priority two—protect classified and/or sensitive data (as regulated by your site or by government regulations).

- Priority three—protect other data, including proprietary, scientific, managerial and other data, because loss of data is costly in terms of resources.

- Priority four—prevent damage to systems (e.g., loss or alteration of system files, damage to disk drives, etc.); damage to systems can result in costly down time and recovery.

- Priority five—minimize disruption of computing resources; it is better in many cases to shut a system down or disconnect from a network than to risk damage to data or systems.

An important implication for defining priorities is that once human life and national security considerations have been addressed, it is generally more important to save data than system software and hardware. Although it is undesirable to have any damage or loss during an incident, systems can be replaced; the loss or compromise of data (especially classified data), however, is usually not an acceptable outcome under any circumstances. Part of handling an incident is being prepared to respond before the incident occurs. This includes establishing a suitable level of protections so that if the incident becomes severe, the damage which can occur is limited. Protection includes preparing incident handling guidelines or a contingency response plan for your organization or site. Written plans eliminate much of the ambiguity which occurs during an incident, and will lead to a more appropriate and thorough set of responses. Second, part of protection is preparing a method of notification so you will know who to call and how to contact them. For example, every member of the Department of Energy's CIAC Team carries a card with every other team member's work and home phone numbers, as well as pager numbers. Third, your organization or site should establish backup procedures for every machine and system. Having backups eliminates much of the threat of even a severe incident, since backups preclude serious data loss. Fourth, you should set up secure systems. This involves eliminating vulnerabilities, establishing an effective password policy, and other procedures, all of which will be explained later in this document. Finally, conducting training activities is part of protection. It is important, for example, to conduct "dry runs," in which your computer security personnel, system administrators, and managers simulate handling an incident.

5.1.4 Local Policies and Regulations Providing Guidance

Any plan for responding to security incidents should be guided by local policies and regulations. Government and private sites that deal with classified material have specific rules that they must follow.

The policies your site makes about how it responds to incidents (as discussed in sections 2.4 and 2.5) will shape your response. For example, it may make little sense to create mechanisms to monitor and trace intruders if your site does not plan to take action against the intruders if they are caught. Other organizations may have policies that affect your plans. Telephone companies often release information about telephone traces only to law enforcement agencies.

Section 5.5 also notes that if any legal action is planned, there are specific guidelines that must be followed to make sure that any information collected can be used as evidence.

5.2 Evaluation

5.2.1 Is It Real?

This stage involves determining the exact problem. Of course many, if not most, signs often associated with virus infections, system intrusions, etc., are simply anomalies such as hardware failures. To assist in identifying whether there really is an incident, it is usually helpful to obtain and use any detection software which may be available. For example, widely available software packages can greatly assist someone who thinks there may be a virus in a Macintosh computer. Audit information is also extremely useful, especially in determining whether there is a network attack. It is extremely important to obtain a system snapshot as soon as one suspects that something is wrong. Many incidents cause a dynamic chain of events to occur, and an initial system snapshot may do more good in identifying the problem and any source of attack than most other actions which can be taken at this stage. Finally, it is important to start a log book.

Recording system events, telephone conversations, time stamps, etc., can lead to a more rapid and systematic identification of the problem, and is the basis for subsequent stages of incident handling. There are certain indications or "symptoms" of an incident which deserve special attention:

- System crashes.

- New user accounts (e.g., the account RUMPLESTILTSKIN has unexplainedly been created), or high activity on an account that has had virtually no activity for months.

- New files (usually with novel or strange file names, such as data.xx or k).

- Accounting discrepancies (e.g., in a UNIX system you might notice that the accounting file called /usr/admin/lastlog has shrunk, something that should make you very suspicious that there may be an intruder).

- Changes in file lengths or dates (e.g., a user should be suspicious if he/she observes that the .EXE files in an MS DOS computer have unexplainedly grown by over 1800 bytes).

- Attempts to write to system (e.g., a system manager notices that a privileged user in a VMS system is attempting to alter RIGHTSLIST.DAT).

- Data modification or deletion (e.g., files start to disappear).

■ Denial of service (e.g., a system manager and all other users become locked out of a UNIX system, which has been changed to single user mode).

■ Unexplained, poor system performance (e.g., system response time becomes unusually slow).

■ Anomalies (e.g., "GOTCHA" is displayed on a display terminal or there are frequent unexplained "beeps").

■ Suspicious probes (e.g., there are numerous unsuccessful login attempts from another node).

■ Suspicious browsing (e.g., someone becomes a root user on a UNIX system and accesses file after file in one user's account, then another's).

None of these indications is absolute "proof" that an incident is occurring, nor are all of these indications normally observed when an incident occurs. If you observe any of these indications, however, it is important to suspect that an incident might be occurring, and act accordingly. There is no formula for determining with 100 percent accuracy that an incident is occurring (possible exception: when a virus detection package indicates that your machine has the nVIR virus and you confirm this by examining contents of the nVIR resource in your Macintosh computer, you can be very certain that your machine is infected).

It is best at this point to collaborate with other technical and computer security personnel to make a decision as a group about whether an incident is occurring.

5.2.2 Scope

Along with the identification of the incident is the evaluation of the scope and impact of the problem. It is important to correctly identify the boundaries of the incident in order to effectively deal with it. In addition, the impact of an incident will determine its priority in allocating resources to deal with the event. Without an indication of the scope and impact of the event, it is difficult to determine a correct response.

In order to identify the scope and impact, a set of criteria should be defined which is appropriate to the site and to the type of connections available. Some of the issues are:

■ Is this a multi-site incident?

■ Are many computers at your site effected by this incident?

■ Is sensitive information involved?

■ What is the entry point of the incident (network, phone line, local terminal, etc.)?

■ Is the press involved?

■ What is the potential damage of the incident?

- What is the estimated time to close out the incident?

- What resources could be required to handle the incident?

5.3 Possible Types of Notification

When you have confirmed that an incident is occurring, the appropriate personnel must be notified. Who and how this notification is achieved is very important in keeping the event under control both from a technical and emotional standpoint.

5.3.1 Explicit

First of all, any notification to either local or off-site personnel must be explicit. This requires that any statement (be it an electronic mail message, phone call, or fax) provides information about the incident that is clear, concise, and fully qualified. When you are notifying others that will help you to handle an event, a "smoke screen" will only divide the effort and create confusion. If a division of labor is suggested, it is helpful to provide information to each section about what is being accomplished in other efforts. This will not only reduce duplication of effort, but allow people working on parts of the problem to know where to obtain other information that would help them resolve a part of the incident.

5.3.2 Factual

Another important consideration when communicating about the incident is to be factual. Attempting to hide aspects of the incident by providing false or incomplete information may not only prevent a successful resolution to the incident, but may even worsen the situation. This is especially true when the press is involved. When an incident severe enough to gain press attention is ongoing, it is likely that any false information you provide will not be substantiated by other sources. This will reflect badly on the site and may create enough ill-will between the site and the press to damage the site's public relations.

5.3.3 Choice of Language

The choice of language used when notifying people about the incident can have a profound effect on the way that information is received. When you use emotional or inflammatory terms, you raise the expectations of damage and negative outcomes of the incident. It is important to remain calm both in written and spoken notifications.

Another issue associated with the choice of language is the notification to non-technical or off-site personnel. It is important to accurately describe the incident without undue alarm or confusing messages. While it is more difficult to describe the incident to a non-technical audience, it is often more important.

A non-technical description may be required for upper-level management, the press, or law enforcement liaisons. The importance of these notifications cannot be underestimated and may make the difference between handling the incident properly and escalating to some higher level of damage.

5.3.4 Notification of Individuals

- Point of Contact (POC) people (Technical, Administrative, Response Teams, Investigative, Legal, Vendors, Service providers), and which POCs are visible to whom.

- Wider community (users).

- Other sites that might be affected.

Finally, there is the question of who should be notified during and after the incident. There are several classes of individuals that need to be considered for notification. These are the technical personnel, administration, appropriate response teams (such as CERT or CIAC), law enforcement, vendors, and other service providers. These issues are important for the central point of contact, since that is the person responsible for the actual notification of others (see section 5.3.6 for further information). A list of people in each of these categories is an important time saver for the POC during an incident. It is much more difficult to find an appropriate person during an incident when many urgent events are ongoing.

In addition to the people responsible for handling part of the incident, there may be other sites affected by the incident (or perhaps simply at risk from the incident). A wider community of users may also benefit from knowledge of the incident. Often, a report of the incident once it is closed out is appropriate for publication to the wider user community.

5.3.5 Public Relations—Press Releases

One of the most important issues to consider is when, who, and how much to release to the general public through the press. There are many issues to consider when deciding this particular issue.

First and foremost, if a public relations office exists for the site, it is important to use this office as liaison to the press.

The public relations office is trained in the type and wording of information released, and will help to assure that the image of the site is protected during and after the incident (if possible).

A public relations office has the advantage that you can communicate candidly with them, and provide a buffer between the constant press attention and the need of the POC to maintain control over the incident.

If a public relations office is not available, the information released to the press must be carefully considered. If the information is sensitive, it may be advantageous to provide only minimal or overview information to the press. It is quite possible that any information provided to the press will be quickly reviewed by the perpetrator of the incident. As a contrast to this consideration, it was discussed above that misleading the press can often backfire and cause more damage than releasing sensitive information.

While it is difficult to determine in advance what level of detail to provide to the press, some guidelines to keep in mind are:

- Keep the technical level of detail low. Detailed information about the incident may provide enough information for copy-cat events or even damage the site's ability to prosecute once the event is over.

- Keep the speculation out of press statements. Speculation of who is causing the incident or the motives are very likely to be in error and may cause an inflamed view of the incident.

- Work with law enforcement professionals to assure that evidence is protected. If prosecution is involved, assure that the evidence collected is not divulged to the press.

- Try not to be forced into a press interview before you are prepared. The popular press is famous for the "2am" interview, where the hope is to catch the interviewee off guard and obtain information otherwise not available.

- Do not allow the press attention to detract from the handling of the event. Always remember that the successful closure of an incident is of primary importance.

5.3.6 Who Needs to Get Involved?

There now exists a number of incident response teams (IRTs) such as the CERT and the CIAC. (See sections 3.9.7.3.1 and 3.9.7.3.4.) Teams exists for many major government agencies and large corporations. If such a team is available for your site, the notification of this team should be of primary importance during the early stages of an incident. These teams are responsible for coordinating computer security incidents over a range of sites and larger entities. Even if the incident is believed to be contained to a single site, it is possible that the information available through a response team could help in closing out the incident.

In setting up a site policy for incident handling, it may be desirable to create an incident handling team (IHT), much like those teams that already exist, that will be responsible for handling computer security incidents for the site (or organization). If such a team is created, it is essential that communication lines be opened between this team and other IHTs.

Once an incident is under way, it is difficult to open a trusted dialogue between other IHTs if none has existed before.

5.4 Response

A major topic still untouched here is how to actually respond to an event. The response to an event will fall into the general categories of containment, eradication, recovery, and follow-up.

Containment

The purpose of containment is to limit the extent of an attack. For example, it is important to limit the spread of a worm attack on a network as quickly as possible. An essential part of containment is decision making (i.e., determining whether to shut a system down, to disconnect from a network, to monitor system or network activity, to set traps, to disable functions such as remote file transfer on a UNIX system, etc.). Sometimes this decision is trivial; shut the system down if the system is classified or sensitive, or if proprietary information is at risk!

In other cases, it is worthwhile to risk having some damage to the system if keeping the system up might enable you to identify an intruder.

The third stage, containment, should involve carrying out predetermined procedures. Your organization or site should, for example, define acceptable risks in dealing with an incident, and should prescribe specific actions and strategies accordingly.

Finally, notification of cognizant authorities should occur during this stage.

Eradication

Once an incident has been detected, it is important to first think about containing the incident. Once the incident has been contained, it is now time to eradicate the cause. Software may be available to help you in this effort. For example, eradication software is available to eliminate most viruses which infect small systems. If any bogus files have been created, it is time to delete them at this point. In the case of virus infections, it is important to clean and reformat any disks containing infected files. Finally, ensure that all backups are clean. Many systems infected with viruses become periodically reinfected simply because people do not systematically eradicate the virus from backups.

Recovery

Once the cause of an incident has been eradicated, the recovery phase defines the next stage of action. The goal of recovery is to return the system to normal. In the case of a network-based attack, it is important to install patches for any operating system vulnerability which was exploited.

Follow-up

One of the most important stages of responding to incidents is also the most often omitted—the follow-up stage. This stage is important because it helps those involved in handling the incident develop a set of "lessons learned" (see section 6.3) to improve future performance in such situations. This stage also provides information which justifies an organization's computer security effort to management, and yields information which may be essential in legal proceedings.

The most important element of the follow-up stage is performing a postmortem analysis. Exactly what happened, and at what times?

How well did the staff involved with the incident perform? What kind of information did the staff need quickly, and how could they have gotten that information as soon as possible? What would the staff do differently next time? A follow-up report is valuable because it provides a reference to be used in case of other similar incidents. Creating a formal chronology of events (including time stamps) is also important for legal reasons. Similarly, it is also important to as quickly obtain a monetary estimate of the amount of damage the incident caused in terms of any loss of software and files, hardware damage, and manpower costs to restore altered files, reconfigure affected systems, and so forth. This estimate may become the basis for subsequent prosecution activity by the FBI, the U.S. Attorney General's Office, etc.

5.4.1 What Will You Do?

- Restore control.

- Relation to policy.

- Which level of service is needed?

- Monitor activity.

- Constrain or shut down system.

5.4.2 Consider Designating a "Single Point of Contact"

When an incident is under way, a major issue is deciding who is in charge of coordinating the activity of the multitude of players.

A major mistake that can be made is to have a number of "points of contact" (POC) that are not pulling their efforts together. This will only add to the confusion of the event, and will probably lead to additional confusion and wasted or ineffective effort.

The single point of contact may or may not be the person "in charge" of the incident. There are two distinct rolls to fill when deciding who shall be the point of contact and the person in charge of the incident. The person in charge will make decisions as to the interpretation of policy applied to the event. The responsibility for the handling of the event falls onto this person. In contrast, the point of contact must coordinate the effort of all the parties involved with handling the event. The point of contact must be a person with the technical expertise to successfully coordinate the effort of the system managers and users involved in monitoring and reacting to the attack. Often the management structure of a site is such that the administrator of a set of resources is not a technically competent person with regard to handling the details of the operations of the computers, but is ultimately responsible for the use of these resources.

Another important function of the POC is to maintain contact with law enforcement and other external agencies (such as the CIA, DoD, U.S. Army, or others) to assure that multi-agency involvement occurs.

Finally, if legal action in the form of prosecution is involved, the POC may be able to speak for the site in court. The alternative is to have multiple witnesses that will be hard to coordinate in a legal sense, and will weaken any case against the attackers. A single POC may also be the single person in charge of evidence collected, which will keep the number of people accounting for evidence to a minimum. As a rule of thumb, the more people that touch a potential piece of evidence, the greater the possibility that it will be inadmissible in court. The section below (Legal/Investigative) will provide more details for consideration on this topic.

5.5 Legal/Investigative

5.5.1 Establishing Contacts with Investigative Agencies

It is important to establish contacts with personnel from investigative agencies such as the FBI and Secret Service as soon as possible, for several reasons. Local law enforcement and local security offices or campus police organizations should also be informed when appropriate. A primary reason is that once a major attack is in progress, there is little time to call various personnel in these agencies to determine exactly who the correct point of contact is. Another reason is that it is important to cooperate with these agencies in a manner that will foster a good working relationship, and that will be in accordance with the working procedures of these agencies. Knowing the working procedures in advance and the expectations of your point of contact is a big step in this direction. For example, it is important to gather evidence that will be admissible in a court of law. If you don't know in advance how to gather admissible evidence, your efforts to collect evidence during an incident are likely to be of no value to the investigative agency with which you deal. A final reason for establishing contacts as soon as possible is that it is impossible to know the particular agency that will assume jurisdiction in any given incident. Making contacts and finding the proper channels early will make responding to an incident go considerably more smoothly. If your organization or site has a legal counsel, you need to notify this office soon after you learn that an incident is in progress. At a minimum, your legal counsel needs to be involved to protect the legal and financial interests of your site or organization. There are many legal and practical issues, a few of which are:

1. Whether your site or organization is willing to risk negative publicity or exposure to cooperate with legal prosecution efforts.

2. Downstream liability—if you leave a compromised system as is so it can be monitored and another computer is damaged because the attack originated from your system, your site or organization may be liable for damages incurred.

3. Distribution of information—if your site or organization distributes information about an attack in which another site or organization may be involved or the vulnerability in a product that may affect ability to market that product, your site or organization may again be liable for any damages (including damage of reputation).

4. Liabilities due to monitoring—your site or organization may be sued if users at your site or elsewhere discover that your site is monitoring account activity without informing users.

Unfortunately, there are no clear precedents yet on the liabilities or responsibilities of organizations involved in a security incident or who might be involved in supporting an investigative effort. Investigators will often encourage organizations to help trace and monitor intruders—indeed, most investigators cannot pursue computer intrusions without extensive support from the organizations involved. However, investigators cannot provide protection from liability claims, and these kinds of efforts may drag out for months and may take lots of effort.

On the other side, an organization's legal council may advise extreme caution and suggest that tracing activities be halted and an intruder shut out of the system. This in itself may not provide protection from liability, and may prevent investigators from identifying anyone.

The balance between supporting investigative activity and limiting liability is tricky; you'll need to consider the advice of your council and the damage the intruder is causing (if any) in making your decision about what to do during any particular incident.

Your legal counsel should also be involved in any decision to contact investigative agencies when an incident occurs at your site. The decision to coordinate efforts with investigative agencies is most properly that of your site or organization.

Involving your legal counsel will also foster the multi-level coordination between your site and the particular investigative agency involved which in turn results in an efficient division of labor. Another result is that you are likely to obtain guidance that will help you avoid future legal mistakes.

Finally, your legal counsel should evaluate your site's written procedures for responding to incidents. It is essential to obtain a "clean bill of health" from a legal perspective before you actually carry out these procedures.

5.5.2 Formal and Informal Legal Procedures

One of the most important considerations in dealing with investigative agencies is verifying that the person who calls asking for information is a legitimate representative from the agency in question. Unfortunately, many well intentioned people have unknowingly leaked sensitive information about incidents, allowed unauthorized people into their systems, etc., because a caller has masqueraded as an FBI or Secret Service agent. A similar consideration is using a secure means of communication.

Because many network attackers can easily reroute electronic mail, avoid using electronic mail to communicate with other agencies (as well as others dealing with the incident at hand). Non-secured phone lines (e.g., the phones normally used in the business world) are also frequent targets for tapping by network intruders, so be careful!

There is no established set of rules for responding to an incident when the U.S. Federal Government becomes involved. Except by court order, no agency can force you to monitor, to disconnect from the network, to avoid telephone contact with the suspected attackers, etc. As discussed in section 5.5.1, you should consult the matter with your legal counsel, especially before taking an action that your organization has never taken. The particular agency involved may ask you to leave an attacked machine on and to monitor activity on this machine, for example.

Your complying with this request will ensure continued cooperation of the agency—usually the best route towards finding the source of the network attacks and, ultimately, terminating these attacks.

Additionally, you may need some information or a favor from the agency involved in the incident. You are likely to get what you need only if you have been cooperative. Of particular importance is avoiding unnecessary or unauthorized disclosure of information about the incident, including any information furnished by the agency involved. The trust between your site and the agency hinges upon your ability to avoid compromising the case the agency will build; keeping "tight lipped" is imperative.

Sometimes your needs and the needs of an investigative agency will differ. Your site may want to get back to normal business by closing an attack route, but the investigative agency may want you to keep this route open. Similarly, your site may want to close a compromised system down to avoid the possibility of negative publicity, but again the investigative agency may want you to continue monitoring. When there is such a conflict, there may be a complex set of tradeoffs (e.g., interests of your site's management, amount of resources you can devote to the problem, jurisdictional boundaries, etc.). An important guiding principle is related to what might be called "Internet citizenship" [22, IAB89, 23] and its responsibilities. Your site can shut a system down, and this will relieve you of the stress, resource demands, and danger of negative exposure. The attacker, however, is likely to simply move on to another system, temporarily leaving others blind to the attacker's intention and actions until another path of attack can be detected. Providing that there is no damage to your systems and others, the most responsible course of action is to cooperate with the participating agency by leaving your compromised system on. This will allow monitoring (and, ultimately, the possibility of terminating the source of the threat to systems just like yours). On the other hand, if there is damage to computers illegally accessed through your system, the choice is more complicated: shutting down the intruder may prevent further damage to systems, but might make it impossible to track down the intruder. If there has been damage, the decision about whether it is important to leave systems up to catch the intruder should involve all the organizations effected. Further complicating the issue of network responsibility is the consideration that if you do not cooperate with the agency involved, you will be less likely to receive help from that agency in the future.

5.6 Documentation Logs

When you respond to an incident, document all details related to the incident. This will provide valuable information to yourself and others as you try to unravel the course of events. Documenting all details will ultimately save you time. If you don't document every relevant phone call, for example, you are likely to forget a good portion of information you obtain, requiring you to contact the source of information once again. This wastes yours and others' time, something you can ill afford. At the same time, recording details will provide evidence for prosecution efforts, providing the case moves in this direction. Documenting an incident also will help you perform a final assessment of damage (something your management as well as law enforcement officers will want to know), and will provide the basis for a follow-up analysis in which you can engage in a valuable "lessons learned" exercise.

During the initial stages of an incident, it is often infeasible to determine whether prosecution is viable, so you should document as if you are gathering evidence for a court case. At a minimum, you should record:

■ All system events (audit records).

■ All actions you take (time tagged).

■ All phone conversations (including the person with whom you talked, the date and time, and the content of the conversation).

The most straightforward way to maintain documentation is keeping a log book. This allows you to go to a centralized, chronological source of information when you need it, instead of requiring you to page through individual sheets of paper. Much of this information is potential evidence in a court of law. Thus, when you initially suspect that an incident will result in prosecution or when an investigative agency becomes involved, you need to regularly (e.g., every day) turn in photocopied, signed copies of your logbook (as well as media you use to record system events) to a document custodian who can store these copied pages in a secure place (e.g., a safe). When you submit information for storage, you should in return receive a signed, dated receipt from the document custodian. Failure to observe these procedures can result in invalidation of any evidence you obtain in a court of law.

6. Establishing Post-Incident Procedures

6.1 Overview

In the wake of an incident, several actions should take place. These actions can be summarized as follows:

1. An inventory should be taken of the systems' assets, i.e., a careful examination should determine how the system was affected by the incident,

2. The lessons learned as a result of the incident should be included in revised security plan to prevent the incident from re-occurring,

3. A new risk analysis should be developed in light of the incident,

4. An investigation and prosecution of the individuals who caused the incident should commence, if it is deemed desirable.

All four steps should provide feedback to the site security policy committee, leading to prompt re-evaluation and amendment of the current policy.

6.2 Removing Vulnerabilities

Removing all vulnerabilities once an incident has occurred is difficult. The key to removing vulnerabilities is knowledge and understanding of the breach. In some cases, it is prudent to remove all access or functionality as soon as possible, and then restore normal operation in limited stages. Bear in mind that removing all access while an incident is in progress will obviously notify all users, including the alleged problem users, that the administrators are aware of a problem; this may have a deleterious effect on an investigation. However, allowing an incident to continue may also open the likelihood of greater damage, loss, aggravation, or liability (civil or criminal).

If it is determined that the breach occurred due to a flaw in the systems' hardware or software, the vendor (or supplier) and the CERT should be notified as soon as possible. Including relevant telephone numbers (also electronic mail addresses and fax numbers) in the site security policy is strongly recommended. To aid prompt acknowledgment and understanding of the problem, the flaw should be described in as much detail as possible, including details about how to exploit the flaw.

As soon as the breach has occurred, the entire system and all its components should be considered suspect. System software is the most probable target. Preparation is key to recovering from a possibly tainted system. This includes checksumming all tapes from the vendor using a checksum algorithm which (hopefully) is resistant to tampering [10]. (See sections 3.9.4.1, 3.9.4.2.) Assuming original vendor distribution tapes are available, an analysis of all system files should commence, and any irregularities should be noted and referred to all parties involved in handling the incident. It can be very difficult, in some cases, to decide which backup tapes to recover from; consider that the incident may have continued for months or years before discovery, and that the suspect may be an employee of the site, or otherwise have intimate knowledge or access to the systems. In all cases, the pre-incident preparation will determine what recovery is possible. At worst-case, restoration from the original manufacturers' media and a re-installation of the systems will be the most prudent solution.

Review the lessons learned from the incident and always update the policy and procedures to reflect changes necessitated by the incident.

6.2.1 Assessing Damage

Before cleanup can begin, the actual system damage must be discerned. This can be quite time consuming, but should lead into some of the insight as to the nature of the incident, and aid investigation and prosecution. It is best to compare previous backups or original tapes when possible; advance preparation is the key. If the system supports centralized logging (most do), go back over the logs and look for abnormalities. If process accounting and connect time accounting is enabled, look for patterns of system usage. To a lesser extent, disk usage may shed light on the incident. Accounting can provide much helpful information in an analysis of an incident and subsequent prosecution.

6.2.2 Cleanup

Once the damage has been assessed, it is necessary to develop a plan for system cleanup. In general, bringing up services in the order of demand to allow a minimum of user inconvenience is the best practice. Understand that the proper recovery procedures for the system are extremely important and should be specific to the site. It may be necessary to go back to the original distributed tapes and recustomize the system. To facilitate this worst case scenario, a record of the original systems setup and each customization change should be kept current with each change to the system.

6.2.3 Follow up

Once you believe that a system has been restored to a "safe" state, it is still possible that holes and even traps could be lurking in the system. In the follow-up stage, the system should be monitored for items that may have been missed during the cleanup stage. It would be prudent to utilize some of the tools mentioned in section 3.9.8.2 (e.g., COPS) as a start. Remember, these tools don't replace continual system monitoring and good systems administration procedures.

6.2.4 Keep a Security Log

As discussed in section 5.6, a security log can be most valuable during this phase of removing vulnerabilities. There are two considerations here; the first is to keep logs of the procedures that have been used to make the system secure again. This should include command procedures (e.g., shell scripts) that can be run on a periodic basis to recheck the security. Second, keep logs of important system events. These can be referenced when trying to determine the extent of the damage of a given incident.

6.3 Capturing Lessons Learned

6.3.1 Understand the Lesson

After an incident, it is prudent to write a report describing the incident, method of discovery, correction procedure, monitoring procedure, and a summary of lesson learned. This will aid in the clear understanding of the problem. Remember, it is difficult to learn from an incident if you don't understand the source.

6.3.2 Resources

6.3.2.1 Other Security Devices, Methods

Security is a dynamic, not static process. Sites are dependent on the nature of security available at each site, and the array of devices and methods that will help promote security.
Keeping up with the security area of the computer industry and their methods will assure a security manager of taking advantage of the latest technology.

6.3.2.2 Repository of Books, Lists, Information Sources

Keep an on site collection of books, lists, information sources, etc., as guides and references for securing the system. Keep this collection up to date. Remember, as systems change, so do security methods and problems.

6.3.2.3 Form a Subgroup

Form a subgroup of system administration personnel that will be the core security staff. This will allow discussions of security problems and multiple views of the site's security issues. This subgroup can also act to develop the site security policy and make suggested changes as necessary to ensure site security.

6.4 Upgrading Policies and Procedures

6.4.1 Establish Mechanisms for Updating Policies, Procedures, and Tools

If an incident is based on poor policy, and unless the policy is changed, then one is doomed to repeat the past. Once a site has recovered from an incident, site policy and procedures should be reviewed to encompass changes to prevent similar incidents. Even without an incident, it would be prudent to review policies and procedures on a regular basis. Reviews are imperative due to today's changing computing environments.

6.4.2 Problem Reporting Procedures

A problem reporting procedure should be implemented to describe, in detail, the incident and the solutions to the incident. Each incident should be reviewed by the site security subgroup to allow understanding of the incident with possible suggestions to the site policy and procedures.

7. References

[1] Quarterman, J., "The Matrix: Computer Networks and Conferencing Systems Worldwide," Pg. 278, Digital Press, Bedford, MA, 1990.

[2] Brand, R., "Coping with the Threat of Computer Security Incidents: A Primer from Prevention through Recovery," R. Brand, available on-line from: cert.sei.cmu.edu:/pub/info/primer, 8 June 1990.

[3] Fites, M., Kratz, P. and A. Brebner, "Control and Security of Computer Information Systems," Computer Science Press, 1989.

[4] Johnson, D., and J. Podesta, "Formulating a Company Policy on Access to and Use and Disclosure of Electronic Mail on Company Computer Systems," Available from: The Electronic Mail Association (EMA) 1555 Wilson Blvd, Suite 555, Arlington VA 22209, (703) 522-7111, 22 October 1990.

[5] Curry, D., "Improving the Security of Your UNIX System," SRI International Report ITSTD-721-FR-90-21, April 1990.

[6] Cheswick, B., "The Design of a Secure Internet Gateway," Proceedings of the Summer Usenix Conference, Anaheim, CA, June 1990.

[7] Linn, J., "Privacy Enhancement for Internet Electronic Mail: Part I—Message Encipherment and Authentication Procedures," RFC 1113, IAB Privacy Task Force, August 1989.

[8] Kent, S., and J. Linn, "Privacy Enhancement for Internet Electronic Mail: Part II—Certificate-Based Key Management," RFC 1114, IAB Privacy Task Force, August 1989.

[9] Linn, J., "Privacy Enhancement for Internet Electronic Mail: Part III—Algorithms, Modes, and Identifiers," RFC 1115, IAB Privacy Task Force, August 1989.

[10] Merkle, R., "A Fast Software One Way Hash Function," Journal of Cryptology, Vol. 3, No. 1.

[11] Postel, J., "Internet Protocol - DARPA Internet Program Protocol Specification," RFC 791, DARPA, September 1981.

[12] Postel, J., "Transmission Control Protocol - DARPA Internet Program Protocol Specification," RFC 793, DARPA, September 1981.

[13] Postel, J., "User Datagram Protocol," RFC 768, USC/Information Sciences Institute, 28 August 1980.

[14] Mogul, J., "Simple and Flexible Datagram Access Controls for UNIX-based Gateways," Digital Western Research Laboratory Research Report 89/4, March 1989.

[15] Bellovin, S., and M. Merritt, "Limitations of the Kerberos Authentication System," Computer Communications Review, October 1990.

[16] Pfleeger, C., "Security in Computing," Prentice-Hall, Englewood Cliffs, N.J., 1989.

[17] Parker, D., Swope, S., and B. Baker, "Ethical Conflicts: Information and Computer Science, Technology and Business," QED Information Sciences, Inc., Wellesley, MA.

[18] Forester, T., and P. Morrison, "Computer Ethics: Tales and Ethical Dilemmas in Computing," MIT Press, Cambridge, MA, 1990.

[19] Postel, J., and J. Reynolds, "Telnet Protocol Specification," RFC 854, USC/Information Sciences Institute, May 1983.

[20] Postel, J., and J. Reynolds, "File Transfer Protocol," RFC 959, USC/Information Sciences Institute, October 1985.

[21] Postel, J., Editor, "IAB Official Protocol Standards," RFC 1200, IAB, April 1991.

[22] Internet Activities Board, "Ethics and the Internet," RFC 1087, Internet Activities Board, January 1989.

[23] Pethia, R., Crocker, S., and B. Fraser, "Policy Guidelines for the Secure Operation of the Internet," CERT, TIS, CERT, RFC in preparation.

[24] Computer Emergency Response Team (CERT/CC), "Unauthorized Password Change Requests," CERT Advisory CA-91:03, April 1991.

[25] Computer Emergency Response Team (CERT/CC), "TELNET Breakin Warning," CERT Advisory CA-89:03, August 1989.

[26] CCITT, Recommendation X.509, "The Directory: Authentication Framework," Annex C.

[27] Farmer, D., and E. Spafford, "The COPS Security Checker System," Proceedings of the Summer 1990 USENIX Conference, Anaheim, CA, Pgs. 165-170, June 1990.

8. Annotated Bibliography

The intent of this annotated bibliography is to offer a representative collection of resources of information that will help the user of this handbook. It is meant provide a starting point for further research in the security area. Included are references to other sources of information for those who wish to pursue issues of the computer security environment.

8.1 Computer Law

[ABA89]

American Bar Association, Section of Science and Technology, "Guide to the Prosecution of Telecommunication Fraud by the Use of Computer Crime Statutes," American Bar Association, 1989.

[BENDER]

Bender, D., "Computer Law: Evidence and Procedure," M. Bender, New York, NY, 1978-present. Kept up to date with supplements. Years covering 1978-1984 focuses on: Computer law, evidence and procedures. The years 1984 to the current focus on general computer law. Bibliographical references and index included.

[BLOOMBECKER]

Bloombecker, B., "Spectacular Computer Crimes," Dow Jones- Irwin, Homewood, IL, 1990.

[CCH]

Commerce Clearing House, "Guide to Computer Law," (Topical Law Reports), Chicago, IL., 1989. Court cases and decisions rendered by federal and state courts throughout the United States on federal and state computer law. Includes Case Table and Topical Index.

[CONLY]

Conly, C., "Organizing for Computer Crime Investigation and Prosecution," U.S. Dept. of Justice, Office of Justice Programs, Under Contract Number OJP-86-C-002, National Institute of Justice, Washington, DC, July 1989.

[FENWICK]

Fenwick, W., Chair, "Computer Litigation, 1985: Trial Tactics and Techniques," Litigation Course Handbook Series No. 280, Prepared for distribution at the Computer Litigation, 1985: Trial Tactics and Techniques Program, February-March 1985.

[GEMIGNANI]

Gemignani, M., "Viruses and Criminal Law," Communications of the ACM, Vol. 32, No. 6, Pgs. 669-671, June 1989.

[HUBAND]

Huband, F., and R. Shelton, Editors, "Protection of Computer Systems and Software: New Approaches for Combating Theft of Software and Unauthorized Intrusion," Papers presented at a workshop sponsored by the National Science Foundation, 1986.

[MCEWEN]

McEwen, J., "Dedicated Computer Crime Units," Report Contributors: D. Fester and H. Nugent, Prepared for the National Institute of Justice, U.S. Department of Justice, by Institute for Law and Justice, Inc., under contract number OJP-85-C-006, Washington, DC, 1989.

[PARKER]

Parker, D., "Computer Crime: Criminal Justice Resource Manual," U.S. Dept. of Justice, National Institute of Justice, Office of Justice Programs, Under Contract Number OJP-86-C-002, Washington, D.C., August 1989.

[SHAW]

Shaw, E., Jr., "Computer Fraud and Abuse Act of 1986," Congressional Record (3 June 1986), Washington, D.C., 3 June 1986.

[TRIBLE]

Trible, P., "The Computer Fraud and Abuse Act of 1986," U.S. Senate Committee on the Judiciary, 1986.

8.2 Computer Security

[BRAND]

Brand, R., "Coping with the Threat of Computer Security Incidents: A Primer from Prevention through Recovery," R. Brand, 8 June 1990.

[CAELLI]

Caelli, W., Editor, "Computer Security in the Age of Information," Proceedings of the Fifth IFIP International Conference on Computer Security, IFIP/Sec '88.

[CARROLL]

Carroll, J., "Computer Security," 2nd Edition, Butterworth Publishers, Stoneham, MA, 1987.

[CHESWICK]

Cheswick, B., "The Design of a Secure Internet Gateway," Proceedings of the Summer Usenix Conference, Anaheim, CA, June 1990.

[COOPER]

Cooper, J., "Computer and Communications Security: Strategies for the 1990s," McGraw-Hill, 1989.

As computer security becomes a more important issue in modern society, it begins to warrant a systematic approach. The vast majority of the computer security problems and the costs associated with them can be prevented with simple inexpensive measures. The most important and cost effective of these measures are available in the prevention and planning phases. These methods are presented in this paper, followed by a simplified guide to incident handling and recovery. Available on-line from:

```
cert.sei.cmu.edu:/pub/info/primer.
```

Brief abstract (slight paraphrase from the original abstract): AT&T maintains a large internal Internet that needs to be protected from outside attacks, while providing useful services between the two. This paper describes AT&T's Internet gateway. This gateway passes mail and many of the common Internet services between AT&T internal machines and the Internet. This is accomplished without IP connectivity using a pair of machines: a trusted internal machine and an untrusted external gateway. These are connected by a private link. The internal machine provides a few carefully-guarded services to the external gateway. This configuration helps protect the internal internet even if the external machine is fully compromised.

This is a very useful and interesting design. Most firewall gateway systems rely on a system that, if compromised, could allow access to the machines behind the firewall. Also, most firewall systems require users who want access to Internet services to have accounts on the firewall machine. AT&T's design allows AT&T internal internet users access to the standard services of TELNET and FTP from their own workstations without accounts on the firewall machine. A very useful paper that shows how to maintain some of the benefits of Internet connectivity while still maintaining strong security.

[CURRY]

Curry, D., "Improving the Security of Your UNIX System," SRI International Report ITSTD-721-FR-90-21, April 1990.

This paper describes measures that you, as a system administrator can take to make your UNIX system(s) more secure. Oriented primarily at SunOS 4.x, most of the information covered applies equally well to any Berkeley UNIX system with or without NFS and/or Yellow Pages (NIS). Some of the information can also be applied to System V, although this is not a primary focus of the paper. A very useful reference, this is also available on the Internet in various locations, including the directory cert.sei.cmu.edu:/pub/info.

[FITES]

Fites, M., Kratz, P. and A. Brebner, "Control and Security of Computer Information Systems," Computer Science Press, 1989.

This book serves as a good guide to the issues encountered in forming computer security policies and procedures. The book is designed as a textbook for an introductory course in information systems security.

The book is divided into five sections: Risk Management (I), Safeguards: security and control measures, organizational and administrative (II), Safeguards: Security and Control Measures, Technical (III), Legal Environment and Professionalism (IV), and CICA Computer Control Guidelines (V).

The book is particularly notable for its straight-forward approach to security, emphasizing that common sense is the first consideration in designing a security program. The authors note that there is a tendency to look to more technical solutions to security problems while overlooking organizational controls which are often cheaper and much more effective. 298 pages, including references and index.

[GARFINKEL]

Garfinkel, S, and E. Spafford, "Practical Unix Security," O'Reilly & Associates, ISBN 0-937175-72-2, May 1991.

Approx 450 pages, $29.95. Orders: 1-800-338-6887

(US & Canada), 1-707-829-0515 (Europe), email: nuts@ora.com

This is one of the most useful books available on Unix security. The first part of the book covers standard Unix and Unix security basics, with particular emphasis on passwords. The second section covers enforcing security on the system. Of particular interest to the Internet user are the sections on network security, which address many of the common security problems that afflict Internet Unix users. Four chapters deal with handling security incidents, and the book concludes with discussions of encryption, physical security, and useful checklists and lists of resources. The book lives up to its name; it is filled with specific references to possible security holes, files to check, and things to do to improve security. This book is an excellent complement to this handbook.

[GREENIA90]

Greenia, M., "Computer Security Information Sourcebook," Lexikon Services, Sacramento, CA, 1989.

A manager's guide to computer security. Contains a sourcebook of key reference materials including access control and computer crimes bibliographies.

[HOFFMAN]

Hoffman, L., "Rogue Programs: Viruses, Worms, and Trojan Horses," Van Nostrand Reinhold, NY, 1990.

(384 pages, includes bibliographical references and index.)

[JOHNSON]

Johnson, D., and J. Podesta, "Formulating A Company Policy on Access to and Use and Disclosure of Electronic Mail on Company Computer Systems."

A white paper prepared for the EMA, written by two experts in privacy law. Gives background on the issues, and presents some policy options.

Available from:

> The Electronic Mail Association (EMA)
> 1555 Wilson Blvd, Suite 555
> Arlington, VA 22209
> (703) 522-7111

[KENT]

Kent, Stephen, "E-Mail Privacy for the Internet: New Software and Strict Registration Procedures will be Implemented this Year," Business Communications Review, Vol. 20, No. 1, Pg. 55, 1 January 1990.

[LU]

Lu, W., and M. Sundareshan, "Secure Communication in Internet Environments: A Hierachical Key Management Scheme for End-to-End Encryption," IEEE Transactions on Communications, Vol. 37, No. 10, Pg. 1014, 1 October 1989.

[LU1]

Lu, W., and M. Sundareshan, "A Model for Multilevel Security in Computer Networks," IEEE Transactions on Software Engineering, Vol. 16, No. 6, Page 647, 1 June 1990.

[NSA]

National Security Agency, "Information Systems Security Products and Services Catalog," NSA, Quarterly Publication. NSA's catalogue contains chapter on: Endorsed Cryptographic Products List; NSA Endorsed Data Encryption Standard (DES) Products List; Protected Services List; Evaluated Products List; Preferred Products List; and Endorsed Tools List. The catalogue is available from the Superintendent of Documents, U.S. Government Printing Office, Washington, D.C. One may place telephone orders by calling: (202) 783-3238.

[OTA]

United States Congress, Office of Technology Assessment, "Defending Secrets, Sharing Data: New Locks and Keys for Electronic Information," OTA-CIT-310, October 1987.

This report, prepared for congressional committee considering Federal policy on the protection of electronic information, is interesting because of the issues it raises regarding the impact of technology used to protect information. It also serves as a reasonable introduction to the various encryption and information protection mechanisms. 185 pages. Available from the U.S. Government Printing Office.

[PALMER]

Palmer, I., and G. Potter, "Computer Security Risk Management," Van Nostrand Reinhold, NY, 1989.

[PFLEEGER]

Pfleeger, C., "Security in Computing," Prentice-Hall, Englewood Cliffs, NJ, 1989.

A general textbook in computer security, this book provides an excellent and very readable introduction to classic computer security problems and solutions, with a particular emphasis on encryption. The encryption coverage serves as a good introduction to the subject. Other topics covered include building secure programs and systems, security of database, personal computer security, network and communications security, physical security, risk analysis and security planning, and legal and ethical issues. 538 pages including index and bibliography.

[SHIREY]

Shirey, R., "Defense Data Network Security Architecture," Computer Communication Review, Vol. 20, No. 2, Page 66, 1 April 1990.

[SPAFFORD]

Spafford, E., Heaphy, K., and D. Ferbrache, "Computer Viruses: Dealing with Electronic Vandalism and Programmed Threats," ADAPSO, 1989. (109 pages.)

This is a good general reference on computer viruses and related concerns. In addition to describing viruses in some detail, it also covers more general security issues, legal recourse in case of security problems, and includes lists of laws, journals focused on computers security, and other security-related resources.

Available from: ADAPSO, 1300 N. 17th St, Suite 300, Arlington VA 22209. (703) 522-5055.

[STOLL88]

Stoll, C., "Stalking the Wily Hacker," Communications of the ACM, Vol. 31, No. 5, Pgs. 484-497, ACM, New York, NY, May 1988.

This article describes some of the technical means used to trace the intruder that was later chronicled in "Cuckoo's Egg" (see below).

[STOLL89]

Stoll, C., "The Cuckoo's Egg," ISBN 00385-24946-2, Doubleday, 1989.

Clifford Stoll, an astronomer turned UNIX System Administrator, recounts an exciting, true story of how he tracked a computer intruder through the maze of American military and research networks. This book is easy to understand and can serve as an interesting introduction to the world of networking. Jon Postel says in a book review, "[this book] ... is absolutely essential reading for anyone that uses or operates any computer connected to the Internet or any other computer network."

[VALLA]

allabhaneni, S., "Auditing Computer Security: A Manual with Case Studies," Wiley, New York, NY, 1989.

8.3 Ethics

[CPSR89]

Computer Professionals for Social Responsibility, "CPSR Statement on the Computer Virus," CPSR, Communications of the ACM, Vol. 32, No. 6, Pg. 699, June 1989.

This memo is a statement on the Internet Computer Virus by the Computer Professionals for Social Responsibility (CPSR).

[DENNING]

Denning, Peter J., Editor, "Computers Under Attack: Intruders, Worms, and Viruses," ACM Press, 1990.

A collection of 40 pieces divided into six sections: the emergence of worldwide computer networks, electronic breakins, worms, viruses, counterculture (articles examining the world of the "hacker"), and finally a section discussing social, legal, and ethical considerations. A thoughtful collection that addresses the phenomenon of attacks on computers. This includes a number of previously published articles and some new ones. The previously published ones are well chosen, and include some references that might be otherwise hard to obtain. This book is a key reference to computer security threats that have generated much of the concern over computer security in recent years.

[ERMANN]

Ermann, D., Williams, M., and C. Gutierrez, Editors, "Computers, Ethics, and Society," Oxford University Press, NY, 1990. (376 pages, includes bibliographical references).

[FORESTER]

Forester, T., and P. Morrison, "Computer Ethics: Tales and Ethical Dilemmas in Computing," MIT Press, Cambridge, MA, 1990. (192 pages including index.)

From the preface: "The aim of this book is two-fold: (1) to describe some of the problems created by society by computers, and (2) to show how these problems present ethical dilemmas for computers professionals and computer users. The problems created by computers arise, in turn, from two main sources: from hardware and software malfunctions and from misuse by human beings. We argue that computer systems by their very nature are insecure, unreliable, and unpredictable—and that society has yet to come to terms with the consequences. We also seek to show how society has become newly vulnerable to human misuse of computers in the form of computer crime, software theft, hacking, the creation of viruses, invasions of privacy, and so on." The eight chapters include "Computer Crime," "Software Theft," "Hacking and Viruses," "Unreliable Computers," "The Invasion of Privacy," "AI and Expert Systems," and "Computerizing the Workplace." Includes extensive notes on sources and an index.

[GOULD]

Gould, C., Editor, "The Information Web: Ethical and Social Implications of Computer Networking," Westview Press, Boulder, CO, 1989.

[IAB89]

Internet Activities Board, "Ethics and the Internet," RFC 1087, IAB, January 1989. Also appears in the Communications of the ACM, Vol. 32, No. 6, Pg. 710, June 1989.

This memo is a statement of policy by the Internet Activities Board (IAB) concerning the proper use of the resources of the Internet. Available on-line on host ftp.nisc.sri.com, directory rfc, filename rfc1087.txt. Also available on host nis.nsf.net, directory RFC, filename RFC1087.TXT-1.

[MARTIN]

Martin, M., and R. Schinzinger, "Ethics in Engineering," McGraw Hill, 2nd Edition, 1989.

[MIT89]

Massachusetts Institute of Technology, "Teaching Students About Responsible Use of Computers," MIT, 1985-1986. Also reprinted in the Communications of the ACM, Vol. 32, No. 6, Pg. 704, Athena Project, MIT, June 1989.

This memo is a statement of policy by the Massachusetts Institute of Technology (MIT) on the responsible use of computers.

[NIST]

National Institute of Standards and Technology, "Computer Viruses and Related Threats: A Management Guide," NIST Special Publication 500-166, August 1989.

[NSF88]

National Science Foundation, "NSF Poses Code of Networking Ethics," Communications of the ACM, Vol. 32, No. 6, Pg. 688, June 1989.

Also appears in the minutes of the regular meeting of the Division Advisory Panel for Networking and Communications Research and Infrastructure, Dave Farber, Chair, November 29-30, 1988.

This memo is a statement of policy by the National Science Foundation (NSF) concerning the ethical use of the Internet.

[PARKER90]

Parker, D., Swope, S., and B. Baker, "Ethical Conflicts: Information and Computer Science, Technology and Business," QED Information Sciences, Inc., Wellesley, MA. (245 pages). Additional publications on Ethics:

The University of New Mexico (UNM)

The UNM has a collection of ethics documents. Included are legislation from several states and policies from many institutions.

Access is via FTP, IP address ariel.umn.edu. Look in the directory /ethics.

8.4 The Internet Worm

[BROCK]

Brock, J., "November 1988 Internet Computer Virus and the Vulnerability of National Telecommunications Networks to Computer Viruses," GAO/T-IMTEC-89-10, Washington, DC, 20 July 1989.

Testimonial statement of Jack L. Brock, Director, U. S. Government Information before the Subcommittee on Telecommunications and Finance, Committee on Energy and Commerce, House of Representatives.

[EICHIN89]

Eichin, M., and J. Rochlis, "With Microscope and Tweezers: An Analysis of the Internet Virus of November 1988," Massachusetts Institute of Technology, February 1989.

Provides a detailed dissection of the worm program. The paper discusses the major points of the worm program then reviews strategies, chronology, lessons and open issues, Acknowledgments; also included are a detailed appendix on the worm program subroutine by subroutine, an appendix on the cast of characters, and a reference section.

[EISENBERG89]

Eisenberg, T., D. Gries, J. Hartmanis, D. Holcomb, M. Lynn, and T. Santoro, "The Computer Worm," Cornell University, 6 February 1989.

A Cornell University Report presented to the Provost of the University on 6 February 1989 on the Internet Worm.

[GAO]

U.S. General Accounting Office, "Computer Security - Virus Highlights Need for Improved Internet Management," United States General Accounting Office, Washington, DC, 1989.

This 36 page report (GAO/IMTEC-89-57), by the U.S. Government Accounting Office, describes the Internet worm and its effects. It gives a good overview of the various U.S. agencies involved in the Internet today and their concerns vis-a-vis computer security and networking. Available on-line on host nnsc.nsf.net, directory pub, filename GAO_RPT; and on nis.nsf.net, directory nsfnet, filename GAO_RPT.TXT.

[REYNOLDS89]

The Helminthiasis of the Internet, RFC 1135, USC/Information Sciences Institute, Marina del Rey, CA, December 1989.

This report looks back at the helminthiasis (infestation with, or disease caused by parasitic worms) of the Internet that was unleashed the evening of 2 November 1988. This document provides a glimpse at the infection, its festering, and cure. The impact of the worm on the Internet community, ethics statements, the role of the news media, crime in the computer world, and future prevention is discussed. A documentation review presents four publications that describe in detail this particular parasitic computer program. Reference and bibliography sections are also included. Available on-line on host ftp.nisc.sri.com directory rfc, filename rfc1135.txt. Also available on host nis.nsf.net, directory RFC, filename RFC1135.TXT-1.

[SEELEY89]

Seeley, D., "A Tour of the Worm," Proceedings of 1989 Winter USENIX Conference, Usenix Association, San Diego, CA, February 1989.

Details are presented as a "walk thru" of this particular worm program. The paper opened with an abstract, introduction, detailed chronology of events upon the discovery of the worm, an overview, the internals of the worm, personal opinions, and conclusion.

[SPAFFORD88]

Spafford, E., "The Internet Worm Program: An Analysis," Computer Communication Review, Vol. 19, No. 1, ACM SIGCOM, January 1989. Also issued as Purdue CS Technical Report CSD-TR-823, 28 November 1988.

Describes the infection of the Internet as a worm program that exploited flaws in utility programs in UNIX based systems. The report gives a detailed description of the components of the worm program: data and functions. Spafford focuses his study on two completely independent reverse-compilations of the worm and a version disassembled to VAX assembly language.

[SPAFFORD89]

Spafford, G., "An Analysis of the Internet Worm," Proceedings of the European Software Engineering Conference 1989, Warwick England, September 1989.

Proceedings published by Springer-Verlag as: Lecture Notes in Computer Science #387. Also issued as Purdue Technical Report #CSD-TR-933.

8.5 National Computer Security Center (NCSC)

All NCSC publications, approved for public release, are available from the NCSC Superintendent of Documents.

NCSC = National Computer Security Center
9800 Savage Road
Ft Meade, MD 20755-6000

CSC = Computer Security Center: an older name for the NCSC

NTISS = National Telecommunications and Information Systems Security

NTISS Committee, National Security Agency
Ft Meade, MD 20755-6000

[CSC]

Department of Defense, "Password Management Guideline," CSC-STD-002-85, 12 April 1985, 31 pages.

The security provided by a password system depends on the passwords being kept secret at all times. Thus, a password is vulnerable to compromise whenever it is used, stored, or even known. In a password-based authentication mechanism implemented on an ADP system, passwords are vulnerable to compromise due to five essential aspects of the password system: 1) a password must be initially assigned to a user when enrolled on the ADP system; 2) a user's password must be changed periodically; 3) the ADP system must maintain a 'password database'; 4) users must remember their passwords; and 5) users must enter their passwords into the ADP system at authentication time. This guideline prescribes steps to be taken to minimize the vulnerability of passwords in each of these circumstances.

[NCSC1]

CSC, "A Guide to Understanding AUDIT in Trusted Systems," NCSC-TG-001, Version-2, 1 June 1988, 25 pages.

Audit trails are used to detect and deter penetration of a computer system and to reveal usage that identifies misuse. At the discretion of the auditor, audit trails may be limited to specific events or may encompass all of the activities on a system. Although not required by the criteria, it should be possible for the target of the audit mechanism to be either a subject or an object. That is to say, the audit mechanism should be capable of monitoring every time John accessed the system as well as every time the nuclear reactor file was accessed; and likewise every time John accessed the nuclear reactor file.

[NCSC2]

NCSC, "A Guide to Understanding DISCRETIONARY ACCESS CONTROL in Trusted Systems," NCSC-TG-003, Version-1, 30 September 1987, 29 pages.

Discretionary control is the most common type of access control mechanism implemented in computer systems today. The basis of this kind of security is that an individual user, or program operating on the user's behalf, is allowed to specify explicitly the types of access other users (or programs executing on their behalf) may have to information under the user's control. [...] Discretionary controls are not a replacement for mandatory controls. In any environment in which information is protected, discretionary security provides for a finer granularity of control within the overall constraints of the mandatory policy.

[NCSC3]

NCSC, "A Guide to Understanding CONFIGURATION MANAGEMENT in Trusted Systems," NCSC-TG-006, Version-1, 28 March 1988, 31 pages.

Configuration management consists of four separate tasks: identification, control, status accounting, and auditing. For every change that is made to an automated data processing (ADP) system, the design and requirements of the changed version of the system should be identified. The control task of configuration management is performed by subjecting every change to documentation, hardware, and software/firmware to review and approval by an authorized authority. Configuration status accounting is responsible for recording and reporting on the configuration of the product throughout the change. Finally, through the process of a configuration audit, the completed change can be verified to be functionally correct, and for trusted systems, consistent with the security policy of the system.

[NTISS]

NTISS, "Advisory Memorandum on Office Automation Security Guideline," NTISSAM CONPUSEC/1-87, 16 January 1987, 58 pages.

This document provides guidance to users, managers, security officers, and procurement officers of Office Automation Systems. Areas addressed include: physical security, personnel security, procedural security, hardware/software security, emanations security (TEMPEST), and communications security for stand-alone OA Systems, OA Systems used as terminals connected to mainframe computer systems, and OA Systems used as hosts in a Local Area Network (LAN). Differentiation is made between those Office Automation Systems equipped with removable storage media only (e.g., floppy disks, cassette tapes, removable hard disks) and those Office Automation Systems equipped with fixed media (e.g., Winchester disks).

Additional NCSC Publications:

[NCSC4]

National Computer Security Center, "Glossary of Computer Security Terms," NCSC-TG-004, NCSC, 21 October 1988.

[NCSC5]

National Computer Security Center, "Trusted Computer System Evaluation Criteria," DoD 5200.28-STD, CSC-STD-001-83, NCSC, December 1985.

[NCSC7]

National Computer Security Center, "Guidance for Applying the Department of Defense Trusted Computer System Evaluation Criteria in Specific Environments," CSC-STD-003-85, NCSC, 25 June 1985.

[NCSC8]

National Computer Security Center, "Technical Rationale Behind CSC-STD-003-85: Computer Security Requirements," CSC-STD-004-85, NCSC, 25 June 85.

[NCSC9]

National Computer Security Center, "Magnetic Remanence Security Guideline," CSC-STD-005-85, NCSC, 15 November 1985.

This guideline is tagged as a "For Official Use Only" exemption under Section 6, Public Law 86-36 (50 U.S. Code 402). Distribution authorized of U.S. Government agencies and their contractors to protect unclassified technical, operational, or administrative data relating to operations of the National Security Agency.

[NCSC10]

National Computer Security Center, "Guidelines for Formal Verification Systems," Shipping list no.: 89-660-P, The Center, Fort George G. Meade, MD, 1 April 1990.

[NCSC11]

National Computer Security Center, "Glossary of Computer Security Terms," Shipping list no.: 89-254-P, The Center, Fort George G. Meade, MD, 21 October 1988.

[NCSC12]

National Computer Security Center, "Trusted UNIX Working Group (TRUSIX) rationale for selecting access control list features for the UNIX system," Shipping list no.: 90-076-P, The Center, Fort George G. Meade, MD, 1990.

[NCSC13]

National Computer Security Center, "Trusted Network Interpretation," NCSC-TG-005, NCSC, 31 July 1987.

[NCSC14]

Tinto, M., "Computer Viruses: Prevention, Detection, and Treatment," National Computer Security Center C1 Technical Report C1-001-89, June 1989.

[NCSC15]

National Computer Security Conference, "12th National Computer Security Conference: Baltimore Convention Center, Baltimore, MD, 10-13 October, 1989: Information Systems Security, Solutions for Today - Concepts for Tomorrow," National Institute of Standards and National Computer Security Center, 1989.

8.6 Security Checklists

[AUCOIN]

Aucoin, R., "Computer Viruses: Checklist for Recovery," Computers in Libraries, Vol. 9, No. 2, Pg. 4, 1 February 1989.

[WOOD]

Wood, C., Banks, W., Guarro, S., Garcia, A., Hampel, V., and H. Sartorio, "Computer Security: A Comprehensive Controls Checklist," John Wiley and Sons, Interscience Publication, 1987.

8.7 Additional Publications

Defense Data Network's Network Information Center (DDN NIC) The DDN NIC maintains DDN Security bulletins and DDN Management bulletins online on the machine:

NIC.DDN.MIL. They are available via anonymous FTP. The DDN Security bulletins are in the directory: SCC, and the DDN Management bulletins are in the directory: DDN-NEWS.

For additional information, you may send a message to:

NIC@NIC.DDN.MIL, or call the DDN NIC at: 1-800-235-3155.

[DDN88]

Defense Data Network, "BSD 4.2 and 4.3 Software Problem Resolution," DDN MGT Bulletin #43, DDN Network Information Center, 3 November 1988.

A Defense Data Network Management Bulletin announcement on the 4.2bsd and 4.3bsd software fixes to the Internet worm.

[DDN89]

DCA DDN Defense Communications System, "DDN Security Bulletin 03," DDN Security Coordination Center, 17 October 1989.

IEEE Proceedings

[IEEE]

"Proceedings of the IEEE Symposium on Security and Privacy," published annually.

IEEE Proceedings are available from:

> Computer Society of the IEEE
> P.O. Box 80452
> Worldway Postal Center
> Los Angeles, CA 90080

Other Publications:

> Computer Law and Tax Report
>
> Computers and Security
>
> Security Management Magazine
>
> Journal of Information Systems Management
>
> Data Processing & Communications Security
>
> SIG Security, Audit & Control Review
>
> Site Security Policy Handbook Working Group

9. Acknowledgments

Thanks to the SSPHWG's illustrious "Outline Squad," who assembled at USC/Information Sciences Institute on 12-June-90: Ray Bates (ISI), Frank Byrum (DEC), Michael A. Contino (PSU), Dave Dalva (Trusted Information Systems, Inc.), Jim Duncan (Penn State Math Department), Bruce Hamilton (Xerox), Sean Kirkpatrick (Unisys), Tom Longstaff (CIAC/LLNL), Fred Ostapik (SRI/NIC), Keith Pilotti (SAIC), and Bjorn Satdeva (/sys/admin, inc.).

Many thanks to Rich Pethia and the Computer Emergency Response Team (CERT); much of the work by Paul Holbrook was done while he was working for CERT. Rich also provided a very thorough review of this document. Thanks also to Jon Postel and USC/Information Sciences Institute for contributing facilities and moral support to this effort.

Last, but NOT least, we would like to thank members of the SSPHWG and Friends for their additional contributions: Vint Cerf (CNRI), Dave Grisham (UNM), Nancy Lee Kirkpatrick (Typist Extraordinaire), Chris McDonald (WSMR), H. Craig McKee (Mitre), Gene Spafford (Purdue), and Aileen Yuan (Mitre).

10. Security Considerations

If security considerations had not been so widely ignored in the Internet, this memo would not have been possible.

11. Authors' Addresses

J. Paul Holbrook
CICNet, Inc.
2901 Hubbard
Ann Arbor, MI 48105
Phone: (313) 998-7680
EMail: holbrook@cic.net

Joyce K. Reynolds
University of Southern California
Information Sciences Institute
4676 Admiralty Way
Marina del Rey, CA 90292
Phone: (213) 822-1511
EMail: JKREY@ISI.EDU

The NCSC Security Rating System

Windows NT was designed from the beginning to be a secure operating system. But secure can have any number of meanings depending on who is using the word. In the case of Windows NT, Microsoft decided to work closely with the U.S. National Computer Security Center to provide a certifiably secure operating system. Thus the C2-level security rating of Windows NT provides a way for evaluating the strength of Windows NT's security.

The U.S. government's official recognition of the importance of information system security began in the late 1960s with a task force assembled to research the issues. Based on the results of the task force, the Department of Defense issued directives regarding the implementation of uniform security policy requirements. Then through the early and mid-1970s, many of the defense agencies, including the Air Force and the Advanced Projects Research Agency, developed and evaluated solutions for managing information security. In an effort to further understand the issues of information security, the Department of Defense formed the Computer Security Initiative in 1977. This lead to symposia and workshops in which the issues were subjected to peer review, analysis, and criticism.

In 1981 the Department of Defense formed the Computer Security Center, now known as the National Computer Security Center, to be the formal government organization for researching computer security issues and for developing standard methods for evaluating the level of security offered by any particular system. The organization has developed a set of criteria for evaluating trusted computer systems. The set of criteria used for evaluating commercially available systems is available in a publication titled *Trusted Computer System Evaluation Criteria*, also known as the *Orange Book*.

The Orange Book classifies computer systems into four divisions named D, C, B, and A, with D being the least secure division and A being the most secure. Each division consists of one or more classes. Windows NT has been designed to conform to class 2 of division C, also known as C2.

The fundamental goal of information security is the prevention of unauthorized information access. The model is of subjects (that is, users or agents) that access objects that may be data or other resources (that is, files, printers, and so on). As such, the Orange Book defines six fundamental requirements:

- **Security policy.** The system must provide a verifiable implementation of a well-defined security policy.

- **Marking.** The system must provide a verifiable implementation of object access control marking such that the system is capable of enforcing the security policy. The marking of an object dictates to the security policy which subjects are allowed to access the object and the type of access allowed.

- **Identification.** Each subject must be identified so that the security policy is capable of enforcing access control to objects. The identification information must be secure.

- **Accountability.** The system must provide a means for auditing security-related events and a means for selecting the types of events that are audited.

■ **Assurance.** The implementation of all security functions must be clearly identifiable and documented so that the correctness and soundness of the implementation can be verified and evaluated.

■ **Continuous protection.** The security system must at all times be secure from tampering.

Consistent with the preceding requirements, a system with C2-level security provides the following four major security features:

■ **Discretionary access control.** The system enforces access control between subjects and objects, and provides a means for authorized users to change the access permissions of objects.

■ **Object reuse.** After an object is released back to the system after its use, the information the object contained is no longer available in the object itself. As an example, memory allocated by a process, used, and then freed, can be wiped with zero values as soon as it is released back to the system. Thus a subsequent process that allocates memory cannot access the information contained in the memory the previous time it was used.

■ **Identification and authentication.** The system has a means for identifying and authenticating each user. In Windows NT, this consists of the user logging on to the system with a name and password before the user is allowed to do anything else on the system.

■ **Audit.** With the capability to identify and authenticate users, the system is capable of auditing security-related events and associating those events with the individual users causing them.

C2-level security implements the fundamental *need to know* security policy with auditing capabilities. Note, however, that it does not address issues such as covert channel prevention, nor does it require extremely formal and rigorous evidence proving the correctness of the security implementation. Such higher levels of security belong to the B2 and higher classes. Windows NT, for example, cannot guarantee that a user could not transmit information through a covert channel created by performing a sequence of reads and writes to memory to generate an electromagnetic wave oscillating at a certain frequency that could be modulated to carry information.

NCSC Security Levels

The Orange Book (officially *Trusted Computer Standards Evaluation Criteria*) lists the following classification levels for computer security.

Level D1

This is the lowest possible level of computer security. The entire computer system is untrusted. The hardware and operating system are easily infiltrated. Additionally, the standard for a D1 level computer system states that there is no authentication for users. In other words, there is no user sign-on or password protection. Anyone can walk up to the computer and start using it.

Examples of D1 level computer systems are

MS-DOS

MS-Windows 3.x and Windows 95 (not in workgroup mode, where user must sign in)

Apple's System 7.x

Compromising all these operating systems is easy because they do not require user authentication.

D1 security is appropriate in situations where both loss exposure and access to other (sensitive) systems is minimal. An example would be a stand-alone workstation connected to a modem that is used by several persons to send nonsensitive data to remote company locations.

Level C1

The Discretionary Security Protection system, or level C1, dictates that the hardware is afforded some level of security, and that the users must log on to the system before use. Additionally, Discretionary Access Control, which is part of C1 protection, enables the system administrator to set access permissions to certain programs or data.

Popular examples of Level C1 compatible computer systems are

Unix systems

XENIX

Novell 3.x or higher

The place where level C1 protection fails is at the point where users gain access to the root level of the operating system. At this level, they can manipulate the configuration of the system and gain further access than the system administrator may desire.

Level C2

Level C2 dictates several features to address the shortcomings of level C1. Level C2 introduces the enhanced feature of controlled-access environment (user authorization levels). Because it is based on more than user permissions, this further restricts users from executing certain system commands.

Level C2 systems may also use system *auditing*. The auditing feature tracks all security events, such as logons and system administrator tasks.

Again, popular operating systems capable of obtaining level C2 certification are

> Unix systems
>
> XENIX
>
> Novell 3.x or higher
>
> Windows NT 3.51 and 4

Level B1

Label Security Protection or level B1 supports multilevel security—security levels such as secret and top secret. These are the computers of real cloak and dagger stuff. At this level, objects under mandatory access control cannot have their permissions changed by the owner.

Examples of computer systems that meet any level B security protection vary by operating system. Government agencies and defense contractor installations house the majority of level B computer systems.

Level B2

This level is also known as Structured Protection. Level B2 security dictates that all objects on the computer system are labeled and that devices (such as workstations, terminals, and disk drives) have security levels assigned to them. A user might have access to a workstation, for example, but he might not have access to a disk subsystem that contains payroll data.

Level B3

Security Domain, or level B3, states that the user's workstation or terminal is connected through a trusted path to the network system. Additionally at this level, hardware is introduced to protect the memory area of the security system.

Level A

This is the highest level of security found in the Orange Book. Sometimes it is also referred to as Verified Design. This level, like all the previous levels, incorporates the features of the levels lower than it. The addition that level A brings is that the design of the security system must undergo scrutiny. Qualified security individuals must analyze and approve the design. Additionally at this level, all the components that comprise the system must come from secured sources, and there must be a guarantee that there is no tampering with the components in distribution. A tape drive is carefully tracked from the factory floor through the distribution process to the computer room at the level A facility.

IP Spoofing and Sniffing

Sniffing and spoofing are security threats that target the lower layers of the networking infrastructure supporting applications that use the Internet. Users do not interact directly with these lower layers and are typically completely unaware that they exist. Without deliberate consideration of these threats, building effective security into the higher levels is impossible.

Sniffing *is a passive security attack in which a machine separate from the intended destination reads data on a network. The term "sniffing" comes from the notion of "sniffing the ether" in an Ethernet network and is a bad pun on the two meanings of the word "ether." Passive security attacks are those that do not alter the normal flow of data on a communication link or inject data into the link.*

Spoofing is an active security attack in which one machine on the network masquerades as a different machine. As an active attack, it disrupts the normal flow of data and may involve injecting data into the communications link between other machines. This masquerade aims to fool other machines on the network into accepting the impostor as an original, either to lure the other machines into sending it data or to allow it to alter data. The meaning of "spoof" here is not "a lighthearted parody," but rather "a deception intended to trick one into accepting as genuine something that is actually false." Such deception can have grave consequences because notions of trust are central to many networking systems. Sniffing may seem innocuous (depending on just how sensitive and confidential you consider the information on your network), some network security attacks use sniffing as a prelude to spoofing. Sniffing gathers sufficient information to make the deception believable.

Sniffing

Sniffing is the use of a network interface to receive data not intended for the machine in which the interface resides. A variety of types of machines need to have this capability. A token-ring bridge, for example, typically has two network interfaces that normally receive all packets traveling on the media on one interface and retransmit some, but not all, of these packets on the other interface. Another example of a device that incorporates sniffing is one typically marketed as a "network analyzer." A network analyzer helps network administrators diagnose a variety of obscure problems that may not be visible on any one particular host. These problems can involve unusual interactions between more than just one or two machines and sometimes involve a variety of protocols interacting in strange ways.

Devices that incorporate sniffing are useful and necessary. However, their very existence implies that a malicious person could use such a device or modify an existing machine to snoop on network traffic. Sniffing programs could be used to gather passwords, read inter-machine e-mail, and examine client-server database records in transit. Besides these high-level data, low-level information might be used to mount an active attack on data in another computer system.

Sniffing: How It Is Done

In a shared media network, such as Ethernet, all network interfaces on a network segment have access to all the data that travels on the media. Each network interface has a hardware-layer address that should differ from all hardware-layer addresses of all other network interfaces on the network. Each network also has at least one broadcast address that corresponds not to an individual network interface, but to the set of all network interfaces. Normally, a network interface only responds to a data frame carrying either its own hardware-layer address in the frame's destination field or the "broadcast address" in the destination field. It responds to these frames by generating a hardware interrupt to the CPU. This interrupt gets the attention of the operating system and passes the data in the frame to the operating system for further processing.

Note The term "broadcast address" is somewhat misleading. When the sender wants to get the attention of the operating systems of all hosts on the network, he or she uses the "broadcast address." Most network interfaces are capable of being put into a "promiscuous mode." In promiscuous mode, network interfaces generate a hardware interrupt to the CPU for every frame they encounter, not just the ones with their own address or the "broadcast address." The term "shared media" indicates to the reader that such networks broadcast all frames—the frames travel on all the physical media that make up the network.

At times, you may hear network administrators talk about their networking trouble spots—when they observe failures in a localized area. They will say a particular area the Ethernet is busier than other areas of the Ethernet where there are no problems. All the packets travel through all parts of the Ethernet segment. Interconnection devices that do not pass all the frames from one side of the device to the other form the boundaries of a segment. Bridges, switches, and routers divide segments from each other, but low-level devices that operate on one bit at a time, such as repeaters and hubs, do not divide segments from each other. If only low-level devices separate two parts of the network, both are part of a single segment. All frames traveling in one part of the segment also travel in the other part.

The broadcast nature of shared media networks affects network performance and reliability so greatly that networking professionals use a network analyzer, or sniffer, to troubleshoot problems. A sniffer puts a network interface in promiscuous mode so that the sniffer can monitor each data packet on the network segment. In the hands of an experienced system administrator, a sniffer is an invaluable aid in determining why a network is behaving (or misbehaving) the way it is. With an analyzer, you can determine how much of the traffic is due to which network protocols, which hosts are the source of most of the traffic, and which hosts are the destination of most of the traffic. You can also examine data traveling between a particular pair of hosts and categorize it by protocol and store it for later analysis offline. With a sufficiently powerful CPU, you can also do the analysis in real time.

Most commercial network sniffers are rather expensive, costing thousands of dollars. When you examine these closely, you notice that they are nothing more than a portable computer with an Ethernet card and some special software. The only item that differentiates a sniffer from an ordinary computer is software. It is also easy to download shareware and freeware sniffing software from the Internet or various bulletin board systems.

The ease of access to sniffing software is great for network administrators because this type of software helps them become better network troubleshooters. However, the availability of this software also means that malicious computer users with access to a network can capture all the data flowing through the network. The sniffer can capture all the data for a short period of time or selected portions of the data for a fairly long period of time. Eventually, the malicious user will run out of space to store the data.

Note   *Esniff.c* is a simple 300-line C language program that works on SunOS 4.x. When run by the root user on a Sun workstation, Esniff captures the first 300 bytes of each TCP/IP connection on the local network. It is quite effective at capturing all usernames and passwords entered by users for telnet, rlogin, and FTP.

TCPDump 3.0.2 is a common, more sophisticated, and more portable Unix sniffing program written by Van Jacobson, a famous developer of high-quality TCP/IP software. It uses the libpcap library for portably interfacing with promiscuous mode network interfaces. The most recent version is available via anonymous FTP to `ftp.ee.lbl.gov`.

NetMan contains a more sophisticated, portable Unix sniffer in several programs in its network management suite. The latest version of NetMan is available via anonymous FTP to `ftp.cs.curtin.edu.au` in the directory /pub/netman.

EthDump is a sniffer that runs under DOS and can be obtained via anonymous FTP from `ftp.eu.germany.net` in the directory /pub/networking/inet/ethernet/.

Warning   On some Unix systems, TCPDump comes bundled with the vendor OS. When run by an ordinary, unprivileged user, it does not put the network interface into promiscuous mode. With this command available, a user can only see data being sent to the Unix host, but is not limited to seeing data sent to processes owned by the user. Systems administrators concerned about sniffing should remove user execution privileges from this program.

Sniffing: How It Threatens Security

Sniffing data from the network leads to loss of privacy of several kinds of information that should be private for a computer network to be secure. These kinds of information include the following:

- Passwords

- Financial account numbers

- Private data

- Low-level protocol information

The following subsections are intended to provide examples of these kinds.

Sniffing Passwords

Perhaps the most common loss of computer privacy is the loss of passwords. Typical users type a password at least once a day. Data is often thought of as secure because access to it requires a password. Users usually are very careful about guarding their password by not sharing it with anyone and not writing it down anywhere.

Passwords are used not only to authenticate users for access to the files they keep in their private accounts but other passwords are often employed within multilevel secure database systems. When the user types any of these passwords, the system does not echo them to the computer screen to ensure that no one will see them. After jealously guarding these passwords and having the computer system reinforce the notion that they are private, a setup that sends each character in a password across the network is extremely easy for any Ethernet sniffer to see. End users do not realize just how easily these passwords can be found by someone using a simple and common piece of software.

Sniffing Financial Account Numbers

Most users are uneasy about sending financial account numbers, such as credit card numbers and checking account numbers, over the Internet. This apprehension may be partly because of the carelessness most retailers display when tearing up or returning carbons of credit card receipts. The privacy of each user's credit card numbers is important. Although the Internet is by no means bulletproof, the most likely location for the loss of privacy to occur is at the endpoints of the transmission. Presumably, businesses making electronic transactions are as fastidious about security as those that make paper transactions, so the highest risk probably comes from the same local network in which the users are typing passwords.

However, much larger potential losses exist for businesses that conduct electronic funds transfer or electronic document interchange over a computer network. These transactions involve the transmission of account numbers that a sniffer could pick up; the thief could then transfer funds into his or her own account or order goods paid for by a corporate account. Most credit card fraud of this kind involves only a few thousand dollars per incident.

Sniffing Private Data

Loss of privacy is also common in e-mail transactions. Many e-mail messages have been publicized without the permission of the sender or receiver. Remember the Iran-Contra affair in which President Reagan's secretary of defense, Caspar Weinberger, was convicted. A crucial piece of evidence was backup tapes of PROFS e-mail on a National Security Agency computer. The e-mail was not intercepted in transit, but in a typical networked system, it could have been. It is not at all uncommon for e-mail to contain confidential business information or personal information. Even routine memos can be embarrassing when they fall into the wrong hands.

Sniffing Low-Level Protocol Information

Information network protocols sent between computers includes hardware addresses of local network interfaces, the IP addresses of remote network interfaces, IP routing information, and sequence numbers assigned to bytes on a TCP connection. Knowledge of any of this information can be misused by someone interested in attacking the security of machines on the network. See the second part of this chapter for more information on how these data can pose risks for the security of a network. A sniffer can obtain any of these data. After an attacker has this kind of information, he or she is in a position to turn a passive attack into an active attack with even greater potential for damage.

Protocol Sniffing: A Case Study

At one point in time, all user access to computing facilities in the organization under study (the university at which the author is employed) was done via terminals. It was not practical to hardwire each terminal to the host, and users needed to use more than one host. To solve these two problems, Central Computing used a switch (an AT&T ISN switch) between the terminals and the hosts. The terminals connected to the switch so that the user had a choice of hosts. When the user chose a host the switch connected the terminal to the chosen host via a very real, physical connection. The switch had several thousand ports and was, in theory, capable of setting up connections between any pair of ports. In practice, however, some ports attached to terminals and other ports attached to hosts. Figure D.1 illustrates this setup.

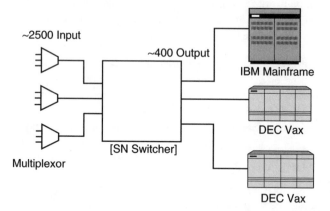

Figure D.1

Case study system before networking.

~2500 Input

~400 Output

IBM Mainframe

DEC Vax

Multiplexor   [SN Switcher]

DEC Vax

To make the system more flexible, the central computing facility was changed to a new system that uses a set of (DEC 550) Ethernet terminal servers with ports connected to the switch, rather than the old system, which used a fixed number of switch ports connected to each host. The new terminal servers are on an Ethernet segment shared by the hosts in the central machine room.

Offices have a cable running from a wallplate to a wiring closet punchdown block. The punchdown block has cables running to multiplexers which in turn connect to the switch. The multiplexers serve to decrease the number of cables that need to be long. With this arrangement sniffing or other forms of security problems are not an issue. No two offices share any media. The switch mediates all interaction between computers, isolating the flow of data away from the physical location of the end users (see fig. D.2).

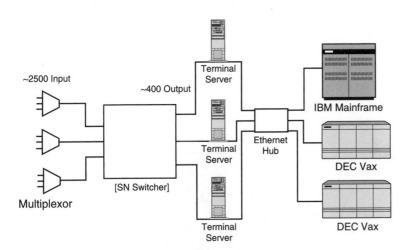

Figure D.2

Case study system after networking of machine room but before networking of user areas.

Rather than using simple terminals, however, most computer users have a computer on their desktop that they use in addition to the Central Computing computers. The switch services these computers as well as simple terminals. The number of computer users, however, has grown rapidly over the past decade and the switch is no longer adequate. Terminal ports are in short supply, host ports are in even shorter supply, and the switch does not supply particularly high-speed connections.

To phase out the switch, Central Computing installed an Ethernet hub in the basement of each building next to the punchdown block used to support both the switch multiplexer and the telephone lines. The hubs in the basements connect to the central facility using fiber-optic cables to prevent signal degradation over long distances. Hubs were also placed in the wiring closets on each floor of each building that connected to the basement hub. Now the cables leading to the wallplates in the offices are being moved from the punchdown block that leads to the multiplexer to a punchdown block that leads to one of these hubs. The new wiring scheme neatly parallels the old and was changed relatively inexpensively. Figure D.3 illustrates the system after the networking of user areas. Figure D.4 shows the user area networking detail.

Figure D.3

Case study system after networking of user areas.

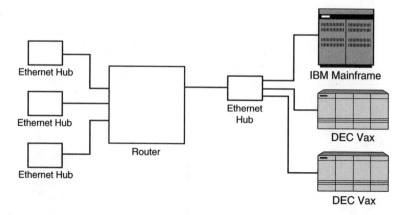

Figure D.4

Case study user area networking detail.

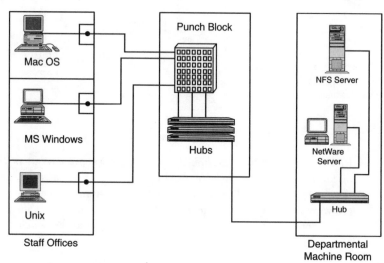

Although the new wiring scheme neatly parallels the old, the data traveling on the new wiring scheme does not neatly parallel its previous path. From a logical standpoint, it can get to the same places, but the data can and does go to many other places as well. Under this scheme, any office can sniff on all the data flowing to Central Computing from all of the other offices in the building. Different departments are located in the same building. These departments compete for resources allocated by upper management and are not above spying on one another. Ordinary staff, the managers that supervise them, and middle management all are located in the same building. A fair amount of potential exists for employees to want to know what other people are sending in e-mail messages, storing in personnel files, and storing in project planning files.

In addition to nosiness and competition, a variety of people sharing the same physical media in the new wiring scheme, could easily misuse the network. Since all occupants of a building share a single set of Ethernet hubs, they broadcast all of their network traffic to every network interface in the entire building. Any sensitive information that they transmit is no longer limited to a direct path between the user's machine and the final destination, anyone in the building can intercept the information with a sniffer. However, some careful planning of network installation or a redesign of an existing network should include security considerations (as well as performance issues) to avoid the risks inherent in shared media networking.

The network in the case study fails miserably in the prevention of sniffing. Any computer in a building is capable of sniffing the network traffic to or from any other computer in the building. The following section describes how to design a network that limits the sharing of media to prevent sniffing by untrustworthy machines.

Sniffing: How to Prevent It

To be able to prevent a sniffing attack, you first need to understand the network segments and trust between computer systems.

Network Segmentation

A *network segment* consists of a set of machines that share low-level devices and wiring and see the same set of data on their network interfaces. The wires on both sides of a repeater are clearly in the same network segment because a repeater simply copies bits from one wire to the other wire. An ordinary hub is essentially a multiport repeater; all the wires attached to it are part of the same segment.

In higher-level devices, such as bridges, something different happens. The wires on opposite sides of a bridge are not part of the same segment because the bridge filters out some of the packets flowing through it. The same data is not flowing on both sides of the bridge. Some packets flow through the bridge, but not all. The two segments are still part of the same physical network. Any device on one side of the bridge can still send packets to any device on the other side of the bridge. However, the exact same sets of data packets do not exist on both sides of the bridge. Just as bridges can be used to set up boundaries between segments, so can switches. Switches are essentially multiport bridges. Because they limit the flow of all data, a careful introduction of bridges and switches can be used to limit the flow of sensitive information and prevent sniffing on untrustworthy machines.

The introduction of switches and bridges into a network is traditionally motivated by factors other than security. They enhance performance by reducing the collision rate of segments, which is much higher without these components. Switches and bridges overcome the time delay problems that occur when wires are too long or when simple repeaters or hubs introduce additional time delay. As one is planning the network infrastructure one should keep these other factors in mind as well. One can use these factors to sell the introduction of additional hardware to parties less concerned with security.

A segment is a subset of machines on the same subnet. Routers are used to partition networks into subnets. Hence, they also form borders between segments in a network. Unlike bridges and switches, which do not interact with software on other devices, routers interact with network layer software on the devices in the network. Machines on different subnets are always part of different segments. Segments are divisions within subnets, although many subnets consist of a single segment in many networks. Dividing a network into subnets with routers is a more radical solution to the sniffing problem than dividing subnets into segments. However, as you will see in a later section, it may help with some spoofing problems.

Segmentation of a network is the primary tool one has in fighting sniffing. Ideally, each machine would be on its own segment and its interface would not have access to network data for which it is not the destination. This ideal can be accomplished by using switches instead of hubs to connect to individual machines in a 10BASE-T network. As a matter of practicality and economics, however, one must often find a less ideal solution. Such solutions all involve the notion of trust between machines. Machines that can trust each other can be on the same segment without worry of one machine sniffing at the other's data.

Understanding Trust

Typically, one thinks of trust at the application layer between file servers and clients. Clearly, the file server trusts its clients to authenticate users. However, this notion of trust extends to lower-level network devices as well. For example, at the network layer, routers are trusted to deliver datagrams and correct routing tables to the hosts on their networks. Hosts are trusting of routers and routers are trusted machines. If you extend the concept of trust down to the data link layer one gets to sniffing. A machine sending data considered private on a particular network segment must trust all machines on that network segment. To be worthy of that trust, the machines on the segment and the wiring between them must have sufficient physical security (locks on doors, armed guards, and such) to ensure that an attacker cannot install a sniffer on that segment.

The threat of sniffing comes from someone installing sniffing software on a machine normally on the network, someone taking a sniffer into a room and jacking it into the network connections available there, or even installing an unauthorized network connection to sniff. To counter these options, you must rely on the security of the operating system itself to prevent the execution of unauthorized sniffing, the personal trustworthiness of the people who have access to the rooms in which network components are located, and physical security to prevent untrustworthy people from gaining access to these rooms.

Hardware Barriers

To create trustworthy segments, you must set up barriers between secure segments and insecure segments. All of the machines on a segment must mutually trust each other with the data traveling on the segment. An example of such a segment would be a segment that does not extend outside the machine room of a computing facility. All machines are under the control of a cooperating and mutually trusting systems staff. The personal trust between staff members is mirrored by the mutual trust between the systems for which they are responsible.

The opposite of this is the belief and understanding that some segments simply must be considered insecure. Insecure segments need not be trusted if those segments carry only public or non-critical data. An example of such a segment is a university laboratory used only by students. No guarantee of absolute security is made for the information stored. Possibly the students realize that for this network drive only reasonable precautions will be taken to maintain privacy by enforcement of password protections, file system access lists, and regular backups.

It is less clear where to draw the line in a more professional business setting. The only basis for trust between machines is for trust between the people who control the machines. Even if a person can be trusted personally in an ethical sense, he or she may not be trustworthy technically to administer a machine in such a way that an attacker could not abuse the machine under his or her control.

Suppose a set of machines has a set of trust relationships as shown in figure D.5 (an arrow points from the trusting machine to the trusted machine). One needs to connect them to the network in such a way that two machines that do not trust each other are on the same segment and provide appropriate physical security to avoid tampering with a trusted machine. One such partitioning is shown in figure D.6 (the lines between segments indicate that the segments are connected by a device that limits data flow, such as a bridge).

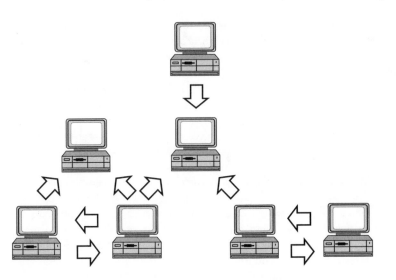

Figure D.5

A simple set of trust relationships between machines An arrow points from the trusting machine to the trusted machines.

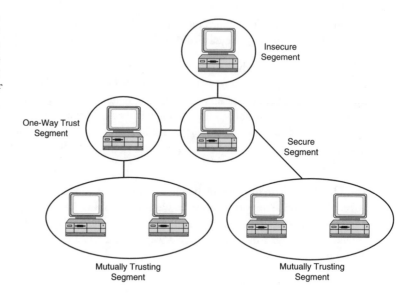

Figure D.6

A partitioning into network segments of the machines in figure D.5 that satisfies the lack of trust between machines.

Insecure Segment

One-Way Trust Segment

Secure Segment

Mutually Trusting Segment

Mutually Trusting Segment

Secure User Segments

Security is a relative thing. How secure you make a segment is related to how much control you take away from the technically untrustworthy end user who uses the network in a location with limited physical security.

In some settings, you may consider it appropriate to remove control of a machine from the end user because you cannot trust the end user from a technical standpoint. However, to actually remove control from the end user and prevent the end user machine from being used for sniffing, the machine on the end user's desk essentially becomes a terminal. This may seem disheartening, but keep in mind that terminals such as X Window System terminals provide the user with all the functionality of a workstation for running most Unix application software—they also have no moving parts and are virtually maintenance free.

If the end user cannot be trusted or if the software on a desktop machine could be altered by the authorized end user because of the machine's physical location, then the machine should not be a personal computer. For the purposes of this discussion, a personal computer is one that runs an operating system such as DOS, Windows 3.1, or Windows 95. These operating systems lack the notion of a privileged user in the sense that any user can run any program without interference from the operating system. Hence, any user can run a sniffer on such a system. PCs have always been popular because they can be customized by the end user. No system administrator can restrict what the end user can and cannot do with one of these machines. In highly secure settings, machines that use these operating systems are set up without local disks to prevent installation of unauthorized software such as a sniffer. Essentially, they become terminals that offload some of the work from the central, physically secure server.

A workstation running an operating system such as Windows NT, Unix, or VMS provides an extra degree of protection because these systems include privileged users, also known as superusers ("administrator" in NT, "root" in Unix, and "system" in VMS) who must know a special password. These operating systems only allow access to certain hardware level operations to superusers. If the end user has ordinary user access to the machine on his or her desk but does not have superuser privileges, then the machine can be trusted to a larger degree than the user. It is still possible to bring alternative boot media to most workstation-class operating systems and obtain superuser privileges without knowing the superuser password. The more secure systems, however, limit the user's ability to install software. Usually the only software that can be installed by the user is the operating system.

Segments with Mutually Trusting Machines

Some research at academic and industrial departments requires that the end user have complete access to the machine on the desktop. In these cases, a secure segment is probably out of the question unless the end users are impeccably ethical and technically competent to maintain system security on the machines they control (a machine administered by someone without security training is likely to be broken into by an attacker and used as a base of operations to attack other machines, including sniffing attacks). If you assume the end users are indeed competent to ensure the security of their own desktop system, all machines on the segment can be considered mutually trusting with respect to sniffing. That is, while any of the machines on the segment *could be* used as a sniffer, the users trust that they will not be based on the following:

- ■ The physical security of the machines

- ■ The technical competence of the other users to prevent outsiders from gaining control of one of the machines remotely

- ■ The personal integrity of the other users

It is possible to build a secure subnet or local area network out of a set of segments that each have mutually trusting machines. You must locate machines that are not mutually trusting on separate segments. Machines that need to communicate across segment boundaries should only do so with data that is not private. You can join mutually trusting segments by secure segments. Such an arrangement presumes that the end users trust the staff operating these central facilities. However, from a practical standpoint all but the most paranoid end users find this acceptable.

Connecting Segments of One-Way Trust

Consider, for example, the simple situation of two segments of mutual trust. Mutual trust exists between the machines on the first segment and mutual trust exists between the machines on the second segment. However, the machines in the first segment are communicating less sensitive information than those in the second segment. The machines in the first segment may trust those in the second segment but not vice versa. In this case, it is allowable for the data from the first segment to flow through the second segment. However, you must use a barrier such as a bridge to prevent the flow of data in the opposite direction.

One-way trust is fairly common between secure segments and other types of segments. The less secure machines must trust the more secure machines, but not vice versa. Similarly, one way trust may exist between a segment of mutual trust and an insecure segment. Connecting segments with one way trust via bridges and routers leads to a hierarchy of segments. Tree diagrams represent hierarchies graphically. In this case, the parent-child relationship in the tree associates the parent with a more secure segment and the child with a less secure segment. Thus, the more secure segments are closer to the root of the tree and less secure segments are closer to the leaves—insecure segments are leaves in the tree representing the one-way trust hierarchy.

Insecure Segments

In many cases, it is not practical to construct the segment boundaries between machines that are not mutually trusting. The reason for this is that such a setup isn't safe from sniffing. Insecure segments might be acceptable in areas where security requirements are also low. However, most users expect a higher level of security than any such setup could provide.

If you must use an insecure segment and still expect a higher degree of security, your only solution is software-based techniques rather than hardware-based techniques, such as encryption technology.

Case Study: A Small Department Subnet

A good case study of a network system at risk is in a university building. Computer Science shares two floors of the building with Mathematics and English. On the lower floor are several rooms with computers that are accessible by clients of Computer Science, offices for professional staff members in each of the three departments, and the Computer Science machine room. On the upper floor are offices for professional staff members of Computer Science and Mathematics and the office suites for the managers and secretarial staff of each.

The rooms in which clients access the network are not secure. Professional staff members in each department are mutually trusting of each other. They are not mutually trusting of all members of other departments. The two management suites cannot trust each other. They cannot trust the professional staff they supervise because they work with sensitive employee records dealing with performance reviews, salary recommendations, and compete for resources provided by higher levels of management.

In fact, the management suites are equipped with a higher level of physical security than the professional staff offices. These suites may be considered secure relative to the offices of the staff they supervise. The machines in each suite can be considered mutually trusting of other machines, because the personnel share sensitive information with each other anyway (see fig. D.7). Finally, the Computer Science machine room is secure.

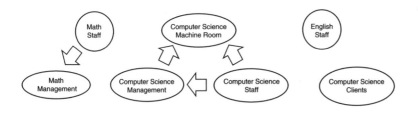

Figure D.7

Trust relationships between groups of machines in case study.

To satisfy the constraints of these trust relationships, the staff members of Computer Science, Mathematics, and English must each be placed on a separate segment. The Mathematics management suite must be placed on a separate segment. However, data to and from the Mathematics staff may flow through the Mathematics management suite without violating the trust constrains. In an exact parallel, the Computer Science management suite can have a segment with data flowing through it to and from the Computer Science staff segment. The machines used by Computer Science clients may transmit through staff and management segments. Notice the fact that we have a hierarchy of trust being in effect here. At the top end of the hierarchy is the Computer Science machine room, which must be on its own segment as well.

Now consider the wiring system available to service these two floors. The lower floor has a single communication closet that contains the connection to the central computing facility. The upper floor has a primary communication closet immediately above it connected by a conduit through the flooring. This primary communication closet on the upper floor is close to the Mathematics management suite. The primary closet connects, via a wiring conduit, to a secondary communication closet on the opposite side of the upper floor close to the Computer Science management suite.

If you do not consider security, you will design the network by looking purely at cost and performance. The minimum cost solution is simply to locate a set of hubs in each communications closet and connect all the hubs together to form a single segment. From a performance standpoint the management personnel do not want to have their network activity slowed by the activity of the staff they supervise or by people from a different department, so one can argue to segment the network on the basis of performance in a way that is close to what is needed for security purposes. If cost is not an issue, each of the proposed segments can simply be connected by a switch.

A realistic solution needs to do the following:

- Balance the issues of cost and performance

- Take into consideration the physical layout of the building

- Maintain security by not violating the trust constraints

Figure D.8 shows such a solution. Mathematics places all of its staff on a single segment by connecting hubs in the upper and lower floor communication closets. The Mathematics management suite has a segment that bears the burden of traffic from the staff segment. While Mathematics has a lower cost solution, Computer Science has a higher performance solution. Computer Science has five separate segments joined by a switch. Computer Science staff are placed on two separate segments, one for the upper floor and one for the lower floor, not to satisfy any security concern, but because separate hubs on each floor simplified the wiring and provide a low-cost opportunity to enhance performance. Computer Science, Mathematics, and English each have a separate subnet. These three subnets are joined into a single network by a router located in the communication closet on the lower floor.

The solution shown in figure D.8 provides for reasonable security against sniffing. Absolute security is not provided since it is still possible for anyone to hook up a sniffer on any of the segments. However, data from areas where more security is needed do not flow through areas where less security is needed. The areas where more security is needed have higher levels of physical security as well. Hence, it is increasingly difficult to physically get to a location where sensitive data is flowing on the wires. Also, except on the insecure Computer Science client segment, there is trust between the authorized users of the machines sharing a segment. Hence, an authorized user of a machine cannot use it to sniff data going to or from someone who does not trust the user.

Figure D.8

Wiring system to satisfy trust constraints and fit the building layout.

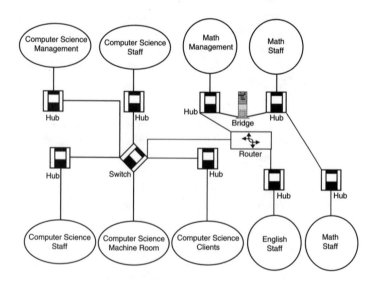

You can learn several things from looking at the case study and its solution:

- A minimum cost solution is not likely to provide for security.

- A totally secure system is prohibitively expensive, but a reasonably secure system is not.

- Different approaches to cost and performance trade-offs may be combined in a secure system. Mathematics and Computer Science have different budgets for equipment and needs for network performance.

- A single solution may provide both security and enhance performance as in the solution shown for Computer Science.

- A solution that provides for security adds significantly to cost. There is almost no cost difference between having a single segment for Mathematics and the solution shown. An extra wire run from the lower floor staff hub to the upper floor staff hub is one extra cost item as is the bridge separating the two segments.

Tip

> A simple hardware barrier that is inexpensive and has the potential for increasing network performance is the installation of a bridge between your machine room and the rest of your facility. In many cases, a great deal of traffic occurs between the computers in the machine room. A bridge placed between the machine room and the rest of the facility prevents this traffic from escaping to less secure areas and reduces the collision rate outside the machine room. Bridges are much less expensive than a router or a switch. In fact, a low-cost personal computer may be configured for this purpose with free software such as Drawbridge.

Drawbridge is a free software package that turns an ordinary PC with a pair of standard Ethernet interfaces into a bridge. Drawbridge is also capable of filtering operations and can act as a cheap alternative to a firewall in small networks. In some cases, you may be able to recycle a used PC considered obsolete for this purpose as the memory and disk requirements of Drawbridge are quite modest.

So far, this section has covered how to avoid sniffing of data from the local part of the Internet. Such an action seems directed toward protection against internal personnel rather than external threats. However, many security breaches are aided either knowingly or unknowingly by internal personnel. In such cases, the hardware barriers described in this section will limit what an intruder, physically present or remote, can do with a sniffer. Not only is physical security greater for the more trusted segments, but so is the technical competence of those in charge of the computer systems. The least technically competent to protect a system from remote intruders must be given systems that cannot be given commands from a remote location (such as a simple personal computer). Systems that can accept commands from remote locations must be administered by those technically competent enough to prevent remote intruders by not making mistakes that will allow remote intruders to gain access to the systems.

Avoiding Transmission of Passwords

In some sense, the prevention of sniffing by installing hardware barriers may be considered the last line of defense in a security system. When building medieval fortresses, the last line of defense was typically the most formidable but could only protect those who would be left inside after the outer defenses had been breached. In dealing with sniffing, the first line of defense is simply not to transmit anything sensitive on the network in the first place. The local hardware defenses may limit intrusion into the local systems. However, if authorized users may access those systems from remote locations, one must not transmit sensitive information over remote parts of the Internet lest the information be sniffed somewhere along the way. One extreme that preserves security is simply not to permit access from remote locations. Also, the most formidable defenses against inward directed attack do nothing to provide for the security of one leaving the area being protected. Legitimate Internet sessions initiated inside a network with those outside must also be protected.

The most glaring security hole beyond simple loss of privacy is the opportunity for a sniffer to gather passwords. The best way to deal with this problem is simply not to transmit cleartext passwords across the network. Simply transmitting an encrypted password that could be captured and replayed by a sniffer is also not acceptable. Several different methods are in use to provide this kind of protection:

- The rlogin family of protocols

- Using encrypted passwords

- Zero knowledge authentication

The rlogin Family of Protocols

The *rlogin protocol*, originally used with Unix-to-Unix terminal sessions, uses end-to-end mutual trust to avoid the transmission of any form of password. The protocol requires that the server trust the client to authenticate the user. The user places a file on the server indicating what combinations of username and hostname may connect to a particular account on machines using the server. The user may connect from these without presenting any further credentials such as a password.

This file is called the *rhosts* file. For the original Unix server, the filename had to be preceded with a dot, ".rhosts," but on non-Unix systems using this protocol, the file may have to have a different name to satisfy the constraints imposed for filenames or different mechanisms used to store the information about what users are accepted on what trusted systems. The user must trust that the server is sufficiently secure, that no one else can alter the rhosts file and that no one else can read the rhosts file. The requirement that the rhosts file not be altered is obvious—if someone modified the rhosts file, he or she could connect to the account via the rlogin protocol without the permission of the legitimate user. The requirement that no one else can read the rhosts file is a bit more obscure, but learned from painful experience. If an attacker gains access to another account on the machine hosting the rlogin server, the attacker can read the rhosts file of a user and target the user for an indirect attack. In an indirect attack, the attacker attempts to gain access to an account listed in the rhosts file on another machine and use it to obtain access to the machine hosting the rlogin server.

Another file used by some servers for the rlogin protocol is called the *host equivalence* file, which is named "/etc/hosts.equiv" in the original Unix implementation. Any user of any host listed in the host equivalence file may access an account with the same username on the machine on which the host equivalence file exists without presenting a password. The use of a host equivalence file adds convenience for the user by relieving individual users from the need to create their own rhosts file. However, it opens up users to the risks of ARP spoofing and name server spoofing (both covered later in this chapter) without the implicit consent they give to that risk when creating their own rhosts file. System administrators are strongly urged not to use a host equivalence file because of those risks. Users without the network savvy to create an rhosts file are being put at risk from a threat they have no possibility of understanding.

Note The rlogin protocol is used by a whole family of programs that use the same authentication protocol. The family is collectively referred to as the *r-commands*. The family includes *rlogin* for terminal sessions, *rsh* for remote shell execution of command-line programs, and *rcp* for remote file copying. rcp is preferred over FTP for its security and ease of use. It is secure because it does not require the transmission of a password and it is easier to use because it can transfer multiple files specified with the same syntax as the local file copying command.

The rlogin protocol remains vulnerable to ARP spoofing and DNS spoofing (discussed later in this chapter). It also does not completely protect a user who uses machines that he or she does not control. For example, when you start an rlogin terminal session from a client's or colleague's office, the client's or colleague's machine is not listed in your rhosts. In these cases, you must remember my password and have it transmitted across the network in plain sight of any sniffers that may be out there.

Note The r-commands are not limited to Unix. DEC VMS has a variety of TCP/IP software available for it including both clients and servers for many of the programs in this family. Many TCP/IP software packages for the PC offer r-command clients. There is a networking suite for Windows NT that provides an rlogin server, enabling you to have access to the command line from a remote location without being logged into it locally. There are many freeware packages that provide a similar server for any PC with winsock.dll.

Problems with rlogin

As mentioned earlier, on a machine with any server for programs in the rlogin protocol family it is critical that only the user can modify his or her rhosts file. If it is possible for someone else to modify it then the ability to modify it can be leveraged into the ability to obtain full access to the account. Note that if your home directory is on an NFS mounted file system exported to someone else's machine your rhosts file is vulnerable to simple attacks on NFS. A standard attack for the superuser of another machine is to give you an account on the other machine and then use the su command to gain access to your account on the other machine. The NFS server is fooled into believing you are accessing your files because it trusts the other machine to authenticate its users. So far, the attacker is limited to accessing your files, but when he alters your rhosts file the attacker can begin to run programs that execute with your privileges and do greater harm.

If an attacker is able to modify the superuser rlogin file or gain access to any account listed in it, such access can be leveraged into a very serious attack. In particular, an attacker can use rsh to subvert the requirement that Unix superuser logins occur from secure terminals. Unlike rlogin or telnet, rsh does not require a pseudo-tty. If protection of your superuser login account involves restricting insecure terminals, you may want to disable or alter the rsh program.

Do not confuse the rexec commands (rexec and rcmd) with the r-commands. The rexec daemon waits for a username and cleartext password to authenticate a client. It will then execute a single shell command. Although this is similar to rsh, rexec requires the transmission of a cleartext password to be sniffed. Also, it provides two distinct error conditions, one for an invalid username and one for an invalid password. Hence, a brute-force attack can be mounted by attempting all possible usernames to both determine what usernames are valid and which users have no password. A standard login program will not provide this distinction and provide a mechanism to prevent rapid-fire attempts to log in. Security conscious system administrators often disable the rexec daemon and rexec commands are so seldom known about by users as not to be missed.

Using Encrypted Passwords

Another solution is to use encrypted passwords over the network. You must use caution, however, when simplifying this technique. Even with encryption, a sniffer can still record the encrypted password and decipher the encrypted password at his or her leisure. One way around this is to use an encryption key that involves the current time. If the sender and receiver are closely synchronized, the sniffer must replay the encrypted password within one tick of the two machines' shared clock. If the sender and receiver are widely separated, however, this technique becomes less practical and effective because shared clocks will lack sufficient time resolution to prevent an attacker from using a quick replay. One way around this lack of close synchronization is to set a limited number of attempts at typing the password correctly.

It also does not suffice to simply encrypt the password with an algorithm using a key that allows an attacker to determine the encryption key. The attacker would decrypt it for repeated use at a later time. Some protocols use an encryption technique equivalent to the one used by the Unix password program when it stores passwords in the password file. This encryption technique is no longer considered particularly secure against brute force cryptographic attacks where all likely passwords are encrypted with the same algorithm used by the password file. Any two words that encrypt the same must be the same. Hence, poorly chosen (for example, dictionary words) or short passwords are particularly easy to crack by brute force.

What is required is the use of public key cryptography such as PGP. In public key cryptography (also called asymmetric cryptography), you use separate keys for encryption and decryption—the decryption key is not computable from the encryption key. The server can send the client its public key and the client can use that key to encrypt the user password. The server then decrypts the password to verify the authenticity of the user. This is a variation on the classic public key system in which a trustworthy third party holds the public keys, but it simplifies the case when no mutually trusted third party is available. It also allows the server to use a time-dependent public key to prevent password replay or brute force decryption of a relatively short password.

Note SRA from Texas A&M provides telnet and FTP without cleartext password exchange. It uses Secure RPC (Remote Procedure Call) authentication. Secure RPC is part of the Sun RPC package distributed along with Secure NFS by many vendors and is quite common on Unix systems. Secure RPC uses public key cryptography using the patented Diffy-Hellman algorithm. SRA uses a new random secret key/public key pair for each connection eliminating the need for a separate keyserver.

SRA can be obtained by anonymous ftp to `coast.cs.purdue.edu` in the directory `/pub/tools/unix/TAMU`.

The use of Kerberos also prevents cleartext passwords from being sent across the network. Kerberos is a comprehensive authentication system using a sophisticated time varying encryption algorithm and requires that both systems at the ends of a communication connection trust a separate security server to negotiate the authentication. This avoids having servers trust clients to do the authentication, as the rlogin protocol must do.

Zero-Knowledge Authentication

Another mechanism for secure authentication without passwords is zero-knowledge proofs. Networks that use this system have a client and a server that share what is in essence a very long sequence of digits. When the client connects to the server, the server queries the client about a set of digits in a small set of positions in the sequence. Because the number of digits in the sequence is very long, knowledge of a few digits by a sniffer is not sufficient. The server will query for a different set of positions each time the client connects.

This type of authentication is growing in popularity. You store the digit sequence held by the client on a credit card sized device or even in a ring worn by the user. No computer needs to be carried by a mobile user of this technique; only a few kilobytes of data storage.

RFC 1704 and RFC 1750 provide a good background in the principles of authentication and the current state of encryption technology for the Internet.

DESlogin 1.3 uses a challenge / response technique in conjunction with DES encryption for authentication. The latest version is available via anonymous FTP from `ftp.uu.net/pub/security/des`.

S/KEY from Bellcore uses the response / challenge technique as well. S/Key is available via anonymous FTP to `thumper.bellcore.com` in the /pub/nmh directory. S/Key has support for a variety of platforms, including Unix, Macintosh, and Windows, to generate the onetime password used as a response to a challenge. It also includes a replacement for /bin/login and the FTP daemon on the Unix host.

RFC 1760 describes the system in technical detail.

Employing Encryption for Entire Connection/Session

Public key cryptography can manage the authentication process to prevent password sniffing but is not practical for entire terminal sessions or TCP/IP connections. Public key cryptography is sometimes called asymmetric because different keys are used for encryption and decryption with no practical way to compute one key from the other key. Classical, symmetric techniques are much more computationally simple and practical for entire sessions. Just as public key cryptography can be used to authenticate a user, it can also be used to solve the key distribution problem of a symmetric encryption technique. Each sender receives the key electronically with the key encrypted by a public key technique. Thus, the key cannot be sniffed and used to decrypt the rest of the session.

One such mechanism employing the RSA public key encryption algorithm is the secure socket layer (SSL) that is being promoted for use with the Web. Because the entire contents of a TCP connection are encrypted, you can send credit card numbers over the Internet without worrying that someone will intercept them at one of the many routers between the user's Web browser and the merchant's Web site. You can use SSL as a layer on top of TCP for any server that might otherwise use raw TCP.

To take advantage of session encryption on the Web, you must have compatible encryption techniques being used on both the browser and the Web server. Typically, encryption is only used for transmission of sensitive information such as passwords and credit card information, not routine HTML and image files. Any vendor doing business on the Web should be quite clear about what encryption techniques the server supports and give a list of some of the browsers that support it so that a user will know in advance if the information being sent is protected by encryption. Conversely, a good browser should indicate if a response to a form on the Web is not going to be encrypted so that vendors who do not provide a compatible encryption technique do not endanger their customers.

Spoofing

Spoofing can occur at all layers of the IP system. The hardware layer, the data link layer, the IP layer, the transport layer, and the application layer are susceptible. All application layer protocols are at risk if the lower layers have been compromised. In this chapter, only the application layer protocols intimately linked to the IP protocol are discussed. This includes routing protocols and the DNS naming protocol. Other application layer protocols depend on these two protocols to provide basic services to almost all applications using the Internet.

Hardware Address Spoofing

At the hardware layer, any network interface for a shared-media network will have a hardware interface address. As you read earlier in the discussion on sniffing, most network interfaces can be put into promiscuous mode and receive frames with any destination address. A much more serious problem occurs if the network interface can alter the source address and send data that appears to come from various source addresses. In the IEEE 802 standards for networking (of which Ethernet is a variant), each network interface has a 48-bit hardware address. It uses this hardware address to match the variety of destination addresses of the frames it sees. The interface copies frames with matching destination addresses into its internal buffer and notifies the operating system that they are available for further processing. Packets coming from the operating system to the interface do not typically specify a source address; the interface always puts its hardware address in the source field.

Most software does not typically control the source field of frames leaving an Ethernet interface. When another host examines a packet containing a hardware source address associated with an interface of a particular machine, it assumes that the packet originated on that machine and accepts it as authentic. An IEEE standards committee assigns each network interface manufacturer a unique 24-bit prefix for the 48-bit hardware address; the manufacturer assigns a unique 24-bit suffix to each interface it makes. Regardless, many interface cards are configurable and allow host software to specify a source address other than the one assigned by the manufacturer. This configurability makes it possible to use them to spoof the source address.

DECNet, for example, uses 16-bit identifiers and requires that the leading 32 bits of the hardware address be set to a fixed value to indicate that the packet is a DECNet packet. Any network interface that is compatible with DECNet can have its hardware source address altered in some way, either by software or switches on the interface board.

To see how common it is for a network interface to be able to spoof the source address, however, recall how a bridge works. A bridge not only puts its interfaces into promiscuous mode, but it also sets the hardware source address of packets sent out on its interfaces to match the hardware source address of the originating interface. A PC with two software configurable interfaces can be configured to be used as a bridge. Clearly, such software configurability has a variety of malicious uses. The drawbridge software mentioned in the previous section on hardware barriers to prevent sniffing is compatible with most Ethernet boards which means most Ethernet boards will permit source address spoofing.

As you can see, it is not entirely safe to base the authenticity of a packet on the hardware source address. Unfortunately, there is very little you can do to protect yourself against such deviousness. One solution is to use digital signatures at the application layer. Unfortunately, currently there are no protections in the IP network layer that will prevent a hardware address spoofer from disguising one machine as another. If the victim machine is trusted (for example, is allowed to NFS mount filesystems from another machine), the spoofer will be able to take advantage of that trust and violate security without being detected. Fortunately, hardware address spoofing is difficult (relative to many other spoofing methods) and requires penetration of physical security.

Countering hardware level spoofing is difficult because it is virtually undetectable without tracing the physical wiring. You need to trace the wiring to be certain no one has connected an unauthorized machine and you also need to check to see if the authorized machines are using the hardware address they should. The latter can be checked using sufficiently "intelligent" hubs in secure locations.

All machines not in physically secure locations can be connected to hubs in secure locations. Some "intelligent" hubs can be configured to accept or send packets or both to or from specific hardware addresses on each port they service. Thus, you can configure the hub to accept only packets with hardware addresses matching the manufacturer-assigned hardware address of the interface on the authorized machine. This interface should be connected to the wall plate on the far side of the wires connected to that port. Clearly, you are still relying on physical security to be sure that the hub, wires, and authorized machine remain as they should.

Note   Devices that perform hardware address verifications cannot be categorized as "hubs" in the traditional sense and are probably actually specialized switches or bridges. However, they are marketed as "active hubs" or "filtering hubs." Such hubs are available from 3Com, HP, and IBM.

ARP Spoofing

A more common form of spoofing that is accidental is ARP spoofing. ARP (Address Resolution Protocol) is part of Ethernet and some other similar protocols (such as token-ring) that associate hardware addresses with IP addresses. ARP is not part of IP but part of these Ethernet-like protocols; ARP supports IP and arbitrary network-layer protocols. When an IP datagram is ready to go out on such a network, the host needs to know the hardware destination address to associate with the given IP destination address. For local IP destinations, the hardware address to use will be the hardware address of the destination interface. For non-local destinations, the hardware address to use will be the hardware address of one of the routers on the local network.

How ARP and ARP Spoofing Work

To find the hardware address, the host sends out an ARP request using the hardware broadcast address. A frame with the hardware broadcast address reaches every network interface on the local network, and each host on the local network has its operating system interrupted by the network interface. The ARP request is essentially asking the question, "What is the hardware address corresponding to the IP address I have here?" Typically, only the host with the matching IP address sends an ARP reply and the remaining hosts ignore the ARP request. The ARP request contains the IP address of the sender of the request and reaches all hosts via a broadcast.

Other hosts could potentially store the association between hardware address and IP address of the sender of the request for future reference. The target of the request certainly would store the association. It will almost certainly send an IP datagram in reply to the IP datagram it is about to receive. The reply will require knowing the association between the IP address and the hardware address of the sender of the ARP broadcast.

The association between the hardware address and the IP address of other machines on a network is stored in an ARP cache on each host. When an IP datagram is about to leave a host, the host consults the ARP cache to find the destination hardware address. If the host finds an entry for the IP destination address, it need not make an ARP request. The entries in an ARP cache expire after a few minutes.

Thus, when the ARP cache entry for a machine expires, an ARP request goes out to refresh the entry. No reply comes back if the target machine goes down. The entries for its interface's hardware will disappear from the ARP caches in the other machines on the network. The other machines will be unable to send out IP datagrams to the downed system after the ARP cache entries expire. Before that point in time, IP datagrams are sent out but are not received. When the machine comes back up, it will again be able to reply to ARP requests. If someone replaces its interface, the now up and running machine will have a new hardware address and will use that new hardware address in ARP replies. ARP caches throughout the network will reflect the change, and IP datagrams go out using the new hardware address.

Because you expect the IP address to hardware address association will change over time, the potential exists that the change may be legitimate. Sometimes it is purely accidental. Someone may inadvertently assign a machine the same IP address held by another machine. On personal computers or special purpose devices such as network printers or X Window System terminals, the end user typically has access to a dialog box, command, or text file that sets the IP address.

On multiuser systems, the system administrator is typically the only one who can set the IP addresses of the network interface(s). This arrangement is changing, however, as more inexperienced IP-based end users with PCs set addresses. In addition, bureaucracies often separate system administrators and network administrators that use the same network. Under such circumstances it is common for two machines to end up with the same IP address. Duplication can occur either by copying the network configuration from one personal computer to another without the end user knowing the need for IP addresses to be unique. Duplication can also occur if system administrators on a network do not work together when configuring system addressing.

When two machines end up with the same IP address, both of them will naturally reply to an ARP request for that address. Two replies to the request come back to the host that originated the request. These replies will arrive in rapid succession, typically separated by at most a few milliseconds. Some operating systems will not realize anything is wrong and simply file each reply in the ARP cache with the slowest response remaining in the ARP cache until the entry for that IP address expires. Other operating systems will discard ARP replies that correspond to IP addresses already in the cache. These may or may not bother to check if the second reply was a harmless duplicate or an indication an ARP spoof may be underway.

Thus, depending on the mechanism used to process duplicate ARP replies, if a spoofer wants to be the target of the IP datagrams being sent to a particular IP address from a particular host, it needs to make sure it is either the first or the last to reply to ARP requests made by that particular host. An easy way to be first or last is to have the *only* machine that replies to the ARP requests. An attacker can simply use a machine assigned, via the normal operating system configuration mechanisms, the same IP address as a machine that is currently not working. An attacker attempting to masquerade his or her machine can simply turn the legitimate machine off. The attacker does not need to have direct access to the power switch on the machine. The machine can be turned off either by unplugging it or flipping the appropriate circuit breaker.

An alternative to disconnecting its power is to disconnect it from the network at some point in the network wiring scheme. Third, the attacker can change the legitimate machine's IP address and leave it turned on if he or she can reconfigure the machine. Doing so is less likely to draw attention or result in confusion from the machine's user or administrator.

A Case Study: Inadvertent ARP Spoofing

At a Department of Computer Services in a midwestern university, a room is set aside for making presentations to groups of clients. The room is equipped with a Unix workstation and a $15,000 ceiling-mounted video projector projecting onto a $2,000 eight-foot diameter screen. One day, the workstation needed to be replaced with a newer model. The new workstation came in and was being configured to match to the configuration of the workstation in the presentation room. One of the first questions asked during the operating system installation process was the IP address. The technician in charge of configuring the new workstation looked up the IP address of the workstation in the presentation room and entered it into the dialog box.

After a short time, the new workstation was up and running. The systems staff wanted to be sure it was working correctly because it was difficult to fix after it was installed in the presentation room. The new workstation was turned off that night after testing the shutdown procedure to be used by the presenters.

The next morning a presentation started in the presentation room with the old workstation. All was going well until the systems staff decided to resume testing of the new workstation. Shortly after the new workstation booted, the presentation came to a complete halt. The person in charge of the presentation was using the X Window System to demonstrate a program running on a better computer. The workstation in the presentation room had established a TCP/IP connection with the better machine and the presenter was creating the illusion that the program was running on the old workstation.

What had happened was the better computer had created an ARP cache entry for the old workstation when the presenter started the TCP/IP connection. As the presentation progressed, the ongoing IP datagrams from the better computer to the old workstation used the cache entry created at the beginning of the presentation. Several minutes into the presentation the ARP cache entry expired and a new ARP request went out from the better computer. The first time the ARP cache entry expired, the old workstation replied appropriately. The next time the ARP cache expired, however, the new workstation had been started. Both the old and new workstations replied to the computer running the demonstration software. The new workstation's hardware address ended up in its ARP cache and the new workstation began receiving the IP datagrams sent to the IP address the old and new workstations shared. The new workstation did not know what to do with these datagrams and promptly sent a TCP/IP reset message in reply, resulting in the shutdown of the demonstration program. From initial appearances, the demonstration program just stopped and the old workstation appeared to have been cut off from the network.

Needless to say, the presenter was upset. When the system administrator figured out what had gone wrong, the technician who used the IP address of an existing machine learned a valuable lesson: two machines with the same IP address cannot be connected to the network at the same time.

A Case Study: Malicious ARP Spoofing

A university where Computer Science allows its clients (students) temporary access to its computers was mentioned earlier. Some Unix workstations using NFS mount a mission-critical filesystem. One of these clients has a laptop running Unix. He already knows the IP address of the workstations that NFS mount the mission-critical filesystems. This particular user has created a copy of the workstation password file on his laptop and has superuser privileges on his own laptop, which runs Unix with NFS.

One day he is left alone in the room with one of our workstations. He shuts down the workstation and jacks his laptop into our network. After a few minutes the file server's ARP cache entry for the workstation expires. Then, he launches an attack by telling his workstation to NFS mount our mission-critical filesystem. The mount daemon on the file server checks the IP address of the machine making this request against the list of authorized IP addresses and finds a match. It then proceeds to send information needed to access the NFS daemon back to the IP address that just made the mount request.

When the mount daemon sends the reply back, the low-level software connecting IP to Ethernet discovers that it does not have an ARP cache entry for this IP address. It puts the reply on hold and makes an ARP broadcast to determine the hardware address to which to send the reply. The attacker's laptop is the only machine to respond. The low-level software takes the response, caches it, and uses it to take the reply out of the holding bin and send it out the Ethernet interface. The attacker succeeds in accessing the mission-critical filesystem as if he were a legitimate user of the workstation that he just turned off.

Preventing an ARP Spoof

It is not particularly satisfying to simply detect ARP spoofing, which only identifies a problem after it has already occurred. Although it may not be possible to prevent ARP spoofing entirely, one simple precaution can be taken where it may count the most. The devious thing about an

ARP spoof is that the attack is really directed at the machine being deceived, not the machine whose IP address is being taken over. Presumably, the machine or machines being deceived contain data that the ARP spoofer wants to get or modify.

The deception is useful to the ARP spoofer because the legitimate holder of the IP address is trusted in some way by the machine being deceived. Perhaps the trusted machine is allowed to NFS mount filesystems, use rlogin, or start a remote shell without being prompted for a password (particularly troublesome for privileged user accounts). Ideally, machines extending such trust should simply not use ARP to identify the hardware addresses of the machines they trust.

Stop Using ARP

Machines extending trust to other machines on the local network based on an IP address should not use ARP to obtain the hardware address of the trusted machines. Instead, the hardware address of the trusted machines should be loaded as permanent entries into the ARP cache of the trusting machine. Unlike normal ARP cache entries, permanent entries do not expire after a few minutes. Sending a datagram to an IP address associated with a permanent ARP cache entry will never result in an ARP request. With no ARP request being sent, an attacker does not have the opportunity to send an ARP reply. It seems unlikely that any operating system would overwrite a permanent ARP cache entry with an unsolicited ARP reply.

With permanent ARP cache entries for trusted machines, the trusting host will not use ARP to determine the correct hardware address and will not be fooled into sending IP data to an ARP spoofer. Of course, it will also send IP data to the machine even if the machine has been down for some time. Another downside to permanent ARP entries is that the cache entries will need revising if the hardware address changes for a legitimate reason. Finally, ARP caches may be of limited size, limiting the number of permanent entries or further limiting the time a dynamic entry spends in the cache.

Displaying ARP Cache Entries

On Unix and Windows 95/NT machines, you use the arp command to manipulate and inspect the ARP cache. This command has several options.

```
arp -a
```

The -a option displays all ARP cache entries for all interfaces of the host. The following output is an example of what you would see on a Windows 95 machine:

```
Interface: 147.226.112.167
Internet Address      Physical Address      Type
147.226.112.1         aa-00-04-00-bc-06     static
147.226.112.88        08-00-20-0b-f0-8d     dynamic
147.226.112.101       08-00-2b-18-93-68     static
147.226.112.102       08-00-2b-1b-d7-fd     static
```

```
147.226.112.103      00-00-c0-63-33-2d      dynamic
147.226.112.104      00-00-c0-d5-da-47      dynamic
147.226.112.105      08-00-20-0b-7b-df      dynamic
147.226.112.106      08-00-20-0e-86-ef      dynamic
147.226.112.124      08-00-2b-1c-08-68      dynamic
147.226.112.169      08-00-09-2a-3c-08      dynamic
```

Deleting an ARP Cache Entry

At some point you may want to delete a permanent ARP cache entry that is no longer valid or delete a dynamic entry that you suspect of being spoofed. The -d option deletes the entry with the given IP address from the ARP cache.

```
arp -d 147.226.112.101
```

Inserting a Permanent ARP Cache Entry

The -s option inserts a permanent (static) ARP cache entry for the given IP address. Typically, the Ethernet address would be obtained by displaying the entire ARP cache as shown previously.

```
arp -s 147.226.112.101 08-00-2b-18-93-68
```

To ensure that the address is in the ARP cache you can first use the ping command to send an ICMP/IP echo request to the IP address in question. A somewhat more secure, but tedious, method is to use an operating system dependent method for querying the machine in question for its own hardware address from its console. You can place a series of such commands into the startup script for the machine that will be extending trust to others.

Inserting Many Permanent ARP Cache Entries

The -f option loads permanent entries into the ARP cache from a file containing an IP address to hardware address database.

```
arp -f arptab
```

In this example, the file is named "arptab," but the name of the file is up to the system administrator using the command. The -f option to the arp command is not available on all systems. In particular, it is missing from the current versions of Windows 95 and Windows NT. However, it is really just a substitute for a series of arp commands with the -s option.

Use an ARP Server

The arp command outlined in the previous section also allows one machine to be an ARP server. An ARP server responds to ARP requests on behalf of another machine by consulting (permanent) entries in its own ARP cache. You can manually configure this ARP cache and configure machines that extend trust based on this IP address to use ARP replies coming from the ARP server rather than ARP replies from other sources. However, configuring a machine to believe only in the ARP server is a difficult task for most operating systems.

Even if you do not configure other machines to trust only the ARP server for ARP replies, the type of server may still be beneficial. The ARP server will send out a reply to the same requests as a potential ARP spoofer. When machines process the ARP replies, there is at least a fair chance that the ARP spoofer's replies will be ignored. You cannot be sure because as you have seen, much depends on the exact timing of the replies and the algorithms used to manage the ARP cache.

Introduce Hardware Barriers

The use of bridges or switches removes the threat of sniffing between network segments; likewise, the use of routers removes the threat of ARP spoofing between IP subnets. You can separate the trusted hosts (those with IP addresses that might benefit an attacker using ARP spoofing) from subnets on which an attacker might obtain access. Subnetting for security is helpful if physical security prevents attachment to the subnet of the trusted machine. Such subnetting prevents a spoofer from powering down one of the trusted machines and attaching to the subnet on which ARP requests from the trusting machine are broadcast.

A temptation when considering using subnetting to protect from ARP spoofing is to place the machine extending trust on a separate subnet from the machines to which it is extending trust. However, this setup simply places the router in the position of being deceived by an ARP spoof. If trust is extended on the basis of IP addresses, the machine extending the trust is in turn trusting the routers to deliver the IP datagrams to the correct machine. If the trusted machines are on a separate subnet that is susceptible to ARP spoofing, the router for that subnet must bear the burden of ensuring that IP datagrams get to their legitimate destination. With this setup, you might need to place permanent ARP cache entries for the trusted machines in the router itself.

Finally, it is also important that trusted machines be protected from an ARP spoofer that is attempting to masquerade as the router. Fortunately, routers are typically physically secure and crash rarely or for very little time, which makes them difficult to impersonate.

Sniffing Case Study Revisited

To illustrate ARP spoofing in a familiar context, recall the solution to the sniffing problem adopted by Computer Science in the case study earlier in the chapter (see fig. D.7). The solution to the sniffing problem was to divide the portion of the network servicing Computer Science into five segments. These segments connect to a switch in the Computer Science machine room. The only router being used is the router that joins Computer Science with the two segment subnet for Mathematics and the one segment subnet for English. All five segments in Computer Science are part of a single subnet.

Within a single subnet an ARP request goes out to all machines on the subnet and a reply may come back from any of them. Thus, an ARP spoof attack may be launched from any of the segments. To prevent this, the segments may be divided into a group of subnets rather than a single larger subnet.

The analysis of the situation for the ARP spoofing problem is analogous to that for the sniffing problem. The trust that a machine will not sniff is replaced by the trust that a machine will not ARP spoof. The hardware barrier used to control ARP spoofing is a router to induce subnetting rather than a bridge or a switch to induce segmenting.

The simple solution to the ARP spoofing problem for Computer Science is to simply place each segment on its own single-segment subnet by replacing the switch with a router. However, the two staff segments that were kept separate for reasons other than satisfying the trust constraints may share a subnet.

One major benefit to this solution is the ease in which routers can perform media conversion. The subnet for the machine room can use high-speed network media such as Fast Ethernet, FDDI, or HyperChannel. The client and staff subnets can use lower speed network media such as 10 Mbps Ethernet or 4 Mbps token ring.

Problems arise, however, with respect to routing protocols. If the Central Computing router controls the router in the communication closet and does not trust the Computer Science router, they cannot exchange routing information. The Central Computing router will refuse to accept the routes advertised by the Computer Science router, cutting off a way for remote machines to send datagrams to machines on subnets not directly attached to the Central Computing router. Machines on the Computer Science subnets not directly connected to the Central Computing router will be forced to interact with the central computing facility by using the hosts in the Computer Science as intermediaries. Such a use of intermediaries is known as a "proxy" arrangement.

A proxy arrangement is actually an attractive setup from a security standpoint, but can be quite awkward for end users. A simple proxy Web server in the Computer Science machine room will reduce this awkwardness. Another, more sophisticated proxy arrangement would be to give IP addresses to Computer Science machines that make them appear to be on the same subnet from the perspective of the Central Computing router. The Central Computing router will make ARP requests to determine where to send the datagrams it is forwarding to a Computer Science segment it is not connected to. The Computer Science router can perform a "proxy ARP" and reply with its own hardware address. The datagrams will be delivered to the Computer Science router for forwarding, while the Central Computing router is led to believe it delivered the datagram to its destination. In essence, the Computer Science router is performing a beneficial ARP spoof: it benefits the machines on the Computer Science subnets, and it spoofs the Central Computing router.

Detecting an ARP Spoof

Unless you have the capability to introduce the kind of hardware barriers described previously, preventing an ARP spoof is probably not practical. The best you can usually hope for is rapid detection followed by some form of intervention. When an anomaly is detected in the ARP protocol it may be legitimate, accidental, or a security breach. Policies and procedures should be in place to handle each type of incident. This chapter limits its discussion to mechanisms; it is up to the reader to decide what policies and procedures to implement after detection of a potentially serious problem takes place.

Several mechanisms exist for detecting an ARP spoof. At the host level, an ordinary host may attempt to detect another machine using its own IP address either by passively examining network broadcasts or by actively probing for such a machine. At the server level, a machine providing a supposedly secure service to the network—perhaps a file server or a router—may also attempt to detect an ARP spoof by one of its clients. Finally, at the network level, a machine under control of the network administrator may examine all ARP requests and replies to check for anomalies indicating an ARP spoof is underway.

Host-Level Passive Detection

As a basic precaution, when an operating system responds to an ARP broadcast, it should inspect both the sender IP address and the target IP address. It only needs to check the target address to see if the target IP address matches its own IP address. If so, it needs to send an ARP reply. However, once the operating system has been interrupted, it takes little extra work to check to see if the sender IP address matches its own. If so, another machine on the network is claiming to have the same IP address. Such an anomaly certainly indicates a serious configuration problem and may be the result of a simplistic ARP spoof in which the attacker simply reset the IP address of the machine being used in the attack. Many Unix systems perform such a check.

Host-Level Active Detection

Another precaution to detect ARP spoofs is to arrange for hosts to send out an ARP request for their own IP address, both on system startup and periodically thereafter. If the host receives an ARP reply for its own IP address, the IP software should report the detection of an ARP spoof to the host user or administrator. Actively querying ARP with one's own IP address will catch inadvertent IP address misconfigurations as well as an attacker who is simply using an ordinary operating system with a deliberately misassigned IP address. However, it is possible to mount a more sophisticated attack that will thwart the active query detection method.

In particular, a technically adept attacker might modify the operating system of the machine being used to mount the attack. A simple modification that thwarts the active query detection method is to not reply to ARP requests originating from the legitimate interface associated with the IP address being used. The availability of such sophisticated software may seem unlikely even to an advanced computer user.

However, freely distributed Unix-like operating systems with freely distributed source code are now very common. It is not particularly difficult for a determined attacker to obtain such an operating system. He or she could then modify its kernel at the source code level, and compile a modified kernel specifically for the purpose of mounting such an attack.

Server-Level Detection

Alternatively, a more elaborate precaution would be to verify an ARP reply by making an RARP request for the hardware address contained in the reply. RARP, the reverse address resolution protocol, uses the same format as ARP and also broadcasts requests. RARP requests ask the question "What is the IP address associated with the hardware address I have here?"

Traditionally, the primary use of RARP is by diskless machines with no permanent modifiable memory. Such machines need to discover their own IP address at boot time. RARP relies on one or more RARP servers that maintain a database of hardware addresses and the corresponding IP addresses. Use of an RARP server is probably overly elaborate when an ARP server would do the same job.

Note The basic idea of checking the validity of the results to a query by making an inverse query is generically useful. That is, in many situations you are querying a system equivalent to a database. Suppose you use one value, X, as a key for a query with the database indexed on one field and get a second value, Y, from a second field as a result. Then, you can use Y as they key for a query with the database indexed on the second field and you should get X as a result. If you do not, then something is wrong with the database or its searching mechanism.

Network-Level Detection: The Motivation

The motivation for network-level detection is that host-level detection may be unable to effectively inform the network staff that a problem exists and that server-level detection probably requires modification of IP software of the operating system source code. When a host detects that it is being impersonated by another machine, it may be able to report the fact to its user, but once an attack is underway it may be unable to inform the network administrator who is presumably using another machine.

Some popular IP system software may very well take the precaution of occasionally making ARP requests for the hardware address associated with the IP address it believes is its own. The active querying precaution is well-known and is a common textbook exercise. Most corporate system staffs are unable to modify the IP software of most of the machines on their network. If that is your situation, you probably want a software detection system that can be deployed on a single machine on your network. Building the system using software already written by someone else is preferable.

Network-Level Detection via Periodic Polling

By periodically inspecting the ARP caches on machines, you should be able to detect changes in the IP address to hardware address association on those machines. It should be routine for the network staff to keep a database of hardware addresses, IP addresses, DNS names, machine types, locations, and responsible persons. At the very least, such an inspection can probably be done manually on most hosts. It could be done more often if hosts could be configured to periodically report the contents of their ARP caches to a centralized machine. A program on that machine could look for inconsistencies between hosts, changes from previous reports, and conflicts between reported ARP cache information and the information in the manually maintained database—any of these may indicate a problem.

Standard mechanisms for periodic reporting of network configuration information from machines on an IP-based network to the network administration staff already exist. One such mechanism is SNMP—the Simple Network Management Protocol.

In SNMP, each machine using IP runs an SNMP agent which both responds to information and configuration requests as well as reports certain conditions to the network management staff. Virtually all current systems provide bundled SNMP agents. To take advantage of SNMP, the network management staff must have SNMP management software to query the agents and react to the agent reports. Finding good SNMP management software may be difficult and expensive to purchase and deploy.

If your network is already employing SNMP for other purposes, including a check on ARP caches may be simple and inexpensive depending on the sophistication of your SNMP management software. The standard SNMP MIB-I contains the address translation group that contains a single table named "at.atTable," which contains the IP address and hardware address of each interface being monitored by the SNMP agent. The address translation group has to be deprecated in SNMP MIB-II to allow for greater flexibility because IP is now no longer the only protocol being controlled with SNMP. For SNMP agents that use MIB-II, you should look in the IP address translation table in the IP group named ip.ipNetToMediaTable.

> **Warning**   SNMPv1 requests use a "community name" to access a particular view of the MIB. Many SNMPv1 agents are configured with a community name of "public" to give a read-only view of all of the objects in the MIB. Writable views should not be used on an SNMPv1 agent if sniffing is a concern. A sniffer could determine the community name for the writable view and use it to alter the state of the device being controlled by the agent.

Network-Level Detection via Continuous Monitoring

A more robust and rapid mechanism for detecting ARP spoofing is to keep an interface on the network in promiscuous mode. A program on the promiscuous interface's host can inspect every packet sent on the network and monitor the network on a continuous basis, not just when troubleshooting. Such a program can monitor network load, the protocol mix—how much of the traffic is IP, how much is IPX, how much is other network-layer protocols—as well as look for anomalies including ARP spoofing. A network monitor can detect a change in the association between a hardware address and an IP address and report such changes immediately when they occur.

Brouters, transparent bridges, and switches are all logical places to locate the type of network monitor described in the previous paragraph. (Brouters are devices that are combination bridges and routers—a hybrid device such as the Cisco AGS that is often found in multiprotocol networks where non-routable protocols must be bridged.) All these devices have their interfaces in promiscuous mode all the time, so the monitor would not dramatically increase the load on one of these machines because they are all routinely examining each packet. Also, they all typically come with SNMP agents that can send a trap message to the network operations center to report the detection of a potential ARP spoof.

These kinds of systems have a reasonable chance of actually getting such a trap message all the way to the network operations center. However, none of these devices may be successful in doing so if the spoofer is masquerading as the network operations center itself. The trap also may be lost if the spoofer is masquerading as a router between the monitor that detects the spoof and the network operations center.

SNMP agents supporting the RMON protocol (as described in RFC 1271) are designed to do low-level monitoring involving sniffing. On a multisegment network, an RMON/SNMP agent needs to be placed on each segment to get full coverage of the network. Locating the RMON agent on devices that connect to more than one segment will reduce the number of agents that need to be fielded.

Note Good, comprehensive, or affordable commercial packages to implement SNMP-based ARP spoofing monitors are rare. However, building your own system using freeware packages such as BTNG and Tricklet provides an alternative to expensive commercial packages.

RFC 1271 describes the RMON protocol.

BTNG (Beholder, The Next Generation) is an RMON agent available from the Delft University of Technology in the Netherlands via anonymous FTP.

Tricklet, an SNMPv1 management system written in the PERL scripting language, was developed by the same group that developed BTNG. The two systems are integrated and are a good place to start to put together an ARP spoofing detection system in a network large enough to require SNMP management.

In smaller networks, simply placing monitoring software on a small number of secure hosts with interfaces in promiscuous mode all the time might be the only ARP spoofing detection you need. Such monitoring software includes "arpmon" and "netlog" from Ohio State University. These two programs are part of a larger set of programs to assist system and network administrators. Another program to do this kind of monitoring is ARPWatch, which is more narrowly focused on the issue of looking for anomalous behavior in the ARP protocol.

■ arpmon is available from `ftp.net.ohio-state.edu:/pub/networking`. It requires tcpdump and PERL.

- netlog is available from `ftp.net.ohio-state.edu:/pub/security`.

- ARPWatch 1.7 is a Unix program for monitoring ARP requests and replies. The most recent version can be obtained via anonymous FTP to `ftp.ee.lbl.gov`.

Spoofing the IP Routing System

On the Internet, every machine that is active at the network layer takes part in routing decisions (bridges and repeaters are only active at lower layers). The decentralization of routing is unlike simpler systems that limit end user machines to delivering data to a single point of entry on the network, isolating the end user machine from the internal complexities of the network. The essential routing decision is "Where should a datagram with a particular IP destination address be sent?" If the destination address matches the (sub)network address of (one of) the machine's interface(s), then the machine routes the datagram directly to the destination hardware address. Otherwise, the machine selects a router to forward the datagram. Each machine keeps a routing table containing a list of destination (sub)networks and the IP address of the router used to forward to that (sub)network. A default router handles destinations not specifically listed.

How Routers and Route Spoofing Work

Route spoofing can take various forms, all of which involve getting Internet machines to send routed IP datagrams somewhere other than where they should. Route spoofing misdirects non-locally delivered IP datagrams and is thus somewhat similar to ARP spoofing, which misdirects directly delivered IP datagrams. Like ARP spoofing, route spoofing can result in a denial of service attack—datagrams do not go to the machine for which they are intended with the result that a machine appears to be unable to communicate with the network. With a little more sophistication, both ARP spoofing and route spoofing can simply intercept all traffic between two pieces of the network. In the process, they can filter through the network traffic, possibly making modifications to it, creating the illusion of a properly working network.

If you start with a single default router and other routers are available on the network, you would expect that for some destination networks the default router would not be the best choice. If the default router is not the best choice, it sends the datagram back over the same network from which the datagram originated to a different router. When a router does so, it uses the Internet Control Message Protocol (ICMP) to send a message to the machine originating the datagram. ICMP includes a variety of types of messages. The type of ICMP message here is a redirect message.

A redirect message essentially says "it would be best to send datagrams to a router with IP address W.X.Y.Z when the destination network is A.B.C.D rather than using me as your router for that destination." A machine receiving an ICMP redirect message typically updates its routing table to avoid making the mistake in the future. Note that the datagram did not become lost and does not need to be re-sent because the router sending the ICMP redirect has already forwarded the datagram to the appropriate router.

ICMP-Based Route Spoofing

If a machine ignores ICMP redirects, its datagrams are still delivered, just not as efficiently. Turning off ICMP redirect processing is one way of avoiding the simplest of route spoofing techniques—sending illegitimate ICMP redirect messages. Many systems simply process ICMP redirect messages without checking for their validity. At the very least, a check hopefully is made to see that the message coming from an IP address corresponds to a known router.

Note Microsoft Windows 95 and Windows NT keep a list of known routers. The first router on the list is the default router; the next router on the list becomes the default router in case the first one appears to be down.

Another minimal safeguard is to ensure the ARP caches on the hosts have permanent entries for the hardware address of all legitimate routers. This prevents an ARP spoof in which a machine masquerades as one of the routers. Such a masquerade would allow such a machine to intercept virtually all traffic leaving the local network just like the attack described in the next paragraph.

If a machine sends ICMP redirect messages to another machine in the network it could cause the other machine to have an invalid routing table. At the very least, an invalid routing table would constitute a denial of service attack—some or all non-local datagrams would not be able to reach their destination. A much more serious situation would arise if a machine poses as a router to intercept IP datagrams to some or all destination networks. In that case, the machine being used to launch the attack could be multihomed and deliver the IP datagrams via its other network interface. Otherwise, it could simply forward the datagrams to the legitimate router over the same network interface on which they arrived (without the usual ICMP redirect to point back to the legitimate router).

The simplest way to avoid ICMP redirect spoofing is to configure hosts not to process ICMP redirect messages. Doing so may be difficult unless your TCP/IP software is configurable. Some systems require source code modifications to prevent these redirect messages. Many Unix System V machines accept a packet filter with no recompilation or relinking of the kernel.

Note ICMPinfo provides specialized monitoring of ICMP packets received by a host.

TAP is an example of a packet filter used for monitoring. It provides an example that helps you put together your own ICMP packet filter to discard suspicious ICMP redirects.

An alternative is to validate ICMP redirect messages, such as checking that the ICMP redirect is from a router you are currently using. This involves checking the IP address of the source of the redirect and verifying that the IP address matches with the hardware address in the ARP cache. The ICMP redirect should contain the header of the IP datagram that was forwarded. The header can be checked for validity but could be forged with the aid of a sniffer. However, such a check may add to your confidence in the validity of the redirect message and may be easier to do than the other checks because neither the routing table nor the ARP cache needs to be consulted.

Understanding Routing Protocols

An alternative to relying on ICMP redirect messages is to use a routing protocol to give machines a better idea of which routers to use for which destination networks. A routing protocol used on an ordinary host is probably not worth the effort because it will probably take more work than processing ICMP redirects unless multiple routers are available on the network. Relying on ICMP messages from a default router will not be effective when the default router fails (which is why Windows 95 and Windows NT have a list of routers as auxiliaries). Of course, routers need routing protocols to exchange routing information with peer routers unless you use manually configured routing tables. Routing protocols may also be vulnerable to an attack leading to corrupted routing tables on both routers and ordinary hosts.

Two categories of protocols used to describe routing protocols: one category separates protocols by intended use; the other category separates protocols by the kind of algorithm used to determine which router to use for a given destination network.

The first category separates internal routing protocols and external routing protocols. Internal routing protocols are used between routers that are within the same corporate network and external routing protocols are used between routers that belong to different companies.

The second category separates protocols that require only local information—no information except information about directly connected routers—from protocols that require global information, or information about the status of every inter-router link in the entire network.

The external protocols are much more limited in the information they share. The technical name for a set of networks of a single company is an "autonomous system." An autonomous system consists of one or more networks that may share detailed and complete routing information with each other, but do not share complete routing information with other autonomous systems. External routing protocols are used to communicate routing information between autonomous systems. Within an autonomous system, the routers have information about how the networks are divided into subnets and about all routes to other autonomous systems.

The internal subnet structure of one company's network almost always should be separate from another company's network. One company may also want to keep its network(s) from carrying datagrams from another company to third parties. For these reasons, external routing protocols are designed specifically to limit the knowledge they convey and to limit the degree of trust put in the information they provide. External protocols are typically only used on "border" routers that connect autonomous systems to each other. At the very least, each site with a network connected to the Internet has a single border router that connects the site with an Internet Service Provider (ISP).

At times, companies with strategic alliances will have border routers connecting their networks to bypass the ISP for IP datagrams that have their source in one company's network and their destination in the other company's network. Clearly, you must limit your trust in routing information provided from other autonomous regions. Today's strategic partner may be tomorrow's primary competitor and you have no control over the level of security provided within another autonomous region. A security breach in another autonomous network could turn into a security breach in your own autonomous region by spoofing the internal routing protocol and then propagating that information using an external routing protocol.

Another category of routing protocols tries to find the best route through the Internet. One type of protocol uses the vector-distance approach in which each router advertises some measure of "distance" or "cost" of delivering datagrams to each destination network for which it advertises a route. Vector-distance routing protocols (also called Bellman-Ford protocols) only require that each router be aware of the routers it can deliver to directly.

Another type of routing protocol is the link-state, also called the Shortest Path First (SPF), in which each router has a complete picture of the corporate network. In link-state routing protocols, each router actively tests the status of its direct links to other routers, propagates change information about the status of such routers to all such routers, and uses an algorithm to compute the best path to all destinations from itself. Such an algorithm is Dijkstra's shortest path algorithm from graph theory.

The most commonly used routing protocol is a vector-distance protocol called simply the Routing Information Protocol (RIP). RIP predates IP: it is part of the Xerox Networking System (XNS), which was a networking protocol in use even before IP. According to some, RIP was introduced to IP by a graduate student at Berkeley who produced the first implementation overnight when he realized the IP would need some form of routing protocol.

RIP works by combining information sent by active participants in the protocol with information on hand in passive participants. Ordinary hosts participate in the protocol passively by listening to UDP broadcasts on port 520 to get information from the routing tables for each router on their network. The hosts then merge these tables to determine which router to use for which destination networks.

Routers participate in protocol actively by broadcasting their entire routing table every 30 seconds. Instead of the destination network being associated with a router IP address as in the actual routing table, these broadcasts contain destination networks and their associated hop count. The hop count is the number of routers between the router making the broadcast and the destination network. A router that can directly deliver to a given network would advertise a hop count of zero to that network.

A router using exactly one intermediary router to reach a network would advertise a hop count of one to that network. RIP treats a hop count of 16 as an infinite distance indicating an inability to deliver to the given network. Using such a low value eliminates routing loops quickly, but limits RIP to networks with at most 16 routers between any two hosts.

Misdirecting IP Datagrams from Hosts

If a machine is a passive participant in the RIP protocol—it listens to RIP broadcasts and uses them to update its routing table—one simple way to route spoof is to broadcast illegitimate route information via UDP on port 520. On a typical Unix system, port 520 is numbered so low that special privileges are required to access it. However, it is possible for almost any personal computer user and anyone with special privileges to use RIP to mount a route spoofing attack on all the passive participants in RIP on a network. A particularly serious situation arises if routers are passive participants in RIP, using it as an internal routing protocol. If so, RIP propagates the illegitimate information throughout a company's portion of the Internet and the damage can be widespread.

A Case Study of a RIP-Based Route Spoof

To illustrate such an attack, assume everyone at the university is well-intentioned and the network seems to be normal. The network as well as the major multiuser systems and many network servers are managed by Central Computing. The university has so many individual systems, however, that some departments, such as Computer Science, have a separate system administration staff. Each departmental system administration staff is responsible for a set of networked hosts and is capable of installing network wiring without the knowledge of Central Computing. Presumably, the Computer Science staff has enough common sense not to modify the wiring installed by Central Computing. Occasionally, however, Computer Science chafes at what seem to be unreasonable policies imposed by Central Computing.

As you can imagine, Computer Science came up with the brilliant idea of installing a network that does not use the wiring installed and maintained by Centralized Computing. After all, Computer Science will have to pay Central Computing to install a network, so why not control the network after it is installed? Of course, the network installation crew is months behind as it is. Network administration does not seem that hard and does not seem particularly distinct from system administration, so the Computer Science staff takes the plunge and tries to do it themselves. They are successful and the new network works wonderfully—they are proud of their work.

The problem comes when the Computer Science head points out that it would really be nice if the new Computer Science network would communicate with the Central Computing network. The solution is obvious to the Computer Science staff: install a router between the Computer Science network and the Central Computing network. The Computer Science staff can control the new router and use RIP to advertise connectivity between the Central Computing network and the Computer Science network. They spend a few dollars on a new network card for one of their workstations and it becomes a router.

At first, the system works fine. The Central Computing routers recognize the availability of the new Computer Science network and forward datagrams in both directions via the newly installed departmental workstation/router. Then, one day, a departmental staff member decides to reconfigure the workstation and makes a small mistake. *He inadvertently changes the*

IP address of the interface connecting the workstation to the Computer Science network. His error prevents machines on the Computer Science network from being able to send IP datagrams to the workstation/router because it no longer responds to their ARP requests. Computer Science use of the Central Computing network is light and network failures on the Central Computing network are common, so no one in Computer Science immediately becomes worried when they can no longer communicate.

This mistake, however, causes much more severe problems than anyone could have predicted. The IP address installed on the Computer Science router makes it appear to belong to a subnet of the Central Computing network. This subnet is really in a building on the far side of campus with several Central Computing routers in between Computer Science and the router in building with this Central Computing subnet. The Computer Science workstation/router begins advertising, via RIP, its direct connection to this subnet with a zero hop count. The nearest Central Computing router decides that it can get to this subnet with a hop count of one via the Computer Science workstation/router instead of using the next Central Computing router that says it has a hop count of three to the subnet in question. The next centrally controlled router gets a RIP broadcast from the first and decides to begin routing datagrams for this subnet through the first.

Within minutes, a large portion of the network can't communicate with the Computer Science network or the Central Computing subnet associated with the misconfigured IP address. These subnets, however, are used by the main multiuser computers and the off-campus Internet link. Complaints are registered with Central Computing from both directions: Computer Science complains its connection to Central Computing is down and the users in the building across campus complain that their link to the multiuser computers and the Internet is down. Initially, the two problems are seen as separate failures because they involve networks in widely separated buildings. The problem was eventually discovered when the routing tables of the routers were examined. To solve the problem, Central Computing made a manual entry in the routing table of the router closest to Computer Science and solved half of the problem. Computer Science fixed the address on its router and solved the other half.

The poor Computer Science system administrator who mistyped a single digit when working on the workstation/router is then chastised. Afterward, Central Computing figures out that someone might do such a thing on purpose, compromising the stability and security of the network.

Preventing Route Spoofing

To prevent spoofing in situations like the case study, you have the following two primary options:

- Stop using RIP passively on routers.

- Use passive RIP carefully on routers.

One way to prevent RIP spoofing is to remove Central Computing routers from passive participation in RIP and use some other routing protocol between them. The Central Computing routers are still active participants in RIP, broadcasting routing information to hosts every 30 seconds. Thus, misinformation from rogue RIP broadcasts is not propagated throughout the entire organization's network. However, individual hosts are still susceptible to attack via RIP if they are passive participants in RIP.

Actually, the problem is not in RIP itself, but in trusting the source of RIP information. To be secure, the passive participant in RIP must only use RIP information from trustworthy sources. The RIP daemon usually distributed with Unix is *routed,* which is overly trusting. A replacement for the standard RIP daemon is *GateD,* developed at Carnegie-Mellon University (CMU), This program consults a configuration file when it starts. The configuration file, among other things, specifies the IP address(es) of trustworthy RIP information.

The GateD software is no longer available directly from CMU. GateD updates are now available from the GateD Consortium at Merit Networking, Inc. The most recent version may be obtained from the World Wide Web at `http://www.gated.merit.edu/~gated` or through anonymous FTP to `ftp.gated.merit.edu` in the directory /net-research/gated.

Rather than abandoning passive participation in RIP, you can use GateD or the equivalent on the routers and hosts. Each router is configured to restrict its sources of trusted RIP information to trusted routers. Similarly, GateD is used on hosts that passively participate in RIP to protect them from rogue RIP broadcasts.

Central Computing in the preceding example still needs to decide if it will configure the router closest to Computer Science to accept the RIP information sent to it from non-Central Computing routers. If it does not, the workstation/router can send IP datagrams from the new departmental subnet to the router. The router, unless specially configured not to do so, will proceed to forward these datagrams to their destinations. When the destination host is ready to send a reply, it will not find the Computer Science network in its routing table. The routing table for the destination host will probably have a default router to use in such a case and send the IP datagram containing the reply to it.

The default router will also not have an entry in its routing table for the destination of the reply. If it does not have a default router to use for such a case, it will send an ICMP message back to the host that was attempting to send back the reply and discard the IP datagram containing the reply. If the routers do have default routers to use, the reply may be sent through a long sequence of routers until it hits one that does not have a default or the time-to-live field on the IP datagram hits zero and the datagram is discarded. In any case, the reply is dropped by a router, an ICMP message goes to the machine that sent the reply, and no reply reaches the Computer Science network.

If the Computer Science workstation/router is ignored by the central routers, it can still be used. In particular it can exchange data between the Computer Science network and the hosts on the Central Computing subnet directly connected to the Computer Science router. The only problem is in getting data from subnets beyond the Central Computing controlled routers.

To give Computer Science access to the rest of the network, Central Computing has several options. First, manual entries for the Computer Science network can be added to the routers closest to the Computer Science router and continue to ignore RIP broadcasts originating from it. This is simple, neat, and clean. However, if the central routers are using a link-state routing protocol rather than RIP to communicate among themselves, a manual entry for the Computer Science router may make it appear that the route to the Computer Science network is always up when, if fact, the route will occasionally be down.

A second option is to have the Central Computing router pay attention to RIP broadcasts from the Computer Science router but limit the information extracted from the broadcast. Specifically, the only thing that the central router really needs to know is if the workstation/ router has a working route to the Computer Science network. Even if the Central Computing routers use a link-state protocol among themselves, the router nearest to Computer Science can use a hybrid approach to manage the oddball workstation/router that is not participating in the link-state protocol.

A Case Study Involving External Routing

Suppose two companies—Apple and IBM, for example—have a direct network link between their respective research networks. Each of them has a "border" router with a direct connection to the other border router. Each of them also has border routers connected to several different Internet Service Providers. An external routing protocol, such as EGP, is used to exchange routing information between the two border routers. Apple's border router tells IBM's border router what internal networks should be reached from which border routers in Apple's autonomous system. IBM's border router inserts these routes in its routing table. It then uses an internal routing protocol to distribute this information within IBM's research network.

Suppose Apple were to use EGP (the External Gateway Protocol—a name that makes it sound like there is no other alternative), a classic external routing protocol, to advertise a route to another company's research network, Intel's, for example, and IBM normally routed IP traffic through an ISP. The IBM routing tables would not have any specific routing information for Intel and would just use the default route to the ISP and let the ISP worry about the delivery route. If all goes as it would normally, the IBM router sees a route to Intel through one of Apple's border routers. It makes a specific entry for Intel's network in its routing table and spreads the reachability information to other IBM routers via its internal routing protocol.

Now, Apple is getting all of the IP traffic sent from IBM to Intel. If no malice is intended in this error, the traffic is routed out to one of Apple's ISPs and on to Intel with only a short added delay and extra traffic on the edge of Apple's internal network. On the other hand, the Apple border router could be configured to discard such datagrams and Apple would have succeeded in a denial of service attack. The attack would be discovered quickly and would be fairly pointless. Alternatively, a sniffer on Apple's internal network would now be able to intercept traffic from IBM to Intel for industrial espionage purposes.

Clearly, a good implementation of an external routing protocol needs to be a bit suspicious of the routing information provided by routers from another organization. A database of network addresses and their associated autonomous system numbers such as the one provided by InterNIC would reveal to IBM's border router that the Intel network has an autonomous system number different from the one Apple was claiming it had when making the EGP advertisement. With millions of networks and thousands of autonomous networks, you merely need to store the part of the InterNIC database that specifies which network numbers are valid for the autonomous systems that are valid peers of the border router.

> **Note** EGP is no longer considered state-of-the-art in external routing protocols, but the principle remains the same for all external routing protocols.

Spoofing Domain Name System Names

Some systems base trust on IP addresses; other systems base trust on Domain Name System (DNS) names. DNS names are easier to remember and easier for most people to work with than dotted decimal IP addresses. Just as the IP address to hardware address correspondence may change over time, the name to address correspondence may change too as different machines are used for a different set of tasks. Unfortunately, the use of names involves yet another layer of software, introducing another point of vulnerability for the security of the systems.

Understanding Name Resolution for Hosts

When software on a host needs to convert a name to an address it sends an address lookup query to a DNS name server. When a client connects to a named host, the client needs to convert the name to an address. The client trusts the DNS system to return the correct address and trusts the routing system to deliver the data to the correct destination. Because virtually all systems place trust in name server, all of the special precautions described previously in this chapter to protect trust should be used to protect that trust. For example, if you go back and see which hosts had permanent ARP cache entries on my Windows 95 machine, one of them was 147.226.112.102—the DNS name server used by my machine. The name server is on the same subnet as my machine, so it would be possible for an ARP spoofer to masquerade as the name server and cause all sorts of mischief by misdirecting datagrams.

Similarly, when a host needs to convert an address to a name it sends a reverse lookup query to a DNS name server. When a server accepts a connection from a prospective client, it can determine the IP address of the prospective client from the IP datagram header. However, the server must rely on the DNS system to perform a reverse lookup query to determine the name of the prospective client. If trust is extended to the client on the basis of the client hostname, the server is trusting the DNS system to perform this reverse lookup properly. If a DNS name server is coerced into providing false data, the security of the system can become compromised.

Understanding DNS Name Servers

The DNS system is complex. To help you understand its structure, think of the DNS system as a distributed database consisting of records with three fields: name, address, and record type. The database is distributed; not all of the records are kept in a centralized location, and no record is kept in only one location. The database is not centralized because it would be impractical to do so—from a technical standpoint and from an administrative standpoint. Technically, such a centralized setup would place an incredible load on one machine, which would have to handle all the name-to-address queries for the entire Internet and create huge amounts of long-distance network traffic. Administratively, this centralized database setup would be horribly awkward to change because thousands of network administrators would need to be checked for authenticity and privileges each time one of them makes a change.

Note The four record types of interest in DNS names are as follows:

- Canonical hostname to address mapping

- Alias hostname to canonical hostname mapping

- Domain name to name server name mapping

- Address to hostname mapping other record types that also exist

The primary purpose of DNS is to break down the authority for a set of names into domains. Each domain is administered independently of each other domain. Each domain can create subdomains that are only loosely related to the domain and administered independently of each other. Each subdomain is responsible for a subset of the names of the whole domain. In turn, subdomains can create subsubdomains and so on. The term "subdomain" is a relative term between a domain and a domain that has control over a piece of the domain.

When a name server receives a query to resolve a name, it may make an authoritative reply based on data it keeps in its own portion of the database, or it may make a non-authoritative reply. Two types of non-local replies are possible: iterative or recursive. If the client asks for recursive resolution (the more common choice), the name server forwards the request to a name server it thinks is more likely to be authoritative than it is and then relays the reply back to the client along with information indicating where the authoritative answer was found. If the client asks for iterative resolution, the name server simply returns the address of the name server it would have forwarded the request to and lets the client query that name server directly.

Efficiency: Caching and Additional Information

Because name resolution is so frequent, efficiency is important. When a name server makes an authoritative response, either to an ordinary client host or another name server, the authoritative response includes a "time to live," which amounts to a claim that the response will continue to be valid for a certain amount of time. When a name server receives a reply from another name server, it caches the reply for the amount of time specified by the "time to live."

Some kinds of DNS replies will clearly lead to a follow-up query. For example, if a reply includes a record specifying the name of a name server for a domain, the client probably will soon make a query to find the address of that name server. Hence, a DNS reply not only has sections for specifying the question, answer, and authority of the answer, but also has a section for additional information. The name server caches additional information records along with the answer records so that it can handle the follow-up queries efficiently without further name server to name server queries.

How DNS Spoofing Can Happen

Suppose a name server somewhere on the Internet has been compromised by a security attack or is being controlled by an intruder. This name server will provide authoritative responses for some domain and all hosts on the Internet will trust those responses. The authoritative responses can direct clients looking up the names of servers to connect to servers under the control of the attacker rather than the legitimate servers. A falsified reverse address lookup can fool servers attempting to determine if the IP address of a prospective client corresponds to the name of an authorized client. Within the DNS system, absolutely nothing can be done about such a direct attack.

A standard attempt at a defense to a DNS spoofing attack is to cross-check all responses to reverse lookup queries by making a forward lookup query. That is, a server queries the DNS system with the IP address of a prospective client via a reverse lookup and receives the DNS name(s) of the prospective client. Then it takes the names and queries the DNS system for the address(es) that corresponds to the name. Cross-checking has become a standard technique with TCP wrapper systems.

Cross-checking may help if the attacker is clumsy and alters the name server files corresponding to reverse lookups, but not those corresponding to forward lookups. Because these tables are kept in separate files, they may also be kept on separate name servers. If the attacker has compromised only one of the two name servers, the cross-checking may discover the inconsistency. Because of potential abuses of the efficiency mechanisms in DNS, the name server may not discover the inconsistency.

Another attempt to stifle DNS spoofing is to make iterative rather than recursive resolution requests so that checks on consistency and authoritativeness can be made more carefully than the name servers themselves do. In particular, when a name server makes a non-authoritative response to an iterative query, it responds with the name of a name server more likely to be authoritative than itself. If the name server has been compromised, it may direct the iterative query to another compromised name server or it may claim authoritativeness when it does not have authoritativeness for the domain being queried. In such cases, a check on authoritativeness should, in principle, detect the attack.

A check on authoritativeness requires querying a root-level name server for the address of the name servers that are authoritative for the base domain of the DNS name. One must then ask the name server at that address for the address of the name server that is authoritative for the next component of the DNS name and so on. Such a procedure is clearly quite time consuming and places considerable load on root-level name servers. Also, it does not help if an authoritative name server has become compromised; it only detects invalid claims to authority.

Note, however, that the plural was used when referring to authoritative name servers. The DNS standards require that data for each domain be replicated on separate computers with no common point of failure, meaning that the name servers with the duplicated data must not be attached to the same network or obtain electrical power from a common source. It seems unlikely that an attacker would be able to compromise all of the authoritative name servers for a given domain.

For this reason, it might seem that you could poll all authoritative name servers when making a query to look for a discrepancy. Unfortunately, one name server is typically designated as the primary authority and the others as secondary authority. The secondary name servers simply make a copy of the data in the primary on a periodic basis after the serial number on the data for a domain has changed. If the primary authoritative name server is compromised, all the secondary authoritative name servers will also contain invalid data after enough time has elapsed. Meanwhile, inconsistencies may simply indicate that the secondary has not copied legitimate changes to the data on the primary.

Efficiency Mechanisms: Downfall of DNS Security

The truly troubling part of the DNS security problem is that when a name server caches invalid data, the invalid data can remain in the cache for a very long time and can misdirect queries that are unrelated to the query that placed the data in the cache in the first place.

For example, suppose one query places the name of a domain and the name of its name server in the cache as well as the name of the name server and its address. All later queries for names in that domain will be referred to the earlier named name server at the earlier specified address. If either of these cached records is invalid, all subsequent queries for this domain will be directed to the wrong place. The responses to these misdirected queries will also be cached. A compromised name server may cause errors in the caches of uncompromised name servers that cause the uncompromised name server to provide invalid data to its clients.

Furthermore, a DNS name server can supply arbitrary information in the additional information section of a response to any query. Thus, it may provide a perfectly valid response to the original query, but arbitrary misinformation provided in the additional information section of the response will be cached by a name server that queries it.

Suppose, for example, that a server (not a name server) attempts to check on the name of a prospective client by making a query that forces the DNS system to do a reverse lookup on the address to find the DNS name of the prospective client. A compromised name server might provide an invalid response, which would seem to make the prospective client legitimate. When the server attempts to cross-check this information, the name server may respond with misinformation provided as additional information to the reverse query. If the server makes an iterative query instead, it will not cause immediate corruption of its name server's cache when the compromised name server is not directly interacting with the local name server, but any client of the local name server may trigger a request that corrupts the cache of the local name server.

Case Study: A Passive Attack

Consider the case of Frank and Mary, who work at Widgets, Inc. Their company runs a name server to support their DNS domain, widget.com. Their workstations consult this name server when looking up the IP addresses of outside networks. One day, Mary is surfing the Web and finds a reference to something that looks interesting at a site in the podunk.edu domain. Her Web browser does a DNS query of the widget.com name server that forwards the query to the podunk.edu name server. The widget.com name server caches the reply from podunk.edu and supplies the requested IP address information to Mary's Web browser.

Unfortunately, the podunk.edu name server has been taken over by a malicious college student. When the reply goes back to the widget.com name server, additional information fields are attached. One of these contains the name "well.sf.ca.us," the DNS name for the Well—an online service provider located in San Francisco. The additional information field says that this name is associated with yet another machine controlled by the malicious college student.

A little while later, Frank decides to telnet to his account on well.sf.ca.us and is greeted with the usual login information and prompt. When he types in his username and password, there is a brief pause, he is presented with his usual menus, and continues his work.

What has happened is that when Frank used telnet, it made a DNS query of the widget.com name server. The widget.com name server found the entry for well.sf.ca.us in its cache and returned the IP address of the college student's machine. Frank's machine established a connection with the college student's machine and it began the classic Trojan horse routine. The student's machine provided the login prompt and stored up the username and password. It then turned around and used a modified version of telnet to connect to well.sf.ca.us and passed packets back and forth between it and Frank's machine at Widgets, Inc. The Trojan horse created the illusion that Frank was directly connected to the Well and gave the college student the password for Frank's account on the Well.

Case Study: An Active Attack

The previous case study is a *passive* attack exploiting DNS weaknesses—the attacker had to wait for someone to stumble into his trap and could not be sure who he would catch. Now examine an *active* attack exploiting this same weakness, and with an attacker who targets a specific individual. Assume that Frank, Mary, and the malicious college student at Podunk University are involved.

Suppose Frank has set up his account at Widgets, Inc. so that he can use rlogin to connect to it from his account on the Well (well.sf.ca.us) without being required to supply a password. Frank trusts that the folks who run the Well are keeping his account secure (he's probably right).

The malicious college student sends a mail message to a mail server at Widgets, Inc. addressed to someone at Podunk University. The mail server performs a DNS lookup for podunk.edu. The compromised name server supplies additional information in its reply that indicates not only that well.sf.ca.us has the college student's IP address but also that the reverse is true: the student's IP address corresponds to the name well.sf.ca.us.

The student then uses rlogin from his machine to connect to Frank's account at Widgets, Inc. His machine starts up the rlogin daemon. The rlogin daemon gets the IP address of the incoming connection and performs a reverse query of the widget.com name server, looking for the name that corresponds to the IP address of the college student's machine. The widget.com name server finds this information in its cache and replies that the IP address corresponds to the name "well.sf.ca.us." The college student gains access to Frank's account at Widgets, Inc. The only thing the logging information indicates is that Frank connected from his account on the Well. The logs on the Well show that Frank was not logged in, however, which would tip Frank off if he ever cross-checked them with his own logs.

> **Warning**   rlogin is handy when you want to keep passwords out of sight of sniffers, but it suffers from the problem outlined here. Do not use rlogin to allow access from machines that do not have authoritative entries in the local name server database. Otherwise, the DNS name of the accessing machine is checked to determine whether it can be trusted to authenticate its users. A DNS spoof will subvert this check.

Defenses against DNS Spoofing

The ultimate defense against DNS spoofing is not to use the DNS. However, DNS style naming is such a part of the way users and system administrators work that it is unthinkable to do without it. On the other hand, many name-to-IP address mappings will not change and, in some cases, it may make as much sense for a system administrator to configure clients to use an IP address as it would to use a DNS name. Every place an IP address is used in place of a DNS name is one less place the system is vulnerable to DNS spoofing.

Many operating systems simplify the process of reducing use of the DNS by having an API for name-to-address and address-to-name mappings. The API is the same whether DNS is being used to implement these mappings or some other standard. Some implementations of the API will consult local data that is believed to be faster or more secure than DNS. The DNS is consulted by these implementations of the API only if the local sources fail to give conclusive results.

Even if the API on your system only implements the naming system via one mechanism (in which case choosing to use DNS may be unavoidable), it may be possible to change the implementation and reap widespread benefit immediately. In particular, many modern operating systems use dynamic linking or shared libraries to reduce the size of executable files. With these systems, replacing the library containing the implementation of the API with an implementation that behaves differently will affect all programs started after the replacement.

Note When using SunOS 4.1 as shipped from Sun, for example, you can choose to have the gethostbyname() and gethostbyaddr() functions use either the /etc/hosts file or the NIS system.

One way to limit the spread of invalid cached entries is to use name server software running on many hosts in your network. If a client on one machine triggers the corruption of the cache on one name server, the use of multiple name servers reduces the likelihood of widespread damage. Placing a name server on every timeshared Unix host, for example, will not only provide quick responses to local clients from the cached entries on the name server, but will also reduce the set of hosts affected by a compromised name server consulted by a set of users on a single timeshared host.

Other hosts can use a different name server that will not have its cache corrupted as long as the name server on the timeshared host does not forward recursive requests to the other name server. An active attacker targeting a particular system may make direct queries of any name server to trigger the corruption of its cache. The technique outlined here limits damage from a passive attacker waiting for victims to come along. You can also add checks to some name servers so that they will respond only to select clients rather than an arbitrary client. Placing such a limitation on a name server does not make it useful for serving requests to the outside world but makes it more secure for internal use.

In the case study of Frank's and Mary's Widget company you read about earlier, the college student would not have been so successful in his attack if Frank and Mary had been running name servers on their own workstations. In the first case study, Mary's cache would have been corrupted but it would not have caused problems for Frank. In the second case, the cache for the name server used by the mail server would have been corrupted, but, again, Frank would not have used the corrupted cache unless his name server consulted with the same one as the mail server.

The use of local name servers on workstations also may reduce total network traffic and aids in fault tolerance. If a network-wide name server goes down, it will not create any delays for information stored in the local name servers.

> **Warning** You are still at risk of a DNS spoof if local name servers on workstations are configured to process queries recursively when they consult the network wide name server. You are also at risk if the local name server refers its local clients to query the network wide name server for names for which the network wide name server is also non-authoritative. In either case, a corrupted network-wide name server cache will affect the workstations.
>
> The use of local name servers will limit, not eliminate, risks. Local name servers are also subject to cache corruption. The reduced risk comes from fewer interactions with any single cache. You should be sure local name servers only process queries from the local machine to prevent an active attacker from directly contaminating their cache. Hiding the workstations behind a firewall will also help.

You might also modify local name server software to be more selective about the information it caches. Again, doing so will be of limited value if the erroneous data is coming from the cache of an unmodified name server being consulted by the local name server. Selective caching by doing such things as ignoring information in the additional information section of DNS replies will certainly have an adverse impact on efficiency. Response times will also be lengthened by any cross-checking or authority checking done by the modified name server, but cached authority checks may ease the problem somewhat.

RFC 1788 proposes an alternative to DNS reverse lookups: all machines would respond to a new ICMP message requesting the set of names that correspond to the IP address on which the ICMP message was received. These responses can then be cross-checked through forward DNS lookups. Although this proposal aims to increase the security of DNS, it is not clear how it would have helped in the case study involving Frank and Mary described earlier. Name-based authentication is fundamentally insecure when the name is not coming directly from a trustworthy source.

The simplest thing a name server administrator can do to prevent a DNS spoof from corrupting the name server cache is to have the most recent version of the operating system's DNS name server software. The most common implementation of a DNS name server is BIND (Berkeley Internet Name Daemon) on Unix. Newer versions of BIND incorporate modifications made with a more security conscious attitude than older versions. For the most current version, consult the Web at http://www.dns.net.dnsrd/servers.html.

Tip

For a more detailed treatment of the security weaknesses of the DNS system, see the paper "Countering Abuses of Name-based Authentication" by Christoph Schuba and Eugene Spafford of the COAST security lab at Purdue University. The COAST department supplies useful security-related information and many useful tools. COAST has a site on the World Wide Web at `http://www.cs.purdue.edu/coast/coast.html`.

Spoofing TCP Connections

TCP builds a connection-oriented, reliable byte stream on top of IP that can send connectionless, unreliable datagrams. It is possible for an attacker's machine to spoof by sending IP datagrams that have an IP source address belonging to another machine. Such spoofing provides a mechanism for an attack on the security of any machine using IP to receive commands.

The attacker's machine can send IP datagrams with a forged source address to other machines while the machine legitimately possessing that IP address is active. It can do so with no intention of getting replies to those datagrams. The other machines will accept these datagrams as coming from the legitimate holder of the IP source address of these forged datagrams. They will carry out actions not actually requested by the user of the legitimate machine.

Typically, IP-based application protocols have some notion of a session with some information exchanged at startup, which is used to identify the two parties to each another during the active part of the session. One effect of the information exchange is that a third party cannot pose as one of the initial two parties. If a sniffer is being used by the attacker, it becomes easy for the attacker to pose as either party. For example, in the NFS protocol, a client will first exchange information with the server's mount daemon. After this exchange, the client will be able to open and read or write files on the server by making requests of the NFS daemon. An attacker can wait for the client to mount a file system and open a file. If the attacker sends out an appropriately formatted UDP datagram, the server will process an NFS request and send the results back to the client. Regardless of the client's reaction to the unexpected reply, if the request was a write request, the attacker will have succeeded in writing some information to the server's disk. If the request was a read request and the attacker has a sniffer between the client and server, the attacker will succeed in finding out some of the contents of the disk via the sniffer.

Through the use of datagrams with forged IP addresses, an attacker can get datagrams holding requests accepted as valid but cannot get replies to those requests without a sniffer. In the NFS scenario described earlier, you were using UDP and assumed the attacker had a sniffer to obtain the credentials that allowed acceptance of the request as valid. You might assume that if you use a connection-oriented protocol, such as TCP, you might be more secure. If you can rule out an attacker having a sniffer between the client and the server, the attacker would be unable to obtain the needed credentials. Unfortunately, these assumptions are valid.

Introduction to TCP/IP End-to-End Handshaking

To understand how an attacker might be able to send datagrams accepted as valid, you need to understand the information exchanged between the parties of a TCP connection. A TCP connection proceeds through three stages:

■ Connection setup

■ Data exchange

■ Connection tear-down

TCP Connection Setup

TCP connection setup requires a three-way handshake between the two parties. Initially, one party is passively waiting for the establishment of a connection. This passive party is said to be "listening." The passive party is typically a server. The other party actively opens the TCP connection by sending the first IP datagram. The active party is typically a client. The definition of client and server is separate from active and passive parties during the setup phase. This discussion refers to the parties as client and server merely to be more suggestive of the typical roles they will play later.

The client starts things off by sending a TCP header with the SYN flag set. SYN stands for "synchronize" and refers to the synchronization of initial sequence numbers. The TCP protocol assigns each data byte sent on a connection its own sequence number. Every TCP header contains a sequence number field corresponding to the sequence number in the first data byte of the field. Initial sequence numbers should be random rather than merely arbitrary. Randomness of initial sequence number is important for handling the situation when a connection is established, the machine on one side crashes, and then attempts to reestablish a connection. The other machine needs to be able to detect wild out-of-range sequence and acknowledgment numbers to close its side of the connection to the program that is no longer running. TCP only sets the SYN flag when the connection is started.

The server replies to the SYN header with a header containing both a SYN and an ACK flag set. ACK stands for "acknowledgment." The SYN lets the client know its initial sequence number—TCP connections are bi-directional. The ACK flag lets the client know that it received the initial sequence number. Whenever the acknowledgment number field is valid, corresponding to the sequence number of the next data byte expected, the TCP sets ACK flag.

To complete the connection, the client responds back to the server with a TCP header that has the ACK flag set. The acknowledgment lets the server know that it is now ready to begin receiving data. Understanding the sequence of events with SYN and ACK flags during the establishment of a connection is also important when configuring firewalls.

TCP Data Exchange

During normal TCP data exchange, one party will send one or more TCP/IP datagrams. The other party will occasionally send back a TCP/IP datagram with the TCP header having the ACK flag set to let the sender know that the data arrived. During establishment of the connection both parties also inform the other how much room they have in their receive buffers. TCP transmits the amount of available room in the window field of the TCP header in each datagram sent to inform the sender how much more data may be sent before the receive buffer fills. As the program on the receiving side empties the receive buffer, the number in the window field increases. The acknowledgment number specifies the lowest sequence number of a data byte that it expects to receive. The acknowledgment number plus the number in the window field specifies the highest sequence number of a data byte that will be placed in the input buffer when received.

Occasionally, IP datagrams will arrive out of order. When a datagram arrives earlier than expected, the early datagram goes into the receiver's input buffer but the receiver does not immediately acknowledge it. When the expected datagram arrives, the receiver may acknowledge both sets of TCP data at once. However, at this point, the receiving program will be able to read both sets of data without waiting for any more action from the sender.

Forged TCP/IP Datagrams

To successfully forge a TCP/IP datagram that will be accepted as part on an existing connection, an attacker only needs to estimate the sequence number to be assigned to the next data byte to be sent by the legitimate sender. Consider the three cases of being exact, being a bit too low with the estimate, and being a bit too high with the estimate.

If the attacker knows or successfully guesses the exact value of the next sequence number of the next byte being sent, the attacker can forge a TCP/IP datagram containing data that will be placed in the receiver's input buffer in the next available position. If the forged datagram arrives after the legitimate datagram, the receiver may completely discard the forged datagram if it contains less data than the legitimate one. However, if the forged datagram contains more data, the receiver will discard only the first part. The receiver will place into its input buffer the part of the forged datagram with data bytes having larger sequence numbers than those received in the earlier legitimate datagram.

On the other hand, if the forged datagram arrives before the legitimate datagram, the legitimate datagram will be discarded by the receiver (at least partially).

If the attacker's guess of the sequence number is a bit too low, it will definitely not get the first part of the data in the forged TCP/IP datagram placed in the receiver's input buffer. However, if the forged datagram contains enough data, the receiver may place the last part of the forged data in its input buffer.

If the attacker's guess of the sequence number is a bit too high, the receiver will consider it to be data that simply arrived out of order and put it into its input buffer. Some of the data bytes at the end of the forged datagram may have sequence numbers that do not fit in the current window, so the receiver will discard these. Later, the legitimate datagram arrives to fill in the gap between the next expected sequence number and the sequence number of the first forged data byte. Then, the whole forged datagram is available to the receiving program.

Sniffing + Forging = Trouble

Clearly, one way to obtain an estimate of the sequence numbers in a TCP/IP connection is to sniff the network somewhere between the client and the server. An attacker could possibly be controlling more than one machine along this path so the machine doing the sniffing need not be the machine doing the forging.

If a machine on the same physical network as the legitimate sender does the forging, then routers will not have much of a chance of stopping the forged datagram. The only possible place to stop the forged datagram would be at the router on the forger's network, where a discrepancy might be detected between the hardware address of the legitimate sender and the forger.

If a machine on the same physical network as the receiver does the forging, the receiver would also have the opportunity to note such a discrepancy. If the forging occurs on neither of the two endpoint networks, then the opportunity to stop the forged datagram decreases. However, in many cases attackers would only have access to physical networks attached to routers with a single legitimate source network. You can protect your network from being the source of a forging attack by configuring these routers not to forward datagrams with impossible IP network addresses.

One particular case deserves special note. If both endpoints are on the same physical network, an attacker might be bold enough to forge a datagram from another physical network. Because only the destination address needs examination to deliver a datagram, the datagram could get to the receiver via the normal routing mechanisms. However, the router would have the opportunity to detect the forged datagram by noting that the IP source network address matches the IP destination network address. Datagrams with matching source and destination network addresses should not be allowed into the router if the network address matches that of an internal network.

Note See the files for CERT Advisory CA:95-01 to find out more about actual attacks based on this special case.

TCP/IP Forging without Sniffing

With four billion possible initial sequence numbers, it should be extremely difficult to guess a valid current sequence number for a TCP/IP connection. However, this assumes assignment of the initial sequence numbers in a completely random manner. If an attacker establishes a TCP/IP connection with the receiving end of another TCP/IP connection, the attacker also obtains an initial sequence number from the receiving end. If the initial sequence numbers of the two connections are related in some way, the attacker will be able to compute the initial sequence number of the other connection.

When the attacker has the initial sequence number of the connection, the next and final step is to estimate how much TCP/IP data has been sent to the receiver. This estimate added to the initial sequence number estimates the current sequence number. An estimate of the current sequence number goes into a forged TCP/IP header.

Some TCP/IP implementations use initial sequence numbers generated by a simple random number generator that generates numbers in a fixed order. If the attacker knows this ordering, the attacker can establish a connection at about the same time as the connection to be spoofed. Knowing that connection's initial sequence number will provide enough information to narrow the plausible initial sequence numbers for the connection to a very few instead of four billion. The way to prevent this attack is to use a TCP/IP implementation that does a good job of generating random initial sequence numbers.

Terminal Hijacking: An Example of TCP/IP Forging

Imagine the following everyday scenario at my workplace. Many workers use windowing systems such as the X Window system or Microsoft Windows to start terminal sessions to one or more of the timesharing systems. The most convenient way to use these systems is to have them start automatically. With this setup, many of the windows will have idle terminal sessions using a TCP/IP-based protocol such as telnet, tn3270, or rlogin.

In fact, some of these sessions never are used after they start. Some of these remain idle for days or weeks at a time. An attacker with ordinary access to one of the timesharing systems can easily detect the time any particular worker starts a terminal session by monitoring the set of users on the timeshared system.

Immediately after the targeted worker logs in to the timesharing system, the attacker determines the initial sequence number of the TCP/IP connection used for the terminal session. The attacker may have received this number using a sniffer running on another host on the network or by taking advantage of the deterministic pattern of initial sequence numbers.

Next, the attacker estimates the number of data bytes the worker's terminal session has sent to the timesharing system. Typically, the worker types in at most a username, password, and a command or two by this time. By simply estimating the number of data bytes to be between zero and one hundred, the attacker will be close enough to hit the window of acceptable sequence numbers.

To do some real damage, the attacker simply has to insert a sequence of characters in the data stream that correspond to a command being typed in at the command prompt. Just to be sure that the command is accepted as an entire command, the attacker could place characters in the data stream that would exit a typical application and get to new command line. Putting "rm -rf *" on the command line in Unix deletes all files in the current directory along with all files in all subdirectories of the current directory.

If the attacker really wants to spook the worker, he or she could wait to see if the terminal session will remain idle overnight while the worker is gone, the office locked, and all the physical security mechanisms in place to ensure no one enters the office.

If the attacker determines the exact initial sequence number for the terminal session, the command is executed by the timesharing system in the worker's absence. The echo of the presumed keystrokes will appear in the worker's terminal window along with a new command prompt indicating that the command has completed. Imagine the surprise the worker gets when he or she shows up in the morning and sees this terminal window. Imagine the horror of realizing that backups were done shortly after the command executed and that a whole backup period of work has been lost.

Reducing the Risks of TCP/IP Spoofing

One way to reduce the threat of this sort of attack is to simply log out of all terminal sessions before they become inactive and only start up terminal sessions when you need them. Inactive terminal sessions are the easiest to hijack.

A second way to reduce the threat is to use an implementation of the terminal session protocol (telnet or rlogin) that inserts extra terminal protocol data transmitted to the timesharing machine. Doing so will not fool a sniffer, but it will make it harder for the attacker who is guessing that the terminal protocol sends only a small, relatively fixed amount of data before the user begins typing commands.

A third way to reduce the threat is to avoid the use of terminal session protocols between the user's desktop and the timesharing machine. For example, with the X Window system, you have the option of running the windowing program (for example, xterm) on the desktop and then starting a remote terminal session with the windowing program.

You can also run the windowing program on the timesharing machine and use the X protocol to have the window displayed on your desktop. Using X may introduce its own set of security problems, but convincing the timesharing system to accept forged data as keystrokes requires a somewhat messier process and it is much harder to make a good guess at a current sequence number without a sniffer.

A fourth way to reduce the threat of TCP/IP spoofing is to use an encryption-based terminal protocol. The use of encryption does not help prevent an attacker from making a good guess at the current sequence number. If the attacker is using a sniffer, the sniffer knows the exact current sequence number. Encrypted protocols, however, can limit the consequences of introducing forged data on the connection. Unless the encryption is broken, the receiver will accept the data as valid but the command interpreter will not be able to make sense of it. When the legitimate sender gets acknowledgments for the forged data it will become confused and may reset the TCP/IP connection, causing the terminal session to be shut down.

The only way to deal with this threat completely with current standardized technology is to use a combination approach. Initial sequence numbers must be unpredictable and fall throughout the full range of four billion. TCP/IP data must be encrypted so that unencrypted or misencrypted data will not be confused with valid commands. You also must simply live with the possibility that an attacker may cause a TCP/IP connection to reset because of garbage injected into a connection by an attacker with a sniffer.

Using Next-Generation Standard IP Encryption Technology

To stop IP address spoofing, you must use encryption on the entire data portion of an IP datagram, including the TCP header. By doing so, you prevent a sniffer from determining the sequence numbers of the TCP connection. See RFCs 1825-1830.

One IP encryption technique currently in use is SwIPe. It encrypts the TCP header and the TCP data, preventing sniffers from finding sequence numbers. This program is considerably more sophisticated than that, and goes well beyond the scope of the kind of coverage provided in this chapter. Because it requires kernel modification the source code is not of general interest; if you are interested, however, use anonymous FTP to access `ftp.csua.berkeley.edu /pub/cypherpunks/swIPe/`.

An emerging standardized IP encryption technique is specified in "RFC 1825: Security Architecture for the Internet Protocol." It is a standards-track specification for an option to the current version of IP (IPv4) and a required part of the next generation of IP (Ipv6). RFC 1825 specifies two parts: an authentication header (AH) and an encapsulating security payload. These two parts may be used separately or in combination. The use of the authentication header prevents the forging of IP datagrams. The encapsulated security payload encrypts the content of the IP datagram, including the TCP header.

The following RFCs detail a proposed standard authored by R. Atkinson of the Naval Research Laboratory and published in August 1995:

- RFC 1825: Security Architecture of the Internet Protocol

- RFC 1826: IP Authentication Header

- RFC 1827: IP Encapsulating Security Payload

The following RFCs detail the mechanisms behind RFC 1826 and RFC 1827, respectively, and are part of the proposed standard. They were authored by Metzger, Karn, and Simpson and published in August 1995. RFC 1851 and RFC 1852, published in September 1995, are follow-ups to these papers. The newer RFCs are, as of this writing, still "experimental" rather than part of a "proposed standard."

- RFC 1828: IP Authentication using Keyed MD5

- RFC 1829: The ESP DES-CBC Transform

INDEX

J-K

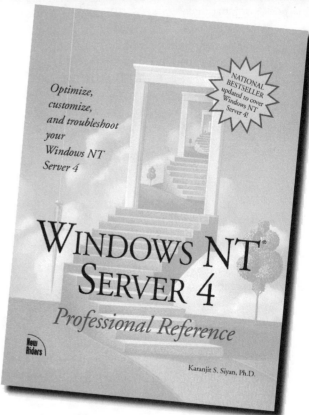

REGISTRATION CARD

Windows NT Server 4: Security, Troubleshooting, and Optimization

Name _____   Title _____

Company _____   Type of business _____

Address _____

City/State/ZIP _____

Have you used these types of books before?   ☐ yes   ☐ no

If yes, which ones? _____

_____

How many computer books do you purchase each year?   ☐ 1–5   ☐ 6 or more

How did you learn about this book? _____

Where did you purchase this book? _____

Which applications do you currently use? _____

_____

Which computer magazines do you subscribe to? _____

_____

What trade shows do you attend? _____

_____

Comments: _____

_____

_____

Would you like to be placed on our preferred mailing list?   ☐ yes   ☐ no

☐ **I would like to see my name in print!** You may use my name and quote me in future New Riders products and promotions. My daytime phone number is: _____

New Riders Publishing   201 West 103rd Street ◆ Indianapolis, Indiana 46290 USA

Fax to 317-581-4670

Fold Here

BUSINESS REPLY MAIL

FIRST-CLASS MAIL PERMIT NO. 9918 INDIANAPOLIS IN

POSTAGE WILL BE PAID BY THE ADDRESSEE

NO POSTAGE
NECESSARY
IF MAILED
IN THE
UNITED STATES

NEW RIDERS PUBLISHING
201 W 103RD ST
INDIANAPOLIS IN 46290-9058

New Riders has emerged as a premier publisher of computer books for the professional computer user. Focusing on CAD/graphics/multimedia, communications/internetworking, and networking/operating systems, New Riders continues to provide expert advice on high-end topics and software.

Check out the online version of *New Riders' Official World Wide Yellow Pages, 1996 Edition* for the most engaging, entertaining, and informative sites on the Web! You can even add your own site!

Brave our site for the finest collection of CAD and 3D imagery produced today. Professionals from all over the world contribute to our gallery, which features new designs every month.

From Novell to Microsoft, New Riders publishes the training guides you need to attain your certification. Visit our site and try your hand at the CNE Endeavor, a test engine created by VFX Technologies, Inc. that enables you to measure what you know—and what you don't!

http://www.mcp.com/newriders

Getting Started with the CD-ROM

This page provides instructions for installing software from the CD-ROM.

Windows 95/NT 4 Installation

Insert the disc into your CD-ROM drive. If autoplay is enabled on your machine, the CD-ROM setup program starts automatically the first time you insert the disc.

If setup does not run automatically, perform these steps:

1. From the Start menu, choose Programs, Windows Explorer.

2. Select your CD-ROM drive under My Computer.

3. Double-click SETUP.EXE in the contents list.

4. Follow the on-screen instructions that appear.

5. Setup adds an icon named CD-ROM Contents to a program group for this book. To explore the CD-ROM, double-click on the CD-ROM Contents icon.

How to Contact New Riders Publishing

If you have a question or comment about this product, there are several ways to contact New Riders Publishing. You can write us at the following address:

New Riders Publishing
Attn: Publishing Manager
201 W. 103rd Street
Indianapolis, IN 46290

If you prefer, you can fax New Riders Publishing at 1-317-817-7448.

To send Internet electronic mail to New Riders, address it to support@mcp.com.

You can also contact us through the Macmillan Computer Publishing CompuServe forum at GO NEWRIDERS. Our World Wide Web address is http://www.mcp.com/newriders.